Plotting for Peace

With Britain by late 1916 facing the prospect of an economic crisis and being increasingly dependent on the United States, rival factions in Asquith's government battled over whether or not to seek a negotiated end to the First World War. In this riveting new account, Daniel Larsen tells the full story for the first time of how Asquith and his supporters secretly sought to end the war. He shows how they supported President Woodrow Wilson's efforts to convene a peace conference and how British intelligence, clandestinely breaking American codes, aimed to sabotage these peace efforts and aided Asquith's rivals. With Britain reading and decrypting all US diplomatic telegrams between Europe and Washington, these decrypts were used in a battle between the Treasury, which was terrified of looming financial catastrophe, and Lloyd George and the generals. This book's findings transform our understanding of British strategy and international diplomacy during the war.

Daniel Larsen is College Lecturer in History at Trinity College, University of Cambridge.

Plotting for Peace

American Peacemakers, British Codebreakers, and Britain at War, 1914–1917

Daniel Larsen

University of Cambridge

CAMBRIDGE
UNIVERSITY PRESS

CAMBRIDGE
UNIVERSITY PRESS

University Printing House, Cambridge CB2 8BS, United Kingdom

One Liberty Plaza, 20th Floor, New York, NY 10006, USA

477 Williamstown Road, Port Melbourne, VIC 3207, Australia

314–321, 3rd Floor, Plot 3, Splendor Forum, Jasola District Centre, New Delhi – 110025, India

79 Anson Road, #06–04/06, Singapore 079906

Cambridge University Press is part of the University of Cambridge.

It furthers the University's mission by disseminating knowledge in the pursuit of education, learning, and research at the highest international levels of excellence.

www.cambridge.org
Information on this title: www.cambridge.org/9781108486682
DOI: 10.1017/9781108761833

First published 2021
Reprinted 2021

Printed in the United Kingdom by TJ Books Limited, Padstow Cornwall

A catalogue record for this publication is available from the British Library.

Library of Congress Cataloging-in-Publication Data
Names: Larsen, Daniel, 1985– author.
Title: Plotting for peace : American peacemakers, British codebreakers, and
  Britain at war, 1914–1917 / Daniel Larsen, University of Cambridge.
Other titles: American peacemakers, British codebreakers, and Britain at war,
  1914–1917
Description: Cambridge ; New York, NY : Cambridge University Press, 2021. |
  Includes bibliographical references and index.
Identifiers: LCCN 2020037949 (print) | LCCN 2020037950 (ebook) |
  ISBN 9781108486682 (hardback) | ISBN 9781108708197 (paperback) |
  ISBN 9781108761833 (epub)
Subjects: LCSH: World War, 1914–1918–Peace. | World War, 1914–1918–
  Diplomatic history. | United States–Foreign relations–Great Britain. | Great
  Britain–Foreign relations–United States. | United States–Foreign relations–
  1913–1921. | Great Britain–Foreign relations–1910–1936. | World War,
  1914–1918–Economic aspects–Great Britain. | World War, 1914–1918–
  Cryptography.
Classification: LCC D619 .L39 2021 (print) | LCC D619 (ebook) | DDC
  940.3/120941–dc23
LC record available at https://lccn.loc.gov/2020037949
LC ebook record available at https://lccn.loc.gov/2020037950

ISBN 978-1-108-48668-2 Hardback

For Mom and Dad

Contents

Figures

Map

Graph and Table

Dramatis Personae

August 1914–April 1917 (Arranged in alphabetical order, may exclude offices not mentioned in the text)

British

† Liberal Party Politician
★ Conservative Party Politician

H. H. Asquith†	Prime Minister (to December 1916) Leader of the Opposition (from December 1916)
Arthur J. Balfour★	First Lord of the Admiralty (May 1915– December 1916) Foreign Secretary (from December 1916)
Francis Bertie	Ambassador to France
Andrew Bonar Law★	Leader of the Conservative Party Colonial Secretary (May 1915– December 1916) Chancellor of the Exchequer (from December 1916)
John Bradbury	Permanent Secretary to the Treasury
Edward Carson★	First Lord of the Admiralty (from December 1916)
Robert Cecil★	Foreign Office Parliamentary Undersecretary (from May 1915) Blockade Minister (from February 1916)
Austen Chamberlain★	Secretary of State for India Manpower Distribution Board Chair (August–December 1916)
Winston Churchill†	First Lord of the Admiralty (to May 1915) Chancellor of the Duchy of Lancaster (May– November 1916)

Lord Crawford*	President of the Board of Agriculture (July–December 1916)
Lord Crewe†	Lord President of the Council (May 1915–December 1916)
Lord Cunliffe	Governor of the Bank of England
Lord Curzon*	Lord Privy Seal (May 1915–December 1916) Shipping Control Committee Chair (January–December 1916) President of the Air Board (May 1916–January 1917) War Cabinet Minister without Portfolio (from December 1916)
Lord Derby*	Director General of Recruiting (October 1915–May 1916)
Eric Drummond	Private Secretary to the Foreign Secretary (from 1915)
Sir Edward Grey†	Foreign Secretary (to December 1916)
Douglas Haig	Commander-in-Chief, British Expeditionary Force (from December 1915)
Reginald Hall	Director of Intelligence Division, Admiralty (from October 1914)
Maurice Hankey	Secretary to the War Council/Committee/Cabinet
Lewis Harcourt†	First Commissioner of Works (May 1915–December 1916)
Lord Hardinge	Foreign Office Permanent Undersecretary (from June 1916)
Arthur Henderson	Leader of the Labour Party President of the Board of Education (May 1915–August 1916) Paymaster General (August–December 1916) War Cabinet Minister without Portfolio (from December 1916)
John Maynard Keynes	Treasury Civil Servant (from January 1915)
Lord Kitchener	War Secretary (to June 1916)
Lord Lansdowne*	Minister without Portfolio (May 1915–December 1916)

David Lloyd George†	Chancellor of the Exchequer (to May 1915) Minister of Munitions (May 1915–July 1916) War Secretary (July–December 1916) Prime Minister (from December 1916)
Walter Long*	President of Local Government Board (May 1915–December 1916)
Reginald McKenna†	Home Secretary (to May 1915) Chancellor of the Exchequer (May 1915–December 1916)
Lord Milner*	War Cabinet Minister without Portfolio (from December 1916)
Edwin Montagu†	Chief Secretary to the Treasury (to February 1915, May 1915–July 1916) Chancellor of the Duchy of Lancaster (February–May 1915, January–July 1916) Minister of Munitions (July–December 1916)
Lord Northcliffe	Newspaper owner, including of *The Times* and *Daily Mail*
Lord Reading†	Lord Chief Justice
William Robertson	Chief of Imperial General Staff (from December 1915)
Walter Runciman†	President of the Board of Trade (to December 1916)
C. P. Scott	Owner and editor of the *Manchester Guardian*
Cecil Spring Rice	Ambassador to the United States
Frances Stevenson	Personal Secretary to Lloyd George
William Wiseman	Head of MI1(c) in the United States (from October 1915)

American

William Jennings Bryan	Secretary of State (to June 1915)
Clifford Carver	Secretary to Edward M. House (January–March 1916)
James Gerard	Ambassador to Germany (to February 1917)
Joseph Grew	First Secretary, US Embassy in Berlin (to February 1917)
Edward M. House	Wilson's advisor and confidant

Roy Howard	President of United Press
Robert Lansing	Secretary of State (from June 1915)
Irwin Laughlin	First Secretary of the US Embassy in London
Walter Page	Ambassador to Britain
Frederic Penfield	Ambassador to Austria-Hungary
Woodrow Wilson	President

German

Count Johann von Bernstorff	Ambassador to the United States (to February 1917)
Theobald von Bethmann Hollweg	Chancellor
Henning von Holtzendorff	Chief of the Admiralty Staff (from September 1915)
Arthur Zimmermann	Foreign Secretary (from November 1916)

Austro-Hungarian

Count Ottokar Czernin	Foreign Minister (from December 1916)
Karl I	Emperor (from November 1916)
Count Adam Tarnowski	Ambassador-Designate to the United States (from January 1917)

Preface

This book began as a project on British codebreaking and Anglo-American relations during the First World War, and now aims to be a combined diplomatic, political, intelligence, and economic study of British war policy and American mediation efforts during the First World War. Its unifying idea is that of an American peace. It argues that a key faction in the coalition of H. H. Asquith favoured the idea and that, owing to British economic policy, the coalition of David Lloyd George had made itself almost powerless to stop one.

This book reconsiders American mediation diplomacy itself. It explores the economic reasons that served as the principal cause of British interest in American mediation. It recounts the political debate within the British government both over this mediation diplomacy and over the fundamental economic concerns that drove British interest in it. Finally, it carefully reconstructs, to the extent possible, the role of British codebreaking and its effects as they relate to an American peace both within the British government and in the United States.

This book aims to augment traditional diplomatic and political history by adding in methodologically robust approaches to economic and intelligence history. The only methodologically comparable work in First World War history, at least in terms of its systematic and detailed consideration of each and all four of these dimensions, is that of Nicholas Lambert in the wartime chapters of his *Planning Armageddon*, which consider the British blockade through the end of 1915 and include a detailed consideration of the economic factors affecting decision-making as well as the intelligence apparatus underpinning the administration of the blockade.[1] This book similarly offers methodological improvement over the existing historiography not only in its combining all four dimensions in detail, but also in its novel approach to both economic and intelligence history. Its methodology concerning economic history benefits considerably from quantitative research, while its robust approach to signals intelligence enables significant historical reconstruction in the face of extensive document destruction and archival loss.

This book's argument arises out of an American diplomatic history core. It re-examines American mediation diplomacy and the British response to it during the period of American neutrality. Previous scholars have concluded that these American efforts were always doomed to failure and that none of the British leaders had any interest in them.[2] This book demonstrates by contrast that a number of leaders in Asquith's coalition showed genuine interest in them at almost every stage in 1916, excepting only a brief period around the month of August. It shows that, after Asquith's fall from power, the peace negotiations between Edward M. House and British intelligence officer Sir William Wiseman in December 1916 and January 1917 were not, as has been universally supposed, a rogue attempt at deceit by Wiseman, but rather formed a genuine attempt by Foreign Secretary Arthur Balfour to keep the possibility of American mediation alive.[3] This enables a fundamental reinterpretation of American mediation diplomacy in this period, showing where it was more effective and where it made mistakes, rather than dismissing it all as pointless.

The fundamental cause of this British interest in American mediation can be explained as a result of this book's approach to economic history. Past consideration of Anglo-American economic history and the balance of trade during the First World War – including both works primarily focussing on economic history and those aiming to combine political, diplomatic, and economic history – has almost universally taken a qualitative approach and looked primarily at the role of economic considerations in decision-making.[4] This book, by contrast, aims to go beyond these qualitative approaches by attempting to evaluate this problem quantitatively as well. Though a lack of a good wartime economic statistics enormously complicates this effort, this book aims not only to consider decision-making, but it also seeks to understand the underlying Anglo-American economics from a numerical point of view – an area of study with an almost completely barren historiography. The only serious existing quantitative study of the British balance of trade in this period is a 1952 work by British economic historian E. V. Morgan.[5] As Appendix I demonstrates, Morgan dramatically underestimated British government payments abroad during the war years, an error that renders his overall estimates of the British balance of trade effectively meaningless. Yet although clear evidence to make this rather straightforward computation has been readily available since the 1970s, previous scholars, in their qualitative approaches, have never detected this. In fact, Morgan's erroneous balance of trade numbers were relatively recently relied upon and reproduced *in toto*.[6]

By developing a clear quantitative understanding of the available data underlying wartime Anglo-American economics and its relationship to the principles of international macroeconomics, this book is able to elucidate more clearly the British Treasury's desired strategy as well as the consequences of the government's refusal to adopt it. By contrast, almost universally, excepting only Martin Farr, previous historians have never taken the Treasury's strategic views particularly seriously, generally seeing the department as obsessed with fiscal rectitude and pessimistically raising false alarms.[7]

This book clearly lays out the fundamental problem: American unwillingness to lend. This forced the liquidation of British assets deployable in the United States. By considering quantitatively the amount and pace of British asset liquidation in the United States,[8] the following chapters are able to demonstrate precisely *why* the alarms the Treasury rose in October 1915 and May 1916 were overly pessimistic at the time: in October 1915, the reason was departmental and allied overestimation of their spending requirements, and in May 1916 it was the Treasury's underestimation of British assets. The Treasury, however, was not wrong about the fundamentals. This quantitative approach is able to show that the Treasury warning in November 1916 about the impending exhaustion of British assets by mid-1917 was in fact accurate: an order for the compulsory seizing of American securities in January 1917 yielded the Treasury only small sums. Britain stood on the brink of financial exhaustion, notwithstanding the confident claims of some of its politicians to the contrary.

By having a clear understanding of the principles of international macroeconomics, this book is also able to make much better sense of the Treasury's economic aims, which focussed above all on maintaining British exports. As explained in Chapter 2, the principle of currency arbitrage in fact lay at the very centre of this strategy in mid-to-late 1915. Without understanding this principle, the Treasury's strategic views simply make no sense. Yet the concept of arbitrage has never before been mentioned in relation to the economics of the war, and in fact one economic historian, neglecting it, wrongly condemned the Treasury for advocating what he saw as a preposterously ineffective strategy.[9]

This book, however, is intended as a work for non-economists and for general readers, and so the presentation of this economic methodology has been approached very carefully. A more robust quantitative approach, despite its seeming complexity, does have some advantages in terms of reader understanding: most numbers in the book are carefully contextualized because they are typically expressed relative to GDP figures, and, wherever practicable, in US dollars.[10] Indeed, it is hoped that by the end of the book the reader will have developed something of an intuitive sense for the amounts of currency under discussion. The terminology, moreover, has been carefully chosen so as to maximize comprehensibility. For example, British efforts to borrow on collateral are purposefully described herein as 'mortgaging operations' to try to make clear that these should be understood principally as a means of disposing of pre-existing British assets. One can either sell a security, or borrow upon it: either way, the security is used up. The term 'collateral loan', by contrast, risks general readers conflating it with 'unsecured loan' as merely two different kinds of loans, and so the term is avoided.[11] Important macroeconomic concepts – including trade deficits, the gold standard, and currency arbitrage – are introduced as the narrative requires, and are explained, it is hoped, in straightforward and easily intelligible terms. Appendix I offers a fuller discussion of the economics involved and is directed more principally at economic historians.

Having thus established the fundamentals of the Anglo-American economic situation, this book reframes British political history during this period. Previous historians have divided the British Cabinet into two camps, pitting a prevailing group that favoured a consumptionist strategy against an unsuccessful group that favoured an alternative economic strategy. The historiography, moreover, has tended to favour strongly the consumptionist camp.[12]

This book, by contrast, styles the fundamental divide within the government as being instead between 'realists' and 'maximalists'. The 'realist' camp includes all of those who favoured one of three possible and reasonable strategies, which can be summed up in the following phrase: 'A total war army, colossal war supplies from the United States, and a long war: choose any two'. A small group most exemplified by Conservative Austen Chamberlain favoured emphasizing the first two of these three, wanting an all-out effort and a gamble for a win in 1916. The Asquithian Liberals and Conservative Arthur Balfour instead favoured a more economic approach that emphasized the latter two. All of these individuals, however, operated in a shared intellectual space, one that affirmed the necessity of making a choice. The 'maximalist' camp – consisting of Liberal David Lloyd George, most of the rest of the key Conservatives within the Cabinet, and Britain's military leadership – by contrast insisted that Britain did not have to make a choice: it could, they said, maintain both a total war army and these colossal American supplies, and it could maintain both of these indefinitely.

The robustness of this book's economic methodology allows for a clear, key judgement: the realists were correct and the maximalists were wrong. British assets did not, in fact, have the capability to sustain such a war effort as the maximalists demanded. This book's approach to understanding this political history, moreover, allows for the political divide within the British government to be understood with greater nuance. Chamberlain typically is identified only as a consumptionist along with Lloyd George and the rest of the Conservatives,[13] when in fact there was an enormous intellectual divide that separated him from the rest – a divide that grows in clarity over the course of 1916.

By thus reconceptualizing British political history in this period, this book is able to explain the political divide within the British government with respect to American mediation diplomacy. This divide over American mediation exists simultaneously as both a manifestation of the realist–maximalist divide and as an important effect of it. This book shows that the key political quarrels within the Asquith coalition over many seemingly disparate subjects – conscription, strategy, finance, munitions, industry, diplomacy – were in fact all part and parcel of one fundamental political debate playing out over and over again: one that ultimately was about the power of the United States and about Britain's ability to continue to rely on the United States as its key base of supplies. The debate over conscription, for example, is not a story of how the exigencies of war forced reluctant Liberals to overcome their ideology of *laissez-faire*, pitting a Lloyd Georgian faction that favoured 'coordinated state control' against Asquithians 'determined to resist state expansion', as it has often been portrayed.[14] Conscription, rather, merely provided yet another battleground for the realists and maximalists to argue over the limits of British economic power vis-à-vis the United States. As on most such issues, the maximalists eventually carried the day.

The fact that the realists continually failed to prevail in these other debates was a key factor in driving them to favour American mediation. The realists correctly understood that these British choices were increasingly placing the Allies into the hands of the American President and that, even absent American hostility, the extensive Allied dependence on American goods would have to end unless they could bring the United States into the war. Though there were differences amongst the realists in terms of timing, most eventually began to conceive of the war as unwinnable absent American military intervention, and American mediation seemed to offer an escape.

This realist–maximalist political framework is capable of explaining the Asquith coalition Cabinet's divide on American mediation with only two individual exceptions. Edwin Montagu was a realist who firmly rejected

American mediation, though he does not play a key role in the narrative until summer 1916, when his actions as Minister of Munitions become especially significant. His views and role are explored more fully in Chapter 6. More importantly, Lloyd George was a maximalist who tended to see the war as unwinnable on other grounds, and he broadly favoured an eventual end to the war through American mediation until the autumn of 1916, when he abruptly became a vehement opponent. This book relies on a robust intelligence history methodology, discussed below, to explain this key shift.

The fall of Asquith and his replacement by Lloyd George in early December 1916 is therefore a seminal political moment, one of enormous consequence for American mediation diplomacy, because it effectively ended the British political debate over the involvement of the United States. The causes, course, and effects of this key event are therefore reconsidered with the assistance of recently found documents that shed new light on Asquith's perspective and strategy during these crucial days.[15]

This key event also marks a fundamental shift in approach for the final two chapters of this book. The preceding seven chapters largely concern themselves with tracking the evolution of the realist–maximalist divide in Britain and its relationship to American mediation diplomacy. With the maximalists having won control of the British government in December 1916, the emphasis of the final two chapters is on the diplomacy of the United States. The focus on British political decision-making accordingly diminishes, albeit with two exceptions. The first exception lies in the re-examination of Balfour's foreign policy and his rogue efforts, as the key remaining realist in the government, to use Wiseman to quietly keep alive the possibility of American mediation notwithstanding his colleagues' unified rejection of it. The second exception lies in the critique of the political cowardice of the new Chancellor, Andrew Bonar Law. His new responsibilities seem to have awoken him to the gravity of Britain's economic problems after he had rejected their seriousness all year. Yet he remained fundamentally unwilling to alert his colleagues and to force a political confrontation over the radical economic measures that would have been needed absent American entry into the war. As for the measures he did take, they were so weak and ineffectual as to amount to a non-response to the deepening crisis.

Otherwise, the final two chapters return more explicitly to the book's American diplomatic history core, re-examining American mediation efforts between Britain and Germany, and subsequently between Britain and Austria-Hungary. For the former, this book offers a novel interpretation of the House–Wiseman talks. For the latter, it sees these as the most significant peace talks of the war, against a historiography that has tended to neglect them.[16] This book makes clear that the German declaration of unrestricted submarine warfare did not diminish Wilson's diplomatic determination to try to force a peace conference. This book's economic methodology establishes that he had the growing power to compel the Allies to attend one.

The key problem is to explain why he nevertheless abandoned this diplomatic course. Doing so requires turning to intelligence history and to the Zimmermann Telegram. A consensus increasingly sees the Zimmermann Telegram as having had only limited impact in the United States, rating German submarine warfare as more important in leading the Wilson Administration and American public opinion to war.[17] This book, by contrast, offers an innovative argument for the importance of the Zimmermann Telegram in the form of making a novel connection between it and the end of Wilson's mediation diplomacy in late February 1917.

This renewed study of the Zimmermann Telegram exists as the culmination of a robust intelligence history methodology that underlies the entire book. This book carefully reconstructs the signals intelligence dimension in Anglo-American relations, which has required a painstaking methodological approach. Even by usual intelligence history standards, the evidentiary base directly related to this intelligence is extremely fragmentary. Most of the relevant papers have been destroyed, including almost all of the archives of MI1(b) and much of the archives of Room 40. There is no surviving distribution list of who received the diplomatic decrypts that these organizations generated, let alone any clear indications in the surviving intelligence files of their impact. The few decrypts that do survive in ministerial papers do so only because the minister ignored clear instructions to burn them.[18] Most of the personal papers of Reginald Hall, the head of Room 40, have been destroyed, and he left behind only a small, self-serving archival collection.[19]

Yet despite these seemingly insuperable difficulties, extremely careful analysis has nevertheless made it possible to reconstruct much of the overarching intelligence narrative. The intelligence files that survive have been very carefully mined. The utility of these files has been augmented with a strongly developed technical understanding of the relevant American codes employed, of British codebreaking capabilities, and of the then-existing telegraphic communications network.[20] This has rendered it mostly irrelevant as to whether individual decrypts of particular telegrams survive: their texts can rather straightforwardly be reconstructed by consulting original American documentation. One can often gain a sense of the impact of these decrypts by carefully and consistently comparing these American telegrams to the papers of British policymakers. With a sufficiently exhaustive search, fleeting but striking similarities emerge, which can then be integrated into the overall narrative.

By contrast, with the exception of Lambert, most existing studies of British intelligence tend to be narrow ones focussed on intelligence history.[21] Wider studies, when they try to pay attention to intelligence, almost always do so according to the convenience of the limited fragments of evidence that survive in the papers of policymakers.[22] They almost never attempt a thorough, systematic study of the intelligence dimension that incorporates a serious and detailed examination of its technical elements.

This robust methodology allows this book to make four principal intelligence contributions. In order of importance, the first is in the reinterpretation of the Zimmermann Telegram episode in Chapter 9. The second is in the impact of the decrypts on David Lloyd George and their crucial role in wrongly convincing him of the hostility of the United States in the autumn and winter of 1916, which is documented in Chapters 6–8. The third is in showing how Lloyd George misused this intelligence, observing the political objectives that he sought to achieve as well as his recklessness in doing so. Lloyd George came profoundly close to disclosing this secret to Washington, the Anglo-American diplomatic – and therefore economic – consequences of which could have been dire. The fourth is in reconstructing the political efforts of the head of Room 40, Reginald Hall, to undermine American mediation within the British government. There is clear evidence that Hall had the motive, means, and opportunity to move as strongly against American mediation as he could. An exhaustive search of the archives has turned up a handful of fragments of evidence showing him acting to do so. But with such extensive archival loss, the evidence takes us no further than this, and the surviving fragments are insufficient to allow a clear, broad judgement as to the overall impact of his manoeuvring within the British government.

The combining of these four dimensions together allows for a complete and compelling novel understanding of American mediation as it relates to Britain during the First World War. Diplomatic history provides us with the fundamental subject matter. Economic history provides a compelling explanation for the motivations behind the interest within the British government in mediation. Political history allows us to chart the course and evolution of the internal debate over American mediation within the British government and to contextualize it within a much broader British strategic debate. Intelligence history gives us important factors contributing to, and in the end causing, mediation's failure. As the Conclusion summarizes it: diplomacy gives us the *what*; economics the *why*; politics the *how*; and intelligence much of the *why not*. Coalesced, these four approaches form a solid and durable whole.

Acknowledgements

For all his comments, questions, and insights, I would like to thank my former PhD supervisor and mentor, Professor Christopher Andrew. He originally set me loose with two pages from his book *Secret Service*, which provided the impetus for an MPhil, a PhD, this book, and a number of journal articles. I am very grateful for all of his attention and support. I would also like to thank my mentor at Trinity College, Professor Dominic Lieven, and my former PhD advisor, Dr Peter Martland, for their guidance and assistance. I am grateful to Professor Lloyd Ambrosius at the University of Nebraska–Lincoln, who originally started me on this path as my undergraduate mentor. I am very appreciative of Dr John Thompson, who served as internal examiner for my doctoral degree, for a number of stimulating conversations in recent years and for generously reading much of my manuscript and providing extensive comments. For many stimulating presentations and discussions, I thank the members of the Cambridge Intelligence Seminar, including my erstwhile fellow MPhil and PhD student, Dr Christian Schlaepfer. I am similarly grateful to Dr Jim Beach, Dr Gui-Xi Young, Dr Almuth Ebke, Dr Martin Deuerlein, Dr Joe Walmswell, Fergus Rattigan, and the anonymous reviewers for their very helpful comments.

I owe a significant debt to Dr Martin Farr of the University of Newcastle. When I contacted him about access to his PhD thesis on Reginald McKenna as Chancellor of the Exchequer, he very trustingly sent me his only personal hardbound copy. This highly significant and stirringly written thesis, now digitized and available online, played an enormous role in my development of this book's economic dimension, as did our extensive subsequent conversations in person, for which I am exceedingly grateful. I am also grateful to Dr Maren Froemel and Dr Solomos Solomou for their assistance in helping me to gain a deeper understanding of international economics as applied to this period.

I would like to acknowledge very gratefully the support, financial and moral, of Trinity College and Christ's College, Cambridge.

Chapters 3 and 4 of this book contain material derived from two journal articles I previously published with Taylor & Francis journals, which I acknowledge here:

"War Pessimism in Britain and an American Peace in Early 1916", International History Review 34/4 (2012), pp. 795–817. Available online: www.tandfonline.com/10.1080/02684527.2010.537123

"British Intelligence and the 1916 Mediation Mission of Colonel Edward M. House", Intelligence and National Security 25/5 (2010), pp. 682–704. Available online: www.tandfonline.com/10.1080/07075332.2012.702675

I am also grateful to Nevil Hagon for assistance in locating a cover image for this book.

Finally, my deepest gratitude and warmest affection goes to my family, and above all to my parents and grandparents, to whom I am deeply indebted and without whom this book would never have come to completion.

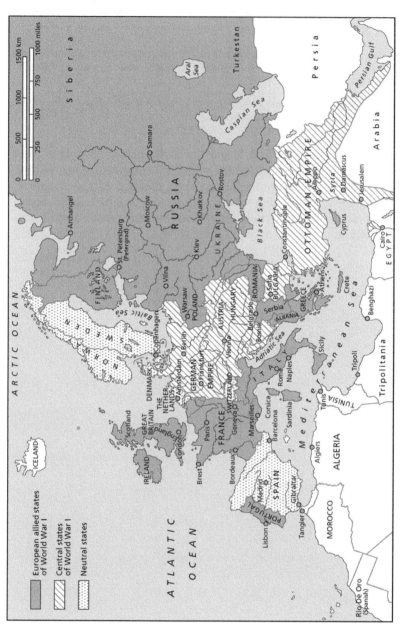

1 Map of First World War Europe

Introduction

In the early years of the Great War, as generals waged such visible carnage that claimed so many young lives, there was another side of the conflict, invisible not only to the public of the day but to history for more than a century. Immense copper cables traversing the Atlantic carried confidential messages destined for the American diplomatic outposts in the capitals of Europe – messages sent in the service of a noble goal: bringing the slaughter to a halt. Only a short walk from the residence of the US Ambassador in London, a nondescript building on Cork Street would house a secret team of British cryptanalysts. A year into the war, that team began working to solve US codes and soon was steadily deciphering American transmissions. As the codebreakers worked, an uneasy political truce hung over the city. Beneath the surface, tension seethed amongst government ministers and unelected military and naval officials, who possessed vastly differing views of how the war was to be won – or if it remained winnable at all.

The war had ground down to a bloody stalemate by 1915. For the next three years, the lines of the Western Front would barely budge. For all their troubles in Europe, however, some British leaders had their minds just as focussed on the other side of the Atlantic. The industry of the United States hummed as the British bought immense quantities of American supplies, but the rising republic's massive, untapped power otherwise remained aloof. Perhaps in other times that building on Cork Street, which would house a secret military intelligence division called MI1(b), might have formed the cornerstone for building the friendliest – if not exactly the most candid – of relationships with Washington. Yet with a right-wing intelligence chief seeking to manipulate leaders as they jockeyed over policy and power, this secret intelligence instead served to provide Whitehall's occupants with ammunition in their skirmishes with one another, and it was very nearly betrayed to the Americans in the process. With the fates of millions hanging in the balance, these British leaders battled over the ultimate question of war and peace – and, at the final key moment, British codebreaking destroyed the best chance for an early end to the First World War.

1

The United States lay at the centre of these leaders' battles, for Britain had never more needed the friendliest of relations with Washington. These supplies from America formed the foundation of Britain's powerful war machine. One can only marvel at the extraordinary British national effort that went into assembling that war machine in the two-and-a-half years before the American entry into the war in April 1917. Not only did the British muster from scratch a large and powerful land army, they deployed their economic might to buttress their alliance on an unprecedented scale. British factories churned out extensive provisions for this massive new military force and for Britain's allies. Even more impressive, however, were the colossal war provisions Britain arranged for the alliance from the United States. Under the aegis of a formidable British financial campaign, by the turn of 1917 the Allies were importing from America about as much as France was spending on its entire war effort. The British did all this without receiving more than modest loans from skittish American bankers and without a dime from the US government. Yet while this financial campaign was formidable – indeed, only the greatest of economic powers could even contemplate attempting such a feat – it was far from inexhaustible. In early 1917, it approached collapse.

Not everyone in the British government, however, looked to the west. A crucial conflict over the United States lay at the very heart of British policy for much of the period of American neutrality. Presaging the role that the United States would come to play in the twentieth century, many of Britain's leaders came to seriously doubt that, without the United States, the war could still be won at all. Taking a realistic view of Britain's capabilities, these leaders dreaded the consequences of exhausting this American supply line and disbelieved that the Allies could prevail before it collapsed. With the war looking increasingly unwinnable, they began looking for an escape: an end to the Great War through a compromise peace negotiated under the auspices of American diplomacy.

Yet those who recognized rising US power were forced to contend with a second, powerful faction that remained wedded to outmoded ideas of America's limited relevance on the global stage. These leaders envisioned the British Empire as the colossus that would continue to bestride the world during the twentieth century. An economically invincible Britain, they insisted, need never worry about such trifles as finance. They refused to accept either the existence of practical limits to British power or the significance of the burgeoning republic across the Atlantic.

As these factions battled for supremacy, the American leadership understood the power it wielded. Seeking to facilitate, and eventually to force, a peace settlement, the Americans pursued an adept diplomatic strategy. The success of their efforts depended fundamentally on European leaders' comprehension of the clout that this growing American leviathan could command. Not all, but some, in Britain were willing to understand. These leaders saw the economic dangers as they approached, and they recognized that British choices were increasingly delivering the Allied war effort into the hands of the American President. By mid-1917, his hands almost certainly held the power, had he desired, to compel the Allies to the peace table. Only a dramatic German decision, and a dramatic British codebreaking coup, stood in the way of that presidential desire. Past historians would have us dismiss these American mediation efforts as little more than an irritant to the belligerents, a mere 'distraction of peace during war'.[1] But the United States in fact loomed far larger in British minds, and it fuelled the fires of British Cabinet politics – fires that raged down an American fault line. The failure of an American peace was never foreordained. There existed a meaningful chance that the world might have escaped the brutality of the second half of the Great War, and been spared its world-shaking events that would reverberate down through the twentieth century.[2] The question is not why the final years of the war became inevitable. The question, rather, is why they had to be fought at all.

Britain marched to war in 1914 with vast global power. Its fleet ruled the world's oceans and immediately drove Germany from the surface of the seas. Powerful British telegraph companies shut down German access to the global communications network. Britain's bankers and manufacturers dominated global markets; the country could commandeer much of the world's productive capacity and press it into Allied service. An enormous British merchant marine worked to deploy that productive capacity into Europe. Only Britain could wall Germany off from the world, and only Britain could marshal the world behind the Allies.

Britain's continental allies in Europe, however, went to war with one thing that Britain lacked: power on land. France and Russia mobilized millions of soldiers in August 1914. The British Expeditionary Force raced across the English Channel numbering only some 250,000. This too Britain sought to transform, assembling millions of men into the New Armies, and the British soon possessed their own formidable share of the military might of the Allies. No one doubted Britain's continuing ability to wall Germany off for as long as the war could last. But as the realization sharpened that the war could last years rather than months, concern began to multiply over whether, even straining every nerve, this British Atlas could hold aloft all that was being asked of it – not merely in Europe but across the globe.

New York City, though an ocean away, held the answer. As the British sought to deploy much of the world's productive capacity on the Allies' behalf, they looked to their Empire, and they looked to neutrals. Above all others, however, they looked to the one great producer outside Europe: the United States. By necessity, London turned to New York. If the power of the budding American financial sector could be harnessed to the Allied cause, the two cities together could form the engine of the Allied global war. Only a few American firms responded to Britain's call, though they did so enthusiastically. The efforts of these firms spawned myths that the malign influence of the American financial class, burning with the need to recoup their investment into the Allies, secretly drove America into the Great War.[3] More recent have been assertions that American investors created a 'mutual dependence' that inextricably linked the United States 'to the fate of the Entente'.[4] But in reality, most American financiers had no desire to risk their balance sheets on the Allied war effort. The enthusiasm and influence of the pro-Allied minority could not make up for their raw lack of numbers. New York's answer to Britain was unmistakable: New York answered 'no'.

With the British pulling ever greater war supplies across the Atlantic, a number of British leaders, led by Chancellor of the Exchequer Reginald McKenna, faced the stark reality of New York's decision. They pressed their colleagues to realize the consequences of the choices they were making. It was still possible, McKenna argued, to continue bringing in such massive supplies from America. The British economy was an international juggernaut. If Britain kept up its global trade, he predicted that it would have the economic wherewithal to keep the financial campaign underwriting those American supplies sustainable for the foreseeable future. But this British Atlas, powerful though he was, had his limits. He could not both sustain a total war British army and keep up Britain's global trade simultaneously. For without sufficient British trade flowing out into the world, Britain had only one way to keep the world's production flowing into Europe. It could seek to liquidate what it could of the country's enormous international reserve of assets, which had been built up over decades. Assets, however, are governed by one ageless, and often inconvenient, maxim: when spent, they run out.

Without direct American government involvement, from 1915 onward the British government was confronted with a stark strategic trilemma. A total war army, colossal war imports from the United States, and a long war: choose any two. Britain could burn through its American assets with abandon to build a massive, abundantly supplied war machine and gamble for a win in 1916 – a strategy that might be termed 'Battle of the Somme or bust'. Alternatively, it could keep indefinitely in the field a very large but more leanly resourced army, while restraining Allied recourse to American provisions. Or it could deploy a significantly smaller but well-supplied army while seeking to coordinate potentially limitless economic assistance to its allies. Each of these three strategies was a reasonable path for a British policymaker to advocate, with arguments for and against each one. There was also room for compromise amongst these, space available in the middle of this triangle or along its edges: the smaller the army or the greater the restraint in their American purchasing, the longer their American assets would last. A difficult choice, however, had to be made.

Previous historians have tended to understand the British leadership by dividing it into two factions, which they have often termed 'economists' and 'consumptionists' – a 'party of caution' on the one hand and those who favoured unleashing British power to the utmost on the other.[5] With the exception of historian Martin Farr,[6] this 'party of caution', led by McKenna, has never been taken particularly seriously. Historians have dismissed it as having a 'fatuous' attitude of 'limited liability', one that 'impeded full British mobilization' out of an unhealthy obsession with 'fiscal prudence'.[7] These critiques, however, underestimate the sheer scale and unsustainability of Britain's economic wartime reliance on the United States. Of the three above-mentioned strategies, McKenna supported the last, wanting to emphasize supplying the Allies' economic needs and preparing for a longer conflict. But more broadly than that, he favoured the Cabinet simply making a choice amongst the three: 'It is no use undertaking to do a thing which you physically cannot do. ... I am looking at the question from the point of view of not attempting to do things which are physically impossible to be done'.[8] Only Martin Farr has treated McKenna's position with the seriousness it deserves: 'The Entente', he writes, 'was an inverted pyramid standing on the Dollar exchange'.[9]

McKenna and his allies in the government grasped this fundamental truth. It may seem deeply counterintuitive to say that the Allied war effort depended above all on something seemingly as trivial as a rate of currency exchange. The exchange rate, however, was merely the surface manifestation of a crucial fact at the heart of the Allied war effort: it depended on importing from the United States far, far more goods than the Allies could ever hope to export in return. Allied imports from the United States exploded from less than $1 billion before the war to at least $3.2 billion in 1916 – a figure that is likely a serious underestimate. The true number may reach some $5 billion.[10] By comparison, France in 1916 was devoting some $4 billion of its economy to its war effort; Britain, about $6 billion.[11] In essence, the British were attempting to marshal and pay for nearly a full extra allied economy's worth of war supplies. Though the French government contributed modestly, until the United States came into the war in 1917 financing this truly abnormal and precarious economic relationship for as long as humanly possible was effectively a British problem.

For those who understood this problem, led by McKenna, it drove their views on almost every aspect of the war. Sustaining this financial campaign depended above all on maintaining the strength of the British economy. The more they disrupted it to feed their ever-growing war machine, the less they could export to neutrals to offset their imports, the less they could supply their allies, and the more the entire alliance had to bring in from America. The more they imported, the more assets they had to liquidate, and the sooner those assets would run out.

Those who faced up to this problem held no illusions about Britain's standing in the world. They recognized that British power – for all its global vastness – had witnessed a generation of relative decline. In 1870, Britain had stood at the apex of the global economic system, its supremacy unrivalled. The United States, its only equal in terms of raw output, possessed none of Britain's financial prowess, and US attention was consumed inward as the British Empire continued to extend across the globe. Four decades later, however, Britain's economy had fallen behind those of the United States and Germany.[12] McKenna faced up frankly to this profound decline in British power: 'We are third of the three', he bluntly told his colleagues.[13] There were a couple of relatively minor members of the British Cabinet who understood this problem as McKenna did and who yet also favoured 'Battle of the Somme or bust' as British strategy. With their eyes fully open to the realities and risks, Britain, they argued, had to make its utmost effort now and gamble for a win in 1916.[14]

But the rest of 'consumptionists', as they have been termed, insisted that the British Empire was economically invincible. They argued for an all-out effort in 1916 while refusing to recognize that this represented any kind of a gamble at all. There was no such strategy, they insisted, of 'Battle of the Somme or bust'. Britain was the world's financial superpower: it would not, and could not ever, bust. Steadfastly denying that they had to make any kind of a strategic choice, they demanded not only that the war be fought on a massive scale for as long as necessary – 1917, 1918, or beyond – but that the gargantuan shipments of war supplies from the United States be continued all the while.

They demanded an impossibility, and they failed to appreciate that this course was to put them increasingly, and eventually completely, at the mercy of the American President. Instead, they fantasized that it was in fact *they* who held the whip in the transatlantic relationship, and not the Americans. They dismissed the importance of the United States as an independent power, refusing to view the American government as much more than a minor player. The Allies, they asserted, could afford to offend the United States with relative impunity. If the United States wished to enter the war on the Allied side, American assistance would of course be helpful. If not, however, it hardly mattered. They rained contempt on their colleagues, accusing them of muddle, of not getting on with the war, of not rising to the profound gravity of the military situation in which the Allies found themselves. McKenna objected to 'Battle of the Somme or bust' because he thought it wrongheaded; he objected to it more fundamentally still because so many of his colleagues insisted on adopting it while firmly shutting their eyes to the realities of its consequences. Few in the British leadership confidently expected to achieve victory in 1916, yet Britain's strategy was predicated on it.

The most fundamental divide within the British government that year, therefore, was not between alternative economic and consumptionist strategies. Rather, it was between those who faced the reality of the limit of British power and those who denied it. A faction of realists comprehended the grave risks that attended an all-out push in 1916. The other faction, of what are more accurately called 'maximalists', wrongly dismissed those grave risks as but figments of their opponents' overly anxious imaginations.

The maximalists' refusal to engage with this problem arose fundamentally out of arrogance and complacency, and was justified by a sense of righteous determination. They insisted on an economic view of the world in which little had changed since 1870, with Britain still able to strut about with the unchallenged swagger it had possessed in their youth. These men had never known London other than as the world's capital of business and banking. The dealings of powerful British financiers had reached for decades into every corner of every inhabited continent. Pound sterling served as the cornerstone of the global financial system: transactions amongst distant countries were routed through London simply as a matter of course. A seemingly unshakeable bedrock of stability, the City had not seen a major banking crisis since 1866, when most of the British leaders during the First World War had been mere children.[15] Even as grave an economic moment as the outbreak of war in 1914, for all its seriousness, caused only a momentary scare, and the British government's successful management of the crisis only helped to reinforce a sense of invulnerability. Few in government understood the intricacies of British finance, but all grasped the profound reservoir of power it gave them. For many, having lived their entire lives with British domination of the global financial system, the notion that this reservoir could ever be emptied seemed beyond the realm of conceivability. And so they dismissed those who forewarned otherwise as mere blinkered bean-counters, ones incomprehensibly obsessed with placing fiscal rectitude ahead of the immediacy of a life-and-death national struggle.

This grave political conflict over Britain's economic invincibility – with the United States at its very centre – governed almost every major debate within the British government before 1917. The realists in the government battled these fantasies of invincibility, seeking desperately to forestall the crash that their opponents denied could ever come. But as the maximalists repeatedly prevailed, those who faced the reality of their situation increasingly realized its impossibility. They had to get the United States into the war, and yet the Americans showed no signs of coming to their rescue. At least in one respect, the maximalists were not entirely wrong: the Allied military situation was indeed grave. In truth, all three of the strategies outlined above probably were inadequate to the task. To win the war, Britain probably needed a total war army, vast American supplies, and a long war – and, quite probably, a large American army as well.

To compound the British strategic thicket, for a number of ministers Britain's military options all seemed to have but the dimmest prospects of success. While a number of civilian leaders retained an unwavering faith in the generals leading Britain's armies, others increasingly saw Western Front offensives as little more than feeding men into an enormous killing field that consumed them to little purpose. To these sceptics, 'Battle of the Somme or bust' looked like a dreadful strategy in every respect: the battle seemed as pointless as the bust. They disbelieved that a large offensive there would produce significant results, yet the military insisted that there were no viable offensive options elsewhere.

Caught between the maximalists' denialism and the military promises they believed to be doomed to failure, many of the realists turned to the Americans. If New York would not help them win the war, then perhaps Washington at least could prevent them from losing it. Pessimism began to drive this faction's decision-making. Historian Brock Millman introduced the concept of 'pessimism' in the discussion of war aims, usefully defining the term not as an emotion, but as a purely rational construct – namely, the specific and serious doubt that victory remains achievable. Pessimism, to be clear, is not defeatism. A defeatist believes that the war is lost, and is prepared to accept whatever conditions the enemy may be disposed to offer, which otherwise would be regarded as intolerable. Though pessimists doubt victory, they are not yet prepared to admit defeat. Rather, a pessimist still hopes a tolerable, even though not victorious, peace can be arranged.[16]

Pessimism defined the outlook of several of the most important British leaders within H. H. Asquith's coalition government for most of 1916, with the exception of a brief period in the later summer. The Allied position was difficult. As Millman observes, the fact that the Allies were losing made any compromise peace in the short term challenging: 'Any peace negotiation, before the Allies had somehow redressed the balance, would simply establish in law what existed in fact – an Allied defeat'.[17] Pessimists no longer look for ways to win the war; they look for pathways to an acceptable peace. These pathways may include limited military offensives with the goal of improving one's negotiating position. They may also include looking to the diplomatic intervention of a friendly and powerful neutral to achieve more favourable terms at the bargaining table than could be obtained on one's own.

By early 1916, the United States was willing to provide precisely that kind of diplomatic intervention, ready to leverage its power in the pursuit of a general peace. Many of the British realists wanted to let them. Not all Europeans recognized it, but the power at the Americans' disposal was profound. Over the previous half-century, an extraordinary transformation had created an American economic powerhouse that had come to tower over its European competitors. The GDP of the United States roughly equalled that of Britain in 1870. By 1913, US GDP was larger than that of Britain and Germany combined.[18] This sheer American economic power, however, was raw and fledgling – tempered by an isolationist streak in American diplomacy, an inward-looking and underdeveloped finance, a relatively modest ability to project military force, and a politically fractious American Congress. Had the United States desired a greater global role, it might already have become the world's foremost geopolitical power. Instead, apart from a few recently acquired colonial possessions in the Pacific, the United States remained content with regional hegemony.[19] Some European leaders recognized the profound change in the transatlantic balance that had happened over the course of their lifetimes. Others did not.

From the moment the war began, the Americans looked for ways to bring it to a halt. Where British policymaking was fractured down a Cabinet of twenty-five, in the United States there were only two men who mattered: President Woodrow Wilson and his close advisor and confidant Colonel Edward M. House. House spearheaded these diplomatic efforts and worked tirelessly with his President to bring the belligerents around a conference table, with a conception of American mediation that steadily grew in ambition. Previous historians have always dismissed these American efforts as a mere fool's errand with no basis in diplomatic reality – 'a Don Quixote tilting at windmills'. They paint a portrait of House as unutterably naïve, susceptible to flattery, and prone to delusions of grandeur. He went to Europe prancing about playing peacemaker; no one had the heart to tell him that they had no interest, and so he deluded himself into thinking that he was succeeding.[20] There is one problem with this picture: none of it is true.

In fact, House had his fingers squarely on the pulse of opinion within the British government. He fostered trust and a surprising degree of honesty, his diplomacy tended to be astute and flexible, and his decision-making was generally sound. A masterful behind-the-scenes political operator and a quiet man of limitless tact, House had helped four consecutive Democratic governors win election in his home state of Texas – one of whom returned the favour by bestowing the honorific title of Colonel on him – before moving to New York and occupying a place on the edge of the national political scene. In the run-up to the 1912 presidential election, he forged an intimate friendship with then-Governor Wilson, who appreciated his talents and increasingly relied upon his advice. A few weeks after they met, their bond had grown so strong that, when House asked him 'if he realized that we had known one another for so short a time', Wilson replied: 'My dear friend, we have known one another always'.[21]

1 Edward M. House and Woodrow Wilson, c. 1915 (Hulton Archive / Getty Images)

House did not possess Wilson's formidable intellect or sharp sense of the public mood, but Wilson lacked House's almost unparalleled expertise in the politics of personal relations. House had an uncanny ability to get people to trust and confide in him, and a keen understanding of how to manage complex webs of human relationships. Deeply introspective and circumspect about his own ego, House sought to keep himself out of the limelight. He wanted no post or title in Wilson's administration, preferring to exercise influence quietly. Not merely did he dislike the public attention, he recognized that it both posed an obstacle to his goal of keeping Wilson's political relationships well-oiled and existed as a potential threat to his elevated position. Despite his status as the President's most valued advisor, his self-effacing manner kept him generally on good terms with Wilson's Cabinet, with most tending to view him as an ally rather than as a rival. Shunning accolades as he exercised global influence, House afforded his ego but one outlet: his diary. Keeping a running, but strictly private, tally of his thoughts and his quiet personal interventions and successes, House hoped to defer his plaudits to history. His efforts proved to be mostly in vain.

Through early 1917, House existed as the centre of the United States's mediation policy, and he and his President came within striking distance of succeeding. Both Wilson and House genuinely desired to bring about a peace settlement. There was never any meaningful breach of intentions between them,[22] but there was one important difference. Throughout 1916, only House tried to grapple seriously with the geopolitical realities of precisely *how* the United States might deploy its power to achieve peace. Only House tried to think through what kind of eventual settlement the United States should want, and about what secondary aims the United States should seek to realize along the way. Wilson, by contrast, tended to be more focussed on the domestic political implications of his foreign policy and on his more immediate diplomatic objectives. The President's thinking about congressional and public opinion could be impressively nuanced – more so than his chief advisor's – and his conduct in the daily rough and tumble of international diplomacy, when American interests and prestige were immediately at stake, have rightly tended to earn him high marks.[23] But at least until the beginning of 1917, the President never stopped to reflect on the complexities of the European war long enough to build a clear sense of how he might be able to stop it, or of what he might want the outcome of his mediation to look like. Wilson understood that a negotiated end to the war was in the best interest of the United States, but it took until the beginning of 1917 for his thinking about American mediation to go much deeper than this. When it came to mediation, everything else seemed to be mere details, and he entrusted the details to House.

Just as House found himself an intimate partner at home, he found a similar one abroad, gaining a close companion in his diplomacy in the ever-realistic – and yet sometimes also idealistic – British Foreign

Secretary, Sir Edward Grey. House counted himself blessed that 'fate has given me two such friends'.[24] Grey came to trust House as 'certainly a very intimate friend',[25] and the two developed a strong rapport, as they shared deeply personal thoughts and reminiscences of their backgrounds. House had grown up as a young, wealthy member of a new, rural Texas aristocracy; Grey had grown up a rural aristocrat at his family seat in Fallodon, Northumberland, before becoming a Liberal MP at the age of 23. Prime Minister William Gladstone had made Grey Undersecretary of State for Foreign Affairs at 30. Grey returned to the Foreign Office in the top post in 1905 and served as the architect of Britain's foreign relations for the next decade, controversially working to form what became known as the 'Triple Entente' with France and Russia and making it the cornerstone of his European policy.[26] Though his handling of the 1914 July Crisis has been debated, a recent magisterial re-examination of the crisis concludes that Grey 'emerges as the "man of action" … consistently work[ing] for a negotiated settlement of the dispute until the very end'. Amongst the key leaders involved in the Crisis, Grey and the German Ambassador to London Prince Lichnowsky 'are the two honourable men', and the 'debate about what Grey could or should have done flows from a later Lloyd Georgeian fabrication'.[27]

2 Sir Edward Grey (Library of Congress / LC-H261–4395)

Despite having worked so hard to preserve the peace, Grey helped lead his Cabinet and his country into the conflagration, but even so, in a private moment of emotion and frustration, Grey was seen slamming his hand upon his desk, exclaiming repeatedly: 'I hate war'.[28] His inability to prevent the conflict weighed heavily on him. To preclude it from ever happening again – and to solidify into place the longstanding British objective of a European balance of power – he repeatedly pressed the Americans to agree to take part in an international league to prevent future conflicts. As the war moved into 1916, Grey's appreciation of America's key role, both with regard to the war and to the global order more generally, led him to prize his connection to House. With their vital American supply link threatening to sputter, he saw this personal relationship as the only viable means of extricating his country from what increasingly looked to be an unwinnable war. A number of leaders in the realist faction joined him.

Britain's American supply link and American mediation existed as the most important of Grey's transatlantic priorities, but they were not his only ones. Grey faced a similar divide with respect to the United States within the government on other day-to-day frictions as well. As Anglo-American controversies emerged, especially over Britain's naval blockade of Germany, Grey consistently battled his colleagues to urge accommodation with the United States: every other issue paled in comparison with keeping the American supplies flowing and preserving the option of American mediation. He took a harder line with Washington only when he felt sure he would pay an acceptably small price in American irritation, or when his colleagues left him no choice. The 'blockade of Germany was essential to the victory of the Allies', Grey later summarized, 'but the ill-will of the United States meant their certain defeat'.[29] Not all of his colleagues, however, saw the threat of American ill-will so starkly – or even necessarily as a significant threat at all. When Grey lost control over the blockade in 1916, its new administrator shared little of Grey's trans-atlantic deference. By autumn, the blockade plunged Anglo-American relations into an ice bath. Wilson pursued his peace diplomacy that winter in a distinctly frostier mood.

Grey's other major problem was that of Britain's alliance. Britain did not fight the war by itself, but as part of a coalition. American peace diplomacy and the Allies' American supply link each held significant diplomatic peril. To hint to its allies that Britain was interested in a negotiated peace risked undermining the alliance and therefore held enormous dangers: Grey dreaded that it could cause 'something like a panic' if Allied governments detected any weakening of the British commitment to the war.[30] At the same time, Allied governments shared the maximalists' views of British capabilities, seeing Britain as an abundant and inexhaustible 'El Dorado' that could pay endlessly for whatever supplies were needed.[31] Despite the British Treasury continually advancing them generous funds for their American purchases, Allied leaders chafed at McKenna's efforts to exert even limited controls, seeing in them only incomprehensible British parsimony. The realists in the British government feared that honestly revealing the impending exhaustion of their American supply link could prove diplomatically catastrophic: 'If we fail to give the assistance they ask of us', worried one, 'they might have to consider the possibility of making a separate peace'.[32] Yet as the economic cliff-edge grew nearer, Grey became adamant that Britain was duty-bound to alert the alliance of the severity of the situation – and to do so *before* their allies took any public stand on peace moves. To an enormous degree, these twin diplomatic perils of finance and mediation were therefore one and the same: it was precisely this cliff-edge that was pushing the British realists towards peace diplomacy. A frank financial warning might push their allies there too.

It is in the Treasury, therefore, not the Foreign Office, that we find the very heart of the problem. As the officials who inhabited the Exchequer well understood, international economics requires equilibrium. It is certainly true that a government, wielding compulsory powers, can reallocate its own economy however it likes. Pressing a foreign economy into one's own service, however, is a different proposition entirely. One cannot get something for nothing. American producers want to be paid in American dollars. If Britain tries to sell the United States more pounds than it wants, ordinarily the system would right itself through a drop in the exchange rate. The pound would continue to plunge until the discrepancy is forced shut and equilibrium is restored. As McKenna tried to simplify the basic economics for his colleagues: 'In normal times the balance of trade would be quickly righted by an increase of exports and a reduction of imports, both stimulated by a fall in the exchange'.[33]

Yet of course, it is possible to sustain a trade deficit. Something, however, must offset it: ordinarily, investment flows would serve this purpose. For much of the nineteenth century, many countries ran large trade deficits with Britain. Being the world's manufacturer, sending its products out to every corner of the globe and getting many fewer goods in return, Britain necessarily became the world's banker. The pound did not go on surging endlessly against everyone else's currencies; instead, British banks invested their country's trade surplus abroad. World demand for British goods was offset by British demand for world investments. Equilibrium was reached – an equilibrium that went on year after year and turned the City of London into the world's financial centre.[34]

The gold standard complicates this simplification of international finance, but the underlying economic truth here remains the same: Britain wanted huge amounts of goods from the United States – much more than it was sending in return – and the deficit had to be offset somehow. Without a sustained, government-organized financial campaign offsetting this deficit, the pound would collapse against the dollar. The pound would drop until the discrepancy was forced shut and the massive flood of American supplies on which the Allied war effort depended fell to a small stream.

McKenna's Treasury explored four principal avenues to artificially offset this massive trade deficit. The first two asked New York to finance the deficit itself: encouraging American capital investment into Britain and obtaining American loans. But New York, it soon became clear, had little interest in providing anything approaching the capital the British required. Instead, the British government organized a massive operation to acquire and then to liquidate whatever British-owned assets that Americans were willing to take, along two principal avenues: shipping enormous amounts of gold while selling or mortgaging the vast British investments that had previously been built up in America. Both were by definition limited resources. What had been massive British investment in the United States, built up by British investors over decades, vanished in only a couple of years. By late spring 1917, Britain had sold or mortgaged almost every available British-owned investment in the United States and was down to its final tranche of gold reserves. The financial campaign keeping the Allies afloat in the United States stood on the verge of collapse, and likely with it the Allied war.

The internal British debate about this impending peril unfolded broadly upon party lines – a debate that took place in a deeply fragile political context of a hung Parliament. The Liberal Party, led by Asquith, had lost its parliamentary majority in 1910. Asquith had held on to his premiership principally by winning over Irish support: the smaller Irish Parliamentary and Labour Parties backed a Liberal government through May 1915.[35] Nine months into the war, Asquith exchanged his minority government for one of national unity. The Conservatives took half the Cabinet.

The two main factions in the government corresponded broadly, though not completely, to the two main parties. The Liberals tended to recognize the limits of Britain's economic capabilities. They understood the centrality of the United States to the Allied war effort and became increasingly pessimistic about Britain's ability to win the war without American assistance. At the same time, many of them became increasingly sceptical about the military's assertions that it could win the war on the Western Front. The Conservatives, by contrast, tended to insist that Britain operated under no meaningful economic constraints, that it could spend and import as it wished, and that the attitude of the United States made little difference. They also accepted the military's strategic choices and their promises of victory largely without question. There were, of course, important exceptions. A few Conservatives tended to share the pessimism of their Liberal colleagues, while there were a few Liberals who adhered strongly to the view that victory remained achievable. Finally, the shifting attitudes of Liberal David Lloyd George, who would become Prime Minister in December 1916, represent a central historical problem all by themselves.

The most important members of the Liberal faction most favourable to the United States were McKenna at the Exchequer and Grey at the Foreign Office. For most of the final year of Asquith's coalition, both men adhered to a pessimistic attitude, which lifted only briefly around August 1916, and both broadly supported convening a peace conference headed by the United States. Though sharply circumscribed by political necessities, their Prime Minister appears to have supported them. In late 1916, as the controversy increasingly spilt into the Cabinet, these individuals were joined by Walter Runciman, the President of the Board of Trade, and at least a few lesser Liberal lights. By the year's end, at least two Conservatives in the Cabinet were also convinced that a negotiated peace should be on the table: Lord Crawford and Lord Lansdowne, the latter of whom penned a famous Cabinet memorandum on the topic in November 1916 – a memorandum that received much more support than historians have recognized. Earlier in 1916 Arthur Balfour, the Conservative First Lord of the Admiralty and former Prime Minister, took a realistic middle position. He was less convinced than McKenna and Grey that the war was unwinnable, but increasingly came around to the possibility as 1916 progressed. The predominantly Conservative faction was led by Andrew Bonar Law, leader of the Conservative Party and Colonial Secretary, whose attitudes were supported by most other Conservatives in the Cabinet.

Driven, temperamental, and above all intensely political, Lloyd George represented a paradoxical faction of one: he was both a maximalist but also much of the time a pessimist. He helped lead the maximalist charge, demanding the largest of army expansions along with unlimited imports from the United States. He blithely and steadfastly refused even to consider the notion that these could not be sustained indefinitely, and he attacked his more realistic colleagues in the most personal of terms, accusing them of 'twiddling their thumbs' while their country's war effort burned.[36] Yet even as he vehemently insisted on Britain's economic invincibility, he simultaneously strongly believed that British military power faced enormous limits on what it could accomplish. He cleaved from his Conservative colleagues, who supported the military leadership's view that the war could and would be won on the Western Front, and he joined those who doubted the wisdom of large offensives there. It seems clear that from late 1915 onwards, except when it suited his political ambitions to say otherwise, Lloyd George believed that only a favourable compromise peace, not victory, could be achieved. Historian Brock Millman has argued that Lloyd George in 1917 and 1918 sought to pursue a military strategy aimed mainly at improving the Allies' negotiating position and not at winning the war.[37] In late 1915 and early 1916, Lloyd George spoke of a similar strategy, but with a key difference. He favoured limited offensives to improve the Allies' negotiating position, and then conducting the peace negotiations through the auspices of friendly American mediation to improve it further still. Yet Lloyd George swung from favouring American mediation at the outset of 1916 to regarding the United States with frosty paranoia by the year's close.

Decrypts produced by British intelligence fuelled Lloyd George's distrust. British intelligence officials deployed these decrypts politically, and while the material did not shake the friendly attitudes other British leaders held towards the United States, they succeeded in moving Lloyd George to outright hostility. British codebreaking's ability to produce these key decrypts arose out of a profound and unique advantage: Britain's control over world communications. A half-century before the war, a telegraph line had connected Europe and North America for the very first time. This transatlantic link had made communication between the continents possible in minutes, rather than days, and as the web of cables multiplied, a telegraphic revolution let loose a wave of globalization that transformed world affairs. Extensive British investment in telegraph technology over the second half of the nineteenth century meant that the world's communications networks converged in Britain by the twentieth. A majority of the planet's telegraph lines were either controlled by British companies or passed through British territory. Though liberal-minded Britain had eschewed any thought of trying to abuse this position for national advantage while the country remained at peace, this changed dramatically in 1914. A curtain of censorship descended, and the world quickly had to contend with British censors deciding which messages would be allowed to pass.[38]

Modern British signals intelligence was born in the opening months of the war, with the founding of two organizations that would later fuse and become Bletchley Park a generation later: the more famous Room 40 in the Admiralty and its lesser-known War Office counterpart, MI1(b).[39] Telegraphic censorship lay at the heart of both organizations' diplomatic decryption capabilities. Because of Britain's place at the centre of the telegraphic universe, huge numbers of diplomatic telegrams to almost every far-flung destination made their way on British-owned cables or across British territory. Even though it was under no obligation to do so, the British government nevertheless allowed neutral and allied governments to send encrypted telegrams over its telegraph lines.[40] Purely in intelligence terms, this concession proved a significant, if perhaps unexpected, advantage. The censors had unfettered access to copies of encrypted diplomatic telegrams, which could readily be made available to the twin signals intelligence organizations. Once MI1(b) or Room 40 had succeeded in cracking a code, the British could easily read large numbers of confidential diplomatic telegrams.

The US Department of State did nothing to make decryption of their telegrams particularly difficult. Reflecting a long-established culture of according little value to the secrecy of their transmissions, American codes were weak and the principal US diplomatic codebook went unchanged from 1910 to 1918.[41] MI1(b) succeeded in solving the American codebooks by the end of 1915, and because of British control over transatlantic communications, MI1(b) had virtually unlimited access to American diplomatic communications between Washington and Europe.

Yet while the cryptanalysts toiled in a relatively methodical fashion – with decryption duties split sensibly, if perhaps not purposely, between the two organizations – what became of the finished products afterwards was anything but orderly. Sharing was selective, discretionary, and often politicized, and the department that had the greatest interest in the material, the Foreign Office, too frequently found itself misled or kept in the dark. An arch-Conservative at the helm of Room 40 had no qualms about misleading his superiors in the pursuit of his own political objectives. Reginald Hall, the Director of Naval Intelligence, took decisions that ought never to have been his, suppressed intelligence for political reasons that his superiors and counterparts in other government departments had every right to see, and frequently engaged in underhanded intrigue in the service of his own political objectives. Known as 'Blinker' to his colleagues and subordinates owing to his rapid blinking,[42] he sometimes evoked a sense of awe in those who knew him. 'For Hall can look through you', the intensely pro-British American Ambassador to London, Walter Page, once wrote to President Wilson, and see the very muscular movements of your immortal soul while he is talking to you. Such eyes as the man has! – which is well, because he hasn't a hair on his head nor a tooth in his mouth. Some dreadful illness once all but killed him and left him a man of genius, a freak, if you will, as I dare say all men of genius are. My Lord!

3 Captain Reginald Hall (Library of Congress / George Grantham Bain Collection / LC-B2-3321-14)

'Now he tells me certain things', Page wrote, 'which he doesn't tell his own Government – that's my claim to distinction'.[43] The British government squelched Hall's plan to publish a memoir during his lifetime, but the self-serving chapters Hall produced before being forced to abandon the project[44] have left popular historians ever since proclaiming Hall a British intelligence hero.[45] Later examinations by scholarly historians, however, have rightly earned him much harsher evaluations.[46]

Just as intelligence was shared with him in a politicized way, Lloyd George had not the slightest compunction about using intelligence to achieve his own political ends, deploying it with an almost shocking degree of recklessness. From mid- to late 1916 onwards, as he received signals intelligence in his capacity as War Secretary, examples abound of Lloyd George misusing intelligence, especially when it suited him politically. Lloyd George's most astonishingly irresponsible intelligence moment came in February 1917, when he revealed to the American Ambassador that he had secretly been reading his communications. Only a tremendous amount of good fortune rescued Lloyd George from what would have almost assuredly been an explosive Anglo-American row.

Although separating Lloyd George's policy desires from his personal ambitions is not always easy, the incomplete and politicized way in which intelligence was shared with Lloyd George is a major factor in explaining his dramatic about face towards American mediation diplomacy during the autumn of 1916 – just as the government began to contend with the reality that 'Battle of the Somme or bust' had, in fact, busted. The assets sustaining Britain's American financial campaign were steadily diminishing and beginning to approach exhaustion. As the year drew to a close, the British again were faced with three paths. The first was to engineer a hard landing in their American expenditure and to fight on. The British would need to radically gut Allied imports from the United States, down to the level British trade could actually sustain, and to hope that their allies would not respond by abandoning them. The second was to end the war, 'presumably', as Grey wrote, 'through the medium of not unsympathetic [American] mediation'.[47] The third was not so much a choice as the inevitable consequence of refusing to choose: experience a sudden crisis as the pound collapsed. When the assets undergirding the financial campaign ran out, the inflexible laws of economics would see to it that the imports stopped. This would likely be accompanied by a financial crash and the destruction of British credit as the country would default on its international obligations. Whether the British liked it or not, unless they got the United States into the war, and soon, the alliance's colossal dependence on American supplies would be coming to an end.

Yet the divide in the British government remained unchanged. The maximalists continued to refuse to accept the necessity of choosing, and rained contempt on those who did. They demanded a fully manned total war army, unlimited imports from the United States, and the gutting of Britain's export industries through 'industrial conscription' – and they denounced any other policy as unacceptable muddle and procrastination. In November 1916, Lloyd George finally decided that he had had enough of Asquith and the other Liberals getting in his way. He became determined either to sideline them within the government or to evict them from it, and, after a series of dramatic and often outrageous political manoeuvres, he succeeded. Almost all of those who recognized the Allies' dependence on the United States were ejected en masse from the government. Any chance of the British government supporting a negotiated end to the carnage went with them.

Lloyd George and the Conservatives who dominated his government then made their denial of economic reality national policy. Though the War Cabinet briefly acknowledged a vague need to limit British orders in America, spending there in fact continued apace, even as the financial campaign sustaining it showed progressing signs of impending collapse. Britain's allies were never told of the gravity of the situation, nor were they instructed to cut back on their purchases. In December 1916, in effect, it became British policy that the United States would be in the war on their side by late spring – full stop. Lloyd George's government made no plans for what Britain would do should the Americans fail to enter the war on schedule, which by that point still showed signs of happening. Indeed, the government denied that it needed the United States to enter the war at all. The only key minister in Lloyd George's government who appears to have recognized the profound peril his country faced was its new Foreign Secretary, Arthur Balfour, who used his new post to try to mitigate the danger. Even as his colleagues firmly rejected even contemplating American mediation, he did all he could to quietly keep it open as an option to turn to should the threatened catastrophe arrive.

The Americans persisted in their peace diplomacy. They possessed profound economic leverage over the Allies in fact, although with the British government refusing to recognize it, not yet in practice. Apart from Balfour's quiet, indirect receptiveness, the remainder of Lloyd George's government saw only troublesome meddling in President Wilson's diplomatic attempts to insert himself between the belligerents over the winter of 1916–1917. Berlin desired a favourable peace, Washington a compromise peace, while London saw no reason for peace at all. In something of a small irony, it nevertheless was Lloyd George who managed to open up a diplomatic advantage with the President after a spate of public peace moves – an advantage that paid a small dividend into the rapidly deteriorating British financial campaign.

The German declaration of unrestricted submarine warfare on 31 January 1917, with its threat to American ships and the lives of their crews, changed everything, though not immediately. Refusing to give up on his desire to force a peace conference, Wilson only broke off diplomatic relations with Germany, while his economic leverage over the Allies continued to grow. The Allies were on their final tranche of assets; for a short time, one sympathetic American bank almost singlehandedly kept the desperate financial campaign afloat. Yet Lloyd George's government, and Britain's allies, continued to spend in America without restraint. Lloyd George was leading the Allies into profoundly dangerous waters, with the rest of the alliance blissfully unaware of the peril they faced. The Allies were almost wholly in Wilson's hands.

Wilson knew this, even if Lloyd George did not, and the American President persisted with his peace efforts by routing them through Germany's junior ally, Austria-Hungary. Its new, young emperor desperately sought the same thing Wilson did: a compromise peace. Both the Americans and the Austro-Hungarians were willing to go far in the pursuit of a settlement. In these quiet negotiations, the world saw its greatest and most serious chance for a peace conference before 1918. The Austro-Hungarians were desperate for one. The Americans stood on the verge of having all the leverage they needed to take Lloyd George to the peace table whether he wanted to go or not.

Yet Reginald Hall delivered the final key blow, one that shattered Wilson's determination to force an end to the war. In a dramatic intelligence coup, Hall obtained a crucial decrypt known to history as the Zimmermann Telegram, in which Germany tried to offer Mexico three American states: Texas, New Mexico, and Arizona. Despite the potential risks of revealing the telegram to the Americans – the decrypt had been obtained only because of Britain's breaking of American codes – Hall manoeuvred to ensure that the American leadership obtained this startling revelation. Despite being the First World War's best-studied intelligence episode, the Telegram affected neither the timing of American entry into the war nor American public opinion, as has usually been supposed. Instead, it blew up this final key chance for peace. The signals intelligence that had been deployed against an American peace within the British government was now deployed even more effectively against the American President. Not yet realizing Vienna's newfound diplomatic independence, Wilson conceived of his negotiations with Austria-Hungary merely as indirect ones with Germany. The Zimmermann Telegram confronted Wilson with proof of German duplicity and treachery in its starkest possible form. There could be no peace conference, he decided, with a German government so deceitful and dishonourable. After two-and-half years of trying, and just as he came nearest to succeeding, British intelligence brought Wilson's efforts to arrange an American peace to an abrupt end.

Soon thereafter, the first American ships were sunk by German unrestricted submarine warfare. The United States entered the war in April 1917 – and massive American government loans suddenly flowed into the British financial campaign just as it was writhing in its death throes. The help Britain could not get from New York, it finally got from Washington. Yet had the United States not entered the war almost precisely when it did, Lloyd George would be remembered today not as the man who won the war, but as the leader who drove his country off a cliff that he had emphatically denied even existed. He was rescued from the consequences of his denial only by the miscalculation of his enemy. The Germans unleashed their submarines on Atlantic shipping with the intent of cutting off the Allies' vital transatlantic supply link. In the ultimate irony, they wound up saving it instead.

For the remainder of the war, the American government lent billions of dollars to keep the link open and the supplies flowing. Once that American aid accelerated in July 1917, the threat at the very heart of the Allied war effort vanished almost overnight. Yet, though some in the British government certainly believed otherwise,[48] the fact that this threat never materialized did not mean that it was never real. For over a year-and-a-half, it loomed over the Allied war effort, governing virtually every important debate within the Asquith coalition, with many of its members anticipating that the threat could well prove fatal. Ultimately, it led to the coalition's collapse. The government that replaced it obliviously barrelled headlong into the danger, and succeeded in escaping it only by the narrowest and luckiest of margins. But it was a closely run thing, and it could just as easily have gone the other way.

This is the story of why it did not, and of why there was no peace before 1918.

1   The First Year of War
August 1914–August 1915

Even from before the moment the war began, the Americans looked for ways to make it stop. On the day of Archduke Franz Ferdinand's assassination in June 1914, Edward House had already been in Europe for a month, getting his first taste of shuttle diplomacy as he attempted to lay the groundwork for a project to decrease tensions and promote disarmament. He had met the Kaiser in Berlin and had then headed over to London for his first meetings with Edward Grey . In early July 1914, his efforts finally may have been getting very slowly off the ground only to suffer one of the most unfortunate cases of poor timing in modern history.[1]

Amidst a tidal wave of war declarations emanating from world capitals, the White House issued its first mediation offer to the belligerents on 4 August 1914.[2] Less than two weeks later, in a neutrality appeal to the American people, Woodrow Wilson declared that the United States stood as 'the one people holding itself ready to play a part of impartial mediation'.[3] Secretary of State William Jennings Bryan tried to get peace talks going in September, but, loathing secret diplomacy, conducted them in 'a blaze of publicity [that] … wrecked [whatever very small] chance of success the negotiations might have had'.[4] House, meanwhile, would next spend a few fruitless months trying to work quietly with the British and German ambassadors in Washington.[5]

With the European bloodshed just beginning, peace as yet had no chance. As the German Army hurtled into Belgium and then France, Britain and the United States most shared worries over finance, not mediation – in an episode that would leave some British leaders learning entirely the wrong lessons. War panic set off a global financial meltdown, above all in the heart of the world economy, the City of London. Fearful London banks refused to lend, and many called in their extensive global short-term loans, including those in the United States. Liquidity evaporated. Panic selling on European stock exchanges forced governments to shut them down as investors desperately sought to move their holdings into cash.[6]

The City cracked its financial whip over New York – the final time in history it would have the power to do so. The American banking sector spiralled into crisis as it sought to comply, urgently seeking to repay the loans the British banks had called in at the same time that Europeans were selling huge amounts of American stocks and bringing their money home. With so many investors trying to sell their dollars so as to buy pounds sterling, the pound surged more than 15 cents to be worth over five US dollars.[7] To modern eyes accustomed to floating exchange rates, with currencies regularly shifting every day, this little strengthening of 3 per cent hardly seems more than a blip – perhaps a minor news story at best.

Under the gold standard, however, this little shift in fact represented a serious financial emergency. Currencies used to be exchangeable for gold, and as a result exchange rates were never supposed to move. One used to be able to take a US dollar to the US Treasury and demand about 23 grains of fine gold. A pound, meanwhile, could be taken to the Bank of England and redeemed for about 113 grains of gold. This ratio determined the exchange rate. A pound was worth just under five times as much gold as a dollar was. A pound should always, therefore, be worth just under five dollars – or to be more precise, $4.86½.[8]

A deviation as small as five cents in either direction from this value represented not an inconsequential momentary fluctuation, but instead revealed a currency to be under constant and considerable pressure. Remove the pressure, and the rate should ease back to its normal value. Under ordinary circumstances, after all, why would traders accept a bad exchange rate when they could simply convert their funds into gold and ship it – and thereby get their money at $4.86½? Normally, it required no more than a deviation of a few cents for it to be advantageous to go through the hassle of converting into gold and shipping it across the Atlantic.[9]

With exchange rates locked in place in this way, these gold flows would offset any momentary trade deficits that might develop. One country would get real useable goods, the other would get shipments of yellow metal. To sustain a deficit, one had to have enough gold to cover it, but in normal times this was rarely a problem. Surpluses would be run with some countries, deficits with others. Complex self-adjustment processes involving prices and money supply helped to keep these relatively small. A bit of gold flowed from this country to that, one year in one direction and the next the other way around. Most of the time, the exchange rates barely budged.[10]

Between 1889 and the start of the war, the pound had never once broken $4.90.[11] An exchange rate holding at more than five dollars per pound meant that American traders were so urgently trying to get their hands on sterling that they were willing to pay a considerable premium to do so. In the midst of the crisis, briefly the rate spiked wildly to as high as seven dollars, a sign of a desperate willingness to get sterling at almost any price.[12] Over the next year, the British would rapidly find out what happens when there was not nearly enough gold to cover their deficit. For now, however, the situation seemed, if anything, to reinforce a sense of British financial invincibility. Most of the time, when a country finds itself in crisis, panicky investors pull their money out, with the currency taking a resulting tumble. Only countries with profound financial strength have the problem of people being desperate to get their money *in*.

In the United States, the Secretary of the Treasury, William McAdoo, acted decisively to stem the crisis. He accelerated the founding and implementation of the Federal Reserve system – one of the crowning achievements of Wilson's 1913 domestic agenda – and he shuttered the New York Stock Exchange for four months, not to prevent a crash in prices, as might be imagined, but to contain the pressure on the exchange. American buyers stood ready to pick up European panic selling of American securities, but if the Europeans were allowed to pull all that money across the Atlantic, the already weak dollar could collapse. For the British, this shuttering would prove an unintentional blessing: Britain soon would sorely need these American securities to offset their trade deficit. Rushing emergency legislation through Congress, McAdoo kept liquidity flowing and, importantly, he resisted pressure to end convertibility with gold, boosting confidence in the relatively fledgling American financial system.[13] The largest US investment bank, J. P. Morgan & Co. ('Morgan's') , joined in by leading a number of banking initiatives to relieve the situation.[14] American gold flowed fitfully into British coffers, trying to maintain the dollar against the enormous amounts of capital flowing out from New York and across the Atlantic.[15] These measures helped ameliorate the situation, but, as the crisis originated in Britain, what Morgan's and McAdoo needed was a restoration of financial calm in London.

The task of coping with the panic gripping the British financial sector fell primarily to David Lloyd George, Chancellor of the Exchequer. Dubbed 'the great outsider' by one of his biographers, Lloyd George grew up speaking Welsh as his first language – the only Prime Minister ever to have done so – and, along with his practical legal education, he stuck out amongst his well-heeled, Oxbridge-educated political contemporaries. Energetic and always embarking on a novel scheme to tackle some unresolved problem, Lloyd George lived impulsively in the political moment. As President of the Board of Trade from 1905 to 1908 and then as Chancellor of the Exchequer until 1915, he pushed through a number of reforms, including the People's Budget, a major series of social measures that laid the foundation for the modern British welfare state. An accomplished mediator, Lloyd George had a gift for persuasive speech and proved an expert conciliator between warring parties – provided, of course, that he was not one of them. When challenged, this ruthless master of political manoeuvre tended to prefer embarking on risky and sometimes outrageous gambits to achieve his goals over compromising. Often devious and deceptive, he tended to regard the truth as a soft and supple thing, often constituting whatever would best suit his political agenda at any given moment. Intensely ambitious and extremely self-confident, he loved the limelight and proved a master manipulator of the British press.[16]

4 David Lloyd George (Library of Congress / George Grantham Bain Collection / LC-B2-3629-3)

Yet for all his effectiveness as a politician, Lloyd George had little patience for the day-to-day managerial duties that formed the mainstay of ministerial responsibility. By the start of the war, he had nearly a decade's combined experience at the two cabinet posts most responsible for the management of the British economy. He ought to have been the closest thing to an economic expert the Cabinet possessed, but instead he had managed to remain deeply ignorant of economic and financial affairs. Leaping from subject to subject seemingly at random – a habit that led his subordinates in the Treasury to label him 'the Goat' – Lloyd George would happily master the most intricate details related to his latest scheme, but otherwise had little interest in the purpose of his departments or the complexities of their operations.[17]

Agile in a crisis, however, his 'innocen[ce] of economics'[18] did Britain no harm in the first month of the war. The Bank of England suffered a domestic run on gold, with its reserve sliding from an already modest nearly £40 million (France had much larger pre-war reserves of around £140 million) to less than £10 million in the first days of the war. Caught up in the general panic swirling around him, initially Lloyd George unwisely wanted to pull Britain off the gold standard, which would have been a severe and unnecessary blow to confidence.[19] Prime Minister Asquith, however, previously a Chancellor himself, refused to approve the suspension of gold payments, and an emergency intervention from the young economist John Maynard Keynes at Cambridge University persuaded Lloyd George against the idea, unless the Bank of England actually were to come completely to the point of running out of gold.[20] Indeed, Britain and the United States were the only countries globally to remain on the gold standard in 1914 – though, to be precise, the British connection to the gold standard would steadily become ever more tenuous. Soon, Britain did all it could to encourage the domestic deposit of gold into the Bank of England for international use, and it would make gaining private access to the bank's gold all but impossible.[21] Staying on the gold standard as everyone else abandoned it, however, gave the world's financial confidence in New York a significant boost and confirmed Britain's position as the global financial superpower.[22]

Once Lloyd George overcame his initial panic, he handled the crisis with aplomb. With a highly competent team of advisors and working well with the Governor of the Bank of England, Lord Cunliffe, Lloyd George deftly handled negotiations with the country's leading banks. Declaring an extended bank holiday to give them time to respond to the crisis, he and his team drove through a number of initiatives that succeeded in getting liquidity unstuck and credit moving again.[23] Famously declaring that Britain remained open for 'business as usual', Lloyd George won the praise of his colleagues[24] – Walter Runciman, the capable President of the Board of Trade, commented admiringly on how Lloyd George, despite understanding virtually nothing about financial markets, nevertheless had led a 'marvellous' rescue of the situation.[25] Lloyd George himself rather implausibly credited his ignorance rather than his advice for the success, later bragging that it was precisely because he 'knew nothing about finance' that the Treasury was able to execute the rescue.[26] Confidence slowly came back, and British markets reverted to a semblance of normality. The Americans felt a deep sense of relief: as calm in Britain returned, the crisis in America passed. The pressure eased, the gold stopped flowing, and the exchange rate slid back to where it was supposed to be.[27]

This crisis, however, left Lloyd George and other British leaders learning all the wrong lessons. The episode seemed to confirm Britain's unassailable global economic position, and it left an impression that there was no crisis that the Treasury could not weather: one needed no more than some financial creativity and competence, and perhaps a dash of flair. The correct combination could always be found, and in the end all would be well. Just over two years later, Lloyd George would harken back to his triumph at this moment to mock a dire Treasury warning: 'The same fears', he said with disdain, 'were expressed on the outbreak of war'.[28] The Chief of the Imperial General Staff would echo the sentiment: 'Before the war', he would write dismissively, finance itself was supposed to be 'a complete bar to a great war ever taking place'.[29] Lloyd George had sorted it all out in 1914 seemingly without much difficulty. There surely was little need for finance to intrude upon Britain's strategy or diplomacy – let alone to justify something as preposterous as seeking a compromise peace because of it.

The executor of this rescue subscribed to this view wholeheartedly even while still Chancellor of the Exchequer. Having successfully calmed the initial financial panic, Lloyd George all but considered his war work as Chancellor complete. Even with Britain's expected role as financial and economic leader of the Entente, soon becoming effectively its paymaster, Lloyd George felt that the financial colossus that was the British Empire would easily 'withstand anything which war might present it' and that it required little more of his attention.[30] Should another crisis present itself, he believed he could solve it just as he had done with the first. Until then, however, he wanted to go and solve real problems, and the Treasury for the moment declined to present any that seemed very serious, and certainly not in comparison with that of the overall war. He all but turned out the lights at the top echelons of the Treasury, expecting it to play no further serious role in the management or direction of the war. The Treasury existed only to pay the bills and get out of the way. Paving the way for later financial crisis, he ordered a complete stop to any Treasury scrutiny of or control over war expenditures. The service departments could spend whatever they wanted, wherever and whenever they liked. Lloyd George all but abandoned his civil servants as he left them to find the way to pay for the war.[31] Many historians have commented, usually with admiration, on Lloyd George's indefatigable energies over the first nine months of the war. They exploded in an omnidirectional burst: speeches rallying the nation, military strategy, munitions and supplies, industrial productivity, labour disputes. Nothing, it seemed, escaped Lloyd George's roving eye. He even found time to combat his colleagues over launching a nationwide campaign to restrict alcohol consumption.[32] All of this, however, came at the expense of the Treasury: by the time of the May 1915 political crisis that resulted in his leaving the Chancellorship, 'Lloyd George had been for months effectively Minister without Portfolio'.[33]

With Lloyd George paying attention to everyone's department but his own, the country found itself without an economic strategy and with a complete mismatch between its military and economic policies. The totality of the country's pre-war planning presupposed a war conducted almost exclusively on a naval and economic basis, with no army commitment beyond that of the initial deployment of the British Expeditionary Force. As War Secretary Lord Kitchener began forming the New Armies, the extensive voluntary recruitment in the first months of the war caused considerable economic disruption. Nearly 1.2 million men enlisted in the first four months of the war[34] out of a total labour force of some 20 million.[35]

For the duration of the wartime Liberal Cabinet, until May 1915, '[n]aval and military policy was decided apart from economic policy'. The formation in November 1914 of the War Council, a leading Cabinet committee on which Lloyd George sat, did nothing to ameliorate the situation. The lack of coordination permeated all aspects of policy: 'For example, there was no discussion of how the Dardanelles operation [against the Ottomans] would be affected by the growing shortage of merchant tonnage in the spring of 1915 or how the operation would affect British trade by diverting merchant ships into war use'. Certainly Asquith must bear some of the blame, but few historians have taken Lloyd George to task for his failures here, so dazzled have they been by his energies elsewhere.[36] But what, after all, is the point of including the Chancellor of the Exchequer in the War Council if not for him to point out and coordinate the key economic aspects of the war?

Perhaps the only major positive financial development during the remainder of Lloyd George's tenure at the Treasury, the appointment of Morgan's as the British commercial agent in the United States, arose not out of Lloyd George's attending to his duties at the Treasury but, if anything, out of his efforts to take charge of munitions.[37] The first few months of the war saw 'confused and costly buying practices' as the War Office, Admiralty, and Lloyd George all competed with each other and with their allies for American contracts – including a particularly embarrassing episode in which Lloyd George nearly found himself competing against the War Office for the very same contract with the same American manufacturer. Morgan's was subsequently appointed as the sole British purchasing agent with a mandate to rationalize what had previously been a disorganized mess and thereby 'sav[e] the government millions of dollars'.[38]

The role of British supplier quickly and naturally evolved into that of British banker, a role that perfectly suited Morgan's, which was by far the most powerful of America's banks. The 'bankers' bank and the leader of Wall Street', as it has been called,[39] Morgan's had almost singlehandedly saved the American economy during a severe financial panic in 1907.[40] In 1913, the bank had demolished its old headquarters at the corner of Wall Street and Broad Street in New York City – some of America's most expensive real estate – and promptly rebuilt it at considerable cost. The elegant new building, an ostentatiously modest four stories set amidst skyscrapers, jutted powerfully out towards the intersection at the heart of America's burgeoning financial centre.[41]

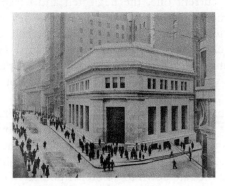

5 Headquarters of J. P. Morgan & Co. (Library of Congress/LC-USZ62-124435)

For most Democrats, including the Wilson Administration, the bank symbolized everything wrong with America. Morgan's epitomized the odious and unaccountable 'money trusts', which were regarded as having a deeply malevolent influence over American life.[42] Loyally Republican, the bank returned the Administration's antipathy twice over.[43] Whatever the political drawbacks of banking with antagonists of the President, the British otherwise found Morgan's ideal for their purposes. With convenient sister firms in London[44] and Paris and enthusiastically Anglophile, the bank's knowledge of American markets and suppliers proved invaluable. As did its assets: Morgan's genuinely and fervently supported the

Allied cause[45] – eventually to the point in 1917 of being willing to back
Britain with massive financing when the country found itself in the
deepest throes of crisis. J. P. Morgan himself would soon take two bullets
for the Allies, surviving an assassination attempt by a pro-German fanatic
in July 1915.[46]

Try as it might, however, Morgan's could not get Lloyd George to pay
attention. Mere finance did not satisfy Lloyd George's 'restless itch for
achievement and accomplishment'.[47] Apart from his obligatory presence
at financial talks with the Allies, his only real task was to prepare and
present two war budgets, which generally went poorly, and he purposefully ignored the advice of his civil servants to increase taxes.[48] As
historian Martin Farr has put it: 'It has been offered in mitigation that
the Chancellor was too occupied elsewhere to attend to his budget: a
defence for a Chancellor voluntarily relinquishing direction and control
of the economy without parallel'.[49] In the meantime, he 'presided over
the near collapse of morale amongst his officials'. His previous permanent secretary had quit in 1913 over Lloyd George misleading the
House of Commons. His current one, the neglected and exasperated
Sir John Bradbury, effectively had been left to run the department
himself. Bradbury very quickly had enough, telling Asquith during
the May 1915 political crisis that he would quit if Lloyd George
were re-appointed.[50] For his part, Lloyd George regarded his separation
from his top civil servant with equanimity: 'Bradbury', he wrote, 'can
go to hell'.[51]

The financial whip was passing from London to New York. While the
pound had surged against the dollar at the outbreak of war, by early
1915 the pound came – as it would remain for the duration of the war –
under significant pressure. As British war orders in America multiplied,
demand for dollars pressed the rate down to $4.80 per pound. Worrying
Morgan immensely, the weight only showed signs of intensifying. Some
gold was being shipped to America, and Lloyd George airily waved
through a small loan scheme involving Morgan's and a couple of other
American banks to support the exchange, but these could offer no more
than temporary relief. Despite having the support of the Governor of the
Bank of England for stronger steps, neither the Governor nor Morgan's
could get the busy Lloyd George, who was consumed with other war
matters, even to consider the problem. The Chancellor was '"fully occupied" with other pressing matters'. '[K]nowing [the] mentality of the
Chancellor', they wrote, it came as no surprise that they could not get
him 'to appreciate a difficult situation especially on such [a] complicated
matter'. Morgan's concluded that the problem probably 'would have to
become worse' before Lloyd George would even look at it.[52]

Undoubtedly, Morgan's was right, though it would not get the chance to find out.

As Britain neglected its growing transatlantic economic problems, on the other side of the Atlantic House refused to give up on his efforts to mediate the war. Though he quickly discovered that it remained far too early, House was beginning to lay the diplomatic foundations for American mediation the following year – by which time Britain's economic problems with America would be at the forefront. In late January 1915, Wilson and House decided to dispatch House to Europe to see whether, as one historian put it, 'the prospect [of peace] was quite as gloomy as it looked'.[53] House almost immediately discovered that it was, in fact, every bit as gloomy as it looked. House instead set about trying to build closer relations with Britain, France, and Germany, aiming to convince all three to make use of the good offices of the President when the time came to make peace. The Allies and Germany had no direct diplomatic relations with each other. A neutral country, therefore, would eventually be needed to facilitate peace negotiations, whatever the military conditions might then be. House sought to ensure that this neutral country would be the United States, and he worked to undermine Wilson's two principal diplomatic rivals, the King of Spain (Alfonso XIII) and Pope Benedict XV: if he could get the two of them 'safely out of the way, there is no one else I can think of in sight'.[54]

At this early stage of the war, House still put strict limits on how far the United States could possibly go in its involvement in peace negotiations. Grey delicately but forthrightly told House that there was no prospect of any kind of peace negotiations in the near future. Once the Allies had made far more military progress, however, Grey actually wanted Wilson to be present at the table for the peace negotiations. Even more importantly, to ensure that this horrible war would never be repeated – and to lock in a European balance of power – Grey wanted the United States to become a guarantor of the peace settlement, perhaps as part of some international organization dedicated to preserving a permanent peace. Both of these possibilities House rejected out of hand. It was 'not only the unwritten law of our country', he told Grey, 'but also our fixed policy not to become involved in European affairs'. 'Mediation' at this point meant only that House wanted the United States – and not Spain or the Vatican – to play the key role in setting up the peace negotiations. Once the conference had been convened, it would be up to the belligerents to sort out the peace terms themselves. Then, after a peace treaty had been agreed, House wanted a second convention bringing the belligerents and neutral countries together. This second convention would establish new rules for any future wars while also discussing methods of preventing such wars altogether.[55]

All the while, House was telegraphing the President detailed reports of his talks.[56] The pair trusted their insecure coding arrangements completely, which involved combining a State Department code with an additional set of private codewords. House and the President often personally encoded and decoded the telegrams themselves to prevent any possibility of leaks to the press.[57]

As House transmitted his reports, however, British intelligence was hard at work crafting a new tool, one that under different political circumstances might have helped British policymakers to better manage and control their spiralling transatlantic vulnerabilities: solving the American diplomatic codebooks. Instead, this seemingly enormous intelligence advantage actually would serve only to damage Britain's relationship with the United States. The twin British signals intelligence agencies, MI1(b) in the War Office and Room 40 in the Admiralty, began their lives as small teams, and only slowly geared up into the highly organized, complex machinery that they would become. Originally tasked with attacking German military and naval codes, the two agencies steadily acquired more staff and in 1915 began to take on decryption responsibilities going beyond the War Office's and Admiralty's immediate tactical needs. Room 40, named after the group's main room in the Old Admiralty Building, developed out of a need for accurate information about German naval movements. At the war's outbreak, the Director of the Royal Navy's intelligence division, Captain Henry Oliver, tasked his old friend Alfred Ewing with creating a group to work on breaking German naval codes. When Oliver was promoted, Captain Reginald Hall took his place. Hall battled Ewing for control of Room 40, with Hall eventually pushing out Ewing entirely in late 1916.[58] Early in the war, Room 40 focussed almost exclusively on decrypting intercepts of German naval wireless transmissions. Despite some problems with the effective distribution and use of this material, Room 40 generally succeeded in keeping close tabs on the German High Seas Fleet, providing accurate intelligence whenever it set out to sea.[59]

In the autumn of 1915, a separate "political" cryptanalytic division was created, and its primary focus was on German diplomatic codes. This new division essentially reported directly to Hall, leaving Ewing to focus on naval decryption for the next year. While this new division worked on several important German channels of diplomatic communication, including between Berlin and Madrid, it was the Berlin–Washington link that proved the most important to Britain's relationship with America.[60] The problem of how the German Ambassador in Washington, Count

Bernstorff, was communicating with the German Foreign Office bedev-illed Room 40's political division for nearly a year, until the late summer of 1916.[61]

From practically the beginning of the war, the Swedes, who were officially neutral, had been covertly helping the Germans with their communications. At first, Bernstorff gave his messages directly to the Swedish legation in Washington, which evaded British cable censorship by disguising them as Swedish diplomatic telegrams to Stockholm. The Foreign Ministry there then retransmitted them to Berlin. In early 1915 – before the political division of Room 40 had been created – the British Foreign Office caught wind of this procedure and issued a complaint, bringing this practice to an abrupt halt.[62] The Swedes, however, would continue to help the Germans by a more indirect route. First Bernstorff would transmit his telegrams to the German legation in Argentina. The Swedish legation there would then transmit the messages to Stockholm, which would then pass them on to Berlin – the 'Swedish Roundabout', as it would come to be known. After all, who in Britain would think to carefully scrutinize encoded Swedish communications with South America? Until the summer of 1916, the scheme would work precisely as intended.[63]

MI1(b), meanwhile, can ultimately trace its origins to a primitive pre-war intelligence group. A three-man team was formed at the beginning of the twentieth century within the Military Operations Directorate, which came to be known as 'MO5a' and was tasked with studying ciphers 'among many "odds and ends"'.[64] After war broke out, with the German military on the march in late 1914, the British Army found itself 'intercept[ing] enemy wireless' messages, which this group became tasked with deciphering. The Military Intelligence Directorate would be founded in December 1915. The slowly expanding team, which in the interim had confusingly been redesignated MO5e and then MO6b, would immediately be relocated into the new directorate and given the designation that would follow it until 1919: MI1(b).[65]

Its efforts to compile the three US diplomatic codes began sometime 'early in 1915', at the same time that the Western Front was becoming static and the Germans were steadily replacing their army wireless com-munications with telegraph wires. Since those telegraph wires could not be tapped, the work that had consumed the group from the beginning of the war 'practically dried up'. With spare time on their hands, the budding codebreakers decided to turn their attention to neutral diplo-matic codes. Even with the weakness of American codes, an internal official history makes clear that the efforts to solve them were slow going: 'The work was entirely fresh to all members of the staff, there were no past records as guidance, and the problem of how to solve large code books had to be thought out ab initio'.[66] By September, the military intelligence organization largely solved the principal American diplomatic codebooks. By the end of the year, it would be able to read all American telegraphic communications passing between Washington and its diplomatic posts throughout Europe.

When it came to accessing transatlantic communications, MI1(b) and Room 40 enjoyed a massive advantage over their continental rivals. Thanks to the enormous investment of British telegraph companies in the technology over the previous half-century, almost all of the numerous transatlantic cables to North America were under direct British control, as they were connected either to Cornwall, England, or to Kerry, Ireland. This effective British monopoly over the transatlantic telegraph meant that all American diplomatic telegrams to and from Europe had to be routed through Britain – with the cable censors carefully making a copy as they went by. French codebreakers could only get copies of those telegrams sent across France, and German codebreakers could only get ones sent from Germany. MI1(b), by contrast, would get everything.[67]

Fortunately for House, his detailed telegrams to the President this time around seem to have done him no harm. Though MI1(b) would be reading everything when the Texan would next embark on European travels, by the time House sailed home in June 1915, the group, though hard at work on the problem, did not yet seem to have managed any success against his telegrams.[68]

After four months in Europe, House returned seemingly empty-handed. He had, however, established good relations with leaders in London, Paris, and Berlin, laying the groundwork for future mediation initiatives,[69] and he believed that he had succeeded in seeing off the King of Spain and the Pope as potential diplomatic rivals.[70] In particular, he was on warm, intimate terms with Grey – so much so that the Foreign Secretary often talked with House more freely than he did with members of his own government. When significant portions of House's diary were published in 1926,[71] Maurice Hankey, the trusted Secretary to the War Committee, was 'horrified' to discover in the diary matters so sensitive that they could be found in the War Committee minutes that Hankey himself had been recording. These matters even included secret British military plans. House was treated 'on the footing of a Cabinet colleague', Hankey wrote, and 'undoubtedly this was carried too far'.[72] Grey even made secret arrangements to allow himself and House to communicate by telegraph directly, bypassing the ambassadors in London and Washington,[73] and Grey continued to press House about American participation in an international league. 'Germany is the peril today', Grey counselled House as he was preparing to depart, 'but the peril will recur every century in Europe, if Europe is left to itself. And the peril now cannot be confined to one continent – the world is too closely knit together'.[74]

While House was shuttling about, the war ground on. The Germans announced the beginning of unrestricted submarine warfare for the first time, and the shocking sinking of the passenger ship *Lusitania* in May 1915, killing nearly 1,200 people of whom 128 were Americans, sent German–American relations into a tailspin from which they would only ever partially recover.[75] Germany's dramatic actions on the Atlantic grievously offended the Americans; British policy on the seas by contrast annoyed Washington rather as a consistent, irritating hum. Britain's efforts to close off Germany's access to the sea lanes provoked a steady drone of American complaints. For now, the Allies' transatlantic vulnerabilities remained limited. Yet even though these American complaints were not yet backed up by potentially war-ending American economic leverage, Grey proved presciently sensitive to growing US power.

Seeking to mute the irritation as best he could, Grey consistently worked to minimize Anglo-American diplomatic conflict, even at the expense of the efficacy of the British blockade. A recent in-depth, albeit academically controversial, study of the blockade goes so far as to argue that Grey's deference to the Americans fatally undermined an intended British strategy of economic warfare against Germany.[76] The academic controversy notwithstanding, it is certainly true that Grey made the case repeatedly within the British government about the need to accommodate American concerns, and he often overrode American protests only when the Cabinet ordered him, even from the very beginning of the war. In the earliest example, when Wilson in August 1914 wanted the American government to buy up the German mercantile vessels interned in American ports, a palpable violation of international law, Grey preferred doing nothing. The Cabinet, worried these vessels would be used to ferry Germany supplies, overruled him and insisted he issue a protest; the scheme subsequently died in the US Senate.[77] So began a near-constant buzz of irritation between the State Department and the British government, with Grey typically trying to play intermediary, generally with success. Indeed, a pair of studies focussing on the US perspective marvel at how much of the blockade Grey was able to get the Wilson Administration to acquiesce to. The Americans, they say, would certainly have been within their rights to have put up far stiffer resistance and probably could have forced the British to back down. But both Grey and Wilson tended to prefer accommodation over confrontation, and Grey manoeuvred carefully to try to keep the blockade from becoming anything more than an annoying Anglo-American buzzing.[78] Its noise level certainly varied, but the din nevertheless would continue almost without interruption through the American entry into the war.

Over on the mainland of Europe, a surprise invasion of the Dardanelles, led by Britain and supported by France, Australia, and New Zealand, aimed to knock the Ottomans out of the war by capturing Constantinople. It failed miserably.[79] The stalemate on the Western Front continued to consolidate, despite offensives on both sides,[80] including for the British a partial success in a relatively small attack at Neuve-Chapelle in March and then a failure in an equally limited offensive at Aubers Ridge in May.[81] The Commander of the British Expeditionary Force, Sir John French, provoked a serious political crisis following the May defeat. He had assured the War Office that he had sufficient guns and ammunition before the attack, but then afterwards, in a politically devastating leak to *The Times*, he blamed the loss on the government, charging that it had failed to equip his troops with adequate weaponry. Under threat of open Conservative attack in Parliament amidst the resulting 'Shells Scandal', Asquith moved to bring the Conservatives and the much smaller Labour Party into a government of national unity, with a necessary reshuffle.[82]

Heeding Bradbury's advice, Asquith got Lloyd George away from the Treasury, compensating him with the privilege of being Man of the Hour by putting him in charge of new Ministry of Munitions. Keen to avoid any appearance of being demoted, Lloyd George insisted that he was being moved out of the prestigious Exchequer only 'temporarily', a contention that has been rightly rejected on '[t]he grounds … that it makes no sense'.[83] Lloyd George's Liberal arch-rival, a man in whom the Prime Minister had far greater financial confidence, Reginald McKenna, rose to the Chancellorship.

When McKenna stepped into the Treasury for the first time on 25 May 1915, the bureaucrats rejoiced 'with an ecstasy'. 'It is glorious to see how happy the civil servants are', reported Edwin Montagu, returning to his post as Financial Secretary, the second-ranking ministerial job, after a four-month hiatus. 'They at last believe they can trust this Chancellor not to give them away and to do business instead of avoiding it'.[84] The Liberal McKenna's promotion to Chancellor, when Asquith's new Conservative coalition partners had a strong claim to the office, represented Asquith's lack of trust in the abilities of the Conservative leadership as well as his determination to show that the new coalition was being formed on his terms.[85] Asquith regarded McKenna as one of the most capable men in his Cabinet, and certainly so on matters of finance. A competent and reliable manager who happily delved into his department's day-to-day work, McKenna had previous experience at the Treasury, enjoying success as Financial Secretary beginning in late 1905 under Asquith as Chancellor.[86] Though some found Asquith and McKenna 'in some ways a curious pairing',[87] they complemented each other well. Abrasive and blunt, McKenna had a sharp edge that the ever-tactful and socially adept Asquith frequently found himself needing to smooth over. Unlike his Prime Minister, McKenna could be awkward and was generally unpopular – except with his civil servants, in whom he consistently inspired devotion.

6 Reginald McKenna (Library of Congress / George Grantham Bain Collection / LC-B2-6056-2)

Whatever their differences of personality, Asquith and McKenna shared a similar temperament, proceeding always in a deliberate and considered way. They found that they liked each other immensely and formed a close political partnership. So impressed had Asquith been with his deputy's work that, when Asquith took the premiership in 1908,

McKenna was the top choice at the Exchequer for both the new Prime Minister and the civil servants at the Treasury. The ambitious and ever-intriguing Lloyd George outmanoeuvred them. Lloyd George had been an energetic President of the Board of Trade, and, always taking care that his successes were widely publicized, he had already began building up a significant personal following in the country. Lloyd George 'put a pistol to Asquith's head', demanding the Exchequer for himself and threatening to resign if not promoted. Throwing up his hands, Asquith handed McKenna the Admiralty instead, and then the Home Office in 1911, both offices in which he excelled.[88]

That incident in 1908, however, began a spiralling deterioration in relations between Lloyd George and McKenna, which by 1915 had descended to a point of mutual hatred. As historian Martin Farr has put it, the 'feud between McKenna and Lloyd George reached a malevolence exceptional even for the ill-tempered and antagonistic coven of which it was the centre'.[89] Where McKenna and Asquith made for a complementary pairing, McKenna and Lloyd George were polar opposites in almost every way. When it suited Lloyd George's purposes, he had no compunction about saying one thing to one person at breakfast and the opposite to another before lunch (such a situation is discussed in Chapter 7). Although McKenna could stay quiet when he needed to, Lloyd George's more scrupulous rival would prefer to say precisely what he thought at both meals, usually not much caring if he offended at either or both. He loathed Lloyd George's belief in malleable truth and referred to him as 'Lliar George' when writing to anyone he trusted. He detested Lloyd George's impulsiveness: 'Prevision is not Lloyd George's strong point', he complained. 'His peculiar genius is an exact appreciation of public feeling at the moment', with no regard for future consequences. Lloyd George, in turn, found his colleague's staid manner intolerable. Referring to another even-tempered colleague, Lloyd George wrote that this other colleague nevertheless 'has a quixotic strain, say 20%. But it is there. McKenna has no 20%!'[90] Lloyd George craved and lapped up public adoration, after the war penning some 3,500 pages of memoirs spanning six volumes.[91] McKenna viewed the public with indifference, and the public tended to view him the same way. After the war, he refused a knighthood and a peerage, declined interviews, and beat away publishers. After the publication of a particularly venomous volume of Lloyd George's memoirs – even Lloyd George worried he may have included 'too many digs at McKenna' – McKenna wrote to a friend about his refusal to engage publicly with 'Lliar George': 'My own view is to disregard everything he says. Don't forget the old warning – "never get into a fisticuffs with a chimney sweep."'[92]

Seeking to remedy what he saw as the 'hopeless financial disorder' left in his predecessor's wake at the Exchequer, McKenna went immediately about turning the lights back on.[93] Ten months late, the Treasury was finally mobilizing as a key department in the war. The new Chancellor, 'a little rattled and overwhelmed by the magnitude of the task',[94] struggled amidst an avalanche of responsibilities, including in his first days an obligatory but ill-timed mission to meet with his country's newest ally, the Italians, who had just been induced to join the Allies with dangled promises of swathes of Austro-Hungarian territory.[95]

Soon, the Treasury would be completely consumed with the problem of sustaining the alliance's insatiable demand for American supplies, to the point that McKenna and his allies in the Cabinet would favour completely reorienting British strategy around it and eventually seeking to end the war. For now, however, with everything else going on, though attuned to the problem of the American exchange, at first McKenna and his subordinates underrated it. They believed it could be solved as part of a larger, urgent British fiscal initiative, the Second War Loan, and that the problem needed nothing more than temporary expedients until this larger scheme got off the ground. The loan sought to raise an unlimited sum, and upped the interest rate from Lloyd George's previous issue by a percentage point to 4.5 per cent.[96] Lloyd George later slammed the higher interest rate as unnecessary and wasteful[97] – a particularly rich critique given that Lloyd George's previous attempt to raise funds, the First War Loan, had barely managed to raise a bit more than half of its announced £350 million target. The Bank of England had helped Lloyd George cover up the failure, secretly providing the rest of the funds so that the Treasury could falsely claim the loan was oversubscribed.[98] In any case, Lloyd George's criticism 'assumed the loan was concerned with investors' money, whereas its objectives were deflationary, political, and determinedly Atlanticist'.[99] McKenna sought primarily to sop up spending power amongst the public so as to reduce inflation and imports, to boost confidence, and, especially, to encourage American investment capital into British coffers. The interest rate needed to be, as one civil servant wrote, 'dear enough to tempt New York to invest in sterling',[100] where prevailing interest rates for long-term bonds were similarly around 4 per cent.[101] McKenna expected the resulting investment flows from America to effect a 'substantial rebound' in the exchange.[102] The loan, he planned, would solve all of Britain's financial problems at a stroke.

7 British war loan poster from 1915 (Library of Congress / POS-WWI-Gt Brit, no. 198)

It did not work out that way. The loan provided a massive £570 million boost to the government's domestic funds, diverting into government coffers funds equivalent to about one-fifth of UK GDP, but very little of that came from New York. What little that did come across the Atlantic was able to provide only 'modest and temporary relief' on the exchange.[103] As the *Wall Street Journal* put it, 'our bankers do not care to invest'.[104] This pursuit of capital inflows from America to offset the British trade deficit proved not so much a financial avenue as a dead end. Given the massive sums required, at best this could only help at the margins. Perhaps the flipside of this situation was more important: nothing should be done to spook Americans into pulling any monies already in Britain home and making a grave situation that much worse. American capital in Britain may have paled in comparison to the reverse, but it was not exactly trivial. The Bank of England estimated that foreign deposits in Britain totalled at least $500 million and 'probably reach a much higher figure'.[105] The spectre of a collapse in confidence triggering capital flight sharply circumscribed the Treasury's options. Any draconian solutions to Britain's financial problems, were they to set off a panic, would carry the considerable risk of doing far more damage than good. 'Confidence is essential at all costs', the Bank of England was warned.[106] Even worse, this worry formed one axe of many that the American government constantly held over McKenna's head, as a simple adverse US government statement could easily frighten American capital into taking flight. American money already in Britain needed to stay there.

The day after the Second War Loan applications closed in mid-July, a Morgan's representative was already meeting with McKenna to warn that the situation required urgent action. The loan making little difference, continuing demand for dollars had pressed the exchange rate down to $4.77, a deviation of nine cents from par, and despite Morgan's attempts to support sterling at that level, the situation seemed only likely to worsen. At the moment, conditions seemed abnormal and under pressure but stable. Morgan's worried: were the rate to break the psychologically important ten-cent deviation barrier, American markets might begin to wonder whether something was quite wrong, and then move accordingly. Though the British were alert to the problem – Morgan's even had a meeting with an attentive and troubled Asquith over the issue – the government nevertheless found itself paralyzed by debate and infighting. The 'autocratic' and strong-willed Governor of the Bank of England, Lord Cunliffe, whose relations with the abrasive McKenna were already severely strained, continued to insist that foreign exchange, traditionally the bank's responsibility, should remain the bank's responsibility, and he resisted McKenna's attempts to take charge. A frustrated Morgan's wished a 'pox on all their houses', believing that none of them were taking their country's predicament seriously enough.[107]

Predicament became crisis on 21–22 July, when Morgan's warned that their previously agreed-upon measures for containing the pressure to $4.77 had reached exhaustion. The government could either act or allow the barrier to be breached. At an emergency meeting, Cunliffe asked McKenna what they should do; McKenna sarcastically replied that he thought that 'this is what you call a matter of exchange. Is it not for you', but then moved quickly. McKenna arranged a gentleman's agreement with Prudential Assurance, an insurance company, whose headquarters lay less than two miles from the Treasury and which had $40 million in American investments. The Treasury got permission to mortgage these securities, which it did with Morgan's help, and topped them up with a modest Canadian loan and further gold shipments. Morgan's continued to be able to contain the ongoing pressure to $4.77, at least for another few weeks.[108]

This financial avenue – the selling or mortgaging of American investments owned by British citizens or companies – would form the principal boulevard on which the British would travel in offsetting their trade deficit over the next two years. Britain's decades of acting as the world's banker gave them an enormous reservoir of foreign investment upon which to draw. Possessing a sprawling commercial empire, Britain had foreign investments in 1913 approaching $18 billion,[109] a massive sum equal to over a year-and-a-half of Britain's entire economic output. Of this, about $4.25 billion had been invested in the United States, a majority of which in its railroads. The ability to liquidate this economic empire provided the British with an extraordinary international reserve. Had the United States been a more outward-looking country – with adventurous investors eager to snap up Britain's worldwide commercial holdings – this reserve could have easily provided the Allies with a number of years' worth of massive American war imports. The United States, however, had long been a debtor nation, not a creditor one. American investors were a provincial lot. For most of them, their interest in opportunities outside their own borders could, on occasion, be made to reach as far as Canada.[110] As one Canadian observer wrote after the war:

Borrowing in New York is very different from borrowing in London. London has been for generations an international money market … The public in the United States had no such experience. They found all the investments they needed in their own country and had little knowledge of foreign investments. Canada they knew [only] because we were their next-door neighbour.[111]

The usefulness in New York of Britain's international reserve, therefore, did not much extend beyond British investment in American rail. But this supply was still formidable, and, with American investors more than happy to have these assets, they formed a large and reliable source of funds. Indeed, a key problem was, as the *New York Times* put it, 'no one kn[ew]' precisely how large this source was.[112] The figure of $4.25 billion was carefully tabulated by economic historians years later. The only thorough estimate at the time, from 1910, put the total at only $3.3 billion – meaning that Britain had a moderately larger US investments reserve than it thought.[113] Of course, as a tool of trade these investments had some limitations. If sold, the investments had to be sold at a careful pace: if too many were sold too quickly, their price would collapse. If mortgaged, someone had to be found that was willing to lend upon them. Above all, like gold, these investments were a limited resource: once exhausted, they could not be renewed.

If McKenna and his colleagues at the Treasury had underestimated the gargantuan task that lay in front of him before these difficulties, distracted by the sudden sea of work – McKenna had, after all, been in post for only eight weeks – they would never make that mistake again. Even in the midst of the crisis, McKenna recognized its wider implications, warning his colleagues that further disruption to the British economy 'would render our financial task so difficult and burdensome as disastrously to impair our financial position and imperil the supply of food, raw materials, and munitions to this country and our Allies'.[114] He complained that the Treasury had neither 'control nor precise know-ledge' of munitions purchasing in the Unitesd States, and asked Lloyd George to curtail his American orders. Lloyd George, who considered the situation little more than a temporary aberration worsened by McKenna's incompetence – after all, they had had no such problems when Lloyd George had headed up the Treasury – refused to comply.[115]

For the next few weeks, McKenna and his team devoted their energies to carefully studying the problem. Morgan grew impatient. It was bearing the immediate brunt of the situation, privately slamming McKenna in frustration for relying on his team of 'second class advisers who really cannot do anything for him'.[116] Considering that his team included the highly competent John Maynard Keynes, soon to become one of the greatest economists of the twentieth century, Morgan's assessment seems to have been more emotional than considered. The Treasury's delay was due not to 'complacency, but rather deliberation in lieu of precedent', a not unreasonable defence considering the complexity of the technical issues involved as well as the completely unchartered waters in which it found itself.[117] Perhaps moving with careful deliberation was wise, for it seemed to have come into the next crisis with a strategy to respond. But the Treasury did little to head it off.

While the Treasury cogitated, Lloyd George did everything in his power to make the next crisis much worse. Lloyd George has been heralded as the 'wizard' at the new Ministry of Munitions; he waved his organizing wand and commanded British munitions production to soar – and soar it did.[118] Lloyd George, however, had precisely the same attitude to the United States, without any regard for the financial conse-quences. Upon taking office, Lloyd George looked across the Atlantic and just about wrung his hands with glee: 'From what I hear we can enormously increase the American output, and what is equally import-ant, we can expedite it'.[119] The new Munitions Minister 'has absolutely no knowledge of what millions mean', Morgan's concluded after a meet-ing in his new office, with the investment bank 'expect[ing] him to order several thousand million sterling of various articles' both in Britain and in America.[120]

Having ended the Treasury's control over war expenditures, Lloyd George now made use of that absence of restraint to the utmost. 'Plac[ing] more and still larger orders with American manufacturers, giving little thought to how they were to be paid',[121] an explosive orgy of spending followed as Lloyd George sought to press American capacity fully into Allied service. By October, the Ministry of Munitions had already placed orders in the United States amounting to $500 million and hoped to place many more.[122] (For context, US GDP in 1914 was about $37 billion, Britain's about $12 billion.)[123] There was only so much Morgan's could do to cut costs. It is difficult to shop around effectively for bargains when one has been instructed to go into every store and buy out their contents. And these munitions were expensive: 'Munitions bought in the United States were always costly as compared with prices and costs in the United Kingdom'.[124] By the end of the year, both Morgan's and Lloyd George's own personal American representative, who had just returned to Britain, agreed that 'the ministry should refrain from placing any further munition orders in the United States at all, since the capacity of currently capable firms was fully taken up'.[125] Even then, Lloyd George remained determined to keep on spending. His next American representative, the abrasive E. W. Moir, would be dispatched with plenary power to place still further orders without even going through Morgan's.[126]

And so Lloyd George spent as McKenna studied. All the while, the purchasing in America of Britain's allies, especially Russia, kept growing, with Britain increasingly picking up the tab.[127] A surge in world food prices at harvest time – Britain imported a majority of its food – compounded the situation.[128] The British were importing more goods at higher prices from the United States than ever before, with imports soaring from $674 million in 1914 to at least, and probably well over, $1.1 billion in 1915.[129] Grey, ever sensitive to American opinion, had no choice but to add to the Treasury's anxiety. Since the beginning of the war, British blockade policy had been to buy, rather than confiscate, intercepted American contraband headed to Germany. Amid a heavy Conservative press campaign, the coalition Cabinet decided in July 1915 to add cotton, which was used in the making of explosives, to the list of forbidden goods. They did so over Grey's objections. Grey had consistently resisted earlier pleas to add cotton to the list of contraband, and for good reason: the likelihood of a collapse in cotton prices imperilled powerful producers in the American South.

The predictable ensuing political storm in America – worsened by a pair of smaller but ill-timed British blockade actions simultaneously offending the Midwest and East – swirled so malevolently that there was open talk of Congress imposing an arms embargo against the British.[130] 'Should [the] British Government do this Congress probably would retaliate', House warned bluntly in a cable he dispatched across the Atlantic. 'The matter is of extreme urgency'.[131] Even if the

Americans did not go that far, the Anglo-American economic balance of power was rapidly shifting, and the US government was increasingly in possession of plenty of ways of making life very difficult for the British. House counselled restraint to the President, but astutely noted the difficulty of Grey's position, telling Wilson that Grey 'will go to almost any limit rather than [let things] come to the breaking point'.[132] The Foreign Secretary tried without success to get the Cabinet to back down, but in the end he salvaged the situation with a potentially expensive promise: to buy vast amounts of American cotton to support its price at ten cents per pound, at a projected cost of $100 million.[133] Morgan's initially blanched at the additional undertaking, thinking the task 'impossible',[134] but the burden on British expenditure actually would prove surprisingly short-lived. Amid an unexpected surge of US domestic demand, within two months cotton hit twelve cents per pound. Indeed, soon the British would have the reverse problem: the price of cotton surged to twenty-four cents by the end of 1916, making army uniforms all the more expensive.[135] For the moment, however, this obligation merely added to the 'heavy pressure' weighing on the pound. The pound slipped a cent during the first half of August to $4.76. Even the US Treasury was getting nervous: the exchange rate remained distressed, sitting ten cents away from where it ought to be, with no sign of an easing back to normality in sight.[136]

Distress, rather, was becoming normal. In only a year, the two countries' longstanding economic relationship had abruptly lurched into reverse. British investors had for decades been willing to finance an American deficit as they steadily acquired billions of dollars' worth in US investments. This gave the British an enormous reservoir of American railroads and other holdings that would provide them with a crucial cushion in the time of trial ahead. Now that the British were finding themselves in the reverse situation, however, American investors seemed to have no enthusiasm to return the favour. If the British intended to settle in for a long war and to use the United States as their crucial supply base, they needed a strategy.

2 Strategy
August–December 1915

On 13 August, all of the financial pressure through the pipe finally caused it to burst. Despite the arrival of a massive $54 million shipment of British gold and securities the previous day, which under 'ordinary conditions ... would have immediately caused a violent upward turn of the exchange market',[1] Morgan's found itself unable to soak up all the pounds being sold for dollars, so fast were the orders coming in. The pound broke through the ten-cent barrier to $4.73, and by the end of the following day smashed through the fifteen-cent one, to fall to $4.70. Compounding everything, on the evening of Saturday, 14 August, Morgan's ran out of authorized funds to prop up the rate. Morgan's proposed to lend the British $100 million if collateral could be promised – importantly, American banking law forbade banks from making direct loans without collateral, which sharply limited Morgan's ability to help – but Lord Cunliffe never responded to the offer. The 'foolhardy' Bank of England governor was determined to end the Treasury's cogitation, probably trying 'to embarrass McKenna and buttress his own claim of control over the exchange'. Cunliffe went ahead and told Morgan's it could pull the plug.[2]

At the same time, however, only ten weeks into McKenna's tenure at the Treasury, we start to see a coherent economic strategy emerging for sustaining the massive war imports the Allies were bringing in from America – one that, if implemented, would make importing those supplies maintainable for a much longer time and possibly indefinitely. The trade deficit had exploded so massively that the purely financial avenues of offsetting it could not hope to sustain it in the long term. McKenna's economic strategy sought to reorientate British policy around maintaining the vital Allied supply link with America. The Treasury's aims can be grouped around four main pillars.

First, Britain had to restore its flow of exports to the neutral world. British exports to the neutral world – defined here as all neutral countries apart from Germany's neighbours (the Netherlands, Switzerland, Denmark, Sweden, and Norway) – had collapsed in 1915 by

48

approximately a third as compared with before the war.[3] It is true, of course, that British exports solely to the United States never had any chance of offsetting the trade deficit: British exports to the United States before the war totalled just under $300 million, as compared with imports in 1915 of well over $1.1 billion. Some historians accordingly have condemned McKenna's desire to boost exports as being completely irrelevant to Britain's problems.[4]

In reality, however, it hardly mattered where in the neutral world British exports were sent. As a British financial report would put it the following year, the entire 'balance of trade of the British Empire and the allies tends to be settled over New York'.[5] Unlike everywhere else, the exchange rate between Britain and America was fixed, and so *arbitrage* forces meant that sending exports to other neutral countries helped Britain's dollar exchange as much as sending them directly to the United States.

To explain arbitrage briefly, Britain would soon re-establish the currency peg with the US dollar at about $4.77 – a distressed position nine cents away from where it ought to be, but one that was stable. To keep it fixed, Britain sought to stockpile as many dollars as it could, and Morgan's would be instructed to spend from that stockpile to buy up British pounds whenever the rate slipped below that value. Now suppose Britain increased its exports to other neutral countries while those countries' trade with America remained unchanged. If those other countries defended their currencies by shipping gold, the British could then put that gold to use in the United States. If those countries did not, ordinarily the pound should rise against those currencies, but the dollar should remain where it is. Yet the existence of the currency peg tells us that this is impossible: the pound must always be worth exactly 4.77 times what a dollar is worth. So if the British pound strengthens against, say, the Brazilian real, the dollar should also rise against the Brazilian real by the same proportion – regardless of whether the trade balance between the United States and Brazil would support that increase ordinarily.

Currency arbitrage is the force that makes this happen, snapping shut any divergences that ought to exist. Suppose a sudden surge in British exports to Brazil caused the pound to jump to, say, over five times the price of the dollar in the Brazilian market. An arbitrage trader could buy pounds sterling in New York at $4.77 and then convert them back into dollars in Brazil, pocketing a tidy profit. With sufficient arbitrage transactions, the rates would equalize. In the process, large amounts of sterling would have been bought in New York – exactly the same end result as if those exports had been sent to the United States itself. The larger the 'natural' difference between the pound and the dollar that ought to exist in other neutral countries, the greater the arbitrage effect. If Britain could strengthen its export position in regards to the rest of the neutral world, the arbitrage relief on the dollar exchange would be magnified because America's neutral trade position was deteriorating. The Allies were soaking up so much of American production that US exports to the rest of the world dropped by more than a fifth between 1913 and 1915 (from $1.55 billion to $1.22 billion).[6] If Britain could generate trade surpluses with the rest of the neutral world, the arbitrage relief on the dollar–pound exchange could be very substantial.

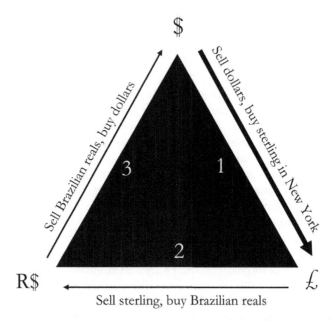

8 Triangular arbitrage, showing an example of a trader taking advantage of a price difference caused by a strong pound in the Brazilian financial market. The first leg is the most important from the British perspective, generating relief on the dollar–pound exchange.

Second, Britain had to tamp down its imports as much as possible and enforce austerity at home. It needed above all to cut back its imports from America, but the same arbitrage forces that applied to British exports also worked in the other direction. As McKenna would put it the following year: 'In whatever country we buy, the arbitrage of exchange is brought into the dollar exchange, and we [end up having] to buy the whole mass of the imports ... with cash in dollars'.[7] Britain had to control its appetite for war supplies from other neutral countries besides the United States. British imports from Argentina, Spain, Chile, and Cuba rose by more than two-thirds between 1914 and 1915.[8] If British trade with the rest of the neutral world moved into deficit, instead of into surplus, arbitrage forces would put additional strain on the dollar exchange, not relieve it.

Third, Britain had to maintain and expand its own productive capacities both for itself and so as to boost its exports to its European allies. Of course, running massive trade surpluses with the Allies, as it was doing, provided no help for the American exchange. Britain was financing these Allied exports itself, providing mammoth loans so its allies could take what they needed. But whatever Britain could make at home for the war, either for itself or its allies, did not need to be imported from America.

Fourth, though of lesser importance than the other three pillars, Britain could rely on, or, depending on one's point of view, exploit, its empire more heavily. To some degree, it could run large trade deficits with its colonies without necessarily having to worry about immediate economic consequences, as the Empire could often be induced or forced to finance those exports itself. To be sure, none of the colonies had the industrial capabilities of the metropole, but unlike neutral countries, whatever they produced for the Allies for the war did not necessarily need to be compensated for by comparable exports – at least if political relations permitted.

These four pillars could reduce the trade deficit to a manageable level, McKenna believed, but what remained of that deficit still needed to be offset, and so McKenna simultaneously and rigorously pursued the purely financial avenues available to him. The Allies had to make better use of their gold resources. France and Russia had large reserves – much larger than Britain's – and yet Britain was shipping off its gold to New York to pay for their American supplies while the other two kept their massive gold chests hidden away in vaults. The Americans certainly would continue shipping away their war supplies in exchange for stocks of the yellow metal, if only the French and the Russians could be 'convinced that gold was better used than hoarded'.[9] Additionally, massive amounts of American investments owned by British citizens remained with their private owners, when the British needed to be putting them to use facilitating American imports. Prying American railroads out of private British hands and into those of the state remained a priority.

Lastly, the final avenue of finance, as yet untried, needed to be pursued: going to New York and seeking American loans. The scale of

Britain's financial problem would be reduced massively if American banks and investors would simply finance much of the trade deficit themselves. While the failure of the Second War Loan in the United States showed that Americans had no interest in sending their money off to London, perhaps they could be induced to provide financing if the British came to them and sought a loan in American dollars.

By reorienting British strategy around maintaining the Allies' American supply link, McKenna hoped to keep the supplies flowing for as long as possible, potentially even for years if necessary. To reject this strategy was to pin any long-term hopes on American lenders in New York and other American cities being willing to provide extensive funding. If American lenders did not come through, the supply link would last only as long as British assets did. As Allied dependence on this link steadily increased, the grave diplomatic, military, and economic consequences of exhausting it would begin to prove a terrible spectre for much of the British leadership.

McKenna had a difficult road ahead of him in getting his strategy implemented: the fractious, ill-tempered, and yet fragile beast that was Asquith's coalition could agree on virtually nothing. The Prime Minister had his hands more than full trying to keep it in check. From relatively humble origins in the Yorkshire middle class, the highly intelligent Asquith had rapidly climbed the social ladder, winning a scholarship in Classics to Balliol College, Oxford, working as a barrister for a decade, and then taking a seat in Parliament at the age of 34. He made such an impression that when the Liberals won back control of the government six years later, in 1892, Prime Minister William Gladstone promoted him directly to Home Secretary. He existed as a lion in the Liberal Party for the next three-and-a-half decades and as its leader for nearly two of those from 1908 until 1926. Tactful and charming with a fondness for drink and a soft spot for young women, Asquith had mastered politics as an art, and he regularly conjured his masterpieces before the House of Commons. While his success as a peacetime prime minister is undisputed, his wartime tenure has proved far more controversial. A natural chairman with a cautious and conciliatory temperament, Asquith was skilled at forging compromise, and his personal reputation for integrity helped glue his coalition government together. Though naturally inclined towards accommodation and consensus,[10] here he had no choice:

[F]or all the condemnation of Asquith's lack of leadership, the real trouble was not administrative but political. The only way to get a straightforward decision out of the Coalition Cabinet would have been to sack the dissentient minority: in which event, which minority ... was to go?[11]

9 Herbert Henry Asquith (Library of Congress / George Grantham
Bain Collection / LC-B2-3629-5)

Yet none of the minorities could be sacked, as without any one of them
the coalition would tumble and shatter. If Asquith had tried to impose his
strategic views – which were effectively McKenna's strategic views – on
his colleagues, his coalition would have collapsed as quickly as it had
been formed. Arriving at consensus, however muddled, was a compulsory feature of the political structure in which the Prime Minister found
himself. No one was better at finding it than Asquith.

Though the Conservatives controlled about half the Cabinet,
Asquith's deft political manoeuvring had sharply limited their control
over key government ministries. With the exception of Balfour, whom he
placed at the Admiralty, Asquith frankly had no faith in the governance
capabilities of his usual political opponents, and he was determined to
keep as much power as possible in hands he trusted. Andrew Bonar Law,
the leader of the Conservative Party, was 'bitter at being given such a
second-class post' after having been made Colonial Secretary (he had,
after all, been born in Canada), when by rights he might have expected
McKenna's post at the Exchequer or Lloyd George's at Munitions.[12]

As the exchange crisis in mid-August gathered pace – a 'welter of
trouble', Asquith called it[13] – McKenna struggled to make his case to

the Conservatives. He failed entirely to persuade Lloyd George. So uninformed was the Treasury that it was caught off-guard when Britain accidentally came close to default: the week of 16 August, Britain owed $17 million for munitions purchases and Morgan's had only $4 million on hand to pay for it.[14] McKenna blamed Lloyd George for failing to keep the Treasury informed, but Lloyd George told the Cabinet flatly that 'no information [had been] refused to the Treasury upon any point on which they have asked me'.[15] Infuriated, McKenna tasked one of his deputies with proving Lloyd George a liar, only to be told that it could not be done, as much of previous communications had either been 'oral' or only 'semi-official'; the few 'official' requests had been responded to.[16]

Munitions spending in the United States continued to explode: the Ministry of Munitions, to the Treasury's alarm, pursued an 'exceedingly lavish' policy of 'all of everything'. It ordered well in excess of 'the war office's own estimate of requirements' – so much so that the War Office did not know if it could 'take all the big guns the M. M. are pressing them to have'.[17] The War Office doubted it had sufficient trained men to fire them all and worried that the ministry's extensive American orders would crowd out the market for Allied and especially Russian munitions manufacture. Nor could McKenna get Lloyd George to take his concerns seriously. Though McKenna could not prove Lloyd George a liar, he nevertheless took advantage of Lloyd George's Cabinet statement, promptly sending over a sweeping and now 'official' demand that the ministry consult with the Treasury on any 'orders involving large immediate payments in America'. The ministry agreed to comply for two months. Reserving the right to make contracts freely so long as payment was needed only after that two-month period, the Munitions Ministry 'warn[ed]' the Treasury icily that it required 'further resort to the resources of America' and that the Treasury could 'not count unduly on this means of influencing the rate of Exchange'.[18]

The two-month respite was intended to give the Treasury time to seek an American loan. In the aftermath of Cunliffe's foolhardy action, the pound endured wild gyrations of a kind never before seen, reaching an unprecedented low of $4.48 on 1 September.[19] Lord Reading, the Lord Chief Justice, was dispatched as the British head of a joint Anglo-French finance mission to the United States in early September 1915. An ally of Lloyd George but nevertheless on good terms with most within the Liberal Party, Reading had a difficult yet crucial task ahead of him.[20] Reading was about to ask the Americans whether they would be willing to fund the Allies' transatlantic purchases themselves. Britain's strategic calculous depended hugely on the answer.

The very first difficulty to be overcome was an official American discouragement of 'war loans'. While Wilson would not rescind this policy, his troubled Secretaries of the Treasury and of State pressed him on the severity of the financial situation. Sufficiently concerned about the effect of the exchange rate situation on American trade, Wilson consented to allowing a loan for 'the maintenance of America's foreign trade'. The British made a pretence of adhering to Wilson's position by promising that the loan proceeds would not fund munitions exports. Given how fungible money is, this distinction made not the slightest bit of difference.[21] Any loan was a war loan.

The mission departed for New York thinking that it could net a loan from American banks and investors of $1 billion – a massive sum (British GDP in 1915 was only $13.5 billion). Reading ran into opposition from Morgan's, which frankly doubted the possibility of raising so much money. If the British attempted an overambitious loan and it failed, Britain would be severely embarrassed and its credit damaged. When the mission arrived in New York in mid-September, Morgan's put forward a counter-proposal, already endorsed by a handful of American banks, that tried to chop down the mission's ambitious target by three quarters. The flabbergasted mission eventually compromised at half, $500 million, still an 'amount staggered the financial markets in the United States', to be offered on extremely generous terms. By making the loan interest free from British tax, the effective interest rate approached 7 per cent, which was significantly higher than the 4 per cent or so then prevailing in America. In this period, loans of this nature first were *underwritten* by banks and large investors at a slightly higher effective interest rate and then *sold* to the general public at a slightly lower one. Whatever could not be sold to the public the underwriters committed to take themselves.

Morgan's vigorously pursued investors, but it barely succeeded in cobbling together an underwriting syndicate, managing only because the bank itself put up $30 million. Despite a massive and expensive publicity campaign, the public sale was virtually a complete failure. The underwriters had hoped to sell over $200 million of the total loan to the general public. They sold about $12 million. On the day that the loan closed, a number of the underwriters sought to offload some of their loans at steep discounts. With the price of the bonds plunging, the British mortgaged enough US securities with Morgan's to get $25 million, and they used the funds to quietly buy back some of their own bonds, trying to prevent the slide from becoming a damaging embarrassment. Some of the underwriters, in effect, had decided they had made a mistake and now wanted their money back, even if it meant suffering a loss on the transaction. The British, reluctantly, obliged them.[22]

Anglo-French Bond Price, 1915-April 1917

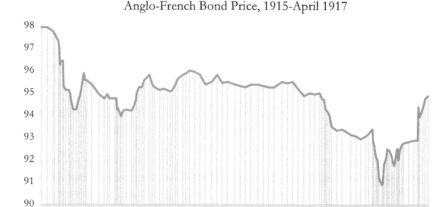

Graph 1 Price in dollars of the 1915 Anglo-French five-year bonds in
the United States, which serves as a barometer of the confidence of US
investors in Britain's ability to repay its debts. Any price below $98
represents a loss for members of the general public who invested; below
$96 represents a loss for the large financial institutions that served as
underwriters for the loan. There was little movement in US interest
rates for long-term loans int his period, so the bond price serves as a
reasonable barometer of US investor confidence in Britain. (*New York
Times*, 1915–1917. Average of low and high sales prices reported, data
points taken at least four times per month, with additional data points
during periods of higher volatility. For US interest rates in this period,
see Kemmerer, 'The War and Interest Rates', 102).

American markets had sent the Allies a clear signal. As Morgan's later
put it, American investors 'did not want to buy' any more Allied loans
'on any scale' – no matter how generous the terms.[23] Morgan's did an
excellent job in covering up that signal from the general public, telling
everyone that the loan in fact had been oversubscribed (because of
Morgan's intervention, technically it had been, just barely). The firm
managed to generate an impression that the loan had been a success.[24]
The clarity of the signal, however, had not been lost on Morgan's, which
concluded that the experience could not be repeated.[25] Nor could it just
try again with a higher interest rate, which could do more harm than
good – too high a rate, and the American investor 'will be told we are
bankrupt' (not to mention that the current loan was already being
denounced by ill-informed critics in London for having an unnecessarily
high interest rate).[26] The Allies had almost certainly satiated the entirety
of the American appetite for Allied debt that existed. The consequences
of failure, Morgan's believed, were far too high to risk having another go.

Reading did hold out some hope that Morgan's might have been just slightly too despairing. In making his report back in London, he told a Cabinet committee that he thought the British *might* be able to coax a little more Allied debt down the throats of American investors in 1916. If they waited long enough, if they kept their targets small enough, if attitudes towards the Allies in the United States were sweet enough, and if the Allies were winning the war, then just *maybe* they could pull off another $250 million loan come spring. If their good fortune held out, possibly they could organize one more $250 million loan the following autumn.

Reading, however, cautioned that even this was far from a sure thing, that many of his colleagues thought him overly optimistic, and that – most importantly – even if they did pull this off, the funds generated would be nowhere near what was needed to change the British strategic calculus. This sum paled in comparison with the billions of dollars in the United States they were sure to need to keep the supply link fully open through the following year. 'The situation', he warned starkly, 'fills me with the greatest alarm'.[27]

In the end, though, Morgan's would be right. No further such loans ever became possible. From this point forward, the Allies would be almost fully dependent on gold and British-owned American securities to finance their American imports. McKenna was working hard on those fronts, succeeding in wringing out of the French and Russians a promise to each have $200 million in gold ready to ship.[28] British gold continued to stream into American coffers, for a 1915 year-end total a little less than that same amount. The British government directly arranged for nearly $100 million in British-owned American securities to hit the auction block between July and December.[29] Most important of all, however, were massive private British sales, which the British government had been encouraging, and which for 1915 one estimate pegged at around $850 million.[30] Between the Anglo-French loan, the securities sales, and the gold shipments, the pound slowly began to stabilize. By January, it would firm back up above the ten-cent deviation barrier. It reached what now seemed, at least by comparison with the chaos over the previous few months, only a very mildly distressed $4.77. Morgan's would be instructed to keep the pound there.[31]

The near-failure of the Anglo-French loan, however, drove home an unmistakably clear message, at least for those who understood it. The Allies had asked New York to serve as the Allies' vital financial lifeline, and New York had refused. The Allies were now on a strict time limit. Without drastic economic changes, the flood of supplies from America could be maintained only as long as the gold and securities lasted. Once the last shipment of gold set sail and the final tranche of American investments had been liquidated, the supply link from America would effectively be closed.

The British leadership now had difficult choices to make for the coming year. This should have been a seminal moment in British strategy, with Britain's leaders frankly facing up the stark consequences of New York's decision. But the political debate within the British Cabinet that autumn was not over which of the hard choices it should select for the coming year, but over whether it faced any hard choices at all. Over the final months of 1915, McKenna made the case to reorient British strategy around sustaining this vital American supply link. Two of the four pillars of McKenna's strategy – restoring British exports to the neutral world and increasing British production for itself and its Allies to reduce their need for American supplies – above all depended on maintaining and enhancing British industrial prowess. This sounds uncontroversial until one arrives at its chief and most pressing logical consequence: the British Army, he argued, had to be expanded at a far slower rate than it had been over the first year of the war.

Yet there was huge political pressure on and within the Cabinet to refuse to accept that increasing the size of the Army involved running any economic risks and to push to make the Army far larger still. Within the government, military officials and many Conservatives believed that despite over 700,000 men enlisting during the first six months of 1915 (in addition to the 1.2 million who had enlisted in 1914 and the 250,000-strong British Army at the outbreak of war),[32] the pace of recruiting remained far too slow. The success or failure of loans in New York seemed irrelevant. With the British labour force at about 20 million (of whom 14 million were men),[33] McKenna believed that the economy could only sustain further recruitment at an annualized rate of up to about 500,000 men; conscriptionists within the government wanted about four times as many.[34] Back in July, the Conservatives, joined by Lloyd George and Liberal Winston Churchill, had forced the government to push a National Register Bill through Parliament. Widely seen as a possible precursor to conscription, which remained intensely politically controversial,[35] by August the political winds were increasingly blowing in that direction. Asquith moved to gain time by convening a War Policy Committee to consider the issue, with a 'membership reflecting the by-now preponderant view' – a trio of conscriptionist Conservatives and Churchill – 'tempered by a solid yeoman and a stolid chairman', Arthur Henderson of the Labour Party and the highly capable Asquith lieutenant, Lord Crewe.[36]

McKenna gave his testimony to the Committee on 23 August, trying to engage with a body that plumbed the depths of economic ignorance. Even Lord Crewe, probably the brightest of the lot, began the session by trying to draw a completely irrelevant distinction between Allied loans that were likely to be repaid after the war and those that were not – a topic that, unsurprisingly, made absolutely no difference to anything until after the war. Lord Selborne, the Conservative President of the Board of Agriculture, wanted to know whether the vast national savings of past years was 'in a form in which it can be realised', leaving McKenna testily trying to explain the basics of capital investment: 'It cannot be realised. You cannot realise this house. You cannot spend this house on the war. I cannot take up the London and North Western Railway and convert it into guns'.

McKenna struggled to explain himself in terms his colleagues could understand. The most important concept was to disabuse them of thinking of money as a *thing*: 'Making a loan to an ally does not simply mean letting him have so much money or credit; it means letting him have goods. He wants a loan because he wants to pay for goods'. British pounds could only be spent on British products: lending £50 million to France meant giving France that share of British production. Over the course of the conscription debate, McKenna argued that every labourer turned into a soldier hit the British economy three times over: his production was lost, that of those who worked with him was disrupted, and others had to be reallocated from their own useful economic production to now support an extra soldier instead.[37] Over 30 per cent of the British economy was now being diverted to the British war effort – a tenfold increase in the military's share of GDP compared with 1913.[38]

The conscriptionists, in McKenna's view, were demanding an army so large that the British economy could not cope with everything asked of it: supporting the Army and Navy, providing their allies with the British supplies they expected, generating the exports needed to help offset the world and especially the American imports that the alliance needed, and maintaining the British civilian population:

It is not bankruptcy I am thinking of, it is capacity. It is no use undertaking to do a thing which you physically cannot do. ... I am looking at the question from the point of view of not attempting to do things which are physically impossible to be done. I do not look at it from any other point of view.

McKenna held no illusions about the relative decline in British economic power over the past few decades. He argued that there 'are only three nations which can produce for this war – the United States,

Germany, and ourselves'. With Britain having a population only two-thirds the size of Germany's, and less than half that of the United States, 'we are third of the three. ... If you cripple one of the three producers you cannot win'. Despite the decline, British productive capacity still far outstripped that of its allies: 'If you take one Russian and one Frenchman and one Englishman, and say out of those three two have to fight and one has to produce, it would only be a madman who would set the Frenchman and the Englishman to fight and the Russian to produce'.

Though there were intelligent critiques of McKenna's position to be had, the Chancellor that day did not encounter any. The session rapidly degenerated into a long, muddled discussion of conscripted men's loss of production, which was jumbled about with an even worse discussion of the economic demands facing the country. The conscriptionists objected that women, boys, and older men could fill the role of men conscripted, and when McKenna mentioned a figure of the average contribution to the national income of a male labourer as £200 a year, much of the rest of the meeting was lost quibbling over the meaning and accuracy of that statistic.[39] (Dividing British GDP for 1915 over a labour force of 20 million people gives £147.)[40]

Archconservative Lord Curzon, who did not really understand McKenna's arguments, asked a more intellectually minded friend of his, Lord Milner, who many years before had been the Undersecretary of Finance in Egypt, to help him 'get something' to refute them.[41] The resulting memorandum, which Curzon circulated under his own name, attacked the £200 figure and did provide an intelligent critique of McKenna's argument about lost production – observing, for example, that there were 90,000 actors and musicians who could be conscripted without any real productive loss – but ignored the main thrust of McKenna's argument. Milner took no notice of the fact that those conscripted actors still had to be fed, clothed, equipped, trained, transported, directed, provided with munitions, backed by an elaborate system of logistical support, and, when wounded, nursed back to health. The memorandum's arguments only made sense if the proposal had been to maroon the country's actors on a remote island and leave them to fend for themselves rather than turn them into soldiers. The economic cost of a brigade of actors was not free.[42]

Nor was replacing men of military age in the economy with women, boys, or older men a straightforward solution. McKenna later made clear the effects of the disruption:

Now every time you withdraw men on a large scale you give it a shock. It recovers slowly as new workers, women and older men and boys, are gradually drawn in and slowly made efficient. But then you come and draw more men and industry runs down again ... We can get on as long as only [approximately 250,000–500,000 men annually] are being drawn away, but if it goes much faster exports fall, the exchange goes against us etc. ... There are 100 ways of winning the war and only one of losing – conscription.[43]

Though they may not have understood McKenna's testimony, when the Committee surveyed the wider war, his financial arguments paled in comparison. Everything seemed to be going terribly wrong. Even with reinforcements, an August offensive against the Turks at the Dardanelles failed spectacularly.[44] On the Eastern Front, Russia was faced with outright catastrophe, losing two million men between April and September.[45] Germany was on the march, moving rapidly through Russian Poland and capturing Warsaw at the beginning of August.[46] In the west, a modest French summer offensive in the Alsatian mountains found only further stalemate,[47] while in the south, Austria-Hungary repulsed Italy's repeated attacks seemingly with ease.[48] With the war going so badly, diplomatic efforts to entice Bulgaria into the alliance were doomed from the start, especially with Serbia refusing to countenance any territorial concessions.[49] German diplomatic accommodation with the United States over its submarines, while modestly easing the threat to merchantmen in the Atlantic, removed any chance of the Americans entering the war and resolving the British economic dilemma.[50]

At home, backbenchers in Parliament – mostly Conservatives, but also some Liberals – and the press piled on additional pressure.[51] France and Russia pleaded for greater British economic and military aid, and grew increasingly critical of Britain's seeming military 'inactivity'.[52] For those on the Committee without a strong grasp of the British economic situation, it frankly seemed preposterous that Britain had to turn away France's and Russia's desperate pleas for help simply because the pound might drop against the dollar. Though Crewe and Henderson dissented, the Committee's majority dismissed McKenna's argument in their report as 'too abstract'. '[W]hile admiring its ingenuity', the conscriptionists wrote, 'we think it is inapplicable to the real problems we are trying to solve'.[53]

Yet while Conservative political pressures for conscription were large, at this point Labour and Liberal pressures against conscription – the Trade Union Congress, representing under three million workers, nearly a sixth of the labour force, had very recently passed a resolution rejecting it – remained formidable enough to justify further delay.[54] Whatever accusations of a tendency towards muddle that Asquith has been subjected to, in this instance he purposefully dragged out the process for as

long as humanly possible. Asquith agreed with McKenna, and yet politically he had no chance of imposing the strategy he preferred on a
Cabinet that would not accept it. Procrastination, then, seemed not
merely politically necessary but economically imperative. As Asquith
later wrote:

When you have made adequate provision for the economic needs of a country like
ours in time of war, you may find that you have left for compulsion only a small
residuum of the dregs of the nation: and you will have set aflame a blazing
controversy – for nothing![55]

As he intended, the Cabinet considered the reports only in a desultory
way for the next month. Asquith entreated Balfour, who unlike other
Conservatives took McKenna's position very seriously, to write up his
views, providing cover for further postponement.[56] Balfour's carefully
considered 19 September memorandum, prioritizing ships and money
ahead of soldiers, put forward amongst other arguments that 'it is not
enough to keep at home sufficient men to carry on national services
which are obviously necessary, such as work on munitions ... We must
add to these necessary services others which are in themselves not necessary at all, and are only valuable because they enable us to purchase
necessary commodities from foreign countries'.[57]

While Asquith temporized on conscription, McKenna used his War
Budget to try to promote austerity at home. 'We have to tax now with
objects beyond revenue', McKenna told the Commons. 'We must look
at the state of our foreign exchanges. We must discourage imports ...
[and] have strict regard to the necessity of reducing consumption'.
Correcting what the *Economist* called 'a deplorable piece of weakness'
in the previous budget, McKenna did 'what Mr Lloyd George ought to
have done last May': massively hiked taxes, increasing projected annual
government revenue by 40 per cent. In addition to large increases in
income tax, McKenna abandoned traditional Liberal free trade dogma
by upping excise taxes on a number of non-essential imports, including
sugar, coffee, and tobacco, and introducing a tax on imported luxuries.
These large tax increases had to be introduced carefully, however,
'keep[ing] in view the necessity of not interfering with the trades which
are most lucrative to us and upon which our exports depend'.[58]

Having imposed a degree of austerity on the public – though some
have argued he ought to have gone further – McKenna also aimed to
impose it on the government, forming the Retrenchment Committee.
For such a dull-sounding governmental body, it had what ought to have
been one of the most crucial jobs of the war: helping keep open their vital
American supply lifeline by reducing imports and finding every economy

there was to be found in their expenditure, especially in the United States. As Keynes later would put it: 'Economy at home [is] very nearly as valuable as economy in purchases abroad'.[59] The Committee's reality, however, proved as dreary as its name. McKenna devoted seemingly endless, tedious hours to this 'ineffectual' committee, confiding to his wife that it was 'more than ordinary humanity can bear'. Three times without success the Committee asked the Ministry of Munitions to consult the Treasury before placing orders. Lloyd George's reaction upon receiving these requests from his hated rival is not recorded but may be readily imagined.[60]

The sheer magnitude of the threatened spending made the Treasury sick with worry and amplified the case for delaying conscription for as long as possible – or, better yet, avoiding it altogether. If the Allies and the Ministry of Munitions managed to spend all of the money in the United States that they had been allocated, a horrified Keynes estimated that the British would have an almost unimaginable trade deficit of nearly $2 billion for just the *six months* from October 1915 to March 1916. (Recall that British GDP for the entire year of 1915 was only about $13.5 billion.) Assuming the Allies could get a fresh $1 billion in a second American loan before March – Keynes did not yet know that the near-failure of the current one would preclude it – he estimated that the British could just barely afford to offset this gargantuan deficit between the loans, gold, and securities sales. 'With luck and skill', he wrote, 'we can get through to 31 March. How do we open the next financial year? ... It would be foolish to assert that we have any reasonable security of getting through the six months April–October 1916 without a catastrophe'.[61]

In reality, however, Lloyd George and the Allies would not manage to spend anywhere close to the amounts that they had promised. For one thing, a shortage of shipping obstructed imports. So many merchantmen were being commandeered for military or Allied use that British ship arrivals dropped by a fifth in 1915.[62] McKenna quipped, not without some relief, that 'we were, in fact, engaged in most effectively blockading ourselves'.[63] More importantly, Lloyd George and the Allies had already so saturated American production that, though not for lack of trying, they simply ran out of ways to spend money. With the Allies alone underspending their allowances by nearly a half billion dollars,[64] Keynes's trade deficit estimates would prove grossly inflated. Keynes's calculations, however, had been based on the spending requirements the Treasury had been given. He had no choice but to take the Ministry of Munitions and Britain's allies 'at their word', and their word was truly a terrifying thing: 'If they had spent all they threatened, we should have been ruined'.[65] The Treasury could not know that they would manage to expend only a fraction of what they said they would. Few understood Keynes's figures, but everyone understood his predictions of doom, and when doom did not arrive on schedule, Lloyd George and others took it as firm evidence that doom would never come at all.[66]

Though some Conservatives recognized the political limits Asquith operated under, the Prime Minister's purposeful temporizing on conscription drove Lloyd George and many Conservatives to infuriated distraction. Lloyd George was determined to overcome the opposition of the 'timid and obstructive' McKenna, who was 'making a bogey of the adverse American exchange'. Entirely dismissing the notion that Britain even needed an economy to fight the war, Lloyd George 'was for enlisting *all* the able-bodied men not needed for his munitions work'.[67] He signalled his support for conscription publicly, to Asquith's great annoyance, and launched a Cabinet conspiracy with Churchill and Curzon. The 'Tories are going to approach the P.M. & say that they cannot proceed any longer under the present state of things'. Lloyd George and Churchill 'will throw in their lot with them', and drive conscription through.[68] By mid-October, the Cabinet found itself in a maelstrom of recrimination as Lloyd George and his Conservative allies tried to force the issue. Many leading Liberals rallied behind McKenna. Grey completely accepted the Chancellor's arguments on 'numbers and finance' and condemned 'very bitterly' the conduct of his colleagues. Lloyd George, Churchill, and at least six leading Conservatives threatened to resign if conscription was not imposed; McKenna and at least two other major Liberals threatened to resign if it was.[69]

Though Asquith supported McKenna, even to the point of considering resigning himself, he deftly assembled a compromise proposal to try to hold his government together. Cleverly co-opting the pro-conscription Earl of Derby to lead it, Asquith revealed the 'Derby Scheme' to his colleagues on 15 October: men of military age were to be canvassed and pressured to 'attest' – in essence, to voluntarily consent in advance to being conscripted into the Army if and when their services were required. The Prime Minister manoeuvred amidst his colleagues to rally them behind the compromise, and he resisted a Conservative demand to push legislation through Parliament that would automatically trigger conscription if Derby 'failed' – that is, if the attestation numbers could not meet the conscriptionists' large target.

The Conservatives grumbled but realized that if they pushed any harder, the coalition would collapse, and that, if accommodation could not be reached, a general election might prove unavoidable. Though the Liberals and Conservatives were both committed to avoiding a general election, this did not preclude anxiety about the possibility of one: while an election would probably lead to a Tory majority, the Conservatives worried that a firestorm of 'great bitterness' and 'violent opposition in the new House' would completely destroy national unity and that there would be a 'certainty of strikes in the labour world outside'.[70] Only Lloyd George continued to cause trouble, threatening the Cabinet that he would 'tell the people the truth'. There were two parties in the government, he said, one of which 'realized the seriousness of the situation ... and the urgent need for action'. The other, he said accusingly of McKenna and his allies, was 'satisfied to let things be and sat twiddling their thumbs'.[71] The reality, of course, was almost precisely the reverse.

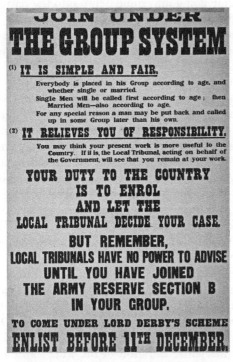

10 Recruitment poster for the Derby Scheme, 1915 (Library of Congress / POS-WWI-Gt Brit, no. 107)

Having introduced the Derby Scheme and quelled the worst of the crisis, Asquith managed to postpone the scheme's implementation for another two weeks by the expedient of a seemingly diplomatic illness: though genuinely suffering from 'overwork', 'Henry is not so ill physically but he is stale & *morally disgusted*', his wife Margot noted. The spell of sickness gave time for tempers to cool, and gave an opening for McKenna and others to continue to expound the case for the economic strategy. Balfour circulated another memorandum on 17 October arguing that there was no 'greater calamity' imaginable for the alliance than 'that Britain should cease to be able to purchase abroad the food and the munitions which she and they so urgently require'.[72] Not all felt charitable about Asquith's absence, however: 'He is a great man', Lord Kitchener, the Secretary of State for War, commented acidly. 'I thought he had exhausted all possible sources of delay; I never thought of the diarrhoea'.[73]

These economic arguments were making no inroads with their detractors. Conservative Leader Andrew Bonar Law hit back against Balfour with a rejoinder that, while going into some depth into the basics of the economic problem, ultimately maintained that they would be able to borrow in America what they needed. The near failure of the Anglo-French loan was irrelevant. 'Our financial stability depends upon our credit', he insisted, 'and our credit depends upon the efficiency with which the war is conducted'.[74]

For the following month and a half, the Derby Scheme kept the economic strategy tottering while providing some modest restraint on the Cabinet's seemingly insatiable need to devour itself. Three of the economic strategy's four pillars were in deep trouble; the only one to see any real kind of success was the least important: Britain did significantly increase its reliance on, and exploitation of, its empire. The absence of large-scale production capabilities prevented a meteoric rise on an American scale, but imports from India, Egypt, Canada, Australia, and New Zealand jumped by at least half from 1914 to 1916 to well over $1 billion.[75] As Britain's balance of trade with its colonies moved into deficit, London imposed certain measures forcing parts of the Empire to finance much of these increases themselves. Initially, India's export earnings were diverted into British war bonds. The following year, India would be pulled off its silver standard. Its currency would become backed by nothing more than British government debt, as was Egypt's. The output of South African gold mines was commandeered by the British government for the entire duration of the war.[76] Britain could not afford to ignore the financial interests of the more politically powerful Australia entirely, but Anglo-Australian financial relations were determined fundamentally by political negotiation, not by the laws of economics.[77] Similarly, Britain and Canada in essence struck a deal: Britain would pay for the cost of Canada's military force in Europe, while domestic Canadian war loans paid for the costs of the Canadian 'munitions, wheat, flour and other Canadian products' that were shipped to support the Allies during the war.[78]

The Cabinet resisted the temptation to destroy itself while Derby did his work, but it nevertheless had more than enough to fight over in the interim. The war continued to go badly. Bulgaria entered the war on the German side in October. It quickly crushed what remained of the Serbian Army and opened up clear supply lines between Germany and the Ottoman Empire,[79] adding further danger to the bottled up Allied force at Gallipoli. As the British political leadership quarrelled seemingly endlessly over whether to withdraw that force and admit defeat in the Dardanelles – it would ultimately withdraw the force in early January[80] – it was also faced with a difficult decision over whether to launch the first major British offensive on the Western Front. Although almost no one in the British leadership, civilian or military, had much faith that it would produce meaningful results, the French were determined to go ahead with another campaign and demanded British support. French and Russian resentment had been multiplying at Britain's 'not doing her share', as House put it (a criticism he thought completely 'unjust'),[81] and so a 'reluctant and apprehensive' Cabinet authorized a large offensive at Loos in support of a simultaneous French attack in Champagne. A 'political gesture designed to reassure the allies of Britain's support for them',[82] the attack failed colossally at the cost of nearly 60,000 British casualties. 'From what I can ascertain', wrote one British commander, 'some of the divisions did actually reach the enemy's trenches, for their bodies can now be seen on the barbed wire'.[83] The French attack failed even more disastrously, with over double the losses.[84] In the east, the Russian line at last stabilized, with a strategic retreat in September leading to formation of a harder line of defence – albeit one that left the Germans now deep in Russian territory.[85] In the south, the Italians continued to bash their forces against the Austro-Hungarians without results. Barely in the war sixth months, in November the Italians launched what was already the Fourth Battle of the Isonzo; the Austro-Hungarians repulsed it just as they had done with the first three.[86]

Germany continued to gravely offend the Americans. Three Americans were amongst the dead after Germany torpedoed a second British passenger liner, the *Arabic*, setting off a fresh diplomatic crisis. Wilson's aggressive diplomacy in the ensuing wrangle, however, ultimately led Germany to back down, and the United States kept itself out of the war.[87] The British blockade, meanwhile, kept up its annoying buzz in the ears of the State Department and of the Foreign Office, with a fresh American protest against the whole British blockade system loudly dispatched in late October. But where Germany threatened American lives, Britain threatened only American wares. This fresh American protest was primarily a declaration of principles, rather than any kind of ultimatum: as House put it, although Britain's blockade was 'entirely illegal', they tolerated it only 'because Germany was so prodigal in larger infractions'. The British made no major changes in response – a fact that did not perturb House, who was in the midst of forming an ambitious new secret plan to end the war.[88]

As the close of 1915 approached, the war was being fought almost exclusively on Allied soil. The Central Powers had taken possession of swathes of French and Russian territory along with virtually the whole of Belgium and Serbia. The smallest of the Allies, Montenegro, would fall within two weeks of the New Year. Amongst the continental Allied powers, only Italy had not yet suffered significant territorial losses. The only gains the Allies could claim, by contrast, were a handful of German colonies, which were largely taken by Britain's dominions.

Given the alliance's dismal military circumstances, the conscriptionists' willingness to continue to submit to Asquith's strategy of delay ended abruptly when Derby submitted his report on 20 December. Though more than two million British men had attested, only some 320,000 of those men were 'actually available' for the Army when considering those in higher-priority occupations, the unfit, and an important self-imposed political restraint: the dominant European custom of not calling up married men when single men remained available. So while a further 400,000 married men would also have been obtainable under the Derby Scheme in terms of their fitness and lesser economic importance, Asquith had promised not to take them unless most single men had attested first – and over a half-million had not done so.[89]

As far as McKenna was concerned, the Derby Scheme was a resounding success and the matter should have been left there. The scheme had occasioned a bump in recruitment, with its concomitant economic disruption, to the tune of about 235,000 during October and November.[90] Limiting the Army's takings to a further 320,000 men would have suited McKenna perfectly. The conscriptionists, however, declared that the scheme was an abject failure. Most Conservatives in the Cabinet along with Lloyd George (Churchill by this time had resigned to pursue military service) would brook no further delay. Lloyd George warned Asquith that he would resign if conscription was not imposed.[91] As an anxious Asquith wrote: 'We seem to be on the brink of a precipice ... shall I be able in the next ten days to devise and build a bridge?'[92]

However much he believed in his Chancellor, if Asquith had tried to impose McKenna's strategy, his government would have collapsed. The Conservatives had been put off by the prospect of winning a divisive general election; losing one provided Asquith still greater deterrence. If the Prime Minister held his ground, he would lose his office, possibly lose his seat, national unity would be destroyed, and the country most likely would still launch itself down the same path, only now with Bonar Law and his Conservatives at the helm. The Prime Minister resigned himself to the inevitable, and on 21 December moved a vote, adopted unanimously, asking Parliament's permission to raise up to a million more troops by the end of March – a move that made conscription all but unavoidable.[93] Asquith now sought only to hold his government together, engaging in some brief delaying tactics on actually imposing conscription. Matters threatened to come to a head at Cabinet on 27 December, but playing for time the Prime Minister brought up Greece instead. By the time it had been fully discussed, five o'clock had rolled around and Asquith announced that conscription would have to wait until the next meeting. A furious Curzon exploded, accusing the Prime Minister of 'wasting time deliberately … in order to avoid giving a decision' – a critique that, while probably true, fails entirely to understand Asquith's reasons.[94]

By the next day, Asquith had run out of breathing room. Hoping that he had sufficiently laid the groundwork to hold his government together, Asquith shepherded conscription for single men – what would become the January 1916 'Bachelors' Bill' – through the Cabinet. The policy's Liberal opponents may have been prevailed upon to let it through, but despite Asquith's best efforts, over the next three days his Chancellor of the Exchequer, Foreign Secretary, Home Secretary, and President of the Board of Trade all submitted their resignations. A grave blow to the integrity of his government, Asquith faced losing the core of his Liberal bloc within the Cabinet – including the only two members who had any good understanding of the British economy. The Home Secretary, John Simon, opposed conscription as a matter of principle. The other three objected not to subordinating individual liberty to the state, but to their colleagues' stubbornly lurching down a path that they thought promised economic catastrophe.[95] 'This is no newly formed opinion on my part', McKenna wrote. '[T]he policy approved by the Cabinet entails the maintaining of an army of a size which will gravely embarrass the country'.[96] Grey wholeheartedly endorsed McKenna and the President of the Board of Trade, Walter Runciman, with 'whose views on the financial and economic needs I am in full accord'.[97]

Asquith pleaded with them all to stay, working them as intensely as he could and mobilizing a number of Liberal loyalists to do so on his behalf. The Prime Minister and his wife, Margot Asquith, both begged McKenna's spouse, Pamela McKenna, to use all her influence 'to keep us united for this terrible war'. Under heavy pressure from all directions,[98] McKenna and Runciman were receptive to a crisis-ending compromise. Maurice Hankey, the trusted civil servant who the following year would become Britain's first Cabinet Secretary, was Secretary to the War Committee (the 'War Council' had after various bureaucratic complications evolved into the 'War Committee' by autumn 1915). Fearing the loss of the 'sanest element' of the Cabinet, Hankey suggested the idea that would soon become the inelegantly named 'Committee for the Co-Ordination of Military and Financial Effort'. While the Cabinet had agreed upon *conscription*, it had not, technically speaking, decided on a target size for the Army. This new committee, uniting the country's military and financial leaderships, could attempt to reconcile the country's military growth with its economic capacity. '[I]f an agreement could be reached', as Hankey put it, 'the great expansion of armies might be limited and means found for McKenna and Runciman to remain in the Cabinet with honour'.[99] The new Chief of the Imperial General Staff, William Robertson, was open to the idea, complaining that 'there has been no co-ordination'. The Treasury thought the country could afford an army of fifty divisions, the Army 'ha[s] been working up to 70 divisions', while 'L[loyd] George has ordered material for 100 div[ision]s'. Robertson appreciated that McKenna 'cannot do impossibilities', and accepted the need to reconcile these competing demands.[100]

At the Cabinet meeting on New Year's Eve, McKenna and Runciman raised the issue of the size of the Army. In a move that Asquith had most likely pre-arranged, Balfour suggested a committee be appointed to thrash out the issue. This sudden manoeuvre could not have pleased Lloyd George and most of the Conservatives, with still further procrastination again stymying their long-postponed victory. With Robertson on the other side, however, they had little choice but to let the proposal through.[101]

Yet they had no need to be cross: this committee would not at all be a means of finding a compromise strategy. Rather, it served as a mechanism for McKenna to negotiate the terms of his strategic defeat. Robertson's sympathy for McKenna's views could only extend so far. With the maximalists outside the committee clamouring for the military to get whatever it wanted, McKenna's position was built upon quicksand. Whatever hopes he may have had upon joining the committee, he came to understand that his task was to contain the growth of the Army just enough for the military to get one big campaign before the finances fell apart. Everything would be pinned on the great 1916 offensive. Their massive, vital supply link from the United States would sputter and quit before the military would have a chance to try again. If the offensive were to fail, so well might the alliance itself.

3   Negotiations
January–March 1916

As the New Year opened, the only real piece of good fortune the Prime Minister could count about his coalition government was that it was still there. Beset by difficulty from without and by division from within, the British government was stuck in a strategic bog. Though about half of the Cabinet believed the country had no need of a coherent economic strategy, Asquith and McKenna nevertheless spent January attempting to devise one. Everyone at least allowed that Britain needed a military strategy, though no one could agree on what that should be. American diplomacy was about to set Asquith's fractious colleagues against each other still further. The President again dispatched House to Europe to resume his quest for a negotiated peace. Wilson's agile advisor this time would find in London an increasingly receptive audience. As Britain settled on a path of gambling on winning the war in 1916 – with many in the Cabinet denying that they were embarking on any kind of a gamble at all – this growing strategic incoherence increasingly drove British leaders into House's arms, and it led House to an even more expansive conception of American mediation than he himself had imagined. By the time he left for home in late February, the possibility of a 1916 peace conference, to be held either immediately or later in the year, suddenly seemed very real. All the while, the watching eyes of British intelligence were reading every secret telegram House sent home.

Over the autumn, on the other side of the Atlantic, House had been working on an ambitious new plan to end the war. Growing increasingly alarmed at the Allies' mounting military losses, House worried that they portended an impending collapse. American diplomacy, he thought, might be able to pull off a masterstroke: rescuing the Allies from defeat while simultaneously bringing the slaughter to a halt.

House's sympathies had always lain with the Allies, but Germany's submarine warfare and the sinking of the *Lusitania*, on which House himself had travelled, had horrified him. House had advised the President to go to the hilt in demanding that Germany back down.[1]

For House, this 'inhuman act'[2] crossed a line, and if Germany crossed it again, it must mean war – a conclusion the President also reached, albeit after some greater initial reluctance.[3] After Germany subsequently sunk the *Arabic*, House preferred escalating the crisis by sending the German Ambassador home to Wilson's course of dispatching another note. In private, he denounced the German leadership as 'bloodthirsty monsters'.[4] A line must be drawn: the 'nation would suffer more in being supine', he felt, 'than in taking a decided stand'.

But House also well understood the 'horrors of this war': he genuinely hoped that Germany would concede rather than drag the United States in.[5] When Germany subsequently yielded under Wilson's pressure, House enthusiastically praised the President for his 'great diplomatic triumph'.[6] So long as Germany refrained from actively killing Americans, House had little desire for the United States to be swallowed up into the conflagration. Before the crisis had even fully wrapped up, House was already trying to resume his mediation efforts. House had a long talk with Ambassador Bernstorff in late September about 'peace overtures, and of when and how they might begin', trying to find a formula that would offer 'a peace free from the menace of another such war'.[7]

House did not mention that he sought not only to end the war but also – if he could – to prevent the Allies from losing it. Watching Germany's submarine barbarity alongside its military successes had only increased House's anxieties about a German victory. If Germany established itself as European hegemon, House feared that this could open up the Americas to German expansionism. Should a victorious Germany, with no significant continental check on its power, set its sights on tearing up the Monroe Doctrine and moving into Latin America, 'we were not only unprepared, but there was no one to help us'.[8]

On 8 October 1915, House 'startled' President Wilson by laying out a dramatic plan for American diplomatic intervention. Earlier, he had merely wanted the President to serve as the necessary clearing house through which the belligerents would eventually end the war. Now, House envisioned leveraging American power to help the Allies stave off defeat. He sought to allow them to lock in an unfavourable compromise peace by forcing Germany to the negotiating table before the Allies were completely overrun. He also aimed to combine this with a demand for international military and naval disarmament, so as to assure the Allies of an end to 'Prussian militarism' and Germany of a reduction in the British naval threat. Ending the war would eliminate any risk of the United States being forced in, and, by preserving a semblance of a European balance of power and achieving a reduction in European armaments, any threat to the Americas would be neutralized.

House suggested to Wilson that they secretly approach the Allies and that, if the Allies agreed, Wilson demand a peace conference on the basis of military and naval disarmament. The United States would take no part in territorial discussions, with the implication that they would therefore be on the basis of the existing military situation. If Germany accepted the overture, the Allies could then pretend to agree reluctantly. Seeking to ensure that the Germans could not reject opening peace negotiations, if Germany refused, the United States 'could then push our insistence to a point where diplomatic relations would first be broken off, and later the whole force of our Government, and perhaps the for[ce] of every neutral, might be brought against them'.[9]

House calculated that the threat of American armed involvement – which had, after all, brought Germany to heel over its submarines – would be a sufficient stick to force the Germans to the table. With the Americans taking no part in the actual territorial negotiations, surely the Germans would prefer general disarmament and securing a favourable peace rather than insisting on pressing their advantage and risking having to fight the United States. Working painstakingly for days, House drafted a letter carefully sounding Grey about the proposal. Though he had Wilson's approval, to test the waters he pretended as if he had not yet approached the President about the idea and asked Grey for his thoughts.[10]

House, however, vastly overestimated the Allies' assessment of their plight in the autumn of 1915. Despite the increasing anxiety over Britain's transatlantic economic problems, no one in the British government yet accepted the proposal's premise that the Allies were knocking on defeat's doorstep and required American diplomatic rescue. Grey all but rejected the proposal out of hand. Before he did so, however, the Foreign Secretary seized on an opportunity. On 9 November, Grey deftly responded to House's letter in an extremely brief telegram sent in their private code, querying whether the 'elimination of militarism and navalism', as House had phrased it, would include American participation in a post-war league. House had completely ruled this out during his last visit, but the submarine crises had illustrated vividly that the Atlantic Ocean no longer protected the United States from being drawn into a European war. Seeing Grey's request, the Colonel now pressured Wilson to consent: 'We should do this not only for the sake of civilization, but for our own welfare, for who may say when we may be involved in such a holocaust as is now devastating Europe?' If adding a league of nations to the proposal would help bring the British on board, all the better. House provided the President with a draft telegram in reply, and a tectonic shift in American foreign policy came back in two words: 'Message approved'.[11]

Having succeeded in this clever diplomatic manoeuvre – committing the Americans to his proposed league without actually having offered anything in return – in his fuller reply Grey now moved, gently, to reject the broader proposal. He tried to dissuade House from taking any immediate action, pointing out that both France and Russia felt that Germany had done its worst and that the military situation could only now improve. 'I wish you were here', Grey wrote, 'but the situation at the moment and the feelings here and among the Allies … do not justify me in urging you to come on the ground that your presence would have any practical result at the moment'.[12] A frustrated House, who believed his proposal had merited a 'warmer response', wanted to postpone any trip to Europe in the wake of this setback, telling Wilson that he wanted to spend January in Texas. With problems of the war so consuming his administration, however, the President thought House should try anyway. Wilson overrode him, summoning him to the White House in mid-December and telling him that he 'should go immediately'. House at once threw himself into preparations for his trip.[13] The lives of millions rested on its outcome.

Aboard the enormous passenger vessel the *S.S. Rotterdam*, ready to press his plan for ending the war, House set sail for Britain on 28 December 1915. House's undertaking has earned him no end of grief from historians, and that grief begins even from before the moment of his departure. House boarded the ship armed explicitly with *carte blanche* from President Wilson, yet historians have consistently asserted that the President dispatched his emissary with a trio of firm instructions, all of which House is accused of violating. Wilson is supposed to have forbidden House from discussing any European territorial questions with the Allies, to have instructed House to promise the Allies absolutely nothing beyond mere diplomatic support, and to have ordered him to press the British hard on their blockade – so much so that dealing with the blockade was to have been his 'primary' task. All of these supposed instructions either misread Wilson's intentions, fundamentally under-estimate the extent to which Wilson trusted and relied on House's judgement, or overestimate the extent to which the President had actually thought through the details of this mediation effort. Moreover, House's preconceived diplomatic strategy would necessarily need to shift and adapt as he conducted his negotiations, and House had an extremely good reason for not consulting the President by telegraph every step of the way: his telegrams were as far from secure as can possibly be imagined.

On 17 December, Wilson wrote unambiguously to House: 'You need no instructions. You know what is in my mind and how to interpret it, and will, I am sure, be able to make it plain to those with whom you may have the privilege of conferring'.[14] Having been given a free hand, House had no obligation to reply to this letter, yet just to confirm that they were entirely on the same page House replied with a request for more detailed instructions, outlining his intended diplomatic strategy. House thought that, tactically, he would have the best chance of success by steering clear of territorial questions or indemnities – which would prevent him from getting embroiled in 'controversies that would be needless and footless' – and focussing instead on the issue of disarmament. On receiving this message, Wilson sent House a letter on Christmas Eve that laid out more complete thoughts.[15]

This Christmas Eve letter has caused House's historical reputation no end of damage, even though Wilson begins his instructions by specifically reiterating his intention to give House *carte blanche*: 'You ask me for instructions as to what attitude and tone you are to take at the several capitals. I feel you do not need any'. Wilson continued simply by parroting House's own advice back at him: 'I agree with you that we have nothing to do with local settlements – territorial questions, indemnities, and the like', concurring that it would be best if House instead focussed on disarmament and a league of nations. Steering clear of 'territorial questions' was a matter of tactics, not policy, and Wilson was perfectly content to rely on House's tactical judgement.[16]

The issue of how far the United States would go against Germany is not quite as clear cut because Wilson himself had not quite made up his mind on this issue and because both House and Wilson wanted to *end* the war, not be dragged into it. Wilson wrote on Christmas Eve that if either party was unreasonable, 'it will clearly be our duty to use our utmost moral force to oblige the other to parley, and I do not see how they could stand in the opinion of the world if they refused'.[17] The phrase 'moral force' has almost universally been distinguished from 'armed force' and interpreted therefore as a strict prohibition on providing anything more than mere rhetorical assistance.[18] Alone amongst historians, David Esposito observes cogently that a different reading is possible: 'Wilson thought in terms of moral force. He never would have tolerated "immoral" or "amoral" force'.[19] And indeed, why should the threat of armed force, in the service of a noble cause, not be considered 'moral force'? Wilson on 18 October, moreover, had authorized House to promise armed force: 'If the Central Powers were still obdurate, it would probably be necessary for us to join the Allies and force the issue'. True, two months later, House 'found the President not quite as belligerent as he was the last time we were together' and thinking that 'we would be able to keep out of the war'.[20] Yet while House wanted action out of his

President, by 'action', he told his diary, 'I mean not to declare war, but to let the Allies know we are definitely on their side and that it is not our intention to permit Germany to win'. The last thing House wanted, however, was for the Allies to have 'decisive success' militarily, for 'it would make our task much more difficult'.[21] The goal was peace, not war. Promising war, however, might be a necessary risk to achieve a negotiated peace. Everything would depend on the specific circumstances, and these the President entrusted to House.

Finally, there is one last line in Wilson's Christmas Eve letter to House that historians have seriously misunderstood. Wilson wrote: 'The errand upon which you are primarily bound you understand as fully and intimately as I do, and the demand in the Senate for further, immediate, and imperative pressure on England and her allies makes the necessity for it the more pressing'.[22] This reference to the Senate has been misinterpreted to suggest that Wilson believed that House was 'primarily' meant to lessen the difficulties of the blockade, or to communicate with Wilson's ambassadors.[23] This interpretation entirely mistakes Wilson's reference to US domestic politics: the preceding paragraph of Wilson's letter is all about arranging a peace conference. The possibility of bringing the war to a halt – the greatest imaginable coup of American diplomacy at this time – cannot be regarded as a mere secondary goal of House's mission. Rather, Wilson was commenting that, if House could pull a rabbit out of his diplomatic hat, the success would also completely obviate Wilson's domestic difficulties with regard to the war. After all, what senator would attempt to exert pressure on the President about Britain's blockade, or indeed about anything else, if Wilson had scored the greatest possible triumph – the convening of a peace conference?

House disembarked from the *Rotterdam*, and he took a train to London on 6 January 1916. Setting immediately to work, he gave advance notice to Grey and then turned up on his doorstep at seven o'clock that evening. House quickly discovered that, while his original plan would not work quite as he had intended, it still might have some potential if it was modestly remoulded. Grey began their talks by telling House 'of the progress of the war and all the misadventures that have befallen the Allies', but even so, the Foreign Secretary threw cold water on any notion of an early end to the war. Barely a week before, Grey had nearly left the Cabinet because he thought his government was lurching down a course promising catastrophe. McKenna's new committee, however, seems to have filled him with renewed optimism: Grey told House flatly that he 'thought things were going better now' and that 'Great Britain was never more resolute to win'.[24]

This, of course, was precisely what Grey had told House before. And so, though the Colonel continued to pursue his scheme, he cast it in a more intermediate-term perspective, dangling American diplomatic intervention as something the Allies could make use of at some future point. House talked about disarmament and ending 'militarism' and 'navalism', and communicated Wilson's newfound willingness to join a 'world agreement' for the 'maintenance of peace'. On 'freedom of the seas', as House phrased his ideas about naval disarmament and rights for nations to conduct their business upon the oceans, House was pleased to find that Grey was willing to 'meet me halfway'.[25] While House does not record exactly what Grey agreed to, Grey's position presumably approximated the nuance he had adopted the previous year, when he rejected the notion that Germany's ships should be able to go about unmolested while Germany itself would 'remain free to make war upon other nations at will'. He was, however, willing to implement new rules for the seas in a post-war order, provided that the United States would join, as he had put it in a September letter to House, in 'a League of Nations binding themselves to side against any Power which broke a Treaty; which broke certain rules of warfare on sea or land ... or which refused, in case of dispute, to adopt some other method of settlement than that of war'.[26]

With Grey still asserting that Britain believed it would win the war, House's approach had a clear diplomatic logic. By framing the situation in the intermediate term and steering clear of territorial questions, the Allies could make use of American diplomatic intervention to force Germany to the negotiating table whenever the time might be right. If the war kept going badly, the proposal could, as originally contemplated, be used to prevent the Allies from being completely overrun and to assure merely an unfavourable peace as an alternative to outright defeat. But if the Allies reversed the military tide, logically it could also be used to impose a favourable peace at a point when Germany might have preferred to fight on. The goal, in effect, was to provide the Allies with a mechanism to propose peace negotiations at a time of their choosing, and one that deprived Germany of the option of rejecting them. By pairing this mechanism with military and naval disarmament and, at Grey's urging, participation in an international league, House hoped to prevent future conflict and to preclude the possibility of a German threat to the Americas. House had but one caveat: he would not allow his scheme for diplomatic intervention to be used in desperation. The Allies could not try to use it once their armies were in full retreat and Germany certain it was at victory's cusp. At that point, no American threat could force the Germans to the negotiating table.

House sought simply to lay the foundation for the scheme, so that it could be activated whenever the time was right. Seen in this light, Grey's willingness to fall into line behind House's idea, as it was then constructed, makes sense. House's plan offered post-war peace and stability, insurance against outright defeat, and it could be used to impose a favourable peace against the Central Powers if and when the military situation shifted to the Allies' advantage later in the year. House's preference, of course, was to organize a peace conference as soon as possible, and to try to speed things up he purposefully embarked on a campaign of exaggerated gloom amongst British leaders that 'endeavored to shake' British confidence in the military situation.[27] House also realized that, as yet, Grey had not heard anything from the President himself about the United States' willingness to join this international league. The Colonel encoded a brief telegram to Wilson, summarizing the conversation and asking for the President to send a cable endorsing a policy 'seeking to bring about and maintain permanent peace among civilized nations' for use in the conference. Wilson replied, as requested, at once.[28]

House and Grey now had to decide who next in the British government it would be best for House to approach, with House observing that the Cabinet was not likely to be particularly cooperative. They quickly agreed on someone who might, they thought, 'be in sympathy with our purposes': the First Lord of the Admiralty, Arthur Balfour.[29] House had good reason to hope that the First Lord might be receptive. A philosophically minded Conservative elder statesman – a biographer dubbed him 'the last grandee' – Balfour had led his party for nine years, the first three as Prime Minister after his uncle's resignation in 1902. The following six years he spent battling the Liberals' programme of reform, which, to the Liberals' fury, he repeatedly obstructed by deploying his party's majority in the House of Lords. Asquith finally broke the tactic with the 1911 Parliament Act – a Liberal victory that also broke Balfour's leadership of his party. Yet despite the prevailing acrimony between the parties, a number of leading Liberals nevertheless developed a profound sense of respect for Balfour, especially on defence matters. Asquith occasionally involved him in the Committee of Imperial Defence; Grey periodically approached him for advice, as did Churchill. In November 1914, still five months away from coalition, Asquith appointed Balfour to his War Council. When coalition came, Balfour was the only Conservative appointed to a key office. By 1916, in many ways he had become closer to Asquith and Grey than to his Conservative colleagues.[30] House certainly conceived of the three men as a clique, and marvelled at Balfour's sharpness: 'It is not possible to allow one's wits to lag when one is in active discussion with him', House wrote admiringly.

'I am inclined to rank him along with the President and Mr. Asquith in intellectuality and this, to my mind, places him at the summit'.[31]

11 Arthur James Balfour (Library of Congress / George Grantham Bain Collection / LC-B2-3537-8)

Over lunch on 10 January, House revealed his scheme to Balfour, while Grey listened quietly. The discussion, however, soon got bogged down in a debate over 'freedom of the seas'. Balfour was not particularly receptive to the notion of accepting limits on British naval power, no matter how formulated. House found him 'not very constructive, but analytical and argumentative'. When the topic turned to the plan for diplomatic intervention, however, House thought he detected 'suppressed excitement' in the both of them, and Balfour showed greater receptiveness to the idea of an international league. Armed with the President's telegram, Balfour was left wondering whether the President could press through such an ambitious scheme that so completely upended America's entire diplomatic tradition. House argued that the President was 'more powerful during his term in office than any sovereign in Europe', noting the sharp contrast between the President's wide-ranging powers and the painstaking consensus-making needed for Britain's governing coalition. While no decisions were made, House found the conference 'entirely satisfactory' and planned to keep pushing.[32]

As House conducted his early negotiations, the increasingly bitter strategic divisions within the British Cabinet were about to give the Colonel's diplomacy an emphatic boost. The War Committee wrangled angrily over military strategy for Britain's prospective 1916 campaign. The military leaders had settled on their preferred course: a grand offensive on the Western Front. The plan, agreed at an Allied military conference at Chantilly in December, was for the Allies to hit the Central Powers hard from the east, west, and south near simultaneously. The British contribution would be the Battle of the Somme. Though Bonar Law immediately threw his support behind the generals' scheme, the rest of the civilians on the War Committee had no such enthusiasm. As the Committee battled over the plan in meetings on 28 December and 13 January, Balfour and Lloyd George argued frankly that any large offensive on the Western Front would fail. The First Lord contended that the 'defensive positions [there] had never been broken, and they were increasing in strength every day'; the military leaders had promised breakthroughs before and 'had been wrong every time'. The military responded flatly that Britain had no practicable military options elsewhere. Bonar Law summed up Britain's quandary succinctly: 'How', he asked pointedly, 'if both lines of thought were correct, [were they] ever to win the war'? A number of his colleagues would soon take his query to its logical conclusion. For now, however, the Committee compromised, allowing preparations for the offensive to go forward, but postponing for the moment any final decision.[33]

Alone amongst the Asquithians, Grey in his overarching strategic thinking at this moment came down squarely, albeit temporarily, on the side of the military authorities. Though technically not a member of the War Committee, Grey was often invited, and the 'paralysis of all strategy' he witnessed at the 13 January meeting filled him with alarm. Despite having moved to resign together with McKenna barely a couple of weeks before, the next day he circulated a memorandum to the War Committee articulating a strategy of 'Battle of the Somme or bust'. He believed that all the powers, Germany included, would be 'exhausted before another year is over' and that there 'will be a sort of general collapse and inconclusive peace before next Winter'. The 'only chance of victory', he wrote, was to 'hammer the Germans hard in the first eight months of this year. If this is impossible, we had better make up our minds to an inconclusive peace'. For now, Grey wanted to take the gamble: 'The plan for a great offensive in the West holds the field ...

[and] it should be proceeded with when the Military Authorities consider that the time has come to begin it'.[34] Grey, it seems, had fought so hard for McKenna's committee mainly to ensure that Britain's economic resources lasted at least through 1916. He still wanted to roll the dice on the Western Front – and then to have the Americans on hand diplomatically to deal with the outcome.

Lloyd George, simultaneously dismissive of Britain's economic constraints and yet deeply sceptical of a great offensive, conceived an even greater role for the Americans to play. Extremely depressed, Lloyd George foresaw only all the belligerents becoming exhausted. 'It was nonsense', Lloyd George had a month earlier told C. P. Scott, editor of the *Manchester Guardian*,

to talk about 'crushing' Germany; it was neither possible nor desirable. The best thing that could happen would be that when the two sides were seen to be evenly matched America should step in and impose terms on both. ... It would be useless for America to intervene now, but when both sides were exhausted her intervention might be decisive.[35]

With House available in London, Lloyd George decided to take his country's diplomacy into his own hands to press his idea. Lord Reading, Lloyd George's close friend, took House aside and asked House to meet exclusively with him and Lloyd George at a private dinner on 14 January.

As soon as the waiters left, Lord Reading sat quietly as Lloyd George, who knew nothing of House's talks with the others, launched into his own initiative for American diplomatic intervention. Remarkably frank, he told House exactly what he thought would happen over the course of the spring and summer – an improvement in the Allied position, with the Germans 'thrown back at many points', but fundamentally a continued stalemate. Lloyd George had given up altogether on the possibility of Allied victory, seeing only a war that would stretch on indefinitely. The war could be ended only by American diplomatic intervention, and he believed that public opinion in the belligerent countries would force the acceptance of Wilson's mediation. But the Allies needed a better stalemate first; and so the President's move could happen only after the summer offensives – 'around September first', Lloyd George ventured.

Where House still conceived of American diplomatic intervention as involving the belligerents sorting out the territorial terms themselves, Lloyd George instead wanted the Americans to take a far more active role. He wanted Wilson at the head of the negotiating table actually imposing the terms of the settlement. The President's moral authority combined with the United States's economic and military power, Lloyd

George said, would give Wilson the ability virtually to dictate a compromise. 'By [Wilson's] mandate', House recorded him saying, 'Russia is
to do this; Germany is to do that, and other nations do as he bids'. House
understandably found Lloyd George's views of Wilson's authority 'fan-
tastic', but was deeply pleased by the proposal. Quickly taking advantage
of this extraordinary conversation, House promptly proposed to Lloyd
George that any tentative agreement be confined to Asquith, Grey,
Balfour, Lloyd George, and Reading – Reading had no great influence,
but since he was sitting right there it would have been awkward to leave
him out. House asked Lloyd George to approach the others about his
idea. Lloyd George agreed.[36]

The next day, 15 January, House had his next conference with Grey
and Balfour. House opened by confiding in detail his remarkable dinner
with Lloyd George and Reading the night before. Predictably, Lloyd
George had told Balfour and Grey nothing of the plan, and the latter
two were irritated that Lloyd George had embarked on such a dramatic
diplomatic overture without having breathed so much as a word of it to
them in advance. Grey could not be too annoyed, however. Lloyd
George's scheme did not differ much from the one House and Grey
had been discussing, adding in only direct American participation in
negotiating the peace terms – which in any case Grey had favoured the
previous year. House told them he had asked Lloyd George to approach
them and Asquith about his idea. The trio then spent the remainder of
the session discussing the conditions that House wanted to encompass
the eventual American diplomatic intervention: military and naval disarmament, including 'freedom of the seas', and a post-war international
league. Grey broadly supported House, especially on a league of nations,
but Balfour again objected repeatedly to imposing international limits on
Britain's projection of sea power. Balfour agreed to think the matter
over,[37] and true to his word he soon produced a lengthy Cabinet memorandum, which, though expressing scepticism about disarmament,
thoughtfully examined how a league of nations might operate and
stressed above all the importance of American participation.[38] The two
of them said they would discuss the matter with Asquith and Lloyd
George while House went to the continent. House and Grey left the
meeting together, and, taking a stroll through London, the two
friends 'moralized upon how difficult it was to do the things that
seemed best, because the people did not understand and would not
permit free action'.[39]

On the evening of 19 January, House saw Grey for the final time before
departing for Germany and France. The two discussed their strategy for
how best to proceed, mainly trying to figure out how to accomplish their

aims without any damaging leaks. Grey thought that Reading should not have been included – he had no particular influence or authority, and his presence only served to increase the possibility of leaks. Both feared that Lloyd George would not be able to keep his mouth shut, but agreed that he was essential. The complexity and delicacy of the situation left House frustrated with the British system, especially in its present coalition setup, wishing he had 'but a single man to deal with here as at home'.[40]

While Lloyd George, Grey, and Balfour contemplated American diplomatic intervention as a possibility for the intermediate future – to impose a favourable peace or to mitigate a stalemate – McKenna had already come to favour it as soon as possible. McKenna, Asquith, and Conservative politician Austen Chamberlain had been taking intellectual command of the war through McKenna's hard-won, if inelegantly named, Committee for the Co-Ordination of Military and Financial Effort. The Committee was certainly not working out as McKenna had hoped. The trio had been plunging into every aspect of the country's war effort, with Hankey as their secretary. A series of officials and ministers was hauled in front of them, and they delved deeply into the figures relating to trade, finance, munitions, intelligence, recruiting, the Army, and the Navy. Though Chamberlain was prepared to run greater risks[41] – Asquith had chosen him because he was both the 'hottest of the conscript Unionists and Big Armyists' and yet also a former Chancellor of the Exchequer[42] – political differences seem to have been quickly set aside. The three worked diligently and earnestly to come to grips with a profoundly complex task: trying to assemble Britain's military and economy into a coherent picture, and then to place that into the wider war as a whole. Asquith, freed from his usual role of playing the mediator amongst rancorous partisans, took the lead as they peppered their interlocutors with intelligent and often difficult questions about the figures being provided and the assumptions underlying them – with Asquith frequently demanding more detailed numbers or that they be recalculated to take into consideration this factor or that.[43]

One understanding underlay everything else: Britain had a limited window to make its great effort before its ability to sustain it would be exhausted. The main question was how great the effort would be and, inversely, how long that effort could last. Asquith's 'personal view was that the world could not stand the strain of this tremendous expenditure for another year'. Unlike most of the Conservatives, Chamberlain 'agreed' with this premise from the outset, saying that they ought to 'concentrate on making a great military effort in 1916, leaving over some of our expenditure till 1917, if necessary'.

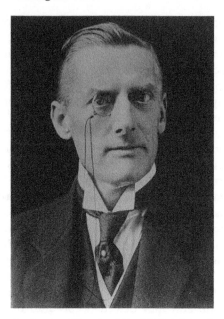

12 Austen Chamberlain (FPG / Getty Images)

A full review of the country's finances in the first meeting drove home those points. They had learnt the lesson of the near failure of their American loan. The Prime Minister bemoaned the 'inability to raise more than [$500 million] in the United States'. McKenna estimated that they still had in reserve ony about $2 billion in British-owned American securities to sell or mortgage. Once that was up, the alliance's reliance on American supplies would be coming to an end. Though this reserve would prove larger than McKenna expected, the problem was still enormous. Keeping France, Russia, and Italy well-supplied – crucial not only militarily but diplomatically – was a massive undertaking. McKenna broke down Britain's financial promises to its allies, a tightly kept secret, which reached nearly $3 billion for 1916 (British GDP in 1915 was only about $13.5 billion). Keynes later estimated that approximately four-fifths of these loans were being spent outside Britain, and mostly in the United States. The Committee well understood its alternatives: a 'smaller army'; an army less lavishly supplied 'for example, [with] less ammunition'; 'pay less to our allies'; or an earlier wind-down of the war effort.[44] As Chamberlain put it starkly to Robertson: would you rather 'maintain our force at a given strength until 1917 or ... have a larger force now and to give up the possibility of maintaining it for long'? For now, Robertson accepted the premise of the question, wanting the larger force now and agreeing that it 'was necessary for us to win this year or not at all'.[45]

Using two different possible schemes to frame the problem – holding the number of British divisions deployed in the field at their present fifty-four, or expanding them as the military wished to sixty-two – the trio delved deep into the problem, examining at length how much an additional division cost, the precise numbers of men the military might require, which men might be spared from what industries, and how quickly. They considered the losses the military might suffer, the details of the military registration and recruiting system, and the country's ports and shipping situation. They sifted through intelligence estimates of the numbers and locations of enemy divisions and the Allied divisions available to counter them. In turn, officials from the Treasury; the military's financial, statistics, recruiting, and registration sections; the Board of Trade; the Munitions Ministry; and Military Intelligence were all summoned,[46] providing 'masses of evidence' for the Committee to work through.[47]

The only real pyrotechnics came when Lloyd George was hauled before the Committee. McKenna felt justified in subjecting him to a rough cross-examination: even Robertson had been critical of Lloyd George's over-ordering, saying he was 'very doubtful whether the Army would be able to find the men to man all the guns that were being made'. It was, Robertson said, 'quite probable they would not be used'.[48] McKenna lit into Lloyd George with a series of hostile questions, demanding that Lloyd George justify what seemed a colossal and reckless waste of the country's preciously finite resources. Lloyd George's principal defence was that over-ordering would allow him to provide the Army what it had requested more quickly. As McKenna worked to pick apart this justification, it rapidly became clear that while Lloyd George understood in depth the different kinds of guns and shells he was charged with providing – the only thing that he thought actually mattered – he comprehended little how much his ministry was spending, and cared even less. Eventually, Asquith called a halt to the acrimonious exchange: it was all 'past history and had been done'. Turning to the future, McKenna then confronted Lloyd George with alarming departmental estimates seeming to show that, just in the past few weeks, the ministry had increased its projected spending requirements by one-third. Lloyd George could not explain the increase, and had to summon in a pair of his subordinates to explain that in fact the larger number represented the ministry's maximum liability and that the smaller number represented its likely actual expenditures.[49]

As the Committee deliberated over its evidence, McKenna argued forcefully for holding the number of divisions at their current level. Further military expansion, he thought, necessitated 'run[ning] grave financial and economic risks' at likely 'very little result' militarily. They would be gambling everything on the 1916 offensive. 'If it was not successful', he warned, 'this would result in our defeat'. Not only this, but it was distinctly possible that their resources might not even last through the end of the offensive, and that 'destruction might be reached during the course of this experiment'.[50] Runciman at the Board of Trade urged his friend to hold the line: 'We must decline to be swindled with our eyes open'.[51]

Chamberlain acknowledged the seriousness and precariousness of their economic position: they were burning through the country's vast stock of American investments at an extraordinary pace. '[T]his could only be done once', he observed sombrely, 'and then we should have used up our securities'. But he still felt inclined to roll the dice. The masses of statistics they had gathered could not predict the course of the war with certainty, and he felt less certain than McKenna that forgoing eight divisions would enhance their staying power for long. Indeed, if it helped them through only for a few extra months, but not actually even long enough to push through a full 1917 campaign, there would be little point.[52]

With his committee divided, Asquith proposed, as an anxious Hankey put it, 'firing the whole thing at the War Committee without a recommendation'. This, at least, would have the advantage of forcing Bonar Law and Lloyd George to spend some time contending with the limits of the country's staying power. Hankey, however, wanted a recommendation out of the trio, and succeeded in getting one.[53]

The result never really was in doubt. Taking intellectual command of the war hardly translated into taking *actual* command of the war. The Committee grappled as best it could with the realities of the conflict, and now had as complete a picture as could be had of where the country's war effort stood, and where it was headed. The political unrealities operating outside it, however, all but determined the outcome from the outset. Whatever Robertson wanted, he would get. The unimpressed general saw only parsimony in McKenna's efforts to explain Britain's economic limitations, airily dismissing the Committee's concerns about labour shortages: 'The streets of England', he told the Committee, seemed 'full of lazy men who were doing nothing'.[54] He did not really understand why McKenna was opposing him. 'The attitude of some ministers', Robertson complained privately, 'is rather to find out what is the smallest amount of money and the smallest number of men with which we may hope, someday, to win the war, or rather not to lose it'.[55] He told the Committee flatly that there was 'no limit to the number of men we ought to place in the field if they were obtainable'.[56]

Asquith evidently persuaded McKenna to yield to political necessity. The Committee's concluding recommendations bowed to the military's demands, approving an effort to have sixty-two divisions in the field while maintaining a further five divisions at home. But the Committee's investigation of the War Office's conscription and recruiting system left them in doubt that the military 'can in practice' assemble the additional divisions very rapidly at all. The Committee warned unambiguously that maintaining this effort required resort to 'financial expedients ... [that could] only be continued for a short period'. If the anticipated delays in recruiting materialized, it would be no bad thing, as it would allow them to keep Britain's war effort at its 'maximum for a longer period'. Backing up its conclusions came a lengthy report assembling many of the detailed figures that the Committee had painstakingly pored over during the previous month.[57] Yet for the Cabinet, accepting the report did not mean accepting its caveats. Those so inclined could, and did, take the recommendation as a victory and dismiss the remainder as defeatist drivel.

Amongst those who favoured an all-out effort in 1916, it seems that only Chamberlain accepted the consequences. The war almost certainly had to be won this year. Chamberlain's position, it should be emphasized, was a perfectly reasonable one. McKenna's approach certainly carried its own diplomatic and military dangers: Britain's allies would have surely resented the British limiting their military deployment, perhaps even to the point that Britain risked one of them seeking a separate peace. Without the extra military forces, Germany might have been able to defeat the Allies on the battlefield. The government faced a difficult choice, and the best answer was far from obvious. 'It was, after all, a question of degree of risk', Asquith commented. '[T]here was a considerable element of speculation in the matter either way'.[58] Though Chamberlain prevailed, he understood that from this point forward the key task of the British government would be to concentrate all of the country's effort as quickly as possible for one short spurt – and then, if it failed, to prepare for a drastic retrenchment.

The maximalists in the government, by contrast, refused to accept the country was embarking on any kind of a gamble at all. Many would begin nonchalant discussion of a 1917 campaign within a few short months. Any notion of an inevitable retrenchment they would dismiss as ridiculous. Chamberlain offered the government a coherent strategy. Lloyd George and his Conservative allies, by contrast, insisted upon an economic fantasy. But for now, Chamberlain's strategy and the maximalists' fantasies could co-exist peacefully. The committee report went through the Cabinet without difficulty. Asquith confidant Edwin Montagu congratulated the Prime Minister on having successfully steered the government 'quite clear of that ditch'. 'Viewed as a method of harmonising Chamberlain and McKenna it seems quite brilliant', Montagu wrote cheerfully. 'All's well that ends well'.[59] Not all were pleased, however. Runciman wrote despairingly: '*We have failed*'.[60]

By mid-January, it seems, McKenna had seen the writing on the wall. With his country on the cusp of gambling everything on a proposed summer offensive he did not believe could succeed, McKenna became the first to look to the Americans for an early way out. He appears to have made some sort of January overture to House, though the precise details are unclear. McKenna's only private meeting with House came on 11 January, when House's young secretary, Clifford Carver – close friends with McKenna and his wife – had set up a social lunch. House's diary, however, records only that McKenna talked somewhat about his battles within the Cabinet and that, clearly mindful of his country's economic position, McKenna cast himself as fervently pro-American. Yet eight days later, House mentions without explanation that Lloyd George 'must have talked to McKenna already' about his plan, 'since McKenna has expressed about the same views to a settlement as Lloyd George has'. Since House records no further private meetings, most likely McKenna had transmitted this through the young Carver.[61]

Appalled at Britain's strategic mire, McKenna confided to Hankey that they 'should probably get a better peace now than later when Germany is wholly on the defensive' – that is, that the *threat* of the summer offensive seemed more likely to get better peace terms out of Germany than would the offensive itself. McKenna, Hankey wrote, 'admitted to me that he had discussed the matter with Colonel House … I know that Grey and Balfour together, and McKenna and Lloyd George secretly and separately have discussed peace possibilities with Col. House. Curious how they all confide in me!'[62] Hankey, though he had expressed personal scepticism about House, wrote that he was personally 'inclined to agree' with the Chancellor's view that an early peace, arranged through the United States, was in the Allies' best interest. Significantly, Hankey had none of Grey's faith that an international league could contain Germany in the future, dismissing the idea a 'dangerous' distraction that would only 'create a sense of security which is wholly fictitious'.[63] Hankey's concurrence was based purely on military and economic calculation – revealing just how bad that calculation had become.

As a number of British leaders moved quietly towards American mediation, British intelligence opened a window into House's negotiations – a window that Reginald Hall attempted to deploy against them. MI1(b) had been systematically decrypting House's telegrams to Wilson, giving others in the government insight into the conversations that House was working so hard to keep tightly concealed. What little evidence that survives centres on the head of Room 40, Reginald Hall, who received copies of the decrypts from MI1(b), and who sought to deploy the intelligence to sabotage House's efforts. Deeply interested in their American visitor, Hall had seen House at two dinners and a luncheon during House's two-week stay in London. Hall had sought to inject himself into the negotiations, writing later that that he had 'endeavoured to convince' House during these meetings 'that we were out to beat the Germans, not by words and treaties, but by horrible deeds of blood!' House, however, took little notice of Hall's views, dismissing these occasions in his diary as unimportant.[64]

By 27 January, Hall had obtained copies from MI1(b) of the three telegrams that House had thus far sent to Wilson. If Hall expected a treasure trove of information, however, he was sorely disappointed. Unlike the previous year, House now dispatched only terse telegrams usually giving only the barest of information. House's faith in his 'absolutely safe' code had obviously been deeply shaken; he wrote repeatedly to Wilson that he had extremely important information that he dared not cable, preferring instead to send letters through the slower but securer American diplomatic pouch.[65] Ironically, Hall probably had his own division to blame for House's newfound wariness. The naval attaché to the United States, Guy Gaunt, Hall's friend and subordinate, had met House for the first time a few months before and thereafter bragged 'constantly' to House of Hall and his activities.[66] The amiable Gaunt chattered so effusively about his work to combat German intelligence efforts that House thought him afflicted by 'the German spy craze'. These conversations had raised the profile of British intelligence considerably. During a courtesy call that House paid to the King, George V, on 14 January, for example, House 'favourably called [the King's] attention to Captain Hall ... and to Captain Gaunt'.[67] Made more vigilant by these encounters, House apparently decided – correctly – that his supposedly impenetrable code might be considerably more vulnerable than he had imagined.

From a traditional intelligence perspective, therefore, House's short telegrams were of extremely limited use. In Grey's hands, they would have told him virtually nothing he did not already know. In fact, it would have likely been to *House's* advantage because all they would have proved was that House was not pursuing a hidden agenda. For an intelligence chief inclined to independent political action, however, the decrypts seem to have provided Hall a limited and secret window through which to observe his government's negotiations with House.

Indeed, House's first cable, sent 7 January, contained a passage that Hall undoubtedly saw as a bombshell: House informed Wilson that 'Grey is now in favour of the freedom of the seas provided it includes the elimination of militarism, and further provided we will join in [a] general covenant to sustain it'.[68] Hall saw in 'freedom of the seas' a German plot to subjugate the Royal Navy. The phrase was a 'dangerous catch term', Hall had written a year before, with which the Germans hoped to 'wrest from us the command of the oceans'.[69] Worse still, the telegram seemed to implicate Balfour, Hall's political master at the Admiralty, as House wrote to Wilson that Balfour's and Grey's 'minds run parallel with ours', though House 'doubt[ed] their colleagues'. Revealing that House was on a peace effort, Hall saw that House had, for use in his negotiations, asked Wilson to cable 'assurance of your willingness to cooperate in a policy seeking to bring about and maintain permanent peace among civilized nations', which Wilson had done promptly.[70]

The next telegrams, from 10 and 15 January, indicated that House had found his conference with Grey and Balfour 'entirely satisfactory'. So far, there had been 'no disagreement', and House wrote that his 'plan [was] to come to a tentative agreement … before going to the Continent'. He gave no sign of what this agreement might consist of, but reported that Grey and Balfour had consented to bring their colleagues around to this mysterious 'tentative agreement' by the time House returned. 'There seems to be some daylight ahead if fortune favours us'.[71]

Rather than having them immediately distributed to relevant individuals and departments, particularly the Foreign Office, Hall deployed the decrypts politically. Since as far as Hall knew Grey and Balfour were already trying to bring their colleagues on board in support of House's proposal, Hall almost certainly began working to oppose House's initiative. We catch a glimpse of his efforts when on 27 January – just two days after the first American decrypts begin to appear in Room 40 files – Hall showed the telegrams to Hankey, calling special attention to the line about freedom of the seas. Hankey had been in the Royal Navy, and his reaction illustrates the internal political nature of the decrypts' use: what they revealed about Grey struck Hankey far more than what they revealed about American diplomacy. Hankey recorded only perfunctorily in his diary that the decrypts confirmed his 'suspicions' that 'House is over here on a peace "stunt."' What 'really horrified' him, however, 'was that Grey seems to have given House the impression that he would bargain the "Freedom of the Seas" against German militarism'. He blasted Grey's willingness to deal at some length, calling it 'a most ridiculous idea' and saying that he could 'imagine no greater folly'.[72]

House's commitment to keeping his messages brief and vague for security reasons was quickly challenged. Wilson and his Secretary of State, Robert Lansing, suddenly blundered into two major diplomatic storms that threatened to undercut his delicate negotiations. First, just as House was leaving Britain, they sent the British a highly unwelcome note proposing a *modus vivendi*: in exchange for the British disarming their seafaring merchantmen, Germany would agree not to torpedo them without warning. This proposal – asking, in effect, for the British to consent to sending more of their shipping to the bottom of the Atlantic in exchange for fewer sailors going down with their ships – received a frosty reception. The British war effort, already straining under a shortage of shipping, frankly cared far more about the survival of its merchant ships than it did about the survival of their crews.[73]

Second, the last that House knew, the lengthy negotiations over Germany's apology concerning the *Lusitania* had at last nearly been settled. Wilson had cabled to that effect as recently as 11 January.[74] Barely two weeks later, House abruptly received a lengthy cable in Berlin saying that Germany refused to admit that the sinking was illegal, and unless they did so, the United States would escalate the crisis and sever diplomatic relations[75] – on the same day that the controversy was exploding into the press.[76]

Observing communications silence because he especially distrusted the security of telegrams sent from Germany,[77] House arrived in Berne on 30 January and immediately fired off a message home. Seeing severing relations 'largely upon the wording of a suitable apology' over 'a nine months' old issue' as a serious mistake, he decided to break with his pattern of giving only the barest of information. Careful not to go beyond what was absolutely needed, he explained to Wilson that the German Navy 'believe that England can be effectively blockaded provided Germany can use their new and powerful submarines indiscriminately' and that the naval leaders blamed the failure to do so on 'our interference and Germany's endeavour to conform to our demands'. The Navy almost openly preferred war with the United States if it meant they could use their submarines to break and reverse the British blockade. 'The civil government believe that if the blockade continues', he wrote,

they may be forced to yield to the navy; consequently they are unwilling to admit to the illegality of their under-sea warfare. They will yield anything but this. If you insist on that point, I believe war will follow.

House urged strongly against any definitive action until he could confer with Wilson personally.[78] Sensing the urgency and gravity of the situation, he again pressed the President, two days later from Paris, not to break over the *Lusitania*: 'I doubt whether a crisis with Germany can long be avoided. … The blockade will make the demand imperative that an attempt be made to break it by transcendent sea warfare', at which point the Americans would 'be compelled to sever relations' in a 'far better' diplomatic position.[79] House succeeded in squelching the controversy, and Wilson quickly reversed course.[80]

When Hankey visited the Admiralty again on 1 February, Hall definitely already had the decrypt of House's 30 January cable to Wilson, probably had the cable from Lansing that House received on 28 January, and possibly had House's 1 February cable to Wilson. Hankey wrote of the telegrams:

Their trend was to indicate, firstly, that the Germans will not agree to the proposals of the U.S.A. for settlement of the Lusitania episode; secondly that the reason for this is that the German Adty. have built big submarines, and seriously believe that they can blockade England …; thirdly that this may force America to break off negotiations and produce war with the U.S.A.

Hankey describes the information as 'priceless'[81] – or, at least, it might have been, had House not simply given this information to Grey himself, and likely in greater detail, when he returned soon thereafter.[82]

More striking, however, is that both Hall and the War Office suppressed this potentially 'priceless' intelligence from their political masters. Hankey records that Hall had not shown the decrypts 'even' to Balfour – likely because Hall believed that Balfour was implicated in the business over freedom of the seas.[83] Perhaps even more importantly, Grey received none of this intelligence, even though as Foreign Secretary he of anyone had the greatest right to it. On 2 February, Lansing cabled House about the merchantmen disarmament proposal, telling him in no uncertain terms that 'the proposal has no relation to [the] *Lusitania* settlement and [has] not yet [been] mentioned to Germany'.[84] Showing clearly that he did not receive a decrypt of this telegram, Grey prepared a memorandum between 13 and 15 February, writing that he 'cannot help feeling that the American [merchantmen disarmament] proposals form part of a *transaction*' between the United States and Germany concerning the *Lusitania*.[85] The suppression of this intelligence allowed the Foreign Office to suspect conspiracies where none existed.

House had gone to Berlin primarily to listen and to take the temperature there.[86] In Paris, however, House worked to pave the way for the British to move on his proposal. All peace talk within a wartime alliance carries significant diplomatic risk. House directly discussing his ideas with the French would reduce the dangers should the British follow up on his conversation. On 7 February, laid out the plan to the French Prime Minister, Aristide Briand, with Jules Cambon, former French Ambassador to the United States, acting as translator. 'In the event the Allies are successful during the next few months', House recorded, 'I promised that the President would not intervene. In the event they were losing ground, I promised the President would intervene'. House still conceived of the plan only as giving a mechanism for the Allies to stave off defeat. If the Allies were gaining ground, the French would have no need of the scheme, but, if they were losing, the United States could intervene diplomatically, threatening to enter the war to force Germany to the negotiating table and thereby prevent a full collapse. House assured them that 'the lower the fortunes of the Allies ebbed, the closer the United States would stand by them', but at the same time he warned them 'not to let the fortunes of the Allies recede beyond a point where our intervention could save them', emphasizing 'the danger of delay and of too much optimism'. It seems that House had decided to abandon connecting American diplomatic intervention to disarmament and freedom of the seas. Apparently deeming them more trouble than they were worth, he made no mention of them.[87]

Yet House's proposal seems to have gotten seriously lost in translation. The French record of the meeting badly mangled the scheme: if the Allies were to have '*un petit succès*' by the summer, Cambon wrote, 'the United States will intervene in favor of peace'. But if they suffered '*un revers*', then 'the United States will intervene militarily and take part in the war against Germany'.[88] Though some historians have treated the French record as a more reliable account of what House said than House's own diary,[89] there is every reason to believe that Cambon had seriously misunderstood House's meaning. While House had left Germany worried that the Germans might soon launch unrestricted submarine warfare, in no other instance did House ever indicate that a US military intervention could be in the cards unless first preceded by a diplomatic one. And House was trying to sell the scheme to the French on the basis that it could prevent their defeat – as such, it made no sense for him to say that the Americans intended to intervene diplomatically against Allied wishes if the Allies were gaining ground. House left Paris thinking he had settled a useful possible path forward with France. The reality proved almost precisely the opposite.

Two days later, House journeyed back to London. He quickly discovered that three weeks could prove an eternity in war: Grey had now changed his mind entirely. The Foreign Secretary had clearly been dissuaded from hanging his hopes on the planned summer offensive and joined the ranks of its sceptics. With McKenna's economic strategy discarded and the British now hurtling down the path of 'Battle of the Somme or bust', Grey joined McKenna and Hankey in looking for an escape. The Americans must be brought into the war or it must be ended. House and Grey met on 10 February. House told him in detail of what he had seen in the meantime. Grey noted the recent re-eruption of the *Lusitania* crisis and tried to persuade House that the United States should enter the war on the Allied side, but when House took this off the table, the two reverted to discussing the plan for diplomatic intervention. House gave way and dropped disarmament and freedom of the seas, 'agree[ing] that it was best for the President not to set any conditions whatever, but merely to demand that war cease'.

House's raising his intervention scheme in Paris mildly eased the profound diplomatic dangers of mediation talk within the alliance, and Grey expressed particular gratitude when House mentioned discussing it, as Grey could now talk to the French about House without causing 'something like a panic'. The two planned out the details of the next few days. First, the two would lunch with Asquith and Balfour the following day. House would then go from there to have dinner with Lloyd George and Reading. Then, in three days' time, all six would gather together.[90]

The first group gathered around the table at Grey's home. After allowing the other three to state their thinking as they ate their lunch, House began working on them. The ministers were particularly concerned about their allies, wondering how they could endorse American diplomatic intervention without causing alarm, but House believed his arguments were making an impression. Though the meeting was 'inconclusive', House felt pleased with his progress.[91] Additionally, though House makes no mention of it in his diary, at some point during the previous few days he apparently promised to try to squelch the merchantmen disarmament controversy. House dispatched a telegram to Wilson strongly urging that 'no further notes or protests be sent' until House returned, and the President quickly dropped the proposal.[92]

That evening, 'like an old sheepdog nudging his flock toward the pen',[93] House saw the other side, showing up at Lord Reading's home at eight o'clock. The three quickly got down to business. Lloyd George preferred to have the United States simply enter the war over the *Lusitania* or another issue, but once House took this off the table, Lloyd George and Reading accepted American diplomatic intervention, at least eventually and in principle.[94]

On the morning of 14 February, House had one final session with Grey to work on their strategy for the key conference that night. For the first time, and evidently with Grey's encouragement, House began to talk about American diplomatic intervention involving not merely setting up peace negotiations, but having President Wilson actually come to the Hague and preside over them himself. In a profound shift from the previous month, Grey confided to House that not only did he favour House's plan, but he also personally believed that the time had already come to implement it. Grey told House that, if the others favoured the plan, they had not dared to express it. The public was completely against peace, and they could 'even go so far as to smash his windows' if the government pursued it, but that was something that Grey was willing to face.[95]

That night, the full group gathered around the table at Reading's home. After the butler withdrew, House used a general discussion of the war to stoke gloom about the Allied outlook. House's efforts here by now were beginning to have a significant effect.[96] Lloyd George's secretary and mistress, Frances Stevenson, recorded in her diary how 'very depressed' and 'pessimistic about us ever pulling it off' Lloyd George had become, and Lloyd George after the meeting gave her House's alarming assessment in detail.[97] Two days before the meeting, Hankey similarly had found Balfour 'depressed', with the First Lord telling him of House's report that the 'German Navy & Army are stronger than we calculate', and that Germany 'may outlast the allies notwithstanding their economic difficulties'.[98] Strikingly, House offered up a prediction 'that the Germans would probably attack the Allies in the west and perhaps at Verdun, and would attack quickly, not waiting for the spring weather to open' – a prediction that very soon would be proven right.[99]

At about half past ten, House directed the conversation back to a future American diplomatic intervention. Lloyd George, contemplating a conference at The Hague presided over by President Wilson, led a lengthy discussion about possible peace terms. House drew him out and got him to commit categorically to the plan, though Lloyd George was now 'chary' of naming a definite time for intervention. Grey signalled that he favoured 'an immediate venture in this direction'. Asquith asked House when he thought the proper time would be; House ventured that, 'if the Allies could make an impression on the German lines of sufficient importance to discourage Germany, that would be the psychological moment'. Asquith agreed 'heartily', confiding that an especially 'deep dent in the German lines' was 'success ... greater than he now considered possible'. Lloyd George and Balfour accepted the idea in principle, but both were 'inclined to take the risk ... and postpone action until sometime later'. The discussion continued until midnight, when at last they made a move to go. House summarized the evening in his diary:

While the conference was not conclusive, there was at least a common agreement reached ... [that] the President should at some time, to be later agreed upon, call a halt and demand a conference. I did not expect to go beyond that, and I was quite content.[100]

In a brief letter to a friend, Asquith described the meeting in guarded terms – understandably, given its potentially explosive content –but without a trace of cynicism: 'We had rather an interesting talk with Col. House at your friend Lord R[eading]'s last night. Ll[oyd] George was particularly good, and A. J. B[alfour] also contributed'.[101]

House turned up at Grey's home the next morning. House found Grey overwhelmed with the historical import of the previous evening. Showing considerable emotion, Grey paced the room as he told House that the government 'had not faced so momentous a decision ... since July 1914'. Grey personally wanted the proposal implemented at once, 'so that the lives of millions of men might be saved and the havoc which would follow another spring and summer campaign might be avoided'. Grey knew that the plan would be unpopular – and fully expected to have a mob attacking his home if his colleagues went through with it – but said he was 'ready to face it'. He especially congratulated House for having gotten Lloyd George so thoroughly committed to the plan, as Grey had not been sure how he might have brought Lloyd George on board, and he had unusually kind words for Lloyd George himself. The two continued by discussing how best to wrap up their agreement, deciding to write up a memorandum of their understanding and to inform the rest of the Cabinet of what had transpired only after House had returned to the United States.[102]

The day after, 16 February, House saw Balfour for a few minutes of private conversation as the two drove to the House of Commons. Balfour was 'satisfied' with the results of the conference. Like Grey, he had kind words for the 'breadth of vision' and 'courage' that Lloyd George had displayed – he had not thought the man had it in him.[103] Balfour's positive reaction is confirmed in a brief personal letter that Balfour wrote to the British Ambassador to the United States, Cecil Spring Rice, that same day. Balfour reported himself pleased by the 'very agreeable' conferences he had taken part in with Colonel House, though he wrote that he felt that the conferences had not 'thoroughly cleared' Anglo-American difficulties, and the confused overall situation seemed 'in many respects as obscure as ever' – likely a reference to the disarmament imbroglio and the ongoing shipping difficulties.[104] Hankey corroborates Balfour's candour with House, writing that Balfour told him that 'he talked to House with almost complete openness on all aspects of the war'.[105]

On 17 February, Lord Reading visited House in the morning, calling the conference three days earlier 'a great success'. He complimented House's diplomacy, saying that a 'great work had been accomplished by getting them all committed to the general proposition in the presence of each other' as there 'was no way now by which one could attack the other to his disadvantage'. Reading said that he thought that 'the Prime Minister had committed himself more strongly than he had any idea he would'.[106]

House went directly from this meeting to Grey's home. The Foreign Secretary reiterated his support for fast action. Charged with emotion, Grey told him that 'history will lay a great charge against those of us who refuse to accept your proffered services at this time'. The extraordinary relationship House had cultivated with Grey continued to bear fruit as Grey showed him the memorandum that the French had written up of House's key conference in Paris on 7 February. Finding to his dismay that the French had believed that he had said the United States would enter the war when asked, no matter how dismal the Allies' fortune became, House asked Grey to clear up that misperception.[107]

The two of them started drafting what would become known as the House-Grey Memorandum, which provided that President Wilson would, 'on hearing from France and England that the moment was opportune, ... propose that a conference should be summoned'. Should Germany refuse to attend, the 'United States would probably enter the war against Germany'. The conference, chaired by the President, would secure 'terms not unfavourable to the Allies'. These would involve 'the restoration of Belgium, the transfer of Alsace and Lorraine to France, and the acquisition by Russia of an outlet to the sea, though ... the loss of territory incurred by Germany ... would have to be compensated to her by concessions to her in other places outside Europe'. If Germany was 'unreasonable', the United States 'would[108] leave the conference as a belligerent on the side of the Allies'. If the Allies too long delayed and the war went wrong, however, 'the United States would probably disinterest themselves in Europe and look to their own protection'.[109]

The following Monday, 21 February, House again met with Grey. Although Grey continued to believe that American intervention should be sought at once, the two discussed how quickly the plan might actually be implemented. Grey told House that he thought that the timing would depend on the opinion of the military authorities. 'If they considered the situation warranted waiting a few months for military success', Grey said, 'it would be necessary to yield to this opinion'. Grey showed him a revised version of their memorandum and reported that he had seen the French Ambassador, who had asked how serious Grey believed it to be, with Grey telling him that it was indeed very serious. 'I was convinced', Grey reiterated to the Ambassador the following day,

that President Wilson really was prepared, if the Allies desired it, to take the action that Colonel House stated. I believed that the Allies could, if they desired it, have a Conference now, presided over by President Wilson, on the lines described by Colonel House in Paris and here; and that, if Germany refused such a Conference, President Wilson would intervene [militarily] on the side of the Allies.[110]

That morning, Lord Reading visited House, eager to tell him of a private conversation with the Prime Minister. Asquith had talked 'more strongly in favor of the agreement than he had at the conference', even going so far as considering altering military strategy to 'make a push in the west at the earliest possible date, so that the President's proposal may come as soon as possible', a revelation that weighed on House heavily. Reading had also seen Lloyd George, who was 'cordial in his support of the understanding, though he does not believe with Asquith and Grey that the time will be auspicious as soon as they think'.[111] Though Lloyd George, like Balfour, contemplated a later intervention, the Munitions Minister nevertheless was deeply serious about it eventually taking place: later that night, Lloyd George 'could not keep his mind off work,' his secretary and mistress, Frances Stevenson, wrote in her diary. He was

preparing a Memorandum to show that the Germans have *not* yet come to the end of their resources and that we cannot count on being superior to them either in men or material ... D[avid] says that unless the U.S.A. come in to help us, we cannot hope for victory.[112]

House's mediation plan had been steadily gaining steam within the British government. At a War Committee meeting the next day, 22 February, however, that momentum suddenly lurched into reverse. The War Committee began by continuing to resist authorizing the proposed Western Front offensive. Lloyd George, while confident in meeting his munitions production targets, doubted that they could 'catch up' with the Germans and 'did not understand how we could decide on offensive action'. McKenna stubbornly demanded historical analyses of previous offensives there, strongly doubting that another one would produce different results. The Committee postponed any decisions, pending additional information.

Grey then made a transparent move to pin down Lloyd George on American mediation in front of Bonar Law and the military

leadership.[113] Half of those present still did not know of House's proposal – House would not depart until the following day, and Grey stuck
to his promise not to reveal it until House left.[114] Instead, using a general
discussion of diplomacy with neutrals, Grey painted the broadest outlines of a hypothetical American diplomatic intervention for a peace
based more or less on the *status quo ante*. The Allies should not turn to
Wilson unless they had 'given up all idea of being able to finish the War'
on their own, he said, and then he pointedly 'referred to Mr Lloyd
George for his opinion'.[115]

It was a pivotal moment. Lloyd George now had the chance to force a
genuine discussion of his doubts that the war remained winnable – and to
provide important political cover for those who felt the same way. Yet
House had seen the mistrust, noting how 'evident' it was that 'Lloyd
George is somewhat distrustful of the Prime Minister, Grey and Balfour,
and they are equally so of him. Neither group wants the other to have the
advantage ... for fear capital might be made of it by the others'.[116]

Lloyd George refused to take the risk. He evaded the probe and
refused to answer the question, replying that he 'thought it would be
far better to leave the United States alone'. With Lloyd George seeming
to renege on everything he had said in the conference with House the
week before, the political danger in the meeting minutes at this point is
palpable. An apprehensive Asquith, having already signalled his support
for early action on the plan to Lloyd George through Reading, rejoined
immediately that he 'was certain that the United States Government was
determined not to come into the War'. Grey, no doubt a bit alarmed at
having his manoeuvre backfiring so spectacularly, decided to show Lloyd
George he was prepared to come out into the open. The Foreign
Secretary told the Cabinet that he 'did not agree, and thought by not
contemplating what he had suggested we might be missing a great
opportunity'. Asquith carefully and partially walked back his previous
statement, saying that 'there was no harm in endeavouring to bring the
United States in' – giving Lloyd George a second chance to open up
about his views. Lloyd George again declined. Perhaps attempting to hint
that the time remained far from ripe for this conversation, Lloyd George
said vaguely only that 'he thought the American Government might like
to come in *later*' – consistent with his view that the intervention scheme
was more appropriate at a later date. Grey and Asquith then rowed back
fully, with both now expressing further notes of scepticism, and Lloyd
George closed the discussion with a suggestion 'that nothing should be
done at present'.[117]

The next morning, Grey had his last conversation with House before
the Colonel returned home. Grey said nothing of the disaster he had

encountered in the War Committee the day before, which would have risked confessing both that the pact may have been unravelling just as House was preparing to leave and that he had skirted House's injunction not to say anything until House had left. Grey gave his friend the final version of the memorandum to take home, and the two of them shared an intimate moment as they said their goodbyes:

Grey expressed the hope that the time would not be far distant when I would visit him in his Northumberland home, when we could arise each morning and greet each other with the salutation, 'the war is over'. He was affectionate in his expressions of friendship, saying I could never know how much my coming into his life has meant.[118]

Grey likely hoped that he could rescue the previous day's debacle at a private lunch with McKenna and Lloyd George that afternoon. Given the extent to which Grey's interlocutors loathed each other, this was clearly no ordinary social call. The only account is that which Lloyd George gave to Frances Stevenson, who wrote that the main topic was 'the prospects of the war'. Distorted though this second-hand account may be, she wrote that Grey and McKenna both supported early negotiations. 'Grey is frankly pessimistic, and is for making peace at once', while 'McKenna was for treating for peace now – getting President Wilson to intervene & mediate'. Lloyd George, it seems, held firm in his retreat, having no intention of risking being seen to support American diplomatic intervention before it became necessary. He 'reminded [Grey] that there are our Allies to be dealt with, and that France will never make peace until Alsace & Lorraine are restored to her', while he 'took [McKenna] up sharply. "Public opinion will not stand it", [Lloyd George] said'.[119] Yet though Lloyd George would not open up to his colleagues about his views, his private opinions remained unchanged: the war remained unwinnable, and American diplomacy would prove the eventual and inevitable end of the war. '[A]s usual strong pessimistic', *Manchester Guardian* editor C. P. Scott would note after another confidential conversation less than a week later. 'Reverted to the suggestion he had thrown out when I last saw him of a possible intervention by the United States when both sides were getting exhausted. Said he had seen Colonel House and implied that House had given some encouragement to the idea'.[120]

That night, House and his party packed their things and took the night train to Falmouth, returning across the Atlantic via the same ship, the *S.S. Rotterdam*.[121] Amongst the files that House packed away were copies of the handful of telegrams he had sent Wilson over the past weeks[122] – copies that also assuredly were in the hands of British military and naval intelligence. House had restrained himself admirably. He had confined his detailed reports to the safe but slow diplomatic pouch, continuing to telegraph repeatedly that he 'dare[d] not cable' in more detail.[123] Even so, in addition to providing some information on his efforts to quash the merchantmen disarmament issue, House provided unmistakable signs in his telegrams that he had been pressing the British leadership on a peace proposal, and that it was getting a rather warmer reception than his unintended recipients in British intelligence would have wished. Grey had 'agree [d] to practically all the programme suggested by me', House had telegraphed after his first meeting on his return to London. 'Tomorrow we will bring the substance of our understanding before Asquith and [Balfour], and if they consent it should mark the beginning of the end of the war'.[124] A few days later, House confirmed a 'satisfactory conference' with Lloyd George, writing mysteriously that 'a complete understanding can be had before I leave looking to action by you at the proper time'.[125] His most revealing telegram came after the conference with all four British leaders, when House reported on 15 February that he was

satisfied with the result. They cordially accept the suggestion that you preside over the convention when it is held, provided our general understanding is carried out. No action however is to be taken until they signify their readiness. There is a difference of opinion only as to the time.[126]

While it seems safe to assume that Hall and his War Office counterparts sought to deploy this intelligence against House and his mediation efforts, the only surviving evidence hinting at this comes in the form of a letter from Hall to the British Ambassador to the United States, Cecil Spring Rice. A frustrated Hall bemoaned House's 'very happy knack of concealing what he is thinking and also what he proposes to do' – clearly a reference to House's telegraphic discipline – but even so, Hall thought that he had 'a pretty firm idea of what [House] is really after, and I do not think he will get it!' If House 'thinks we are going to agree to any such catch term as "freedom of the seas"', Hall wrote icily, 'he will also be undeceived on that point'. Most pointedly, however, after Hall mentioned his efforts to convince House that Britain was determined to 'beat the Germans', 'nothing is more certain', Hall added menacingly, than

that any vacillation shown on the part of our Government would bring the wrath of the people down in a form they never thought of ... A certain class in London, mostly in the higher circles, are fearfully depressed, and go about with faces as long as a main-top-bowline. They do an awful lot of harm with their grousings, but it gives me great pleasure when I get alongside some of them to blow off some of the steam which I dare not put on paper. As a fact, things are really going very well.[127]

Even after House's departure, Hall's interest in him continued
unabated. Only a relatively small number of US decrypts generated by
MI1(b) from this period survive in Room 40 files, and all of these
concern either House personally or American mediation more
generally.[128]

Weathering a severe snowstorm just before completing its journey, the
Rotterdam steamed into New York harbour on 5 March.
Notwithstanding the snow, House had largely enjoyed a 'restful' week
at sea – though receiving regular news updates from the ship's wireless
system, he lamented the Administration's having waded into 'deep
waters' with its 'ill-timed' extra diplomacy.[129] Not only had the
President pointlessly antagonized both London and Berlin, the moves
had triggered an unnecessary domestic showdown with Wilson's nervous
critics in Congress. Amongst the trio of controversies Wilson emerged
victorious in only the last, with decisive votes in both houses backing the
President.[130] 'In precipitating this controversy with Congress and by
making the situation so acute with Germany', however, an aggrieved
House wrote, 'I feel that the President and Lansing have largely inter-
fered with my efforts abroad'.[131]

Summoned immediately to Washington, House headed down on the
overnight train and arrived at the White House early the following
morning. He spent most of the afternoon and evening with Wilson,
recounting his journey in detail and presenting him with the
memorandum he had concluded with Grey. The President endorsed
the document, though with a scholar's eagle-eyed attention to detail,
noticed a small drafting error – the memo committed the United States
to 'probably enter the war' if Germany refused a peace conference, but to
certainly enter it if Germany proved unreasonable in negotiating. Wilson
asked that the latter promise be qualified with a 'probably', so that the
commitments matched.[132]

Deeply pleased at House's achievement, Wilson put his arm around
his trusted advisor's shoulders and told him that 'he could not imagine a
more difficult task than the one placed in your hands, but you have
accomplished it in a way beyond any expectations'. Wilson's expressions
of kindness touched House deeply. Certainly, that House had succeeded
at all in getting talk of negotiations going was a major diplomatic achievement. House's concept of 'American mediation' had evolved enormously
over the past year from the original aspiration merely to serve as the
neutral power through which official notes would be exchanged. Even
just two months before, House had conceived only of a dramatic diplomatic demand that the belligerents end the war and convene a peace
conference. Now, British economic and strategic worries had driven a

number of British leaders into seeking a far more ambitious form of American mediation. Largely at British encouragement, the Americans saw themselves as at the very centre of a negotiated end to the conflict. House told Wilson of the tremendous pride he felt as he envisaged his President 'sitting at the head of the counsel table at the Hague'.

The plan, of course, had its risks, and the changes the British had wrought dramatically increased the odds of a German rejection if the plan were ever implemented. Germany later in 1916 would seek American mediation along the lines of House's earlier conceptions. They had no desire at all to have the Americans at the negotiating table itself. And by guaranteeing comparatively generous minimum terms for the Allies – which certainly did not reflect Germany's current battlefield advantage – Germany had plenty of reasons to walk away from any American attempt to impose such a compromise. Yet even so, if certain ministers in Whitehall had their way, serious peace overtures could be opened within months, or even sooner. And, for the Americans, risks for peace seemed worth taking: the Germans might at any time force the United States into the war with their submarines. For a man who had thought his winter would be best spent at home in Texas, House had achieved more than he or his President had dreamed possible. 'My dear friend', Wilson replied to his trusted advisor, 'you should be proud of yourself and not of me since you have done it all'.[133]

4   Deliberations
March–May 1916

As spring approached, the possibility of an early peace conference glistened for the first time in the war. Grey made a strong push for sounding the French about activating the House-Grey Memorandum – only to be outmanoeuvred. At the same time, the economic underpinnings of British strategy, so tenuously established in February, started to come apart. The Asquithians had coalesced reluctantly around Chamberlain's strategy. The great gamble on a victory in 1916 was now decided. Yet though the strategy was decided, debate in the government continued: not over whether the gamble should be taken, but over whether its consequences were real. The military, most of the Conservatives in the government, and Lloyd George all fantasized that Britain's massive economic effort could be continued on the same scale into 1917 and, if necessary, beyond. Although Robertson had assured Asquith in January that he understood that it 'was necessary for us to win this year or not at all',[1] it seems that the military leadership had never actually believed this. The British commander on the Western Front, Sir Douglas Haig, himself ceased to talk about winning the war with the Somme Offensive, telling one of his subordinates at the end of May that its principal objective in fact was only to put 'troops in favourable positions' and to lay foundations for a 'campaign in 1917 so as to make sure of success next year'.[2]

In April, the military authorities moved to replace Chamberlain's carefully considered strategy with this economic fantasy. They set off an unnecessary political crisis by demanding general conscription – a demand they justified on the necessity of continuing the war well beyond the 1916 campaign. Though compromise was reached in the Cabinet, the House of Commons sided with the generals and summarily blew up the accords that had briefly reconciled British military strategy with Britain's economic capacity.

The government then lurched from an unnecessary political crisis to an equally unnecessary financial scare. For once, Lloyd George's charges of Treasury timidity had merit. The department had hesitated to impose stiffer measures to assemble the country's stock of American investments for fear of triggering capital flight. As a consequence, the Treasury dramatically underestimated the country's staying power, projecting the collapse of the British financial campaign in the United States by autumn. Tardily, McKenna found the right combination of measures at the end of May, and the scare receded. But this was not before the economic anxiety that he provoked resurrected the House-Grey Memorandum. House and Wilson pushed for an autumn implementation of the agreement, and, with British war strategy now in tatters, the British leaders battled over whether to signal their willingness to go along – only this time, the Memorandum's proponents were foiled, unintentionally, by the President himself.

In March, Grey gave the House-Grey Memorandum a great push and the fractious British leadership found itself in the throes of another contentious debate. For a matter of the utmost secrecy and explosiveness, a surprising number of traces of that debate survive in the archives – and all point to serious manoeuvring taking place behind the scenes. Grey's approach, seeking to push House's proposal without wrecking the coalition government, lay in introducing a careful hedge: emphasizing the importance of the military's assessment of the war's outlook. He sought to neutralize military opposition by asking for concrete guarantees – ones that surely he knew no fair-minded general could possibly give.

At the centre of the British debate over the House-Grey Memorandum in March lay concerns over the alliance. In fact, the whole of the political manoeuvring was over merely *broaching* the subject with the French government at an impending conference. House's journey to Paris had mitigated some of the diplomatic risks of doing this, and there were plenty of ways of sounding the French leaders about House's visit obliquely and informally. But raising the possibility of peace with an ally, however indirectly, was seen as such a dangerous diplomatic step that only the War Committee could authorize it. Grey and a number of other British leaders were so alarmed about the state of the Allied war effort that they were prepared to chance the diplomatic dangers.

House was still aboard ship when the British Ambassador in Paris, Lord Bertie, a hard-line Conservative, opened up a salvo against his proposal. In letters to Grey, Bertie blisteringly dismissed House as a 'sheep-faced but fox-minded gentleman' who had been sent 'on an electioneering mission'.[3] Grey, who had to be especially delicate with Bertie, given that he was both a hard-liner and Grey's conduit to the French government, vigorously defended his American friend. 'I like

[House] and am convinced he is genuinely friendly', Grey told Bertie, replying carefully that as long as the military

say they can beat the Germans there need be no talk of mediation: but if the war gets to a stalemate the question to be asked will not be whether mediation is good electioneering for President Wilson, but whether it will secure better terms for the Allies than can be secured without it. It is ... a great mistake not to treat Colonel House seriously; though if the Allies can dictate terms of peace in Berlin without the help of the United States nothing will come of Colonel House's proposals. These however do not seem to me to be times in which to neglect any possible friend.[4]

Fundamentally, implementation of the House-Grey Memorandum would depend on French support. Bertie was unequivocal on this point, telling Grey: 'I understand that Colonel House when in London spoke of the possibility of Germany consenting to Peace on the terms that Alsace Lorraine should be ceded to France in return for some French Colonies. No such conditions would be listened to here'.[5] Grey's persistence in urging his colleagues to consult the French directly about the House-Grey Memorandum, however, shows that he distrusted Bertie's assessment – or that he believed that giving them an honest assessment of Britain's economic predicament might change French minds. Even if the French were tempted by the Memorandum, moreover, they would naturally be reticent about sharing it with Bertie for fear of undermining the alliance. Additionally, Bertie might very well have been projecting his own hard-line, pro-war views onto the French leadership. The fiercely pro-Allied and equally pro-war US Ambassador in London, Walter Page, had precisely that problem. Just as the British leadership would be seriously revisiting the House-Grey Memorandum in May, he was writing to House that '[e]xcept the half-dozen peace cranks in the House [of Commons] ... you can't find a man, a woman, a child, a dog that isn't fired with determination to see the war through'.[6]

By the beginning of March, support for moving on the House-Grey Memorandum was regaining momentum. Germany's failure at Verdun was becoming increasingly apparent, and it seems that many of the British leaders regarded this failure as being sufficiently discouraging to Germany to be the 'psychological moment' of which House had spoken. Balfour, who had told House he contemplated a later implementation of the plan, on 3 March sent House a letter unmistakably hinting that the pact could be activated at some point, writing that he was very sorry to have missed saying 'Goodbye' to the Colonel and his wife. '*Unless, however, I am making a mistake, it will not be very long before I have again the pleasure of meeting you,* and discussing with an open heart some of the great problems raised by the world crisis through which we are living'.[7]

The hint was not lost on House, who wrote in his diary that 'there was a significant sentence in Balfour's letter intimating, if his judgment was correct, that it would not be long before he should see me again'.[8] House quickly replied: 'I am much heartened by your prediction that it will not be long before we are together again. I eagerly await the summons'.[9]

Much more than anyone else in the British leadership, however, Asquith was playing dangerously with political fire. Coming out strongly in favour of the House-Grey Memorandum and failing to push it through would be to hand his Cabinet opponents a flame-thrower. Yet in addition to the strong support Reading reported, on 6 March Hankey met with Edwin Montagu, the Financial Secretary to the Treasury and Asquith's confidant. Montagu believed in 'smashing Germany'[10] and strongly opposed the House plan. Hankey's diary reads: 'Montagu lunched with me at [the] club. He seems to think peace not very distant'. A subsequent entry explicitly links this to the House proposal. Given the tightness with which the secret of the House-Grey Memorandum was being kept – even Hankey would not see the document for more than another week – Montagu's close relationship with Asquith is the only conceivable source for Montagu's statement.[11] Particularly given that this was *before* Wilson had even telegraphed his confirmation of the agreement, this strongly suggests that Asquith believed that it could be implemented, which in turn implies his support.

House's short telegram communicating Wilson's endorsement of the scheme, with his minor correction, arrived two days later.[12] Lloyd George in his memoirs would blame this correction – the word 'prob- ably' – for the plan's failure.[13] A contention rightly dismissed as 'com- pletely erroneous',[14] Lloyd George himself in 1927 privately confirmed to House that the correction had 'in no way lessened' the agreement's value before going on to write precisely the opposite in his memoirs.[15]

On 11 March, Hankey had lunch with Montagu again. Hankey briefly jotted down afterwards that Montagu 'told me that following our talk at lunch last Monday he had urged' – to the Prime Minister, presumably – 'that Sir William Robertson should be told of Col. House's proposal'. Hankey agreed about informing Robertson but came down himself squarely in favour of the agreement. For those who accepted the realities of Britain's economic limitations, Hankey's conclusion could be difficult to escape. The summer would mark the high point of Britain's war effort, and Hankey wanted Robertson warned unmistakably that afterwards 'economic pressure would probably compel a reduction in our maximum effort'. If the alliance stood on the cusp of victory and Robertson could promise 'defeat[ing] the Germans this summer', House's proposal could be ignored. But 'otherwise in my view they ought to test Col. House's suggestion, in order either (1) to discuss peace before we passed our zenith or (2) to get the U.S.A. behind us in which case we could go on forever'.[16]

Two days later, Hankey caught Asquith himself for a few minutes' conversation, and 'he told me that Sir E. Grey had asked to bring Col. House's suggestion before [the] War [Committee]'. Hankey on his own initiative met with Robertson 'to warn him that the Col. House question was coming up, and that the decision would largely depend upon what he and [First Sea Lord] Sir Henry Jackson thought about the prospects of the war'.[17]

On 15 March, Hankey finally got to see the secret House documents himself when Grey sent a note to the members of the War Committee, informing them that he had 'a cable from Colonel House saying that the President substantially confirms' the House-Grey Memorandum. Grey carefully put the question before the others:

> We ought to come to some decision as to whether President Wilson's suggestion should be discarded, or regarded as premature, or encouraged. This decision depends, I imagine, upon the opinion of the military and naval authorities on the prospects of the War. I should therefore be glad of a meeting of the War Committee to consider the question.[18]

The next day, Hankey saw a bedridden Asquith, who was taken down by a nasty bout of bronchitis. The illness forced a four-day delay in the meeting of the War Committee, giving plenty of time for additional mischief. The Prime Minister put on a front of scepticism towards the House proposal. Hankey, however, saw through this, writing that Asquith merely 'affects to regard the whole thing as humbug, and a mere manoeuvre of American politics'. Hankey's word choice strongly suggests that Hankey did not believe him – almost certainly because Montagu had given him a very different account. Asquith asked Hankey to arrange an informal discussion between Grey and Robertson to discuss the proposal.

Hankey duly went to see Grey, and the two discussed the situation at length, with Grey giving him the 'whole story'. Hankey saw the Foreign Secretary agonizing over the 'heavy responsibility' laid upon him. 'If he took no notice of it, and the war went wrong, he would have missed a great opportunity either to get a decent peace or to bring in the U.S.A.', while if they postponed they risked 'miss[ing] our opportunity'. Only if 'we were likely to be completely victorious it would be better to ignore it'; much, therefore, 'depended on the anticipation of the military and naval authorities in regard to the course of the war'.[19] That same day, Robertson wrote to Hankey, no doubt with a touch of irony, that he was 'glad to hear that Sir Edward Grey's question is to be discussed by the departments chiefly concerned before it comes before the War Committee'. Robertson undoubtedly had had access to the House decrypts from MI1(b) for the past two months, but had only been told officially about the matter in the past two days.

The delay forced by Asquith's illness gave Montagu time to open up a broadside against the proposal in a private letter to the Prime Minister. He penned Asquith a lengthy, 'passionate denunciation' of House's proposal. Previous historians thought it probably 'reflect[ed] Asquith's opinions'.[20] The letter, however, goes on for a dozen pages, laying out in great detail all of the risks involved in House's plan. If Asquith opposed the proposal and believed it would not be adopted, his closest confidant would have no reason to pen such an exhaustive condemnation of it at such extraordinary length – particularly given that the two had already had multiple conversations about it. Montagu clearly identifies as 'the question at hand' *whether* House's proposal should be rejected, not merely *how*. He refers to the 'many who believe implicitly in the good faith of both Wilson and House' and acknowledges that his criticisms would be 'hotly contested by some men of excellent judgment'.[21]

Much more likely is that Montagu believed that Asquith supported, or was seriously contemplating supporting, House's plan, and that Montagu wrote this letter in a frantic bid to dissuade him. If Montagu's arguments had any effect, however, this owed in part to the limited distribution of the decrypts of House's telegrams, an unbiased reading of which would have undermined many of Montagu's points. Montagu imputed to the Americans a shocking capacity for duplicity, suggesting that they had struck a similar bargain with the Germans and would betray the Allies at the peace conference. Montagu argued that, at the very least, consideration of the proposal should be postponed – a curious tack to take if its rejection was certain. The assumptions that underlie everything Montagu wrote make it clear that they took the Memorandum extremely seriously.[22]

Showing the gravity of the deliberations, Hankey had one final conversation with Grey about House's proposal on 20 March, but his diary gives no details of the conversation. The traces that survive in the historical record, recounted above, can represent only a fraction of the behind-the-scenes manoeuvring leading up to the meeting on 21 March. What the evidence makes clear, however, is that the British leadership examined House's proposal extremely carefully. Hankey, after all, was the only one keeping a diary, and the House matter is a dominant theme in his entries for the ten days before the meeting. It is difficult to imagine that the intensity of his focus on the question was unique.

Asquith having recovered, the War Committee convened on 21 March and went into an especially secret session to consider the House proposal. Grey began the meeting by attempting a lengthy and careful framing of their predicament. British economic strategy now staked everything on the summer offensive. If the military authorities could promise that the Allies could 'dictate terms', or, at the very least, that they could 'improve considerably their military position' within the next six months, the matter could be dropped. But the country was operating on borrowed time: in six months, 'our financial and economic power to meet the demands of our Allies' would be significantly curtailed. So 'if there was a prospect of a deadlock' – or worse – facing them come autumn, then Grey considered it 'imperative to consult the French Government' about House's proposal, and to do so 'now'. In any case, in less than a week, the British leaders would be in Paris for an inter-Allied conference, and if the French brought up Colonel House, Grey needed to know how he should reply.

The Prime Minister referred the question to Robertson for a military assessment. The general had had nearly a week to contemplate his answer, and he knocked the legs out from under Grey's strategy for the meeting entirely. Rather than being forced, as Grey might have expected, to offer up a range of possible outcomes for the summer offensive and assigning them probabilities, Robertson simply declared that he could not make any attempt at a forecast at all without first consulting the French military leadership. While of course he 'knew our position', it was too 'difficult' to 'form a judgment' as to the overall Allied situation without consultations. Nevertheless, he emphasized that 'all his own instincts were opposed' to the proposal. In a stroke, Robertson had left Grey trapped. The very point of the meeting, after all, was to decide whether to consult the French about the agreement. Grey had said that the French should only be consulted if the military offered a forecast of deadlock. Robertson rejoined that he could not offer any forecast at all unless the French had been consulted already. The manoeuvre may have been deeply underhanded and unhelpful, but even so one cannot help but admire its brilliance.[23]

Bonar Law immediately jumped in to add his opposition to the plan. Ignoring the actual peace terms stated in the House-Grey Memorandum – which Grey, perhaps unwisely, had not reviewed as part of his opening speech – Bonar Law argued that any 'peace negotiations must be based on the *status quo* before the war'. These terms 'would be equivalent to defeat', and 'public opinion' would not permit it. Lloyd George, however, went the furthest he would ever go towards supporting House's pact in the War Committee. Lloyd George's preferred strategy had been predicated on progress on the Eastern Front combined with pressure on the Western Front, which would improve the Allies' negotiating position for when they brought in the Americans to arrange the settlement. In the past month, however, his hopes for results on the Eastern Front had vanished. He cautiously backed Grey by venturing a pessimistic assessment of the Russian military situation. Their position 'in regard to munitions', he told the War Committee, 'was not such as to justify hopes of a successful offensive'. McKenna also cautiously offered tentative support for implementing the pact by emphasizing that he could guarantee a 'perfectly safe' financial position only until July.[24]

Asquith, however, either decided that the opposition of Robertson and Bonar Law made the plan politically impossible or else he had been genuinely dissuaded about it. He asserted 'that the proposal ought to be put aside for the present', doubting whether Wilson was 'strong enough ... to carry through this policy'. Trying to salvage the situation, Grey rejoined that Wilson 'would have the support of the whole nation ... to end the war by a Conference if the Allies agreed'. Balfour then drove the nail into the coffin by dismissing House's proposal as 'at present not worth five minutes' thought'. Earlier in the meeting, Balfour had enquired of Grey whether House had not said that the 'offer would be repeated' and 'might be taken advantage of at some later date'. Balfour evidently stuck to his view that American diplomatic intervention should be kept for autumn. Saying that he could not see 'any dark spot' except 'money and ships' – and perhaps having been nobbled by Hall behind the scenes – the clear implication is that Balfour did not yet think the situation urgent enough to justify looking to the Americans.[25] The Americans, after all, might well end up in the war whether they liked it or not. Hall had a decrypt of House saying that he thought German submarines were likely to force the United States in eventually. There remained a decent chance this could happen before their American supplies reached the point of financial collapse.[26]

The Committee decided 'that no action should be taken' for now and that only Asquith would be able to bring back the matter for reconsideration.[27] Reeling, Grey moved to mitigate the damage he did to himself by drafting a memorandum to, as one might say today, 'clarify' his position. He now emphasized that he brought the proposal before the Committee only because the 'military authorities ought to know' about it, and that it should not be implemented unless they had thought 'the Allies had reached the high water mark'. Yet, in a clear bout of frustration, Grey obtained Hankey's minutes of the secret part of the meeting and pored over the document making extensive corrections – the only time during the war a minister would ever take out his dissatisfaction with a decision on Hankey's minutes – before having these secret minutes secured in Hankey's special 'Magnum Opus' files. While the memorandum was a necessary attempt at damage control, the minutes, by contrast, would safely disappear and Grey could be honest about his views. Historian John Milton Cooper, Jr., thought these corrections made Grey sound like a 'passionate advocate' of the plan,[28] and so they do. Clearly upset by the outcome, where Hankey had written that Grey had said it would be 'better policy' to now approach the French about House's proposal if a deadlock was expected, Grey struck this out and inserted 'imperative'. Hankey had Grey saying that the French were not interested in the proposal 'so far as his information went'; Grey pointedly added 'hitherto' – again showing his distrust of Bertie's assessment. The line about Wilson having 'the support of the whole nation' had been added by Grey himself. Hankey took the extraordinarily unusual step of sealing the minutes in an envelope marked '*Most Secret* – This envelope is not to [be] opened except by authority of the Secretary or Acting Secretary'. According to a note on it, the envelope was opened but once, in 1922.

Grey did not give up. He could not raise the proposal with the French himself, but he could do everything in his power to try to get the French to bring the matter up, and, of course, House still could approach the French himself. To his colleagues, Grey affirmed that 'it was unnecessary to send [House] an answer',[29] but he secretly wrote his American friend a private letter anyway. Grey explained the decision to House, though he presented it as if it had been a united one. Grey detailed to House his plan to let the French leadership know through the French Embassy that the House proposal had been confirmed and to assure it that Russia would not be informed about the matter. Since Grey, Asquith, and a few other key Cabinet members would be going to Paris for a conference on 30 March, if the French had any views on the matter, they could then raise them there. Grey closed his letter by all but openly pleading with House to support his initiative, writing: 'Of course there is nothing in this to prevent your making any communication to the French that you think opportune'.[30]

Grey's plans were scuppered by the slowness of the mail. His letter to House did not arrive until 8 April, after Grey had already returned to London. House moved immediately to do as Grey asked, writing at once to the President suggesting a frank talk with the French Ambassador informing him of Wilson's desire that the pact be activated. Awkwardly, House and Wilson had telegraphed Grey just two days earlier, enquiring whether the Allies planned to move for an early implementation of the Memorandum. As he was about to send his letter to the President with Grey's letter enclosed, House received a cable from Grey reporting that the French had not raised the topic at the conference.[31] Grey wrote

House a letter at the same time, giving a more detailed account of the conference and deflecting the enquiry about implementing the House-Grey Memorandum. It had been less than three weeks since his defeat in the War Committee, and he was not about to repeat the experience.[32]

As Grey dealt with the Americans, Robertson had a couple of unwelcome gifts waiting for the Prime Minister when he returned from Paris. The British military leadership had determined to force through the plan for the Battle of the Somme while simultaneously seeking to detonate the overall British war strategy agreed just a couple of months before. Then, the military had agreed to an all-out effort that sought to win the war this year, before the exhaustion of Britain's vital American supply link. The military's new approach called for an all-out effort this year and another all-out effort next year. Continuing the alliance's American supply link through the 1917 campaign was to be the Treasury's problem, which it ought to sort out, somehow. The debate now was not over two competing strategic visions. It was between adhering to the strategy already decided or replacing it with a fantasy untethered from economic reality – one that would make the Allied war effort completely dependent on a timely American entry into the war.

13 William Robertson, left (Print Collector / Hulton Archive / Getty Images), and Douglas Haig, right (Hulton Archive / Getty Images)

Robertson's first gift for Asquith was a message from the British commander on the Western Front, Sir Douglas Haig, designed to force immediate approval of the Somme Offensive. Leveraging alliance considerations to force a political decision, Haig wrote that the French military needed to know whether they could count on British support, and he demanded to be 'definitely informed with the least possible delay' whether he had authorization to proceed. The War Committee met the morning after the ministers returned. They gave in.[33] Their authorization was, as Hankey noted, 'so worded as not to give the impression the War Committee liked it', but they could hardly have done otherwise. There is no evidence that any of the civilians but Bonar Law believed that the offensive would produce significant results, but they had no other options from which to choose. Every other military scheme had been shot down as impractical. The Committee itself had set aside its only significant diplomatic alternative. Haig's letter made further postponement impossible. Their only remaining option was simply to cancel the offensive and indefinitely adopt a defensive posture – a decision that would seriously upset their allies and that would be at dramatic odds with Britain's economic strategy of gambling for a win in 1916. All of their efforts over the past months to craft an alternative had come to naught. It was not out of confidence in their strategy, out of resolve and determination to see the war through to victory, that the British leaders committed the lives of their soldiers to the greatest sacrifice they would ever be called upon to make. Rather, these leaders slid ungracefully, filled with prescient doubt, into a campaign they did not want. They distrusted their generals' promises, but they could not find a way out, and had little choice but to yield.[34]

Robertson's first gift was disposed of in under an hour. The second would consume the Prime Minister for a month. Asquith returned to a Cabinet plunged into a fresh political crisis. He and his delegation had barely left for Paris when Robertson lobbed a bomb of a memorandum into his fragile government. The short document seems to be written as if that was precisely the intention. After a summary of the earlier agreed conscription arrangements, a single paragraph gave the Cabinet an update on the situation. The contents were explosive:

The number of men actually received by the Army has, however, fallen far short of the number demanded ... At the present time the infantry serving abroad is 78,000 below its establishment; the 13 Territorial Divisions at Home are also deficient of about 50,000 men; and the men under training as reserves to make good wastage are far below requirements.

Bereft of detail, it considered neither the causes of the problem nor possible solutions.[35] The impression it left, however, was that the existing conscription measures were inadequate. Demands for conscription of married men began almost immediately. The Army Council itself insisted on it the day the Prime Minister returned.[36]

With his Cabinet in an uproar, Asquith went from authorizing the Somme Offensive in the morning to reconvening his inelegantly named Committee for the Co-Ordination of Military and Financial Effort that afternoon. The Cabinet had added to its membership Lord Lansdowne, a Conservative elder statesman and a minister without portfolio.[37] Over the next week, the Committee again delved deep into the same matters it had examined a few months before. As the Committee poured over the statistics, it emerged within a few meetings that the crisis had been almost entirely artificially concocted by the military. The source of the overall manpower shortage was the War Office's own machinery, which was exactly as the Committee had 'foreseen and foretold' in January. There were plenty of men yet available for the War Office to take. In fact, the Board of Trade was almost beside itself with relief at how relatively few men the War Office had succeeded in conscripting over the past few months. As Hankey commented, 'so far compulsory service has proved such a failure and has produced so few men that trade has not yet suffered. Perhaps after all compulsory service will save the nation!'[38] The pool that the War Office could still yet work through was expected to yield the roughly one million men for the Army that it had demanded. Extending conscription to married men was expected to add to that number a mere 200,000.[39] The only major part of the recruiting system outside War Office control was the 'Tribunals' system, which consisted of local bodies designed to adjudicate temporary exemption claims, and these were in the hands of Conservative and arch-conscriptionist Walter Long.[40]

The cause of the shortage in the infantry serving abroad the Committee found even more perverse. The government had given clear orders that no men were to be added to the home forces until the forces abroad were at their full complement. The Committee discovered that those orders had been ignored. 'The alleged deficit of 78,000 is purely artificial', Asquith fumed. He found the War Office's subsequent explanation wholly unsatisfactory: the 'decision of the War Committee was not in fact carried out', he told the Committee.[41]

The effect – and likely the intent – of the crisis was twofold. First, the military was able to saddle the Prime Minister and the Cabinet with the political blame for the manpower shortage. The focus on general conscription created a distraction that, both at the time and in the century since, led people to believe that the fault lay with the Cabinet's conscription policy, rather than with the War Office machinery. Second, and more important, the military could now choose to reopen and repudiate the economic caveats of the Committee's January report. That entire report had been predicated on giving the military one big push in 1916. The Committee had warned emphatically that, by burning through their American assets with such abandon, it was almost certainly making Robertson true to his promise to win the war with the summer offensive. It would, indeed, be necessary for them to win this year, or not at all. Yet though everyone had agreed to the report, neither the military nor the maximalists in the Cabinet had much believed the accompanying caution. Haig had now decided on the necessity of a 1917 campaign, and so did the military leadership in London. They now moved to disregard the warning.

Despite the political crisis swirling in the Cabinet, and in Parliament outside,[42] the Committee held firm, and it held together. Conservative Austen Chamberlain still believed in the work he had done together with the Prime Minister and McKenna a few months before. They had battled it out then, and Chamberlain had prevailed. Then, his coherent strategy could co-exist peacefully with the maximalists' fantasies. Now it could not. With his strategy under attack, Chamberlain sought to rise to the challenge: he was not about to stick his head into a hole in the ground on military command. He led the pushback, drafting a memorandum that served as the basis of the Committee's final report. Rapidly persuaded by the carefulness and seriousness of the debate unfolding around him, Lord Lansdowne was equally convinced. There was nothing unexpected, Chamberlain wrote, about the delays in processing conscripts. The original Committee members had never believed that the War Office would be able to carry out its schedule, and they had been proven right. There were plenty of men still available for conscription, and extending it to married men, Chamberlain argued, 'affords no remedy. The difficulty is not that the raw material is deficient, but that the machinery cannot turn it out quickly enough'. Should the available pool of men dry up later on, he noted, at that point extending conscription might well prove necessary, albeit as a part of a significant retrenchment. For the 1916 campaign, however, it would accomplish little, and it was the campaign this year that mattered above all else. Instead of general conscription, there were a few other steps that should be taken – ones that would actually have an immediate impact on the coming offensive, including cancelling the expiration dates of all enlistments so as to force men to serve until the end of the war.[43] ('Cromwellian', Asquith commented, but 'necessary'.)[44]

Lloyd George, however, was determined to force the acceptance of the Army Council's position, and believed that, if he resigned over conscription, he could take most of the Conservatives with him. 'There is no grip', Lloyd George complained. 'Asquith and Balfour do not seem to realise the serious nature of the situation'.[45] The Munitions Minister led a firestorm of criticism when the report was presented to the Cabinet the next day, refusing to give his approval until the Army Council assented to it. Bonar Law asked the Committee to meet with the Army men, and with a key faction of the Cabinet in all but open rebellion, Asquith reluctantly agreed. Hankey thought this an 'absurdity' – the 'whole object of the Coordination C[ommit]tee had been to coordinate conflicting interests' and to serve as arbiter among them. Now one of those interests was to get a veto over the decision of the arbiter.[46]

The Committee's frustration with the Army Council at their joint meeting was palpable. The Army Council repeated its demands for general conscription. But the military men could not agree whether they were increasing their overall demand for men from January. Lord Kitchener, the War Secretary, said that they were not. Robertson said they might be, but he could not say by how much. McKenna and Chamberlain in turn demanded that the military men explain exactly what good general conscription would achieve when there were still hundreds of thousands of available men yet to process. Their efforts proved in vain. Kitchener spoke vaguely of adding 'an extra pipe to our reservoir'. When Asquith demanded that he drop the metaphor, Kitchener again spoke nebulously of being able to 'get ahead more quickly', without explaining how. Asquith then tried to force an answer out of them. Speaking of general conscription, *'Can we, by this means, provide Sir Douglas Haig with the force he needs at the time when he needs it?'* Asquith asked, in a passage underlined as if to communicate the Prime Minister's exasperation. He explained that he did not believe that Parliament would be willing to pass such a bill, and, given British strategy, he asked pointedly: 'What possible use would such legislation be?' Kitchener refused to answer the question. His response, in its entirety, was simply: 'We fully appreciate the political difficulties, but our business is, of course, to look at this question from a purely military point of view'. There was no elaboration.[47]

An evidently very annoyed Chamberlain then broke in to point out that the 'military point of view' must include 'the whole problem facing us as a nation at war, in all its aspects':

[O]ur military effort is a comparatively small part of our general effort. Our assistance in other ways than the provision of Armies in the Field is really vital to our Allies … [T]he nation can only stand the financial strain of raising, equipping, supplying and moving these forces for a very short period, and this period would be followed by a very rapid decline afterwards.

The 'whole problem' included as a vital part Britain's financing of its allies, which was essential not only militarily but diplomatically. He asked McKenna's permission to give the total amounts being lent to each of the Allies – a closely guarded secret. McKenna provided them. Chamberlain continued, giving what Hankey called an 'extraordinarily eloquent appeal':

You are now in possession of the figures, and you are aware of the extent of our financial commitments so far as our Allies are concerned. These financial considerations are just as much part of the military problem as are men. For the War Office to demand more men is to deprive this nation of its power of keeping Russia and France in the field. If we fail to give the assistance they ask of us they might have to consider the possibility of making a separate peace.

Yet even the prospect of one of their allies abandoning them failed to make any impression on the military leadership. Kitchener said that these concerns did not apply, because they were not asking for more men. Chamberlain then repeated that there were plenty of men left to take, the only problem being that the War Office's machinery was too slow. So if they were not asking for more men, why did they need general conscription? The discussion was going around in circles. Kitchener repeated, without explaining how, that general conscription would somehow allow them to speed things up. At this point, the Army Council got up and left the meeting.[48]

The 'woolly headed soldiers', as an unimpressed Hankey called them, then went away to have their own meeting, 'and of course plonked again for general conscription'.[49] More than this, however, the Army Council issued a memorandum that served as its repudiation of the joint military and economic strategy agreed a few months before. It rejected the Committee's April report and decided to actually increase its manpower demands, insisting on having 'every man of military age who is physically fit and can be spared'. This, it said, 'represents the only maximum which the Council have ever contemplated'. It admitted that there were 'no fresh steps that might be taken now' to produce more men in time for the summer offensive. But the Army Council, it said, 'have to look beyond that time'. It asserted that, without general conscription, further recruits at the current pace would not be forthcoming from October onwards. It did not say so, but it was immediately evident: given the necessary three to four months of training, these further men could not be made fighting fit before February 1917. The Army was all but admitting that it was now looking to fight a 1917 campaign on the same expansive scale. The Army Council demanded that conscription be immediately extended to married men, and it declared that any postponement of this 'would involve serious consequences to the successful prosecution of the war'.[50]

This declaration immediately sent the Cabinet spiralling into a full-blown political crisis. There still had yet to be any clear explanation as to how making available 200,000 married men from general conscription could possibly do any immediate good when there remained almost one million men that the Army could get its hands on first. But by now the facts of the matter had become all but completely divorced from the politics of it. Lloyd George said that he thought the military's demand was 'moderate' and that '[t]he soldiers are the best judges & he accepted their figures'. If the government did not yield, he said, he would resign.[51]

As contemptuous as Lloyd George was of his colleagues' economic concerns, the Munitions Minister had his eye on a much larger and more personal prize, and he was willing to contemplate an outrageous plan to achieve it. His loyal undersecretary, Christopher Addison, recorded that, after Lloyd George would resign, his 'idea is ... that he would go out and conduct a campaign in the country' in a bid to collapse the government and force a general election – an election that Lloyd George planned to win. Lloyd George would 'come in' as Prime Minister, and then he would win the war.[52] The rest of Britain's political leadership regarded a wartime general election as a politically divisive calamity to be avoided at almost any cost. Lloyd George thought it a suitable objective. Less than eight months later, Lloyd George would move to put this extreme plan into action. For now, however, the time could not quite yet be made ripe.

The Conservative leaders met in conclave. It seems reasonably clear that Chamberlain and Lansdowne convinced them that, whatever they believed about the broader economic situation, the immediate problem was the slowness of the War Office machinery, not insufficient conscription. Bonar Law frankly acknowledged that he 'd[id] not agree' with the military about the urgency of the situation – an extraordinary statement coming from the usually very deferent Conservative leader. In the lengthy letter that he subsequently sent the Prime Minister, Bonar Law admitted that the Army's demand was likely inappropriate, the issue being one 'which the Government and not the military authorities, should decide'. He conceded that 'general compulsion may not in itself be of sufficient military importance in the immediate future to justify the breaking up of the Government'. The Conservative leaders supported extending conscription to married men in principle, Bonar Law wrote, but they nevertheless had been 'prepared to face our Party and declare that in the interest of national unity it would not be right to press this question now'. But the military's memorandum, he wrote, had created a new political fact. He could not ask his MPs to reject the military view, and they were unlikely to follow him if he did. Asquith, on the other hand, probably would be at least somewhat more successful in imploring Liberal MPs to vote for conscription,[53] and so, as one furious Liberal Cabinet member put it, '[h]e (B.L.) therefore suggested the latter as the course of least resistance!!! What a man! A cur!'[54]

The Asquithians in the Cabinet thought the whole 'crisis' a political absurdity. One told Kitchener bluntly that 'he would be a fool if he played into Ll[oyd] Geo[rge]'s hands' and bemoaned the fact that the government somehow had found itself on the edge of a precipice for 'the sake of a problematical 200,000 men' – none of whom would make any difference to the all-important summer offensive. Yet the stakes seemed extraordinarily high. If the government collapsed into the farce of a mid-war general election, this 'might end the war to our damage: Roumania might join Austria; America would be discouraged; Labour here would revolt with a good chance of a general strike; the finance, munitions, and shipping of the Allies would fail and Germany would triumph'.[55]

The Cabinet settled on scrapping the Committee report and setting up a new committee, this time including Lloyd George, Bonar Law, and the small Labour Party's leader, Arthur Henderson. The Committee on the Size of the Army met just once. The contrast with the eminently business-like committee that it replaced was stark. The discussion meandered all over the place. The upshot, however, was that Henderson told the Committee flatly that the working class would not accept extending conscription to married men at this time, and certainly would not until and unless the military could show that it actually needed it. Most of the Conservative leaders were eager for a bargain. With them having 'ratted almost to a man', Lloyd George decided that the time was not right to try to set off a smash.[56] Lloyd George told *Manchester Guardian* editor C. P. Scott that it was 'either too soon or too late' for him to resign.[57] He did not explain, but his meaning seems clear. The Conservatives wanted to end the crisis because the military's case did not, in fact, seem particularly urgent. Its case seemed so flimsy, in fact, that even Lloyd George's loyal undersecretary was unpersuaded.[58] But the underlying divide within the government remained unchanged. There is no indication that Chamberlain and Balfour had succeeded in winning over any new Conservative converts, except Lansdowne, to the idea that Britain's present war effort faced a meaningful American time limit. The real battle within the Cabinet seemed yet to come, probably when a convincing case could be made that the metrics had fallen short. That would be the time to strike. With its conscriptionist political patrons moving to deal, the Army Council relented. The Cabinet agreed on a compromise: to postpone extending conscription, pending close examination of War Office numbers. If the numbers were insufficient, the

Cabinet then would look to extend conscription to married men. Asquith had succeeded once more in defusing a crisis and keeping his Cabinet together.[59]

The only task that remained was to persuade the House of Commons in a 25 April Secret Session to back the plan. Asquith and Hankey worked hard to prepare the Prime Minister's address. It gave a detailed exposition of the full British war effort – which went far beyond the Western Front. Unlike their continental allies, Britain had unique responsibilities upon which the entire alliance depended. Asquith laid out Britain's naval effort, which included both the Royal Navy's control of the seas and the Mercantile Marine's operation of the vital economic sea lanes. Britain simultaneously served as the Allies' financial and economic paymaster. 'It must not be supposed that this service consists merely in sending cheques to our Allies', Asquith warned the House of Commons. 'The sum is granted in the form of credits and is delivered in the form of goods'. They had to consider Britain's manpower needs broadly. 'If we so reduce our supplies of labour that we cannot produce the commodities they require they will be unable to carry on the war'. Equally as crucial was their financial position in the United States:

Some considerable part of the credits supplied by the British Government is furnished in America. These purchases in America can be paid for to some extent in American Securities, of which we hold large quantities ... Beyond this, however, they cannot be paid for except by counterbalancing exports from this country, and if labour is withdrawn in too excessive quantities, our trade balances, which are essential no less to our Allies than to ourselves, cannot be maintained.

The Prime Minister then moved on to a detailed discussion of recruiting figures, and laid out in summary form the measures agreed on in the Cabinet. Asquith's speech was nuanced, and it was balanced – and it went over like a lead balloon. The House of Commons did not want nuance or balance; it wanted someone to take that lead balloon and to smash the Germans with it. In the absence of any Germans in the chamber, MP Edward Carson, the government's leading Conservative critic, settled for the Prime Minister. Hankey found Asquith the next morning worried and 'very flushed' about his experience.[60] That afternoon, Conservative Walter Long introduced the government's bill. Almost every corner of the Commons reacted with outright hostility. 'The bill was dead right away and not a soul got up except to condemn it', one Conservative MP gleefully observed. The Prime Minister and his Cabinet bowed to political necessity. The bill was withdrawn, and a new one was introduced that extended conscription to married men. The crisis, at last, was over.[61]

January's brief reconciliation of Britain's military and economic strategies had now collapsed into complete incoherence. Economically, Britain was locking itself into needing to win the war in 1916. But militarily, it was already moving on to measures that made no sense except as preparations for a 1917 campaign. 'It really is an astonishing situation', Hankey fumed to his diary. 'The only real military case for this bill is the great offensive'. But given the time it would take to process and train the married men being conscripted, none of them would be in France by the time the offensive was over. The offensive, moreover, would probably fail:

The Cabinet have yielded to a demand based solely on carrying out the plan for a great offensive, a plan which no member of the Cabinet and none of the regimental soldiers who will have to carry it out believe in, a plan conceived in the heads of the red-hatted, brass-bound brigade behind … [T]he French did it all last summer, with the result that they are now bled white and have no reserves left … Yet we are asked by the 'scientific' soldier to repeat the process, notwithstanding that it may jeopardise the financial stability of this country on which the whole future of the Allies rests![62]

For the Prime Minister, the only upside would be political. By intervening now, the House of Commons spared the Cabinet a fresh crisis whenever the numbers would come up short – and thus deprived Lloyd George of a renewed opportunity to blow up the government.

The conscriptionists, however, celebrated their triumph over the naysayers. Robertson exulted to Lloyd George: 'The great thing is to get the Bill, and for it the Empire's thanks are due to you – alone'.[63] When questioned about the long-term financial considerations when the bill was considered in Parliament, Lloyd George dismissed any concerns. 'I always took the view that this was going to be a long war', he reassured the Commons. Britain could, he said, 'outstay, and outstay for years, anything Germany could do'.[64]

As the political crisis facing the Cabinet diminished, the anxiety in the Treasury was in the midst of a renewed crescendo. The Treasury's goal had been to sustain the Allies' American supply link through to the end of the year and to give the military until then to win the war. Now McKenna was panicking that Britain was actually facing financial exhaustion by the autumn, before the campaigning season had even finished. Back in January, McKenna had finalized additional initiatives to mobilize the country's American investments for the war effort. With the help of Morgan's, the Treasury put together a plan, later called 'Scheme A', to encourage the deposit of these investments with the government, on reasonably generous terms. A new American Dollar Securities Committee was set up to collect the investment certificates and to ship them across the Atlantic. There, Morgan's was charged with disposing of them. The Committee did good work, sending Morgan's 'cases upon cases' of certificates, and the bank faced a 'mammoth undertaking' in coping with the avalanche of paperwork.[65] The Treasury, moreover, finally forced some economy on the War Office in the form of the Committee on War Office Expenditure, which was chaired by the impeccably Conservative Walter Long. Finding that the War Office had 'no efficient system for checking expenditure', with the Army Council having completely sidelined its own Finance Member, Long's body seems to have had rather more luck than McKenna's ineffectual Retrenchment Committee in restoring a degree of internal controls and rooting out some inefficiencies and waste.[66] A similar committee for Admiralty expenditure was also convened, but with the economy-minded Balfour already at the Admiralty's helm, the committee had much less work to do.[67] The Treasury had far less success with Lloyd George's Munitions Ministry. Again, it asked Lloyd George to show restraint in his American expenditure. The minister and his chief deputy dismissed the request as 'utter nonsense'. A fuming Lloyd George 'absolutely declined even to discuss the proposition that American manufacturers ... would decline to supply goods on the credit of the British Empire; the Russian Empire; the French Republic and the Italian Kingdom all joined in one guarantee'. He ordered his subordinates to ignore the Treasury and continue to 'place whatever orders we thought were necessary'. If McKenna wished to object, Lloyd George said, the Chancellor could take it to Cabinet.[68] Lloyd George lampooned as ridiculous any notion that Britain could not import as much as it wished for as long as it wanted: 'Put the British Empire at one end of the scale and the 31st March [the end of the financial year] at the other', Lloyd George later wrote caustically, 'and the latter would win every time. That was Mr. M'Kenna's view'.[69] Unfortunately for the Treasury, the War Office and Admiralty economies could help their American problem only indirectly. It was Lloyd George's direct spending in the United States that most needed checking. By July, the War Office would have active contracts in the United States costing a total of $1 million; the Admiralty, $2 million; the Munitions Ministry, $727 million.[70]

Britain's allies, after having underspent their allowances earlier, now again added to the strain. France, which to this point had been relying to a considerable extent on its own assets and on its share of the Anglo-French loan, suddenly demanded an urgent injection of the equivalent of $600 million. (British GDP in 1916 was $15.3 billion; France,

$10.1 billion.) Not all of this would be spent outside Britain, but most of it would be, and generally in the United States. The Treasury was able to negotiate this down by half and to get its hands on $100 million in French gold for use in New York, but this financial 'collapse of France' added to the Treasury's pressures.[71] Russia also was demanding more money to cover its spending in America. With Russia already receiving about as much British financial assistance as the rest of the Allies combined, the Treasury held the line, agreeing only to an extra $10 million per month.[72]

Their allies had the same unrealistic expectations of British finance as Lloyd George did. Not once does the possibility of British financial exhaustion appear even to have crossed their minds: 'Britain's international financial supremacy was a given'.[73] The modest efforts of the Treasury to keep its mammoth assistance within some kind of bounds generated only resentment, even as Britain's allies simultaneously demanded ever greater British military efforts. When the French discovered that McKenna had used France's application for urgent assistance as an additional reason to oppose general conscription, this only made them doubt him all the more. As Lloyd George put it: 'The French think they are making all the sacrifices and we are endeavouring to preserve our trade and carry on as usual'.[74]

The realists in the British leadership never meaningfully tried to dispel their allies' assumption that Britain's financial assistance was inexhaustible. France, Russia, and Italy never appreciated that their vast American purchasing ever faced any serious danger. The diplomatic consequences of Britain explaining this could be dire. Chamberlain had worried that one of their allies could seek a separate peace – similarly to how the British realists were showing increasing inclination towards American mediation diplomacy. But there is also real doubt that Britain's allies could have been convinced of this even if they had tried, at least at this point. After all, so strong was the presumption of British economic invincibility that the realists could not even convince their own colleagues. France or Russia likely would have been more inclined to see such an attempt at this stage simply as an excuse for an intolerable British tendency towards miserliness – a development that would have given them only more reason to doubt the trustworthiness of their British ally.[75]

Despite these fantasies of British financial invincibility, the Treasury at the moment simply was not generating sufficient funds to sustain all these American war supplies. With the Treasury foreseeing a possible payments crisis as early as June,[76] McKenna decided to sound the alarm. Circulating a memorandum to his colleagues on 19 May, he pleaded for imposing restraint on the Munitions Minister. McKenna tried not to make it personal, referring to the three 'War Departments' as a group, but one needed only the briefest glance at the numbers to know exactly whom he meant. The Treasury estimated it needed to find $795 million in the United States by 30 September – $315 million for the Allies, $80 million for miscellaneous expenditures, and the rest to cover 'the War Departments'. Shipping across the Atlantic every ounce of Allied gold they had available would only cover just under half the total. McKenna thought he would need to be 'extraordinarily fortunate' to come up with the remainder through securities, or, even less probable, loans. 'We are likely', he warned ominously, 'to face the last quarter of the calendar year without resources in sight'.[77]

But the Treasury did not need extraordinary luck to sustain its American supply line through September; all it needed was a bit of coercion. When the Treasury had predicted doom in the autumn of 1915, the fault for the mistaken timing lay with the Ministry of Munitions and with the Allies, who had vastly overestimated their ability to spend. They had spent only a fraction of what they said they would, and doomsday was accordingly delayed. Now, however, the Munitions Ministry and Britain's allies had gotten a far better grip on their estimates. The Treasury subtracted a generous allowance for underspending in coming up with their new total of $795 million.[78] The actual total turned out to be just shy of $1 billion – matching the original estimates almost exactly.[79]

This time, the fault for the mistaken projection lay entirely with McKenna and the Treasury, who had significantly underestimated the American investments still in private British hands and therefore the ability of the Treasury to pay its way. At the end of May, the Treasury would introduce a special tax on these investments. The only way to avoid the tax was to sell them or to deposit them in the government's scheme. Bonar Law demanded that the government simply commandeer the securities, but the Treasury worried, not unreasonably, that such a drastic move could spook foreign investors and set off a capital flight crisis.[80] Taxing the investments, rather than seizing them, proved a cleverer solution. It appeared merely as a small, dry detail of war finance administration – the press treated it as a minor story, with even the *Economist* relegating it to page five. Yet it had precisely the desired effect. The National Debt Office was rapidly 'besieged' by investors looking to unload their American securities.[81] As historian Martin Farr put it: 'Taxation had an uncanny habit of stimulating patriotism'.[82] Over the summer, a large portion of the American investments that the British did not know they had would pour into government coffers. Some $430 million – almost precisely the sum the Treasury feared it could not raise by the end of September – in fact rolled in by 21 July.[83]

With hindsight, it is clear that the Treasury should have imposed this tax much earlier. Had it been introduced even a month before, the Treasury might have been able to generate a more accurate projection of the country's ability to sustain its American lifeline. Yet although the Treasury badly botched the estimate, this did not mean it was wrong to be worried about the Munition Ministry's extravagant American expenditures. Merely because the country's reservoir of US railroad investments turned out to be somewhat larger than expected did not make that reservoir any less finite. Lloyd George, however, was unstinting in his mockery. The date of Keynes's prediction of doom for 31 March had 'struck and we still bought greater quantities than ever of food, raw material and munitions from abroad … [R]epeated failures discredit the prophet'.[84] Of course, it seems unlikely that a more accurate estimate would have stopped Lloyd George from contemptuously dismissing it. But by incorrectly projecting doom twice, the Treasury did itself no favours – looking as if it had turned itself into a clock perpetually predicting the sky would fall in six months' time.

Yet had McKenna's warning in May turned out to be accurate, with their American supply lifeline already sputtering by summer's end, the war effort could have been in serious jeopardy. Those in the British leadership who understood the implications of McKenna's warning and relied on it were right to be alarmed. The Allies would need to gut their imports of vital American supplies, to get the United States into the war, or to end it. On the very day McKenna issued his warning, House and Wilson dangled before the British leadership a tempting diplomatic escape route.

House and Wilson had met at the beginning of May to talk through the volatile foreign policy situation. Thus far, their plans for an international league after the war had been discussed only privately in House's negotiations. The two men decided that they needed to make them public. House had once vowed he would rather 'lose an arm' than allow electoral considerations to directly influence their foreign policy, but just this once he could not resist. House had heard that the Republicans planned on announcing a rival such scheme at their national nominating convention in early June. (The Republican platform in fact would declare itself in favour of a 'world court'.) House therefore felt it essential for Wilson to pre-empt his Republican challenger and announce his support for an international post-war league by the end of May. Initially, House contemplated only informing Grey of the coming address and to ask for Britain to announce its public support afterwards.[85]

Wilson had then been consumed with the *Sussex* crisis: a German submarine had sunk a French passenger ferry, injuring several Americans. With the resolution of the crisis in early May, however, as Germany backed down in the face of Wilson's threats,[86] House now thought he had a clear opportunity to push the British about an eventual activation of the House-Grey Memorandum at the same time. After getting Wilson's approval, he telegraphed Grey about the President's 'willing[ness] to publicly commit' to participation in a post-war international league. But, he told Grey – not quite honestly – that such a public declaration was conditional on Wilson being able to 'announce at the same time that if the war continued much longer, he purposed calling a conference to discuss peace'.

Asking Grey for his opinion on the 'advisability of such a move', House warned that it was starting to seem to neutral opinion that the Allies sought the 'punishment of Germany' rather than the exaction of 'just' terms. The President was under an 'increasingly insistent demand', he wrote, 'to try to bring the war to a close', and 'steps should be taken now'.[87] Grey, in no hurry to repeat his March defeat so soon, telegraphed House confidentially that, if he took the plan before his colleagues, it was likely to be rejected as 'premature'. He cautioned that Wilson must address his intended peace terms: if the President announced that he intended to call a conference 'without any indication of a basis on which peace might be made', it 'would be construed as instigated by Germany to secure peace on terms unfavourable to the Allies'. He told House, however, that he would take the matter before Asquith – following the procedure the War Committee had agreed on 21 March – if House and Wilson wished.[88]

House preferred a gentle reply to Grey, wanting to assure the British that the statement regarding a peace conference would be 'scarcely more than an intimation', but Wilson insisted on some 'hard pan'. House accordingly toughened up his language, asking Grey to take the matter before his colleagues and warning that 'America has reached a crossroads and if we cannot soon inaugurate some sort of peace discussion, there will come a demand from our people ... that we assert our undeniable rights against the Allies with the same insistence we have used towards the Central Powers'. House offered assurances only that the peace conference would not be called 'immediately'. They would give the Allies 'ample time' for their summer offensives so as 'to demonstrate whether or not ... the deadlock can be broken'.[89] Grey quickly responded, promising to take the matter up with Asquith at once.[90]

This telegram from House was sent on the very day that McKenna issued his warning. Given the dire financial situation, Asquith evidently decided to refer the question to the War Committee as a whole, which was scheduled to meet on 24 May. The military began intriguing as soon as it learnt of Asquith's decision to put the matter back before the War Committee. Giving a glimpse into his manoeuvres, Robertson told his most trusted aide that he was

> *most* anxious the King shall *not* move in the matter for the present, or he will give me away and do himself no good ... I send you to tell [the King's assistant private secretary Clive] *Wigram*. We can keep [the King] afterwards informed of events ... The War Committee conclusions *may* give the King a handle, and if so he can use it if he likes. On the other hand they may *not*. I don't know what will appear. Perhaps very little as the thing is so sub-rosa. Any how His Majesty should not move till he hears of it from some other source than me, unless I tell Wigram the coast is clear ... I think Wigram had best await the War Committee conclusions before saying anything to His Majesty, and when he gets them *if they say nothing*, he had better still wait till he gets the word go from me.[91]

Robertson backed this up with overt threats: the Army Council 'threaten[ed] to resign if the War Committee insisted on an inquiry into the peace question'. The ministers were furious. When the War Committee convened, a 'frightful row' erupted, and the ministers actually threw their advisors out of the meeting. They met in secret for almost an hour, with Hankey, Robertson, and the First Sea Lord waiting outside – the two military men 'very sick at being kept waiting so long'. Hankey caught up afterwards with McKenna, who reported that

> they had not reached a decision, but that he, the P.M., Grey and Balfour had been in favour of accepting President Wilson's good offices, owing to the black financial outlook, while Bonar Law and Ll[oyd] George were averse as they did not admit of the seriousness of the financial situation. They had not reached a decision, but [McKenna] thought there was every prospect of the proposal being accepted.

They had considered a 'draft telegram' prepared by Grey, but Balfour, McKenna said, was going to prepare another for the Committee to consider.[92]

A second account of the meeting – an evidential smoking gun entirely missed by previous historians – comes in a letter to the Prime Minister from Lord Curzon, the pompous and hardline Conservative Lord Privy Seal, who also chaired the Air Board and the Shipping Control Committee. House called him the 'worst jingo I have met'.[93] Curzon frequently attended the War Committee – including this particular meeting – though he would not formally be made a member until July.[94] Perhaps owing to his non-member status, evidently he felt unable to speak up during the discussion itself. Afterwards, however, he was alarmed by what he had just witnessed. Denouncing President Wilson as 'singularly ignoble and un-moral' and 'evidently now thinking almost exclusively of his own re-election', he told Asquith that he was '*much surprised to hear [Wilson] treated this morning as the preordained or inevitable mediator*'. He was even more astonished to learn that Wilson, 'pos[ing] as the Champion of Peace', was not only to 'have a hand in formulating its terms now' but would then 'appear as the head of an organisation to prevent its recurrence in parts of the world where she has no direct interest':

I was further startled to hear that the conditions upon which the War Committee appears not indisposed to consider the question of peace, involve only the

14 Lord Curzon (Photo by E. O. Hoppe / Hulton Archive/Getty Images)

restoration to France of Alsace-Lorraine, the liberation of Belgium (I did not hear Serbia or Poland mentioned), and some other territorial re-adjustments – no mention of indemnity, no recompense to us for the fearful sacrifices to which we have been submitted, no guarantees for the future.

… I am seriously alarmed at the prospect of our being inveigled or frightened into the discussion of terms which I truly believe would be repudiated by the country and would be discreditable to ourselves.

Curzon refused to take seriously any notion of a time limit to Britain's war effort. 'I would sooner go on indefinitely', he told the Prime Minister, 'than contemplate a peace so inglorious' as the one the War Committee was apparently considering. He argued that they should take a far harder line with the Americans. '[W]e should be quite prepared', he wrote, to run 'the risk of more active hostilities'. The cowardly Americans had 'swallowed almost immeasurable dirt sooner tha[n] quarrel with Germany', and so the United States 'need not, I think, be regarded as a probable foe by ourselves'.

Not quite comprehending that the British were trying to finance the importation of billions of dollars' worth of American goods while the Germans were not, Curzon seemed to think that their only transatlantic peril was the possibility of actually going to war with the United States. They had nothing to fear, he argued, because the chance of this happening was remote. 'America does not want, or mean to fight', he wrote, and that 'includes Britain as well as Germany'.

Curzon bluntly told the Prime Minister that he was playing with political fire. The terms being contemplated, he warned, 'fall far short of the conditions repeatedly laid down by yourself as indispensable'. He all but threw down an ultimatum demanding that the whole matter be dropped: 'Not the conclusion only, but even the discussion of a premature and inconclusive peace, would in my opinion wreck the Government, and be a breach of faith with the nation'.[95]

Asquith beat a retreat, writing back a one-line missive two days later: 'I am in general – in fact, I think, complete agreement with your letter of 24th on terms of peace'.[96] Whether this reflected his true opinions is another matter. McKenna had certainly thought that Asquith was on his side. But the Prime Minister clearly was not about to blow up his government over a diplomatic reply concerning a possible peace overture that was still months away.

Grey's draft reply to House, which does not survive, must have proposed giving the Americans a favourable response. There certainly would have been a clear logic for doing so. With their American lifeline apparently in danger within a few months, telling the Americans to go ahead and make the proposed speech would still give the military time to launch their summer offensive. If the push unexpectedly succeeded in breaking the German lines, the Allies could pre-empt the President and impose their terms. But if it did not, either the war would need to be wound up or, to keep the supply link open, the Americans brought in. Invoking the House-Grey Memorandum at that point could be all but unavoidable.

Balfour's subsequent draft has been dismissed as 'weak almost to the point of futility'.[97] More probable, however, is that Balfour's draft telegram in fact was intended as a compromise, which more convincingly explains its muddled nature – it reads as if Balfour was trying to combine the divergent thinking of a half-dozen people. The way that the draft is put together seems to be designed to try to draw Wilson and House into answering the objections that had been raised. Historian John Milton Cooper, Jr., observes correctly that even though

caution struck the dominant note ... the draft did represent a sympathetic response to the House-Grey Memorandum. Renouncing all notions of a Carthaginian peace, Balfour ... endorsed territorial settlements in line with the House and Wilson thinking ... [D]espite its hedging, the draft reply left the way open for mediation and a negotiated settlement of the war.[98]

The first part of Balfour's draft was essentially a request that Wilson reconfirm the contents of the House-Grey Memorandum, asking the Americans to address a fundamental tension at the heart of the document. The Memorandum promised that the Americans would probably enter the war on the Allied side if Germany refused the conference, or if Germany refused the minimum terms specified in the document. But the Germans and their allies were in possession of nearly the whole of Belgium, Serbia, and Montenegro, as well as swathes of France and Russia. Given the military situation, the Memorandum's terms, Balfour noted, were '*not* in the interests of the Central Powers', and they carried real risks. Was the President 'prepared actively to promote [those terms] either by war or the threat of war'? The Americans may have been willing to go to war for the sake of American ships, but was the President *really* willing, as the Memorandum promised, to do so for the sake of Alsace-Lorraine, as well might prove necessary?

Moreover, the only guarantee of extending such a settlement into 'a lasting peace' lay in the success of this proposed new international league. Britain, Balfour assured House, would be these plans' 'chief friend ... who could most be trusted to stand by them in the hour of stress'. But for the league to successfully fulfil its role as global peacekeeper, the new international organization would need to rest on the sound foundations of a stable European peace. The maintenance those foundations would require reliable Anglo-American sea power, as

'Germany', Balfour wrote with evident intended understatement, 'will certainly lack the will to help'. But the Americans' 'diplomatic pressure' against Britain's wartime blockade, if written into international law, would threaten the only means 'by which ... the proposed peace machinery can be made effective':

> The *best* chance for the great scheme is that it should be proposed by the United States in connection with a peace favourable to the Allies, obtained by American aid.
>
> The *worst* chance would be that it should be proposed in connection with an inconclusive or disastrous peace accompanied, perhaps promoted, by diplomatic friction between the Allies and the United States over maritime affairs.
>
> Between these extremes there are endless intermediate possibilities.

Finally, Balfour echoed Grey's warning. The President's speech *had* to make some reference to the terms of peace themselves, otherwise it would be 'interpreted as meaning that he desired peace on the basis of the *status quo ante*', and 'no such peace could lead to an international organisation of the kind he contemplates'.[99]

Balfour appears to have genuinely believed that this new international league could be successful in keeping the peace. In a conversation the day before – showing the extent to which the post-war settlement was on the War Committee's mind – Hankey, to his 'horror', found Balfour 'bitter with the idea of some form of compulsory arbitration after the war with an "international [tribunal]"'. After being unable to dissuade Balfour from supporting this 'vain and impracticable suggestion',[100] Hankey was so concerned that he dispatched a lengthy memorandum to Balfour and Asquith laying out the dangers he saw. He warned that the scheme would give only a false 'sense of security', and because the British had an inherent 'trustful confidence' in institutions, when the next threat arose the country would by then 'have been lulled to sleep'.[101] On Sunday, 28 May, the day before the War Committee was to take back up the House proposal, Hankey got into another lengthy argument with Balfour, who continued to support the idea. Hankey wrote in his diary that it 'appears that part of President Wilson's scheme is to try and force some such hare-brained scheme [that is, international arbitration] on the world as part of the peace terms, and Grey is backing him for all he is worth'.[102]

Across the Atlantic, the date of Wilson's announcement had been fixed for 27 May. He was to give an address before the League to Enforce Peace, an organization dedicated to the principle of compulsory international arbitration, which was chaired by former Republican President William Howard Taft. With still no answer from

London – House fumed that the British 'travel[led] by freight' when the belated British reply finally arrived on 31 May – House and Wilson decided to revert to their original plan. They would announce support for a post-war league and only 'hint at peace', rather than insist on an early conference.[103] The speech was still intended to lay diplomatic foundations for an autumn peace conference to be chaired by the President himself.

Wilson asked House to put together the initial draft. The Colonel rushed to supply the ideas that would form the core of the address, assembling an epoch-making announcement that sought to bring to a close more than a century of American isolationism. Most of House's draft was very welcome to the British leadership. House called for a 'new and more wholesome diplomacy', articulating the idea that has since come to be called collective security: the United States now sought a convention 'reached by the great powers as to what fundamentals they hold to be their common interest and agree to act in concert when any nation or nations violates these fundamentals'. 'Nations in the future', he wrote, 'must be governed by the same high code of honor as we demand of individuals'.[104]

Mystifyingly, however, House concluded his draft with a call for precisely the same pair of ideas that he had purposefully dropped when in Europe: international disarmament and 'freedom of the seas'.[105] Certainly, these had been amongst House's longstanding objectives, even if they had given him no end of grief back in January. He had evidently not given up on them, with a March diary entry casually listing 'future conduct of war, restriction of armaments, freedom of the seas during war, etc. etc.' as amongst his objectives for a peace conference.[106] But oddly House does not seem at all to have taken into account the nature or depth of the British opposition to these ideas – or, if he was going to insist on pursuing them despite that opposition, at least to have reflected on how he might try to frame them in a more careful and palatable way.

After talking it over with House in person, Wilson took House's hasty draft and transformed it into a polished address. He amplified his chief advisor's error by adding an even more serious one of his own. Not only did he include House's call for international disarmament and freedom of the seas, the President also decided it was essential to emphasize his even-handedness as mediator, telling House that he 'was trying to put it in a way that would be very hard for the Allies to reject, as well as for Germany'. But this attempt at impartiality instead struck right at the core of the British concerns – and could even have been construed as a repudiation of the House-Grey Memorandum.

Wilson had never seriously thought through the European geopolitics of his mediation policy, and he was now putting that on full display.

Wilson said of the war: 'With its causes and its objects we are not concerned. The obscure fountains from which its stupendous flood has burst forth we are not interested to search for or explore'.[107] House, who had not seen the final draft before Wilson delivered the speech, winced at this line, writing presciently in his diary: 'The Allies will overlook all the good in it and accentuate this'.[108] The President compounded this by saying he was looking toward a 'settlement … as the *belligerents* may agree upon'. He indicated clearly that he did not intend to get involved in the territorial negotiations himself, saying he was 'quite aware that we are in no sense or degree parties to the present quarrel. Our interest is only in peace and its future guarantees'.[109]

The British had been worried that Wilson did not take seriously the House-Grey Memorandum's commitments about guaranteeing the Allies' minimum peace terms. Wilson's speech played right into their fears and suggested that the President did not even have a basic grasp of the current military situation. Grey and Balfour had been emphatic that the President must address the terms of peace. For the Allies, the whole *point* of the Memorandum was to leverage American power to convert an unfavourable military situation into a tolerable peace. Wilson had to take an active role in the territorial negotiations to make this happen. Not only was the President appearing to renege on House's commitments, with this reference to 'freedom of the seas', the Americans also seemed to be throwing up a threat to British naval power at the same time. Hankey was livid. He immediately fired off an angry minute to Balfour and Asquith, in time for the decisive War Committee meeting, warning that 'the American peace would be more dangerous to the British Empire than the German war'. At lunch later that day with a journalist from the *Daily Telegraph*, Hankey asked the paper to take the line 'hands off our sea power' in reference to the speech.[110]

Just before noon, a telegram from Britain's Ambassador in Washington, Cecil Spring Rice, arrived in the Foreign Office and delivered a blistering assault on the address. The Ambassador wrongly intimated that the speech came out of a secret understanding with Germany, calling it 'based on German suggestions' and noting that it came out on the same day as a 'peace interview' by the German Ambassador. Spring Rice attacked various sections as 'practically a paraphrase of recent German utterances' and told the government that the 'object of [the] speech' was 'plainly to gain German sympathy during [the] elections and to detach [the] Pacificist from [the] Republican Party'.

Grey, finally getting the public commitment from the Americans that he had sought for so long only for it to arrive in such a disagreeable form, scribbled a minute on the telegram:

It is better to leave President Wilson's speech alone ... we should, however, welcome the proposal for an association of nations to prevent aggressive war and secure respect for the sovereignty and territorial integrity of small states.[111]

The British press, which had been leaned on by the government not to criticize American policies,[112] largely did as it was told, with the exception of the *Daily Mail*, which printed an icy editorial:

There is much that every Briton would like to say, but will rightly refrain from saying, about President Wilson's latest speech. We will satisfy ourselves with only one reminder. It is that this is a 'Presidential year' and that Mr. Wilson is a candidate for re-election. To those who know the United States no more need be said.[113]

The speech had upset all of the careful calculations going into the British deliberations. Balfour's draft had wanted to get Wilson to re-affirm explicitly his commitment to at least a minimum set of Allied war aims. Instead, Wilson all but explicitly told them of his indifference to their concerns. However anxious McKenna's projections may have made some members of the War Committee, the House-Grey Memorandum suddenly seemed a far less viable path of escape. When the War Committee convened, Balfour's muddle was turned into an unmistakable rejection, the Committee telling the Americans to try talking to the French.[114]

Grey once more found himself humiliated. In sharp contrast to his muted initial reaction, the damage that Wilson's speech inflicted seemed to be on his mind for months. On 28 June, a wounded Grey reproached House, writing: 'The phrase about not being concerned with the objects and causes of the war was sure to chill the Allies'.[115] Two months after the speech, Grey was still nursing the injury, bringing up the speech specifically and discussing it in some detail. He told a sympathetic Ambassador Page: 'When the President said that the objects of the war did not concern him, that was taken by British public opinion as meaning a condemnation of the British cause, and it produced deep feeling'. In a revealing line that shows the extent of the damage done, Grey said that the speech's contents had 'produced in many minds an unwillingness, he feared, to use the good offices of the President whenever any mediatorial service might be done by a neutral'.[116]

The British rejection – a long, meandering telegram – exasperated House and Wilson. 'It does not get us anywhere', House complained to his diary. The Colonel promptly took up the matter with the French Ambassador, who came for a visit the next day, trying to reassure him that, notwithstanding the President's remarks, the United States could secure Alsace-Lorraine for the French at a peace conference. But the tone of the interview rapidly turned aggressive as the Ambassador flatly rejected any peace talks, accused Wilson of having delivered a speech 'in the German interest', and denounced the American leaders for keeping their country in a flaccid 'state of atony by a regime of procrastination'. (House generously did not report the Ambassador's most severe remarks to the President.)[117] House tried a measure of damage control with Grey, walking back Wilson's blunder by accusing the speech's critics of

pick[ing] out some expression he makes and giving it a meaning and importance he never meant. If we are to take part in maintaining the peace of the world we could hardly be indifferent to the war and its causes and the President never intended to leave such an impression.

The normally deferent House copied this letter to Wilson, which showed that the Colonel clearly believed that the President knew he had bungled and would not mind House's effort to clean up the mess.[118]

Wilson botched the execution of this key address so badly that he provoked a severe backlash of Allied resentment and ruined a promising chance of implementing the House-Grey Memorandum. The Americans recognized that any further peace efforts would now have to wait until after the summer offensive at the earliest – and by then the presidential election campaign would be in full swing. With the Democratic National Convention about to meet in mid-June and nothing else to be done, the President, consumed with domestic politics, did not even bother to reply to House's letters about the diplomatic situation. In early June, Colonel House made his customary retreat north to escape the summer heat, enjoying a long break in rural New Hampshire. It was as if the American pursuit of mediation followed him there and took an identical rest, as suspended in animation as House's diary.

The courses of both countries for the next few months were locked in. Britain's economic and military strategies had now diverged completely. Even though the country's strategy for the war had been fully predicated on winning the war with the summer offensive, Haig now merely hoped that it could lay the foundations for a decisive 1917 campaign – a campaign that certainly could not be fought on the same expansive economic scale, assuming it could be fought at all. But reconciling all this, and any further diplomatic dealings with the Americans, would be a problem for the autumn. '[T]here is nothing to add or to do for the moment', House told Grey in his last letter before his holiday, 'and if the Allies are willing to take the gamble which the future may hold, we must rest content'.[119]

5   The Gamble
June–August 1916

The great gamble was now imminent, a development that seems to have filled some quarters of the British government with an acute sense of dread. Not only was it launching a massive offensive many did not think would work, but, for those who acknowledged Britain's economic ticking clock, it was also doing so in the glum recognition that this might well be Britain's only chance to win the war. Asquith moved to extend that clock for a little longer by making an urgent personnel change: ejecting Lloyd George from the Ministry of Munitions – even if the only way to achieve that was by promoting him. Otherwise, however, while the summer would be anything but quiet for the soldiers mired in the bloodletting on the Somme, any dramatic diplomatic moves were out of the question until the tragedy had finished its unfolding. Startling talk of peace came from the President of France, but otherwise the question of American mediation rumbled only quietly beneath the surface on the British side as everyone awaited the campaign's results. As the Battle of the Somme got underway, the tides of pessimism within the government unexpectedly went out. Dismay over the initial casualties by August gave way to inestimable optimism: as Romania entered the war on the Allied side, even Grey momentarily misplaced his sense. It suddenly appeared as if the Allies might actually win the war on schedule.

The realists continued to try to combat maximalist fantasies of British invincibility, although political realities sharply limited the battlefield. A wartime tragedy, however, unexpectedly gave the Prime Minister some limited room for manoeuvre. On 5 June, the war claimed its first and only casualty from the coalition Cabinet. The *HMS Hampshire* struck a mine in the North Sea and sank; amongst the 643 losing their lives was Lord Kitchener, the War Secretary, who was on his way to Russia. (The Treasury, and twentieth-century economics, had a near-miss – Keynes had been due to accompany Kitchener but was by chance forced to cancel at the last minute.) Seeking to get a better grip on his country's war effort, Asquith assumed control of the vacant War Office himself for

137

the few crucial weeks leading up to the opening of the Somme.[1] Without good evidence of his intentions, historians have long wondered about Asquith's decision-making in his subsequently handing the office over to Lloyd George, tending to chalk up the appointment to a weakened Prime Minister looking to avoid fresh political turmoil.[2] They are surely right that Asquith had no enthusiasm for the appointment. Asquith 'knows the appointment is a bad one', McKenna wrote, and wishing his hated arch-rival could just be turfed out of the government altogether, the Chancellor deplored Asquith's not showing 'strength to resist'.[3] Though a desire to appease Lloyd George may have been part of Asquith's motivation, a different explanation seems more likely: that the Prime Minister was more concerned about removing the profligate Lloyd George from the Ministry of Munitions than about the risks of promoting him.

To be sure, Lloyd George had considerable success at the Ministry he founded. His great feat of organizing prowess had left the Army with plenty of munitions, albeit ones of uneven quality: 'Some 25–30 percent of all shells fired during the preliminary bombardment on the Somme were duds'.[4] Even so, Lloyd George was right to feel pride that '[a]mmunition is pouring in'.[5] Asquith praised Lloyd George in the War Committee for the 'marvellous' accomplishment this represented.[6] But Lloyd George's uncontrolled spending in the United States threatened the war effort. His ministry had given the military every weapon it might hope to get for its one great push. Further American extravagance would only hasten the closure of the alliance's crucial economic lifeline.

Lloyd George's decision to launch a vicious June attack on the Treasury over Russian munitions could only have confirmed Asquith in a desire to remove him. The Russian munitions situation had been in a state of complete disorder since the beginning of the war, with the British and French expending enormous energies to help supply the Russians with what they required without jeopardizing their own needs.[7] The British Treasury had lavished the Russians with extensive credits, especially in the United States, despite their 'careless buying practices' and 'wastefulness'.[8] Russian incompetence knew almost no bounds. 'An already badly muddled situation', one historian has written, 'was made worse by the lack of any informed, consistent [Russian] government authority, faulty or incomplete Russian design specifications and draw-ings, many of which were repeatedly altered during the course of a single order'. Equally dire were the Russian government's technical advisors in America, 'most of whom spoke little or no English, were often inexperi-enced, always difficult, and frequently arbitrary'.[9]

Not only were preciously finite resources being wasted, the resulting delays in deliveries led to crucial shortages in munitions on the Russian

Front. Precisely for the sake of trying to sort out these problems Kitchener had gone and given his life.[10] With the Russians now demanding a fresh influx of British funds, McKenna was determined to impose some better controls. At the very least, he hoped to prevent them from giving orders that could not be transported – their main port city, Archangel, was blocked by ice for half the year.

Lloyd George, unsurprisingly, vehemently opposed any effort to impose controls of any kind on the Russians. The dispute rumbled quietly for some time before surfacing in the War Committee on 30 June. He and McKenna sniped at each other, with Lloyd George accusing McKenna of having 'cut down' on the Russian requests 'by several millions for months'. Bonar Law actually spoke up to defend the Russian cuts, though only 'because transport was not available'. Balfour also supported McKenna, bemoaning that the Russians 'believed we had endless American securities'. McKenna hit back at Lloyd George, commenting on 'our enormous expenditures and requirements' on munitions in the United States 'as compared with France'. Lloyd George said the large British Navy made the two countries not comparable, but McKenna would have none of it, saying that the 'cost of the navy including the pay of all ranks was only half the cost of munitions'. Asquith had to break up the quarrel, and eventually it was decided first to establish what the Russian requirements were, then to decide what of that could be transported, and, finally, to consider what of that could actually be afforded.[11]

Following this meeting, Lloyd George circulated a memorandum, which was written the previous day.[12] In it, Lloyd George claimed to have solved all of their financial and economic problems in the United States at a single stroke. His great idea, which somehow had eluded both the financial experts in the British Treasury and the bankers at Morgan's, meant that the Allies henceforth would be able to get all the American goods they should ever want. He suggested that they threaten American manufacturers with the loss of Allied business, imagining that such threats would force American businessmen to agree to 'mak[e] their own arrangements for financing those contracts', relying 'on the joint credit of the three Allied countries'. If the Allies were to follow through on these threats, he was sure that there would be a 'great crash', and that the US government would 'directly or indirectly see to it that such a disastrous collapse should not take place'. He argued that this not only applied to American manufacturing but also to 'the produce of the American farmer and cotton planter'. If only they took a hard line, he argued, they would get all they wanted for as long as they needed.[13]

Lloyd George was putting his economic illiteracy on full display. It had long been evident that he understood little about the country's financial situation, though he confidently believed the opposite. Six months earlier, Hankey had fumed about Lloyd George's talking 'an awful lot of froth' about American finance at a dinner party. Hankey commented that Lord Reading, who had recently returned from his loan mission, 'was very eloquent by his silence', and Reading later confessed to Hankey that 'he had purposefully remained silent, because he did not want to have a wrangle'.[14]

Lloyd George asserted with airy confidence that his proposal should pose no problem because 'all the business of America is done on credit'. 'No gold passes' from buyer to seller in all these transactions, he wrote, as if this were a profound observation. Americans conduct their business with bank cheques and short-term finance bills, instead of by hauling bags of gold around, and so the logical conclusion, Lloyd George believed, was that long-term loans should be easy to obtain. More serious was his accusation that the Treasury had 'deprived' the Russians 'of heavy guns, heavy shell, railway material – all of them essential to victory – merely because we cannot see our way to financing the necessary orders on the present basis by the present methods'. Victory could 'be assured for 1917', but because of the Treasury, he wrote, now this would be 'put off for another year'. It was vital, he argued, 'not [to] cut down the Russian Requirements', which included 'rails, locomotives, waggons, heavy guns, heavy shell'. His most astonishingly ignorant statement, however, came in his closing sentence: 'To stint them in these things because these three great rich countries cannot afford to incur another [five] hundred million [dollars] debtedness to America is the height of stupidity'.[15]

If I have succeeded in explaining Britain's financial situation with even a modicum of the clarity to which I have aspired, the absurdity of this last statement should need no elaboration. For those of my readers with no previous study of economics, one realization should prove striking: armed with no economic training beyond a few hours in the company of my prose, you have achieved a superior understanding of Britain's financial situation in 1916 than a man with eight years' experience as Chancellor of the Exchequer. Indeed, Lloyd George's experience seems only to have added a sweeping arrogance to his ignorance.

His proposal was at best unworkable and, by adopting such an antagonistic position, very probably seriously counterproductive. Though the United States had suffered recession in 1913 and 1914, the American domestic economy by 1916 was humming to the point of overheating, experiencing real annual GDP growth at a zooming 14 per cent compared with the previous year.[16] Allied orders contributed to this growth, to be sure, but with the American economy more than double that of Britain, there is little indication that withdrawing these orders would give the US economy much more than a bit of a slowdown, and in many key areas not even that. American steel, for example, was one of the Allies' most demanded war imports, but the US Steel Corporation had a backlog of nearly 10 million tons' worth of unfilled orders in May 1916 – and that backlog had been sharply increasing.[17] An Allied threat to cease purchases of food and cotton, meanwhile, would have provoked US government relief, not alarm. Swollen American food prices already were at their highest levels in many years. Over the autumn, amidst a weak harvest, they would climb still higher,[18] to such an extent that there would be demands in Congress to impose a temporary export embargo.[19] American cotton prices similarly were surging to some two-and-a-half times their pre-war levels amidst high domestic demand.[20] American farmers and cotton planters had no shortage of willing buyers.

Though Lloyd George found it incomprehensible, the credit of 'these three great rich countries' frankly was not worth very much in the United States. We have seen the near failure of the $500 million Anglo-French loan the previous year. The prices on those bonds had since fallen, and those Americans who had taken part now possessed investments worth less than what they had paid for them.[21] New York traders had no enthusiasm for more Allied debt. In November 1916, against Morgan's advice, Russia would make its own attempt at a little unsecured public loan in the United States, looking to raise a paltry $50 million. Despite offering generous terms, the Russians could get only half of this sum underwritten. The underwriters who participated all wished they had not, suffering 'heavy losses' on the subsequent public sale.[22] Lloyd George had it entirely the wrong way around: it was the Allies who were gravely economically vulnerable to the United States.

At a meeting of a Cabinet Finance Committee called to consider this proposal and the Russian munitions situation more generally, McKenna restrained himself from launching into a hostile response. He told Lloyd George – who was by now in his final days at the Munitions Ministry – that he could go ahead and have a try with his idea, though he thought 'it would have a very poor time in America'. Much of the meeting got bogged down in discussion of domestic Russian munitions manufacture and questions of transport, but even so, the broader divisions continued to be evident. McKenna doubted that they could get anyone to lend to them except by mortgaging investments. Bonar Law, by contrast, declared his support for Lloyd George, saying that he 'had no doubt that when the United States appreciated the fact that they would not get the business at all unless they helped us financially, they would certainly give way'.[23]

Afterwards, however, McKenna hit back with an even-tempered but brutal written reply, originally drafted by Keynes. Keynes, though appearing to welcome an 'experiment' of Lloyd George's idea, systematically dismantled the ill-conceived plan. He observed that, with the American domestic economy now at full steam, there were only a few 'isolated cases of highly specialised munitions manufacturers' that might even in theory be vulnerable to the kind of pressure Lloyd George suggested. American steel companies were 'booked up for orders many months ahead', so much so that Allied munition orders were actively hindering US railway development. The Munitions Ministry was itself continually coming to the Treasury demanding urgency 'because otherwise prices would rise or other buyers snap up the orders'.

The Treasury vehemently rejected the accusation that the Russians had been 'deprived' or 'stinted', and slammed Lloyd George's ridiculous closing line – painting a 'picture of the allies refusing loans in America for fear of the subsequent burden of indebtedness!' The Treasury, in fact, was desperately 'trying to borrow any penny anyone will lend'. The problem was that there were so few willing to do so. In a dramatic closing flourish of his own, Keynes appended a draft of a telegram to Morgan's, inviting them for their views on Lloyd George's scheme and advising the bank to proceed with it if they though it practicable.[24] Lloyd George moved to the War Office a few days later; the telegram, it seems, was never sent. The Russian munitions situation was subsequently settled, with the imposition of greater British control over their purchasing.[25]

Asquith had been trying for some time to get Lloyd George out of the Munitions Ministry, even before Kitchener drowned. He had offered Lloyd George the Chief Secretaryship of Ireland, even if only 'for a short time', in the tumultuous aftermath of the Easter Rising. But Lloyd George 'd[id] not want to give up his active participation in the war', and agreed to take Ireland on only as a special mission in addition to his current role.[26] After Kitchener's death, Asquith made his opening gambit on 13 June. He offered Lloyd George either the War Office with its reduced powers, or, appealing to Lloyd George's vanity, offered him the grandiose-sounding title of Vice Chairman of the War Committee without Portfolio – the latter a suitable way of harnessing Lloyd George's energies for important projects while trying to contain any collateral damage.[27] Lloyd George intrigued for a time, hoping that he could not only take the War Office with an expansion of the minister's powers, but also to roll the Ministry of Munitions into it. He threatened again to resign and continued to fantasize about taking power from the outside.

'If I went out I should at once form a great Party organization', he bragged to a friend. 'I have promises of all the money necessary'. But Asquith held firm and eventually Lloyd George relented, accepting Asquith's original offer of the War Office on 28 June.[28] Lloyd George, apparently with Bonar Law's support, seems to have argued for installing as his successor at the Munitions Ministry Winston Churchill, who had been Lloyd George's key Liberal maximalist ally in 1915. The Prime Minister, unsurprisingly, would hear none of it.[29]

Asquith's intentions in promoting Lloyd George may be best illustrated in the men he tapped instead. The day after Lloyd George accepted the War Office, Asquith summoned Austen Chamberlain and offered him the Munitions Ministry. Whatever their political differences, Chamberlain had shown himself to be a Conservative who was sound on the war economy and who could be trusted to seek to maintain their American lifeline as long as possible. In a fit of personal pique, however, Chamberlain rejected the office: Lloyd George 'had got all the kudos he could out of it', he told Asquith. The 'limelight' was now 'elsewhere'.[30] With the only suitable Conservative having turned down the post, Asquith was now forced to turn to a reliable Liberal ally to rein in the department. The Tories might not like it, but it could not be helped. He offered the promotion to his friend and confidant Edwin Montagu, the Financial Secretary to the Treasury, who promptly accepted.[31] McKenna was pleased enough: 'To get rid of Ll[oyd] G[eorge] from the Munitions is such a relief that I am quite reconciled to his going to the War Office'. Montagu, McKenna trusted, would 'introduce order and rationality' to the expenditures, especially in the United States,[32] and an initial top-level meeting between the Treasury and the Ministry of Munitions a few days after Montagu's appointment went amicably.[33] Someone recalled that at least one Secretary of State was supposed to be a peer; Grey consented to being kicked upstairs and became Viscount Grey of Fallodon. The deck chairs on the top of the ship of state now stood suitably rearranged, as they would remain until December.[34]

Within the bowels of the ship, another important personnel change took place. Grey took on as his new Permanent Undersecretary something of a saboteur, at least when it came to Grey's policy towards the United States. Charles Hardinge, a conservative, had worked well with Grey as his Permanent Undersecretary from 1906 to 1910, before spending the next six years as Viceroy of India. Grey was only too happy to have him back, as was Hardinge. The two liked each other immensely: five months later, Hardinge would be 'very sorry to lose Grey to whom I was really much attached'.[35] But personal affection did not stand in his way: Hardinge worked behind Grey's back with a close friend, the hardline

British Ambassador to Paris, Lord Bertie, to undermine the Foreign Secretary on a single specific issue: American mediation. 'The views held upstairs', Hardinge wrote to Bertie, 'are utterly rotten'.[36] The two would do their utmost to kill it.

15 Charles Hardinge (Library of Congress / George Grantham Bain Collection/LC-B2-1070-14)

Finally, though Chamberlain would not take on the Munitions Ministry, by the end of the summer the Prime Minister would nevertheless find another important role for him. In early August, Lloyd George would propose what would become the 'Manpower Distribution Board', a body that would be charged with adjudicating competing governmental claims over increasingly scarce manpower. Lloyd George envisioned this as nothing less than the 'germ of [a] machine' that would 'compel all men to work for the nation where they are required' – not only in the military, but in the war workshops as well.[37] Lloyd George believed that Britain could import whatever it wished; the logical corollary of this was that the country's export industries were pointless. The Board of Trade, unsurprisingly, reacted to the proposal with considerable caution. It warned that compared with the demands of the Army or the Munitions Ministry, British trade was no less important but 'much more likely to be forgotten' in the competition for manpower. In principle, the Board of Trade wrote, there was no harm in the proposed manpower board – provided that it 'include[d] members who appreciate the importance of maintaining the economic strength of the country for the purpose of the successful prosecution of the war'.[38] The Asquithians made sure of this. They intercepted Lloyd George's nominee for the chair of the board and handed the job to Chamberlain instead.[39]

Having done his utmost to extend their ticking clock, the only thing for the Prime Minister to do now was to hope his generals could win the war before time was up. There was plenty of doubt in the Cabinet that their generals could succeed. As summer began, Britain's civilian leaders steeled themselves for the offensive. Only Bonar Law in the War Committee had any enthusiasm for the undertaking.[40] In a rare moment of candour, Robertson confessed on 22 June that the Allies 'had a superiority in men, but he thought the Germans had a superiority in guns'. Balfour replied scathingly that then 'our superiority was great except in the one thing that really mattered'.[41] Yet they could only let the offensive go forward and then re-evaluate their position. Three days before the battle began, Grey wrote House a letter that was devoid of even a trace of enthusiasm and that purposely held the door open for American mediation. '[T]he British Army has to make its efforts and its sacrifices', he told House,

before we can be the first to call a halt ... [E]verybody in the next few weeks is going to make their maximum effort; if the result is a distinct sweep to one side or the other the situation will be changed; even if the result is deadlock, the situation will not be the same ... and must be reviewed afresh.[42]

The great guns of July opened, beginning that awful, on-going calamity. Britain was committed; until the offensive had run its course, there was little to be done. When Grey's letter reached New Hampshire two weeks later, House grasped his meaning immediately: 'What he says about a change in conditions after this offensive has been tried out is interesting and important', he wrote to Wilson. 'They should know by September 1st whether it is to be a success or failure. Then would be the time to press some proposal on them'.[43] Until then, all they could do was wait.

The appalling costs of the battle on the Somme became evident very quickly – nearly 40,000 deaths in July alone[44] – with corresponding disquiet in some quarters of the Cabinet. The House-Grey Memorandum, sitting on the shelf with its promise of either 'a decent peace' or inexhaustible American aid, could not have made the initial shock of the horrible casualty lists coming out of France any easier for the Liberal consciences on the War Committee to bear. Walter Runciman, the Liberal President of the Board of Trade, bemoaned on 8 July the 'cruelly heavy losses with only indirect gains'.[45]

16 A British field dressing station in France during the Battle of the
Somme, 1916 (Historica Graphica Collection / Heritage Images /
Hulton Archive via Getty Images)

Robertson, however, continually pumped the government with optimism. Indeed, through the offensive's end in November, the military
consistently told the government that everything on the Western Front
was sunshine and rainbows. In certain quarters, the military's happy talk
was swallowed continually, without either interruption or so much as a
question mark. Reflecting an influential strand of predominantly
Conservative opinion, Hardinge, for example, never wavered in his faith
in the military's assessment: 'It is only a question of time', he asserted in
August, 'before the big collapse will come'.[46] Even though the big
collapse never came, by the end of November he was nevertheless calling
the outcome of the offensive – which after four-and-a-half months had
not even accomplished all of the objectives assigned for its first day – 'a
result to be well satisfied with', and he was 'look[ing] forward to next
Spring full of hope and confidence'.[47]

    In the early days of July, however, not even Robertson believed the
sunbeams coming out of his mouth. Haig saw the almost 20,000 soldiers
killed on 1 July as about what one would expect, and celebrated the
'marvellous advance'. Robertson recognized it for what it was: an unmiti-
gated disaster. Politics, however, came over honesty. He

supported Haig, even when it was ill advised, to prevent the civilians from undermining Britain's commitment to the land war in France and Flanders. Standing apart, Robertson and Haig were vulnerable. Together they seemed invincible because of the political risks of removing them both.

Unwilling to jeopardize the military's dominance of policy and strategy, '[n]one of Robertson's doubts about Haig's leadership were shared with the government'.[48] The politicians had little choice but to rely on Robertson's and Haig's assurances.

Even so, by month's end, the disquiet in some quarters of the Cabinet about the vast quantities of blood being spilt on the Somme was finally threatening to reach a boil. 'The powers that be', Robertson wrote to Haig on 29 July, 'are beginning to get a little uneasy about the situation'. Troublesomely, they 'persist in asking me whether I think a loss of say, 300,000 men will lead to really good results because if not we ought to be content with something less'. 'What is bothering them', he wrote damningly, 'is the probability that we may soon have to face a bill of 2 to 300,000 casualties with no very great gains additional to the present'.[49]

Three days later, on 1 August, the Attorney General, F. E. Smith, circulated a fierce attack by Winston Churchill, then on the backbenches, arguing the futility of the offensive and demanding that the attacks be called off. Smith was careful to distance himself from it personally, saying that he was not 'wholly in agreement' with it and that Churchill in particular 'underrates the importance of our offensive as a contribution to the general strategical situation'. But he wanted his colleagues to 'apply their minds to the situation' with 'both the official and a critical view before them'.[50] Churchill's critique, 'marked by a high level of cogency and command of events', was devastating:

In *personnel* the results of the operation have been disastrous; in *terrain* they have been absolutely barren ... From every point of view, therefore, the British offensive *per se* has been a great failure.[51]

In the absence of a reply from Haig, Robertson nevertheless did his best to hit back. In the past month, Germany had suffered extraordinary casualties, he said, of some 1.25 million – an arresting figure, but one that seems to have been simply invented: British military intelligence estimates at this point put German casualties for July at 130,000–150,000. Over the entire four-and-a-half months of the battle, Germany actually suffered casualties of less than a half million.[52]

When told of Churchill's critique, Haig contemptuously dismissed it. 'Winston's judgement', he speculated to a friend, must be 'impaired from taking drugs'.[53] Robertson soon had Haig's written reply, which he played like a trump card. Haig listed the main accomplishments of the battle as relieving the pressure on Verdun and on the Russian Front, and giving a 'general good moral effect', which had 'brought the Allies forward on the way to victory'. In spite of the fact that the accomplishments were 'sometimes hypothetical', the statement won over most of the Cabinet and effectively silenced those it did not.[54] Buttressing Haig's positivity were a series of optimistic British military intelligence estimates, which assumed that the Germans had only a meagre three divisions left in reserve to reinforce the Somme Front. If the British just kept up the assault, they stood a decent chance of overwhelming the depleted German reserves and inflicting severe losses on the German lines. What British military intelligence did not know, and would not find out until autumn, was that they were constructing their assessments on a foundation of quicksand. The Germans actually had six divisions in reserve, not three, and the German lines were never in any significant danger.[55]

Between Robertson's sunbeams and, at long last, encouraging developments elsewhere, previously pessimistic ministers now found themselves daring to succumb to an unexpected and unfamiliar emotion: hope. The Allies, it suddenly seemed, might actually win the war this year. The Russians, for once, were encountering something other than disaster, having launched what became known as the Brusilov Offensive at the beginning of June. Battling depleted Austro-Hungarian forces – weakened because Vienna had diverted troops for an ill-advised offensive against Italy the previous month – Russian forces broke through the defensive line, starting a 'spectacular collapse' that sent the Austro-Hungarians hurtling into a full retreat. Suffering 'disastrous' casualties of nearly a half-million men in just two months, Austria-Hungary lost control of significant portions of its two north-easternmost provinces, including a key provincial capital, Czernowitz.[56] One of the Allied fronts had finally moved meaningfully into enemy territory.

Allied diplomacy with Romania was also beginning to bear fruit. By late July, British leaders began to grow increasingly optimistic about the prospect of drawing Romania into the war and unleashing twenty-five fresh divisions on Austria-Hungary's south-eastern frontiers. If the Romanians came in as the Russians hammered Austria-Hungary from the north-east, it seemed certain that 'the Austrian difficulties will be overwhelming', as McKenna put it on 21 July. McKenna had another reason for relief: the tax on American securities was working out 'wonderfully' and had allowed him to 'build up quite a substantial reserve against the autumn demand'. McKenna penned a phrase, perhaps for the only time: 'The war is going well'.[57]

His arch-rival, now at the War Office, felt the same way. In early July, House gently sounded Lloyd George about the possibility of invoking the

House-Grey Memorandum, sending along a press clipping and then tacking on a post-script mentioning 'the things we talked of in London' and wondering whether they 'will ever come to fruition'. Lloyd George's reply on 31 July did not close the door to the possibility, calling it only 'premature' now that the 'Allies are winning at last'. He told House that 'although Germany must now be getting anxious, her rulers are not quite convinced as yet that the game is up'.[58]

In the Foreign Office, Grey likewise spent the summer cautiously exploring this unfamiliar feeling of optimism. With financial doomsday pushed off until into the following year, the Allied militaries had some additional months to win the war, and for once it looked as if they might actually pull it off. If the military could win the war by then, there would be no need to turn to American mediation diplomacy – and every reason to try to postpone it. Grey eventually succumbed to this optimism at the end of August. Until then, he continued to insist that the Allies must take seriously any autumn mediation move by the United States – which, it must be remembered, he had thus far done nothing to discourage. Indeed, if anything, his previous letter to House had purposefully kept the door to such a move wide open. Grey continued to insist that the government be prepared for the possibility of ending the war on compromise terms. Beginning in July and continuing for the next couple of months, Asquith's government began to consider specific war aims, which were ultimately manifested in a number of memoranda detailing British wishlists of what they hoped to achieve.[59] A dictated peace – which would remain a fantasy for another two years – lay at the foundation of all but one of these reports. The one that did not, and that included a long section discussing the possibility of a negotiated peace, was at Grey's insistence. On 25 July, he wrote to Bonar Law about a proposed joint committee on peace terms, and Grey insisted that their deliberations must include a scenario in which 'peace terms are more or less a matter of bargaining'.[60]

Yet he also recognized that if the war were to end in a compromise peace, there was no question of it while the Somme Offensive was still going on. The very same day that he wrote to Bonar Law demanding that a compromise peace remain on the table, he also allowed his private secretary, Eric Drummond, to send a letter reassuring the British Ambassador to Washington, Cecil Spring Rice – a vehement opponent of American mediation[61] – that no mediation proposal would 'be entertained for a moment here'.[62]

The tensions in Grey's thinking were on display in a conversation with the American Ambassador. Four days later, Grey confided to US

Ambassador to London Walter Page the great damage that the President's speech to the League to Enforce Peace had done. It

had produced in many minds an unwillingness, he feared, to use the good offices of the President whenever any mediatorial service might be done by a neutral ... Yet Sir Edward carefully abstained from expressing such an unwillingness on his own part; and the inference from his tone and manner, as well as from his habitual attitude, is that he feels no unwillingness to use the President's good offices, if occasion should arise.

These remarks were of course tempered by a few caveats: Grey 'did not expect the President to act on his own initiative', and wished that the President; would not act without ascertaining the feeling of the Allies'. Moreover, he added that he 'didn't think that any considerable group of people in any other country – certainly not in Great Britain' – believed that the war would end 'inconclusively – as a draw'.[63] Considering that he had just asked Bonar Law to consider precisely this scenario, this seems an exaggeration to be sure; yet it also serves as an indication of the creeping optimism within the government. Even so, Grey was fortunate that these comments did not go to Washington by telegraph. Page had been recalled to Washington; the documents accompanied him on his voyage home, and so were safely outside the reach of MI1(b).

Grey's account of the conversation sent to Spring Rice in Washington, moreover, omitted any discussion of 'mediatorial service', though he indirectly rebuked his Ambassador for his constant assertion that 'President Wilson's motive in anything he would do, would be that of getting votes in the United States'. Grey wrote flatly: 'This was not my view of President Wilson'.[64]

Yet even with these growing expressions of optimism, Grey remained profoundly anxious about the war effort – so much so that his new subordinate in the Foreign Office and his Ambassador in Paris felt an increasing need to undermine him. Almost immediately after Hardinge began working at the Foreign Office, he and Lord Bertie in Paris secretly began gossiping about Grey and his relations with House in a series of private letters. After Hardinge mentioned some questionable Russian information showing the Germans would soon be interested in an armistice, possibly to be arranged by President Wilson,[65] Bertie wrote back to him about 'a sheep-faced and fox-minded American, intimate friend of President Wilson, one Colonel House. Grey believed in his pro-Entente sentiments. From what I saw and heard of him here I considered him to be a humbug'. Bertie mentioned House's travels and disclosed House's indication that the United States could possibly join the war 'if the Germans were not reasonable'.[66] Hardinge replied to this with but a single sentence: 'I have naturally said nothing to Grey of your opinion of

Colonel House as he is apparently a great friend of his and a man in whom he has much confidence'.[67]

Sufficiently concerned by Hardinge's response, Bertie decided to bring his close friend in on much of the secret negotiations with House. In a nod to the supreme secrecy of the document, he left out the House–Grey Memorandum itself, but included much of the rest of his earlier correspondence with Grey, in which Bertie had denounced House in vigorous terms and Grey had replied equally forcefully defending him.[68] Hardinge thanked him for the correspondence. Propriety demanded that he not disclose to Bertie his conversations with his minister, but he replied with an unmistakable hint: reiterating again simply that 'great confidence is expressed upstairs in the power and good faith of [Colonel House]'.[69]

Alarmed by this, when Lord Bertie returned to Britain for a short trip a few weeks later, he made squelching any positive response to an American diplomatic move a top priority. The day after his arrival, 10 August, he joined a luncheon with Lloyd George, who was 'all for going on until Germany went on her knees'. American mediation, Bertie thought, would be the Americans 'twisting the tail of the British lion' for electoral purposes. 'The lion', Bertie told Lloyd George, 'ought to show his teeth as soon as we were independent of American supplies'. Bertie recorded that the great proponent of spending with abandon in America replied in the strangest possible way: Lloyd George 'seemed inclined to agree and said that we were already nearly independent of American supplies'. Bertie perhaps mistook Lloyd George's sentiment, which might more accurately be described as wanting Britain to show its teeth *regardless* of its dependence on American supplies.[70]

On 11 August, tipped off by Hardinge that Grey was 'not very sound in the matter of war, peace, and possible American mediation',[71] Bertie spent most of his interview with the Foreign Secretary pressing Grey to take a harder line. Grey was adamant that the Allies could not make a 'blank refusal' to a proposal for American mediation 'and so put America against us'. He would have to tell the Americans that they needed to 'consult our allies' and to 'know the *peace* bases' on which Germany would be 'prepared to treat'. Only after the terms had been proposed, and only after the Allies had been consulted, could the Entente reject the terms if they proved unacceptable. Bertie objected that any mediation proposal 'would be an electoral manoeuvre and we ought', he told Grey, 'to have a stiff upper lip'. Despite Bertie's repeated arguments, however, Grey would not budge from his position that Britain 'must not reject' any American overture. Bertie wrote in disgust that Grey had been 'inoculated by the Colonel House virus'.[72]

Bertie went back and reported on the interview to his close friend. Hardinge was 'glad' that the Ambassador had bluntly made the case against mediation. He told Bertie that he 'passes his time in trying to buck up Grey' and that he had warned Grey that the country would not stand 'giv[ing] way an iota to Germany. The argument which seems to answer best is that the Ministry would be turned out if they gave way at all'.[73]

Whatever the Prime Minister's personal beliefs, that political fact had not been lost on him in the slightest. When Bertie came to see him a few days later, the Ambassador urgently brought up the possibility, 'anticipated by Grey as a certainty', of an American mediation attempt, and asked whether he 'believed in Col House as Grey does'. To Bertie's relief, Asquith 'd[id] not' and 'regard[ed] Col House as merely an electoral wine-puller for Wilson'.[74]

Bertie immediately followed up this conversation by penning Asquith a letter:

With reference to our conversation this morning respecting a possible offer of mediation by America in October as an electoral dodge on the part of President Wilson I suggest that instead of replying to Col House or any other Electoral Agent or Diplomatic Representative … it would be better to tell the Americans that if Germany want peace she must apply direct to all the Entente Allies stating for consideration her suggestions. We should thus avoid a discussion with President Wilson who would like to have a wordy controversy with England for his own electoral purposes.[75]

A far more potentially explosive conversation occurred later that afternoon. For months, Bertie had asserted unequivocally that the French wanted nothing to do with American mediation and would not entertain the idea of peace negotiations. A conversation with the King seemed to shatter these assumptions. The King had seen the French President, Raymond Poincaré, on 12 August on a visit to the British Front in France. Bertie was stunned to learn that Poincaré had been in favour of 'bringing the war to a conclusion as soon as possible' and had said that 'when an offer of American mediation comes, which may be expected to take place in October, the Allies should be ready to state their terms'. Nothing but gloom attended Poincaré's outlook. The French public was 'too optimistic' and would not take kindly to having to 'be shown that a winter campaign will be necessary'. He expressed 'great anxiety in regard to the state of affairs in Russia'. Germany had 'a fresh class of recruits' of a million men, while France did not.[76] The King's decision to share this information with Bertie probably was a political one: the King was one of the military's closest supporters[77] and one of Wilson's greatest detractors. So coldly did he regard the meddling American President that when

Wilson's engagement to Edith Bolling Galt was announced the year before, the King refused to send a telegram of congratulations, and on their marriage the previous December Grey had to intervene personally to get the King to despatch one.[78] The King likely entrusted this information to Bertie, when it should have been reported immediately to Grey, in the knowledge that Bertie would do all he could to bury it. Bertie kept it to himself until he arrived back in Paris, mentioning nothing to Asquith in the letter he wrote him later that day. Even Hardinge was kept out of the loop.

On his return to Paris, he rushed to speak with the French Premier and the Foreign Minister, who entirely dismissed – or thought it best to dismiss to Bertie – the views of their President as 'absolute nonsense' and asserted that the French were determined, as Bertie put it, 'to *aller jusqu'au bout*'. Sufficiently reassured that he had killed any talk of mediation, Bertie at last recounted everything that had happened in a lengthy, 'personal and confidential' letter to Hardinge on 24 August, to which he appended an extensive bromide against the Americans: 'It seems to be thought in London that [American mediation] could not be rejected ... We know and the French know that an offer of mediation by President Wilson would be a Presidential Electoral manoeuvre solicited by Germany'. Why, therefore, he demanded to know,

should we consent to be the intermediary between the United States Government and our Allies and bear the principal burden of the blame for an inevitable failure? Would it not be much better ... to reply that if Germany desire peace she must apply direct to the Entente Allies stating the bases of the terms on which she would be ready to treat[?] This would obviate a wordy controversy with the United States Government which President Wilson would like to have for electoral purposes.

He hit hard against any peace talks with views rooted in the military's assurances of success:

I do not think that the time has yet come for Peace Negotiations ... When Germany has been properly beaten[,] starved of food and of the necessaries for continuing the struggle[,] and brought to her knees[,] as she will be if the Allies persevere, there will be less probability than there would be now of their quarrelling amongst themselves over the Peace terms.

When Hardinge got this letter a few days later, he ignored the 'confidential' label. Deciding he could strike a blow against his superior's American policy, he promptly circulated it to the King and all the members of the War Committee. Undoubtedly embarrassed, Grey scrawled a minute in response to Bertie's charges. 'I have taken steps to let it be known that we cannot be used as a stalking horse for President

Wilson to approach the Allies', he wrote. But at the same time he affirmed that there was no way 'of preventing [Wilson] from approaching the Allies if he means to make his move'.[79]

Grey stuck to his policy, despite the intrigues against it. On 24 August, Grey had assured the French Ambassador that if Germany approached Wilson in October about an armistice, which Grey thought 'almost certain', Britain would act in common with the Allies. Grey warned, however, that a 'direct negative' would allow Germany to blame the continuation of the war on the Allies, and encouraged 'considering what answer we should give', particularly as it related to the conditions of a potential armistice. Grey related this conversation to Bertie in a letter, and Grey arranged to have the letter printed and circulated to the Cabinet. Grey's views on the matter were on record to all of his colleagues.[80]

Fresh intelligence from Room 40 gave Hardinge new urgency to undercut his superior. Room 40 opened up an enormous new window into German-American diplomacy, with particularly fortuitous timing: the intelligence breakthrough came just as Berlin was deciding to seek American mediation for an end to the war. The mediation the Germans wanted, of course, was a far cry from what House had come to envisage. The Germans wanted the Americans to set up direct negotiations between the belligerents – and then to stay entirely out of the way. They did not want Wilson frittering away their hard-earned conquests at the bargaining table.[81] Where the British liberals sought American mediation in order to neutralize a German victory, Germany largely sought mediation in order to impose one. But these distinctions were both lost on, and irrelevant to, the intelligence men: all mediation, in whatever form, was unacceptable. Hall continued to play politics with the decrypts at his disposal to try to achieve that end.

Room 40 had been puzzling all year to discover the route of communications of the German Ambassador to the United States, Count Bernstorff. 'We have traced nearly every route', Hall had written at the beginning of May, 'and I am really reduced to the following: he sends them down to Buenos Aires, thence across to Valparaiso. From there I cannot make out where they are sent, whether via China or Russia through the connivance of a neutral legation or not'.[82] Sometime in mid-July, however, Hall discovered that Bernstorff's telegrams had been sitting in the censor's office the entire time. An intercepted letter from the German Minister in Mexico to the German Chancellor, Theobald von Bethmann Hollweg, apparently revealed the Swedish complicity in arranging German communications. The Swedish Chargé d'Affaires in Mexico would 'every time, often late at night, personally ... go to the telegraph office to hand in the despatches', Hall recounted in his unpublished autobiography. 'It was clear', Hall wrote, that steps would have to be taken to have all Swedish Foreign Office cipher telegrams brought to us for examination. Arrangements were soon made for this to be done, and in many cases it was found that after a few Swedish groups our old friend 13040 [a long-cracked German code] would appear. Our excitement, moreover, may be imagined when through this means we discovered the route by which Bernstorff was communicating with his Government![83]

He had at last tracked down the 'Swedish roundabout': Bernstorff was in fact communicating with Berlin via Buenos Aires, as Hall had earlier suspected – but the messages went from there to Stockholm, having been passed on by the Swedish legation, and then forwarded from there to Berlin. The messages from Berlin went by the same process, only in reverse. It was the Buenos Aires-Stockholm link, however, that was the key one: on its way to Stockholm, the messages had to pass through Britain – meaning that the copies were waiting for Hall in the censor's office, only now they knew where to look.[84]

'In this way', Hall continued, 'we found ourselves in full possession for all practical purposes of the enemy's every move in the diplomatic game of the moment, and knew from the Ambassador's admirably clear despatches the points of greatest importance in Mr Wilson's fluctuating policy'.[85] Two of the first new decrypts intercepted gave Hall evidence of German intentions. Neither decrypt survives, but their text is found in published German documents, and there is clear British evidence that both were decrypted. The first is Bernstorff's most recent major dispatch, which was received in Berlin on 22 June, warning that any 'withdrawal or deviation from the concessions made' in the Sussex Pledge[86] would 'lead to a break and the entrance of the United States into the war'. Bernstorff revealed that he was 'constantly in communication with House with regard to the questions of peace mediation and blockade'. Mediation, Bernstorff said, 'is to be definitely expected in the course of the summer, from election prospects if for no other reason'.[87]

Even more importantly, the second decrypt was of a telegram from Bethmann Hollweg to Bernstorff, dated 18 August, and revealed that Germany 'would be glad to accept mediation by the President with a view to initiate peace negotiations between the belligerents', and asked Bernstorff to '[k]indly encourage the President in his activities along this line'. Hall lost no time in revealing these decrypts to Balfour, who on 25 August saw Hankey. Hankey recorded in his diary that

the German foreign office communicated with the United States via Sweden, the Swedish Foreign Office forwarding their messages, sometimes through Russia[88] & sometimes through England. As we had got their cipher we knew exactly what was passing. E. G. we now knew for a fact that Bernsdorf had most solemnly told

Germany that their submarine blockade must cease, or the U.S.A. would inevitably be drawn into the war. Also that the German Foreign Office had told Bernsdorf to keep in friendly relations with President Wilson in order to secure his intervention when required.[89]

Hall appears to have circulated this information as widely as possible – passing it even on to his pro-British friends in the American Embassy. First Secretary Irwin Laughlin, in charge while Page was away, wrote Page a lengthy letter revealing it on 30 August. Laughlin began by discussing the 'persistent rumours, which indeed are more than rumours ... of an approaching movement by Germany toward an early armistice'. He believed that Germany hoped 'it may result in peace – a peace more or less favourable to her, of course'. He continued,

I finally fastened on Hall of the Admiralty as a man with whom I could talk profitably and confidentially, and he told me positively that his information showed that Germany was looking in the direction I have indicated, and that she would soon approach the President on the subject – even if she had not already taken the first steps toward preparing her advance to him.

Hall pushed his American friend to take the matter up with Hardinge in the Foreign Office – Laughlin initially had suggested Grey, but Hall discouraged this, probably for political reasons. Hardinge could be trusted to spurn mediation, while the Foreign Secretary could not. Laughlin did so, and Hardinge, though 'wary at the outset', soon 'warmed up'. Laughlin continued:

I then finally asked him point blank if he thought the Germans would approach the President for an armistice, and, if so, when. He said he was inclined to think they might do so perhaps about October. On my asking him if he was disposed to let me communicate his opinion privately to the Government in Washington he replied after some hesitation that he had no objection, but he quickly added that I must make it clear at the same time that the British Government would not listen to any such proposals.
... Hardinge was very emphatic in what he said of the attitude of his government and the British people toward continuing the war to an absolutely conclusive end, and I was much impressed.[90]

In making these representations to Laughlin, Hardinge directly undermined his superior's settled policy.

Hardinge, however, did not need to have gone to the trouble. On 27 August, Romania finally declared war on the side of the Entente, immediately unleashing twenty-five divisions on the Central Powers' south-eastern frontiers – an event that 'caused the civilian members of the War Committee to experience new heights of optimism'.[91] At long last, they thought, they would break the stalemate. Between Romania's entry and Robertson's assurances, Asquith was now satisfied: 'Haig is I think doing very well: sticking to his original plan and not allowing himself to be hustled'. The entry of the Romanians, who were 'going ahead in good style', was a considerable 'coup' from which 'about anything may happen'.[92] Amidst all the enthusiasm, even Grey's usual good sense abandoned him. Romania's entry, combined with Robertson's optimism and the successful Russian offensive, convinced Grey that the Entente at long last was winning the war – and, for the first time, he made a deliberate move to put American mediation on hold.

In mid-July, House had answered Grey's previous letter. An admirable missive, House struck dulcet tones seeking to appeal to Grey's idealism, while aiming to reinforce the weakened assumptions that undergirded the House-Grey Memorandum. House indirectly queried the lack of response to Wilson's speech before the League to Enforce Peace, in which Wilson had announced his intention to join a post-war international league, while reaffirming their commitment to it, noting that it had even been incorporated into the Democratic Party platform – so that 'if the President is re-elected the people will have endorsed his position'. He also argued the strength of Wilson's position, contending that '[h]is successful duel with Germany has given the people so large a measure of confidence in him that they would, I think, follow wherever he might think it wise to go'– in other words, that Wilson had the power to implement the House-Grey Memorandum if they would only consent to invoking it. 'We are standing it seems at the roads of destiny', he told Grey, 'waiting to see which way to turn'.[93]

As well-constructed as the letter may have been, it arrived at the worst possible time. Grey received the letter likely sometime mid-month, but he put off replying until 28 August – the day after Romania entered the war. Finally confident in the military situation, Grey moved to head off any early mediation move. In reply to House's indirect query about a post-war league, Grey replied bluntly that the unfortunate lines in the President's May speech to the League to Enforce Peace had produced 'great obstacles to a response here'. 'There is nothing more that I can do at the moment', he told House. 'The utmost I can do is to stand by what I have said when I am challenged and that I should do'. The German attack at Verdun 'has failed and the Allies have had considerable successes elsewhere. The military situation has changed very much in their favour'. Britain would not consider peace until her Allies were willing to consider it, and he informed House that '[n]one of the Allies are likely to consider peace as long as the military situation continues to improve in their favour, or there is good prospect of it doing so'.[94] Written at perhaps the very peak of British optimism in 1916, within a few weeks Grey almost certainly wished he could have taken it back.

In America, meanwhile, a well-rested House continued to enjoy his quiet summer. 'The international situation', he wrote one correspondent near the end of August, 'has simmered down to a degree of calm that I have not known since the summer began'.[95] It would not remain calm for long.

6 The Knock-Out Blow
September–October 1916

As autumn approached, the optimism of August receded within the British government as rapidly as it had arrived: the Cabinet now began to grapple with the stark military reality that the Battle of the Somme would not win them the war. Romania's entry proved not a great coup, but an unutterable disaster. At the same time, the great flow of British-owned American investments into government coffers was slowing. Morgan's worked to stretch the British assets that remained. They would be to able sustain the flood of American supplies into the spring. Continuing it through a full 1917 campaign, however, seemed impossible. Britain's strategy for the war was failing.

For the realists, as this truth steadily became more apparent its terrible consequences loomed ever larger. The British leadership would soon be facing some extraordinarily hard choices. But with most Conservatives still siding with Lloyd George and half the Cabinet in emphatic denial, the debate was not over which choice for 1917 would be the least detrimental, but over whether they in fact faced any difficult choices at all.

With the Cabinet suffering strategic paralysis, Montagu, the new Munitions Minister, aimed to create a new way forward. Montagu's views occupied a unique position in the government: he both understood the Allies' economic quandary and yet also shared the hardliners' determination to carry on the war at almost any cost. His solution was to envision engineering a hard landing in their American expenditure and fighting on. He worked to remould his department around this prospect, aiming to sharply curb its dependence on the United States while vastly expanding its productive capacities. The American supplies might have to stop, but he sought to provide his country the weapons it would need for a 1917 campaign – even if that campaign had to be fought on a radically reduced economic scale. Engineering such a landing was a dangerous and risky strategy, not only economically and militarily, but diplomatically: Montagu acknowledged that one or more of their allies might abandon them

159

when told their American spigot would be switched off. Even then, he argued, Britain must fight on. He regarded it as the country's only option. American mediation, he believed, provided no suitable alternative.

For others in the government, however, Wilson's mediation remained viable. Continuing the war without their American supply link would be hugely difficult. Continuing it without a major ally seemed impossible. The House-Grey Memorandum, promising a decent peace or American entry, still sat seductively on the shelf.

Lloyd George, in a dramatic public intervention, aimed to tear up the Memorandum and to commit his government to an indefinite war. His extraordinary *volte-face* on American mediation – considering that Lloyd George himself back in February had suggested a mediation move to House – was due to seemingly sensational intelligence from MI1(b). Convinced that there existed a burgeoning German-American diplomatic conspiracy, Lloyd George decided to act at once, and, even better, he sought to strike a blow at McKenna's cowardly insistence that their war effort faced any kind of time constraint in the process. Deprived of further signals intelligence that would have shown this 'conspiracy' to be but a figment of his imagination, Lloyd George delivered a blow to Anglo-American relations as unnecessary as it was severe. He declared in a public interview that the war would be a fight to a 'knock-out blow', even if this took years, and then he wielded the decrypt as a political shield within the Cabinet to protect himself from any consequences. He sought to use the newspapers to impose his views on the government, and he lied to Parliament to try to impose them further, earning extensive Conservative praise in the process. At the same time, he urged his colleagues to spend ever greater sums in the United States, declaring that he thought there was little likelihood of Anglo-American trouble and obstinately refusing to acknowledge even the existence of a problem. Lloyd George's actions horrified his Asquithian colleagues, who rather saw themselves as if trapped on a sinking ship with a madman – one who not only was actively urging everyone to bucket water onto the decks, but who then, just for good measure, detonated one of their only decent lifeboats.

The optimism of August had not gone undetected across the Atlantic. As much as the Americans wished they could act, there was nothing to be done while the Romanian die was still being cast. Following that, an even more serious obstacle to action was the poor timing of the American political calendar. The all-consuming election madness that descends punctually upon the American republic every four years was now approaching its nadir. A crass opportunist of a president would have had no compunction about launching an 'October surprise' of a dramatic mediation move just before the election.

Wilson's detractors believed that the President was precisely that sort of man – a group that included the British Ambassador in Washington. Spring Rice found himself caught up in the frenzy and entirely disregarded Grey's sound rebuke about assuming Wilson's motives were always governed by domestic political considerations. A lousy amateur pundit on American politics, the Ambassador kept up a steady stream of speculation about the President's diplomatic intentions – always assuming that Wilson's only thought was the first Tuesday in November. Typical of his attitude, on 6 September Spring Rice cabled: 'It is quite possible that [the] Germans may be making, or have already made, a bargain with Wilson ... What is required is ... to counteract [the] weight of [the] German vote which at present is [the] prevailing factor. Change the wind and you will change the weathercock'.[1] He could hardly have been more wrong. When a fellow Democrat urged a peace move just before the election to help Wilson's campaign, House flatly rejected the advice: 'This was impossible', House told him, precisely 'because it would be construed as an electioneering move'.[2] As one historian put it, the 'British ambassador may have been right in thinking that trouble with Britain would be good politics for Wilson. Where he and so many other observers fell into error was in supposing that this was an area in which Wilson played politics'.[3]

House and Wilson remained committed to pursuing a negotiated peace. When Page paid House a visit in early September, the ardently pro-British ambassador argued for immediately entering the war on the Allied side, and he accused House in disgust of having been 'sent abroad as the special emissary of the President in order to find some crevice in the armor where we might make an entering wedge toward peace'. An exasperated House commented wryly: 'I did not think this was as ignoble an effort as it seemed to Page'.[4]

Moreover, while House preferred arranging a settlement in accordance with Allied wishes, his patience with the Allies, like the President's, was wearing thin. Back at the end of July, House had already begun to consider their next mediation move once the Somme offensive had finished. Regardless of whether the Allies were ready, he advised the President that, if a diplomatic opening presented itself, 'I believe you should seriously consider making the proposal without their consent'.[5]

An enormous spike in Anglo-American controversy over the summer no doubt had contributed to this American impatience. The aftermath of the Easter Rising in Ireland caused a series of problems, especially over the fate of one of the Rising's key leaders, Sir Roger Casement. With a large Irish-American population in the United States, Grey pleaded with his colleagues for a deft touch. 'If Ireland gets worse', he warned starkly, or if anti-British sentiment continued to increase, 'the American Govt. might bring us down in finance or on blockade by convoying in their own ships'. As the Cabinet debated whether to let the execution of Casement go forward, Grey was adamant that the execution's effect 'will be *most deplorable* in [the] U.S.'. There had been a deluge of American pleas, including even a resolution approved by the US Senate, asking the British not to execute him, and Grey read the Cabinet a series of telegrams urging clemency. But even those who acknowledged the depth of British dependence on the United States thought that the execution could not be stopped. Balfour wrung his hands about it all, but concluded that the 'execution cannot be avoided', and it went forward as scheduled.[6] Hall, meanwhile, had worked to ensure the execution, privately sharing extracts from Casement's so-called 'Black Diaries', with their record of Casement's same-sex romances and sexual encounters, to try to undermine American support for clemency. The stomachs in the American Embassy evidently were easily upset by the contemplation of male homosexuality; Ambassador Page said he felt faint after reading a short passage.[7]

At the same time, the ever-present Anglo-American din of the blockade had grown into a deafening roar. Back in January, amidst a vicious newspaper campaign accusing Grey of laxity over the blockade, Grey had voluntarily surrendered control of it to a new Blockade Ministry run by the intelligent though high-handed Conservative Robert Cecil.[8] Cecil threw himself into his work, creating a significantly tighter blockade, but one that also showed a much more cavalier attitude towards offending the United States.[9] In his first months, this attitude towards the United States did not inflict too much damage, despite the controversies Cecil generated. At the end of March, a new Order-in-Council stiffening the blockade rules, issued without any effort to prepare the way diplomatically, drew State Department protests. A couple of months later, Lansing dispatched a complaint concerning British interference with American mails.[10]

Summer, however, saw much more serious diplomatic consequences from Grey's loss of control over the blockade. A poorly timed quintet of blockade-related controversies hit within the span of just a few weeks. A move by Cecil targeting American tobacco was announced at the end of June. Shortly thereafter, another Order-in-Council from his ministry was issued, explicitly repudiating American demands that the blockade adhere to the rules set out in the 1909 Declaration of London. Previously, the British had maintained an increasingly strained pretence that they were adhering to the Declaration 'with modifications'. Cecil, in an unnecessarily honest move, dropped the pretence altogether. Within a few days of that, the arrival of a German cargo submarine in the United States set off a spat, with the State Department rejecting Allied demands that it be detained. The cargo submarine was still in its port in Baltimore when Grey gave an interim reply to Lansing's complaint over the mails that failed to address any of the Americans' concerns.[11]

The most serious of the quintet, however, came when Cecil's department decided to publish a blacklist of eighty-seven American firms accused of trading with Germany. The publication set off a storm of American indignation, with particularly threatening lightning bolts emanating from the White House. Cecil was squandering much of the President's considerable goodwill towards the Allies. Wilson told House that he was at the end of his patience. 'This black list business is the last straw'. The State Department fired off an irate protest at the President's behest.[12]

Intransigent, Cecil defended his policy. Even the fiercely pro-Allied Ambassador Page thought Cecil's move an unnecessary act of 'sheer stupidity', but when Cecil subsequently spoke to reporters, he categorically rejected even the possibility of concessions. An angry Congress began working on measures giving Wilson the authority to retaliate. Added as an amendment to a revenue bill, Congress handed the President considerable diplomatic leverage, including the ability to limit Allied exports to the United States as well as a nuclear option: the power to close American ports to Allied ships. London jolted, but Cecil remained obdurate.[13] In an act of supreme arrogance from an otherwise intelligent man, Cecil even had a hysterical message transmitted to an unimpressed House, in which Cecil threatened that Britain would break off diplomatic relations and withdraw all trade if Wilson made use of his new powers.[14] Grey, alarmed at these developments, quickly sought to convene a broad interdepartmental committee to confirm what he already knew: that the Allies were almost completely dependent on the United States and that Britain had no meaningful ability to retaliate in turn.[15] Cecil's stronger, better blockade was running colossal diplomatic and economic risks with the Allies' crucial transatlantic relationship.

Even so, this nosedive in the overall Anglo-American relationship had no immediate effect on American mediation diplomacy. Although House had been impatient for action in late July amidst the uproar over the blacklist, a month later Romania loomed much larger in his mind. When House returned to New York in early September, he realized that Romania's entry had transformed the diplomatic situation. There was no prospect of a successful mediation move until some of the military uncertainty had been resolved, and by then the impending American election would make a move impossible. Bernstorff arranged a meeting with House, in which the German Ambassador continued to press for a peace move, but House told him flatly that nothing could happen until after the election. House considered it so utterly obvious that he did not even bother to record having said it in his diary.[16] Bernstorff, however, rushed to inform Berlin. 'Wilson's peace activities have been postponed', Bernstorff telegraphed,

because at the present moment they would lead to nothing on account of Roumania's entrance into the war and because of the confidence of victory on the part of our enemies resulting therefrom. Wilson believes that he will not be able to accomplish anything more before the election ... But in case Wilson wins the election, the prospects of which are now favorable, and if [by][17] that time there is a lull in military operations, the President will immediately take steps towards mediation. He believes that then he will be strong enough to force a peace conference.

Wilson considers it important to American interests that neither belligerent should win a decisive victory.

German Chancellor Bethmann Hollweg received this telegram on 13 September.[18] Reginald Hall in Room 40 had a decrypt of it five days earlier, accurately, and in its entirety.

While Hall had evidently arranged as wide a distribution net as possible for those earlier German decrypts discussing mediation, he now took precisely the opposite course. Hall now had before him crucial intelligence showing that, at least until early November, there was no prospect of an American mediation move.[19] A second telegram from Bernstorff, decrypted two days later, clearly worked from the assumption that there would be nothing done until after the election. 'If Wilson is re-elected', Bernstorff telegraphed, 'I am of the opinion that his mediation, even before the end of the year [,] would probably be fruitful'.[20]

Yet this intelligence seems never to have seen the light of day – buried, until now, in an obscure Admiralty file. Certainly, neither the Foreign Office nor the War Office saw it. Hall's reasons for suppressing it can only be inferred. It appears, however, that Hall desired his government to mistrust the Americans and that he found this information inconvenient for his narrative. This was not the only signals intelligence pointing in this direction. Back in mid-July, MI1(b) had decrypted a telegram from the American Ambassador in Madrid to Washington revealing an initiative from the King of Spain to enlist Wilson's help for a joint mediation project.[21] On 23 August, MI1(b) intercepted the reply. Secretary of State Lansing wrote back that confidential information ... indicated that it would be unacceptable to the Allied Governments to receive from a neutral any suggestion looking towards the restoration of peace ... the President does not judge that the Governments of the Entente, have, up to the present time, changed their attitude.[22]

Taken with the decrypt of Bernstorff's telegram two weeks later, the decrypts plainly showed the intention of the US government. A failure of the British Embassy to keep in close contact with the President's chief advisor enormously amplified the importance of withholding this decrypt. The only reason Germany had this information and Britain did not was because Bernstorff took an early opportunity to sojourn up to see House in New York. Spring Rice, by contrast, put off seeing House for another month.[23] Only Hall, it appears, had the opportunity to put this intelligence together. Lloyd George certainly did not.

Over the course of September, British optimism about the military picture steadily receded, just as the financial picture again began to darken. After a visit to the Western Front early in the month, Asquith's report to the War Committee, although he sought to remain hopeful, 'was largely negative'. Asquith doubted whether they would push through the enemy line before Christmas, at which point Grey observed that 'the situation was not much affected [that is, improved] if the Germans were not pushed back'. With Britain's economic clock ticking ever louder, Grey conceded that 'we must keep going, but he wanted to know what it leads to'. Robertson was far from reassuring, stating simply that '[t]here was nothing else to be done'.[24] Hardinge, meanwhile, detected growing doubts as early as 8 September. 'The lower classes', he wrote to Spring Rice,

are absolutely sound and solid in their judgment – far more so than our rulers. It is, I believe, the same in Russia, where, although people in high places may have a hankering for peace, the peasants and army are determined to have their revenge and to carry on the war to the bitter end. The Russian losses have been hideous, but they don't mind a bit.[25]

Events, it would seem, would soon disprove his assertions.

Near the end of the month, a military intelligence coup on the Western Front finally revealed Germany's extra divisions of reserves behind their lines. The implications were clear immediately: the Germans were in a much better military position than the British had thought.[26] Romania's entry, meanwhile, far from being the decisive event that would break the stalemate, was rapidly becoming an Allied catastrophe. Once a massive German counterattack began on 18 September, the confidence Romania had evoked quickly vanished.[27] Lloyd George demanded that British forces be sent to rescue the hapless Romanians, provoking a quarrel with

Robertson, who insisted that there were no forces to spare, that even if spared would arrive too late, and that Russia was the only power able to offer aid. In the end, Lloyd George's manoeuvres succeeded in having a division dispatched, but the German advances continued. The Romanian capital, Bucharest, would fall in December.[28]

Across the Atlantic, British finances were again showing signs of strain. After the rosy summer influx of funds, the flow of American investments into government coffers slowed significantly as autumn began. The British cut down on the sale of these investments in New York and looked for ways to stretch what remained of this vital reservoir.[29] Provincial American investors still had little interest in owning non-US securities. Unable to sell off the vast stock of British world investments in New York, Morgan's thought up a clever way to use them to help make Britain's American investments go a bit further. In September, the British looked to borrow $250 million – covering about a month's worth of their American supplies – by mortgaging a *blend* of investments. The British put up as collateral $100 million in American securities, $100 million in Canadian securities, and $100 million in investments from other neutral countries. (American law required a 20 per cent margin.) In short, the British hoped to convert $100 million in US investments into $250 million in British cash. Offering a generous interest rate to sweeten the deal, Morgan's thought the borrowing operation would be 'irresistible' to American investors. It was not. Morgan's had to put up nearly $90 million itself to complete the underwriting for the operation. The subsequent public sale was slow.[30]

It was, however, just barely enough of a success for Morgan's to justify trying again the next month. This time it sought to convert $100 million of American securities into $300 million in cash, with the rest of the mortgaging operation rounded out with Canadian, neutral, and Empire investments. The British upped the already generous interest rate by half a point. Even still, applications remained 'sluggish'. Morgan's again had to put up the final $30 million of underwriting to stave off the embarrassment of coming up short. The subsequent public sale went even more poorly than the one the month before. To unload their share, Morgan's had to sell it off for less than it paid for it.[31] Morgan's was not the only one. Come January, Morgan's would write that 'all underwriters' of the two operations had suffered 'material loss'.[32] But between these mortgaging operations and further gold shipments, the British would have enough dollars to make it through the winter. Spring, however, seemed another question entirely.

Despite the darkening picture, Lloyd George abruptly moved to blow up American mediation as a possible escape route – a move fuelled by alarming intelligence. The man most responsible for facilitating Lloyd George's interview, Lord Northcliffe, owned the *Daily Mail* and *The Times*, amongst other papers. Northcliffe was not content merely to use his newspapers to influence politics indirectly, but instead injected himself personally into politics. He had no compunction about bursting into a minister's office and threatening to have his papers launch an attack if his opinions were ignored.[33] His influence impressed Roy Howard, the prominent American newspaperman to whom Lloyd George would give his famous interview, who hyperbolically described Northcliffe as 'the biggest man and ... the most powerful man in the British Empire today. I should say that his power of accomplishment in England is comparable with nothing so much as the Kaiser's power of accomplishment in Germany'.[34]

17 Lord Northcliffe (Alfred Harmsworth) (Library of Congress / Harris & Ewing Photographs / LC-H261-8941)

Northcliffe's tentacles reached extensively. He was secretly in touch with both Robertson and Haig – Haig, to his surprise, found that he 'quite like[d]' the press baron. Northcliffe struck Haig as a man with 'the courage of his opinions' who 'thinks only of doing his utmost to help to win the war'.[35] Northcliffe, particularly after a stay at the Western Front of more than two weeks beginning in late July, supported the two men unconditionally. Haig stuffed him with stories of how his incremental gains were far more significant than they appeared, because the trenches and dugouts they had taken over were really giant 'German subterranean fortresses'[36] and 'vast underground strongholds'. Northcliffe quickly and willingly became a vigorous proponent of the ongoing Somme Offensive and the results it was supposedly producing. '[C]ompared with the disgraceful waste of life at Loos where nothing was gained', Northcliffe wrote to Lloyd George on 6 August: 'the one hundred and fifty thousand casualties of the battles of the Somme ... are trivial'.[37]

After his visit to the front, Northcliffe stayed in close touch with Haig's personal secretary, Philip Sassoon, both men writing sometimes several times a week. Northcliffe provided information on the political goings-on in London, while Haig attempted to steer – usually, but not always, with success – the line that Northcliffe's papers took on the battle. The happy talk Haig was providing his superiors in London Northcliffe obligingly provided to the British public at large. 'I must write to tell you how much we all liked the Times leader of the 18th', Sassoon gushed to Northcliffe on 19 September. 'It must have made people realise for the first time the true significance of our victory of the 15th. The C[ommander] in C[hief] was quite delighted with it ... We are going on *well*. Steadily every day with comparatively few casualties – all according to plan and nothing haphazard'.[38] 'I am doing my best', Northcliffe assured Sassoon, 'to dispel the idea that our victories are accompanied by great losses'.[39]

Although Northcliffe suspected that a German peace move was in the air, as late as 23 September, he saw no particular urgency about it. 'Personally, I expect a big peace proposal from Germany before Christmas ... probably com[ing] from the United States', he wrote Sassoon.[40] Two days later, things had changed. 'The Germans are preparing for a great peace squeal through the United States, as I have already told you. I have heard further details in the last two days'.[41] That same day, he wrote to Lloyd George: 'A propos our conversation last week ... I think you ought to see Mr. Roy Howard, the head of the United Press of the United States, who has told me certain disquieting things'.[42]

In addition to whatever inaccurate rumours Howard may have possessed, two other pieces of information appear to have reached Lloyd George before their meeting the next day. The first was a telegram from Spring Rice, which appears to have advocated a statement from London as a means of heading off an American mediation move.[43] The second, and most significant according to Lloyd George, was a dramatic decrypt from MI1(b) of a telegram sent on 25 September from US Ambassador to Germany James Gerard to Washington. Lloyd George's copy does not survive, but Hall obtained a copy as well, which read:

Germany is anxious to make peace. I can state on the best authority that if the President will make an offer of mediation in General terms, somewhat in terms of the President's despatch of June 8th, 1905 to Russia and Japan, [that is, with the President doing nothing more than arranging negotiations, and taking no direct part in the settlement of the peace terms] Germany will accept in general terms immediately and state her readiness to send delegates to (a?) Peace Conference.

To-day von Jagow will ask me to forward a cipher message to Bernsdorff through the State Department. Int-which (omission) he says will.......... message and matter. [sic]

Of course the utmost secrecy is desirable for if any hint is given that [the] suggestion comes from Berlin and not as the spontaneous act of the President the whole matter will fail and be denied.

I desire to know whether the message may be forwarded for delivery to Bernsdorff.

Colonel House should be informed of the above.[44]

Joseph Grew, First Secretary of the American Embassy in Berlin, recalled that it 'was regarded as so confidential that it was cabled to the Department in our special secret code, Winslow and I being the only members of the Embassy in on the secret. It was said that if the intimation should leak out, Germany would immediately disavow any connection with it'.[45] The telegram was not deciphered in the State Department until 26 September at twenty past one in the afternoon, Washington time.[46] It was almost certainly in Lloyd George's hands several hours before then. It is unclear who gave the decrypt to Lloyd George, but it had to have been from within the War Office. Robertson, it is clear, exerted significant control over what his minister was allowed to see: Lloyd George complained to Haig the next month that the 'Gen. Staff at the War Office don't let him know *everything* but only feed him with what *they think* is suitable for him to know'.[47]

Lloyd George plainly distrusted Grey to take sufficiently vigorous action in response. Roy Howard arrived in Lloyd George's office on 26 September, hoping to talk 'over the possibility of an interview'.[48] Howard was delighted when he got much more. Convinced that something needed to be done to head off an imminent German-American move, Lloyd George listened to what Howard had to say and then proceeded to give him an interview fiercely denouncing the possibility of neutral mediation. Howard promptly wrote up the interview and gave it to Northcliffe. Ecstatic, Northcliffe sent a copy to Lloyd George the next day, urgently recommending 'instant publication'.[49] Lloyd George approved.[50]

None of his colleagues had the slightest suspicion that anything was afoot. The War Committee met on the morning of 28 September at half past eleven, entirely unaware that Lloyd George had planted a bomb underneath their feet set to explode some twelve hours later. American mediation was discussed briefly in the context of a paper that had been prepared for the eventuality of armistice negotiations. Lord Crawford, the Conservative President of the Board of Agriculture, argued that Wilson, 'whose recent action shows how deeply he is obsessed by electioneering ambition', would likely make a peace move shortly before the election.[51]

Asquith, apparently referring to a 19 September speech given by the French Premier,[52] said he now 'thought that President Wilson would be less likely than before to come forward with any peace proposal'. Grey agreed, saying 'the best thing to do was to lie low'. No one raised a contrary view. The War Office was evidently sitting on the Gerard decrypt, certainly for political reasons. Plainly, neither the Prime Minister nor the Foreign Office had seen it. Lloyd George sat, perhaps smirking, in silence.[53]

Lloyd George took no chances that the Americans would mistake his meaning. He made a 'special request' to Roy Howard to have a 'complete, exact copy' of the interview delivered directly to House as quickly as possible and before the interview had even gone to press. Probably only an hour or two after the War Committee finished meeting, Howard had a copy delivered directly to House in New York, with a note pointedly saying that it was being sent at Lloyd George's express instructions. A copy was also dispatched directly to the White House by special messenger. Howard took the opportunity to ask House for 'a little comment' – one that he might be able to include before the article hit the presses that afternoon. An undoubtedly stunned House declined to respond.[54]

The interview hit Howard's US, Canadian, and Latin American papers that evening.[55] As Northcliffe had organized, most other papers followed suit the next morning. It caused an immediate sensation. 'There is no end of the war in sight', the interview opened breathlessly. 'Any step at this time', it declared, 'by the United States, the Vatican or any other neutral in the direction of peace would be construed by England as an unneutral, pro-German move'.

'Britain has only begun to fight', Lloyd George announced. He continued in rather crass terms and took indirect aim at the Prime Minister in the process:

Sporting terms are pretty well understood wherever English is spoken ... The British soldier is a good sportsman ... For two years [he] had a bad time – no one knows so well as he what a bad time. He was sadly inferior in equipment. The vast majority of the British soldiers were inferior in training. He saw the Allied causes beaten all about the ring. But he didn't appeal either to spectators or referee to stop the fight on the ground that it was brutal. Nor did he ask that the rules be changed.

'He took his punishment', Lloyd George said, mixing his metaphors, 'even when he was beaten like a dog. He was a game dog ... The fight', he declared, 'must be to a finish – to a knockout'. He warned off Wilson and House all but by name. 'The whole world', he said 'including neutrals of the highest purposes and humanitarians with the best of motives[,] must know that there can be no outside interference at this stage'.

He continued with an assault on his Cabinet colleagues, publicly rejecting the view that the country faced any kind of time limit on its war effort:

There is neither clock nor calendar in the British Army to-day ... Time is the least vital factor. Only the result counts – not the time consumed in achieving it. It took England 20 years to defeat Napoleon, and the first 15 of those were black with British defeat. It will not take 20 years to win this war, but whatever time is required it will be done.

And I say this recognizing that we have only begun to win. There is no disposition on our side to fix the hour of ultimate victory after the first success. We have no delusion that the war is near an end. We have not the slightest doubt as to *how* it is to end.[56]

The interview constituted a complete reversal of what Lloyd George had told House earlier that year, and amounted to a total repudiation of House's entire diplomatic policy. The suddenness and vehemence of the interview must have bewildered the Texan – particularly as he and Wilson had no immediate plans to do anything. Though we have no direct evidence of House's reaction, we can be sure that Lloyd George's public rejection proved a painful and humiliating experience. House's diary contains a detailed record of House's thoughts on every significant diplomatic development of the war – except this one. Curiously silent for 28 and 29 September, his diary does not resume until the following day and completely ignores the entire episode.[57]

What became of the telegram that put these events in motion, the supposedly grave threat that Lloyd George needed to head off so quickly? After being decrypted in the State Department code room, it spent four days lost in the bureaucracy. On 30 September, Lansing forwarded it to the President with a brief note:

By some oversight this flimsy was not forwarded to you promptly. Perhaps, however, it is just as well; since it came Mr. Lloyd George has given out an authorized statement that the war is to be 'a fight to the finish' and that any suggestion of peace from neutrals would be considered as more or less unfriendly.[58]

The Americans never put the connection between the two together.

In London, Lloyd George's outburst struck Grey 'as a bolt from the blue'.[59] Grey, the Secretary of State for Foreign Affairs, had pronounced in Britain's most powerful council that the government's policy should be to sit quietly and do nothing to upset the United States. No one, including Lloyd George, had raised any objection. Grey had every reason to go to bed on the evening of 28 September believing his views had been confirmed as British policy. House and Wilson had almost certainly learned of Britain's total rejection of their mediation efforts nearly a full day before its Foreign Secretary did.

The next morning, Grey awoke to discover Lloyd George's interview plastered in nearly every London newspaper. 'HANDS OFF THE WAR!' and 'Lloyd George to Neutrals: "Keep out of the Ring!"' screamed seven column headlines in the *Daily Mail* and *Daily Express*.[60] Furious and humiliated, Grey wrote at once to Lloyd George in protest. Hurt by Lloyd George's complete rejection of his policy, stung by Lloyd George's underhanded intrigue, and fearful of the consequences that the interview would have, Grey's missive is as close to enraged as the even-tempered man could muster. He deplored the interview as 'unnecessary', warned of it pushing Wilson and Germany closer together, and feared that it would have the result of causing Wilson to put more pressure on the British – which, after the election, would be precisely what the President would do. 'It has always been my view', Grey wrote,

that until the Allies were sure of victory the door should be kept open for Wilson's mediation. It is now closed for ever as far as we are concerned ... A public warning to the President of the United States is an important step, and I wish I had had an opportunity of putting these considerations before you and discussing them with you.

He ended his letter brusquely. 'No answer needed now as nothing more can be done till we see the effect'.[61] Grey confided to Runciman that he was 'much disturbed' by Lloyd George's action, and that he 'dread[ed] the political consequences of it'.[62]

An incensed McKenna was far less restrained– but only with those he trusted. The day after the interview appeared, McKenna carefully censored himself in a confidential talk with a right-wing journalist from

Northcliffe's *The Times*.[63] To a sympathetic C. P. Scott, the editor of the liberal *Manchester Guardian*, he let himself go. 'Sheer lunacy', he vented. 'Lloyd George thought he could say what he liked and nothing would happen because the war profits reaped in the U.S. were so great', McKenna fumed to Scott. 'I am in the position now of [having to finance in] America [spending of] two million pounds a day'. Britain's mortgaging operations in New York required American investors being willing to participate, and the results so far had not been encouraging. Britain could not afford to gratuitously offend the United States right now. Lloyd George could 'easily go too far ... How am I to pay', McKenna demanded to know, 'if I can no longer borrow?'[64]

Nor did McKenna believe that such a knock-out blow was even possible. 'What good can come of that sort of wild talk about the war[?]', McKenna raged. The people, McKenna asserted, *'don't want an indefinite war, but a reasonable peace*. They have no desire to sacrifice their lives or the lives of those dear to them'.[65]

Above all, it was Lloyd George's unadulterated *arrogance* that most infuriated McKenna. The Chancellor had also been around the table at the War Committee meeting on 28 September, listening in silent agreement as Grey had laid out a policy of 'lying low' when it came to the United States.[66] He had been as unaware as Grey that Lloyd George's silence signified anything but agreement. How could a government govern when one of its members believed he could freely dictate policy to his colleagues from the pages of the newspapers? 'There was no redress for such things', McKenna spat. 'The fact was that George ought to be "suppressed"; there was nothing else for it'.[67]

'As for Lloyd George himself', he seethed, 'he risks very little. His sons are well-sheltered'.[68] The editor of C. P. Scott's papers refused to include this 'cruel and slighting remark' in the published version of the diary entry.[69] Lloyd George's hypocrisy, however, galled the Chancellor. Lloyd George had personally intervened to get his sons safe staff appointments well away from the dangers of the front line.[70] Lloyd George was calling for much more loss of life – which McKenna believed amounted only to 'indefinite' loss of life – and all the while Lloyd George spoke as if the war were no more serious than a particularly protracted game of football. Lloyd George's call for far greater, even endless sacrifice would come only at the expense of other families' sons.

The contrast with the Prime Minister, who McKenna believed shared his views,[71] could scarcely have been starker. In the late evening of 17 September, barely a week before Lloyd George gave his interview, Asquith had sat for hours in an arm chair, surrounded by his family, grieving the news of the loss of his eldest son, Raymond, who had been killed in the heavy fighting on the Somme. '[H]is poor face set with tears but quite simple and natural – a wonderful exhibition of emotion, self-mastery, and unselfconsciousness', his wife Margot Asquith later recalled in her diary. 'I was never more struck by the size and depth of his nature, the absence of bitterness and largeness of his heart and purpose than that night'.[72] It was, she later said, only the second time in her life that she had seen her husband break down.[73] Raymond's younger brother, Arthur, had been wounded in action at Gallipoli the year before and awarded a medal for his bravery. As Lloyd George spoke with Roy Howard, Arthur remained on the Somme, obstinately refusing his stepmother's attempts to have him moved out of the line of fire in the wake of his brother's death.[74] The tragedy still very fresh – Raymond's memorial service would not be until 13 October – Asquith could not have been pleased to see Lloyd George describing the war in such a puerile way. War, to Asquith, was not some mere sport to be played with the lives of others' sons. As far as McKenna was concerned, Lloyd George had disloyally upended the Prime Minister's and Foreign Secretary's settled policy, wrongly laid the blame for Britain's lack of success in the war at the Prime Minister's feet, dismissed the country's losses – and, by extension, Asquith's loss – as no more significant than a boxer having had a bad first couple of rounds, and called for far more British blood to be shed while hypocritically ensuring that his family risked no consequences as a result of that call. What loyal lieutenant of the Prime Minister would not be appalled by such conduct?

The interview, however, delighted most Conservatives. Though the Liberal press either criticized Lloyd George's interview or effectively ignored it,[75] the Conservative press gushed its support, calling it 'impressive and clear-sighted', [76] an 'historic manifesto'[77] that 'needed saying'.[78] Bertie in Paris enthused that the interview would serve as an 'effective scarecrow to the American electoral bird'[79] and hoped that Lloyd George would 'bring over to a determined attitude towards American intervention or mediation those who are weak-kneed'.[80] Hardinge wrote, plainly with the decrypt in mind, that the interview would 'be very useful in staving off inconvenient proposals for mediation, which really a week ago were beginning to be threatening' – a line that is also a clear indication that he had not received the Room 40 material showing that there would be no mediation move until after the election.[81] Indeed, in another letter, Hardinge clearly believed that it was precisely *because* of Lloyd George's interview that 'President Wilson is not likely to make any proposals'.[82] Calling the interview 'splendid and most opportune', he confided to Bertie that this was not the opinion upstairs. Between you and me, I think the views held upstairs about Col. House, the Pres. of the U.S., and peace terms are utterly rotten, but I am consoled by the knowledge that they will not prevail. The P.M. is not much sounder, but Lloyd George is all right and he can hold his own as I have seen more than once at the War Co[mmittee].[83]

Bertie told Hardinge that Grey 'is not sound on the question of American mediation. He is at heart a pacifist. I think he is what the Americans term 'a sick man'".[84] Hardinge did not challenge the assessment.[85]

In an almost shocking display of pro-British sentiment, the American Embassy in London not only failed to be offended by Lloyd George's gratuitous affront to their President, but it was actually gratified by it. Clifford Carver, who had served as Colonel House's personal secretary on his mission earlier that year, was in London at the time. Carver was stunned by Irwin Laughlin's 'unlimited approval' of the interview,[86] tactfully reporting to House, with considerable under-statement, that Laughlin had 'ideas which are not quite coincident with ours'.[87]

Spring Rice over in the United States finally managed his first conversation with Colonel House in months on 2 October.[88] House confirmed that the President had no intention of making a mediation move before the election. This, of course, had been settled American policy for some time, but Spring Rice erroneously attributed it to the interview. He promptly cabled London celebrating Lloyd George's interview as 'ha[ving] had a great effect'.[89] A much more accurate assessment came from Bernstorff to Berlin. In the aftermath of the interview, Bernstorff informed his superiors – and Room 40 – that the situation 'was unchanged' and reaffirmed that Wilson 'would only attempt intervention after he has been re-elected'.[90]

Lloyd George relished the ruckus that the interview had caused. In less than seventy-two hours after Gerard's telegram had been dispatched – and in less than forty-eight hours after that telegram had been received (and misplaced) at the State Department[91] – Lloyd George had not only had successfully headed off the German-American 'plot' but landed a public assault to the views of his hated Cabinet arch-rival in the process. On 30 September, he confided the story of the interview to his secretary and mistress, Frances Stevenson, telling her of Grey's letter of protest. She wrote in her diary that

D[avid] in reply sent [Grey] a copy of a secret message intercepted from von Bethmann Hollweg to America asking them to propose a peace conference. We have discovered a wireless installation, [and] are intercepting all their messages,

176 Plotting for Peace

but they do not know it. This is a great find. Had D[avid] not given his interview, Wilson would most probably have made the proposal to us, [and] it would have been difficult for us to refuse to discuss terms. This would spoil all chances of a decisive victory for us. Now D[avid]'s interview has made peace proposals impossible for some time to come. The enemy are furious, and are gnashing their teeth with rage.[92]

There are obviously some problems with the details here. Although it is evident from this passage that Lloyd George drafted his reply to Grey almost immediately, he would sit on it over the weekend before dispatching it. The reference to a wireless installation is in error: it was a telegraphic intercept, not a wireless one. Either Lloyd George had decided to recount all he knew of the entire British signals intelligence operation to Stevenson, and she got mixed up in the particular details of what prompted the interview, or Lloyd George himself had not been told how the MI1(b) information had been obtained. The direct connection between the decrypt and the interview, however, is clear from Stevenson's entry, as is the political role of the decrypt in protecting Lloyd George from any consequences from his action.

Politically, Lloyd George was delighted that the interview proved popular with Conservative opinion. Letters of congratulation came 'pouring in'. 'On every hand', Stevenson exulted, 'we hear that D[avid] never stood so high in the eyes of the nation. The French adore him. They say he is the one man in England who counts'.[93]

Lloyd George sent his reply to Grey on 2 October. The first thing he did was play the decrypt like a trump card. 'I wonder whether you are still of the same opinion after reading M.I.1's secret information?" he opened his letter to Grey, apparently attaching the decrypt, which was presumably entering the Foreign Office for the first time. 'Have you seen it?' Brazenly, he even went so far as to suggest that he had been doing Grey a favour. 'Any cessation of hostilities now would be a disaster … You could not have warned off the United States without doing it formally. I could commit a serviceable indiscretion; you could not. It would ruin you; I am inoculated!' He repeated the same, tired charge: 'I know the American politician. He has no international conscience. He thinks of nothing but the ticket, and he has not given the least thought to the effect of his action upon European affairs'.[94]

Grey was unimpressed. He recognized the decrypt for what it was: an ambassador transmitting a German proposal, not an American endorsement of the proposal. A week later, he wrote to a friend: 'We believe Wilson to be as friendly to the Allies as he thinks public opinion in the U.S.A. will allow him to be'. Though he disapproved of the United

States' declining to 'play a great part' in the war by not entering it on the Allied side, he plainly disbelieved Lloyd George's contention that the Americans and the Germans were secretly conspiring together.[95] The decrypt, it seems, protected Lloyd George from any challenge in the War Committee. McKenna had certainly been spoiling for a fight, but Grey may well have shared the decrypt with key colleagues before the War Committee's next meeting on 3 October. The interview never came up. Instead, Balfour took indirect aim at Lloyd George's call for open-ended warfare by demanding that the War Committee 'survey our resources'. They needed 'to make a forecast and to decide to what extent we could continue to expend men and money ... We could not go on indefinitely pouring out capital and suffering heavy casualties which required replacing'. Grey and McKenna supported him, with Grey insisting that they needed to carefully 'take stock of their military, naval, and financial position'. Grey argued that it was 'most necessary that our own resources, and those of our Allies, as well as those of the enemy, and also the probable period of exhaustion of each Power, should be very carefully surveyed'. Asquith directed the Treasury, the Board of Trade, the Admiralty, and the General Staff all to draft and circulate papers prior to a more general discussion.[96]

Two days later, Chamberlain forced a first, albeit oblique, debate as to whether the government could, in fact, continue the war after their looming financial exhaustion in the United States. Chamberlain clearly thought not. On 5 October, the War Committee took up an initial list of suggestions from Chamberlain's Manpower Distribution Board. Anxiety pervades the list, but none more so than in Chamberlain's taking aim at Montagu at the Ministry of Munitions. Where Lloyd George formed a paradoxical faction of one as both a maximalist and yet most of the time a pessimist, Montagu occupied the opposite pole: he was, uniquely, an economic realist and yet an optimist. One of the two main factions in the government treated the exhaustion of their American supply lifeline as a war-ending catastrophe; the other denied that this lifeline could ever be exhausted. Only Montagu, it seems, both recognized the reality of the time limit to Britain's American supplies and yet remained untroubled by it. Montagu firmly rejected the possibility of American mediation. Earlier, in August, Montagu circulated a Cabinet memorandum denouncing 'the American politician' as 'contemptible and untrustworthy'. He demanded that any offer of American mediation be rejected and that the war be continued until Germany was 'crush[ed]'. The Allies must, he argued, 'exact from her everything that can be exacted'. Yet he acknowledged that the time was coming when Britain 'cannot help [its allies] as much as they require financially', and even that withdrawing this financial support could cause one or more of their allies to seek a separate peace. Even then he was determined to continue the war, urging that contingency plans be drawn up for 'continu[ing] to fight without each of our Allies individually'.[97]

18 Edwin Montagu (Hulton Archive / Stringer / Getty Images)

When their American resources were exhausted, Montagu envisioned engineering a hard landing in their American supplies and fighting on, and he worked to impose this strategy for 1917 on his department. He aimed to dramatically reduce the Munitions Ministry's American expenditure and sought to launch a major factory-building programme. This programme looked to reduce the burden on 'our exchange with the United States'; it was intended to end British reliance on costly American munitions manufacturers and to allow Britain to become 'independent ... for the production of the finished article'. These new British arms factories were designed to become operational over the next year. As the Allies would cease to be able to afford their flood of American supplies, Montagu hoped these new factories could at least provide them with much of the necessary weapons – allowing the Allies to continue the war, albeit on a much more limited economic scale, through 1917 and, if necessary, beyond.[98]

Chamberlain, however, did not see it that way. Adhering to his strategy decided in January, 'the time has been reached', Chamberlain declared, 'when new factories cannot generally be expected to begin production in time to be of service in this war'. Chamberlain proposed that Montagu's factory programme be cancelled. Lloyd George likewise announced himself 'absolutely opposed' to Montagu's plans – albeit for a very different reason. McKenna had complained that Lloyd George 'thought he could say what he liked' without any consequences in the United States. This was, in fact, absolutely the case. Without a trace of irony, Lloyd George declared that his view 'was that the United States should be utilised as far as possible' and that he 'did not believe there was much chance of trouble between this country and the United States'. McKenna replied that he 'had always maintained that we could only finance the war at our present rate up to a certain time'. Lloyd George dismissed McKenna's answer, retorting that the time 'was always being extended' and telling the War Committee flatly that he had 'never shared the pessimistic views of the Chancellor of the Exchequer'. Lloyd George 'repeated that he was definitely opposed to limiting our orders in the United States'. But as much as Lloyd George rejected the reasoning behind Montagu's plans, he even more emphatically rejected the reasoning behind Chamberlain's recommendation: escalating his language, Lloyd George declared that 'it would be a most serious matter' if the government attempted to fix any kind of time limit to the war.

Perhaps sensing that Chamberlain's recommendation was beginning to pose a fundamental political threat to his government, Asquith decided that the recommendation had to be put aside. Lloyd George had no objection to the factories themselves; he merely wanted them to produce weapons *in addition* to the vast amounts they were importing from America, rather than to substitute for them. Montagu's factory programme therefore could go ahead for now, and the confrontation was defused.[99] Notwithstanding Lloyd George's objections, however, Montagu proceeded to carry out his urgent American economy drive, and it had the desired effect. Though the reductions were more than offset by other government purchases, by March 1917 Keynes at the Treasury was praising the Munitions Ministry for having its American commitments 'substantially reduced and their character changed', while at the same time noting very large increases in domestic shell production[100] – about which Montagu was very proud indeed.[101] With politics making an honest reckoning about Britain's strategic position impossible, the British leadership was drifting almost by accident into Montagu's strategy for continuing the war into 1917.

The contrast between Lloyd George and Grey scarcely could have been sharper. A few weeks before, following the US Congress' authorizing of retaliatory measures against the British blockade, Grey had asked an array of government departments to name representatives to a special committee to consider the extent of British dependence on the United States. The committee was tasked with two questions: how much damage the Americans could do to the British war effort if they wished, and whether the British had any counter-retaliatory options available in response.[102] The Foreign Office had wanted to get the committee off the ground quickly,[103] but as the threat of dramatic American action against the British blockade seemed to wane, a number of departments were dilatory in sending in their replies.[104]

After Lloyd George's interview, however, the matter took on much more urgency: the final department responded on 2 October,[105] and the committee convened the very next day. The preliminary report, issued two days later, revealed Lloyd George to be completely divorced from reality:

It developed at once at the conference that there was really nothing to deliberate about because our dependence was so vital and complete in every possible respect that it was folly even to consider reprisals ... [which] while they would produce tremendous distress in America, would also practically stop the war ...

[O]ur job is not merely to maintain decently friendly relations with the United States, but to keep sentiment in America so sweet that it will lend us practically unlimited money. And so far as I can see, eventually the sentiment will have to be so sweet as to be prepared to lend us the money without any collateral at all[.][106]

When the committee reconvened around 13 October,[107] it approved a 'considered resolution' that was an unmistakeable reproach to the War Secretary, declaring that Britain had an 'extremely weak' negotiating position vis-à-vis the United States and no meaningful option of reprisal.

Attached to the resolution was an even more forthright statement by Keynes at the Treasury, which was endorsed by the committee's War Office representative. It emphasized that their current mortgaging operations in New York were *public* lending operations, and that favourable American public opinion was therefore crucial to their success. It warned that a disapproving statement from Wilson would have a calamitous effect, but even if Wilson did not take action, 'any feeling of irritation or lack of sympathy' with Britain on the part of the American public could seriously undermine them. Keynes concluded:

It is hardly an exaggeration to say that in a few months' time the American Executive and the American public will be in a position to dictate to this country on matters that affect us more nearly than them.

It is, therefore, the view of the Treasury ... that the policy of this country towards the United States of America should be so directed as not only to avoid any form of reprisal or active irritation, but also to conciliate and to please.

The resolution and the appendix were approved and specifically sent to the Army Council, which was chaired by Lloyd George. Grey and McKenna won their rebuke. It was as close to a unanimous telling off of the War Secretary as two ministers could hope to achieve.[108] Lloyd George must have been aware that the rebuke was coming. It did nothing to stop him.

On 11 October, Lloyd George faced down his critics in a dramatic session of Parliament. The House of Commons was scheduled to debate a supplementary vote of credit necessary to continue the war. Although the measure would pass unanimously, Asquith was expected to address the status of the war, and questions were put to ministers. A group of Liberal MPs led by Richard Holt – Holt wanted 'peace as soon as possible'[109] – had heard that the Cabinet had had nothing to do with the interview, and they decided to force the issue in open session: had the interview been authorized by the Foreign Secretary or the Cabinet? The day before, the *Manchester Guardian* announced that the question was expected, and, for the first time, the divisions in the government seeped into the press. The *Guardian* wrote, on 'trustworthy authority', that 'the interview was not seen or approved by the Government or the Foreign Secretary, and that it was a purely spontaneous expression of Lloyd George's private opinions'.[110] Later that day, Holt's group of MPs discussed the issue with House's former secretary, Clifford Carver. Holt asked whether Carver 'had any objection to his raising a question' on it. Carver approved, though he urged Holt to focus on the 'question of taste', fearing 'trouble' might result from a more direct challenge.[111] The Liberal MPs no doubt believed that they had the War Secretary cornered, and the *Guardian* expected 'interesting examples of diplomatic phrasing' when the question was asked.[112] They had not counted on Lloyd George deploying the politician's ultimate escape hatch: perjuring himself before Parliament.

Asquith opened the debate with a long, sober assessment of the finances of the war and of the state of the various theatres in which it was being fought – 'a trying and difficult speech', Asquith described it, 'especially the last part'. The Prime Minister ended his speech with a moving, dignified, and artfully worded declaration on the fundamental question of war and peace, trying to keep the country united in the wake of Lloyd George's outburst. He spoke poignantly of the 'long and sombre procession of cruelty and suffering' that the conflict had caused. 'War is, as we now know too well' – and, for Asquith, personally so – 'a terrible and wasteful thing, justified only by the greatness of its cause'. For his Conservative colleagues, he affirmed it was not time 'for faint hearts, faltering purpose or wavering counsel' and that the war 'cannot be allowed to end in some patched-up, precarious, dishonouring compromise, masquerading under the name of Peace'. Yet moderately minded Liberals could not have failed to notice that words like 'victory' and 'triumph' were entirely absent from the address.[113] President Wilson himself had in December 1915 spoken against a 'patched-up peace', wanting a peace instead that 'will endure'.[114] A negotiated settlement that was not 'precarious' or 'dishonouring' was, by implication, not ruled out. Asquith spoke of British aims in a moderate way:

The ends of the Allies are well known; they have been frequently and precisely stated. They are not selfish ends, they are not vindictive ends, but they require that there shall be adequate reparation for the past and adequate security for the future.[115]

Lloyd George, however, had no time for Asquith's finesse. Holt rose to confront Lloyd George on his interview. The backbencher praised the Prime Minister's address effusively, and then proceeded not only to challenge the language that Lloyd George had employed, but, ignoring Carver's opinion, to directly attack Lloyd George's desire for a 'knock-out blow'. Holt returned to the Prime Minister's famous declaration of British war aims at the outset of the war in which Asquith had spoken of restoring Belgium and crushing Prussian militarism.[116] Holt argued that Prussian militarism could be said to be crushed far short of inflicting a complete and utter 'knock-out blow' on Germany: 'Surely Prussian militarism will have been crushed when the German Emperor has been made to see that it does not pay, when the Germans have discovered that ... they are unable to obtain that which in justice is not theirs?' Holt insisted that if 'peace were made to-morrow', German militarism would have nothing to show for its efforts 'but a bloody record of failure'. He asserted that if Germany were 'made to assent to a League of Peace among the nations ... [s]urely then Prussian militarism would be as effectually crushed as anyone could desire to see'. He gave Lloyd George a stark warning. 'We desire peace as soon as we can get it consistently with attaining our objects ... Let us be very careful that in the prosecution of this War we do not allow our objects to degenerate'.[117]

Lloyd George, ever crafty on his feet, parried Holt's challenge to his language with typical jocularity:

The interview was not a speech. It was not a letter. It was an interview. An interview is a public report of a private conversation. I do not know how my hon.

Friend talks to his friends in private. Surely he does not address his acquaintances in private as he does this assembly? If he does, God help his friends!

Yet Lloyd George went much further. He said that his interview was nothing less than a continuation of what had been government policy since the outset of the war. He falsely declared to Parliament that he had consulted with his colleagues about the interview, saying that it was given with their knowledge and approval. 'I proclaimed no new policy', he lied, but had only repeated 'that of the Prime Minister' and 'the policy of the government'. He told Holt that it was actually *Holt* who was at odds with the policy of the Prime Minister, and not himself. Lloyd George was unrepentant, and even referred obliquely to the decrypt in open session:

I do not withdraw a single syllable. *It was essential. I could tell the hon. Member how timely it was.* I can tell the hon. Member it was not merely the expression of my own opinion, but the expression of the opinion of the Cabinet, of the War Committee, and of our military advisers.[118]

In an attack on the *Manchester Guardian*, referring to the newspaper correspondents who wrote the stories saying that Lloyd George's interview had been unauthorized, Lloyd George declared to the Commons that the correspondents were liars, 'trying to sow and spread disaffection'. They only 'pretend they have got it from my colleagues', he said, when they 'suggest that I made this declaration without consulting my colleagues and that I was speaking only for myself'. 'Do not believe it!' he deceitfully implored his fellow MPs. 'It is a pure invention of theirs'. He shamelessly trotted out the decrypt's ability to silence his colleagues, telling Parliament: 'I cannot believe my colleagues would tell correspondents what they have never said in the Cabinet, or in the War Office'.[119]

There is no record of Asquith's, McKenna's, or Grey's reactions – Asquith and McKenna sitting on the very same front bench behind Lloyd George as their War Secretary brazenly lied to the Commons. Asquith had in his speech sought to keep his country united. However angry he might have felt, confronting Lloyd George's fabrications would have meant repudiating the interview and putting the divisions in the government on embarrassingly public display – a course that risked blowing the coalition apart. Lloyd George knew this and was exploiting it to the utmost. The others could only seethe in silence as Lloyd George took it upon himself to declare the policy of the government.

Despite Lloyd George's efforts to upset the Prime Minister's nuance, Asquith's speech nevertheless received near universal praise from all wings of the press. The Prime Minister certainly succeeded at his goal of preserving national unity: everyone interpreted the Prime Minister's speech as saying what they wanted it to. The Liberals were not convinced by Lloyd George's claims that he and Asquith spoke with one voice. The *Manchester Guardian* – which, of course, knew directly of Lloyd George's mendacity – praised Asquith's speech as a 'finely tempered' address, rejecting any notion that it called for 'crush[ing]' or 'maim[ing]' Germany.[120] It simultaneously dismissed Lloyd George's eruption in his exchange with Holt as nothing more than a 'fiery little philippic',[121] and objected to Lloyd George's claims that the interview had been approved by the Cabinet and Foreign Secretary.[122] The rest of the Liberal press either took a similar line, or tended to follow that of the Asquithian *Westminster Gazette*, which ignored Lloyd George entirely – as if Lloyd George had said nothing at all.[123]

Both Labour to Asquith's left and the Conservatives to his right found no fault with Asquith's address, for contradictory reasons. The socialist newspaper the *Labour Leader* called the speech 'satisfactory', noting the 'striking contrast' it made with the pronouncements of Lloyd George.[124] The right, however, saw Asquith's words as an *endorsement* of Lloyd George. The *Daily Mail* celebrated Asquith's speech as a 'rebuke to those mischievous busybodies' who had been saying that Lloyd George spoke only for himself,[125] while the rabid *National Review* called Asquith's speech 'admirable' – although, presumably with the Liberals' praise of the speech in mind, it warned that 'unless [it] means the same thing as Mr. Lloyd George it means nothing'.[126]

Asquith's speech pleased not only the Conservative press, but hardline Conservatives within the government as well. Lord Bertie congratulated Asquith on his 'splendid' speech that 'confirmed the declarations made by the Secretary of State for War to the American Pressman'.[127] When Bertie visited London a couple of weeks later, he cornered Asquith, wanting to know if mediation was 'dead'". Bertie was deeply pleased when Asquith said it was.[128] Asquith did not, however, mention his increasing doubts over the military leadership, which he confided to a close friend on 21 October, writing about a dinner with Haig at which 'I tried to extract from him some definite statement as to his present and future objectives. I found him rather nebulous (entre nous) and as usual very tongue-tied'.[129]

Lloyd George's reference to the decrypt sent the press atwitter, no doubt to the horror of military and naval intelligence. The *Daily Mail* noted that 'members pricked their ears and waited for revelations from secret history, but Mr. Lloyd George had only whetted their appetite without satisfying it'.[130] The *Daily News* wrote that 'it was the reference to the "timeliness" of the interview that most obviously interested the

House'.[131] Perhaps most worrisome, however, was the American coverage of the interview. A large headline on page two in the *New York Times* blazed that Lloyd George 'Defends "Fight-to-a-Finish" Interview, But Can't Disclose How Timely It Was'.[132] Lloyd George was fortunate that the White House took no notice.

No doubt spurred on by Lloyd George's oblique reference to the decrypt, pacifist Liberal MP William Byles demanded to know in an official question whether the Foreign Office 'has any official information that Mr. Gerard is conveying from the German Government to the United States Government suggestions of mediation in the interests of peace'. Gerard had left for home for a holiday at the end of September, shortly after dispatching the telegram. Byles thought perhaps this might be the 'timely' intervention that Lloyd George spoke of. There is no record of the Foreign Office's horror at Lloyd George's playing fast and loose with one of Britain's most tightly kept secrets for his own political purposes. The Foreign Office issued only a six-word reply, which was of course not true: 'The answer is in the negative'.[133]

The Allies, moreover, may have been much less enthusiastic about Lloyd George's interview than Lloyd George thought. On 11 October, the *Guardian*'s Paris correspondent, Robert Dell, filed a report with his superiors:

The United Press interview with Lloyd George has caused great annoyance here; [French Prime Minister Aristide] Briand is very angry about it. Lloyd George's habit of running over uninvited to Paris has already made him unpopular in official circles; it is said that he interferes too much with everything and everybody. Now he is posing as the mouthpiece of the Allies. The general public has not taken very much notice of the interview; the French press gave a summary of it, but there has hardly been a word of comment, no doubt because the Government has asked for silence. So far, however, as the interview has made an impression, the impression is deplorable. To say to France just now that time does not count is not exactly tactful.[134]

The *Guardian* ran a short report based on this, though rather less frank, on 16 October.[135] A furious Lloyd George immediately penned a letter to Scott accusing the *Guardian* of 'utterly misstat[ing] facts in order to discredit someone they do not approve of', and gave a short list of primarily right-wing French papers that had endorsed the interview. Scott denied any personal animus, replying that 'there is a great deal of opinion which does not find expression in the [French] newspapers and I did not feel justified in suppressing [Dell's] report'. Lloyd George answered by again accusing Scott of 'gross misstatements' and, referring to the decrypt, retorted that he was confident that 'if you had the information which I have … you would have approved entirely of my interposition'.[136] The next month, Lloyd George would give that information to Scott in a bid to bring the *Manchester Guardian* back on his side.

Grey now faced the formidable task of trying to clean up what had become an enormous Anglo-American mess. The first step was to try prevent the Blockade Ministry from doing more damage. Although he had lost control over the blockade, Grey used the interdepartmental committee's conclusions on their dependence on the United States to press Cecil's Blockade Ministry to show the 'greatest possible consideration' for American interests. Rating the financial dangers far ahead of Wilson's new retaliatory powers – 'weapons too big for them to use', except in case of a serious escalation – Grey warned that the United States might prefer 'a speedy peace'. Despite these perils, he acknowledged that, unless things took yet another turn for the worse, there was no present need for any concessions 'on any matter of principle'. (Nor would Cecil have been likely to agree to any such concessions even if Grey had urged them.) But even so, Grey pleaded for 'greater civility' and for anything else that could be done to placate the Americans.[137] It seems that Cecil took the plea to heart; the noise level over the blockade stayed relatively quiet for the remainder of the period of American neutrality.[138]

The second step was to seek to heal the divisions that Lloyd George had created. Grey still had one salve he could apply to the Anglo-American relationship: the post-war international league. Grey gave a speech to the Foreign Press Association in London on 23 October. Previously, he had told House that he could not publicly endorse Wilson's call for a league because of the serious missteps in Wilson's speech to the League to Enforce Peace back in May. Grey now took the opportunity to do so. At the same time, he swallowed his serious objections to Lloyd George's interview. The damage to Anglo-American relations was done. Lloyd George already had single-handedly put Grey's imprimatur on the interview, whether the Foreign Secretary liked it or not. Understandably not willing to put the divisions in the government on display, all Grey could do was attempt to put the episode behind him and pull his party, the coalition, and the Allies together in its aftermath. Lumping Lloyd George's interview with Asquith's speech, along with a recent speech of the French Premier, Grey said, very briefly, 'I endorse all that they have said' – the words no doubt leaving a bad taste as they left his mouth.

Attempting to restore good relations with the United States, Grey at last gave full-throated public support to Wilson's earlier call for a post-war league of nations, noting that Wilson's opponent in the election had endorsed the idea as well. He encouraged the United States to take a more proactive approach in putting together a proposal for a workable league. '[I]f we seem to have little time to give to such ideas ourselves', he said, 'that is a work in neutral countries to which we should all look with confidence and hope'. Adopting Lloyd George's use of colloquialisms, he told the Americans: 'Get on with this question; we are in favour of it'.[139]

The speech angered some Conservatives – the arch-Conservative *Morning Post* denounced Grey's faith in an international league as 'pathetic' and shrieked that, if Grey's proposal were implemented, 'our ultimate destruction would be certain'[140] – but it pleased the Americans. A delighted House, otherwise consumed with the President's re-election campaign, immediately wrote Grey a letter, the first since Grey had rejected mediation in August amidst Romania's entry. House praised Grey's speech as being of 'far-reaching importance'. The pending election, however, put everything on hold. House forthrightly told Grey that 'it seems futile to forecast any action until we know whether or not our Government shall continue as it is'.[141]

Anglo-American relations again went into suspended animation for a couple of weeks as everyone awaited the results of 7 November. Yet despite Bertie's joy at mediation being 'dead', and despite Grey's 'endorsement' of Lloyd George's interview, it certainly does not seem that Grey had closed the door altogether. On 2 November – House's letter had yet to arrive – Grey sent House a copy of the speech, fearing that perhaps in the 'turmoil of the election it had not reached the United States'. He affectionately asked his friend, no matter the result of the election, to 'remember that I hope always to maintain the friendship and to see you again whenever there is opportunity'. He continued with a curious paragraph, containing a curious reference, that certainly seemed to suggest that mediation was not nearly as dead to Grey as Lloyd George would have liked:

It seems of little use to write about public matters such as *mediation* or submarines till the Election is over and we know what the President's position is, but I should like to hear from you after the Election, especially as to the prospect of a League of Nations to keep future peace being effectively supported and pressed by the United States.[142]

Indeed, over the next month, mediation would be very much alive, and it would play its role in tearing the government apart.

7   The Fall of Asquith
October–December 1916

In November, the battle that the Cabinet had been fighting all year reached its apex. The wells of British finance in America were beginning to run dry, and their American supply link would soon be in palpable danger. A serious financial crisis at the end of the month only underlined Britain's vulnerability. Yet the Cabinet continued to divide on the same lines it had done all year. One faction recognized that soon the British either would have to make some very difficult economic choices, or else they would need to wind up the war. The other side insisted that the government should not only stay the course, but that it should intensify it, demanding a 1917 campaign fought on an even more expansive economic scale. Britain, they believed, must stint neither itself nor its allies any supplies they required. There needed to be a serious further turn of the domestic economic screw, with a massive diversion of more men not only into the Army but also into the war industries supporting it.

The Prime Minister faced an unenviable, even impossible task: accommodating political necessity when it stood opposed to economic reality. Yet by all appearances come the first of December, he succeeded. Asquith engineered a series of deft compromises. Neither faction was happy, to be sure, but all of his ministers – save one – were mollified, at least for the moment. Lloyd George, however, was through with compromise. He had had enough of financial threats that he regarded as fictional being deployed to excuse a prosecution of the war that he considered lax. He determined to stop at nothing to eject Asquith and his allies from the levers of power.

The debate about whether the war remained winnable that had rumbled periodically in the War Committee burst suddenly and openly into the Cabinet in mid-November. A crescendo of pessimism about Britain's staying power led Conservative elder statesman and Minister without Portfolio Lord Lansdowne – who importantly had no direct knowledge of the decrypt that had sparked it – to launch a belated but direct attack on Lloyd George's interview by issuing a key Cabinet memorandum. Previous historians have consistently asserted that

Lansdowne represented only a 'solitary' faction of one in the Cabinet.[1] But Lansdowne in reality found broad and meaningful support amongst leading Liberals in the Cabinet as he argued in favour of testing the waters for a tolerable negotiated peace.

Aware to some extent of Lloyd George's manoeuvres against him, Asquith moved to contain the debate that Lansdowne had started until his government had landed on safer political ground. The Prime Minister did his utmost to preserve national unity, a task that was becoming increasingly difficult. Further pressures added to his problems. Military reverses damaged the government's standing. There were labour troubles at home. All these problems combined with a number of smaller ones – in particular, a nasty turf war concerning airplanes between Balfour and Curzon. Asquith's usual practice was to allow his ministers wide latitude in making their cases and voicing their opinions. Members of his government threatened resignation sufficiently often that Asquith did not need to add bruised egos to their list of grievances. In November, however, the volume of business, Asquith's low-key leadership style, and his colleagues' love of talk all combined to overwhelm the decision-making apparatus of Asquith's government. To this point, Asquith had needed to convene his War Committee only about a half-dozen times per month. Between 24 October and 1 December, however, the War Committee met no fewer than 21 times – the meetings often lasting hours – and yet Hankey still complained that the Committee was not getting through its work.[2]

Sensing weakness, Lloyd George was determined to seize power for himself and did his utmost to put further strain on the coalition. Taking advantage of a Conservative Party drifting into two camps under Bonar Law and Edward Carson, a leading right-wing backbencher and critic of the government, Lloyd George aimed to create a new parliamentary majority by creating a pact amongst himself, Bonar Law, Carson, and the small Labour Party – a pact that Lloyd George planned to dominate. Asquith could stay on as Prime Minister, but only as an impotent one that would bend to Lloyd George's will. If Asquith became an irritant, the pact could then easily enough bounce him from office.

Yet Asquith outmanoeuvred him. As November closed, his government held together, while Lloyd George stood isolated and alone. Unwilling to admit defeat, Lloyd George launched a desperate and outrageous gambit to resurrect his plan. When the dust settled, he was in Downing Street.

British intelligence continued its efforts to undermine American mediation within the government, intercepting German and American telegrams – telegrams that seemed to show strong German interest in

American mediation. Hall, who had suppressed the decrypts in September showing that the Americans would not move on mediation until after the election, now ensured that these decrypts saw distribution. He had positively delighted in Lloyd George's interview, even though he no doubt guessed what had triggered it, and he alone possessed crucial intelligence showing that it had been completely unnecessary. 'You will have seen by Lloyd George's speech', Hall wrote gleefully, 'that for once in our lives we hold the same views. It has been a struggle to get the ministers out in the open and say exactly what the people of England think, and not what the politicians would like them to think'.[3]

Ever since Hall uncovered the Swedish roundabout in the summer, the decryption of German messages proceeded steadily in two directions. Room 40 kept up with any new messages being sent via the Swedish roundabout, all of which were dispatched in long-cracked codes. They also worked backwards from the date of the roundabout's discovery, gradually working their way back into 1915 when the Swedish roundabout had been inaugurated.[4] Over the course of October, Hall had a strong insight into German foreign policy – and at least some of these decrypts made their way into the hands of the Foreign Office.

Despite Bernstorff's assessments and Lloyd George's interview, Berlin continued to encourage Bernstorff to press Wilson to push ahead with a 'spontaneous appeal for peace' before the election. If Wilson could not 'make up his mind to reach this decision alone', Bethmann Hollweg suggested to Bernstorff, 'he should put himself in touch with the Pope, the King of Spain, and the European neutral nations'. This would 'assure him of reelection and a place in history, because it could not be rejected by the Entente'.[5] Only the file of decrypts of Bernstorff's telegrams to Berlin survives; the file of decrypts of Berlin's replies does not.[6] Yet there is unmistakable evidence not only that the latter existed, but that this one particular telegram was distributed to the Foreign Office: on 25 October, Hardinge wrote to the British Ambassador in Rome: 'There is absolutely no doubt – in fact we have incontestable proof – that the Germans are doing all they can at the present moment to obtain peace through the mediation of President Wilson or of a combination of President Wilson, the Pope, and the King of Spain'.[7]

Bernstorff replied flatly that Wilson would not make any moves before the election, although he thought it 'very likely' that Wilson would afterwards.[8] It is difficult to say whether the Foreign Office received this or very many of the other decrypts. On Election Day in America, 7 November, Hardinge wrote his cousin, the Ambassador at Madrid, that he 'cannot help feeling that if Wilson wins the election that is going on to-day, he will come forward before long with some sort of proposal' – an uncertain, speculative wording ('cannot help feeling') that perhaps suggests that he did not see Bernstorff's reply.[9] In any case, however, it is clear that the Foreign Office saw only what Hall wanted it to see.

The decrypts also showed a growing conflict within the German government over submarines. 'The one question of paramount importance' from the naval point of view, Hall later recalled, 'was this: at what date would the Germans open their campaign of unrestricted submarine warfare?' Hall had been convinced at the end of September that the Americans' rebuff of the Germans' peace attempts, combined with Lloyd George's interview, would provoke Germany into launching the campaign 'in the next few weeks'.[10] This expectation proved mistaken. Bernstorff and the German civilian leadership succeeded in getting the Kaiser to postpone a decision until after the American election. Hall saw that Bernstorff urgently recommended this course to Berlin on 5 October,[11] and though Berlin confided to Bernstorff that the 'demands here for unrestricted U-boat war are growing', the government nevertheless informed him definitely on 9 October that 'unrestricted U-boat warfare will not be carried on for the present'.[12]

Room 40 also worked to clear the backlog of intercepts of Bernstorff's communications with Berlin from earlier in 1916 – a process that had begun in August and which appears to have been completed by early November. The contents were damning to House, and Hall no doubt took them as confirmation that House was a German agent. Bernstorff's close relations with House were discussed frequently, and two decrypts in particular seemed very damaging indeed. One decrypt, dated 30 August, of a telegram from May seemed to show that Wilson's major speech to the League to Enforce Peace in May was coordinated with Berlin. 'House tells me that ... Wilson will open his peace propaganda with a speech to the Peace League meeting on the 27th of this month', Bernstorff wrote. 'It is desirable that this should be taken up in a friendly spirit at home'.[13] Even worse, in a decrypt dated 20 October, Hall learned that on 6 June Bernstorff had telegraphed Berlin:

Colonel House is working continually in accordance with your telegram No. 41, as Wilson is especially anxious to remove the impression that Germany is urgently wanting peace, and [House] wishes for that reason to secure Wilson for our interests ...

House asks that you should be influenced in the sense that Germany should show no great desire for peace as in that case our enemies will stiffen their attitude.[14]

We can be sure that Hall circulated this 'proof' of House as a German agent as widely as he dared.

A major cryptological development took Room 40 by surprise at the beginning of November. A German cargo submarine landed in Connecticut; its deliveries included a new, somewhat more secure code for the German Embassy in Washington.[15] The Germans' main diplomatic code was replaced with the brand new Code 7500.[16] For the next couple of months, the most secure German telegrams would be completely unreadable in London, although given the Americans' diplomatic inaction, there certainly was little intelligence at this point to be had about possible peace moves, either from German or American sources. 'We have heard little from America', Hardinge wrote in mid-November, 'as to any schemes of mediation that Wilson may be thinking of but perhaps these are early days'.[17]

Some parts of some German messages, however, continued to be sent in old codes. One in particular, sent from Washington on 17 November, contained a cryptic reference that no doubt concerned Hall immensely. Bernstorff warned Berlin 'not to reopen the armed merchantmen question, especially in light of Wilson's peace plan'.[18] Bernstorff's apparent knowledge of 'Wilson's peace plan' – of which Spring Rice knew nothing – undoubtedly could have seemed to suggest that Berlin and Washington were cooperating. In reality, this was mere exaggeration on Bernstorff's part. He had no special information. He simply was desperate to keep his government from starting unrestricted submarine warfare and bringing the United States into the war.[19]

Hall, it seems clear, promptly showed this decrypt to Balfour. On 18 November, Hankey went for tea with Balfour, who gave Hankey '*absolutely reliable but very secret information* that the German Chancellor is trying to get American mediation' – no doubt telling him of this decrypt, perhaps along with some of the October decrypts from before the Germans had changed their codes.[20] Two days later, Hankey briefly notes in his diary, he went to see Asquith and passed along this information. This is one of only a very few known pieces of direct evidence of Asquith ever receiving information obviously gleaned from decrypts.[21]

With another chunk of an important telegram, also inexplicably sent in an old code, Hall found further, and even more explicit, seeming confirmation of his suspicions that House was essentially a German agent. In a telegram decrypted in London on 23 November, Bernstorff assured Berlin: 'House I keep in strict control'. Referring to two controversial cases of ships sunk by German submarines, Bernstorff wrote of growing German-American cooperation, saying that he 'believe[d] that I can with House's help bury the two outstanding cases with comparative inconspicuousness as Wilson wishes this himself'.[22] While Bernstorff's statement that he was 'control[ling]' House would have startled the Colonel immensely, we can be sure that Hall would have spared no effort to get this decrypt as wide a circulation as he thought wise.

Other sensitive information found its way into Hall's hands through the Germans' use of old codes. 'I urgently request', Bernstorff asked Berlin on 19 November, 'that no change in submarine warfare may be allowed to come into operation until it is decided whether Wilson will enter on Peace mediation. I judge this (viz. such action on his part) to be imminent'.[23]

Around mid-November, meanwhile, MI1(b) began picking up decrypts from the American Embassy in Germany concerning potential peace moves. A series of decrypts dating from 16 to 28 November, the first to appear in Hall's files since the dramatic decrypt in late September, gave advance warning of a 'peace interview' between the German Chancellor and an American newspaper correspondent. In a decrypt dated 17 November, the American *chargé d'affaires* Joseph Grew (Gerard had yet to return) cabled that an interview had taken place and was 'in the nature of an informal suggestion to the President, whose response is awaited with eagerness'.[24] Grew managed his own interview with the Chancellor on 22 November, cabling that Bethmann Hollweg 'clearly intimated disappointment that the U.S. had not taken steps leading to peace'.[25] This information, it seems, served to heighten the tension within a British political leadership already gripped in the throes of acrimony.

Across the Atlantic, American peace diplomacy was slowly coming out of its months-long stupor. One thing after another had prevented any American action on this front since May. First came the summer fighting, then Romania's entry, then the presidential campaign, and now the presidential election itself: Wilson's re-election victory hung by a single Californian thread. Though Wilson comfortably won the national popular tally, the count in the Electoral College was one of the closest in American history, with the whole election hinging on California's thirteen electoral votes. After a few tense days of counting, Wilson finally carried the state by a razor-thin margin – only a few thousand votes – and with it the presidency. The Democrats then spent a few more days celebrating and recovering from the drama. It was not until a full week after the election, on 14 November, that the Wilson Administration's foreign policy machinery slowly began to grind back into gear as Wilson summoned House to Washington to plan their next moves.[26]

Wilson had yet to settle on any course of action. Lloyd George's interview and its aftermath led House to reach entirely the wrong conclusion about how to advance mediation – and, much by accident, the President's instincts surpassed those of his chief advisor's. The declarations from London notwithstanding, Wilson wanted to take the dramatic step of writing a note to the belligerents demanding that the war cease. He rested his hopes on 'sufficient peace sentiment' amongst the Allied peoples to make their governments consent. Yet Lloyd George's startling and humiliating public rebuke, which House had very good reason to believe was directed at him personally, convinced the Colonel that they should simply wait and see for the time being. House replied by virtually repeating Lloyd George's words, saying the 'Allies would consider it an unfriendly act if done at a time when they are beginning to be successful after two years of war'.[27] The President suggested sending House back to Europe. When he arrived, Wilson thought, the President would announce his peace move. Based on what he believed to be Allied opinion, House shuddered at the thought. 'I was entirely willing to do this if it were thought best', he recorded, 'although my feeling was that I should prefer [H]ades for the moment rather than those countries when such a proposal was put up to them'. House argued that they should merely 'sit tight and await further developments'. Wilson was not entirely convinced, but House's arguments had left the President 'deeply disturbed'. The President decided that he would first draft a note and then hash things out with his chief advisor further.[28]

House's counsel in mid-November stands as almost certainly his most serious diplomatic error to this point. The window was open for a mediation move, but it would close within the next three weeks. To be sure, the Colonel's advice was sensible if the situation that House believed existed *had* existed. Lloyd George's pronouncement was hardly equivocal, and Asquith's and Grey's speeches as reported in the papers were certainly easy to read as endorsements of Lloyd George's position. Yet House also had information from the young Clifford Carver that the interview was issued 'quite independently by Mr. L-G. and without the sanction or approval of the Cabinet in any manner – in fact several members of the Government with whom I have discussed it have not considered it in the least expressive of public feeling and in some cases have frankly regretted it'.[29] House must have discounted this information in light of Asquith's and Grey's speeches, as well as other more bellicose reports, such as that from Roy Howard, that 'Lloyd George not only voiced the official but the popular British attitude'.[30]

At the same time, however, one cannot help but wonder: had House been in London in November, while the Lansdowne Memorandum was under consideration, might things have played out differently? Though it is impossible to know what might have happened, it certainly makes for a fascinating counterfactual: House, flitting gracefully across the various factions of the British government, as he had ten months before, providing assurances as he strengthened the spines and the hands of those wanting to consider an American-mediated peace.

As things would transpire, the first draft of the President's note would not be ready for nearly another two weeks, on 25 November, when Wilson would summon House to Washington.[31] House was not particularly pleased with the piece. Yet even though House disagreed with the President over tactics, he did not differ with Wilson over policy. House believed, just as the President did, that the war could be wound up on reasonable terms, and House was as willing as the President to begin tightening the screws on the Allies to make this happen. Grey's pre-election letter to House, discussed at the end of Chapter 6, finally arrived on 23 November. House's reply, drafted in conjunction with and approved by the President,[32] was a renewal of their earlier policy of offering American assistance to ensure a peace acceptable to the Allies – only without the warmth. It warned the British that American patience was wearing thin. Blunt almost to the point of unfriendly, after a short introductory preface House opened with a threat. 'There is a growing discontent in America over the high cost of living', he flatly told the Foreign Secretary, 'and there is certain to be a demand to place some sort of restriction upon the exportation of foodstuffs'. 'Contrary to common report', he wrote with unmistakable indignation, 'this country is willing to do its share towards bringing about a proper adjustment of affairs'. He told Grey that he believed that a suitable compromise peace could be reached. 'There is', he wrote frankly, 'a feeling that Germany is now ready to largely meet the conditions laid down by Mr Asquith'. He also implied that the House-Grey Memorandum remained on the table:

With the weight of this Government thrown into the scales on the right side (and every other neutral would probably join us) Germany would yield everything that could properly be demanded of her.

Because of this cooperation between ourselves and the Allies the working out of an insurance against future wars would not be difficult.

He assured Grey that 'this country is thoroughly committed' to a post-war league of nations to maintain the peace. 'It was in the Democratic Platform and the President made it one of the issues of the campaign. His re-election places the people's seal of approval upon it, so now it is merely a question of how to do it'. He concluded with a brief lecture that can only be read as a belated rebuke to Lloyd George's interview: 'I think it is the part of statesmanship now to keep down passion, as far as possible, for it will obscure the vision and prevent the accomplishment of those things which seem necessary for the welfare of humanity in the future'.[33] Perhaps realizing in retrospect that the missive was rather harsh, he tacked on a friendly handwritten post-script: 'I greatly value your assurances of friendship. It is one of the few consolations the war has brought me'.[34] House took the opportunity to send a letter to Balfour at the same time, approved by the President, that was shorter and blunter still. He told Balfour that he had 'often thought' of their conferences in January and February and that he still hoped that the British would 'let us extend a helping hand along the line that we discussed'. In the very next line, he reiterated the same threat he made to Grey, speaking of the 'great pressure' on the US government to restrict food exports because of rising prices.[35]

Neither of these letters, however, would arrive until after the Asquith government had fallen. Page in London, of course, was completely oblivious to the unfolding debate in the Cabinet, unshakeable as ever in his errant belief that 'the British war spirit continues to be resolute'.[36] As the deliberations about the Lansdowne Memorandum unfolded, the most prominent American personalities stood entirely on the sidelines.

The rising tide of pessimism within the British government came into the open in the Cabinet beginning in late October. The stock-taking that Grey and Balfour had demanded a few weeks before led to a rapid succession of crisis memoranda, now reaching well beyond the financial situation. The shipping situation and the food supply, each a long-standing source of concern, threatened their own catastrophes. German submarines were sinking British merchant ships at an unsustainable rate, disrupting the transport of crucial materiel and supplies from across the world and especially from the United States – amongst them food. The ability of the British to feed their home population through the next harvest was rapidly being called into question. At the same time, the deteriorating American financial picture was reaching ever more dire proportions. The British were rapidly exhausting their remaining dollar reserves, and they soon would be at the mercy of the American President – a man who Lloyd George had, only a short time ago, offended in spectacular fashion at a time when Britain's blockade measures had already put him in a particularly sour mood. Meanwhile, although the military's assurances that all was well on the Western Front continued to satisfy the bulk of hardline Conservative opinion within the Cabinet, others increasingly recognized the Somme Offensive for what it was: negligible results at enormous cost in British blood and treasure.

McKenna sounded the first warning blast. The British financial outlook in the United States had been steadily deteriorating. In a telegram to Morgan's later that month, McKenna reliably could count up only $1 billion remaining in British assets deployable in the United States.[37]

There was more than this left in the till, but not much more. A few more mortgaging operations to stretch their final reserve of American investments would be essential. Better yet would be if they could figure out a way to raise at least some sort of unsecured loan, notwithstanding the near failure the previous year. At the current rate of spending, however, the British were on track to need to find $3–$4 billion in the United States to get through a full 1917 campaign. The odds of finding this colossal sum seemed frankly zero.[38] Unless they could get the United States into the war and soon, either engineering a hard landing in their American expenditure or an end to the war were the Allies' only feasible options. Morgan's bluntly warned the Treasury that it needed urgently to 'reconsider [the] whole subject' of the Allies' American spending 'with a view to rigid economy' if the alliance's American supply link was to survive much into 1917.[39]

In his warning memorandum, McKenna reminded the Cabinet of the seemingly forgotten Committee for Co-Ordination of Military and Financial Effort earlier in the year, which then had warned that their 'financial expedients' in the United States could 'only be continued for a short period'. He told the Cabinet that their allies expected 'lavish and increasing financial assistance' in the United States, and that what remained of British assets deployable there should last at least through March, when the next round of Allied financial conferences would be due. But if the British government did not begin a sharp reduction in its American spending, there would be almost nothing left for their allies afterwards. '[W]hat will be my position' at those conferences, he asked, 'if our assets in sight are already completely pledged?' Moreover, he had wrung out of their allies all of the gold he was likely to wring, and he had had 'to exercise pressure which went dangerously far' to do it. There was 'no likelihood', he told the Cabinet, of their allies being willing to furnish anything more. McKenna's conclusion was stark and disquieting:

If things go on as at present, I venture to say with certainty that by next June or earlier the President of the American Republic will be in a position, if he wishes, to dictate his own terms to us.

The Treasury appeared to recognize that its credibility had been damaged by its previous gloomy warnings not having come to pass. In a vain attempt to win over those who might disbelieve the message because of a disdain for the messenger, McKenna appended a report to support his conclusions from an 'outside committee of great weight, in whose deliberations I have taken no part', whose membership included Lloyd George's confidant Lord Reading. (In reality, both documents almost certainly had been originally drafted by Keynes, so the distinction between them is more notional than real.)

This outside committee echoed McKenna's conclusions in more detail and at greater length. Principally, its members clung to a hope that, in future mortgaging operations, they could change the blend of the collateral. If they could get American investors to accept a blend that included more world investments and less American ones – a debatable proposition at best, given the mixed results so far – their remaining assets would stretch much further. But even assuming this worked, the British still would face an enormous problem with the 'possible *pace of borrowing*'. There seemed little likelihood that 'the money can be turned over in America and brought back to us ... as fast as we are spending it'. And this course, moreover, would put them almost completely at the mercy of the American President, who could shut these operations down on a whim.

Finally, this committee felt obliged to reject the fantasy that the United States was now 'so deeply committed to the Allied cause, that it cannot afford to let us fall into difficulties'. The government 'cannot expect', the report wrote flatly, 'that these influences will induce the United States to finance anything approaching the total requirements of ourselves and our allies'.[40]

The President of the Board of Trade, Walter Runciman, sounded the next alarm bell over shipping. The message was simple but bleak: 'Our shipbuilding is not keeping pace with our losses', he warned his colleagues, while the demands of the war 'require more vessels rather than less'. The situation was distinctly not helped by a disappointing American wheat crop, which meant that the British had to dispatch their ships to Australia instead. Nor was it helped by the failure of the military and naval authorities to comply with a direct order from the War Committee to release 200 steamers from military service and put them to shipping work instead. Finally, the British 'depend[ed] more and more on neutral ships for our existence' – in particular, American ships, whose willingness to make the voyage across the Atlantic depended enormously upon the seriousness of the German submarine menace.[41]

Runciman participated in a short discussion over shipping in the War Committee on 9 November. The Conservative President of the Board of Agriculture, Lord Crawford, also invited, pithily summarized the situation: 'By June either munitions, raw material or foodstuffs must be limited – owing to shortage of ships'. He wondered: 'How long can we last – or Germany?' Lloyd George turned to what would become his stock solution of the month and demanded the appointment of a 'shipping dictator', but even Crawford, sympathetic to such calls for more government power, recognized that 'his scheme wasn't thought out' – there already was a Shipping Control Committee under Curzon. The problem was that the Army and Navy ignored the Committee's decisions – and a 'dictator' would only be confronted with the same problem.[42] Hankey bluntly called Lloyd George's proposal 'undigested and stupid', writing in his diary that Lloyd George had 'wasted the whole meeting'.[43]

Lloyd George, with nothing but contempt for McKenna's warning about their finances, then turned to his other favourite panacea. Could they not, he demanded to know, simply buy more ships by placing 'orders in America for steamers'? If Runciman was startled by this suggestion – that, at a time when British finances were already in serious peril, the government should casually put in a costly order for a fresh fleet of American merchantmen – the meeting minutes give no sign of it. Runciman explained patiently that his experts had examined the question, and in addition to other problems, to put it mildly, '[i]f we were to buy we should have to pay prodigious prices'. Lloyd George retorted scathingly that buying the ships 'would be better than losing the war'. McKenna broke in and calmly pointed out that it would be far more cost-effective simply to let the Americans build the ships themselves, since it would expand the market of neutral ships for hire. Lloyd George let the point lie.[44]

Feeling that he was not sufficiently clear about the gravity of the situation, Runciman followed up with another memorandum later that day. 'My expert advisors believe that I am far too sanguine in advising the War Committee that the complete breakdown in shipping will come in June 1917', he told the Committee. 'They are convinced it will come much sooner than June'.[45]

Next in line was Lord Crawford, who warned of an agricultural crisis. Not only were they running out of enough shipping to meet Britain's usual food import requirements, compounding that problem was the failure of their previous potato crop and, even more serious, the massive risks to their next harvest caused by conscription. Zealous to satisfy Haig's thirst for more men, the War Office had snapped up vast numbers of the agricultural labourers that the country needed to produce the next harvest – so many that, unless more farm labourers were found, 'land will go derelict, yield will decline, and live stock must be greatly diminished'. 'The outlook grows more difficult', he informed the War Committee:

Our own requirements are larger; the Allies can export nothing to us; and, while France and Italy look to us for assisting their importation, we have to meet an increasing demand for larger exports of coal and munitions of war [to the Allies].[46]

'Land', Crawford explained emphatically to Lloyd George and Asquith, was simply 'going out of cultivation' because of a lack of manpower.[47] 'Not before August 1917', he warned starkly, 'will war policy be free to dissociate itself from the influence of home food supply'.[48]

Apart from trying to work with Lloyd George to free up labour for the harvest, Crawford was short on detailed solutions. He had a meeting with Asquith on 4 November to press the urgency of the problem, during which he suggested appointing a 'food commission'. When Asquith asked Crawford to submit a memorandum on the subject, Crawford rather unhelpfully accused Asquith of not having read his earlier memorandum – buried at the end of it, Crawford had included a single sentence suggesting that 'it may prove desirable to establish some central food department', with almost no elaboration. Asquith no doubt had in mind Crawford drawing up a detailed proposal of the composition and powers of such a food commission, answering straightforward bureaucratic issues like the relationship between the proposed commission and Crawford's own Board of Agriculture. Instead, Crawford sent Asquith an indignant letter with a copy of that short sentence from his earlier memorandum, adding arrogantly and unconstructively that he had 'very little to add to the proposal'.[49] Crawford then proceeded to bemoan Asquith's 'weak and undecided' nature.[50] Such were the egos with which the Prime Minister had to contend.

Lloyd George followed up with a brief memorandum demanding the appointment of a 'food dictator' who would be given unlimited control over every farm in the country and whose 'responsibilities' consisted mostly of a wish – providing more food at lower prices. In another pointed jab at McKenna, and at reality, the 'dictator' would be directed to purchase large quantities of agricultural equipment in the United States.[51] With the looming threat of a group of Conservative MPs planning to offer a resolution demanding more food controls, Lloyd George pushed his memorandum in the War Committee on 13 November, haranguing the others at considerable length.[52]

The War Committee toned down the proposal, and, after clearing it with the Cabinet later that same day,[53] Asquith left its implementation in Runciman's charge, who toned it down still further while hurriedly drafting more specific proposals that could actually be implemented as policy. When the Conservative MPs offered their resolution in the House of Commons on 15 November, Runciman announced a new post of 'Food Controller', along with a number of new economy measures, such as the banning of white bread, which wastes part of the wheat grain.[54] The controller would be primarily responsible for coordinating the existing bodies in the government responsible for food, not dictating to the country's farmers, and under questioning from the Conservatives

Runciman explicitly denied that it would be a 'food dictator' – no doubt to Lloyd George's considerable displeasure.[55] Many Conservatives, led by Carson, believed that Runciman's pronouncements did not nearly go far enough, demanding effectively the nationalization of agriculture.[56] They regarded Runciman's measures, however, as better than nothing, and Parliament adopted the proposals unanimously.[57]

With the stock-taking memoranda producing a diverse mass of departmental perspectives, Hankey worked to write them up together into a single 'general review of the war'. Hankey warned that the Allies' 'weakest point ... is their staying power, owing to the prodigious strain of the American orders on their financial resources', which now gave 'grave cause for anxiety'. It was essential, therefore, to 'diminish the dependence of the Allies on the United States of America'. Yet with a significant faction of the Cabinet still in emphatic denial that a problem existed at all, Hankey's position as a neutral advisor prevented him from putting forward the only plausible path to achieving this: a hard landing. They needed to gut their American expenditure and hope their Allies would remain onside. Instead, Hankey's only proposed solution was entirely inadequate to the problem. He suggested opening the political Pandora's Box of importing foreign labour to ease the manpower situation. This would probably set off its own political crisis with labour and the trades unions, but more men could generate more production, allowing the British to reduce imports and 'increase exports ... an essential element in the maintenance of our foreign exchanges, on which the whole financial power and staying power of the Allies depends'.[58]

All these memoranda were circulated to the Cabinet on 6 and 7 November. A week later, around 15 November,[59] the doubts that had quietly consumed the government for most of the year finally burst into the open with the first direct attack on Lloyd George's interview. Conservative elder statesman Lord Lansdowne put forward a sombre memorandum that challenged Lloyd George and openly questioned the wisdom of continuing the war.

Lansdowne – who, it should be remembered, had been on Asquith's Committee for Co-Ordination of Military and Financial Effort back in April – was one of only a handful of members of the Cabinet who could have done so. His good standing as a Conservative meant that he could put forward his views without the Conservatives accusing the Liberals of being weak on the war. Lansdowne had strongly supported conscription and had almost single-handedly destroyed Lloyd George's attempts to bring home rule to Ireland earlier that summer.[60] His fellow Conservatives could not dismiss him out of hand – and he gave at least some degree of political cover to the Liberals who shared his views. Perhaps most importantly, Lansdowne's ignorance of the decrypt that had provoked

Lloyd George's interview allowed him to challenge it. That interview had 'produced an impression', he wrote, that 'will not be easy to efface':

There may have been circumstances of which I am unaware,[61] connected perhaps with the Presidential election, which made it necessary to announce that at that particular moment any intervention, however well meant, would be distasteful to us or inopportune. [Lloyd George] said, indeed, that 'the world must know that there can be no outside interference *at this stage*'[62] – a very momentous limitation.

Lansdowne's memorandum was a carefully reasoned assault on Lloyd George's 'knock-out blow'. He began by referring to the various wishlists for peace terms that had been compiled (most of which had been written in the sunnier days of August), almost all of which were predicated on the assumption of a 'dictated' peace. He took the Cabinet on a brief tour of the information that they had recently received. Employing a massive degree of understatement, he called the overall situation 'far from reassuring'. He pointed to evidence suggesting that the determination to continue the war in France and in Italy was beginning to falter, and asked whether the War Committee was 'quite sure' that the Allies were 'entirely to be depended upon'. Nor were their troubles with neutrals likely to ease:

We have been within an ace of grave complications with Sweden and the United States. As time goes on the neutrals are likely to become more and more restive and intolerant of the belligerents, whose right to go on disturbing the peace of the civilised world they will refuse to admit.

19 Lord Lansdowne (Library of Congress / George Grantham Bain Collection / LC-B2-593-10)

Horrified by the 'appalling' casualties that they had suffered so far, he observed that they were 'slowly but surely killing off the best of the male population of these islands'. Generations, he wrote, 'will have to come and go before the country recovers from the loss which it has sustained in human beings, and from the financial ruin and the destruction of the means of production which are taking place'.

He acknowledged that it was 'no doubt our duty to bear' these terrible costs if the war could be won, but if it could not, he declared, 'the responsibility of those who needlessly prolong such a war is not less than that of those who needlessly provoked it'. The war, it seemed, would go on for at least another year – if not two or three. 'What will that year have cost us?' Lansdowne demanded to know:

How much better will our position be at the end of it? Shall we even then be strong enough to 'dictate' terms?

... No one for a moment believes that we are going to lose the war; but what is our chance of winning it in such a manner, and within such limits of time, as will enable us to beat our enemy to the ground and impose upon him the kind of terms which we so freely discuss?

Unless the military and naval authorities could show his concerns to be 'groundless', he urged his colleagues 'not to discourage any movement, no matter where originating, in favour of an interchange of views as to the possibility of a settlement'. It was 'inconceivable' that they would get through the winter without being 'sounded by some one' about peace terms or an armistice. He argued that an 'unconditional refusal would be inadmissible'. He put forth an interpretation of the Prime Minister's speech the previous month that lined up with that of the Liberal press:

As to peace terms, I hope we shall adhere stedfastly to the main principle laid down by the Prime Minister ... [in his] declaration that we could agree to no peace which did not afford adequate reparation for the past and adequate security for the future, but the outline was broadly sketched and might be filled up in many different ways.

The same, he wrote, could be said of the 'temperate speeches' of the Foreign Secretary. He declared it 'unfortunate', because of Lloyd George's interview,

that in spite of these utterances [by Asquith and Grey], it should be possible to represent us and our Allies as committed to a policy partly vindictive and partly selfish, and so irreconcilably committed to that policy that we should regard as unfriendly any attempt, however sincere, to extricate us from the impasse.

Lansdowne threw down the gauntlet at Lloyd George. 'To *many of us*', he wrote flatly, believing he spoke for others in the Cabinet, 'it seems as if the prospect of a "knock out" was, to say the least of it, remote'.[63]

Cabinet reactions to Lansdowne's memorandum largely broke down along now familiar Liberal-Conservative lines. For the Conservative camp, no evidence has emerged about Balfour's or Chamberlain's views, and so only Lord Crawford can be confirmed as a significant Lansdowne ally. In a conversation with Lansdowne on 14 November, Crawford reacted with similar fears. He had no disapproval of Lansdowne's questioning 'whether the country is strong enough to stand out for all we have threatened and guaranteed'. Instead, Crawford listed the challenges facing the Allies: 'The submarine danger menaces our whole position. Russia is still unprepared, France exhausted, Italy fatigued – Germany increasing her strength internally to compensate for military failures'. Crawford asked bluntly: 'How long can we last?'[64]

In September, in discussions about a possible armistice, Crawford had maintained that the conditions demanded should not be, as the generals insisted, 'so difficult to achieve as to amount to a refusal to enter upon negotiations', mostly because he was worried about the effect on the neutrals. He did, however, argue that they should insist on terms that would nevertheless be 'denounced as harsh and unreasonable' and would 'give us overwhelming advantages in the event of the later negotiations breaking down'. Even still, the armistice terms that Crawford had then proposed were rather moderate, leaving nearly all of Belgium in German hands while peace negotiations would take place.[65]

Now, however, Crawford was mainly concerned to get negotiations opened, telling Lansdowne that 'it would be folly to impose terms so impossible of achievement that no discussion could ensue'.[66] When Germany's peace note would come out the next month, Crawford would pen a personal memorandum on the topic. Gone were the discussions of 'overwhelming advantages'. Instead, Crawford emphasized, 'prompt evacuation of portions of occupied territory' – and small portions, at that – would be demanded only 'as a guarantee of German good faith, and to ensure that [the Germans] treat our counterproposals with a wholesome respect'.[67]

Amongst the Liberals, as we will see, there is evidence that Lansdowne's memorandum found support at least from Grey, Runciman, and McKenna, as well as from some of the lesser Liberal lights of the Cabinet. Finally, while we have only the briefest evidence of Asquith's attitude towards the memorandum, we can be sure that he was not hostile.

Grey had in mind a similar approach to Crawford of stating minimum terms for beginning negotiations, telling Spring Rice on 26 November that if [Wilson] made any proposal I should personally advise His Majesty's Government to suggest to the Allies that they should state the minimum conditions to be laid down on which they would accept mediation or begin discussion of peace terms.[68]

Grey, moreover, appears to have been supportive of working with Lansdowne. In a key document in the Walter Runciman Papers, Grey wrote the following to Runciman on 20 November:

If you do not think this overstated, I propose to show it to Lansdowne and one or two others and perhaps to circulate it eventually to the whole Cabinet and C in C. Please return it and let no other eye see it meanwhile.[69]

There is no direct indication of which document this was. By far the most likely candidate, however, is an early draft of what would become Grey's reply to Robertson's rebuke of Lansdowne. This reply, discussed below, reads in large part as the fusion of two distinct papers – one a direct reply to Robertson, the other an independent paper that focuses on shipping and submarines, which could easily have predated Robertson's memorandum. It seems reasonable that the second half of this paper was the document that Grey refers to. In any case, however, Grey's letter shows that he, and by implication, Runciman, were working in cooperation with Lansdowne, not at odds with him. Two days later, the Cabinet would have its first, and only, debate over Lansdowne's memorandum. The body stood divided – a fire that Lloyd George was determined to stoke.

The tale of the fall of Asquith has been told countless times. The conflict in the main, we are usually told, was over leadership style and the governmental mechanisms administering the war. The War Committee was too big, Asquith too indecisive, the machinery of government too slow. While noting disagreements over policy, historian David French sums up what has been written by speaking of Lloyd George's 'frustration' with 'inertia' and 'inefficiency', and 'endless debate'.[70] Lloyd George was determined to get things running more efficiently, and when Asquith stood in the way, Lloyd George took him down. In believing this to be the case, however, historians have fallen for the feints of the key actor in the drama. The form and the machinery of government was the field on which the fight played out because, for tactical reasons, Lloyd George selected it as his preferred battleground.

Certainly these criticisms of Asquith counted amongst the complaints of the discontented. In the main, however, the conflict was over policy and power. Lloyd George himself admitted to his friend George Riddell of the *News of the World* that the key defect of the current War Committee 'is the number of able men with strong opinions'.[71] He wanted McKenna and the other Liberals out of his way. He wanted restrictions on British spending in the United States lifted and the British economy remoulded to his conception of a total war footing – which assuredly did not include what he saw as unnecessary export industries. He wanted those who would contemplate a negotiated peace through the United States made powerless. Grey he regarded with considerable suspicion: in discussing a proposed trip to Russia, Lloyd George asserted to Hankey that 'the French didn't want Grey to go, as they regarded him as rather inclined to make peace', which, Hankey noted, was 'a view of [Grey] which Lloyd George seemed inclined to share'.[72]

In his memoirs, Lloyd George put forward a story of how Hankey supposedly approached him on 16 November while in Paris and urged him to insist on a new, smaller War Committee to be chaired by Lloyd George and from which the Prime Minister would be excluded. This new War Committee would be 'independent of the Cabinet' and would take over 'the day-to-day conduct of the war'. Hankey graciously declined to challenge Lloyd George's account in his own memoirs, but the story was almost certainly concocted.[73] Hankey's detailed diary entry for that date makes no mention of making such a government-shaking proposal. A subsequent entry on 22 November, when Lloyd George revealed the scheme, similarly makes no mention of a prior conversation and specifically refers to the scheme as being '*his* [i.e. Lloyd George's] proposal'.[74] But Lloyd George's account tells us a great deal as to how he wanted his coup to be remembered – that its origins arose out of Hankey's domain, the machinery of government, and not out of politics or policy or, least of all, ambition. Lloyd George's efforts to rewrite history have largely been successful, with most accounts of the crisis typically writing as if Lloyd George merely envisioned leading a small committee of talented technocrats and wanted nothing more than to streamline decision-making.

One central fact, however, has tended to get overlooked: in selecting his 'small' war committee, Lloyd George sought not to provide technocrats, but to amass a parliamentary majority. If Lloyd George had been serious about nominating able administrators, he might have chosen, for example, Conservative Robert Cecil, who was showing talent in running the blockade against Germany and who broadly agreed with Lloyd George's economic views.[75] He could also have chosen a Liberal friendly to Asquith – Montagu would have been an inspired choice. Hankey was 'enormously impressed with Montagu and his administration of the Munitions Dep[artment]'.[76] And unlike many of the other Liberals, Montagu was committedly hostile to American mediation.[77] At the very least, with these nominees Asquith would have been able to regard Lloyd George's scheme as a genuine attempt to improve the machinery of the government.

With Lloyd George's actual proposal, however, Asquith certainly could not have believed that for an instant. When Lloyd George told Hankey on 22 November about his intention of having a war committee made up of Lloyd George, 'Carson (!), Bonar Law, and Henderson', Hankey was thunderstruck. None of the latter three had shown the slightest ounce of administrative talent.[78] Carson's only appreciable skill was in agitating against the government; Lloyd George later would toss him out of the Admiralty after only seven months for incompetence and indecision.[79] Lloyd George himself panned a 'limp and lifeless' Bonar Law as being someone who 'ought to be kept in cold storage and brought out when you want him to make a speech. He makes good speeches, but in Council he is not so good'.[80] Henderson's most recent wartime posts had been as President of the Board of Education and Paymaster General. With the weakness of the other three members, Hankey immediately recognized that the scheme's 'net result would be to put absolute power in [Lloyd George's] hands'.[81] This was, it seems clear, precisely the aim. About the only thing these three men could deliver was parliamentary support. One Liberal Cabinet member soon would call this proposed War Committee arrangement 'absurd as composed merely of politicians who commanded votes'.[82] Bonar Law and Carson could offer reasonably unified Conservative support, Lloyd George seemed to think, while Henderson could deliver most of the Labour MPs. Lloyd George himself could muster at least a small rump of Liberal backing in the House of Commons. Amongst them, Lloyd George thought, they could muster at least a slim parliamentary majority.

With these men in his War Committee, Lloyd George intended to sideline Asquith, McKenna, and the rest of the main body of Liberals in the Cabinet and to seize power for himself. The new committee would in theory be responsible to the Cabinet, but, as long as the four of them agreed, they would have their way. A simple threat to resign if the Cabinet sought to reverse them would be enough to keep Asquith and the other Liberals at bay. It could be useful to keep Asquith as Prime Minister and his camp around as national unity window dressing – but if they got in the way, they could easily enough be bounced from office.

That is precisely the way Hankey saw it. As the crisis reached its climax, Hankey deeply resented Lloyd George's presenting this scheme, clearly intended for his own aggrandizement, as if he were simply seeking to streamline the government's operations. Describing Lloyd George's personnel choices as 'really ridiculous', he wrote that the three men were 'merely representatives of the noisiest groups in the House of Commons to prop him up'. Lloyd George 'wants to be virtually "dictator"', and to achieve this he was resorting to a 'mere political expedient of the most transparent kind'.[83] That is, moreover, precisely how Lloyd George described it to Frances Stevenson. 'If Carson came in', he told her on 22 November, '[Carson], Bonar Law, and [Lloyd George] could arrange to run the War Committee and leave the P.M. to run "his show", i.e. the Cabinet which would not then count for much'.[84] From the moment, therefore, that Lloyd George disclosed this proposed personnel of his War Committee to the Prime Minister, Asquith could not have failed to recognize it for the deeply hostile measure it was – a transparent attempt at a coup.

20 Edward Carson and Andrew Bonar Law (Hulton Archive / Stringer / Getty Images)

In a series of meetings mostly facilitated by Max Aitken (soon to become Lord Beaverbrook) of the right-wing *Daily Express* – Page colourfully described him as a 'Canadian scoundrel of brilliant criminality'[85] – Lloyd George, Bonar Law, and Carson had put aside their differences and formed something of a working relationship. In the so-called 'Nigeria Debate' on 8 November, Carson had demonstrated that, as one historian put it, '[e]ven on a poorly chosen issue, with an ill-framed motion and a badly judged speech', Carson could, in a direct challenge to Bonar Law, command 'close to majority support' amongst Conservative MPs.[86] Putting Conservative Party unity ahead of his own dislike of Carson's agitation, Bonar Law wanted to try to reconcile with him, struggling to find a compromise that would keep the government and his party together. Above all, however, he was not willing to tear his party asunder. Lloyd George, by contrast, in his pursuit of power, had no qualms about doing so.

Asquith had believed something to be afoot as early as 10 November. He had heard, perhaps inaccurately,[87] that on the 'very evening' of Carson's rebellion two days before, Lloyd George had dined with him. The Prime Minister certainly resented Lloyd George's adding to the government's problems when it was already buried under a backlog of urgent issues. Hankey described the Prime Minister as 'very patient' but 'rather annoyed' with his ever-intriguing, troublesome lieutenant. Asquith, however, had more than enough to worry about at the moment, and, for now, decided that his War Secretary was 'so erratic and change-able that too much attention must not be paid to him'.[88]

Two weeks later, however, Lloyd George was determined to follow through. Showing the extent of his political manoeuvring, on 22 November Lloyd George managed to take diametrically opposite positions on 'the knock-out blow' within the span of a few hours. *Manchester Guardian* editor C. P. Scott, after irately refusing to see Lloyd George on his visit to London in early October, finally breakfasted with him that morning. Even after almost two months, Scott still remained angry with Lloyd George, recording that he 'had felt a strong disinclination to see Lloyd George because of his violent outbreak, in his interview with an American journalist, against America as a possible peace-maker and for an indefinite continuance of war to the death (to say nothing of a rather insolent letter he wrote me at the time)'.

As they ate, Lloyd George made a play to win back Scott's support. Some two months after the 'knock-out blow' interview, Lloyd George had not finished using the Gerard decrypt that had sparked it for his own political purposes. The War Secretary carefully distanced himself from the episode. 'The violence' of the interview, Scott seemed to think after speaking with Lloyd George, 'was at least in part calculated' and, most importantly, 'George himself appeared a good deal better than his words'. Lloyd George stressed to Scott that

he had positive and documentary evidence that Gerard ... had gone to America with a proposal to Wilson that he should propose mediation and Wilson would be under very strong temptation to do this in order to conciliate German-American opposition to his re-election which would probably turn the scale. Once mediation were proposed it would have been very difficult to refuse, and once the war was stopped it would have been impossible to resume it. But the time for a settlement was for us extremely unfavourable and for the Germans favourable.

This explanation did not completely satisfy Scott – Lloyd George, Scott observed, 'did not explain why he had thought it necessary to use such violent language or why he rather than the Prime Minister or the Foreign Secretary should have felt called upon to make this declaration'. Yet Scott 'thought much better of [Lloyd George] after hearing what he had to say'. After this talk, Scott, who had grown increasingly frustrated with the performance of Asquith's government, put aside his doubts about Lloyd George and decided to support the Welshman in any struggle with the Prime Minister. This conversation played a crucial role in restoring the alliance between Lloyd George and the newspaper, which may have helped encourage Lloyd George to set off his coalition-ending political crisis barely a week later. Playing the decrypt card won Lloyd George the important support of the *Manchester Guardian*.[89]

After carefully distancing himself from the interview at breakfast, he vehemently defended it before lunch to further stoke the building pressure on the coalition. The Cabinet convened for a long, winding discussion to confront the problems before it. British intelligence made the issue of a possible peace move all the more pressing: Asquith and Lloyd George, clearly with diplomatic decrypts in mind, told the Cabinet that there were 'overtures for peace in the air, certainly from Germany via President Wilson'. As they began to confront the agenda, however, the Liberal Lord Chancellor, Lord Buckmaster, broke in to say that it was 'no use discussing these things until we had faced our own situation and capacities'. Showing that Lansdowne had meaningful support amongst the Liberal lesser lights, Buckmaster emphasized his view that the Lansdowne Memorandum was of 'capital importance' and 'could not be ignored'.[90] Lord Crewe, the Lord President of the Council and Leader in the House of Lords, similarly would praise the Lansdowne Memorandum a few weeks later as 'a plain and courageous exposition of the facts ... displaying no poverty of spirit or lack of determination'.[91]

Lloyd George now stressed that 'he thought a knock-out blow is possible', and declared that he wanted 'a special Cabinet called' specifically for the purpose of discussing Lansdowne's memorandum. If the Cabinet concluded over Lloyd George's vigorous objections that a knock-out was not possible then 'we ought to consider what terms of peace we could offer or accept'. Lloyd George was right to note that 'if we don't settle our policy' as to whether a knoc-out blow was possible, 'there will be hesitating counsels, divergence of aim'. That said, this proposed 'special Cabinet' would have the political advantage of further increasing the friction between the Conservatives and Liberals just as Lloyd George was doing his utmost to blow them apart.

The other Liberals feeling ready for the fight, there was 'general agreement to this'. 'We ask for a special Cabinet on this', wrote Lewis Harcourt, the Liberal First Commissioner of Works.

[The] military authorities [are] to give us their view as to the probabilities of a knock out. We also want statements as to future *finance* and *shipping* – both very bad. I think the latter will be critical and perhaps conclusive by next spring.

Crawford 'says we shall shortly be "besieged" as regards food'. Grey stressed that he thought 'the submarine was the real menace', while Runciman discussed the incoming 'shipping breakdown'. McKenna, meanwhile, re-emphasized the dangers of their financial position. 'To conduct war for six months on our present financial powers', he declared, 'will be difficult, for 12 months almost impossible. Quite apart from our willingness [the] USA will be able to call a halt next summer or autumn'.[92]

Two days later, Robertson circulated the promised military memorandum. Described as 'the most bellicose document ever inflicted on a British Cabinet',[93] it was far from the sober assessment of probabilities the Cabinet had expected. Robertson later recalled that Lloyd George had encouraged him to 'speak out' and 'not "be afraid to let yourself go"'.[94] A century on, the memorandum still makes for extraordinary reading. The Cabinet had, not unreasonably, asked for a careful attempt to project the Allies' likely military position in a year's time. It is difficult to imagine a more useless answer. The closest Robertson came to answering Lansdowne's request for a forecast was: 'I have always warned His Majesty's Government that this country had before it a time of strain far greater than any experienced in the past. This time of additional strain is now beginning[.]' The Cabinet could hardly be faulted for finding this distinctly unenlightening.

The memorandum is riddled with transparent mendacities. Robertson opens by professing 'surprise that the question [of the possibility of a "knock-out blow"] should be asked. The idea had not before entered my mind that any member of His Majesty's Government had a doubt on the matter. His Majesty's Army has none'. At one point, he concedes that 'it is not for me to discuss either the financial or the naval situation'. He then immediately continued by slating McKenna's assessment of their serious financial problems. '[B]efore the war', he wrote almost mockingly, 'we were told by those supposed to know that finance itself was a

complete bar to a great war ever taking place'. Having disclaimed the
ability to speak for the Navy, he then does precisely that, declaring that he
'will not insult it by thinking that the sailor's views as to the ultimate
result of the war are less optimistic than those of the soldier'. Having
usurped the Treasury and the Admiralty, Robertson then acknowledges
that it is not his place 'to say what terms of peace should or should not be
accepted' – a decision that belongs with the ministers collectively. He
immediately proceeds to imply that anything short of a knock-out blow
'would be to estrange our Over-seas Dominions, to betray our Allies, to
sacrifice our own interests, and to dishonour the memory of those who
have laid down their lives for the Empire'.[95]

The rhetorical flourishes are breathtaking. He lectures Lansdowne that
every single soldier in the British Army would be 'disappointed and
astonished if they were aware of the reasons for which this paper is being
written'. Robertson indirectly insults him in astoundingly insolent terms:

As for ourselves, there are amongst us, as in all communities, a certain number of
cranks, cowards, and philosophers, some of whom are afraid of their own skins
being hurt, whilst others are capable of proving to those sufficiently weak-minded
to listen to them that we stand to gain more by losing the war than by winning
it ... We need pay no attention to these miserable members of society.[96]

On and on he thunders, one vacuous expression following another.
'The whole art of making war', he actually wrote near the end of his
harangue, as if it were a profound observation, 'may be summed up in
three words – courage, action, and determination'. He concludes with
one final inane platitude. 'We shall win if we deserve to win'.

Robertson appended a statement from Haig that was no more reassuring. 'It is true', Haig wrote, 'that the amount of ground gained is not
great. That is nothing'. He proceeds with a very short, and unconvincing,
explanation as to why this is 'nothing' – repeating the same line he had
earlier given Northcliffe about having defeated 'the strongest fortifica-
tions' and having inflicted supposedly grievous damage on the German
troops' morale. Then he tells the Cabinet that 'the prospects of success
on this front next year are most favourable'. He gives no more details –
'success' goes completely undefined – and then, having so fully enlight-
ened his government on his campaign's progress and prognosis, he
proceeds to give the government seven paragraphs of 'requirements' for
next year's campaign.[97]

Had any ordinary Chief of the Imperial General Staff (CIGS) inflicted
such an insubordinate and profoundly unserious document on any
ordinary Cabinet, such a general could only expect to promptly have
the Prime Minister demanding his resignation. These, however, were not

ordinary times, Robertson was no ordinary CIGS, and the fragile coalition was certainly no ordinary government.

If Asquith had not yet detected grave political peril in Lloyd George's actions – Bonar Law had given Asquith some indication of what was afoot on 15 November[98] – the Prime Minister certainly did on the morning of 23 November when the pro-Carson and arch-Conservative *Morning Post* published a bizarre editorial leader. The *Post*, which almost never had anything remotely complimentary to say about Lloyd George, forthrightly admitted that it had 'never liked' him as it suddenly came out championing him. The *Post* blamed Britain's lack of success on the war in part on 'what we can only describe as the undefined treachery of the Liberal mind', which, it said, had been 'full of maggots'. Contrasting him with his weak-kneed Liberal colleagues, Lloyd George's 'whole mind and heart', it declared, 'are now set upon victory', and for that reason 'we advise our friends who think with us to back Mr. Lloyd George'. In an ominous and unmistakeable hint that intrigues were well under way, it wrote emphatically: 'Let us inform our readers, without lifting too much of the veil, that Mr. Lloyd George and the cause he has at heart need all the support they can get'. If Lloyd George was successful, it assured its readership, victory in 1917 would be the inevitable consequence.[99]

Asquith, understandably, held off on scheduling the special Cabinet on the Lansdowne Memorandum. In the interim, he continued to have more than enough to worry about. McKenna and Grey were demanding that 'the whole country ought to be rationed in food', but Runciman was not yet ready to take that step, wanting to 'first prohibit brewing of beer and save all the barley tonnage'. Asquith decided that all this would be a matter for the new Food Controller,[100] but having announced the position Asquith found it impossible to find one. Crawford had recommended James Lowther, the Speaker of the House of Commons. Asquith, though a bit sceptical of the choice, went along with it. He sent Lowther a 'very strong' letter asking him to take up the post, along with endorsements from Grey and Balfour, and Asquith deployed Runciman to pressure him. Lowther sat on the request for four days before turning it down. By early December, Asquith had asked at least five others, including the Conservative Alfred Milner – and apparently Asquith fell before Milner gave his answer.[101] Adding insult to injury, the lack of an appointment was treated as proof of Asquith's indecision. Crawford laid all the blame squarely at Asquith's feet, faulting him for having failed to have 'pressed [Lowther] in a manner which would have made it impossible for him' to refuse.[102]

A torrent of other poorly timed misfortunes weighed heavily on Asquith's government. The military situation on all fronts remained deadlocked – except for the Allies' newest ally, Romania, which faced disaster. Britain's Battle of the Somme was finally brought to a close on 18 November. After more than four-and-a-half months, the military had not even succeeded in taking the objectives it had set for 1 July. Even so, a visiting Haig on 23 November reassured the War Committee that all was well, giving 'quite an optimistic estimate of the military position'. As Crawford pointedly noted, however, 'it is not in France that our danger really lies'.[103] In the east, any further Russian progress into Austria-Hungary remained halted,[104] while in the south the Italians had launched what was now the Ninth Battle of the Isonzo. Though the Austro-Hungarian forces there showed increasing signs of strain, they checked the Italians there yet again.[105] In the southeast, however, Romania's entry into the war had escalated into a full-blown calamity. The Battle of Bucharest began on 25 November. The Central Powers would have control of the Romanian capital by the time of Asquith's resignation, with almost daily articles in the British press warning of German progress. By the end of the year, two-thirds of Romania would be in enemy hands, a handsome addition to Germany's list of conquests.[106]

In addition to this military disaster, the government simultaneously faced embarrassing episodes in Parliament. A poorly prepared 'fiasco' of a government pensions bill, spearheaded by Henderson as Paymaster General – the very man Lloyd George was determined to include in his new War Committee – had to be withdrawn back to committee after a hostile reception in the Commons.[107] In the Lords, the government saw two minor but troubling defeats on amendments, ones that were 'less on merits', Crawford observed, 'than as a proof of contempt'.[108]

Bonar Law, unsure of his footing, went to see Asquith on 25 November and revealed Lloyd George's plans almost fully – suggesting a War Committee of Asquith, Bonar Law, Lloyd George, Carson, and Henderson. He concealed only the exclusion of Asquith from the War Committee, the wisdom of which Bonar Law himself had begun to doubt. Asquith must have felt only contempt for the impractical absurdity of the proposal. Nevertheless, he replied at length in a gentle, patient letter in which he tried to open Bonar Law's eyes to the dangers of the scheme. Demonstrating his usual mastery of political analysis, he wrote that 'there is one construction, and one only, that could be put on the new arrangement', which is 'that it has been engineered by [Lloyd George] with the purpose … as soon as a fitting pretext could be found, of his displacing me'.

Even more worrisome, however, Bonar Law seemed blind to the risks of provoking not only Liberal resignations from the government, but Conservative ones as well. Asquith gently pointed out, with significant understatement, that it could cause 'resentment' if Balfour, Curzon, and McKenna were passed over to get Carson in the government.[109] The prediction was an accurate one: in a few days, both McKenna and Curzon would threaten to resign if excluded from the new War Committee. McKenna saw the scheme for what it was – a means of depriving him of his remaining control over Britain's finances – while Curzon frankly distrusted Bonar Law and Carson to serve as adequate counterweights to Lloyd George. As events would play out, Balfour never threatened to resign if excluded from the War Committee, but Asquith had no way of knowing that he would not. Moreover, if McKenna and Curzon left, the tide seemed unlikely to stop there: Chamberlain said that both he and Cecil would have jumped ship if Lloyd George had gotten his way.[110] Quite probably following McKenna out would have been Grey and Runciman; the three men had nearly resigned as a bloc a year before.[111] Lansdowne seems unlikely to have stayed. Who could know where the exodus would end – or whether the government could possible survive it?

From the point of view of parliamentary support for the coalition, at best it would be a wash; at worst, a disaster: whatever support from MPs Carson could deliver would likely be offset by these resignations. As far as effective governance was concerned, the scheme seemed simply madness. How could it possibly be a good idea to risk losing at least a half-dozen individuals – each individually more talented than Carson – merely, as Asquith put it, to 'shut the mouth of our most formidable parliamentary critic'?

Finally, Asquith refused to take a dim view of the current War Committee. While 'open to suggestions for its improvement', the current committee included the heads of the departments most crucial to prosecuting the war as well as the political diversity needed to command the confidence of the wide ideological range of the Cabinet. Reshuffling the War Committee would be a delicate task in any event. Getting Carson in it while at the same time trying to shrink it would be as foolish as it was impossible.[112]

Grey and Lansdowne struck back against Robertson with memoranda of their own on 27 November. Grey's contribution has been fundamentally misunderstood. Historians have regarded the first half of the memorandum, in which Grey resents Robertson's dismissal of diplomacy's usefulness, as 'disappointing', while the second has been seen, oddly, as an attack on Lansdowne's position.[113] The first half of the memorandum certainly exhibits some touchiness, rebuking Robertson at length for his rather brief remark that 'diplomacy seriously failed to assist us with regard to Bulgaria and Turkey'. This should, however, be understood in the context of the inappropriately sweeping nature of Robertson's memorandum, which had made so many pronouncements affecting so many government departments well beyond the domain of the War Office. This reproach is better understood as aimed at knocking Robertson back into his own sphere – and making clear that the military takes orders from the government and not the other way around.

The second half of the document (an earlier version of which likely had been the document that Grey had previously discussed with Lansdowne and Runciman) lays out, in a highly guarded fashion, Grey's views on 'the general question of peace', and it plainly shows that Grey's worries about submarines were driving him to contemplate a negotiated peace through American mediation. Employing the same formula that he had used earlier in the year, Grey hid behind the opinion of the 'military and naval authorities'. He contemplated three different scenarios: military and naval advice that victory remained probable, advice that the Allied position would probably improve though outright victory was doubtful, and advice that the Allied position would probably not much improve.

He then carefully distinguished between the military situation, about which he was not (or, more likely, in the wake of Robertson's outburst, pretended not to be) unduly negative, and the naval situation, about which he most certainly was. Grey unambiguously rejected Robertson's attempt to speak for the Admiralty. Grey demanded a paper from the naval authorities, the Board of Trade, and the Shipping Control Committee – in which Robertson would have no input – giving an 'estimate whether a breakdown in shipping, sufficient to paralyse ourselves or the Allies, is likely to bring us to our knees before military operations in the field can bring Germany to her knees'. He sternly reminded them that the 'future of this country depends upon our giving a correct answer to this question'. As the government considered the matter, it needed to do so 'without emotion, certainly without sentiment, and without rhetoric' – a further rebuke to Robertson – and instead regard the question as one of 'cold, hard fact'.

If the report returned with a pessimistic answer, Grey advised contemplating 'wind[ing] up the war at once on the best terms obtainable, *presumably through the medium of not unsympathetic mediation*', warning gravely that 'if they did not do so, they would be responsible for future disaster to their countries'.[114] This was, of course, a clear reference to the United States – meaning that Grey either was not seeing the decrypts supposedly showing German-American cooperation, or, more likely, that he correctly rejected the others' misinterpretations of them. For those who *did see* the decrypts and believed that the United States and Germany were secretly cooperating, this willingness to contemplate an

American-mediated compromise peace must have seemed simply madness; Lloyd George in particular, having already headed off a German-
American conspiracy, must have been aghast.

As Grey demanded this report on the shipping situation, moreover, he
would have known that the likelihood of a pessimistic answer was very
high. Runciman's experts had already forecast a shipping breakdown well
before the middle of the following year. Runciman himself believed that
'shipping may prove to be the breaking point in the Allied strength'.[115]
The Admiralty, moreover, had been making anything but positive noises
about its ability to control the growing submarine problem. Less than
two weeks before, it had sent the War Committee a melancholy paper
that, as one historian put it, 'amounted to an admission that [it] had no
solution'.[116] It warned that it could not 'actually protect by escort even a
small proportion of the sailings' while writing that 'naval resources are
practically exhausted' as far as hunting submarines are concerned. The
Navy's only new 'idea', if it can even be called that, was that of asking the
Army to solve its problems – wondering whether the War Committee
could order Robertson and Haig to try to recapture the Belgian ports,
which would deprive the Germans of their most important submarine
bases.[117] Considering the dearth of progress on the Western Front to
date, this was not exactly the most promising of schemes. Looking to
shake up the Admiralty, Asquith had insisted that Balfour reshuffle his
top admirals. Balfour reluctantly complied.[118]

It is worth noting, however, the battle that Grey did not try to fight.
The financial situation was no less grave than the shipping one, yet
Grey's paper made no mention of it. Certainly, Grey continued to
understand the seriousness of the problem. 'In this war', he had
explained to the Italian Ambassador less than a week before, not only
were the British providing extensive 'naval and financial' support, 'we
had for the first time created a large army ... Our resources were very
considerable, but they were not inexhaustible'.[119] We can only speculate
as to the reason why his carefully crafted push for renewed contemplation
of American mediation omitted any discussion of financing their
American supplies. The likeliest explanation, however, is simply that he
did not believe McKenna could prevail. The division in the coalition on
this issue had become so entrenched as to be insurmountable. Amongst
the denialists, the Treasury's premature predictions of doom five and
thirteen months earlier seem to have irreparably damaged the department's credibility. The reasons why those predictions had not come to
pass were immaterial. The Treasury was accused of having 'cried wolf
too soon', as Keynes put it, and so could not be trusted.[120] As Lloyd
George later wrote mockingly in his memoirs, 'the Cabinet as a whole

were not, therefore, at this time unduly depressed by Mr. M'Kenna's pictures of approaching famine, because they had ceased to believe in the impish Baxter [that is, Keynes] who at the Chancellor's invitation had wandered into the Treasury'.[121] This was the first time, however, that the Board of Trade had sounded such an alarm over shipping. And if the Shipping Control Committee, led by the arch-Conservative Curzon concurred, the divide plaguing the government all year might finally be transcended.

Lansdowne separately lit into Robertson's reply. In a paper also sent around the Cabinet, Lansdowne attacked Robertson's message as 'surely not a very helpful contribution'. His queries, he sternly told Robertson, deserved a proper answer, and he could not be fobbed off 'by confident assertions as to the temper of the Army, which no one ever doubted, by moving exhortations to stedfastness, and still less by vehement denunciations'. Lansdowne re-emphasized that he was not proposing peace on any terms, but only an 'interchange of views'. He wanted a peace that provided 'adequate reparation' and 'adequate security', as Asquith had demanded, but reiterated that this was only a 'broadly-sketched outline' that 'could be filled up in many different ways'. He spotlighted Robertson's serious insubordination by observing that *'[t]hese suggestions the Cabinet treated as so little deserving of peremptory rejection that they authorised a full enquiry'*. 'Those who ask questions which the Cabinet think worthy of a respectful answer', he wrote pointedly, 'will not consider that they are answered when they are told that such questions are an "insult" to the fighting services'.[122]

The very next day, 28 November, Asquith promptly wrote Lansdowne a brief note: 'I write at once to assure you of my complete concurrence in what you say'.[123] This debate surely was not one that Asquith wanted to be having at this particular moment, not when the government was struggling to cope with its workload and certainly not with Lloyd George's and Carson's falcons circling overhead. The unambiguous nature, however, of Asquith's missive cannot be dismissed. Most historians have simply ignored this letter outright.[124] Historian Andrew Adonis, trying to reconcile it with the conventional contention that Lansdowne received no support, rejects it as nothing more than 'characteristic of [Asquith's] readiness to appease strongly expressed views'.[125] To be sure, Asquith did have this characteristic, but at the same time he should not be treated as some sort of burnt-out half-wit unable to control the words that his hand was putting to paper. The Prime Minister's appeasement almost always went in one direction: the one leading away from political danger. In this case, however, Asquith's 'complete concurrence' was to commit himself to Lansdowne's profoundly politically perilous views. Lansdowne had written a Cabinet memorandum, not a letter to the Prime Minister that demanded a reply. Asquith's missive was not only unnecessary, it also exposed him to meaningful political hazard. Plainly, he agreed that there needed to be a careful analysis of the country's remaining staying power, and he clearly shared Lansdowne's contempt for the military's scornful refusal to cooperate with this. The letter to Lansdowne strongly suggests that Asquith was very much open to an 'interchange of views', with the possibility of a negotiated peace.

Weighing in for the main body of Conservatives, two more Cabinet responses to Robertson's memorandum came in from Cecil and Walter Long, a leading Conservative politician. Where Lansdowne, Grey, and Asquith regarded Robertson's 'contribution' with derision, Cecil and Long took Robertson's assurances at face value. Cecil wrote that if 'we can carry on for another year[,] we have a reasonable prospect of victory', and, for that reason, '[a] peace now could only be disastrous'. He felt they were thus 'bound to continue the war'. Long, similarly, accepted Robertson's contention that 'we can win if only we take the necessary measures to give us success, and take them in time', and he accused the government of failing to do everything it could to win the war. Both wanted drastic measures to extend far greater government control over the economy. They wanted to seize various sectors – shipping and coal mines, in particular. Long wanted worker protections for the coal industry, in particular the eight-hour working day, stripped. Both wanted to impose rationing to reduce imports. Long reiterated his support for the long-standing Conservative demand to impose conscription on Ireland. Cecil suggested 'industrial compulsion'; Long demanded it.[126] Lloyd George had been pushing for it since the summer.[127]

Robertson now joined them. In a further memorandum, Robertson now demanded a further million men for the Army and an additional 150,000–200,000 men for the Ministry of Munitions. Two-and-half 'million men of military age' still remained 'in Civil life', so Robertson saw 'no reason why ... the men should not be forthcoming'. The only possible solution, he wrote, was 'national service'. Military conscription had to be paired with industrial compulsion so as to 'introduce some better system of utilizing the manhood of the nation'.[128]

Industrial compulsion – which was, in effect, to declare every able-bodied male of the kingdom a slave of the state – ran contrary to every ideological impulse a Liberal could possess. Asquith in particular had in previous debates over conscription explicitly forsworn any recourse to such an extreme measure.[129] But the Asquithian Liberals had repeatedly set aside ideology in the name of the war. Instead, they had far more pressing reasons to be sceptical of such a radical move: could a 'manpower dictator' truly improve the situation? Runciman thought that it would lead to 'confusion and not to efficiency', denying that there could possibly be 'any advantages that can arise from industrial compulsion'.[130] There were also political reasons to worry. The seemingly inevitable labour troubles that would ensue, Runciman warned, would be highly 'detrimental' to the war effort. The government had already had to deal with multiple strikes, including a serious one in Sheffield just that month.[131] Adding additional fuel to that fire seemed foolish and dangerous.

The gravest threat, however, would be to Britain's export industries. Within months, the resources sustaining Britain's financial campaign in the United States would be exhausted. From that point forward, there would be almost no war industry more crucial than that of ordinary British trade. Every import would have to be matched with an export. Yet the very people peddling 'industrial compulsion' as a cure to Britain's ailments were precisely the same ones who refused to take this problem seriously. Everyone agreed that Britain faced a serious manpower shortage. The premise behind the proposal, however – that there remained vast sectors of the economy devoted to pointless endeavours – seems doubtful at best. Runciman believed industrial conscription would 'hamper' his work, and no wonder: the 1.2 million men Robertson demanded would have to come from somewhere. Runciman's Board of Trade surely would bear the brunt of it.[132]

To push through these new measures, Cecil made a proposal that completely upended Lloyd George's political strategy. Knowing nothing of Bonar Law's secret negotiations, Cecil proposed a new executive 'Civil Committee', separate from the War Committee, although 'one member of the War Committee' should also be on the Civil Committee – meaning, plainly, Lloyd George. From the Conservative perspective, this proposal had considerable advantages. Lloyd George would be free to use this new committee to push through these measures, but it would give him no ability to press his own ideas about military strategy, which would continue to be carefully checked in the existing War Committee.[133] Completely unaware of Lloyd George's manoeuvres, Cecil was about to stop them dead in their tracks.

Across the Atlantic, an increasingly apprehensive Morgan's was trying to extend Britain's financial campaign a little longer into 1917. The Treasury had been frantically pitching to Morgan's every expedient it could conceive of to generate even a small amount of additional dollars – as an example, dreaming up a convoluted scheme involving trying to raise and sell commercial paper denominated in Japanese yen. (There being 'practically no market for it' in New York, Morgan's kiboshed the idea.)[134] If they were going to stave off the seemingly inevitable crash, the British needed simple old-fashioned loans, ones backed by nothing more than a simple promise to repay. Yet every indication remained that another attempt at such a long-term loan would fail.

In a creative though desperate financial manoeuvre, Morgan's planned to try to get the British these loans, albeit in a different form: offering short-term British Treasury bills denominated in dollars. That is, rather than aiming for an ordinary loan with a promise of repayment years later, the British would instead seek to raise a large amount in very short-term loans, with a promise to repay in a few weeks or months. The plan was that, as each bill became due, the British would issue a fresh one to replace it – paying off the previous lender with money from the next. Morgan's conceived of starting a juggling operation that might soon get $500 million, and perhaps even as much as $1 billion, in these short-term British loans up in the air. A fresh, billion-dollar influx into Allied finance would extend their American supply link by at least a few months. The British needed it urgently.

Yet Morgan's botched its political handling of the idea, badly. Morgan's partner Henry Davidson spearheaded the plan, and when it came to dealing with the powerful new Federal Reserve Board about the scheme, 'rather than entreating, Davidson notified'. Davison's meeting with the Board on 18 November proved three solid hours of disaster. The British blamed Morgan's for the fiasco; Morgan's blamed German-born Federal Reserve Board member Paul Warburg.[135] Yet, it is easy to see why the Board hated the plan, German-borns notwithstanding, and why even the sweetest of political approaches may not have fared any better. A billion dollars was a colossal sum, amounting to a few percentage points of US GDP. (British GDP in 1916 was about $15 billion.)[136] The Board immediately saw the danger in Britain's relying on new lenders to pay off old ones. If sentiment should shift, and the new lenders refuse to lend, US finance could be faced with a huge, sudden default. Potentially, this could even set off a liquidity crisis and pose a systemic risk to the entire American financial sector. As Warburg put it: 'While you thought you have the bull by the tail, as a matter of fact the bull had you by the tail. In this case it is *John Bull* who would have us by the tail'.[137]

It was not only the Americans who were nervous. Canada's Finance Minister observed that the 'New York Market is peculiarly subject to panic and ... is a most dangerous market in which to have afloat large liabilities in the form of short-term securities'.[138] The Reserve Board's worries were magnified by a faulty presumption that American finance *already* faced considerable exposure to this kind of short-term foreign debt, and would only discover a few weeks later that there was actually less than $250 million of it in the system. That is not to say, however, as historians have, that the Federal Reserve was wrong to be worried.[139] Increasing that sum by up to $1 billion should still have made any responsible banker nervous.

If Morgan's had taken a more tactful approach, aimed at a less ambitious target, and waited to correct the faulty presumption, the bank might have been able to get a smaller version of the scheme through and net the British a bit of extra breathing room. Instead, Morgan's unwisely decided to forge ahead, and it publicly announced the scheme on 22 November, with sales to begin in less than two weeks. Three days later, an unhappy Federal Reserve deliberated over issuing a public statement cautioning against investing too much in this kind of foreign debt. The Board took a proposed draft to the President that afternoon. Wilson wrote back, asking that it be made 'a little stronger and more pointed' and that it contain 'explicit advice against these investments ... rather than convey a mere caution'. Unmentioned went Wilson's real purpose: this statement would serve perfectly as a diplomatic warning shot across Britain's bow. Wilson wanted peace, and he had no qualms about placing financial pressure on the Allies to make it happen.[140]

The Federal Reserve issued the warning on 27 November. McKenna learned of the action the next day. The War Committee convened twice that day, with Asquith trying finally to clear Curzon's and Balfour's wretched airplane turf war from the Committee's docket. After five hours of deliberation and despite Asquith's nudging mediation, the two men obstinately refused to come to an agreement. With so many other problems pressing, Asquith was left seriously frustrated by this 'most waste of time he had participated in for years',[141] fuming to a friend that 'Ll[oyd] G[eorge], McKenna, and I could have settled the whole thing in less than an hour'.[142] At the evening meeting, however, McKenna broke in to announce 'a very serious situation arising owing to the apparent intention of the United States withholding their further financial support from the Allies'.

The War Committee immediately divided along despairingly familiar lines. Except for Balfour, the Conservatives refused to take the action seriously. Curzon dismissed it as merely a 'long-winded disquisition of advice', without much authority. Bonar Law frankly could not see what the problem was, declaring it a 'fact' that 'people who had money to lend would always be prepared to lend it in order to make a profit'. McKenna warned that the Treasury would need to get its hands on $3–$4 billion to get through the next year if they kept on spending as they were. They still had some gold and securities but nothing on the order of this phenomenal sum, and now the Americans were choking off fresh operations: 'Our finances and credit would not stand it'. Bonar Law wearisomely saw only a renewed claim that the sky was falling, accusing McKenna of tiresomely trotting out the 'same argument' that had 'come up before the War Committee on various occasions, notably about 12 months previously'.

Balfour, on the other hand, recognized the peril at once, declaring it 'the most serious matter which had come ... before the War Committee. It was infinitely more serious even than the submarine menace'. And rightly so: the submarines threatened Britain's ability to ship its imports across the Atlantic. That threat was irrelevant if they could not finance those imports to begin with. With these twin dangers of finance and submarines threatening their vital American supplies, both Grey and McKenna believed that, whether the others liked it or not, the Committee soon 'might have to consider the question of terms'.

McKenna patiently explained that they could still go on by gutting their American expenditure down to sustainable levels. But the problem of the alliance had to be dealt with: if they ended their financial support to their allies, this probably could allow them just enough American supplies to continue the British war effort at its current level 'practically indefinitely'. The diplomatic consequences of this, however, would be dire. In any case, however, they simply could not keep on providing themselves and their allies with everything they wanted at anything like the present pace. The American action meant that no further lending operations – mortgaging or otherwise – could be attempted until January at the earliest, assuming Wilson did not interfere with those as well. 'Facts must be faced', McKenna declared. 'The Allies must take stock immediately'. He asked Montagu to state how long he could go without placing any further munitions orders in America. Montagu, at this point, sprung some bad news: a British investigation of the French train network had discovered that the situation was far worse than anyone had realized. He had just been told that they needed to place a massive order for railway wagons.[143]

Without even pausing to ask how much the order would cost, Bonar Law immediately and ominously warned McKenna that 'these orders must be placed. Any cessation could offer but one alternative'. An exasperated McKenna replied frankly that he thought Morgan's would simply 'refuse further orders'. Bonar Law angrily refused to accept this. 'There could be no slackening of the pace', he declared. 'We must go on as long as we could'. McKenna explained that, yes, 'we could go on', but that 'it all depended on the *rate* at which we proceeded'. Bonar Law would have none of it, solving the problem before them with a slogan: 'We must face victory or bankruptcy', he thundered.[144]

Grey tried to explain the foreign policy context of this move. 'President Wilson', he explained, 'believed that the war could be wound up now on reasonable terms', but those terms were ones that, ideally speaking, the Allies regarded as 'unsatisfactory and inconclusive'. This financial move was, it seemed likely, designed to 'bring pressure to bear'. McKenna chimed in that, if Wilson's foreign policy was actually behind this move – hiding behind the Federal Reserve as a pretext to cut off financial support, as was in fact almost precisely the case – then 'unless President Wilson was prepared to render further financial assistance[,] we could look for no further credits in America'.[145] 'Apparently attending another meeting, or war', as historian Martin Farr blisteringly commented,[146] Bonar Law then asserted that he 'thought there was still a means by which we could retaliate upon the United States', despite the considered Committee conclusion from two months before that the British had no such options. Unusually for Lloyd George, he did not utter a single word during this whole discussion, sitting in what must have been a thoroughly disgusted silence – and leaving it to Bonar Law to realize the depth of the spinelessness they were dealing with.[147]

The Cabinet convened the next day, 29 November. Robert Cecil brought up his Civil Committee proposal and pressed for its adoption. This new committee scheme was deeply disruptive to Lloyd George's plans, and the War Secretary instead tried to argue that they should consider Lansdowne's memorandum first. Lansdowne, however, perhaps realizing the conniving political calculations behind this request – as well as the dangerous potential explosiveness that could result – intercepted this and insisted that 'whatever we do hereafter let's get our machinery organised if the present system is inefficient'. Presented with a perfectly timed opportunity to head off Lloyd George's demands, Asquith came out strongly for Cecil's proposal, and agreed that the War Committee 'must be reconstructed or reformed'. Leery though Runciman and some of the other Liberals may have been of what Cecil's proposal portended, with their chief endorsing it they swallowed whatever reservations they may have had. Lloyd George and Bonar Law could scarcely spring their secret plan on the Cabinet now, and they remained quiet as well.[148] Asquith would later report to the King that the Cabinet had adopted the proposal unanimously.[149]

The Cabinet had barely moved on from this when McKenna, who had been called out of the room, burst back into the meeting and announced that 'a financial crisis of the greatest magnitude seemed imminent'.[150]

Because of the Federal Reserve Board statement, the Treasury's greatest fear appeared to be materializing: American capital was taking flight out of London. Morgan's had burned through some $20 million on each of the previous two days, offsetting the American money being brought home.[151] The bank advised that the situation was 'very grave ... we cannot maintain this pace for even a few days'. At the same time, it pleaded its powerlessness: 'We must ask you to understand that for the time being our hands are almost completely tied'. All the British could do in the face of 'great excitement' in the financial markets was to continue shipping their available stocks of gold and pray that the quantities in hand would meet the current crisis. 'The present outlook', Morgan's warned, 'is very dark'.[152]

Fear gripped the financial authorities in London. If the capital flight intensified, the Cabinet was told, 'any panic today (business in N.Y. opens at 3 p.m. of our time) we might have to sell 100 million dollars!' This would 'exhaust all our gold there' – and leave nothing if the sell-off continued into the next day.[153] The Exchange Committee, led by the Bank of England,[154] panicked at the prospect. It urged an immediate announcement, before markets opened in New York, terminating what remained of the pound's tenuous link to the gold standard by ending the currency peg to the dollar. The Treasury blanched at the recommendation. No American, it seemed certain, would even consider participating in any future British lending operations if they resorted to such a measure. The financial consequences for Britain sustaining its allies would be calamitous: 'If we do this we gravely damage our credit and cannot finance the Allies after March next', McKenna told the Cabinet – not to mention that taking this step seemed very likely to intensify the financial panic.[155]

Lloyd George merely rolled his eyes at McKenna's alarm: 'The same fears were expressed on the outbreak of war'.[156] McKenna asked that the Cabinet resolve into the War Committee to consider the crisis; Asquith instead opted to put it in the hands of the Cabinet's 'financial experts' – himself, McKenna, and Austen Chamberlain, along with Grey 'for [the] allies', and then Lloyd George and Bonar Law.[157] The Prime Minister's calculation here is evident: the knowledgeable Chamberlain and his Conservative pedigree would stand the best shot of convincing the pair of denialists of the seriousness of the problem, assuming it could be done at all. The Committee held its nerve, ordering Morgan's to maintain the pound and to 'pay out ... to the last bean'. If the line could be held, they would hold it.[158]

At the same time, Asquith sensed the political danger rapidly building within his government. If industrial conscription at least in principle did not go through, the Conservative support upon which Asquith depended could rapidly evaporate. Asquith moved quickly. We have no evidence of his manoeuvring amongst his Liberal colleagues before the 'epoch-making'[159] War Committee meeting on the morning of 30 November, but for the measure to go through so easily we can be sure there must have been a considerable amount of it. Runciman and the Labour Party representatives were, it seems clear, told nothing in advance and purposefully excluded from this portion of the meeting, despite – or rather, because of – their opposition.[160] They would need to be consulted when it came time to turn principle into practice, but for the moment Asquith simply needed to get the principle through. In perhaps a quarter of an hour, it was done. Asquith said that he wanted legislation drafted promptly so that he could press it through Parliament before the Christmas recess.[161]

The problem of the almost inevitable Liberal and Labour backbench revolts could be dealt with later. For now, he needed to keep his Cabinet together. In a pre-emptive attempt to pacify Runciman, he moved to prevent industrial conscription from doing too much damage. Asquith carefully checked Lloyd George, who was to chair the new Civil Committee, with people the Prime Minister could count on. For the Liberals, he appointed Runciman along with Herbert Samuel, the Home Secretary. He rounded out the Committee with two Conservatives well respected by their colleagues. Asquith picked Cecil, the able Minister for Blockade, and – as one by now would expect – the economically sound Chamberlain. Cecil would be Lloyd George's only truly maximalist ally on the Committee, but Cecil at least had a reputation for intelligence and reasonableness and would be open to arguments from the other side.[162] Even so, an angry Runciman insisted on turning up at the War Committee the next day – what would be the last War Committee of Asquith's premiership – to have it 'placed on the record' that he was not present for the decision and did not agree with it. ('Quite fair', Asquith commented.) Crucially, however, Runciman would not challenge the decision, and Asquith affirmed unambiguously that industrial conscription 'had been accepted in principle'.[163]

Asquith had thus calmed any immediate risk of revolt from his right and left flanks. The Conservative ministers were still disgruntled with their Liberal counterparts for not taking these stiff measures sooner, while his Liberal wing was discontented with what these bitter pills might portend. Yet, for the moment, Asquith had made important political steps towards mollifying everyone – everyone, that is, except Lloyd George. The War Secretary was to be handed the chairmanship of a committee with significant but far from universal jurisdiction. Crucially, it excluded the matter of war strategy, and would be filled with people sure to seek to water down his measures for stiffer control and economic reallocation. It was a sensible compromise, but this was a very far cry from the coup in effect, if not in name, that Lloyd George had in mind.

With Cecil accidentally having upended Bonar Law's secret plans on 29 November, the next day Bonar Law finally had to come clean to his fellow Conservatives about his dealings with Lloyd George. Except perhaps for Walter Long, the others were startled and dismayed, and they promptly torpedoed the scheme. They did not trust Lloyd George and openly questioned Bonar Law's judgement in getting involved with the War Secretary's plotting.[164] The Civil Committee would give Lloyd George greater ability to push through additional measures of control, and Asquith had already made the monumental concession of industrial conscription. They were still uneasy with the Liberals in the government, but for the moment they had been placated. Lansdowne insisted that 'we all of us owe it to Asquith to avoid any action which might be regarded by him as a concerted attempt to oust him', and for now this view held the field.[165] Bonar Law had been trying to rebuild Conservative unity. Much as he may have been disturbed by his colleagues' attitudes, he would not override them.

That evening, then, by all appearances Lloyd George's plan was in tatters. The Cabinet had unanimously approved a rival committee scheme, the membership of which had already been appointed. Conservative support for Lloyd George's coup was almost non-existent, and it certainly seemed unlikely that Bonar Law would act independently of the others. In the Cabinet, Lloyd George practically stood isolated and alone. He had found himself in a nearly identical position in April, and then had decided to back down. A less foolhardy minister would have simply accepted that his Prime Minister had just outmanoeuvred him. There would be later opportunities to build Conservative support for taking down Asquith – after a confrontation over the Lansdowne Memorandum, for example, or if there was Liberal obstruction of his new committee, or about the Allies' American expenditure. Lloyd George instead embarked on a reckless, desperate gambit to resurrect his original plan.

Asquith's last War Committee met on Friday, 1 December. The first thing it did was dispose of the railway wagons problem. McKenna and Runciman had cooperated to come up with a scheme to get the wagons from existing British supplies instead of ordering them from America. Bonar Law grumbled that he wanted the order placed anyway – 'Would it not be wise to have a surplus to fall back upon? – but the plan went through, and this particular confrontation was defused. Lloyd George, meanwhile, reported that the Romanian capital was all but doomed to defeat, and he attacked his colleagues for not dispatching more forces there earlier. This time, the Conservatives led the pushback. Curzon warned ominously that Lloyd George was criticizing 'the military policy of our advisors' and a 'decision of the War Committee'. Asquith emphasized that there was 'no doubt of the military advice which had been given to the War Committee'. Bonar Law said flatly that 'condemnation of the Committee was condemnation of the military staff'. Lloyd George, pointedly accepting the challenge, agreed. The discussion went no further than this, but this sharply reminded the Conservatives that Lloyd George did not at all share their deference to their military advisors.[166]

Hankey found the Prime Minister 'a bit piano' during this meeting, and for good reason. Earlier that morning, Lloyd George had commenced his desperate gamble to seize control of the government. He had marched into Asquith's office with a five-point memorandum that laid out his plan to reconstruct the government and demanded that it be accepted.[167] There can be no greater evidence for Lloyd George's unadulterated contempt for the gravity of Britain's economic situation than in this act: the ambitious Welshman was plunging his country into the most paralyzing of political crises at the same time it was trying to cope with a serious financial one. Indeed, if anything, his colleagues' apprehensions about the unfolding financial crisis appears to have accelerated Lloyd George's determination to eject them from power.

With the government politically incapacitated by its War Secretary by the day's end, for the next week the responsibility for dealing with the financial crisis would fall to Morgan's, the Treasury's civil servants, and the Bank of England, who worked frantically to stem the tide. Morgan's pleaded for more gold; shipments were organized and dispatched immediately.[168] Asquith and his colleagues' decision to hold firm would prove the right choice: the crisis never escalated into the full-scale panic the Exchange Committee feared. The capital flight continued for the next week and a half, but only in a steady stream rather than the feared flood. Some $140 million would be pulled across the Atlantic before that stream finally started to dry up on 8 December, just as the government's decapitation was coming to a close.[169] The British would make it through, but the crisis left the Treasury frantic with worry: had the flight continued for another week, it could have 'cleaned us out completely'.[170] The civil servants fumed at Morgan's for the colossal screw-up. The bank's scheme to net the British $1 billion in fresh supplies had instead blown a $140 million hole in their finances – and choked off the prospect of any new lending operations of any kind anytime soon – at a time when the British could least afford it.[171] The British made it through the crisis, but the political decapitation left British decision-making paralyzed at a fraught moment: still in the throes of the financial crisis on 5 December, Morgan's demanded immediate, firm instructions regarding the exchange. The Bank of England decided it had no choice but to ignore the bank's urgent telegram. Morgan's would just have to improvise on the basis of the Asquith Committee instructions the week before. The decisions Morgan's demanded belonged not to the Bank but 'rather, with the government'.[172]

Only Britain at that moment had no government. Completely over-shadowing the financial crisis simultaneously taking place, the political one had now begun. With Lloyd George's memorandum, Asquith learned for the first time that Lloyd George intended to exclude him from the new War Committee, which would consist of Lloyd George as War Secretary, Carson as First Lord of the Admiralty, and Bonar Law as Minister without Portfolio. The Prime Minister nominally would retain 'supreme control' of the war by being able to refer War Committee decisions to the Cabinet for reversal, but it was plain that the War Committee could threaten to resign if he did so, rendering this authority effectively useless.[173]

Lloyd George refused to accept that he was insisting on a proposal that, politically, was entirely unworkable – even had Asquith been willing to accept defeat and swallow this humiliation. The risks of this particular War Committee constellation provoking several resignations of disgruntled ministers, Liberal and Conservative alike, had not diminished in the slightest. It is no accident that Lloyd George as Prime Minister would not be able to build a working coalition with a War Committee along these lines. Given a dilemma impossible for him to resolve, Asquith did his best to send Lloyd George a conciliatory reply – 'considered and not unfriendly' Crawford later called it[174] – but aside from the concession that the War Committee should be shrunk, Asquith could go little further. Pointedly, he insisted on retaining the chairmanship of the War Committee, and continued to support the decision of the Cabinet for the Civil Committee taken the day before.[175]

With his plan rejected by the Prime Minister and by most of his Conservative colleagues, Lloyd George then made the most extreme and shocking move a politician could make in a time of war and especially at a moment of crisis. He decided not only to resign, but to commit himself publicly to destroying the government by whatever means necessary. Lloyd George forwarded Asquith's letter to Bonar Law with the melodramatic message: 'The life of the country depends on resolute action by you now'. Bonar Law, realizing that this portended Lloyd George's resignation, called a meeting of his Conservative colleagues for the next day. He hoped that he could convince his colleagues to let him resign on his own so as to get out ahead of Lloyd George in the eyes of the press and of Conservative MPs.[176]

Not waiting for Bonar Law's answer, Lloyd George then sent in his reply to Asquith – through the press. He spoke extensively with the editor of *Reynolds's Newspaper*, a Sunday weekly. Whatever the paper had intended to have on its front page was hastily moved to make way for a large photograph of Lloyd George and one of the most explosive newspaper articles in British political history. Historians when referring to this article typically mention its telegraphing of Lloyd George's intention to resign.[177] But the article did far more than that: it announced that Lloyd George intended to pursue a 'campaign in the country', waging war on his colleagues, criss-crossing Britain delivering angry speeches, 'ask[ing] the people of the country to save themselves from the blunders and delays of this government'. Lloyd George would dispense altogether with the usual practice of giving a resignation statement in the House of Commons, and instead immediately would launch his public campaign to destroy Asquith's government 'in one of the largest towns of the midlands' or possibly 'in his own constituency'. From the article, it is clear that Lloyd George regarded this as no mere bluff: he still believed that Asquith would retain enough Conservative support for the present Cabinet to 'continue to carry on' and that even Bonar Law's resignation was only 'possible, though not at the moment probable'.[178]

The Conservatives that Bonar Law called together on 3 December were stunned and furious that Lloyd George could possibly commit himself to such an outrageous course of action. When Bonar Law expressed his desire to resign, the other Conservatives insisted that they would all resign as well. Only two outcomes could seem likely: either Asquith, with Lloyd George's gun pointed at his head, would capitulate to Lloyd George's terms, or Lloyd George would resign and begin his public campaign to destroy the government. Neither course could be permitted. There was only one thing to be done, whether Asquith liked it or not: Lloyd George must be forced to try to form a government. Then he would, as Curzon later explained to Lansdowne (who was not present), 'for the first time, be confronted with the difficulties of the situation. He will cease to be a merely destructive and disloyal force. He will have to make terms with the Prime Minister and with all the rest of us'. Either he would fail to form a government and be brought to heel, or he would succeed – in which case he would discover that his proposed quasi-dictatorial War Committee arrangement was completely unworkable. He would have to negotiate with Asquith and the rest of the Conservatives: Lloyd George's government would be 'dictated to him by others, not shaped exclusively by himself'.[179]

In either case, the air would be cleared. The Conservatives approved a resolution declaring that 'the publicity given to the intentions of Mr Lloyd George makes reconstruction from within no longer possible' and advising the Prime Minister 'to tender the resignation of the Government'. If Asquith was unwilling to resign, the Conservatives would make him: authorizing 'Bonar Law to tender our resignation' as a bloc.[180] Chamberlain did not even think a Lloyd George government was a possibility, telling Liberal Cabinet member Lewis Harcourt that their 'object was that by Asquith's resignation Lloyd George should be "put in his place" by Friday [so] that he could not form a Gov[ernment]'. Chamberlain assured him that 'their decision was in no way unfriendly to Asq[uith]'. Yet by either misunderstanding or design, Bonar Law failed to communicate the Conservatives' intentions to the Prime Minster – as Asquith put it, he was told only of the Conservatives' 'general dissatisfaction with the conduct of the war', and so he 'thought he was deserted by all his [Conservative] Colleagues'.[181]

Asquith met with Lloyd George to try to arrange a compromise. For a century, a key mystery at the centre of this episode has been Asquith's account of this meeting. New evidence finally gives us an answer. The Prime Minister told his Liberal colleagues the following day that he and Lloyd George had struck a deal. Asquith conceded that 'a smaller War Committee was desirable: that it ought to sit every day and twice or thrice a day and that he could not devote the time necessary for this'. As such, Lloyd George could be designated the chairman of the committee. But the chairmanship was in practice to be a kind of exalted vice-chairmanship: Asquith was to 'remain a member', he would 'attend when he could', and 'when he did he took the chair'. When he could not attend, 'the agenda [would be] submitted to him before its meeting, and its decisions afterward', and the Prime Minister would retain 'an absolute veto over all its decisions'. In exchange for this limited chairmanship, Lloyd George would drop his demands on personnel. The Prime Minister told him flatly 'that he would not dismiss Balfour and that he would not agree to a War Committee so constituted' of the people Lloyd George demanded. Lloyd George, Asquith said, 'agreed to all this and Asq[uith] thought he might proceed on those lines'.[182]

Asquith's biggest mistake was that he failed to pin down Lloyd George in writing on the spot. Lloyd George went around telling everyone not that they had struck a compromise, but that the Prime Minister had surrendered. Lloyd George told Hankey that Asquith had fully agreed to 'reconstruct[ing] [the government] on the basis of the Lloyd George plan'. The 'new War C[omit]tee is really ridiculous', a horrified Hankey wrote in his diary. '[N]o one would say that these four were the wisest heads to win the war – two are really feather heads'. Asquith, supposedly, would now defer to his War Secretary, would give up his membership in the War Committee, and had 'agreed that Ll[oyd] G[eorge] should have a free hand'.[183] Lloyd George gave precisely the same story of the Prime Minister's complete capitulation at least to C. P. Scott of the *Manchester Guardian* the next day and, apparently, to one of his subordinates at the Ministry of Munitions.[184]

Lloyd George was deliberately lying about Asquith agreeing to his demands about the personnel of the War Committee. He admitted as much, perhaps inadvertently, in his resignation letter to Asquith two days later: 'It is true', he wrote, 'that on Sunday I expressed views as to the constitution of the Committee, but these were for discussion'.[185] There is also evidence that Lloyd George was lying about the Committee's structure. It comes in the form of Carson's private recollection after the fact. Such evidence, like that from memoirs, is highly unreliable; historians should be very careful with it, and should make a general rule of excluding it when trying to understand the unfolding of specific events. In this instance, however, the fact that Carson remembers that Lloyd George confided to him precisely the opposite of what he was telling everyone else – and that this memory lines up precisely with the contemporaneous account of the Prime Minister, whom Carson despised – gives one pause. Carson recalled that Asquith at this meeting 'got all he required; that if the Prime Minister cared to attend and preside over every sitting no one could have prevented him'. Even so, as Lady Carson wrote in her diary, Lloyd George assured Carson that he was fighting for a War Committee of 'only Lloyd George, Edward [Carson], and Bonar Law'.[186]

Asquith never had any intention of giving Lloyd George his committee of Bonar Law, Carson, and Henderson. Nor should he have. The risks of his government falling apart if he had accepted this demand were as unchanged as ever. Curzon had declared that he 'could not serve under Ll[oyd] G[eorge] as dictator'.[187] Chamberlain soon would affirm that he 'certainly would not have served under such a committee'.[188] McKenna threatened to resign unless 'included in the War Council'.[189] Henry Duke, the Conservative Chief Secretary for Ireland, asserted that 'none of us [Conservatives] are inclined to say ditto to Ll[oyd] Geo[rge] *or Carson*'.[190] Hankey, believing Lloyd George's report, feared an immediately ensuing wave of Cabinet resignations from Conservatives and Liberals alike, and he worried that his own position as the Committee's Secretary was about to become very awkward: 'If they do foolish things', he wrote, 'I shall be bound to go to the P. M. about it and Ll[oyd] G[eorge] will always be suspicious of me'.[191]

The Prime Minister, however, had every reason to think that his meeting with Lloyd George had settled the matter. He had dealt with 'a "Crisis" – this time with a very big C', he wrote to a friend that night, but it now 'shows every sign of following its many predecessors to an early and unhonoured grave. But there were many wigs very nearly on the green'.[192] On Bonar Law's advice, he saw the King and secured permission to have the entire Cabinet resign pending reconstruction of the government, and released a public statement to that effect.[193]

The Prime Minister only discovered in the next morning's papers that Lloyd George had reneged on the deal they had struck. The leader in Northcliffe's *The Times* discussed Lloyd George's demands and, noting the announcement for reconstruction, speculated that Asquith had accepted them. Asquith, *The Times* said, was 'not to be a member' of the War Committee, and it implied that Lloyd George would henceforth become the *de facto* Prime Minister.[194] *The Times'* information had come from Carson,[195] but Asquith blamed Lloyd George for the article. Supposedly this 'misunderstanding' of who was responsible greatly affected the course of events.[196] But generally ignored by historians is the editorial leader that morning in the *Manchester Guardian*. Lloyd George had seen Scott before his meeting with Asquith the previous day. Lloyd George had laid out his full demands and told Scott he could write up their conversation. Importantly, Lloyd George made no move to intercept the article after he and Asquith struck their deal.

Though penned in Scott's dulcet Liberal tones, the *Guardian*'s account of Lloyd George's demands was even more explicit than the article in *The Times*. It declared that Lloyd George's handpicked War Committee of four, which would exclude the Prime Minister, 'would be in fact, if not in name, the effective government of the country', calling it a 'covert', 'fundamental redistribution of power'. Asquith, if he disagreed with the Committee, would retain only the power to refer matters to Cabinet, and even this 'could not be done often'. Even more worrisomely for Asquith, the paper gave this scheme a measure of support.[197] It seems unlikely that the Prime Minister missed the *Guardian*'s editorial; probably he believed that both newspapers' articles were inspired by Lloyd George. But that Lloyd George did not speak to *The Times* himself should not lead us to conclude that any significant 'misunderstanding' occurred. Lloyd George was delighted, not dismayed, by these newspaper articles. C. P. Scott wrote that Lloyd George '[c]ongratulated himself on "a very good press" that morning'.[198] The message Lloyd George intended to transmit through that morning's papers was precisely the message the Prime Minister received.

234   Plotting for Peace

Faced with yet another reminder of Lloyd George's bad faith and capacity for intrigue, the Prime Minister promptly sent a letter demanding that Lloyd George acknowledge Asquith's 'supreme and effective control of War Policy' and threw down an ultimatum: unless 'the impression is corrected at once that I am being relegated to the position of an irresponsible spectator of the War, I cannot possibly go on'. Asquith then briefly summarized their deal as to the structure of the War Committee – in which, unwisely, he omitted any mention of personnel or to add explicitly that he was to chair the War Committee when he attended. Asquith probably assumed that this was implicit in the demand that he have 'supreme and effective control'.[199] After all, how else could the control be either supreme or effective?

Lloyd George decided to respond by treating Asquith's ultimatum as if it had never been issued, and instead answered only Asquith's description of the new War Committee. He sent back a brief letter that ignored the ultimatum and acknowledged that he 'fully accept[ed] in letter and in spirit your summary of the suggested arrangement'.[200] Disingenuously playing the victim, Lloyd George blamed the article on Northcliffe, giving a transparently mendacious denial of not even having 'seen the "*Times*" article'. 'I have had these misrepresentations to put up with for months', he claimed with extraordinary chutzpah. 'Northcliffe wants a smash', Lloyd George wrote. 'I do not'. Pointedly, however, Lloyd George made explicit that his agreement was 'subject of course to personnel'.[201]

There is every reason to reject the sincerity of this letter. Lloyd George, it seems clear, intended to have his victory made complete or to resign. Lloyd George purposefully ignored Asquith's ultimatum to publicly correct the 'misrepresentations' in the morning's papers. When Lloyd George showed Asquith's letter to C. P. Scott, he told Scott to skip the paragraph containing the ultimatum because it 'relates to another matter and is of no consequence'.[202] That afternoon, Asquith gave a short statement in Parliament announcing the impending reconstruction of the government. 'The Prime Minister was supported by Mr. Bonar Law, Mr. McKenna, and a bench full of ministers'. Lloyd George, however, was nowhere to be found.[203] *The Times* would sum up the day's events by reporting that it 'is understood that [Lloyd George] adheres strictly to his proposals for reconstruction, which were accurately recorded in these columns yesterday'.[204] The *Guardian* would report the same, adding, outrageously, that even when the Prime Minister would attend the War Committee, 'he should not have the right of taking part in its decisions'.[205] Given that Hankey found Lloyd George's 'anteroom crowded with a mob' of journalists,[206] it seems reasonable to assume that Lloyd George inspired these reports. But even if not, Lloyd George certainly had ample opportunity to correct the record and reassert the Prime Minister's supreme and effective control. He chose to either do the opposite or do nothing at all.

Over the course of the day, Asquith took counsel from his Liberal colleagues, who were convinced that a final confrontation was inevitable. Lloyd George, gaining greater powers through manoeuvres of this sort, would surely not be dissuaded from attempting to repeat the experience. It seemed better to force matters to a head now. They advised Asquith to take precisely the same step the Conservatives had wanted him to take two days before:

We all concluded and pressed on Asq[uith] that the best way to reassert his authority and (probably) bring Ll[oyd] G[eorge] down was to resign and recommend the King to send for Ll[oyd] G[eorge] to form a Gov[ernment].

... Asquith said that for himself our suggestion of resignation was much the most agreeable, but he had to think of the country and the war and (subsidiary) the Liberal Party. I think we convinced him as to resignation but I do not feel quite sure.

The group agreed not to join a Lloyd George government, and 'it was thought that most of the Tories w[oul]d do so too'. Henderson promised Labour would stick with Asquith, while Lloyd George could command only a fraction of Liberal support. The possibility that Lloyd George might succeed was acknowledged, but the likeliest endgame seemed to be that Lloyd George would reluctantly rejoin an Asquith government and that the Prime Minister, whose 'position w[oul]d be greatly strengthened', would at long last have established some discipline over his troublesome and wayward colleague.[207] Further reassuring news came from the House of Commons that evening, as a meeting of Liberal MPs passed a vote of confidence in Asquith, although, as the *Manchester Guardian* noted, 'there were dissentient voices, some dissentient votes, and not a few abstentions'.[208]

Faced that night with Lloyd George having ignored his ultimatum for a public correction, Asquith decided that, instead of resigning, he would push forward with a middle course. Lloyd George's own creative middle course – disregarding the ultimatum but sending in an otherwise conciliatory reply – had chipped away somewhat at a suitable basis for Asquith to resign. Moreover, Asquith clearly felt a strong sense of duty not to leave office if it could possibly be helped. He decided to give Lloyd George one last chance, looking to see whether he could salvage their deal in a manner that reasserted his authority over the situation. Asquith belatedly put to paper the full details of what he believed to be his deal with Lloyd George the day before. He modified it only slightly. Lloyd George's 'chairmanship' of the War Committee had been intended in practice to be a kind of exalted vice-chairmanship, with Asquith taking the chair when he could attend. So much mischief had been made that Asquith decided that he needed to make that vice-chairmanship explicit. Instead of Lloyd George taking the title of 'chairman' of the Committee, he wrote to Lloyd George, to prevent any misunderstanding, that the title and the 'permanent presiden[cy]' of the War Committee must remain with the Prime Minister. For Asquith not to take the title of chairman would be 'incompatible with the Prime Minister's final and supreme control'. But nevertheless Asquith would need 'to delegate from time to time the Chairmanship to another Minister as his representative and *locum tenens*' – and this powerful vice-chairman, Asquith implied, would be Lloyd George. Asquith reaffirmed that Balfour must remain as First Lord with a seat on the War Committee '(as I told you yesterday)', that Carson could not join the government, and that the Prime Minister alone would decide the personnel of the War Committee.[209]

Every detail of this letter matches precisely the deal that Asquith said he had struck with Lloyd George the day before. The only difference is that, instead of being the chairman who does not chair when the Prime Minister attends, Lloyd George was to be the vice-chairman who chairs when the Prime Minister does not attend. Surely, Asquith must have imagined that, if Lloyd George meant a word of what he had said, he could not reject such a minimal amendment to their arrangement, and especially not after conceding that the Prime Minister must retain 'supreme and effective control' of the war. At the very least, this step would clarify once and for all where he and Lloyd George stood.

Lloyd George in the morning turned the tables, sending in a reply portraying Asquith's minor alteration as a complete repudiation. After having spent the whole of the previous two days undermining the bargain that they had struck, Lloyd George now accused the Prime Minister of being the one who had reneged entirely on their accord. 'Today you have gone back on your own proposals', Lloyd George wrote censoriously. This, he asserted, gave him no choice but to resign.[210] Lloyd George twisted Asquith's conciliatory firmness into proof of 'indecision and vacillation'.[211] Asquith had agreed, Lloyd George wrote, that the 'executive functions' of the war should be 'left to others', then reversed himself, then agreed to it, and now reversed himself again. Lloyd George selectively quoted Asquith's letter the previous morning, carefully omitting the passage containing Asquith's ultimatum. Lloyd George actually had the gall to claim that '[y]ou yourself proposed that I should be the [War Committee] chairman … though as you know I never put forward that demand'.[212] (Lest there be any doubt, Montagu records that on 2 December Lloyd George had 'insist[ed] upon the Chairmanship of the War Committee'.)[213] Lloyd George then continued with a lengthy diatribe against Asquith, accusing him of 'delay, hesitation, lack of forethought and vision'. He declared he would follow through on his threat to launch a campaign in the country and to wage war on the Prime Minister. 'It is my duty', he wrote, 'to leave the Government in order to inform the people of the real condition of affairs and give them an opportunity before it is too late to save their country from a disaster'.[214]

Even though it was not in the least clear what would happen, Lloyd George was 'much happier' now that Asquith had handed him the gift of easy, albeit disingenuous, grounds for resignation.[215] Asquith wrote back, calling Lloyd George a liar in the most dignified way possible, saying that he 'could not accept [Lloyd George's] version of what had taken place between us', especially in that Lloyd George had omitted 'the most material part', that containing the ultimatum, of Asquith's letter the previous morning.[216] Asquith's catastrophic attempt to salvage their deal merely served to strengthen Lloyd George's hand. Not only had the Prime Minister allowed Lloyd George to resign first, and to resign explicitly upon the chairmanship of the War Committee, instead of upon its personnel, he had gifted Lloyd George a set of politically powerful accusations. The truth of the matter, of course, was irrelevant.

In the aftermath of this disaster, Asquith's Liberal colleagues continued to advise immediate resignation. Liberal Cabinet member Lewis Harcourt fumed that Asquith 'did *not* resign last night as we advised him'. Now Lloyd George 'will appear to the public to have compelled Asquith's *later* resignation. Asq[uith]'s delay [is] very foolish and unintelligible'.[217] Asquith decided to probe Conservative intentions before making any final decisions. At three o'clock in the afternoon, Asquith summoned to a crucial meeting the three Conservatives besides Lansdowne and Balfour that he felt would be most likely to support him against Lloyd George – Curzon, Cecil, and Chamberlain.[218] The three, however, refused to continue in office without Lloyd George and 'press[ed] him to resign in order to counter the Ll[oyd] Geo[rge] manoeuvres', as Asquith put it to his Liberal colleagues a couple of hours later. Moreover, while the three of them were not willing to serve under Lloyd George's proposed 'dictatorship', they would not promise they would decline, under any circumstances, to serve under Lloyd George.[219]

Balfour, meanwhile, had been ill for most of the crisis. Around midday, he wrote to Asquith admitting that he could 'collect no very complete idea of what has been going on'. The idea that he did have, however, was that the crisis was all about the machinery of the War Committee and Lloyd George's wish to have Balfour removed from it. Believing that it had been decided that Lloyd George was now to be the 'working chairman' of the War Committee, Balfour was more than willing to put his ego aside and resign. Asquith immediately sent over his letter to Lloyd George of the previous evening. Balfour wrote back, again seeming to think that Lloyd George only wanted control over the 'day-to-day work of the War Committee'. Balfour was inclined to let him have it. Otherwise, Balfour feared, Lloyd George might resign, and this would cause the profound 'misfortune' of a 'break-up of the government'. It seemed worth giving Lloyd George's proposed machinery a try. Going on with the existing War Committee arrangements had now become politically impossible. 'We cannot, I think, go on in the old way. An open breach with Lloyd George will not improve matters'. If the government was to be preserved, Balfour believed, he had to give way.[220]

Asquith told his Liberal colleagues of his meeting with the Conservatives, and read them Balfour's letters. As Harcourt exclaimed, 'Balfour did not seem to realize the exact position!' Asquith continued to hesitate to resign: he feared 'the great division which would occur in the country and the impression [it would have] on the Allies (and enemies)'. Harcourt told him bluntly that

'by not resigning last night and writing your letter to Ll[oyd] G[eorge] you have allowed *him* to get in first with his resignation and now you will follow as if *yours* was the result of his; but yours must come and must come tonight and be in tomorrow's papers. You cannot contemplate going on without the 11 [Conservatives] and Lloyd George – with only a Liberal rump: argument is out of the question'. All my colleagues agreed with me, and pressed the same view on Asq[uith].

The calamitous past twenty-four hours, moreover, had significantly shifted the political winds. Most of those at the meeting now 'believed that Ll[oyd] G[eorge] would try to form a gov[ernment] and would succeed in getting something together though it might be a scratch affair'.

In the middle of the meeting, Curzon arrived at Downing Street armed with a fresh resolution from the Conservative ministers insisting on Asquith's resignation. Asquith told him that his Liberal colleagues had reached the same conclusion.[221] Asquith went to the King and resigned. Three questions remained: Would Lloyd George be able to get the Conservatives behind him? Would he be able to get the Labour Party to defect? And, finally, what level of support would Lloyd George be able to command within the Liberal ranks?

Convention dictated that the outgoing Prime Minister advised the King as to who next should be invited to form a government. Convention also dictated that the leader of the other largest party ought to have the right of first refusal. The King, on Asquith's advice,[222] first sent for Bonar Law and asked him to attempt to form a government. Bonar Law declined, and advised the King to send for Lloyd George. The King, who was 'intensely indignant' about Lloyd George's behaviour and regarded him as a 'blackmailer', wrote in his diary that the loss of Asquith would be 'a great blow to me, and will I fear buck up the Germans'.[223] He also worried that, if he invited Lloyd George to form a government, Lloyd George would immediately try to have him dissolve Parliament and call a general election. The King sought emergency legal advice as to whether constitutionally he could refuse. The reply was that only an *actual* Prime Minister and not merely a 'possible Prime Minister' could advise the King to dissolve Parliament.[224] So at least until Lloyd George succeeded in forming a government, the King not only could but should ignore any demand for an election.

Rather than immediately inviting Lloyd George to form a government as convention dictated, the King decided instead to convene a conference of party leaders. The King even wondered whether he should 'perhaps take a more active share in the Gov[ernmen]t of the country'; Hankey urged the King's chief advisor against it: 'The War outlook was so doubtful from a financial and economic point of view that ... the King ought on no account to take a hand, though I added that I wished he could'.[225] At the conference of party leaders, Bonar Law asked Asquith if he would serve under him, or potentially under Balfour, as an alternative to a Lloyd George government. Asquith refused.[226]

The King was then obliged to invite Lloyd George to form a government. Lloyd George gave Carson the Admiralty, as promised, but unsurprisingly he found his original plans for personnel unworkable. Bonar Law, in addition to a seat on the War Cabinet, finally got the office to match his station and became Chancellor of the Exchequer. But to get the establishment Conservatives united behind him, Lloyd George had to renege on his promises to Carson and keep him out of the new 'War Cabinet', a humiliation that Carson decided to swallow. Instead, he was replaced by Curzon and by Lord Milner, a leading Conservative not part of the previous coalition. This satisfied the other Conservative leaders that they would be the ones who would control Lloyd George, and not the other way around.

Balfour was offered and accepted the Foreign Office, to Grey's profound 'relie[f]'. A dramatic speech by Lloyd George and a sizeable increase in allotted government posts, including a new Ministry of

Labour, won over most Labour MPs. A number of Liberals defected to support the new coalition. Lloyd George had cobbled together a government that could command a majority in the Commons. On 7 December, Lloyd George kissed hands at Buckingham Palace as Prime Minister, while Asquith assumed the leadership of the opposition.[227]

Both contemporaries and historians have roundly criticized Asquith for his refusals to serve under Bonar Law, Balfour, and Lloyd George. The claim made by Asquith confidant Lord Crewe that these decisions were made not out of any 'amour propre'[228] have been dismissed as virtually farcical.[229] To be sure, Asquith's ego had been bruised and battered over the past few days. Yet these criticisms of Asquith's refusals to participate seek to divorce Asquith's refusals from the *terms* under which Asquith and the other Liberals would take part in those governments.

From the beginning of the coalition, even though Asquith had deprived the Conservatives, with the exception of Balfour, of any the great offices of state, Asquith had always run the coalition on the principle of consensus. Asquith's distrust of the Conservatives' abilities and intentions left him certain that it was for good reasons that the Foreign Office and the Exchequer should be in Grey's and McKenna's charge. Yet even though they had been excluded from major office, Bonar Law, and later Curzon, had been carefully included in the War Committee, even though they only held the relatively minor offices of Colonial Secretary and Lord Privy Seal. Under Asquith, important decisions were always made collectively, with cross-party approval. Asquith strived genuinely to preserve national unity. But precisely the *point* of Lloyd George's scheme was to exclude Asquith and the main body of Liberals from a significant role in the decision-making. Whatever offices the Asquithian Liberals could have negotiated if they stayed, any Lloyd George government would be constructed so as to try to deprive them as much as possible of access to the levers of power. It also seemed likely that Lloyd George might move to have them expelled at the earliest possible moment. As Harcourt put it, they risked in 'a few weeks be[ing] forced out by Ll[oyd] G[eorge] and Northcliffe and [would then] be in an even worse position than today'.[230] Unsurprisingly, Asquith and the other Liberals concluded that, under such terms, they could do more good from the ranks of the opposition. There, at least, they would have the ability to speak out, to influence the government through criticism or the threat of it, and to provide a credible government-in-waiting should the worst should come to pass.

Accounts of Asquith's premiership have too frequently divorced the performance of his coalition from the difficulty – one might say impossibility – of his task. Preserving national unity for as long as he did required skill and finesse, and these Asquith possessed in abundance. To be sure, he had his faults. By all accounts, he was tired and worn down by the length of his time in office, as well as his own personal tragedy. He had good reasons for allowing his colleagues wide latitude to speak their minds during meetings, yet he possessed more than enough tact to have held a firmer grasp on the reins without alienating them.

Still, Asquith stood in the middle of a balance. To keep men like Curzon and Runciman in the same government for over a year and a half is no mean feat. The disagreements within the government were numerous; the tension put upon the coalition was extreme. Yet Asquith held them together through tactful skill, conciliating compromises, and his ability to inspire personal loyalty. It is difficult to imagine anyone else – certainly not Lloyd George – occupying Asquith's fragile position and succeeding even half as well.

Even unto his final days in Downing Street, there were few in the government who preferred to turn him out. To be sure, the Conservatives found themselves angered and impatient by the Liberals' economic approach, and they were dismayed by Grey's and others' willingness to consider a negotiated peace through American mediation. Yet while they cheered Lloyd George's enthusiasm for a maximal war effort and his determination to fight for a 'knock-out blow', they regarded his ideas about military strategy with suspicion. Above all, he inspired such great personal mistrust. As Chamberlain put it: 'I take no pleasure in a change which gives me a chief whom I profoundly distrust', calling Lloyd George a man 'who doesn't run crooked because he wants to, but because he doesn't know how to run straight'.[231] Cecil's solution – giving Lloyd George greater power over the domestic economy, but not over the conduct of the war itself – was broadly preferred compared with elevating him over Asquith. On 1 December, the risk of a spontaneous Conservative revolt was at its lowest ebb in some time. The Liberals' acceptance of industrial compulsion and of a Civil Committee under Lloyd George went a long way towards assuaging Conservative discontent. Had Lloyd George felt obligated to act in concert with, rather than independently of, the Conservatives who would come to dominate his government, his coup certainly would not have come when it did. It may never have come at all.

Lloyd George's coup was certainly brilliantly executed. His campaign of deceit succeeded in keeping the Prime Minister entirely off-balance throughout the crisis. Lloyd George's use of the press to achieve his own objectives was certainly formidable. Yet few ministers in history have been willing, in time of war, to leak so violently against their own government. No doubt Lloyd George believed that the ends justified the means, but even so, his depth of determination to stop at nothing to seize power is breath-taking. Lloyd George was perfectly willing to destroy his party and divide his country in the pursuit of his ascendency atop the British war machine. The public declaration of an influential minister of his intention not only to resign, but then, as the government tries to fight a war, to stump across the country bitterly attacking that government in a bid to force its collapse, is simply without historical analogy. Hankey condemned Lloyd George's plan of action as a grave betrayal of the national interest: if Lloyd George carried out his threat to 'stump the country with hysterical speeches', he would 'give away an enormous lot to the enemy, encouraging him beyond measure, and every sort of national unity will be broken'.[232]

Asquith made a number of mistakes throughout the crisis, almost all of which stemmed from his willingness to trust what Lloyd George told him. These mistakes likely cost him his premiership. Had Asquith resigned immediately on the publication of the *Reynolds's Newspaper* article and tarred Lloyd George with the outrageousness of his planned course of action, this dramatic manoeuvre may well have succeeded in bringing his troublesome subordinate to heel. Instead, the expert conciliator tried to negotiate a settlement, and he let himself be duped into thinking he had succeeded. He should never have allowed Lloyd George to leave the room on 3 December without a full written record of their compromise. This mistake allowed Lloyd George to spread a false account of that meeting. It seems reasonable to surmise that Lloyd George was purposefully seeking to set up a resignation scenario, intending to accuse Asquith of reneging on a deal that the Prime Minister had never agreed to. Asquith's subsequent attempts to salvage that deal could not have better played into Lloyd George's hands.

Despite the viciousness of the coup, even as Asquith moved into opposition, he remained committed to doing what he could to maintain Liberal and national unity. Over the next two years, he would steadfastly refuse to criticize Lloyd George. Only on one occasion, and with good reason, would he challenge Lloyd George's leadership in the Commons; the Prime Minister successfully turned back the criticism with 'distortions and bald-faced lies'.[233] Lloyd George rewarded Asquith's efforts to preserve national unity by, as soon as Allied military success in 1918 ensured his own personal popularity, beginning to draft plans for a general election before the fighting had even stopped, and then watching gleefully as Asquith and his supporters were immolated at the polls.[234]

Asquith's dramatic fall from power in December 1916 ended any chance of the British government endorsing a negotiated peace or dealing with the country's hazardous economic trajectory. Bold moves for peace would take place only days after his ejection from office. Without Asquith and his Liberal followers in the government, there was no chance of these moves being taken seriously. Amongst the realists, only Balfour, Hankey, and Chamberlain remained. Balfour secretly would do his best to keep the possibility of a negotiated peace alive. None of these, however, had the power to force Lloyd George to alter course. Britain was hurtling towards the most crucial turning point of the war, and the men who realized its gravity had abruptly been left powerless.

In the end, then, what did Lloyd George actually think? Historian Brock Millman – focussing almost exclusively on military grand strategy, and generally ignoring politics – contends that by the time Lloyd George took power he had already given up achieving anything resembling a total triumph in the war. He argues that when Lloyd George spoke of 'victory' he was merely employing a tortured and 'eccentric' definition of the term. From the moment the new Prime Minister took office, Millman says, he was already angling for a favourable negotiated peace through military action in the east – what would become the 'New Eastern critique' in 1917–1918. Yet Millman entirely ignores the 'knock-out blow' interview and Lloyd George's continuing efforts to defend it over the following months.[235] As one observer noted at the time, Lloyd George irrationally seemed to combine the gloomiest 'view of the condition of the war with the most extreme view of the victory to be aimed at'.[236]

For Millman to be right, the 'knock-out blow' must have been nothing more than cynical and perverse politicking at work. Was it all, then, merely a mendacious political strategy to undermine Asquith – to detach the Conservatives from him and seize power for himself – all the while not believing a single word of it? Lloyd George was an intensely ambitious, power-hungry man. Yet Lloyd George was also a politician with a tendency to shoot from the hip, and the idea of him secretly and patiently pursuing such a strategy over three months seems doubtful at best. Nor is there any evidence to support this contention.

Is Millman wrong about the timing, then? Had Lloyd George become convinced that complete victory was possible in the autumn and early winter, and did his pessimism only resume sometime in early 1917? To be sure, there was an element of the arrogance of power in Lloyd George's gloominess. Like many ambitious men, Lloyd George fell prey to the conceit that *if only I were completely in charge, I could set everything right*. Lloyd George certainly believed that if he could get the troublemakers out of his way, he personally could fix many of the serious problems ailing the British war effort. The whole war on the home front could be easily fixed with a vigorous expansion of government powers and a reallocation of the British economy, along with unlimited spending in the United States.

At the same time, however, Millman is certainly right that, when it comes to military grand strategy, Lloyd George's ideas were hardly likely to see Allied armies marching triumphantly deep into German territory. Lloyd George had more or less given up on the Western Front, and the main purpose of the operations in the east that he favoured could only be to improve the Allies' position at the bargaining table, not to destroy Germany as a great power. Did Lloyd George simply overestimate the effectiveness of his own ideas about military strategy and their ability to deliver results? It is possible. Lloyd George was by no means plagued with self-doubt or lacking in confidence in the efficacy of his own ideas.

It is easy to lose sight of the fact that the conflict over the Lansdowne Memorandum was, in many ways, a conflict over the trustworthiness of the United States – or, more specifically, the trustworthiness of Woodrow Wilson and Colonel House. Even though both men's names go unmentioned throughout the debate, Lloyd George was well aware that, so long as Grey remained in charge of diplomacy, any peace would be negotiated under the auspices of American mediation. Grey made this abundantly clear in his 27 November memorandum – this despite ample decrypts from Room 40 and MI1(b) seeming to show Washington conspiring with Berlin. Lloyd George had certainly seen enough to conclude that the Americans could not be trusted. Indeed, the next chapter shows conclusively that Lloyd George's decrypt-fuelled paranoia of the United States had become serious in the extreme. Yet it was precisely *through* the United States that Grey hoped to obtain what he had earlier called 'a decent peace'. If one accepts the premise that any peace negotiated directly with Germany would be to accept an Allied defeat – and if one rules out American mediation as a reliable means of escaping this defeat – then a call to carry on the war is all that remains.

One can reach a convincing middle ground by viewing the 'knock-out blow' as an exaggerated metaphor. Robertson, after all, embraced the phrase, yet his conception of Allied victory would be when they pushed Germany back 'inside its pre-war frontiers' and forced it to 'surrender a certain portion' of its fleet. He was perfectly willing to have a post-war continental balance that included a 'strong Central European power', rather than to crush Germany entirely.[237] Hankey wrote that on 9 November he told Lloyd George that 'the best I had ever hoped for at any time was a draw in our favour, and a favourable peace extorted by economic pressure'. Instead of disagreeing, Lloyd George simply replied: 'We are going to lose this war'.[238]

Lloyd George probably overestimated the ability of his premiership to produce results, but at the same time almost certainly considered the term 'knock-out blow' to represent something well short of Allied troops marching victoriously into Berlin. A negotiated peace, on terms favourable to the Allies, made obtainable through Allied military progress – and, pointedly, not through American diplomacy – it seems, had become Lloyd George's vision of the knock-out blow.

8   Peace Moves

December 1916–January 1917

Though their ejection from office seemed in every sense a 'cataclysm', as Asquith put it,[1] he and his Liberal allies could only go on with a sense of betrayal and dread. In effect, it was now the firmly established economic policy of the British government that the United States would be in the war before the summer. It was now also the settled policy of the British government to think that this was not, in fact, their policy. Lloyd George's new 'War Cabinet', as he styled it, made no preparation for the alternative. Spending in the United States went on unchecked. Britain's allies were given no warning that the vast American spigot on which they depended could suddenly be switched off. No preparations were made for a sudden wind-down of their American purchases to prevent a potentially war-ending financial crisis. Any kind of engineered landing, hard or otherwise, was off the table. So complete was the government's refusal to engage with this problem that most historical accounts of Lloyd George's premiership ignore it entirely.[2] Yet if the Americans did not oblige Britain's new twin policies of dependence and delusion, the allies of the former Prime Minister had reason to believe that the melancholy responsibility of dealing with the seemingly inevitable catastrophe might well be returned to them. And so they took up the mantle of the opposition, fearing the events that might return Asquith to office and hoping that they would not come to pass.

As the Christmas season of 1916 opened, the armies on the Western Front were settling into their winter holding patterns. The slaughter on the Western Front slowed; the possibility of peace moves hung palpably in the air. Within days of Lloyd George's triumph, an overture burst forth from Berlin. Within days of that overture, the note that had been slowly winding its way together on Wilson's desk at last sprung across the Atlantic. With Asquith and his followers relegated to the opposition benches and pro-negotiation Conservatives like Lansdowne and Crawford[3] pointedly excluded from taking part in the new government, the window for any favourable British response to these moves had abruptly slammed shut. The British leadership debated only tactics, not policy, in deciding how to answer these peace overtures. While Bonar Law's new responsibilities as Chancellor opened his eyes and gave him a wobble, he did little to head off the impending crisis: his denialism merely gave way to ineffectual cowardice. Only Balfour in the new government took action to respond to the reality of the situation, secretly using his new post at the Foreign Office to try to keep open the option of American mediation. Lloyd George and his new War Cabinet gave no especially earnest consideration to either note's substance and merely sought how best to manoeuvre around them. But the Americans' determination to force a settlement was growing, and Britain's time for manoeuvre was starting to run out.

Though the War Cabinet's course was fixed, the two fathers of the House-Grey Memorandum sought in vain to keep the ailing pact alive. In the waning days of his tenure at the Foreign Office, Grey had drafted a Cabinet memorandum that tried to resurrect the agreement. This memorandum was – or, more precisely, would have been – an effort to breathe new life into the Anglo-American pact by placing it in the hands of the Cabinet, instead of the War Committee. Most of Asquith's Cabinet would have learnt about the existence and text of the agreement for the first time. The pact would very likely have found new friends: Lansdowne, Crawford, Runciman, and some of the lesser Liberal lights. The agreement had been kept from the full Cabinet for a reason: if it leaked, the consequences could well have been dire. To get it reconsidered, Grey was now prepared to take this risk. It is unclear whether he had cleared the memorandum with Asquith before he wrote it, but in light of their good working relationship and Grey's general lack of a reputation for engaging in underhanded intrigue, it seems more likely than not that he had. This action was being taken, however, without the permission of Asquith's War Committee as a whole.[4]

    This memorandum has always been misunderstood, with the platitudes Grey uttered for the sake of Asquith's coalition mistaken for Grey's actual opinions.[5] Grey had been part of an intended month-long Anglo-French mission to Russia that, until Lloyd George made his dramatic manoeuvres to take down the government, had been shortly due to leave. Grey intended to have this memorandum distributed on his departure. Using his voyage as an excuse, Grey pretended that he was 'not raising the question of mediation now', but was 'submitting this paper to my colleagues only because I shall be ... out of touch with them for so long'.[6]

    This explanation that Grey hides behind fails to make the slightest bit of sense. Asquith's War Committee had been well aware of the House-Grey Memorandum all year. Grey's departure would not cause that knowledge to disappear magically from that body. There was no sudden need to inform the entire Cabinet. For all of Grey's platitudes about working towards the 'defeat of Germany', plainly designed to reassure Conservative opinion, the crux of it came to this: 'What I fear most', Grey wrote,

is that one of the Great Allies, when told, *as they ought to be told now*, that our support in shipping and finance, one or both, has to be curtailed in a few months, will abandon hope of ultimate victory, and demand that the war be wound up on the best terms available ... we cannot force the Great Allies to continue the war against their will, or beyond their strength. And if their action makes peace inevitable before Germany is defeated, then I would submit that the intervention of President Wilson – (if it is still available in the spirit described) – should be seriously considered.

Britain's alliance lay at the centre of Grey's worries. Even as McKenna had sought to impose a degree of spending control and get the Allies to put their gold to use in America, no one had let loose the secret to their allies that the American spigot on which they depended would soon be drying up. It was now time, Grey believed, for Britain to have a frank conversation with its friends. Peace moves during the winter lull in fighting seemed inevitable. Britain, Grey believed, had a duty to let its allies know the true state of affairs beforehand. If any of them then decided it was time to accept a peace overture, the British could not stand in the way – and American mediation then still could be pulled off the shelf.

He included the text of the House-Grey Memorandum so that his Cabinet colleagues could make up their own minds. Grey had devised what would have been an effective way of giving the pact a new lease on life while trying to minimize the immediate political danger to himself or Asquith's coalition.[7] Still further evidence of Grey's support of Lansdowne's memorandum comes in a letter from Grey to Lansdowne on 6 December 1916. Curiously, historians have never located this letter in Lansdowne's papers, but in an article in 1934 Lansdowne's son cited it to support a statement – likely over-interpreted, but nevertheless indicative of Grey's positive attitude – that 'the Foreign Secretary (Lord Grey) was about to ask for a secret session of the House of Lords for the purpose of [the Lansdowne memorandum's] discussion'.[8]

Yet Grey's calculations and plans, along with any new potential friends the House-Grey Memorandum might have found, were all swept away with Lloyd George's destructive tide. Suddenly ejected from office, Grey was reduced to meekly forwarding his memorandum to Balfour and

Cecil. 'What has occurred this week', Grey wrote gravely, 'makes me feel that the matter dealt with in the paper is likely to become more and not less important'.[9]

House's carefully crafted letter to Grey from late November, implicitly renewing the terms of the House-Grey Memorandum, arrived a couple of days later. Grey promptly forwarded it to the Foreign Office, calling special attention to the fact that it 'indicate[s] clearly that the President will adhere to his previous attitude'.[10] Cecil gave Grey the courtesy of apprising Lloyd George of these messages, which the Prime Minister appears to have ignored entirely.[11]

Grey's efforts in London were mirrored by House in America. Just as Lloyd George was succeeding in putting his government together, the Colonel petitioned his President for permission to send a letter to the new Prime Minister reminding him of their extraordinary February conversation. He wanted to urge Lloyd George to have 'the courage and the force to do great things' and work to end the war. Wilson, however, was content to allow the pact to pass into history. 'We cannot go back to those old plans', the President told his friend. 'We must shape new ones'.[12]

As for Wilson's own note, almost as quickly as Wilson had made up his mind to follow House's counsel of delay did he change it, on an evening replete with symbolic meaning. The Statue of Liberty had its inaugural illumination on 2 December, transforming it from a distant, night-time shadow into a resplendent emblem of freedom's march into the darkness. Before, a small light in her torch served as a little beacon for shipping in New York's harbour; now, at Wilson's command aboard the presidential yacht *Mayflower*, surrounded by a squadron of powerful American battle-ships, *Liberty Enlightening the World* lit up radiantly against the night sky. (A night that almost encapsulates Wilson's entire presidency: someone had forgotten to invite New York's congressional delegation, who were left seething that the local organizers 'lack[ed] all knowledge of what is usual or proper'.)[13] Under the glow of Lady Liberty, Wilson spoke with Ambassador Gerard, still home from Germany and amongst the invited dignitaries aboard the *Mayflower*. Gerard advised immediate action on a peace note and left Wilson convinced, as he put it to House the next day, that 'if we are going to do the proposed thing effectively we must do it very soon'. But between his trip to New York and his State of the Union address on 5 December, the presidential agenda that week did not offer Wilson much time for quiet diplomatic contemplation. Then, with the political crisis in Britain, it must have seemed useless to move forward until the dust had settled.[14]

21 The illumination of the Statue of Liberty, drawn by Charles Graham
(Photo by © CORBIS / Corbis via Getty Images)

Little Belgium added to the pressure for a brief delay. In mid- and
late November, amidst a world outcry, King Albert had asked Wilson,
the Pope, and the King of Spain to intervene diplomatically and object to
a new German policy of deporting Belgians into Germany and forcing
them to labour for the German military machine.[15] Though hesitant to
get involved, Wilson acceded to the request, firing off a strong protest.
Wilson complained to Berlin that he wanted to move for peace but was
'repeatedly distressed to have his hopes frustrated by such unhappy
incidents as the sinking of the *Marina* and the *Arabia*' – Germany had
also recently sunk two ships it ought not to have – 'and the Belgian
deportations'. Exasperatedly, Wilson wrote that he 'is now earnestly
desiring ... practical cooperation on the part of the German authorities
in creating a favourable opportunity for some affirmative action by him in
the interest of an early peace'.[16] Not until 9 December – the same day
that an intransigent public statement from Germany hit the press
defending their deportation policy and refusing even to consider
changing it[17] – did Wilson send a revised draft of his peace note to his
Secretary of State requesting comments.[18]

Wilson had told the Germans that he could not act until after the
election; a full month had now gone by and still nothing emanated from

Washington. Germany was under pressure from Austria-Hungary to seek direct negotiations, and with growing demand both inside the German government and outside it to begin unrestricted submarine warfare, Berlin decided it had waited long enough. On 12 December, Germany publicly issued its own direct peace offer, which it asked Washington to forward formally to the Allies. As historian Patrick Devlin has observed, this note had to 'be pitched high lest it be interpreted as coming from weakness', but even so the tone of the note seemed all but a trumpet call to surrender, almost needing to be seen to be believed:

[The Central Powers] have given proof of their indestructible strength in winning considerable successes at war. Their unshakable lines resist ceaseless attacks of their enemies' arms. The recent diversion in the Balkans was speedily and victoriously thwarted. The latest events have demonstrated that a continuation of the war cannot break their resisting power. The general situation much rather justifies their hope of fresh successes.

On it rambled, before jarringly shifting from jingoism to requesting direct negotiations in the very same sentence. Though Bethmann Hollweg genuinely hoped the offer would be accepted, it reads almost as if it had been designed to be rejected, not least with its grave warning that, if the offer was refused, the Central Powers would triumph victoriously 'while solemnly disclaiming any responsibility before mankind and history' for the war's continuance.[19] While still welcoming the move, even Scott's *Manchester Guardian* – which had practically rejoiced at the news of the overture before any details were released – nevertheless had its nose put rather out of joint by its pugnacious tone.[20] In an explanatory note to Bernstorff, Berlin ingeniously turned Wilson's request for 'practical cooperation' on its head: instead of Germany desisting from frustrating Wilson's peace attempts through ill-timed inhumane acts, the Ambassador was to explain that this peace note was precisely how the German government sought to best answer Wilson's call to cooperate in promoting peace.[21]

Signals intelligence gave the British some advance warning of Germany's peace note of 12 December 1916, and it may have helped to strengthen the prevailing notion that the move was a purely cynical one. On 10 December, the German government had abruptly summoned a meeting of the Reichstag for an important announcement, but observers could only guess at its purpose.[22] Grew in Berlin informed Washington – and MI1(b) – that he had heard

that the Chancellor will probably say ... that now is the time for peace and that he will give the general outline of the terms which would be acceptable to Germany.

It is not felt that this will bring any immediate result but it is intended to strengthen the hands of peace parties in Russia, England and France.[23]

Grey could not resist weighing in on this sudden diplomatic development. Again showing the centrality of their alliance in his mind, he urged his successors to let the Allies take the lead on any reply. He was adamant, however, that the Allies must be told 'the exact prospects as regards shipping and finance before a final decision is taken' – even though such an economic warning may well have led to one or more of their allies to want to accept Germany's offer.[24]

The new War Cabinet agreed on letting the Allies take the lead with the diplomatic reply, but it would give their allies no such economic warning. Certainly, the last thing to be done now was to risk frightening the alliance with pessimistic projections. At their first meeting, unsurprisingly, Britain's new masters swept their severe financial problems under the rug, squelching a proposed telegram to the Allies asking them to curtail their US orders – perhaps McKenna's final proposal as Chancellor, jointly with the Bank of England – lest such a warning cause unnecessary 'alarm'.[25] Yet having bellowed at McKenna that the British would have 'victory or bankruptcy', a crash course in international finance at the Treasury jolted Bonar Law to the very real danger that bankruptcy posed. Within two days of taking power, Lloyd George and Bonar Law now seemingly endorsed the very policy they had condemned. The War Cabinet decided that McKenna's 'policy of curtailing the orders in the United States ... should be continued without making any announcement'.[26]

This War Cabinet decision, however, did not herald the beginning of an effort to engineer a landing – hard or otherwise – in their American expenditure. Rather, it proved little more than bare lip service to the existence of the problem. Bonar Law and the War Cabinet did nothing to enforce it, and the spending departments appear to have ignored it entirely – in fact, 'new British and French orders actually peaked in December 1916', with 214 contracts with American firms signed that month alone.[27] The Allies were making pledges to pay American firms with dollars they did not have, and, unless Wilson entered the war on their side, with dollars they could not get.

Bonar Law's new responsibilities gave him enough of a jolt, however, that when the German peace note came forward he genuinely considered the possibility of its leading to a peace conference. General Sir Henry Wilson found a depressed Bonar Law 'half in love with peace proposals'. The new Chancellor confided to him precisely the same thing McKenna had said – and Bonar Law had sneered at – less than two weeks before: 'If

America liked to refuse us money and ammunition, then we *must* make peace'.[28] Lloyd George had delegated the role of Leader of the House of Commons to Bonar Law, and so it fell to the new Chancellor to make the first public comments on the overture. While necessarily circumspect, as the government still awaited the formal delivery of the note from the American Ambassador, he gave the pacific Liberal press hope when he spoke with 'simple and sober' reserve,[29] saying only that

my right hon. Friend the ex-Prime Minister ... used these words: 'They (the Allies) require that there shall be adequate reparation for the past and adequate security for the future'. That is still the policy, that is still the determination of His Majesty's Government.[30]

Besides Bonar Law's wobble – seemingly under control by the end of the month[31] – of those in the British government who favoured considering a compromise peace, only a small faction in the Foreign Office survived. The day after Germany issued its peace note, Eric Drummond, Grey's private secretary whom Balfour retained, followed up on Grey's communications with a memorandum to Cecil (Balfour was still ill) urging renewed consideration of 'invit[ing] the President of the United States to act as mediator'.[32] The recommendation, of course, was ignored.

That faction, however, had not completely given up. Certainly, they could not carry on peace diplomacy with Washington, even unofficially. With just the right person, however, they might be able to open up a back channel to the Americans. They needed someone so positioned that the Americans would not realize that he was, in fact, acting as a back channel – a person who could help keep the option of mediation open while keeping any direct link with the Foreign Office carefully concealed. British intelligence provided precisely the perfect channel in the person of Sir William Wiseman, who headed up the New York outpost of MI1 (c), the organization today known as the Secret Intelligence Service (SIS). Sporting a small moustache, round-faced, and young for his post at the age of 31, Wiseman appeared even younger still – one British politician thought he looked 'the merest boy'.[33] A baronet with a boxing blue from Cambridge, Wiseman had served on the Western Front but, after a wound left him with impaired vision, Mansfield Cumming, the head of MI1 (c), tapped him for service in America. Wiseman had been in post for a little over a year, working to thwart German operations and trying to keep an eye on groups supporting Indian and Irish independence.[34] In the final months of American neutrality, he began a relationship with House that would become the closest Anglo-American partnership of the war.

The beginning of that partnership, however, has always posed something of a historical conundrum. For six weeks, Wiseman negotiated with House about a compromise peace settlement – a subject in which, historians have contended, the British government had not the slightest interest. These historians have tried to resolve this seemingly puzzling contradiction by arguing that these talks were not, in fact, negotiations at all. Instead, they chastise a gullible House for being deceived. Wiseman, they say, acted as no emissary of the British government. Rather, a young man dissembled out of ambition, lying to House when he said that he represented the Foreign Office and whispering sweet peaceable nothings in his ear. He sought to seduce the Colonel into making Wiseman his link to the British and he succeeded: what would eventually become the strongest personal partnership in First World War Anglo-American relations, they argue, began from a meeting of purest happenstance and was subsequently exploited by a wily intelligence officer's lies.[35]

In reality, however, an unnoticed folder in Wiseman's papers proves that the seduction very much went the other way around.[36] Wiseman's link to the Foreign Office was absolutely genuine. Even with this folder, the evidence is still fragmentary, but it all points in one direction: the Foreign Office decided to quietly use Wiseman to keep alive the possibility of a negotiated peace – with the link to the Foreign Office, crucially, Wiseman was very much not supposed to disclose. Yet House would succeed in wheedling the secret out of him. The young man confessed the truth to him and then lied to his London superiors to cover up the indiscretion.

The day Germany issued its peace note, Cumming telegraphed Wiseman in Washington – perhaps with the connivance of the Foreign Office, since the telegram is pencilled with a 'D', possibly for 'Drummond' – asking Wiseman to 'do your utmost to find what is at the back of' Germany's move and to 'use utmost endeavours to discover what terms Germany is asking'.[37] Wiseman's telegram in reply, marked with pencil 'Willie to C', is a reasonably astute piece of political analysis. He wrote that the Germans sought to cause the Allies to be 'forced into peace', and estimated that Germany would be willing to evacuate France, Belgium, and Poland. He reported that Wilson was 'being strongly pressed to take steps' of his own, and that the belief that the war would inevitably end in a draw was widely held in the administration.[38]

The influenza that had taken down Balfour at the height of the Cabinet crisis had not yet fully relented. Yet Balfour attached such importance to sounding out Germany's terms that he took personal charge from his sickbed of asking Wiseman to find out. The next telegram to Wiseman on 16 December, pencilled with 'AJB', Balfour's initials, asked Wiseman to 'use House or any other prominent American to obtain details' of the terms that Germany would be prepared to offer. 'Please do your utmost to effect scoop', Wiseman was told, and to 'cable if you want money'.[39] The next day, Wiseman went to House with a letter of introduction from the British Ambassador, and on the pretence of seeing him on a 'relatively unimportant matter' left a pleasantly surprised and excited House convinced that he had just had 'the most important caller I have had for some time'.[40]

The two jointly drafted a telegram to London. With Wiseman reporting that no one on his side of the Atlantic knew what Germany's terms were, House said he could ask Bernstorff to find out – but on one condition. Lloyd George, who had been taken down with a bad cold for the past week, was scheduled to give his inaugural speech to the House of Commons as Prime Minister a few days later. House knew that Lloyd George would be expected to speak about the peace offer, and, most likely for fear of what Lloyd George might say, House asked for the speech to be postponed for just a short while longer to give him a chance to make the enquiry through Bernstorff. Once House had the terms, he would pass them to Wiseman. Wiseman warned specifically that the assurance that the speech would be delayed was essential: 'Until hearing from me he will make no move. Please understand if you wish House to try to get terms I must be able to tell him that [the] P.M.'s [speech] will be postponed'.[41] A hopeful House wrote Wilson that it 'looks as though you might soon be having the belligerents talking – at least there is hope'.[42]

House's delay demand, however, ended this quiet sounding before it had even begun. Lloyd George almost certainly knew nothing about Balfour's initiative and would hardly be willing to countenance postponing his great triumph – his first address to the House of Commons as the Prime Minister – in order to facilitate it. Balfour dropped the matter instantly, telegraphing back that the 'Prime Minister's statement cannot be postponed and in any case Secretary of State for Foreign Affairs thinks it better that no action should be taken'.[43] House had overreached in insisting on the delay, and as a consequence it would take another week and a half for him to get a request to Berlin for its terms off the ground. A contradiction stood at the centre of House's assumptions: if Lloyd George intended to speak harshly about the German offer, he would hardly be willing to postpone the speech, while if he did not intend to speak harshly, House had no need for him to postpone it. Perhaps House hoped that the mere fact that *he* had asked for it would get him the delay – because, of course, House had every right to be worried.

When Lloyd George took the floor, he poured scorn on the German offer. Taking issue with a line in which Germany asserted that its own interests were 'not in any degree incompatible' with 'the respect for the rights of other nations', Lloyd George retorted sarcastically:

When did they discover that? Where was the respect for the rights of other nations in Belgium and Serbia? Oh, that was self-defence! Menaced, I suppose, by the overwhelming armies of Belgium, the Germans had been intimidated into invading that country, to the burning of Belgian cities and villages ... to the carrying of the survivors ... into slavery at the very moment when this precious Note was being written!

'What are the proposals?' he demanded to know. 'There are none. To enter at the invitation of Germany, proclaiming herself victorious, without any knowledge of the proposals she proposes to make, into a conference, is to put our heads into a noose with the rope end in the hands of Germany'.[44]

When Lloyd George sat down, Asquith rose from the opposite bench and gave a dignified speech that was firm concerning the German note and yet lacked Lloyd George's hostility – an approach that surely would have reflected his attitude had he remained where Lloyd George sat. He challenged Germany to state their terms: 'If they are prepared to give us reparation for the past and security for the future, let them say so'. Yet, unlike the man who displaced him, Asquith remained fully aware of the perilous economic waters in which the government was sailing. 'The gigantic imports of food, munitions and a hundred other necessaries of war', he warned, remained a profound British responsibility for the entire alliance. The prospect of a 'breakdown' remained 'very serious'.

In public, Asquith tempered his remarks, assuring Parliament that there was no immediate cause for 'alarm'.[45] In private, however, Runciman fumed about Lloyd George's 'contempt for the shortage of tonnage, & the exhaustion of British credit in America'. 'Disaster', he wrote, 'will pursue us as surely as it now pursues Germany'.[46] McKenna was telling Keynes 'that peace must come soon, and all this note exchanging amounts after all to negotiation'.[47]

The pacific *Manchester Guardian* and *Nation* tried to interpret Lloyd George's speech as if it were Asquith's, arguing that the Prime Minister had not completely 'closed the door to peace' (though admitting the signs were 'not encouraging').[48] In reality, however, the War Cabinet had already, and wrongly, deemed the peace note 'disingenuous', with Lloyd George leading the charge. Yet that body disagreed about whether or not the Allies should respond by challenging Germany to state its terms, postponing a decision by agreeing to await further views from Paris.[49]

Unbeknownst to them, Wilson had already decided to resolve that debate for them. The President hastily redrafted his planned note and delivered it to the State Department for simultaneous dispatch to all the belligerents on 18 December. Wilson demanded that both sides state the 'precise objects' and 'definitive results' they sought. So far, both alliance blocs had proffered only glittering generalities, and 'stated in general terms, they seem the same on both sides'. He denied his overture having any connection with the German note – he was in fact 'somewhat embarrassed' by the timing – and asserted that 'he is not proposing peace; he is not even offering mediation'. Yet in addition to the 'million after million of human lives' being given up, the belligerents' quarrel had profoundly disturbed the 'life of the world' for more than two long years. The rest of the world, Wilson asserted, now deserved to know for what reasons the nations at war insisted on continuing to do so.[50]

Wilson's penchant for giving unintentional offense did not fail him. The note deeply offended almost everyone in Britain. Few could see beyond the words 'seem the same on both sides' as meaning that the President drew a full moral equivalence between Britain and its adversaries, rather than a simple observation that each side's generalities glittered so meaninglessly as to be indistinguishable. The moment House saw the note he fumed at Wilson's blunder in phrasing, correctly predicting that 'that one sentence will enrage' the Allies.[51] Even the strongly pro-American *Manchester Guardian*, while welcoming the note, initially took umbrage at the line before 'carefully read[ing]' it again and finally figuring out what the President intended the next day.[52] Only the Asquithian *Westminster Gazette* correctly understood Wilson's meaning from the beginning, with Page reporting that the 'article was directly suggested by Asquith'.[53]

Wilson's intervention offended the British public, but it enraged their Prime Minister. The intelligence he had received over the past week – selectively chosen decrypts almost certainly designed to mislead – had led him to continue his astounding misbelief that a hostile United States was actively conspiring with Germany. Two decrypts had landed on Lloyd George's desk on 14 and 15 December. The first was an incredibly incomplete Room 40 decrypt of a lengthy German telegram from Berlin to Bernstorff.[54] The lengthy original telegram, dispatched from Berlin on 9 December as an explanatory note to the German peace move, contained Berlin's ingenious turning of Wilson's request for 'practical cooperation', described above, on its head:

On the occasion of an interview with the Imperial Chancel[l]or on the 5th of December, the American Chargé representing the President made, in confidence, the following statements among others: '**What the President now** most earnestly desires is a practical cooperation on the part of German authorities in bringing about a favorable opportunity for early and affirmative action by the President looking to an immediate restoration of peace'. The Imperial Chancel[l]or answered the American Chargé d'Affaires that he was 'extremely gratified to see from the President's message that in the given moment he could count upon the sincere and practical cooperation of the President in the restoration of peace, just as the President could count upon the practical cooperation of the German authorities'.[55]

Though the overall telegram had been dispatched in Code 7500, the two passages in bold above were quotes from documents in American possession, so they would have been encoded in a different, older code, in order to protect the new code. Room 40 still had made no meaningful progress on 7500, but the older codes it had long solved. This meant that, of this lengthy telegram, Room 40 produced a decrypt that consisted *only* of the two bolded sentences above – which it mendaciously passed off to its own government as if they were two separate telegrams:

Dec. 9, 1916

Message of Mr Grew to German Government.

What the President now most earnestly desires is the practical co-operation on part of the German authorities in bringing about a favourable opportunity for early and affirmative action by President aiming at earliest restoration of peace.

Reply of German Government.

Extremely gratified to see from President's message that at given moment we could count upon sincere and practical co-operation of President in restoration of peace as much as the President can count upon practical co-operation of German authorities.

Hardinge received the decrypt in this highly misleading form, sending it on to Lloyd George with the comment: 'I enclose to you copies of telegrams received from a certain source of which I believe you are aware'.[56] Others probably saw the decrypt as well: Hall's copy of the decrypt, filed away in his folder of MI1(b) American decrypts, is marked 'To be returned', suggesting that it had been lent outside his office.[57]

A different decrypt, from MI1(b) and forwarded on by Robertson, landed on Lloyd George's desk that same day. For good measure, Hardinge would send an additional copy to Lloyd George the day after. Both rushed to get Lloyd George a copy of an MI1(b) decrypt of a confidential message that the German Chancellor sent to Washington through the US Embassy in Berlin. This decrypt no doubt also reinforced the false impression of German-American collaboration. On Robertson's copy, one particular passage of the Chancellor's message is marked for special attention:

I believe that mutual respect and good will between the nations is likely to be the (logical) aim of the President of the United States, whose recent message, in which he asked for the co-operation of the German authorities to bring about a situation enabling him to take early action in this direction, you were kind enough to deliver to me on December 5th. It is my sincere hope that this formal and solemn offer [of peace to the Allies] ... will coincide with the wishes of the President of the United States.[58]

These are the only two wartime decrypts that survive in a British policymaker's papers; all three letters ask Lloyd George to 'burn' or 'destroy' the decrypts after reading them. Although the next chapter establishes conclusively that the Prime Minister continued to receive subsequent decrypts, it is difficult to discern precisely how much was being forwarded to him. There are two possibilities, however, as to why these three *particular* letters happen to survive in Lloyd George's papers. The first is pure historical accident. The second, much likelier, possibility is that Lloyd George did not burn these decrypts because he wanted to be able to use them to demonstrate the untrustworthiness of the United States.[59]

Divorced from their contexts, these provided Lloyd George – already inclined to view American actions in the worst possible light – with seemingly ironclad proof of a devious and dangerous German-American conspiracy. When Wilson subsequently made his move, a furious Lloyd George wanted to send Wilson a strong and prompt message to mind his own business. Through Scott's friend James Bone, Lloyd George sought unsuccessfully to pressure the *Manchester Guardian*. Bone reported to Scott that Lloyd George had denounced the American note as a 'German move' and said that the British would refuse it outright. 'They *knew, absolutely knew*', Bone wrote, 'that it was put forward at the inspiration of Bernstorff and [Lloyd George] implied that America had done a deal with Germany'. Hyper-suspicious, Lloyd George angrily asserted that 'Wilson's note was meant to embarrass us' and said flatly that it was 'impossible for us to state definitely our terms just now'.[60] Even six weeks later, Lloyd George's deep distrust of Wilson had not abated in the slightest. He later told Scott that Wilson's note was a 'pro-German move' that 'was sent in fulfilment of a definite pledge given during the course of the recent Presidential election to certain pro-German Jews in exchange for cash for the Election Fund which was running very low'. 'The government', Lloyd George declared, 'had positive evidence of this'.[61]

Historian Sterling Kernek dismisses Lloyd George's vehement reaction as of 'doubtful significance': the new Prime Minister, he says, was just blowing off a bit of steam.[62] Yet Lloyd George's hostile stance fits in precisely with his attitudes over the past few months. In large part because of signals intelligence, Lloyd George considered the American leadership unfriendly, and yet he also regarded it as impotent. In Lloyd George's mind, the United States had arms to sell and money to lend. However much Wilson might pretend at rattling his sabre, the President would not dare damage his own economy by cutting down his exports. Believing this, there was no reason Lloyd George would feel any need to conceal his contempt and make a conciliatory reply.

The War Cabinet convened on 21 December to consider its answer to Wilson's note. Hankey's minutes are of little help in establishing what actually was said – his previous practice of recording each minister's remarks in near-verbatim fashion was now abandoned[63] – but the small body appears to have disagreed vehemently. A subsequent memorandum by Cecil reveals that Lloyd George had reiterated the line from his speech and argued that Wilson had 'ask[ed] us to put our heads into a noose'.[64] Whatever exactly happened, Lloyd George's desire to snub Wilson clearly ran into stiff opposition. In the end, the War Cabinet decided only to instruct Hankey to prepare a paper on Britain's dependence on the United States 'at the earliest possible date'.[65] Initially, Lloyd George even wanted it done that evening.[66] Considering that a British interdepartmental committee only two months before had considered the same subject at length, this decision of the War Cabinet only makes sense recalling the context in which that earlier committee had convened. Lloyd George evidently reviled that earlier committee's product as little more than a personal attack by his enemies that was precipitated by his 'knock-out blow' interview. With those weak-kneed ministers ejected from office, he appears to have (wrongly) expected the trustworthy Hankey to return quickly with an assessment that would validate his dismissal of Wilson's ability to damage the Allied war effort. Yet while the demand for the assessment worked as a compromise that allowed the War Cabinet to put off a decision for a short while, the document was only of marginal importance to any actual decision – even if America *could* hurt Britain, that did not mean that Lloyd George could be convinced that it *would*. When the War Cabinet reconvened two days later, none of its members had actually looked at the assessment that Hankey's office had heroically managed to cobble together. The Secretary was left spluttering in fury to his diary:

The new War Cabinet are very tiresome and exacting. They are making the mistake of 'bustle for business'. ... [Concerning the US note] I at once put on Young, the best man I had free, and by a tremendous effort he produced a very good paper, which by a great effort was reproduced and circulated. Although on Thursday morning [21 December] they had insisted that this was an essential to their discussion, when they tackled the question on Saturday [23 December], they seemed to have forgotten all about it. Not one of them had read it, and Lord Milner told me he thought they had been rather premature in demanding it! Yet this work had tremendously upset half the Departments in the Govt. and placed an almost intolerable strain on my office![67]

As the War Cabinet struggled with its response, Drummond pushed again, asking for permission to cable House to confirm whether the House-Grey Memorandum still held good. He also urged that the agreement be circulated to the War Cabinet, as Henderson and Milner, and possibly Curzon, were still ignorant of it.[68] Cecil – Balfour would not return to work for another couple of days – accepted Drummond's advice only as to the latter.[69]

Yet despite his illness, Balfour continued to quietly use Wiseman to probe the possibility of American mediation. Without the War Cabinet's permission, he evidently went ahead and asked Wiseman to approach House. Wiseman telegraphed back on 22 December, although, because Balfour's original cable is missing, it is somewhat unclear precisely what he means. House, Wiseman wrote,

to whom I deprecated the proposal, has positively assured me that the attitude of the Administration towards Britain has not changed from that which he explained to Balfour in February. I cable you as Balfour is reported absent.[70]

It is not entirely clear who the 'you' is that Wiseman is cabling – Drummond, probably. Nor is it clear what 'proposal' Wiseman 'deprecated'. It might refer to the House-Grey Memorandum, but it seems unlikely that Wiseman would have been privy to that secret. The most reasonable interpretation is that Wiseman had been asked whether the Americans still adhered to the attitude that House had explained 'to Balfour in February', probably without an explanation of what that meant, and House confirmed that they remained willing, also without explaining to Wiseman what that meant.[71] Nothing became of this. The House-Grey Memorandum had finally breathed its last.

At the Saturday meeting, the War Cabinet remained far from united. Those who favoured giving the United States a direct answer, however, made progress in convincing Lloyd George. Regardless of whether the United States was hostile or impotent, Britain could still state its aims in a way that would be to its advantage. To explore this, Cecil was to put together a 'preliminary draft' reply to the US note in this vein and to inform the Russians that Britain, though still non-committal, was starting to lean in this direction.[72]

A brief diplomatic lull in London took place over Christmas. An Anglo-French conference in London had previously been scheduled for 26–28

December, and matters would be decided there. Grey had believed Britain owed a frank financial warning to its Allies, whatever diplomatic consequences might result. Bonar Law, by contrast, the only one in the War Cabinet now grasping the Allies' economic problem, chose to demonstrate the rawest possible political cowardice. Evidently unable to endure the embarrassment of admitting he had been completely wrong for the whole of the past year, he refused to confront his colleagues with the seriousness of the situation. The War Cabinet still happily ensconced in its delusions, the chance of it authorizing such a warning to the Allies was zero.

In theory, this Anglo-French conference was to be an economic one. It had been decided on at the very first War Cabinet meeting.[73] This could have been a pivotal moment in the history of the war: if there was ever a moment for the British to be honest with France about the severity of the situation and about the imminent need for drastic American cutbacks, now was it. Instead, most of the conference was spent discussing Wilson's note and the military situation. Finance was left until the very end, as if a mere afterthought, and the only important French politician asked to stay for the discussion was the French Finance Minister. Bonar Law did nothing more than to ask him to help out by shipping another $100 million in French gold to the United States – a sum that, even had France been willing to provide it, paled insignificantly in comparison with the billions required to sustain their American supply link through 1917. Bonar Law's argument to the French shows that he understood the problem: 'The President of the United States', he told them, 'might use the inability of the Allies to pay in gold to enforce peace'. But McKenna had doubted that their allies would be willing to ship any more gold, and he was right. The French Finance Minister refused, while at the same time pointedly warning the British that they needed 'to buy freely in the United States'. He also asked for additional help financing French purchases of British coal; Lloyd George told the Treasury to consider it. On that brief note, the Minister headed back to Paris. The record of the conference's conclusions fail even to mention finance.[74] Though Bonar Law evidently now understood something of the Allies' economic problem, he was completely unwilling to confront either the rest of the new British leadership or their allies with the gravity of it. Instead, he timidly pleaded for trifles, and he could not even get that. Disaster was on their doorstep, and yet denial remained the order of the day.

A couple of days earlier, Berlin on Boxing Day had unexpectedly handed the Allied conference an especially genial diplomatic gift: an outright rejection of Wilson's note. Though the Germans tried to give it the friendliest possible tone, they nevertheless refused to disclose their terms, insisting a direct peace conference amongst the belligerents was the only way forward.[75]

Germany's snub horrified the German Ambassador in Washington, who rushed off to catch a train to New York within hours of the note's arrival. (Under no other American president, it might be added, has the first instinct of an ambassador in crisis been to race to New York, but then House had no ordinary role). The next morning, Bernstorff was standing on the doorstep of House's apartment, seeing the only man who could help him extricate his country from a serious diplomatic predicament of its own making. Desperate to undo the damage, Bernstorff worked with the Colonel to hatch a scheme to try to get Berlin to state its terms confidentially only to Wilson and House, and to keep the potentially leaky State Department out of things.[76] Even if Germany could not state its terms publicly, entrusting them to the Americans would still be major progress: it would get the two sides actually talking terms, however fleetingly, and with the Americans as their conduit.

Speed seemed of the essence. Their best chance was to wring the terms from Berlin – or, at least to wring a *promise* of terms from Berlin – before the Allies could publicly reject the German move. A day was spent securing the President's blessing, and House then signalled Bernstorff to contact his government.[77] Yet when Bernstorff delivered an urgent coded message to the State Department for Berlin on 29 December, Secretary of State Lansing stopped it going through, informing Bernstorff a day later that he refused to send it because he could see 'no peculiar necessity' for the message. Bernstorff, trying to reach House frantically by telephone, successfully appealed to him to get Lansing to send the message.[78]

Though House makes no mention of it in his diary, evidently he and Bernstorff came to some agreement about the State Department's transmitting Bernstorff's coded messages. Having Gerard deliver the messages would be much quicker than having them loiter around South America. The State Department had extended this privilege to Bernstorff on occasions in the past – during the 1915 *Lusitania* negotiations, most notably, and at times in 1916.[79] Over the next month, most communication between Bernstorff and Berlin would go via the State Department, with significant numbers of encoded transmissions. This pattern of Lansing's obstruction and House's intervention would be repeated, with Lansing trying to block the messages and House getting them let through.[80]

House's decision would result in one of the most poignant ironies in diplomatic history: Germany's January 1917 offer of an alliance to Mexico against the United States, the infamous Zimmermann

Telegram, would be transmitted via the good offices of the US State Department itself. Historian Barbara Tuchman savages House for committing an error so 'dangerous' that 'for us to accept it requires what the poets call a willing suspension of disbelief'.[81] Yet though the irony is poignant, House's support of allowing Bernstorff access to this privilege is far from the madness it appears on first glance. House never left behind a direct explanation for this decision, but his reason is clear enough: on the most important issues in German-American relations, and despite Bernstorff's assertion of the opposite, House practically had Bernstorff in his pocket. Bernstorff trusted House implicitly, believing (*exceptionally* inaccurately) that House was 'absolutely neutral' and could be trusted to be even-handed when it came to the belligerents.[82] Bernstorff's advocacy to Berlin aligned almost entirely with the United States' major objectives. The Ambassador doggedly opposed unrestricted submarine warfare and consistently fought any decision that risked a rupture. Bernstorff had, as one scholar put it, 'one major goal: a negotiated peace, initiated through the mediation of President Wilson'. Only this, Bernstorff believed, could 'save his country from a catastrophic defeat'.[83]

Lansing's supposedly wise hindering of Bernstorff's telegrams mostly served to obstruct Bernstorff's valiant last-ditch efforts on the Americans' behalf. Had Lansing prevailed, the Zimmermann Telegram would still have made its way to Mexico (albeit more slowly) via the Swedish Roundabout. Even with the benefit of hindsight, the mere chance that Bernstorff could have persuaded his superiors to take a more pro-American line, impossible without the speed of the American privilege, seems easily worth the cost of allowing the Zimmermann Telegram through.

Lansing's obstruction delayed the arrival of Bernstorff's detailed and well-argued message in Berlin until 3 January – nearly a week after Bernstorff delivered it to the State Department.[84] The Allies' strident rejection of the German peace note, agreed at the Paris conference,[85] arrived in Washington around the time Bernstorff's telegram was finally being sent off.[86] Even with the Allied rejection, however, Bernstorff's message divided opinions in Berlin. Bethmann Hollweg initially wanted to accept Bernstorff's scheme, and he started on a draft accepting his ambassador's initiative. He staked out what would have been a very tough opening negotiating position, laying out a number of terms that were obviously unacceptable to the Allies, including unspecified Belgian 'guarantees' and the German annexation of Liege, where the valiant resistance of a network of Belgian forts had single-handedly stymied the 1914 German advance for nearly a week. But the draft nevertheless showed a willingness to negotiate using President Wilson as a channel for negotiations, and the Chancellor did not frame the terms as an ultimatum, suggesting that there could be room for negotiation and compromise.[87]

Yet this halting advance towards an opening of peace discussions was stifled before it had even begun. The stiff Allied rejection of the German note hardened uncompromising attitudes; hostility to Wilson already pervaded Berlin's halls of power. Unrestricted submarine warfare – madness by any other name – steadily advanced.[88] The Imperial German Navy's Chief of the Admiralty Staff, Henning von Holtzendorff, submitted a key memorandum promising that his submarines could deliver victory by the end of 1917, but only if they abandoned the restrictions they had agreed upon with the United States.[89] The Chancellor, standing effectively alone, abandoned his draft and left it to his relatively new Foreign Minister, Arthur Zimmermann (of Zimmermann Telegram fame), to put together Berlin's reply.[90]

The first part of Zimmermann's answer, received in Washington on 10 January, frustrated Bernstorff immensely. Zimmermann instructed the Ambassador flatly that Germany would have nothing to do with anything that would directly involve the Americans in any discussion of peace terms. Bernstorff, he wrote, should be 'dilatory' in dealing with the 'disclosure of our peace conditions'. Yet Berlin gave Bernstorff material to work with: after the belligerents' conference settled the terms, a 'second convention' with neutrals could be held to consider Wilson's programme. Here, Germany promised that Wilson could set the conference's agenda with Germany's full support: a league of nations, disarmament, arbitration in international disputes. Without providing details, Germany's peace terms were assured to be 'very moderate' and 'kept within reasonable bounds', including a promise 'not to annex' the country of Belgium.[91]

Bernstorff nominally complied with the instruction to delay by doing nothing involving peace discussions for a full three days. While he impatiently sat on his hands, the long-awaited Allied reply to Wilson's note at last arrived in Washington. Opening up a significant diplomatic advantage in America, the Allies stated their terms. They demanded the evacuation and restoration, with reparation and indemnity, of all Allied countries who had lost territory – France, Russia, Romania, Belgium, Serbia, and Montenegro – and the return of Alsace-Lorraine. They supported a Russian plan for Poland, which entailed significant territorial losses for Germany and Austria-Hungary. The Dual Monarchy's losses would not stop there: the Allies effectively called for the Empire's breakup, seeking 'the liberation of Italians, of Slavs, of Roumanians and of Czecho-Slovaks from foreign domination' – leaving behind only a rump state of Austrians and Hungarians, perhaps one-third the size of the pre-war Empire. Finally, they called for a significant curtailment of Ottoman power.[92]

Wilson welcomed the fact that, unlike the Central Powers, the Allies had at least replied as he had requested, though he was 'taken aback' at the sweeping nature of the terms, particularly those involving Austria-Hungary.[93] After a talk with House, Wiseman reported home, somewhat exaggeratedly, that Wilson was 'well satisfied with the reply' and believed 'his action is justified as having given to the Allies a splendid opportunity to state their position'.[94]

The most important dividend from this British diplomacy came in financial form: ever since Wilson had damaged British credit in America at the end of November, every expedient had been considered to pay Britain's American obligations and to prevent the pound from collapsing.[95] Having opened up a significant diplomatic advantage over the Central Powers, Britain moved swiftly. Within a week of the Allied note's arrival, Morgan's was already announcing a new mortgaging operation, again using a blend of investments – mixing some $100 million of US and the highest-grade Canadian investments with other Canadian and world securities in a bid to borrow $250 million.[96] With Morgan's having so badly botched the political dealings with the Federal Reserve in November, this time the British commercial attaché took the lead, seeking the go-ahead from the US Secretary of the Treasury and the Chairman of the Federal Reserve. His meetings went successfully. The British made the borrowing terms even more generous than before, and for once American investors actually reacted positively.[97] Economic historians previously have emphasized a shift in British negotiating tactics in the success of this loan, with the very amiable commercial attaché replacing more disagreeable Morgan's officials whom the administration seriously disliked. Yet while this tactical shift probably helped, this loan would have been almost unthinkable were it not for the successful British diplomacy that had preceded it.[98]

In addition to these efforts, Bonar Law tried to put his own mark on British finance, but with weak measures that remained completely inadequate to the problem. Britain was still headed for a 1917 crash and taking none of the hard decisions needed to prevent one. Months earlier, Bonar Law had demanded without success that McKenna commandeer the country's American securities. With the Bank of England urging him on, Bonar Law now did so, making it compulsory to sell them to the government. Since this move was seen as 'merely another step in the process already inaugurated', no panic ensued.[99] The main problem was that there were few securities left. This time, no one was besieging the

National Debt Offices. From January to March, the government bought up a mere $160 million in American investments.[100] For the entire following year, barely $90 million.[101] As Keynes put it in mid-February: 'A good many of our past resources are now exhausted'. If President Wilson continued to 'stand aloof', Keynes wrote, 'I do not see how we can possibly get through this summer'.[102] There would be no hidden reserve of American securities to save them this time. The government had drained the reserve dry.

Keynes himself had been thrust the forbidding responsibility of trying to save the government from itself, being made the head of a new 'A' division to handle external finance. 'I am filled with perpetual contempt and detestation of the new gov[ernmen]t', he confessed to a friend on 14 January. 'I pray for the most absolute financial crash (and yet strive to prevent it – so that all I do is a contradiction with all I feel)'. His loathing of the new Prime Minister was absolute: 'God curse [Lloyd George]'.[103] The Prime Minister returned the feeling. Keynes's name had been put up for inclusion in the February publication of the New Year Honours. Lloyd George struck it out.[104]

Unable to sit on his hands any longer, Bernstorff, desperate to try something – anything – to resurrect peace negotiations, made an appointment to see House in New York on the morning of Monday, 15 January. Arriving yet again at the Texan's apartment, Bernstorff showered House with all of the good news his government was allowing him to deliver. Almost certainly on purpose, the Ambassador managed to elide completely the distinction between the main peace conference amongst the belligerents only and the 'second convention' to which the Americans would be invited. House was left with the distinct impression that Germany welcomed Wilson 'nam[ing] the terms upon which the peace conference is to be called' and that if 'there should be *mutual* restoration, reparation and indemnity, his Government would have agreed to enter negotiation on those terms'. With that precondition, Germany would then even be willing to 'submit to arbitration as a means of ending the war'. Bernstorff further 'interpreted' Berlin's promise not to annex the *country* of Belgium into an undertaking not to annex *any part* of Belgium. Just to make sure, House jotted down some notes of the conversation and read them aloud to Bernstorff, who declared them accurate. Considering that House's notes included the line '[The Germans] propose that [Wilson] submit a *program* for a peace conference and they agree to give it their approval', it seems unlikely that the miscommunication could have been anything other than deliberate.[105] Given the difficulty and desperation of Bernstorff's position, it clearly did not much matter to the Ambassador what the Americans (mis)understood, just so long as they did something with it. Bernstorff soon would confess to House – rather too frankly and in direct violation of his instructions – that he 'had hoped that some step, statement or note might be forthcoming right away, so that the whole world and especially our people would know that President Wilson's movement for peace is still going on'.[106]

After keeping in reasonably close touch since their initial meeting,[107] Wiseman visited House that same afternoon. House sought to prime the British for the talks that he hoped would ensue. He told Wiseman that he could not possibly 'divulge what had passed' that morning, but then did precisely that:

[Bernstorff], he said[,] made proposals of an astonishing character. From hints which he dropped, perhaps purposely, I gather [Bernstorff]'s communication was something of the following nature: That the Liberal party in Germany, with the support of the Emperor, has secured ascendency over the Military Party, and is determined to make peace … The United States will be asked to be one of the Trustees to see that Germany carries out the reparation and guarantees demanded by the Allies. My idea is that they are [tr]ying to avoid undue material punishment by extreme sentimental efforts. Whatever the communication was, [House] is much impressed and says the President will be also.[108]

Confronted with this seemingly extraordinary German proposal, House was prepared to go to the limit to compel the Allies to accept it. If he had any doubts before, an indiscretion from McKenna that reached House at about this time left the Americans in no uncertain terms as to the financial power they held over the British: it would only be a short time before that economic leverage would enable the Americans to force the British to the negotiating table. Norman Hapgood, who served as a foreign correspondent for a number of American periodicals and who was a confidant of Colonel House, reported a private talk with McKenna to House. The former Chancellor allowed his bitterness at Lloyd George to consume him, saying that 'the President could force the Allies to their knees any time in a moment' – a line that House called especial attention to as he passed it along promptly to the President.[109]

The Colonel immediately communicated to Wilson his seemingly extraordinary conversation with Bernstorff. The question of how to press the proposal 'to the best advantage' initially puzzled them, but within a couple of days House settled on a course, the outlines of which Wilson endorsed: House would cable Bernstorff's message to Balfour and Lloyd George. If even a hint of positivity returned, then House would at once again set sail for Britain; if not – crucially demonstrating the pressure House was willing to put on the Allies – the Americans would flex their considerable economic muscles: House told Wilson that he 'would be justified in forcing the Allies to consider it'.[110]

Bernstorff undoubtedly would have been delighted if the Americans had set this diplomatic train in motion, happily enduring any inevitably resulting reprimand from Berlin if it meant a resumption in efforts for peace. Yet House prudently, though perhaps uncreatively, did not exploit the opening that Bernstorff's misrepresentation had given them. First wanting to make sure the ground was solid beneath his feet, House decided to demand confirmation of the German proposal from the Ambassador in writing.[111]

The game was now up. With nothing actually on paper but House's jottings from a conversation, the Ambassador could plead a mix-up if anything resulted from his desperate ploy. Bernstorff's manoeuvre, however, depended above all upon the fiction that the Americans had simply misunderstood what he had said. House's diplomatic prudence had now made this impossible. Bernstorff had no choice but to confess that everything he had said applied only to a second convention, after peace had already been concluded amongst the belligerents themselves. House was left seriously frustrated but undaunted. Bernstorff's confession extinguished the possibility of a fresh, immediate approach to the Allies: the Americans now needed more from Berlin. House again pressed Bernstorff to wring 'more specific information' on Germany's actual peace terms from his government.[112]

At this point, courtesy of an obliging US State Department and to Bernstorff's horror, two most unwelcome diplomatic grenades arrived at the German Embassy in Washington. Berlin dispatched the encoded telegrams numbers 157 and 158 through Gerard in Berlin, lying to him by saying that they were related to Wilson's peace initiative. Telegram 157 ordered Bernstorff to declare the resumption of unrestricted submarine warfare on 31 January. Telegram 158 was the infamous Zimmermann Telegram; Berlin directed Bernstorff to send it on to Mexico.[113] Bernstorff carried out his instructions, but until he had no choice but to present the declaration of unrestricted submarine warfare, the Ambassador 'strained every nerve' fighting a frantic rear-guard action, seeking to get his superiors to reverse the decision and pursue a negotiated peace instead. The grenades arrived on Friday, 19 January – giving Bernstorff a mere twelve days to stop his government from ending all his hopes of a peace settlement and dooming his country to defeat.[114]

The encoded version of the Zimmermann Telegram had landed in Room 40 two days before Bernstorff received it, with codebreakers Nigel de Grey and 'Dilly' Knox having the first go at a solution. Room 40 had made major breakthroughs in solving the new German Code

7500 between mid-December[115] and mid-January. Building on the progress made over the past month, the two men painstakingly pieced together a fragmentary decrypt, one that nevertheless captured the gist of the original:

> We propose to begin on the 1st February unrestricted submarine warfare. In doing so however we shall endeavour to keep America neutral..... ? If we should not (succeed in doing so) we propose to (?Mexico) an alliance upon the following basis.
>
> (joint) conduct of war (joint) conduct of peace
>
> Your Excellency should for the present inform the President secretly (that we expect) war with the U.S.A. (possibly) (...... Japan) and at the same time to negotiate between us and Japan.....
>
> (Indecipherable sentence opening please tell the President) that.....our submarines...... will compel England to peace in a few months. Acknowledge receipt.
>
> Zimmermann

Hall records in his unpublished autobiography, with melodramatic flair, that the two men came to him: 'D.I.D.', de Grey is supposed to have asked, 'd'you want to bring America into the war?' 'Yes, my boy', Hall replied, 'Why?' The two men explained, and gave him a copy. At once, Hall decided that the material was not to be shared outside of Room 40. He would sit on it at least until 1 February to seewhether Wilson would join the Allies after the German declaration. 'Not a soul outside this room', Hall decided, 'is to be told anything at all'.[116]

As much as the telegrams excited Hall, they alarmed Bernstorff. At once, the German Ambassador managed to get an urgent, short message sent through the State Department pleading for postponement and warning categorically that 'war [is] unavoidable if we proceed as contemplated'.[117] He quickly phoned House, who happened to be in the middle of an appointment with Wiseman at the time. When a disturbed House got off the telephone, he explained the situation to Wiseman. The intelligence officer informed London on 20 January that the 'situation in [Germany] is getting out of [Bernstorff's] control'. House had correctly interpreted this to mean that 'unrestricted submarine warfare must be commenced' – with Hall sitting on the decrypt, this gave the British Foreign Office its first documented intimation of what would happen less than two weeks later. Wiseman emphasized that House 'does not know that I cable you our conversations, in addition to reporting them to [Spring Rice], and that if he did, he would probably not speak so freely'.[118]

Bernstorff made clear the seriousness of the situation in a letter to House the following day, which House promptly passed on to the

President. Bernstorff's frantic, overly honest plea in this letter to have a 'step ... forthcoming right away' was about to be answered. Unbeknownst to the German Ambassador, Wilson had a major address in the works. It had been conceived on 3 January and completed on 12 January. The Americans were taking elaborate steps to maximize its publicity: the State Department sent a copy of the text to a number of American embassies in Europe with instructions that it be released to every country's press at the same time as the delivery of the address itself. Wilson planned to spring it on the world on Monday, 22 January, taking every precaution to keep even the existence of the address a secret.[119]

The day before the address, with House's mediation efforts with Germany having imploded, the Colonel shifted his peace efforts to Britain, seeking to hatch a scheme with Wiseman. Receptive and genuinely cooperative, Wiseman quickly reported this conversation to London:

I discussed with [House] the following idea:

That a conference of belligerents should be proposed by [Britain] and that [the United States] should agree to join the conference on certain conditions. These conditions, which would have to be very carefully drawn up, would provide that the war should go on just the same while the conference was sitting; that the belligerents should both agree that in principle they would consent to limitation of armaments and arbitration, and the readjustment of the disputed territories of Europe on the basis of nationalities. Such essentials as a warm sea port for [Russia] should also be included. The main point of the provisions should be a very strict undertaking by all the neutrals concerned in the conference that, if either of the belligerents committed any breach of international law during the time the conference was sitting, the whole of the neutrals would pledge themselves without more ado to enter the war against such belligerent. What constitutes any breach of international law would probably have to be defined.

House promised Wilson's support for the independence of Poland and for 'the adjustment of Alsace Loraine [*sic*] on the basis of nationalities'. Importantly, the earnestness of Wiseman's report makes no sense if Wiseman was wilily trying to deceive House.

House presented Wiseman with the arguments of Wilson's speech, though without telling Wiseman of the address itself. But he did tip off Wiseman that some kind of major event was in the offing: without telling him why, House mysteriously told Wiseman to come back the next day at exactly half past two, and to book a ticket for the Monday afternoon train to Washington an hour later.[120]

When Wiseman turned up, House revealed that the President had just finished delivering a major surprise address – only an hour's notice had been given – to the Senate. House gave Wiseman a copy of the speech to read on the train and, dispatching the intelligence officer as his uniquely well-suited errand boy, asked him to report back on the 'consensus of opinion of the Allied representatives'. With any luck, the speech would lay the groundwork for implementing the scheme for peace they had crafted the previous day.[121]

As his train rumbled to Washington, Wiseman had as his onboard reading one of the most significant speeches of Wilson's presidency, which was most remembered for its most memorable phrase: 'peace without victory'. The world had now united in a conviction, Wilson announced, that there must be 'some definite concert of power' after the war that would prevent such a terrible event from ever again recurring. He declared it 'inconceivable' that this concert would not include the United States. While disclaiming a right to any 'voice in what th[e peace] terms shall be', the United States, he said, nevertheless had the right to pass judgement upon them. Contrasting significantly with his address the previous May, if the belligerents wanted the United States to guarantee the peace, the war had to be ended on terms that the Americans found acceptable. The United States could not take part in a concert guaranteeing an unjust, unstable peace of 'victor's terms imposed upon the vanquished'. If the Americans were to participate, then the settlement terms could only be those of 'a peace between equals' – necessarily, 'a peace without victory'. For the first time, the President was beginning to engage seriously with the geopolitical realities of a European peace settlement. He laid out some of the ideas that would find fuller expression in his famous 'fourteen points' address a year later: the equality of the rights of nations; 'a united, independent, and autonomous Poland'; the freedom of the seas; and the right of every nation to an 'outlet to the great highways of the sea' by neutralization of rights if not by territory.

The speech existed not only as a call to Americans to rally behind the idea of American participation in a post-war international concert and as a quasi-diplomatic note to the belligerent governments, but also – and in some ways primarily – as an appeal to the belligerent peoples. Wilson told the Senate that he 'hope[d] and believe[d] that' he was 'speaking for liberals and friends of humanity in every nation and of every program of liberty',[122] later writing to a friend that the 'real people I was speaking to was neither the Senate nor foreign governments … but the *people* of the countries now at war'.[123]

While Wiseman was canvassing the response of the Allied embassies in Washington, the German Embassy saw the speech as a welcome opportunity to hurriedly draft a new dispatch for Berlin. Sensing that another raw plea to postpone unrestricted submarine warfare would only fall on deaf ears, Bernstorff nevertheless did his best to detail an alternative course, which was still available if only his superiors would listen. They could still lay out Germany's peace conditions 'either publicly or confidentially'. If they did, Wilson had promised 'at once [to] propose a peace conference' – a bit of an exaggeration, to be sure, but Bernstorff clearly felt that the urgency of the situation justified desperate measures. The morning papers gave Bernstorff additional ammunition: 'Our opponents', he reported, were savagely 'denouncing the President as pro-German'. Above all, if Berlin persisted in its determination to begin unrestricted submarine warfare, he warned, all of these peace efforts would come to a 'complete standstill'.[124]

Lansing, however, again threw up his roadblocks: House yet again was called to give permission. Exasperated by Lansing's obduracy and wanting the matter 'settle[d] once and for all' (in reality, for exactly one more week), the Colonel told the State Department it should consult the President, which then took it another couple of days.[125] The delay practically obviated the point of the message: the telegram would not arrive in Berlin until Saturday, 27 January – leaving Germany all of four days to change course.[126]

Wiseman's two-day embassy survey complete, the intelligence officer had a telegram from Hall waiting for him on his return to New York. As might be expected, the speech had failed to impress Hall in the slightest. In yet another display of his love of playing politics, Hall urged Wiseman to try to get an American newspaper to raise the sceptical question: 'Will President W[ilson] state what steps the projected peace league will take should Germany and Russia decide at some future date to divide Poland again'[?][127]

House saw Wiseman that Wednesday afternoon. Entirely too honestly, Wiseman gave House a 'depressing story' of the feeling of the Allied ambassadors in Washington. Wiseman, House wrote to Wilson, reported that for the Allied representatives, 'on the surface and officially your address was accepted with cordiality, but that underneath there was a deep feeling of resentment'.[128] Yet despite this seeming rebuff, the Americans persevered: on Wilson's instructions, House summoned Bernstorff to New York.[129]

Where the mid-week had brought such disappointment, Friday (26 January) put House in a much more hopeful mood. Bernstorff arrived in the morning and had a much franker conversation with House than his superiors would have certainly liked. The depressed Ambassador confessed that now the 'military have complete control in Germany' and that, in his view, 'none of the belligerent governments' – including his own – 'can survive such a peace as must necessarily be made'. When House suggested that Germany should propose '*mutual* "restoration, reparation and indemnity"', Bernstorff now 'shied at this ... although in a former conversation he suggested it himself'. The two settled on Bernstorff sending off a fresh dispatch to Berlin asking for 'definite terms', with Bernstorff agreeing that they should be 'on the basis of [Wilson's] address to the Senate', including the 'complete evacuation of Belgium and France' – and that, 'if their terms were moderate, there was reason to believe something might be done towards bringing about an early peace'.[130]

With Lansing no longer in the way, the Ambassador rushed away from this meeting and fired off a screaming telegram to Berlin: 'Your 157 most urgent! After having had [a] very important conference, request most urgently postponement until my next two messages received'.[131] Bernstorff continued to play the role of the desperate middleman, again distorting the truth in the hopes of getting anyone to play ball. He offered Berlin Wilson's 'peace mediation based on his message to the Senate, that is, without interfering in the matter of the territorial conditions of peace' – an interpretation of the address that the Americans might have been a touch surprised to see. Gone was any mention of the evacuation of France and Belgium that he had promised House. He gave a detailed exposition as to why the Americans wanted to know Germany's terms, and warned that commencing unrestricted submarine warfare now would be seen as a 'slap in the face' that would 'unavoidabl[y]' result in war. 'We can get a better peace by means of conferences', he urged, 'than if the United States should join our enemies'. He pleaded desperately, at the very least, for a tactical 'brief delay' to 'improve our diplomatic position' – trying to get Berlin to give him some breathing room by disingenuously dangling the possibility that, with just a bit more diplomatic manoeuvring, Germany might be able both to unleash its submarines *and* to keep the United States out of the war.[132]

If the morning brought House a glimmer of hope, an afternoon visit from Wiseman seemed to bring rays of it. Wiseman's 'whole tone had changed', with Wiseman telling House that 'the atmosphere had cleared wonderfully' in the past forty-eight hours. To House's surprise and delight – House called it 'the most hopeful conversation I have had with anyone representing the British' – the two men had 'a discussion of actual peace terms, and the conference which [Wiseman] seemed to now think could be brought about in the event that Germany returns a favorable reply'. Wiseman even discussed such specifics as to where the conference might be held, with Wiseman proposing Spain and House favouring the Netherlands or Norway.[133]

The only thing that could explain this sudden lurch in the British position is an intervening message from London – likely from Balfour – to Wiseman giving some sort of positive indication towards peace talks. This was precisely House's interpretation: 'I take it he has heard directly from his government ... for he seemed to speak with authority'.[134] This message from London, combined with Wiseman's new closeness with House, would explain why Wiseman now decided to reveal his secret link with the Foreign Office, even though he had been firmly instructed not to. Given the vehemence of Spring Rice's reaction against Wilson's speech, the intelligence officer had to have *some* explanation for how everything had 'cleared wonderfully' so abruptly and mysteriously. House wrote to Wilson afterwards that Wiseman had confided to him 'in the *gravest confidence*, a thing which I had already suspected and that is that he is in direct communication with the Foreign Office, and that the Ambassador and other members of the Embassy are not aware of it'.[135]

While Wiseman's subsequent report to the Foreign Office confirms Wiseman's genuineness in the conversation, it also suggests that he probably exceeded his instructions in talking with House about such specifics as locations for the conference. Wiseman's account of the conversation reads as only half of it, detailing what House told him but saying nothing of what he told House. Like Bernstorff with Berlin, House also sought to play the role of the creative middleman between Bernstorff and London. Notwithstanding his conversation that very morning, he told Wiseman that 'the Liberal party in Germany is now in control' and that the 'Military Party has lost its prestige'. Berlin, supposedly, was willing to offer the 'evacuation of Belgium and France; to give up some part of Alsace Loraine; [sic] and ... to accept the term "mutual compensation, reparation and guarantees"' – even though Bernstorff had been evasive on that phrase just hours before. House and Wilson, Wiseman reported, had agreed 'to practically all the Allies' main terms', while the Americans now even regarded it as 'unlikely' that the Germans would 'commit some flagrant submarine frightfulness'.[136]

Yet while Wiseman was becoming closer to House than his government intended, it appears that House also may have been becoming too close to Wiseman. The next day, perhaps feeling guilty for having omitted it initially, Wiseman telegraphed London with a key part of the conversation he had concealed:

[House] informs me very confidentially that, acting on official instructions from [Wilson], he yesterday asked [Bernstorff] to obtain German terms. [Bernstorff]'s only comment was to ask [House] (a) if [the] request was official, (b) if [the] matter would be made public. He then said he would cable Berlin as requested without comment. All this will be published soon.

It is important [House] should not know I have communicated this to you.[137]

We will probably never know what the crucial message from London giving Wiseman a positive response to Wilson's speech said precisely, or ever have proof of the authorization on which it had been sent. Most probably, it was at the instigation of Balfour himself. Piecing together what was happening in the Foreign Office at this moment, or the information that it was receiving, is no easy task. Historian Arthur Link has raised the possibility that the British were playing cleverly and seductively with House thanks to Room 40: the British knew all about the coming declaration of unrestricted submarine warfare, and they cynically encouraged American mediation hopes as a 'cheap and safe way to earn badly needed credit with the Washington Administration'.[138]

While a tempting explanation, it seems unlikely. Hall held on tightly to the Zimmermann Telegram; we do not know how complete the rest of the partial decrypts in his possession might have been, nor do we have any reason to believe that he would have been in an especially sharing mood with them. Had he been sharing the rest, it could have raised uncomfortable questions about why the Zimmermann Telegram had been the only one withheld. Moreover, even if he had been forwarding them to the Foreign Office, the intelligence picture would have been far from clear: Balfour would have seen not only Berlin's intent to declare unrestricted submarine warfare but also Bernstorff's frantic efforts to stop it.

The Foreign Office believed it likely that unrestricted submarine warfare was coming, even before Wiseman's uncertain report on 20 January. Our best indication of their thinking is from a letter penned by Hardinge four days before that:

The all-important question to my mind is that of sea transport ... I confess I am somewhat alarmed at what may happen when the Germans start sinking everything at sight, which, according to all indications, is to take place next month. Of course it may be only [a] bluff, though I am inclined to think not.[139]

Crucially, however, no matter the intelligence shared, the Foreign Office could not have been completely sure about what was going to happen: cynically encouraging American mediation solely for the sake of 'cheap credit' was to be gambling terribly that there would not be some last-minute accommodation, as had been the case in every German-American crisis so far. Moreover, the Foreign Office would also have been deceiving Wiseman, which they would have had no reason to do – failing to tell him that he was only supposed to be *pretending* to encourage House.

Most likely, Balfour was hedging his bets: if the Germans did launch unrestricted submarine warfare, Wiseman's encouragement would give the British their much-needed credit just as Germany forced the Americans firmly into the Allied orbit. If the Americans succeeded in staying out of the war, however, with financial Armageddon evidently no more than a few months away, Balfour clearly wanted to keep American mediation open as a fallback option. Using Wiseman must have appeared a safe way to do this: as long as House remained ignorant of the direct link between Wiseman and the Foreign Office, Wiseman could freely be instructed to encourage mediation. Any resulting peace proposals could be brought before the War Cabinet without their hands having been tied beforehand. Balfour could not have known that Wiseman would confess to House his secret link with the Foreign Office. Indeed, Wiseman seems to have recognized the significance of his confession, immediately lying to cover it up: Wiseman reported to the Foreign Office immediately after that conversation that House 'may suspect that I cable to you, but I doubt it'.[140]

The last few days of the month were as quiet for the Americans as they were anxious for Bernstorff, who was awaiting Berlin's final decision with terrible trepidation. Germany's submarines, however, had received their instructions. A countermand, for many of them, might arrive too late. Nor was there much point in Bethmann Hollweg asking for one: the hardliners had made up their minds. Bethmann's lone 'success', if it may be called that, lay in persuading his colleagues to send a list of peace terms to the United States, for Wilson's confidential information, in the vain and totally unrealistic hope that it would have 'the effect that America totally loses her desire' to enter the war.[141]

As an attempt to sound some pleasant tones of diplomatic euphony to the Americans' ears – ones that, Berlin thought, might even offset the jarring, dissonant blast of the submarines – this German note could not have been more poorly conceived. Its list of terms was as stiff as the one Bethmann had briefly flirted with in his abandoned draft earlier in the month; those, however, at least had the virtue of being seen as a starting place for negotiations. These, on the other hand, were styled as the very moderate and generous terms that *would have been available* to the Allies, if only the Allies had had the sense to accept Germany's December peace offer. Not a single concession was listed amongst them, with the Germans even demanding back the sparsely populated sliver of the Alsatian mountains that the French Army had managed to occupy.[142] Effectively, they were the terms of a German victory. As House observed with some disgust: 'They might have made them much more liberal, because they could have evaded them since they mean nothing'.[143]

278 Plotting for Peace

Bernstorff much later wrote, restrainedly, that the terms were without 'diplomatic value';[144] at the time, they almost certainly left him aghast. He tried to describe them somewhat optimistically to House over the telephone as 'half good and half bad' as he hurriedly dispatched them to New York on 31 January,[145] but as historian Patrick Devlin observes, the terms 'were hardly those which he had led House to expect nor those that [Bernstorff] believed that Germany could get'.[146]

Britain managed to escape diplomatically unscathed from the past two months of peace moves, despite the inclinations of its new Prime Minister. The Allies had significantly improved their position in Washington. The resulting mortgaging operation in New York netted British finance a couple of weeks of extra breathing room. Intelligence, however, continued to serve the British poorly. Its politicized nature impaired, rather than improved, British decision-making. Lloyd George's paranoid initial reaction to the American note demonstrates how intelligence can lead to incorrect assumptions that, because of the quality of the intelligence, become very strongly held. The final gasps of receptiveness to American mediation reinforce the conclusions of the previous chapters, showing just how deeply pessimism reached.

The Asquithians, however, had lost the political battle, and economic denial had now become British policy. If the British were going to continue the war both without the United States and until the 'knock-out blow', they needed to be making some very difficult economic choices. An axe would have to be taken to their American expenditure. Allied militaries would need to be weaned off their vast American supplies, and the Allied peoples would need to be prepared for far more serious levels of privation. The Allied governments needed to be kept onside. Successfully engineering a hard landing would be a profoundly difficult undertaking. Instead, the new government blithely insisted that it did not need to do anything. Spending went on. Choices went unmade. The Allies were told nothing. The government was headed straight towards a cliff and only picking up speed.

Fortunately for Britain, the Germans had now decided to make a race of it. Despite the perhaps too valiant efforts of their envoy in Washington, the Germans were now headed off their own cliff. The only real question was which government would get there first. Bernstorff had barely gotten the disastrous set of 'peace terms' sent off to House when the time arrived for the Ambassador to present the declaration that he had worked so hard to postpone – an act that brought all of these talks screeching to an abrupt halt. With intense reluctance, he went to the State Department and delivered the German thunderclap. Emotional and apologetic,

Bernstorff gave a startled Lansing the documents officially informing the US government of the resumption of unrestricted submarine warfare. The Ambassador now played his final part: after a brief conversation with the Secretary of State, Bernstorff bowed, and with a 'ghost of a smile' he turned and left the room.[147]

9   The Zimmermann Telegram and Wilson's Move to War

February–April 1917

The diplomatic universe had been transformed: the Americans having drawn their line in the sand, Germany could not be allowed to step across it. Yet while the Americans could no longer have any official dealings with Berlin, Wilson would not yet give up. For the month thereafter, his mediation efforts suddenly thrust Vienna into the diplomatic spotlight – a move that seemed to teem with promise. The new Austro-Hungarian leadership could not have been more horrified at their ally's giving up on peace. The elderly Franz Joseph had passed away in November; his grandnephew, the young and newly crowned Emperor Karl, urgently sought to end the war, not to escalate it still further. A relative liberal amongst Europe's staunchly conservative monarchical class, the handsome and moustachioed new Emperor ascended to the throne at the age of 29, and had about him a youthful glow that made him appear still younger. A devout Catholic who was beatified by the Pope in 2004 for his peace efforts, Karl saw ending the war as not only a practical but a religious imperative. He had come to power amidst chaos and crisis, and adding the United States to the already lengthy list of his country's enemies was the last thing Karl and his new 'modest brain trust' of advisors wanted.[1] With Germany's submarine warfare, Austria-Hungary faced an unenviable task: appeasing its much stronger ally while at the same time trying to prevent it from flinging the both of them off a cliff.[2]

Austria-Hungary may have been locked in Berlin's orbit, but Vienna's new leadership was determined to try to pull out far enough to be able to mediate an end to the war. Karl had appointed a new foreign minister, the 'complex, often contradictory' Count Czernin, precisely because he hoped that Czernin would help him exercise the degree of independence he believed that Austria-Hungary needed.[3] An outright separate peace, of course, was out of the question. Karl especially – much more so than Czernin – was willing to go particularly far in his pursuit of a general peace, however, even to the point of soon secretly offering to the French to 'use all my personal influence … to exact from my Allies a settlement of the just claims of France in Alsace-Lorraine'.[4] As historian David Stevenson has astutely observed: 'Discussing a general settlement on conditions he knew to be unacceptable to his ally ... may not constitute willingness for a separate peace, but the distinction becomes fine'.[5] And indeed, one strongly suspects that if a general peace conference could have been convened, Karl would have had little compunction about threatening Berlin with a separate peace at the pivotal moment – but only if he felt the move was guaranteed to seal a deal and end the war. For until the pivotal moment, such an extreme tactic was far too dangerous to be used: threatening an ally with a separate peace exists as amongst the highest-risk wartime diplomatic moves imaginable. It is only to be deployed when it is sure to obtain the objective desired, for it destroys utterly the trust needed to carry on a war together.

22 Karl I of Austria-Hungary (Library of Congress / George Grantham Bain Collection / LC-B2-3173-6)

Though riddled with its share of paradoxes and complications, Vienna's basic diplomatic strategy sought to arrange a general peace amongst the great powers based largely around Romanian and Montenegrin defeat. The essential idea was for Austria-Hungary to transfer some of its own territory to Germany – Polish Austria-Hungary. This, it was hoped, would induce Germany to give Alsace-Lorraine to the French and to restore Belgium. To maximize Austro-Hungarian aims and placate any domestic critics of this loss of territory, Vienna would absorb significant portions of defeated Romania and Montenegro: 'In effect, Poland was not going to be exchanged just for Rumania, but for an end to the war itself'. Under Vienna's plans, most of the great powers would end up with some sort of concrete gain: Britain, a restored Belgium; France, Alsace-Lorraine; Russia, a restoration of defeated Serbia; Italy, some modest territorial concession in southwest Austria; Germany, Austrian Poland; and Austria-Hungary, parts of Romania and Montenegro. Only Romania and Montenegro would come out significantly worse off. Surely, the Austro-Hungarians thought, the Allies would not want to continue the war solely for the sake of their two small friends in the Balkans. The Romanians had made such a catastrophic mess of their war that they hardly deserved much sympathy; many Western Europeans were hardly aware that the tiny and totally defeated Montenegro even existed, let alone able to find it on a map.[6]

Of course, while on paper a seemingly elegant starting point for general negotiations, this strategy had a central problem: the gains it promised the various European powers seemed such pale things in comparison with the vast amounts of blood and treasure that each had shed to achieve them. Given the sacrifices that had been made, Berlin certainly saw no reason to give up Alsace-Lorraine with or without Austrian Poland;[7] Many Italians wanted vast tracts of Austrian territory, not modest concessions;[8] and so on.

For a general peace to have a chance, it needed leverage: if the other belligerents were to accept it, they needed to be made to. Might Austria-Hungary and the United States, working together, have had the leverage to make it work? From the standpoint of an all-knowing observer, a new Austro-American peace axis certainly appeared possible. Karl sought desperately to get his country out of the war just as much as Wilson hoped to keep his from joining it.

Vienna's leverage over the Central Powers may have been limited, but it was there; whether the British recognized it or not, Washington's financial influence over the Allies grew day by day. Whether between them they would have had enough leverage to force a settlement is a debatable question, but certainly the two countries would have stood a better chance working together than they would working apart. What is surprising, however, is not that Austria-Hungary and the United States failed to force a peace settlement in 1917. It is that they never tried. How did two countries whose interests so closely aligned fail to realize that they stood a much greater chance of success together than apart? For the Americans had never held so much economic power over the Allies as they did at this moment – a fact that Lloyd George would have to deal with eventually. For the first half of 1917, Morgan's alone stood between the Allies and financial catastrophe in the United States. For a few months, the bank in some ways existed as another Allied power – non-state and minor but crucial – in its own right. The British shipped nearly a half-billion dollars' worth of gold from January to June, but this came nowhere close to providing the funds that the British needed.[9] To stagger on through early 1917, the British sunk most of their final tranche of American securities into allowing Morgan's to offer the British a massive overdraft. The bank had previously made arrangements for the British to have some overdraft protection, setting up a syndicate of banks, led by itself, to provide a 'demand loan' that the British could tap into if their funds temporarily ran short. Intended to be only a short-term liquidity buffer, for the first half of 1917 it became Britain's primary way of paying its bills. Indeed, by the end of January the overdraft had ballooned such that the mortgaging operation discussed in the previous chapter did not raise a dime of unspent funds: it merely pushed the overdraft back down to a manageable $72 million, from where it would swell yet again. With the uncertainties generated by the German submarine declaration, however, this time Morgan's found the syndicate much less willing to play its role. By early March, the overdraft had already ballooned back to $266 million. A couple of months earlier, the syndicate had borne a large majority of it, but now nearly two-thirds of the loan had to be provided by Morgan's itself – a sum that the increasingly nervous bank called 'far too much and unwise both from the point of view of the British government as well as ourselves'.[10]

Yet the bank kept on lending: by April, the overdraft reached $437 million – a colossal sum just shy of a full percentage point of then-US GDP. (For context, 1 per cent of US GDP in 2019 would be over $210 billion.)[11] In the end, the firm would stand to make a tidy profit, and while Morgan's was taking on some short-term liquidity risks in lending so much, with the securities for collateral the bank's long-term safety was never really in question. But even so, as one British admirer put it, when the situation got difficult 'Messrs. Morgan never flinched but placed their whole fortune into the balance'.[12] The previous hope of arranging a fresh mortgaging operation to stretch out what remained of their American investments evaporated: the US Treasury wanted the market kept clear for their own loans in case the United States entered the war.[13] In the final tranche of their American securities, Britain had, just barely, the collateral they needed to cover this overdraft. Otherwise, perhaps $200 million in these investments, covering a mere few weeks of Allied spending, remained undeployed. And there was no more to be had.[14]

Morgan's financial might pushed them along for an extra few months, but Britain had come to the end of its financial rope. It needed simple, unsecured loans to stave off financial catastrophe, and it needed them in huge amounts. When Morgan's would be left with no choice but to put a stop to their assistance, only one entity could provide those kinds of loans in the quantity Britain needed: the American government. Just as Morgan's at the beginning of May called its halt on the supposedly temporary overdraft (which would in fact not be fully repaid until 1919), US government loan assistance was finally getting started. From late April to early July, a mere two-and-half months, the US Treasury would provide the Allies with an extraordinary series of advances totalling $1.1 billion – a staggering amount equal to some one-and-a-half times the entire 1916 American federal budget.[15]

23 Signing the British War Loan, 1917. Left to right: Lord Cunliffe, Ambassador Cecil Spring-Rice, Secretary of the Treasury William McAdoo, Sir Hardman Lever, Sir Richard Crawford. (Library of Congress / National Photo Company Collection / LC-F82-10282)

Even this mammoth financial assistance would barely plug the Allied fiscal haemorrhage. In July, the moment McKenna had feared for so long – and the one that his detractors had denied could ever come – would arrive. On 20 July, Bonar Law flung himself at the Americans' feet: 'Our resources available for payments in America are exhausted. Unless the United States Government can meet in full our expenses in America, the whole financial fabric of the alliance will collapse. This conclusion will be a matter not of months but of days'.[16]

McKenna had predicted back in November that Wilson would be able to call an end to the war by summer 1917. And this time, he was right: financially, the Allies were almost totally in Wilson's hands by May. Had the President not permitted the $250 million mortgaging operation in January, that moment may well have arrived even earlier. Lloyd George's government had done nothing to preserve the possibility of engineering a hard landing in their American expenditure. Denial is a powerful force, but it must contend with reality eventually. If Wilson had wished to arrange a peace conference together with Austria-Hungary, the Allies would have been virtually powerless to stop him.

Yet despite a diplomatic alignment between Vienna and Washington seeming to hold so much promise, it never materialized. Neither country appreciated just how far the other was prepared to go in the pursuit of peace. Initially, the Austro-Hungarian leadership saw the Americans as too pro-Allied, and it had no way of knowing either the economic power Wilson and House held over the Allies or their willingness to use it. Czernin pursued mediation with the King of Spain instead, failing to appreciate that, unlike Washington, Madrid had no meaningful leverage over anyone.[17] Perhaps more importantly, Vienna knew virtually nothing of all of the behind-the-scenes peace diplomacy that had dominated House's efforts for so much of the war. House had never included the Austro-Hungarians in any of his discussions with Bernstorff; Berlin, certainly, had never seen fit to inform Vienna. On neither of his peace missions to Europe had House ever visited Austria-Hungary. He had never seen the point. The closest he ever got was to meet personally with the US Ambassador to Vienna Frederic Penfield in Geneva in 1916: Penfield 'confirmed our belief that Austria-Hungary and Turkey are now but little more than provinces of Germany'.[18]

The sea change in Austro-Hungarian policy following Karl's ascension to power went almost completely unnoticed in Washington. Perhaps based on information ultimately derived from British decrypts of Austro-Hungarian telegrams, Wiseman in late January seems to have belatedly planted the idea in House that Vienna was not quite so beholden to Berlin as it seemed.[19] Wilson, however, never much bought into the notion.

The President worked the Austro-Hungarian route in February 1917, primarily, it seems, as a means of continuing to pursue peace with *Germany* – the only country in the Central Powers that he believed mattered – not because he appreciated Vienna's newfound independence. For a month, Wilson worked this angle assiduously, acting as an intermediary between Austria-Hungary and Britain. Though the Austro-Hungarian leadership had no way of knowing it, its diplomacy would lead Lloyd George to make one of the most irresponsible confessions imaginable, one that could have introduced a fatal wedge in the Anglo-American relationship. Once that month was up, however, Wilson's interest in continuing to pursue mediation with Vienna suddenly evaporated. The decrypts that had been deployed so effectively to undermine peace talks within the British government were deployed to even greater effect against the American President. As Hall would have wanted it, American mediation died there and then.

As soon as House heard about Germany's declaration of unrestricted submarine warfare on 31 January, he summoned Wiseman to a quick meeting before dashing down on the overnight train to Washington. House told Wiseman of the result of Bernstorff's efforts – a set of preposterous terms that, as Wiseman reported to London, 'would not be acceptable to [the] Allies either in spirit or details'.[20] As soon as his train pulled into Washington, House went directly to breakfast at the White House. He showed the President the terms that Bernstorff had given him; the 'perfectly shallow' missive failed to impress Wilson in the slightest. A straightforward decision confronted them: diplomatic relations with Germany had to be broken. To give them time to lay the necessary groundwork, they would keep Germany waiting two more days. What to do after the break in relations, however, proved a much more difficult question. Wilson felt 'as if the world had suddenly reversed itself; that after going from east to west, it had begun to go from west to east and that he could not get his balance'.[21]

House suggested now making a pivot to see instead 'whether we could not make peace proposals through the Austrians'[22] – a suggestion that seems to stem from Wiseman's excessive honesty. Over the past month, Czernin had sought to get mediation going via Spain, and it seems that Britain had found out. The source of Wiseman's information remains unknown – possibly it was Room 40's success with Austro-Hungarian codes,[23] though we have no direct evidence of the precise decrypts – but Wiseman told House 'in deepest confidence' that 'there was some ground to think that the Pope might be able to get Austria to consent to a separate peace'. Though it did not occur to House immediately, when Wiseman specifically proposed Madrid as a location for a peace conference, in a remarkable leap of intuition, House guessed that there must have been some sort of talks going on:

[I]t seems to me likely that a trade is going on with the Vatican and Austria (with the approval of the allies) looking to the holding of the peace conference in a Catholic country and a country favourable to Austria, and perhaps with Al[f]onso [King of Spain] as sponsor. I shall watch this lead closely and try to follow it further.[24]

Not entirely accurate, of course. But it was not bad, considering how little he had to work with. The appearance of Count Adam Tarnowski, the long-delayed new Austro-Hungarian Ambassador-Designate, a man of liberal reputation who, with impeccable timing, stepped off a ship onto American soil on the very day Bernstorff delivered the submarine declaration, gave additional reason for hope.

There had seemed to be good reasons for House and Wilson to focus their efforts primarily on Britain and Germany, but with Wiseman's suggestions and Tarnowski's arrival it now occurred to House that he and his President 'ha[d] made a mistake in confining ourselves so wholly to the English and the Germans, for ... neither one will likely listen to a reasonable peace unless their allies force them to it'.[25] In Austria-Hungary's case, the self-criticism was largely justified. House ought not to have left Vienna out of his peace efforts over the past two months. With Karl's ascension, House had certainly missed the opportunity to add in some harmonious lines of Viennese counterpoint to Bernstorff's pacific tenor. Austro-Hungarian involvement in House's talks undoubtedly would have made them more complicated for Berlin – the German government likely could not have so swiftly rejected out of hand Bernstorff's first plea to pass its peace terms confidentially to Wilson, for example. Nor would the Austro-Hungarian leadership have been pleased with the set of preposterous German terms that arrived in Washington just before the break in relations.

Yet while House had made a mistake in not including Vienna in the talks, Austria-Hungary nevertheless had sharp limits on what it could accomplish: when the Germans were deciding on unrestricted submarine warfare, Vienna had blasted protest after furious protest, proactively dispatching a special emissary to Berlin to try to head off the move and then arguing stridently after the decision had been made. On a decision of this import, Austria-Hungary mattered enough to Berlin to merit the Kaiser and Zimmermann making personal trips to Vienna to appeal for their ally's support. But the balance of power in the *Zweibund* alliance can be summed up in a single fact: Germany had already issued the orders for unrestricted warfare to its submarines before Vienna had even been asked to give its approval.[26]

When Ambassador-Designate Tarnowski first visited the State Department on 3 February, in part to arrange the obligatory presentation of his diplomatic credentials and his formal reception as Ambassador by the President, he made a stirringly good first impression. The newly arrived Austrian diplomat gave Lansing every sign of the genuine rift that the submarine question had opened up between the two allies. Tarnowski confessed to being 'much disturbed' over Germany's action and indicated that Vienna likely would oppose the move. He asked for permission, which Lansing gave, to send via the State Department two encoded telegrams urging his government to break publicly with Berlin on the issue and move decisively for peace negotiations.

Tarnowski's good impression, however, imploded within minutes. He had barely left the building when a telegram arrived that destroyed any assumption that he had spoken with the authority of his government: not only had the Austro-Hungarians decided to give Berlin their full public diplomatic support, but in a note that copied sections of Germany's declaration verbatim, they announced that their submarines in the Adriatic would also abandon some restrictions previously agreed upon with the United States.[27]

Austria-Hungary had caved. When the Kaiser and Zimmermann had arrived in Vienna on 20 January, the Austro-Hungarians showered them with arguments. Czernin made the case for continuing the submarine campaign using the existing 'cruiser rules' of warning merchant ships before sinking them. Substantial growth in German submarine numbers had already led to a significant increase in tonnage sunk – surely whatever further increase unrestricted warfare could produce would not be worth adding the world's only remaining neutral great power to the ranks of their enemies? With the ministers at loggerheads, the decision fell to the two emperors. After a key meeting, Karl capitulated: bowing to the reality that the Germans would go forward with the campaign regardless of Vienna's position, alliance solidarity had to come first. Nothing good could come, he decided, of public opposition or even 'ostentatious non-participation'. Picking a public fight with Germany on this would achieve nothing and, of incalculably greater importance, might even jeopardize Karl's ability to arrange a general peace. Germany was determined to dive off a cliff and demanded that the Austro-Hungarians jump with them. The only thing, Karl decided, that grasping at the air would accomplish would be to compromise his efforts to search for a parachute on their way down.[28]

A few hours after Tarnowski's visit, at exactly two o'clock, State Department officials arrived at the German Embassy with the Germans' passports in hand – an act that was choreographed to match the precise moment President Wilson took the podium before a joint session of Congress. Wilson took his supportive audience through the pledges that Germany had made and had now withdrawn from, and then sought to play for time to carry on his diplomacy: 'I refuse to believe that it is the intention of the German authorities to do in fact what they have warned us they will feel at liberty to do ... Only actual overt acts on their part can make me believe it even now'. Until the Germans actually carried out their threat, peace would remain Wilson's first priority.[29] The State Department rapidly cleared Bernstorff's safe return back to Germany with London – the Foreign Office, 'anxious to get Bernstorff and his crew away from where mischief can be done with as little delay as possible', quickly obliged[30] – and on 14 February, an 'inexpressibly sad' Bernstorff embarked on his journey home.[31]

As soon as he heard about Wilson's speech, the British Naval Attaché in Washington, Guy Gaunt, fired off an exultant telegram to Hall in London: 'Bernstorff has just been given his passports. I shall probably get drunk tonight'.[32] Hall went straight to the American Embassy to give the news to a jubilant Page, and the Embassy immediately served celebratory 'whiskies and soda'.[33] It quickly became clear, however, that Washington would only break off relations, not declare war. Having kept the Zimmermann Telegram firmly under wraps, Hall now finally brought the Foreign Office into the loop, finding Hardinge 'interested but cautious' and with strong doubts that any 'immediate decision ... could be taken'. 'For this', however, Hall 'had been prepared'. Earlier that morning, Hall had begun working with Gaunt to get the British Consul in Mexico City to obtain an encoded copy of the version of the telegram that had been sent on from Washington to Mexico. This version most likely would have been in the old and long-cracked code, 13040. As one might expect, the two of them were tasking the Consul almost certainly without bothering to obtain Foreign Office approval.[34]

With Bernstorff sent packing and Gerard on his way home, the awkwardness of Austria-Hungary's near-identical declaration flustered the Americans as much as it did Tarnowski. Logically, having expelled the Germans for the same offense, it was difficult to justify keeping the Austro-Hungarians around. The Americans took a creative middle course: letting the Ambassador-Designate stay but indefinitely postponing the formal presentation of his diplomatic credentials needed to make him officially an ambassador.[35] House had previously probed Wiseman about pursuing an Austro-Hungarian peace route and describes Wiseman in his diary as 'in thorough sympathy with it',[36] but with the Austro-Hungarian declaration, the Colonel now wrote to the President on 7 February that 'if Austria holds to Germany's new submarine policy, if I were you, I would send the whole lot home with the Germans'. He had not yet completely given up on peace, adding mysteriously: 'I have another plan to suggest to you which Wiseman and I think might prove more effective than if Tarnowski were retained. It may not be workable but Wiseman thinks it might be'.[37]

There is no indication of what this plan might have been – whatever it was, House abandoned it promptly in favour of the President's approach – but from this point on House, who had been at the centre of the United States' peace efforts throughout the war, now stood on the sidelines, limited to occasionally phoning a friend in the State Department for news. Certainly, his increasing conviction that the United States was 'drifting into [war]' played a part. Mostly, however, it stemmed from the fact that, for whatever reason – most likely simply his ignorance of House's previously assiduous involvement in peace efforts – Tarnowski never made the journey to New York. House's unofficial role did not permit him to just turn up unannounced on the doorstep of an embassy in Washington; he had to be sought out, and Tarnowski never did so.[38]

Yet if Wilson was at all tempted to follow House's counsel and expel the Austro-Hungarians, the fruits of Tarnowski's cables home rescued the situation. While staying firm on submarines, Czernin's reply endorsed Wilson's call for a 'peace without victory'. Though Czernin did not say so explicitly, at this point, Vienna did not yet look to Wilson to play mediator. Czernin sought mediation via Madrid, and he also would soon dispatch Count Albert von Mensdorff – Vienna's former Ambassador to London – to Scandinavia to secretly pursue direct talks with Britain.[39] The Foreign Minister nevertheless sought to use Wilson to apply pressure on the Allies, in the hopes it might make them more receptive to his other avenues of approach. He accused the Allies of having announced 'a programme which aims at the dismemberment of Austria-Hungary', which made it 'impossible for us to talk about peace', and asked Wilson to 'use his influence with the powers of the Entente to make them accept' a peace without victory. The American Ambassador, Frederic Penfield, added his own stark assessment of Austria-Hungary's situation:

Long period of freezing weather with interruption of traffic is accentuating scarcity of food. Economic life of Austria-Hungary seems paralyzed. Intelligent persons assure me [the] Monarchy has food for but two or three months. Nearly every street in Vienna has [a] bread line and misery and destitution [are] visible everywhere. People [of] all classes [are] praying for peace.[40]

Once these telegrams arrived in Washington on 7 February, Wilson moved creatively and speedily that same evening to draft a telegram to Page in London. The President all but converted this carefully worded request into a peace overture, instructing Page to probe 'informally' whether the British could reassure Vienna that they did not intend to break up Austria-Hungary. This was, Wilson wrote, the 'chief if not only obstacle' to the Austro-Hungarians being willing to discuss peace. Wilson wanted a reassurance from the Allies that they did not intend a 'radical dismemberment' of Austria-Hungary, and he told Page that he had 'reason to believe that ... he could in a very short time force the acceptance of peace upon terms *which would follow the general lines of [Wilson's] recent address to the Senate*' – that is to say, a *general* peace. The diplomatic strategy at the heart of this move was clear: Wilson intended to re-route his peace efforts to Berlin through Vienna. He could no longer talk directly to Germany, but Berlin, he thought, still sought a negotiated settlement. If he could get Austria-Hungary discussing peace, the Germans would follow. Peace remained the most important objective, no matter the circumstances: the 'effort of this Government will be constantly for peace even should it become itself involved'. Even with the awkwardness of the Austrian submarine note, Wilson would do his best to overlook it, deciding to keep diplomatic relations with Austria-Hungary 'so that', as his instructions to Page explained, 'he may use her for peace'.[41]

Despite Wilson's clear instructions about his intentions, Page seized on this message at once for a very different purpose: arranging a separate peace with Austria-Hungary so that the Allies could more easily defeat Germany. By the time Wilson's message arrived at his country's London Embassy, the War Cabinet had already decided on its desire for a separate peace with Austria-Hungary. Peace with Berlin, of course, remained out of the question, but if Vienna could be isolated and removed from the equation the War Cabinet was all for it: on 18 January, it had decided that a separate peace would be a 'decided advantage', for it would remove a significant number of enemy divisions from the Western Front.[42]

The clearest British intelligence on Austro-Hungarian policy, moreover, seems to have increased, rather than eliminated, the British leadership's mistaken belief that a separate peace might be on offer.[43] In addition to Room 40's earlier Austrian decrypts, MI1(b) had almost certainly decrypted all of these American telegrams, although the only decrypt to survive is that of Wilson's dispatch to Page.[44] Importantly, while the 5 February telegram from Vienna to Washington was couched in terms that envisioned a general peace, it did not unambiguously rule out a separate one.[45] This information appears now to have been directly available to the War Cabinet – Hankey recorded soon thereafter that he had set aside some space in his office, 'where they come every day to read the secret telegrams'.[46] Because Lloyd George wanted a separate peace with Austria-Hungary, he saw what he wanted to see in the intelligence.

Page secured an interview with the Prime Minister on 10 February. Lloyd George had clearly seen Page's instructions, and, most likely, the other American telegrams as well. After Page made a few brief introductory remarks, Lloyd George, who seemed to have known more than Page did about the Austro-American overture, interrupted the Ambassador and launched into a long discourse about the situation. 'Before I could mention [any] details', Page noted, Lloyd George had 'answered every question I had prepared to ask him'. Page was deeply puzzled, however, by Lloyd George's absolute refusal to discuss receiving a peace offer from Austria-Hungary, with Lloyd George giving Page mystifying arguments for how a separate peace 'might bring especial disadvantages to the Entente', saying that 'Austria was a greater hindrance to Germany as an ally than she would be as a neutral'. Lloyd George, however, agreed to discuss the matter with others in the government and get back to Page.[47]

Of course, no sudden change of heart about wanting Austria-Hungary out of the war had abruptly gripped the Prime Minister. In reality, Lloyd George was stalling because the British were pursuing their own direct talks with Austria-Hungary: if at all possible, the Prime Minister hoped to keep the Americans out of it. London had caught wind of former Ambassador Mensdorff's presence in Scandinavia and had dispatched British civil servant Sir Francis Hopwood to pursue the feeler. Lloyd George was determined to play for time with Page to give Hopwood a chance. When Page tried to corner Lloyd George at two dinner parties in the next week, Lloyd George artfully dodged the topic, giving Page an array of excuses.[48]

While Lloyd George waited on Hopwood, everything that Hall had hoped for arrived from Mexico on 19 February. The British Consul there had succeeded in getting his hands on the encoded copy of the Zimmermann Telegram that had been sent from Washington to Mexico City. As hoped and expected, this copy was in code 13040; Room 40 decrypted it at once, able to fill in all of the pieces missing from the 7500 version. Not only did Hall now have the complete decrypt, he could present it to the Americans without their ever needing to suspect that the British were decrypting American telegrams. Indeed, he could (and would) even invite the Americans to get from Western Union a copy of the encoded telegram sent on to Mexico so as to confirm its authenticity.

Without even bothering to consult the Foreign Office, Hall at once summoned to his office Edward Bell, a close contact that Hall had cultivated in the American Embassy. When Hall gave Bell a copy of the Zimmermann Telegram, explaining how the British had broken German codes and obtained the message in Mexico, Bell exploded in indignation. Having already done it, Hall only *then* approached the Foreign Office for authorization 'to give the substance to Mr. Bell of the United States Embassy'. Hall explained to Bell that he would be waiting on the Foreign Office to give him formal authorization: 'What I want you to do', Hall asked of him, 'is to tell your Ambassador what you have seen and beg him to make no use of the information until Mr. Balfour has made his decision'.[49]

The next day, Hall received a memorandum from the Foreign Office now giving him permission to do what he had already done. A reluctant Hardinge had emphasized the 'great care [that] would be necessary', feeling that 'it would be difficult to explain … how we came to be in possession of this news' and worried about convincing the Americans 'of its authenticity'. Balfour, however, gave Hall *carte blanche*: 'He knows the ropes better than anyone'.[50] Hall marched over to the American Embassy and this time 'officially' presented it to the Americans. Diplomat Irwin Laughlin had a rather unusual response to discovering a possible invasion plot against his own country. Delighted to have something that might help push the United States into the war on the British side, he exclaimed: 'This is wonderful!' Page appears to have feigned surprise for the sake of his subordinates, banged his hand on his desk, and pronounced that the telegram must quickly be sent to Washington.[51]

On that very same day, Page received another major, and much more reckless, intelligence disclosure from the British government. The Ambassador went to see the Prime Minister, and by this time Hopwood had reported back: Hopwood believed (wrongly, as it turned out) that the Germans had found out about his efforts. With secrecy so central to any negotiations for a separate peace, London scrubbed his talks and Lloyd George fell back to using the American route instead.[52] Lloyd George now 'yielded at once – gracefully, easily, almost unbidden' to the Ambassador's carefully prepared arguments as to why a separate peace with Austria-Hungary would be highly advantageous. (The bewildered Ambassador could only conclude that the fickle Welshman was obviously guided by 'moods, sometimes, instead of reason'.)

Lloyd George authorized the Americans to pursue further talks, 'provided, provided, provided the greatest secrecy could be maintained'. Beyond the obvious reason that 'if the Germans realize it' they would torpedo a separate peace, Lloyd George had another consideration on his mind. 'No doubt if he could announce Austria's surrender, that would be a great stroke', Page wrote, 'but if it got [about] that he were "dickering" with Austria or anybody else about peace, he would lose his Dictatorship over night'.[53] The concern was a valid one. Indistinct reports of peace talks could well cause papers like Northcliffe's *Daily Mail* or the arch-conservative *Morning Post* to flip angrily against Lloyd George – and perhaps take enough right-wing Conservative MPs with them to collapse the government.

Lloyd George then made a confession that should have rocked the Anglo-American relationship to its core. The Prime Minister 'showed an almost morbid fear of publicity', which was, Page continued in an astonishing passage in a draft letter to Wilson,

based also on apprehension of a 'leak' at Washington. *He knows that news of your instructions to me got out at Washington somehow and was telegraphed here by someone in the British Embassy or in the British spy service. Although this implies a compliment to their service, he is afraid that other persons also may hear of it.* This leak has added to the fear which the British Government has often shown of the danger of publicity at Washington. Of course I reassured him as best I could but ... he continued to harp on the danger of a leak. It is unfortunate that this news fell into some British hands in the U.S.[54]

By any interpretation, this was a monstrously and dangerously indiscreet act on the Prime Minister's part. Two possibilities exist. The first is that Lloyd George, caught up in the excitement of having this great secret, made this revelation in the spur of the moment and then hastily invented this fear of a leak to cover up the fact that Britain was decrypting American cables. The second possibility, which seems to make the most sense in this context, is that Lloyd George did not actually know how the American cables were obtained. Neglecting the possibility of decryption, Lloyd George assumed the cables were leaking out in Washington – and while the intelligence was welcome, this also suggested the likelihood of serious problems with maintaining the secrecy of any negotiations occurring via the American capital. Lloyd George, carelessly, would have given up this source of invaluable intelligence simply to assure the confidentiality of these communications with Vienna. If British intelligence organizations had concealed the true nature of the secret from the Prime Minister in a bid to safeguard it, they ironically had made him more likely to leak it.

And yet, at least in his drawing the conclusion that he ought to be concerned about American secrecy after receiving numerous copies of American telegrams, Lloyd George was actually a bit ahead of his principal adversary: we have seen how Germany, without having the slightest realization that there could be a secrecy issue in doing so, had foolishly asked Gerard to transmit the telegram that had provoked Lloyd George's knock-out blow interview. Had Lloyd George been properly briefed, he might have comprehended that the key to the problem of secrecy in using American communications in 1917 was not in urging the Americans to prevent leaks, it was in understanding the route of American telegraphic communications. The Americans' Vienna Embassy communicated with Washington via the US legation in Berne, Switzerland, and then from there through France across the channel to Britain, where it was repeated across the transatlantic cable to America. Lloyd George needed to grasp that, through a simple matter of geography and the feebleness of American codes, the capital that would be most likely able to read these communications was Paris. Lloyd George ought not to have been fretting about leaks in Washington, but about anticipating France's reaction when the British response to the Austro-Hungarians would come over French telegraph lines.

Lloyd George's senseless confession could only portend explosive diplomatic – and therefore potentially economic – consequences with the United States: intense suspicion of the British and a thorough leak investigation, culminating in the firing of some hapless scapegoat, or, far more perilously, in the American realization that the British were breaking not only German codes but American ones as well. Whether Wilson would have been willing to provide Britain with billions of dollars in American government loans in the aftermath of such a realization seems very much questionable. Indeed, the Prime Minister had a profoundly lucky stroke in that his interlocutor so obtusely failed to put it together on the spot, considering that Page had only just been told about British codebreaking efforts against Germany in the past couple of days.

But Lloyd George's luck that day went much further. Ambassador Page's obtuseness was matched only by his magnanimity, sparing Lloyd George any consequences at all. So enraptured had Page become with the cause of his host country that he forgot his duty to his own. Page had for so long sought to bring the United States in the war on the side of his British friends. With the Zimmermann Telegram in hand and the United States at the brink of war, the thought of triggering a scandal that might jeopardize everything he had worked so hard for clearly proved too much for him. Page decided where his loyalty now lay. Given that he suspected

British espionage might have been at work, it clearly was not with his President. After penning the above passage in a draft of a personal letter to Wilson, he crossed the page out multiple times, set it aside in his personal files, and evidently never spoke of the matter again.[55] In comparison with the great, manifest justness of the British cause, after all, what was a little spying between friends?

The British offer of a separate peace sped back to Washington. It contained the proviso that Germany could not be informed and only provided the most meagre sweetener imaginable, reversing the previous pledge to free the Czecho-Slovaks. It proposed to guarantee the continued unity of Austria, Hungary, and Bohemia – with, by clear implication, the Polish, Slovakian, Ukrainian, Romanian, Italian, and South Slavic parts of Austria-Hungary (about half its territory) all up for negotiation. Page's diplomatic 'accomplishment' bore almost no resemblance to what Wilson had been looking for. Even still, the President and Lansing acted at once, dispatching a message to Vienna on 22 February. Wilson heavily and creatively massaged the British offer to try to make it more palatable, and he even did not disclose that it had in fact come from Britain to try to allay Lloyd George's concerns about secrecy. The Americans informed Czernin of the Allies' meagre sweetener, and then they told the Austro-Hungarians that the Allies welcomed 'any comments, suggestions or proposals' concerning peace, provided that they be kept secret from the public and from 'any other government'. In essence, Wilson sought to leave the misleading impression that, though it was a request to begin separate confidential discussions, these separate talks nevertheless would be a precursor to *general* peace negotiations.[56]

As this overture was making its way to Vienna, Hall was busily planting a number of lies and red herrings with Page and Bell as the three of them discussed how to most effectively present the Zimmermann Telegram to the President. Hall confided to Page the existence of the Swedish Roundabout (though only identifying 'a neutral country' as the culprit), to throw them even further off the scent that the Zimmermann Telegram had been initially decrypted from an American cable. He spun a story about how a German codebook had been pilfered from the luggage of a German consul in Persia, rather than patiently assembled by a team of dedicated codebreakers. Page never suspected – or, perhaps more precisely, never *allowed* himself to suspect – a thing.[57]

The three of them worked together to craft a strategy to maximize the telegram's pro-British and anti-German diplomatic impact on the President, deciding that the best way to convince Wilson of its authenticity lay in Balfour's reputation for integrity. In a carefully choreographed meeting on 23 February, 'as dramatic a moment as I remember in all my life', Balfour later wrote, the Foreign Secretary presented the telegram to Page – this time *officially* officially – emphasizing how it had been 'bought in Mexico' and authorizing the Americans to publish it. Having now been presented with the telegram for the third time, Page only now moved to inform Wilson and Lansing, toiling until at least two o'clock in the morning drafting and redrafting his telegram home, which was finally dispatched the following afternoon. In a particularly (and likely deliberately) dull-witted passage, he commented that the British government was 'so greatly exercised ... that they lost no time in communicating it to me' so that the Americans would be able to act swiftly to head off 'the threatened invasion of our territory', Page wrote.[58] For forestalling 'the threatened invasion' as urgently as possible was *obviously* the matter of foremost importance in all their minds. (Indeed, it is striking how little the whole Zimmermann Affair had to do with the Zimmermann Telegram's *actual* proposal.)

MI1(b) and the War Office – which to this point had plainly been kept in the dark – only first learnt of what was going on when they decrypted Page's telegram to Washington, to their considerable shock. While we have no evidence of War Office reaction beyond one of initial surprise,[59] it seems reasonably safe to assume that it displeased MI1(b) to learn that Hall had revealed the existence of British diplomatic codebreaking to the Americans – 'Persian codebook' story or no – without even bothering to first consult his military counterparts. Nevertheless, MI1(b) took it in stride, later cheerfully sending Hall 'a copy for your file' of a decrypt of a US telegram expressing the President's 'very great appreciation of so marked an act of friendliness on the part of the British Government'.[60]

MI1(b) also captured Vienna's reply to Britain's peace offer, providing the British with their first clear evidence of Austria-Hungary's unwillingness for a separate peace. Czernin sought desperately to keep the negotiations going. With his Spanish and Swedish routes having gone nowhere, he made a crucial concession to the Americans: for the first time, he accepted the role of the United States as mediator, telling Ambassador Penfield that peace 'must eventually come through President Wilson'. Vienna would accept this at any time: it was 'always ready to end this war'. Implicitly rejecting the request for separate talks ahead of general peace negotiations, Czernin said that Vienna 'could only enter into negotiations for peace simultaneously with her allies' – thereby clearly ruling out a separate peace, but then Wilson had never sought a separate peace, nor had he even told Austria-Hungary that the Allies expected it. The Foreign Minister had only two peace conditions. First, he insisted 'that the Monarchy will remain intact' – a likely deliberately ambiguous phrasing that could refer equally to Austria-Hungary's form of government or to its territorial integrity. Second, in what must by then have seemed like a reference to ancient history, the 'cessation of [the] propaganda ... which led to the assassination at Sarajevo'. Penfield commented that Czernin 'was deeply desirous of peace', that his 'bona fides' could not be doubted, and he urgently asked Lansing and Wilson to 'rush a telegram that may continue the negotiations'. The Foreign Minister had not delivered with a little bow the tidy surrender that Lloyd George had wanted, but at the same time he certainly gave Wilson plenty to keep working with. Czernin did not know, however, that Wilson very soon no longer would want to.

The sensation unleashed by the Zimmermann Telegram has sometimes been credited with transforming the American political scene: supposedly, it sped the administration to war and united a previously divided and pacific American public. One particularly melodramatic popular biography of Hall carries the subtitle 'The Man Who Brought America into World War I'.[61] Very little of this is true. For the American public, as sensational as the story was, it did not survive much beyond a single news cycle and then quickly became old news. By mid-March, the American people largely seem to have already forgotten about it. So 'ephemeral' was the impact on US public opinion that, when the country entered the war a couple of weeks later, hardly any American newspapers bothered even to mention the telegram amongst the reasons justifying or explaining the American entry.[62] As for the timing of the US war declaration, one recent study concluded that it accelerated Wilson's move to war, 'if only by a few weeks'.[63] Even this explanation has been accused of significantly overstating the telegram's importance,[64] and not unreasonably so: Germany would begin committing its 'overt acts' by sinking a handful of American ships without warning beginning on 12 March.[65] Postponing moving for a joint session of Congress for an additional few weeks would have looked belated and weak.

The far more decisive impact of the Zimmermann Telegram, however, was on Wilson's pursuit of peace. Page's explosive missive arrived at the State Department on the evening of Sunday, 25 February. Frank Polk, the top official at the State Department – Lansing was away on a long weekend – swiftly handed the document to the President. Polk rang up House the next day and told him what was going on, saying that the President 'was much disturbed and a plan is being considered as to what is best to do'. Wilson himself quickly sent a copy of the Zimmermann Telegram to House, calling it an 'astounding dispatch'.[66]

When Lansing returned on Tuesday, he found the President puzzling over just how the telegram had reached Bernstorff, given the

Ambassador's difficulties in communicating with Berlin. The Secretary of State must have felt vindicated in all his previous obstruction. He relished explaining that the State Department had handed Bernstorff a long telegram from Berlin on 18 January, which Berlin had promised was a reply to House's peace initiative. The next day, Bernstorff had delivered the Zimmermann Telegram to Western Union to be transmitted to Mexico. Only one conclusion could present itself. Wilson 'exclaimed "Good Lord" and ... showed much resentment at the German Government for having imposed upon our kindness in this way and for having made us the innocent agents to advance a conspiracy against this country'.[67]

After pursuing it the entire war, Wilson now no longer believed that mediation had a chance. The revelations eliminated the remaining value of Bernstorff's reassurances about Germany's fundamentally pacific intentions. On 28 February, the day before the telegram was published, Wilson met with a number of peace societies. Two independent recollections attest that Wilson referred to the telegram: 'If you knew what I know at this present moment, and what you will see reported in tomorrow morning's newspapers, you would not ask me to attempt further peaceful dealings with the Germans', remembered one participant; 'the President's mood was stern ... as he told us of recent disclosures of German machinations in Mexico and announced the impossibility of any form of adjudication', recalled another.[68] The telegram hit the national press the next morning. Soon thereafter, Zimmermann incomprehensibly cleared up any lingering doubts about its authenticity by confessing to it publicly.[69] Wilson had been trying to get measures to begin arming American merchant ships – 'armed neutrality' – through Congress, and the momentary outrage did help Wilson to shepherd his armed ships bill decisively through the House. Were it not for a determined filibuster in the dying days of the congressional session, the bill would have sailed through the Senate. Wilson adopted the measures anyway.[70]

Czernin, who had been horrified by the Zimmermann Telegram and who denounced it privately as a 'colossal stupidity',[71] had his desperate plea to continue peace negotiations arrive right in the midst of the Zimmermann Affair. So far, Wilson had pursued this Austro-Hungarian avenue of negotiations urgently and creatively, always responding at once and milking every possible opening to the last diplomatic drop. This time, however, Vienna's reply sat in his inbox for four days before Wilson got around to answering, and despite Czernin giving him plenty of material to work with, Wilson's previous inventiveness evaporated entirely.

To this point, Wilson seems to have earnestly believed, despite the absurdity of Germany's proposed peace terms in January, that 'peace is intensely desired by the Teutonic powers', as he had put it in his instructions to Page on 8 February.[72] Austria-Hungary could help to moderate Germany's terms and get it to the negotiating table, but – especially given that so far he had received hardly a hint of diplomatic independence emanating from Vienna – everything fundamentally rested on an underlying assumption of a German willingness to pursue peace for any of it to have a chance. The 'perfidy of the German Government in talking peace and friendship with this country and at the same time plotting a hostile coalition against it',[73] as Lansing put it, shattered Wilson's hopes of arranging peace with Germany. Bernstorff's desperate final peace attempts now backfired spectacularly; the Zimmermann Telegram made them all look like nothing more than conniving lies. Historian Arthur Link reasonably concludes that Wilson must have thought it 'almost incredible that any government could be so evil and intriguing'.[74] As Wilson himself would put it in his war message to Congress:

[Germany] has filled our unsuspecting communities and even our offices of government with spies and set criminal intrigues everywhere afoot ... [These] have played their part in serving to convince us at last that that Government entertains no real friendship for us and means to act against our peace and security at its convenience. That it means to stir up enemies against us at our very doors the intercepted note to the German Minister at Mexico City is eloquent evidence ... in such a government, following such methods, we can never have a friend.[75]

With Germany's peace talk exposed in Wilson's mind as only the most sinister of deceit, his strategy of trying to use Vienna as a route to pursue peace with Berlin now seemed unworkable and hopeless. Continuing to attempt negotiations with Austria-Hungary now only made the slightest sense if Vienna was willing to separate completely from Berlin, and the only way to find that out was to take a hard line. He observed to Lansing that their freedom to act had now been significantly curtailed: the reply they sent the Austro-Hungarians was 'the most we are at liberty to attempt'. He toned down a couple of passages from a draft Lansing had provided to 'avoid the use of any words which might ... be understood to indicate an attempt on our part to bargain with Austria-Hungary for her separation from her dominating ally', but Wilson's subsequent actions show that only a separate peace would satisfy him. He had, moreover, evidently decided that Vienna had to spontaneously make its break, and that it could not even be told that a separate peace was now expected. Without actually telling the Austro-Hungarians what he expected them to do, Wilson wrote insistently that he 'earnestly hopes that Count Czernin will reconsider the subject', given that the Foreign Minister could secure 'for his country certain advantages which this government feels might be obtained under existing conditions which may not continue long'. They gave Czernin no openings other than to make a complete u-turn.[76]

Wilson's demand set off a frenzy of diplomatic activity in Vienna, with four conferences between Penfield and Czernin, the latter having extensive consultations with the Emperor. With Wilson's 22 February message having purposefully obscured that the Allies wanted a separate peace, the two Austro-Hungarian leaders now made the u-turn that they believed Wilson was asking for – without realizing that it was now insufficient. Though Czernin again firmly rejected the possibility of a separate peace, he made a further extraordinary and crucial concession. He accepted Wilson's proposal to open up separate and secret negotiations, about which Germany would know nothing, provided that they were designed to lead eventually to a general peace conference:

Count Czernin would be disposed to send a man in his confidence to a neutral country to meet a representative of the Entente. The two gentlemen would discuss secretly and freely the basis and the conditions of negotiations for peace.[77]

A month earlier, such an opening would have sent Wilson spinning with excitement. Vienna had just offered, in essence, to secretly fix up the terms of peace with the Allies in advance, and then to pressure Germany into accepting those terms at a general peace conference. Wilson had previously hoped to accomplish precisely this – the only thing more he could have wanted might have been to make it 'three gentlemen', adding into the mix an American to mediate.

Around the same time, Vienna also proposed a last-ditch effort to Berlin to stave off war with the United States, suggesting that German submarines might simply happen to 'overlook' American vessels, notwithstanding Berlin's public declaration.[78] Though smacking of desperation, such an unofficial policy could have given Germany virtually all of the benefits of unrestricted submarine warfare without any of its costs. The American merchant marine had been growing enormously, but in 1917 it was still only a sixth the size of that of the Allies – 20 million tons of shipping for Britain, along with another 4 million for France and Italy combined, compared with 4 million for the United States.[79] In the face of crisis, Wilson had tacitly retreated from his previous position on submarines. He had previously always insisted that attacks on *all* merchant ships, neutral or not, had to obey 'cruiser rules' and give advance warning so the crew could escape into lifeboats. Now, he had 'indicated, both through press leaks and through his own inaction' that Allied merchant-men could be sunk indiscriminately and without warning.[80]

The red line had moved enormously: barring another *Lusitania*-style outrage, it would now take attacks without warning only on *American* ships to draw the ire of the American government. Unbeknownst to the Americans, the German Admiralty had given neutral shipping a grace period until the end of February, during which it would continue to obey 'cruiser rules'. Yet it would take Germany nearly another two weeks thereafter to sink an American ship without warning, in large part because so few American ships were venturing upon the seas. 'The great majority have remained in port', noted Spring Rice, 'and the German threat appears to be entirely effective. She has not committed murder, but the threat of murder has kept America off the seas'. Only a minority of ships – either profit-hungry or ardently pro-Allied or both – were risking the now especially treacherous journey across the Atlantic.[81]

It is impossible to exaggerate the foolishness of Germany's submarine policy. Germany was waking the American giant for the sake of sinking an infinitesimal quantity of Allied imports. Germany could quietly have continued its grace period of following cruiser rules regarding American ships indefinitely. Berlin had virtually nothing to gain from actually carrying through on its threat against the United States. They could have left Wilson twisting in the wind, awaiting an overt act for months, just as the British raced off the cliff of financial catastrophe. The American merchant marine constituted perhaps a bit over 10 per cent of the shipping available to the Allies. A large fraction of that was now bottled up in American ports, and Germany was now free to attack the non-American remainder effectively at will. Germany brought America into the war for the sake of sinking only a modestly greater fraction of the American ships that were actually at sea, which by now constituted but a small percentage of the merchant marine supplying the Allies. To sink this extra little fraction, Germany was willing to risk fighting an enormous American Expeditionary Force and risk the Allies receiving billions of dollars in American government loans. Utter madness, yet the German leadership could not handle policies of nuance. The German Admiralty denounced any notion of extending the grace period for whatever reason as a 'flippant and rascally game'. 'Now, once and for all', the Kaiser wrote, 'an *end* to negotiations with America. If Wilson wants war, let him make it, and let him then have it'.[82]

Wilson lay on his sickbed, taken down by a nasty cold, when the Austro-Hungarian peace offer arrived back in Washington on 15 March – just as the news and outrage about the first German 'overt acts' against

American ships was spreading across the country. The deaths of American sailors combined with the Zimmermann Affair left the President so hardened that he read Vienna's note with disappointment and tossed it into the fire. Austria-Hungary had handed him on a silver platter almost everything he had hoped to gain just the previous month, but he now found this so useless that it did not even merit a reply. Until and unless Austria-Hungary was prepared to start discussing a separate peace, there was now no point in even continuing the conversation. Even Lansing tried to change the President's mind two days later. Sending along another copy of Penfield's message to replace the one that he assumed Wilson had burned, the Secretary argued that once general peace negotiations began they might 'gradually drift into a discussion of a separate peace'. They should take the opening: 'We may accomplish nothing or we may accomplish more than we expect. If we fail, I do not see that anything has been lost'.[83]

The President could not now be moved, and no answer to the overture was ever returned. Berlin had no interest in peace, Vienna would do nothing without Berlin, and so now even separate talks with Vienna had no point unless a separate peace was actually on offer. A reply from Austria-Hungary on submarine warfare shortly before could not have helped their case. The Americans had formally asked whether Vienna really intended to follow through on unrestricted submarine warfare. After the Austro-Hungarians temporized for a couple of weeks, Washington received on 4 March a rambling, agonizingly tortured reply. The note twisted itself into a pretzel as it sought both to claim that it was joining Germany in unrestricted submarine warfare while at the same time continuing to adhere to the pledges on submarine warfare that it had previously given the United States. The whole thing, of course, was academic: Penfield soon after reported unofficial assurances that Austro-Hungarian submarines 'will never molest American vessels' in the unlikely case they should ever encounter any.[84] But if Austria-Hungary felt so obliged to bend to the will of its senior partner that it could not even pursue an independent policy on a question that was purely theoretical, Wilson must have concluded, what hope did the Americans have of using Austria-Hungary to force Germany to begin peace talks?

In reality, however, a despairing Wilson had chosen to disengage with Vienna just as Austria-Hungary found itself in the middle of the very same secret talks that it had asked the Americans to set up. The only difference was that now Wilson would never be told anything about them. With Czernin's Spanish, Swedish, and now American routes all having failed, Karl took his country's peace diplomacy wholly into his own hands. His greatest hopes now lay in his own family connections amidst Europe's sprawling noble class. He had in his wife's brother, the young and charismatic Prince Sixte, the perfect intermediary. Sixte, despite having grown up in Austria, had been studying law in Paris when the war broke out and decided his loyalties lay with France. Unable to join the French Army on account of his nobility, he joined that of the Belgians and served as an officer in their artillery.[85]

The preparations for Sixte's role had been in play for months. In December, Sixte's mother – the imperial mother-in-law – had pleaded with the King and Queen of the Belgians, with whom Sixte had happened to be spending Christmas Eve, that her son urgently should be given leave to visit her in Switzerland. Europe's nobility looked out for its own; permission was granted, and he left towards the end of January. Sixte shuttled between Switzerland and Paris for a month and a half to lay the groundwork before taking a crucial trip to Vienna on 22 March for secret meetings with the Emperor. Karl secretly promised him Austria-Hungary's support for general peace terms involving the return of Alsace-Lorraine to France, amidst other concessions.[86]

24 Prince Sixtus of Bourbon-Parma in 1914 (Austrian Archives / Imagno / Getty Images)

Sixte shuttled for another few months, engaging in some creative diplomacy of his own by dangling the possibility of a separate peace to the Allies and doing all he could to emphasize common ground. Italy, however, scuppered the talks: Rome's uncompromising Foreign Minister, Baron Sonnino, would have nothing less than the ambitious territorial gains from Austria-Hungary – which included not only Italian-speaking areas but plenty of German-speaking ones as well – that Italy had been promised in the 1915 Treaty of London. The Southern Front still existed effectively in a stalemate, with neither side having achieved any meaningful advantage; Karl, though open to a few modest territorial concessions, could see little reason to offer Italy more than this. Tragically, a significant faction of ministers in the Italian Cabinet was prepared to settle for far less than Sonnino wanted. They had even dispatched an emissary to Vienna without Sonnino's knowledge to pursue it. Unwisely, Karl refused the overture so as not to complicate Sixte's diplomacy. The Allies, however, had no choice but to talk to Rome through Sonnino, and Sonnino refused to budge. London and Paris decided that pursuing these talks was not worth risking the support of their Italian ally, and that was the end of it.[87]

Of course, the Allies never saw fit to inform the United States of these negotiations – and given Wilson's disengagement, neither did Austria-Hungary. We cannot know whether even this astonishing Austro-Hungarian diplomacy would have gone far enough to satisfy the hard line that Wilson had decided to take in the aftermath of the Zimmermann Affair. In February, it would have certainly electrified the White House with excitement. Wilson then would never have tolerated this important overture failing simply because Sonnino could not do without large tracts of German-speaking Austrian territory. If the Allies wanted America's bottomless pockets, they would have to do better. Now, however, as the drumbeats of war roared ever louder, the Wilson who had previously sworn that the 'effort of this Government will be constantly for peace even should it become itself involved' had disappeared. The possibility of an early peace, which had hung so palpably in the air for so long, now met a final, ignominious end. Though Wilson did not want war, he would now make it, and Germany would then have it.

Of course, even had Wilson and Karl been working hand in glove to arrange a peace settlement, formidable obstacles would still have confronted them. They may not have succeeded, but they certainly would have come much closer. For the dead men who littered Europe's killing fields in 1917 and 1918, it remains a tragedy that the two leaders did not try. As these telegrams sped back and forth across the Atlantic, Reginald Hall in London read them all. Whether he understood that, with his great coup in the Zimmermann Telegram, he largely had himself to thank for the sudden and final collapse of Wilson's peace pursuits, we cannot know. If he did, of course, he would have only felt keen patriotic satisfaction at having rendered his country such an inestimable service.

Amidst a steady proliferation of sunken American ships and drowned American sailors, Wilson convened his Cabinet on 20 March. The next day, he called Congress into special session for the first practicable date: Monday, 2 April.[88] He told only House of his decision for war, but everyone could now guess. Congressmen streamed back into Washington over that weekend; House took the Sunday overnight train down from New York and joined the President in his study the morning of that momentous day. The two of them cloistered in the White House as Wilson showed his friend the final draft. There was one line that House convinced his President to remove: 'until the German people have a government we can trust'. However true, it smacked too much of 'inciting revolution'.[89]

That evening, Wilson took the podium in the Capitol. His silent friend stepped out from the shadows, watching his President with pride from the public gallery. 'Wilson unfurled a creed for his time and for thereafter', as historian Patrick Devlin put it: 'Each sentence was a pennant and every word a blazoning and all of it a banner flown in a rushing mighty Pentecostal wind'.[90] 'The right is more precious than peace', Wilson pronounced,

and we shall fight for the things which we have always carried nearest our hearts – for democracy, for the right of those who submit to authority to have a voice in their own Governments, for the rights and liberties of small nations, for a universal dominion of right by such a concert of free peoples as shall bring peace and safety to all nations and make the world itself at last free.

To such a task we can dedicate our lives and our fortunes, everything that we are and everything that we have, with the pride of those who know that the day has come when America is privileged to spend her blood and her might for the principles that gave her birth and happiness and the peace which she has treasured. God helping her, she can do no other.[91]

Conclusion

The Americans thus took their first steps into the global spotlight, the world's largest economy commencing its transformation into the world's dominant power. This transformation would require another few decades and a second world war to complete. The twentieth century, however, would belong to the United States. Some European leaders sensed something of what was to come, and saw the Great War as standing on an American pivot. No matter the ocean in between, the outcome of the war could as readily be decided in Washington as on the various European fronts. Others, blinded by nationalism and arrogance, refused to see what was happening before their eyes.

For the war, ultimately, was decided in Washington in the spring of 1917. Up until that moment, parallel debates about the United States had been taking place within the British and German governments. Their internal quarrels over American finance and over submarine warfare were, at their cores, one and the same: between those who recognized and respected the power the Americans could come to wield in the twentieth century, and those deluded by fantasies of wielding such power themselves. In both countries, those who discounted the Americans' importance prevailed. Yet although the British and the Germans were both wrong about the United States in almost identical ways, the German error rescued the British from the consequences of their own. As historian Martin Farr put it: 'Fortunately, the Germans had Lloyd George's grasp of economics'.[1] The colossal stupidity of the German decision to unleash unrestricted submarine warfare cannot be overstated. Germany launched its submarine campaign precisely with the intention of cutting off Britain's imported supplies. Had the Germans simply waited a few more months for British assets in America to run out, the loss in supplies inflicted on the Allies would have been far more severe and consequential than what their submarines ever could have hoped to achieve.

In many ways, the war was a contest of the staying power of Asquith, McKenna, and Grey on the one hand against Bethmann Hollweg and

307

Bernstorff on the other. Each correctly assessed the fundamentals of their transatlantic realities, and each faced sharp internal opposition bent upon denying them. They suffered ridicule from hardliners, who derided them for weakness, hesitation, and muddle. Foresight was mistaken for infirmity, a lack of determination, and a lax unwillingness to take the steps necessary for victory. Both sets of hardliners carried the day, and at nearly the same time. Within a month of each other, each country began hurtling down a path promising catastrophe. It was merely a question of which catastrophe would unfold first. The Germans would hardly follow through on submarine warfare if the pound collapsed; the British could spend all they wanted in America if Germany provoked the United States into the war.

Ultimately, Asquith emerged victorious. He and his loyal lieutenants succeeded in keeping Britain's transatlantic ship of state afloat just long enough to witness Germany torpedoing its own. A profoundly relieved McKenna praised the American entry as of 'transcendent value'.[2] From that moment forward, the ultimate outcome of the war never really was in doubt. Yet Asquith's success had been by the narrowest of margins. Reverse events by a mere couple of months and Bernstorff might have been the one watching on with relief, and Asquith resuming his premiership amidst national disaster.

One set of hardliners was certain to lead their alliance to calamity; the second to be rescued by the other's folly. Fortunately for Lloyd George, Holtzendorff struck first. History, privileging the victors, has made its judgements accordingly. Those in Berlin who launched unrestricted submarine warfare are condemned for dooming their country to defeat, while their beleaguered opponents are praised for their prudence. Lloyd George, by contrast, triumphed as the 'Man Who Won the War',[3] while Asquith became something of a damp squib, remembered most for preceding his successor. Bernstorff and McKenna manifest something of a historical maxim: fail to prevent a disaster and be proclaimed a sage, succeed in doing so and be dismissed as a hysteric. Yet shift the past but slightly, and Lloyd George would instead be the arrogant denialist who briefly ran his country's war effort right into the ground – and Asquith the beleaguered statesman who foresaw events and was left picking up the pieces.

Lloyd George's economic denialism did not arise out of a uniquely personal recklessness. Most Conservatives in the government shared his sense of the country's economic invulnerability. In some ways, their attitudes reflect an almost distinctively British hubris: having once been the world's economic and imperial leader, British politics ever since has struggled over the country's sense of its place in the world and clashed over the extent and meaning of its relative decline.[4] Lloyd George is hardly the only British leader in the modern era to dismiss caution and restraint in favour of the conviction that, if only Britain was bold, an exceptional Britain was bound to prevail. Whether because of that boldness or simple luck, or both, this conviction is one that has, by and large, been seen as tending to work out in modern British history. Prime Minister Winston Churchill spurned the possibility of peace with Germany amidst fantasies that Britain militarily standing alone was still capable of defeating Adolf Hitler in 1940–1941, before the entries into the war of the Soviet Union and the United States made that a realistic prospect.[5] Margaret Thatcher ignored counsels of caution, responding to Argentina's invasion of the Falklands with a devastating counter-invasion of her own that routed the Argentinians in a decisive victory.[6]

Merely because that conviction has worked out for Britain, however, is no guarantee that it must. We have seen how close Lloyd George brought his country to disaster. The frantic efforts of Asquith and his allies may have been all that stood between Lloyd George and his achieving it. Where Lloyd George and most of his Conservative allies were happily and imperviously ensconced in their delusions about Britain's power and its standing in the world, the Asquithians' grim realism helped to provide Britain the pivotal window of time it needed for the United States to come to its rescue.

Ultimately, it turned out to be a combination of Asquith's grim realism and Lloyd George's delusional boldness that won Britain the war. In terms of achieving Allied victory, in many ways Britain was profoundly fortunate that its new Prime Minister assumed power precisely when he did. Lloyd George unwittingly pursued almost precisely the best course possible. The British could hardly have better exploited their American assets. There was little advantage to having unspent resources in the United States after the Americans entered the war. To time Britain's financial exhaustion to within a couple of months of American entry could scarcely have been more perfect. Lloyd George left the Asquithians in power just long enough to prevent disaster, and then he bounced them from office just as any further restraint would no longer prove useful.

Had Asquith beaten back his challenger in the early days of December 1916, his government certainly would have remained riven by division. Asquith likely would have had to manage paralyzing debates over the Lansdowne Memorandum, brutal Cabinet rows over whether to begin engineering a hard landing in their American expenditure, potentially very serious diplomatic fallout from warning their allies that their American supply spigot would soon be switched off, ugly internal conflict over the German and American peace notes. The government would have continued to fray, and possibly the alliance as well – with a chance of events playing right into Woodrow Wilson's peacemaking hands. Instead, Lloyd George and the Conservatives were able to get on with the war. They solved the most important problem before them by denying the problem existed, and by chance it proved the most effective solution of all. The supplies continued uninterrupted; the alliance was never endangered; and the government found itself more united than ever before.

Lloyd George's new government's immediate decision to conceal the gravity of their transatlantic difficulties from their allies (and from itself) during the winter peace moves of 1916–1917 may have been of monumental consequence. It is difficult to imagine Asquith being willing to countenance such a decision. Grey was adamant that Britain's allies deserved to be informed of 'the exact prospects as regards shipping and finance before a final decision is taken'.[7] The impact of informing France, Russia, and Italy that their accustomed flood of American war supplies was about to dry up is unknowable. Certainly, there was grave anxiety in the British government over the prospect. 'If we fail to give the assistance they ask of us', Chamberlain had worried, 'they might have to consider the possibility of making a separate peace'.[8] McKenna wrote in October 1916 that their allies 'did not conceal' from him that lavish British financing was 'a necessary condition of their continuance'.[9] Keynes was sure that 'without our money the Allies will make peace whether we like it or not'.[10]

Of course, the fact that this flood of American supplies seemed so crucial at the time is not to say that it was utterly indispensable. Montagu, certainly, regarded its loss without serious anxiety, though he appears to have been the only one. The others either regarded a hard landing with dread or blithely denied they had any need to engineer one. The alliance might even have continued the fight after a financial crash, persisting through the crisis, albeit with far greater economic, political, and diplomatic dislocation. The Central Powers, despite the blockade, certainly made do to a surprising extent. Historians have made the grisly calculation as to how each corpse Germany managed to inflict on the Allies came at significantly lower expenditure than the reverse.[11] The civilian populations in Central Europe suffered and starved, yet continued to fight on. Life inside the 'ring of steel' was marked by awful hardship; the brutal 'turnip winter' of 1916–1917 was the worst of the war.[12] Outside that ring, British-funded imports buffeted the war's impact on the home front. Keynes estimated that 'not half of what we give [to the Allies] has the smallest direct military significance. The rest is a *douceur*. Food for Italy, pigs for Paris'.[13] In sharp contrast to German suffering, the British working class actually enjoyed a meaningful rise in living standards during the war – although British social historians have neglected to notice that this rise owed enormously to the flood of imports that Britain was bringing in from the United States.[14] Allied civilians and especially their working classes may have learnt some of the grim endurance of their Central European counterparts. But even uninterrupted American imports were not enough to save Russia from the jaws of revolution.

Perhaps British fears of Allied abandonment at the close of 1916 were unwarranted, at least immediately. Their allies may possibly have insisted on a hardline rejection of Germany's December 1916 overture, notwithstanding a financial warning. The Allied leaderships may have accepted the loss of these supplies with grace and fought on. Historians, after all, have been sure that none of the Allies had any interest in a negotiated settlement. Those who have studied the French war effort tell us that the French government was united against the possibility.[15] Even so, it seems worth observing that the decision of French President Poincaré in summer 1916 to broach a compromise peace with the British King was a major diplomatic act. These historians may say that Poincaré represented a solitary faction of one, and they may well be right – but then British historians have said the same of Lansdowne for decades. Poincaré would have had to have been exceptionally foolish to undertake such an extraordinarily risky diplomatic move without at least some quiet support within the French government behind him. Foolishness in the First World War was not uncommon, of course, but even so, renewed historical examination of the subject may well be indicated. To believe the war unwinnable in 1916 was a sentiment of profound political and diplomatic peril. If such a belief existed, it would rumble quietly beneath the surface, with only the bravest articulating it boldly. For the British, such rumblings were easy to miss, and even the most careful of historians have missed them. But the rumblings were there, and when assembled together they prove unmistakable. Britain may not have been unique amongst the Allies in this regard – and even if it was, the prospect of the impending loss of these American supplies may have significantly altered their allies' calculations.

The alliance might well have held together, at least immediately, and fought on. But fighting on is not the same as prevailing. Any counterfactual prognosis of the war into 1917 and 1918 depriving the Allies of American supplies, an American army, and Russia as an effective ally, can only appear as the grimmest of scenarios.

Nor can one take seriously the argument, made so passionately by Lloyd George and others, that the United States would not permit Britain to go bankrupt because it would harm America's own economic prosperity. As we have seen, American financial markets refused to lend the British meaningfully large sums in unsecured debt, so the US Treasury, and therefore the US Congress, would have been the Allies' only hope. The notion that Congress would grant any kind of foreign loan while the United States remained neutral is frankly delusional, and even more so considering the colossal sums required for the Allies to go on purchasing without interruption. The United States, only involved in the war for a year and a half, lent the Allied governments nearly $11 billion[16] – some fifteen times the entire 1916 US federal budget.[17] A sudden British default might have given the American economy a bit of a cold, but the economic output of the United States was more than double that of Britain. By 1917, the American domestic economy was humming, even overheated, and was 'already at full employment'.[18] To that point, American investors were on the hook only for rather a limited amount of unsecured loans; everything else, including the Morgan's overdraft, had been lent on collateral. A British default would not come without some advantages: the collateral would simply be taken. The war boom would have to come to an end eventually. Whatever economic slowdown that may have resulted from a British default could not have been any worse than the pair of post-war recessions that rocked the United States in 1919–1921, as the US economy absorbed the shock of abruptly lurching to a total war footing and back again within a short two-year span.[19]

Lloyd George was profoundly wrong about the United States during the period of American neutrality in a way that could easily have cost the Allies the war. This is not to say, of course, that he did not have his share of successes during the conflict. Certainly he did, and they are well recounted by his more sympathetic biographers. He was an effective organizer and campaigner. He had energy and zeal. Hankey called him 'more gifted with ideas than any member of the War Committee'. These traits made him a crucial member of the Asquith government. Had he been less dishonest, more of a team player, and, more accepting of the realities of Britain's transatlantic economic constraints, he would have been even more so. Even despite his flaws, both Hankey and Balfour were willing to see Lloyd George handed responsibility for the 'day-to-day' details of the war in December 1916. This certainly did not mean, however, that they wanted him left with absolute authority. Lloyd George was a man of ideas, 'but', Hankey wrote, 'they are not always good ideas'. He needed the Asquithians to prevent him from 'do[ing] foolish things'.[20] The only significant realists left in the government in early 1917, Hankey and Balfour commiserated on the fact that 'our military effort' seemed to be 'so far exhaust[ing] us that we cannot maintain our sea power and our economic position'.[21]

For all of Lloyd George's supposed emphasis on 'push and go', moreover, his new government hardly ushered in an abrupt new era of efficient decision-making. By ejecting the Asquithians, he ought to have had an immediate and profound administrative advantage over his predecessor. He had removed the fundamental fault line in Asquith's coalition. He and his Conservative colleagues were determined to ignore their American economic problem, and so no longer had any need to have policymaking gummed up battling those who sought to force them to face it. Four months into Lloyd George's administration, however, Hankey's verdict on the new regime was dire. Hankey may have grown irritated with Asquith's letter-writing and bridge-playing,[22] but he slammed the new government and its 'hasty and unbusinesslike methods', recording on 18 March that the War Cabinet 'never discuss their agenda paper at all – in fact they have not done so probably for a fortnight'. They always 'allow themselves to be side-tracked', and 'consequently all the work is dreadfully congested – far worse than it was under the so-called "wait-and-see" government'. Lloyd George could be seriously derelict in his responsibilities. Hankey blasted him for not 'initial[ling] the conclusions' of the War Cabinets, 'without which they do not become operative'. 'All the business of the War Cabinet gets in arrears', Hankey fumed, which left 'the Departments tired of waiting for [War Cabinet] decisions'. Hankey sought to shunt as much business as possible away from the paralyzed War Cabinet, recording that he had 'only got the work along at all this week by a wide delegation of decisions to Committees, to which with some difficulty I persuaded Ll[oyd] G[eorge] to assent'.[23] A few weeks later, in early April, the Prime Minister 'shipped off to Walton Heath', his weekend retreat beside his favoured golf course, leaving Hankey spluttering in fury to his diary about Lloyd George's 'refusing to look at, much less to initial, three lots of War Cabinet Minutes'.[24]

Lloyd George's ascendancy also came with meaningful longer-term diplomatic costs. His intelligence-fuelled anti-American actions in the autumn and winter of 1916–1917, coupled with his Conservative-dominated government, gave rise to a lasting mistrust on the part of House and Wilson. Common interests forced the two governments into partnership following Washington's declaration of war, but this partnership came with none of the Anglo-American warmth that the Asquithian Liberals had inspired. House repeatedly bemoaned the loss of Grey at the

Foreign Office and Britain's lurch to the right; Wilson told House emphatically in July 1917 that American objectives for the post-war peace diverged completely from those of Britain and France. Later that year, when Herbert Hoover's Food Administration began putting up war posters referring to 'our allies', Wilson coldly insisted the phrasing be abandoned: 'We have no allies'.[25]

Asquith, of course, also had his faults, and these also have been well recounted. With fresh eyes, however, some of his supposed weaknesses now instead appear as strengths. He showed determination and fortitude, resisting to the best of his ability policies he knew to be unwise and yet holding his government together with considerable political skill. The brakes that he and his lieutenants sought to impose on the British war effort may well have saved it. Most consequential of all may have been his successful dislodging of Lloyd George from the Ministry of Munitions in June 1916. The economies that Montagu subsequently imposed helped extend Britain's American assets, possibly by just long enough to prove decisive. A few days after Asquith's resignation, Hankey wrote the former Prime Minister a stirring tribute. 'The country at present', Hankey wrote, 'has only a slight conception of what it owes to your courage, nerve, tact, unswerving straightness, incredible patience, and indomitable perseverance. History however will record it'.[26] Now, perhaps, at long last, it may.

Of anyone, however, the man who best understood the power that the United States wielded was Edward House. His plan to arrange a compromise peace existed not as a farfetched plot or a diplomatic flight of fancy. His fundamental idea, leveraging American power to force a negotiated settlement, was sound. The problem was not that the United States had insufficient power to leverage; the problem was that crucial European decision-makers failed to recognize the profound power that was there. His diplomatic idea tempted the Allies with the siren song of a resolution to their economic conundrum. It threatened the Central Powers with an all but guaranteed military defeat. But blinded statesmen refused to see either the existence of the conundrum or the certainty of the defeat.

House has been accused of 'disregard[ing] domestic politics' in pursuing his mediation plans. Congress, it has been said, would never have gone along with the House-Grey Memorandum's promises to enter the war.[27] To be sure, there is some validity to this critique. House held strongly to a belief in the transformative power of a peace conference. The mere convening of one, he thought, could bridge the chasms between the belligerents. No doubt, he also believed that a dramatic failure, if the President blamed it on Germany, could shake previous

presumptions about what was and was not politically possible in the
United States. House thought that Congress as a rule falls into line when
it came to questions of war: in a discussion of presidential powers, House
once explained to the King that the 'President could so frame his notes to
foreign governments that war would become inevitable and Congress
must necessarily sustain the President'.[28] But we should not surmise that
the value of the House-Grey Memorandum hinged wholly on the cor-
rectness of this conviction. A full alignment between the Wilson
Administration and the Allies, short of war, could still have eased the
Allied strategic predicament considerably. Diplomatically, such an alignment would have offered greater benevolence towards the Allies, particularly over the British blockade, and a stiffer American line against
Germany. More importantly, the prospect of open Administration support for British finance in the United States would have sent paroxysms
of relief shuddering through the British Treasury: the hard landing in the
Allies' American expenditure might have been softened considerably.
Even if Wilson could not push Allied loans through Congress, he could
still have offered public encouragement to British mortgaging operations
and to its short-term Treasury bills. With Wilson's blessing, the possibility of floating a second large long-term loan might even have emerged.

There were those in the British government who were cognizant that
the United States' significance to the Allies went far beyond the troops it
could eventually hope to dispatch across the Atlantic. 'We must', Hankey
wrote in February 1916, 'educate Col. House that America's role, if she
becomes involved in the war, will be one of finance and supplier to the
Allies; not military'.[29] Similarly, Keynes in early 1917 thought that if
Wilson offered the British Treasury his help, even if only 'behind the
scenes', it 'would enable us to struggle on for the present'.[30] Most
importantly, of course, all of this would have substantially increased the
chances of an escalation in German-American tensions and the likelihood of a subsequent American entry into the war. President Wilson
might not have been able immediately to deliver on the Memorandum's
military promises in the aftermath of a failed peace conference, but he
still had plenty that he could deliver – at least for those in the British
government who understood the profound value of what Wilson had to
offer.

Grey in particular comprehended the overriding importance of good
diplomatic relations with the United States ahead of almost any other
priority. Most previous writings about the British blockade conclude that
Grey's management of it was a disaster: his solicitousness of the United
States reduced the blockade's effectiveness and allowed more goods to
slip into Germany. Cecil's willingness to court American anger, they say,

led him to a significantly tighter operation and therefore much greater success.[31] But such judgements depend on one's priorities. Perhaps Grey had his in the correct order after all.

House failed. That did not mean, however, that he never stood a chance of success. Peace was possible. There were those in Britain who heard his economic siren song and those in Germany who saw their defeat written on the wall, and these men occupied powerful positions. That their internal opponents prevailed may always have been a likely outcome, but it was not an inevitable one. Amidst the many, myriad alternative paths history might have taken, one can see at least a handful ending in a peace conference before 1919, and at least a few of those in a successful peace. This is not to say that a majority of these alternative paths would end there; that peace was possible is not to say that it was necessarily probable. But there were moments when its potentiality seemed to glisten a bit brighter: in March and in May 1916, in the peace moves the following winter, in the Austro-Hungarian negotiations the following spring. In each, the taking of any further steps forward was foiled by the decisions of a few key actors. In March 1916, a few important British politicians and military officials aligned to block consultations with the French over the House-Grey Memorandum. In May, they aligned again, and received powerful, unintentional assistance from President Wilson himself. The following winter, with many in the British leadership beginning to see peace negotiations as almost inevitable, Lloyd George succeeded in ejecting them from office mere days before the issue again became salient. The ensuing spring, the Zimmermann Telegram scuppered it once more.

Indeed, of these four moments, the possibilities of the last perhaps glistened brightest. The best chance for peace lay in a diplomatic alignment between Austria-Hungary and the United States. Had it been allowed to fully form, it seems difficult to imagine how some sort of general peace conference could have been avoided. The February Revolution in Russia seriously compromised the effectiveness of the Allied Eastern Front.[32] The denialism of the Lloyd George government would have crashed into economic reality soon thereafter. Germany had been assuring Austria-Hungary of its willingness to attend a peace conference for months. Whether such a conference could have succeeded, of course, is another matter. The gulf between the belligerents was enormous. Austria-Hungary, however, felt sure that 'neutral mediation might possibly bring together a peace conference, and then popular opinion would make it impossible for any power to leave it'.[33] House, similarly, had no doubt that 'if a conference is once started it can never break up without peace'.[34] It was not only the would-be mediators who believed this: even Lloyd George said that 'once mediation were proposed it would have been very difficult to refuse, and once the war was stopped it would have been impossible to resume it'.[35] Whether they were right is, of course, unknowable.

The Zimmermann Telegram blew up this diplomatic alignment in its nascency. Though the telegram's decryption and presentation has proven the First World War's best studied intelligence episode, its greatest importance lies not in the American entry into the war, nor in its impact on American public opinion. It lies instead in the termination of these negotiations, and with them the best chance for an early peace. The revelation radically altered Wilson's diplomacy.

Intelligence, it is clear, can provide a powerful weapon and imbue those who control it with considerable influence. The twin British signals intelligence organizations played a key role throughout this entire arc. In addition to the Zimmermann Telegram, it appears almost certain that it was signals intelligence that led Lloyd George to such profound hostility towards the United States in the autumn of 1916. Earlier in the spring, even as he scorned his colleagues' economic anxieties, he had neverthe- less seen the United States as offering a crucial diplomatic escape hatch to the Western-Front-orientated military strategy that he so strongly opposed. Wilson's May 1916 speech to the League to Enforce Peace no doubt did some damage, but even so, at the end of July, Lloyd George merely called the possibility of invoking American mediation 'prema- ture'.[36] Two months later, however, he abruptly and violently rejected it in the most public of interventions, telling or hinting to everyone and anyone about the crucial secret evidence that had made this necessary. Led astray by a dramatic but misleading decrypt, and deprived of crucial, unambiguous intelligence pointing in the opposite direction, he aban- doned any willingness to consider American mediation as a potential means of ending the war. With more and more intelligence feeding his paranoia, he became convinced that the United States was conspiring with Germany. No doubt his political acuity also helped to feed this paranoia – his embrace of the 'knock-out blow' proved popular amongst Conservatives – but even so, intelligence clearly had a marked impact. Indeed, had Lloyd George retained his earlier view that the United States should eventually 'step in and impose terms'[37] into autumn 1916, events may well have played out very differently. Beyond intelligence's effect on Lloyd George, Hall's machinations probably had at least some additional political impact behind the scenes, although the rareness of the docu- mentary traces of this makes that impact difficult to quantify.

More broadly, I have shown in this book the crucial importance of paying close historical attention to intelligence. This study began its life as an intelligence project, examining the British breaking of American diplomatic codes. Despite the fountains of ink devoted to Anglo-American diplomacy in this period, this codebreaking had been entirely neglected as unimportant or irrelevant or impossible to study. This book has shown not only that intelligence is none of these, but that it can be the most vital of threads – one that in this case when pulled has unravelled more than a half-century of scholarship.

Indeed, for those involved in the historical craft, this book has shown that politics, diplomacy, economics, and intelligence must all be considered together. Too often they are examined in isolation by historians operating in narrow silos. Certainly, this study has benefitted enormously from the previous research undertaken within, and occasionally across, these silos and has built on it. But to remove any of these four crucial dimensions would be to introduce a massive hole in this book. Diplomacy gives us the *what*; economics, the *why*; politics, the *how*; and intelligence, much of the *why not*. Coalesced, they form a solid and durable whole.

For a century, our collective understanding of the First World War has tended to see July 1914 as the one defining turning point on the path between peace and war. Once the war declarations swept through Europe, we have usually been told, the continent had locked itself into a brutal and unyielding fight to the death. One side would triumph; the other would suffer the bitter consequences of defeat. The only questions that remained after that fateful July were which alliance bloc would be which, and how many corpses over how many years would prove necessary to reach that end.

As if to illustrate that presumption, in 2014 one of the most poignant of the centenary commemorations came at the Tower of London. Nearly nine hundred thousand ceramic poppies, one for every British and colonial soldier killed in the conflict, were planted around the Tower. A transient monument to the enormity of the war, it captured the scale of the death and pain of the British war effort. Each poppy symbolized a human story, a life snuffed out before its time, a family left behind to grieve. The Tower became encompassed in a sea of red flowers, flowing far outside it, leaving those who viewed it with an awful and indelible imprint of the misery that the war inflicted. The poppies were put up to mark the outbreak of the war and taken down a few months later – a reflection of a notion of the war as a tragedy in every classical sense of the word: a calamity that, once set in motion, could not be stopped. It sees the war as one of cosmic forces, forces that arrogant men in July 1914 briefly imagined that they held in their power, that then escaped and consumed their world. A Pandora's Box was opened; the powers

25 'Blood Swept Lands and Seas of Red' exhibition at the Tower of London, November 2014 (Photo by Tolga Akmen / Anadolu Agency / Getty Images)

unleashed ravaged a continent until at long last they spent themselves into exhaustion, and they then returned from whence they came for a generation's-long sleep.

But the number of poppies in that sea of pain was not fixed in 1914. The people that those poppies represented were not put into the ground by some impersonal force swirling beyond mortal control. They continued to be put there for more than four long years by the decisions of men – decisions taken in the fullness of the knowledge that other paths laid open to them. They saw these other paths, and they scorned them. They rained contempt on those who did not share their scorn. They clung to a fantasy that another British Century lay before them, just as it had lain behind. For the sake of that fantasy, they were willing to ignore every risk and to pay every cost, to swell the field of poppies that would surround the Tower of London and then to swell it again. They cast these untravelled paths aside.

Revealed, these paths now tantalize us. Where and how they might have ended, of course, we cannot know. But even so, when we look, we cannot help but to picture a glimpse of the poppies that might have gone unplanted. There were those leaders at the time who saw those glimpses as much as we see them. They pursued them – a sentiment, of course, borne as much of calculation as of sentimentality, one grounded in a firm awareness of the reality of Britain's and America's places in a changing world. They failed. But their efforts show us the essential humanity of the First World War: that it was, ultimately, always a human conflict – of forces under human control – marshalled and channelled by men.

Appendix I The Gold Standard and the Fixed Exchange Rate

It has been suggested, both at the time and since, that the gold standard (or, more properly, the attempt to continue to fix the dollar–pound exchange rate at approximately $4.77, since gold was nearly impossible to obtain on private account)[1] was a key source of Britain's difficulties. 'Undoubtedly, leaving gold would occasion a further slide in the exchange', one historian has written dismissively of the Treasury's urgent attempts to maintain the exchange rate. 'The questions of how far sterling would fall and where it would stabilize were and are unanswerable'.[2]

The problem with these critiques such as this is that they assume that, under war circumstances, there was some benefit to be derived from abandoning the $4.77 peg to the dollar. Having the pound drop against the dollar would not somehow have allowed the British to eke out a bit more in American supplies. Precisely the opposite: the pound's fall would have been the symptom of the economic imbalance trying to right itself. The pound would fall to *force* the British to take less in foreign supplies. Ordinarily, a drop in the exchange rate should stimulate exports and discourage imports. But with the British war machine consuming so much of the economy, British export industries scarcely would have had much ability to take advantage and export more goods. For imports, a drop in the exchange rate only discourages imports made on private account – not those on government account. Indeed, to reduce imports on government account, all one needs to do is order government departments to stop importing so much.

Discouragement of imports made on private account would, of course, have been beneficial to the overall wartime economic situation in a purely numerical sense, even though these imports included crucial staples such as food. But attempting to achieve a reduction in imports on private account through abandoning the fixed exchange rate risked a number of serious disadvantages that may well have offset any gains altogether. These risks Keynes detailed at considerable length. In addition to the potentially serious damage to British credit – recall that by autumn

1916 collateral loans had taken a central place in the British financial campaign – and the possibly serious international economic dislocation such a measure could cause, large amounts of foreign money would likely be withdrawn from the country. If the British tried to prevent this by taking the extraordinary measure of freezing all foreign balances held in London, not only would this risk serious diplomatic consequences, but no one would send any money through London at least for the duration of the war. The most disastrous outcome for the British war effort, of course, would have been that Germany, seeing the plunge in the pound, might have reconsidered going forward with its unrestricted submarine warfare campaign.[3]

There were other, less destructive, methods to achieve a reduction of imports on private account. Excise taxes, tariffs, and other import and shipping restrictions could work towards the same outcome, and these measures the government was already extensively engaged in. Additionally, with the severe transatlantic shipping shortage and the extensive powers of the government to commandeer shipping, purely private imports had the lowest shipping priority. Perhaps these government measures might have been made more stringent, but an argument that the British government's fundamental problem in its adverse trade balance was merely a laxity in private import controls is far from a straightforward one.

Attempting to evaluate this problem quantitatively is almost impossible without considerable additional research into developing a more accurate set of British wartime economic statistics. The only existing effort at calculating British balance of payments during the war is a 1952 estimate by British economic historian E. V. Morgan (no relation to J. P. Morgan). He attempted to do so without having any data whatever on British government payments abroad. We can be sure that he grievously underestimated them. He estimated total British government direct payments abroad in 1916 at about $250 million.[4] In fact, from April to December that year, the British government spent over $1.8 billion in the United States alone (about $1.2 billion in direct payments and about $600 million in propping up the exchange rate)[5] – a figure that excludes both the first three months of the year as well as all direct British government payments in other countries. Additionally, British government loans to its allies in 1916 have been put at approximately $2.5 billion.[6] Keynes estimated that approximately four-fifths of these loans were being spent outside Britain, and mostly in the United States.[7] French trade statistics, for example, put French imports from the United States in 1916 at just over $1 billion.[8]

By contrast, British imports on private account from the United States in 1916 are given by Board of Trade figures, which seem to be reasonably reliable, at $1.39 billion. These would be the only British imports from the United States outside government control that would have been discouraged by a drop in the exchange rate. Yet even this is problematic, as a large amount of what were in practice British government imports would have been counted in these Board of Trade figures. Any imports ordered by private British firms that were serving government contracts – for example, cotton imports for military uniforms – are likely to have been included in these figures as imports on private, and not government, account. Of this $1.39 billion total, moreover, more than half, $770 million, was being spent on food and cotton alone.[9] After one would subtract out the imports of private British firms serving government contracts from the remaining $620 million, it is far from clear that there existed a very significant amount of non-essential imports from the United States on private account that remained for the British government to suppress. Perhaps amounting at most to a few hundred million dollars per year, this seems hardly to be a sum that could justify the potentially serious wartime consequences of abandoning the fixed exchange rate.

Nor were the sums spent in the United States propping up the exchange rate simply being wasted, as has been implied.[10] They were crucial to offsetting the 'sterling credits placed at the disposal of the allies', as Keynes put it.[11] Not only did these funds also facilitate the indirect British government purchases described in the previous paragraph, they facilitated all British government purchases, direct and indirect, from all other neutral countries. By 1917, British trade relations with the rest of the neutral world had moved significantly into deficit – though exactly to what extent is impossible to say. Arbitrage processes, however, as described in Chapter 2, meant that these deficits were being offset by the funds being expended on exchange in New York.[12]

It is worth pausing to note that summing up British government direct payments in the United States from April to December, British imports from the United States on private account, and French imports from the United States gives a total of at least $3.6 billion for 1916. This total excludes Russian and Italian imports from the United States as well as British direct government payments for the first quarter of the year. Yet US trade figures give total exports to all four major Allies in 1916 of only $3.2 billion, a figure that itself was revised upward from $2.7 billion.[13] These US trade figures therefore appear to be significant underestimates.

Possibly, there remained meaningful quantities of unnecessary British imports on private account in 1916 that the government could have been more actively supressing. And, possibly, suppression of these might have been of consequence. Actually demonstrating that, however, is far from straightforward. And in any case, abandoning the fixed exchange rate seems to have been amongst the worst possible methods of trying to achieve that aim. Keynes had no emotional attachment to the gold standard. He argued vehemently against its reintroduction in the 1920s.[14] But he was absolutely convinced, both at the time and in retrospect, that maintaining the fixed exchange rate during the war was absolutely the right course of action. 'The abandonment of the gold standard', he wrote in January 1917, to discourage Bonar Law from considering it,

'does not afford the means to discharge a single liability; it does not furnish a new instrument of economy except through the consternation it creates; it diminishes our assets by involving the abdication of our position as the world's banker; it is gravely injurious to our credit; and it affords encouragement to the enemy. It is not so much a possible policy for deliberate adoption, as the symptom, if it occurs, of a grave disease'.[15]

A much more powerful case than has thus far been put forward would need to be made to demonstrate that he was wrong.

Appendix II GDP of the United States, Britain, and France, 1914–1918

To contextualize the figures in this book – securities sales, gold shipments, loans, etc. – comparable GDP figures for the United States, Britain, and France are helpful. Each country experienced high but different levels of inflation, with the United States experiencing relatively lower levels than the other two.

The table below gives the nominal GDP in billions of dollars for the United States. The GDP figures of Britain and France have been converted into constant 1913 dollars at par and then adjusted for US inflation.

Like all wartime statistics, these should be treated with caution, and are provided primarily for the purpose of illustration and contextualization. It should be noted that other computations of GDP levels show a somewhat less dramatic advantage for the United States. Angus Maddison puts UK GDP in 1913 – calculated in 1990 dollars, and therefore not comparable with the figures below – at $224.6 billion, compared with $517.4 billion for the United States and $144.5 billion for France. Maddison, however, was seeking to compute GDP levels primarily from the perspective of determining relative productive capacity and estimating total world economic output.[1] This book, by

Table 1 *US, British, and French GDP, 1914–1918 ($ bil)*

	United States	Britain	France
1914	$36.8	$12.4	$8.8
1915	$39.0	$13.5	$7.6
1916	$50.1	$15.3	$10.1
1917	$60.3	$18.8	$12.4
1918	$76.6	$22.3	$12.3

Sources: Samuel H. Williamson, 'What Was the U.K. GDP Then?', *MeasuringWorth.com*, University of Illinois-Chicago, 2017; Hautcoeur, 'Economics of World War I in France', 171.

contrast, is interested in GDP levels mostly in order to contextualize figures associated with international trade. The figures computed here, using exchange rates rather than parity purchasing power, are therefore best adapted to the purpose of this book. For other purposes, however, a different set of computations could be more appropriate, and great care should be exercised in adapting the figures above to other contexts.

Notes

Preface

1 Lambert, *Planning Armageddon*, Chs. 5–11. This work has set off considerable academic debate. See, in particular, Coogan, 'The Short-War Illusion Resurrected'.
2 For a full historiographical discussion, see Larsen, 'War Pessimism'.
3 Cf. Fowler, *British-American Relations*, Chs. 1–2; Andrew, *For the President's Eyes Only*, Ch. 2; Lockhart, 'Sir William Wiseman'; Murray, *Master and Brother*, 154; Murray, *At Close Quarters*, 2; Devlin, *Too Proud to Fight*, 611–612; Burk, *Old World, New World*, 450–451; Jeffery, *MI6*, 114; Kernek, *Distractions of Peace*, 35–36.
4 Though many of these works quote numerical figures, and sometimes do so extensively, they are almost universally numbers found in archival documents, rather than products of the authors' computation and analysis, and are thus fundamentally qualitative in nature. See, for example, Burk, *Britain, America, and the Sinews of War*; Soutou, *L'or et le sang*; French, *British Strategy*; Clarke, *Locomotive of War*; Farr, 'Reginald McKenna as Chancellor'; Farr, 'A Compelling Case'; and Neilson, *Strategy and Supply*. Martin Horn attempts to grapple in more depth with his numbers, but not in a comprehensive fashion. For example, he never quotes the crucial figure of Britain's pre-war American securities as $4.25 billion or engages with E. V. Morgan's balance of trade figures, and his import and export figures do not identify whether they are those on private account, government account, or both. See Horn, *Britain, France, and the Financing of the First World War*, Ch. 2; cf. Appendix I.
5 Morgan, *Studies in British Financial Policy*, Ch. 9.
6 Broadberry and Howlett, 'United Kingdom during World War I', 220–222.
7 See Strachan, 'Battle of the Somme', 87–92; Philpott, *Bloody Victory*, 131; French, *British Strategy*, 136; Clarke, *Locomotive of War*, Chs. 5, 7; and French, *British Economic and Strategic Planning*, Chs. 7–11. For a fuller historiographical discussion, see Farr, 'A Compelling Case', 279–283. Only Martin Farr has rejected this consensus. See Farr, 'Reginald McKenna as Chancellor'; and Farr, 'A Compelling Case'.

8 In an economic history article, currently in preparation, I am attempting to construct full numerical estimates of the pace of British asset liquidation, with a detailed quantitative, chronological breakdown from the outbreak of the war to mid-1917.

9 Horn, *Britain, France, and the Financing of the First World War*, 106.

10 By contrast, amounts of currency in much of the existing historiography are very rarely made meaningful to any reader who is not already an economic specialist. For example, Peter Clarke mistakenly states that Britain raised £800 million (that is, $3.8 billion) across three loans in the United States, rather than $800 million – a nearly five-fold difference. But neither the error nor the correction can be said to make much difference to readers' comprehension of the text, which does not offer a contextualization of these figures. See Clarke, *Locomotive of War*, 178–179. In reality, had the Treasury been able to raise a further $3 billion in loans in the United States, the Anglo-American economic situation would have been completely transformed.

11 Adam Tooze elides this crucial distinction when he asserts that 'American investors had wagered two billion dollars on an Entente victory'. See Tooze, *Deluge*, 38. A significant majority of this sum was lent upon collateral; the collateral would have been seized in the event of a British default.

12 See note 7.

13 For example, French, *British Strategy*, 174–175.

14 For example, DeGroot, *Blighty*, 80.

15 That is, Harcourt Cabinet Minutes/Diary, Harcourt Papers, MS. Eng. c. 8271, Bodleian Library, Oxford.

16 For example, Stevenson, *1917*, Ch. 9.

17 See Chapter 9 for a full discussion.

18 Robertson to Lloyd George, 14 December 1916, Lloyd George Papers, F/44/3/3, Parliamentary Archive, Westminster; Hardinge to Lloyd George, 14 December 1916, US Decrypt, 9 December 1916, Lloyd George Papers, F/3/2/1, Parliamentary Archive, Westminster; Hardinge to Lloyd George, 15 December 1916, F/3/2/2, Parliamentary Archive, Westminster.

19 That is, Hall Papers, Churchill College Archive Centre, Cambridge.

20 With much of this detail considerably too technical in nature to be publishable in book form, it has instead been made available elsewhere – see Larsen, 'British Intelligence'; Larsen, 'British Codebreaking'; Larsen, 'British Signals Intelligence'; and Larsen, 'Creating an American Culture of Secrecy'.

21 See Larsen, 'Intelligence in the First World War'.

22 For example, Kernek, 'British Government's Reactions', 731.

Introduction

1 Kernek, *Distractions of Peace*.

2 See, in particular, Stevenson, *1917*.

3 For example, Tansill, *America Goes to War*.

4 Tooze, *Deluge*, 49.

5 French, *British Strategy*, xii.

6 Farr, 'Reginald McKenna as Chancellor'; Farr, *Reginald McKenna*; Farr, 'A Compelling Case'.

7 Strachan, 'Battle of the Somme', 87–92; Philpott, *Bloody Victory*, 131. Similarly see French, *British Strategy*, 136; Clarke, *Locomotive of War*, Chs. 5, 7; and French, *British Economic and Strategic Planning*, Chs. 7–11. For a fuller historiographical discussion, see Farr, 'A Compelling Case', 279–283.

8 War Policy Committee Meeting Minutes, 23 August 1915, CAB 27/2, The National Archives, Kew.

9 Farr, 'A Compelling Case', 302–303; Farr, 'Reginald McKenna as Chancellor', 196–197.

10 The $3.2 billion figure comes from American trade statistics, but seems a serious underestimate, and was itself revised upward from $2.7 billion. See US Senate, *Munitions Industry*, 8701; War Trade Board Bureau of Research, *Export Trade Policy of the United Kingdom*, 43. For further discussion of these statistics, see Appendix I.

11 Estimated from Broadberry and Howlett, 'United Kingdom during World War I', 216; and Hautcoeur, 'Economics of World War I in France', 184 in conjunction with Appendix II and its sources.

12 Maddison, *Contours of the World Economy*, 379. See also Appendix II.

13 War Policy Committee Meeting Minutes, 23 August 1915, CAB 27/2, The National Archives, Kew.

14 That is, Conservative Secretary of State for India Austen Chamberlain and, later, Conservative Minister without Portfolio Lord Lansdowne. See Chapters 3 and 4.

15 Dimsdale and Hotson, *British Financial Crises since 1825*.

16 Millman, *Pessimism*. Previous historians, by contrast, have insisted that pessimism – thus defined – played no role in British decision-making before 1917. For a fuller historiographical discussion, see Larsen, 'War Pessimism'.

17 Millman, *Pessimism*, 3.

18 Maddison, *Contours of the World Economy*, 379. See also Appendix II.

19 Thompson, *A Sense of Power*, 1–55.

20 For a full historiographical discussion of this view, see Larsen, 'War Pessimism'. Quote taken from Zeman, *A Diplomatic History*, 182.

21 Neu, *Colonel House*, quoted at 58. See also Hodgson, *Woodrow Wilson's Right Hand*, Ch. 5.

22 Several historians have taken an opposing view. See Link, *Wilson: Confusions and Crises*, 113; Devlin, *Too Proud to Fight*, Chs. 13–14; Williams, *Colonel House and Sir Edward Grey*, 80; Cooper, *Woodrow Wilson*, 316–318; Knock, *To End All Wars*, 73; French, *British Strategy and War Aims*, 191–192; Link, *Woodrow Wilson: Revolution, War, and Peace*, 36–38; Doenecke, *Nothing Less than War*, 138–145; Tucker, *Woodrow Wilson*, Ch. 7; Esposito, 'Imagined Power', 747–748; Ambrosius, *Woodrow Wilson and the American Diplomatic Tradition*, 19–21; and Taylor, *Struggle for Mastery in Europe*, 554.

23 See, for example, and in particular, Thompson, *Woodrow Wilson*.

24 Edward House Diaries, 30 April 1915, Yale University Library, New Haven, Connecticut.

25 Trevelyan, *Grey of Fallodon*, 33.

26 See, for example, Hinsley, *British Foreign Policy under Sir Edward Grey*.
27 Otte, *July Crisis*, 520–521.
28 Valone, 'There Must Be Some Misunderstanding', 424.
29 Grey, *Twenty-Five Years*, Vol. 2, 107.
30 Edward House Diaries, 10 February 1916, Yale University Library, New Haven, Connecticut; Link, *Papers of Woodrow Wilson*, Vol. 36, 166–168.
31 Lieven, 'Keith Neilson. *Strategy and Supply*', 150.
32 Proceedings of the Cabinet Committee on the Co-ordination of Military and Financial Effort, April 1916, pp. 356–358, CAB 27/4, The National Archives, Kew.
33 McKenna Memorandum, 22 July 1915, CAB 37/131/37, The National Archives, Kew.
34 See, for example, Imlah, 'British Balance of Payments'; and Davis and Huttenback, 'Export of British Finance'.
35 See, for example and in particular, Blewett, *The Peers, the Parties and the People*.
36 Cassar, *Asquith as War Leader*, 155.
37 Millman, *Pessimism*.
38 See Winkler, *Nexus*; Winkler, 'Information Warfare'; Headrick, *Invisible Weapon*, Chs. 8–9; and [UK] Report on Cable Censorship during the Great War (1914–1919), Record Group 25 f8, Volume 1073, File #81, National Archives Canada, Ottawa, Ontario.
39 Ferris correctly points out that there were precursors to these organizations in the years before the war. See Ferris, 'Before "Room 40"'.
40 See [UK] Report on Cable Censorship during the Great War (1914–1919), Record Group 25 f8, Volume 1073, File #81, National Archives Canada, Ottawa, Ontario.
41 Larsen, 'Creating an American Culture of Secrecy'.
42 Andrew, *Secret Service*, 91.
43 Page to Wilson, 17 March 1918, Woodrow Wilson Papers, Reel 95, Library of Congress, Washington, DC. See also Larsen, 'Abandoning Democracy', 488–489. For more on Page, see Gregory, *Walter Hines Page*; and Cooper, *Walter Hines Page*. Most of the literature on Hall cites this quote, but invariably uses a bowdlerized version of it: see Andrew, *Secret Service*, 91; Andrew, *For the President's Eyes Only*, 35; Boghardt, *Zimmermann Telegram*, 83; Beesly, *Room 40*, 37; Kahn, *Codebreakers*, 276; McMahon, *British Spies and Irish Rebels*, 18; and Devlin, *Too Proud to Fight*, 649. The bowdlerized version they cite is from James, *Eyes of the Navy*, xvii. James, without citing his source, took the quote from Hendrick, *Life and Letters*, Vol. 3, 361.
44 Hall unpublished autobiography, Reginald Hall Papers, HALL 3, Churchill College Archive Centre, Cambridge.
45 Ramsay, '*Blinker*' Hall; Beesly, *Room 40*; Gannon, *Inside Room 40*.
46 For example, Andrew, *Secret Service*, esp. Ch. 3; Boghardt, *Zimmermann Telegram*; Larsen, 'British Intelligence'; and Richards, 'Room 40 and German Intrigues in Morocco'.
47 Grey Memorandum, 27 November 1916, CAB 37/160, The National Archives, Kew.
48 See, especially, Lloyd George, *War Memoirs*, Vol. 2, 682–686.

Chapter 1

1 Hodgson, *Woodrow Wilson's Right Hand*, Ch. 8; Devlin, *Too Proud to Fight*, 220–225; Link, *Wilson: The New Freedom*, 314–318.
2 *FRUS, 1914 Supplement*, 42.
3 Link, *Papers of Woodrow Wilson*, Vol. 30, 394.
4 Devlin, *Too Proud to Fight*, 229.
5 Ibid., 230–237, 244–249; Neu, *Colonel House*, 147–150, 163–168.
6 For accounts of the crisis, see Lambert, *Planning Armageddon*, Ch. 5; Horn, *Britain, France, and the Financing of the First World War*, Ch. 2; De Cecco, *International Gold Standard*, Ch. 7; Silber, *When Washington Shut Down Wall Street*; Brown, *Monetary Chaos in Europe*, Ch. 1; and Morgan, *Studies in British Financial Policy*, Ch. 1.
7 Carosso, 'The Morgan Partnerships', Unfinished Manuscript, pp. II-16 to II-17, Vincent Carosso Papers, ARC 1214, Pierpont Morgan Library, New York; Silber, *When Washington Shut Down Wall Street*, Chs. 1–2, 5.
8 Schwartz, *Money in Historical Perspective*, 365. Technically, it was $4.8665.
9 Silber, *When Washington Shut Down Wall Street*, Ch. 2; Schwartz, *Money in Historical Perspective*, 366. In practice this activity was mostly carried out by arbitrage houses devoted to this purpose.
10 Schwartz, *Money in Historical Perspective*, 366. See also Silber, *When Washington Shut Down Wall Street*, Ch. 2.
11 Silber, *When Washington Shut Down Wall Street*, 32.
12 Burk, *Britain, America, and the Sinews of War*, 56; Carosso, 'The Morgan Partnerships', Unfinished Manuscript, pp. 4–7, Vincent Carosso Papers, ARC 1214, Pierpont Morgan Library, New York.
13 Silber, *When Washington Shut Down Wall Street*; Wilkins, *History of Foreign Investment (1914–1945)*, 8–9.
14 Carosso, 'The Morgan Partnerships', Unfinished Manuscript, Ch. II, Vincent Carosso Papers, ARC 1214, Pierpont Morgan Library, New York.
15 Silber, *When Washington Shut Down Wall Street*; *The Bank of England, 1914–1921*, Unpublished War History, pp. V-246 to V-250, M7/157, Bank of England Archive, London.
16 Hattersley, *The Great Outsider*. Additional relevant biographies of Lloyd George include Crosby, *Unknown Lloyd George*; Fry, *Lloyd George and Foreign Policy*; Gilbert, *Organizer of Victory*; Grigg, *From Peace to War*; Pugh, *Lloyd George*; and Rowland, *Lloyd George*.
17 Pugh, *Lloyd George*, 45. Similarly, see Horn, *Britain, France, and the Financing of the First World War*, 15; Crosby, *Unknown Lloyd George*, 176; and Farr, 'Reginald McKenna as Chancellor', 132.
18 De Cecco, *International Gold Standard*, 170.
19 Morgan, *Studies in British Financial Policy*, 10, 160; Horn, *Britain, France, and the Financing of the First World War*, 23.
20 De Cecco, *International Gold Standard*, 150–152; Lambert, *Planning Armageddon*, 189–190.
21 *The Bank of England, 1914–1921*, Unpublished War History, pp. V-147 to V-157, M7/157, Bank of England Archive, London.

22 Silber, *When Washington Shut Down Wall Street*, 2; 'Increased Gold Holdings of European Central Banks', *Wall Street Journal*, 25 August 1915 (Morning Edition), 8.

23 Roberts, *Saving the City*; Peters, 'British Government'; De Cecco, *International Gold Standard*, Ch. 6; Morgan, *Studies in British Financial Policy*, Ch. 1; Strachan, *Financing the First World War*, 5–15; Lambert, *Planning Armageddon*, 185–195; Horn, *Britain, France, and the Financing of the First World War*, 28–37; Crosby, *Unknown Lloyd George*, 175–177; Hazlehurst, *Politicians at War*, Ch. 7.

24 French, 'Business as Usual', 19.

25 Crosby, *Unknown Lloyd George*, 176–177.

26 Farr, 'Reginald McKenna as Chancellor', 343, n. 75.

27 Carosso, 'The Morgan Partnerships', Unfinished Manuscript, pp. II-16 to II-29, Vincent Carosso Papers, ARC 1214, Pierpont Morgan Library, New York.

28 Vincent, *Crawford Papers*, 368–369.

29 Robertson Memorandum, 24 November 1916, CAB 37/160/15, The National Archives, Kew.

30 Farr, 'McKenna as Chancellor', 346, n. 109.

31 *History of the Ministry of Munitions*, Vol. 2, Pt. 1, 3, 13–15; Farr, 'Reginald McKenna as Chancellor', 123–129; Farr, *Reginald McKenna*, 285–286; Burk, 'The Treasury', 86; French, *British Strategy*, 121; Strachan, *Financing the First World War*, 58.

32 For example, Crosby, *Unknown Lloyd George*, 178–189; Grigg, *From Peace to War*, 155–248; Hazlehurst, *Politicians at War*, Ch. 12; and Heffer, *Staring at God*, 166–173.

33 Farr, 'Reginald McKenna as Chancellor', 116.

34 United Kingdom War Office, *Statistics of the Military Effort*, 364.

35 LCES, *British Economy*, 8; Booth, *British Economy*, 124.

36 See French, 'Business as Usual', 24–27, quoted at 26. Having originally laid the principal blame on Asquith, French later offered one of the few negative critiques of Lloyd George as Chancellor early in the war: see French, *British Strategy*, 89–91.

37 See Lloyd-Jones, *Arming the Western Front*, Chs. 4–5; and Hazlehurst, *Politicians at War*, Ch. 10.

38 Carosso, 'The Morgan Partnerships', Unfinished Manuscript, Ch. 3, quoted at 3-156, Vincent Carosso Papers, ARC 1214, Pierpont Morgan Library, New York. See also Burk, *Britain, America, and the Sinews of War*, Ch. 1; and Horn, *Britain, France, and the Financing of the First World War*, Ch. 3.

39 Burk, 'Mobilization of Anglo-American Finance', 27.

40 Carosso, *Morgans*, Ch. 15; Silber, *When Washington Shut Down Wall Street*, Ch. 3; Burk, *Morgan Grenfell*, Ch. 2.

41 Carosso, 'The Morgan Partnerships', Unfinished Manuscript, pp. II-57 to II-60, Vincent Carosso Papers, ARC 1214, Pierpont Morgan Library, New York.

42 Burk, *Britain, America, and the Sinews of War*, 68.

43 Burk, 'Mobilization of Anglo-American Finance', 34.

44 See Burk, *Morgan Grenfell*.
45 See, for example, Burk, 'Mobilization of Anglo-American Finance', 27.
46 'J. P. Morgan Shot by Man Who Set the Capitol Bomb, Hit by Two Bullets before Wife Disarms Assailant', *New York Times*, 4 July 1915, 1.
47 Crosby, *Unknown Lloyd George*, 182.
48 French, *British Economic and Strategic Planning*, 106; Farr, 'Reginald McKenna as Chancellor', Ch. 6; Horn, *Britain, France, and the Financing of the First World War*, 43–56.
49 Farr, 'Reginald McKenna as Chancellor', 128–129.
50 Horn, *Britain, France, and the Financing of the First World War*, 14; Farr, 'Reginald McKenna as Chancellor', 124; Farr, *Reginald McKenna*, 285–286.
51 Farr, 'Reginald McKenna as Chancellor', 342 n. 65.
52 Carosso, 'The Morgan Partnerships', Unfinished Manuscript, pp. 4-8 to 4-14 quoted at pp. 4-11 to 4-12, Vincent Carosso Papers, ARC 1214, Pierpont Morgan Library, New York.
53 Devlin, *Too Proud to Fight*, 249.
54 Edward House Diaries, 19 April 1915, Yale University Library, New Haven, Connecticut. House's aims in these negotiations have tended to be misunderstood, with a contention that House falsely reported to the President that he had gotten France and Germany to agree in principle to a compromise peace. See, in particular, Neu, *Colonel House*, Ch. 14. House's objectives were in fact far more limited.
55 Edward House Diaries, 10 February 1915, Yale University Library, New Haven, Connecticut; Neu, *Colonel House*, 172. See also Yearwood, *Guarantee of Peace*, Ch. 1.
56 Weber, 'State Department Cryptographic Security', 576–577; Link, *Papers of Woodrow Wilson*, Vol. 32, 300–301, 304, 328, 335, 372,403, 422–423, 429, 455–456, 462, 475, 504, 521, 523–524, 531–532; Vol. 33, 10–13, 63–64, 88–89, 105–106, 134, 190, 198, 205, 217, 222–223, 229, 239, 247–248, 253, 257, 266–267, 321.
57 Larsen, 'Creating an American Culture of Secrecy'; Baker, *Woodrow Wilson*, Vol. 6, 52–53; Andrew, *Secret Service*, 108; Weber, 'State Department Cryptographic Security', 572–576; Link, *Papers of Woodrow Wilson*, Vol. 32, 147–148, 297–299; Vol. 33, 237; Edward House Papers, 283:409, Yale University Library, New Haven, Connecticut; Edward House Diaries, 8 May 1915, Yale University Library, New Haven, Connecticut. See also Baker, *Woodrow Wilson*, Vol. 5, 307.
58 See Gannon, *Inside Room 40*, Chs. 2, 10; Andrew, *Secret Service*, Ch. 3; Boghardt, *Zimmermann Telegram*, Ch. 6; Beesly, *Room 40*, Chs. 2, 11; Ewing, *Man of Room 40*; Ewing, 'Some Special War Work Part I'; and Ewing, 'Some Special War Work Part II'.
59 Andrew, *Secret Service*, Ch. 3; Santoni, 'First Ultra Secret'; Hines, 'Sins of Omission'.
60 Draft 'D', Chapter 25, Hall unpublished autobiography, Reginald Hall Papers, HALL 3/6, Churchill College Archive Centre, Cambridge; 'Political Branch of Room 40' Memorandum, ADM 223/773, The National Archives, Kew; Gannon, *Inside Room 40*, Ch. 10; Beesly, *Room 40*, Ch. 8; Larsen, 'British Signals Intelligence'.

61 Larsen, 'British Signals Intelligence'.
62 Nickles, *Under the Wire*, 141; Gannon, *Inside Room 40*, 133–135; Beesly, *Room 40*, 208.
63 Larsen, 'British Signals Intelligence'.
64 Ferris, 'Before "Room 40"', 443–444.
65 Larsen, 'British Codebreaking', 257; Official History of MI1(b), HW 7/35, The National Archives, Kew; R. H. Brade Memorandum No. 803, 12 April 1915, War Office Memorandum, 15 May 1915, War Office Organizational Chart, [1915], Esher Papers, Acc. 2006-11-57, Vol. 1, National Army Museum, London; Ferris, 'Before "Room 40"', 444–445.
66 Larsen, 'British Codebreaking'; Official History of MI1(b), HW 7/35, The National Archives, Kew.
67 Winkler, *Nexus*; [UK] Report on Cable Censorship during the Great War (1914–1919), Record Group 25 f8, Volume 1073, File #81, National Archives Canada, Ottawa, Ontario. The only cables not under British control were a pair of old French transatlantic cables from Brest that 'never worked very well' and that were widely avoided, since they had a terrible reputation for 'very slow' transmission and hopelessly garbling messages, the German transatlantic cables having been cut at the outbreak of the war. See Winkler, 'Information Warfare', 849. While it cannot be entirely ruled out that some miniscule fraction of State Department messages may have gone via the Brest cables and escaped British interception, even this seems doubtful given the unreliability of the cables. The telegrams of the key US outposts in Germany and Scandinavia are even less likely to have gone via the Brest cables. The US embassy in Germany communicated via Copenhagen (see, for example, Egan to State Department, 25 September 1916, Record Group 59, State Department Decimal File 1910–1929, 763.72119/172, US National Archives and Records Administration, College Park) and the 'only alternative' to using British cables to get around the Western Front communications blackout was a single French cable between Denmark and Calais, which is unlikely to have been used. See Larsen, 'British Signals Intelligence', 54; and Larsen, 'British Codebreaking', 259. See also Winkler, *Nexus*, 17, 106; Memorandum on Communications to and from Colonel House and Members of the American Mission and Washington, [1917], Edward House Papers, 180:184, Yale University Library, New Haven, Connecticut; [UK] Report on Cable Censorship during the Great War (1914–1919), p. 10, Record Group 25 f8, Volume 1073, File #81, National Archives Canada, Ottawa, Ontario; and Headrick, *Invisible Weapon*.
68 Larsen, 'British Codebreaking', 260–261.
69 See Devlin, *Too Proud to Fight*, Chs. 8–10; Hodgson, *Woodrow Wilson's Right Hand*, Ch. 9; Neu, *Colonel House*, Ch. 14.
70 Link, *Papers of Woodrow Wilson*, Vol. 32, 522.
71 Seymour, *Intimate Papers*.
72 Devlin, *Too Proud to Fight*, 265; Hankey, *Supreme Command*, Vol. 1, 361; Edward House Diaries, 11, 13 February 1915, Yale University Library, New Haven, Connecticut.

73 Correspondence between Edward House and Sir Eric Drummond, 1915, Edward House Papers, 40:1249, Yale University Library, New Haven, Connecticut; Edward House Diaries, 3–4 June 1915, Yale University Library, New Haven, Connecticut; 'Code Made by British Government for their Confidential Communication with EMH', Edward House Papers, 283:409, Yale University Library, New Haven, Connecticut.

74 Neu, *Colonel House*, 91.

75 See, for example, Link, *Wilson: The Struggle for Neutrality*, Chs. 10–13, 16–17, 19–20; Devlin, *Too Proud to Fight*, Chs. 10–11; Cooper, *Woodrow Wilson*, Chs. 13–14; and May, *World War and American Isolation*, Chs. 6–9.

76 Lambert, *Planning Armageddon*; Cf. in particular Coogan, 'The Short-War Illusion Resurrected'.

77 Lambert, *Planning Armageddon*, 242–248.

78 Coogan, *End of Neutrality*; Floyd, *Abandoning American Neutrality*.

79 Hart, *Gallipoli*, Chs. 1–10; Erickson, *Gallipoli*, Chs. 1–3; Prior, *Gallipoli*, Chs. 1–9; Rogan, *Fall of the Ottomans*, 130–145; French, *British Strategy*, Chs. 4–5.

80 Doughty, *Pyrrhic Victory*, Ch. 3; Greenhalgh, *French Army*, Ch. 3; Sheldon, *The German Army on the Western Front 1915*, Chs. 1–5; Krause, *Early Trench Tactics*.

81 Cassar, *Kitchener's War*, 162–179; French, *British Strategy*, 88.

82 Ibid., Ch. 9; Pugh, 'Asquith, Bonar Law, and the First Coalition'; Turner, *British Politics*, 56–64; Farr, 'Reginald McKenna as Chancellor', 59–61; Hazlehurst, *Politicians at War*, Pt. 3; Heffer, *Staring at God*, 205–238. See also Fraser, 'British "Shells Scandal" of 1915'.

83 Farr, 'Reginald McKenna as Chancellor', 60; Farr, *Reginald McKenna*, 282–284.

84 Farr, *Reginald McKenna*, 287. See also Farr, 'Reginald McKenna as Chancellor', 132.

85 Pugh, 'Asquith, Bonar Law, and the First Coalition'; Turner, *British Politics*, 56–64.

86 Farr, *Reginald McKenna*, Ch. 3.

87 Farr, 'Reginald McKenna as Chancellor', 86.

88 Farr, *Reginald McKenna*, Chs. 3–5; Farr, 'Reginald McKenna as Chancellor', 59.

89 Farr, 'Reginald McKenna as Chancellor', 79.

90 Ibid., 79–81.

91 Lloyd George, *War Memoirs*; Egerton, 'The Lloyd George "War Memoirs"'; Suttie, *Rewriting the First World War*.

92 Farr, 'Reginald McKenna as Chancellor', 197; Farr, *Reginald McKenna*, 7–8.

93 David, *Inside Asquith's Cabinet*, 247; Farr, 'Reginald McKenna as Chancellor', 132. See also Levine, *Politics, Religion, and Love*, 330.

94 Levine, *Politics, Religion, and Love*, 330.

95 Carosso, 'The Morgan Partnerships', Unfinished Manuscript, p. 4–15, Vincent Carosso Papers, ARC 1214, Pierpont Morgan Library, New York; French, *British Strategy*, 84–87.

96 Farr, 'Reginald McKenna as Chancellor', 132–134; see also Farr, *Reginald McKenna*, 291–292.

97 Lloyd George, *War Memoirs*, Vol. 1, 122–123.
98 '"Manipulation": BoE Helped Cover Up War Loan Shortfall', 9 August 2017, *Financial Times*, 2.
99 Farr, 'Reginald McKenna as Chancellor', 133.
100 Ibid., 132–134; see also Farr, *Reginald McKenna*, 291–292.
101 Kemmerer, 'The War and Interest Rates', 102.
102 Carosso, 'The Morgan Partnerships', Unfinished Manuscript, p. 4-24, Vincent Carosso Papers, ARC 1214, Pierpont Morgan Library, New York.
103 Ibid.; Farr, 'Reginald McKenna as Chancellor', 132–134; see also Farr, *Reginald McKenna*, 291–292.
104 'Exchange Market Ignores Stiffer London Money', 28 July 1915, *Wall Street Journal*, 8.
105 Report of the Cabinet Committee on the Co-Ordination of Military and Financial Effort, 4 February 1916, p. 17, CAB 27/4, The National Archives, Kew.
106 McPhail et al. to Cunliffe, 7 December 1915, London Exchange Committee Papers, C91/1, Bank of England Archive, London.
107 Carosso, 'The Morgan Partnerships', Unfinished Manuscript, pp. 4-21 to 4-32, Vincent Carosso Papers, ARC 1214, Pierpont Morgan Library, New York.
108 Farr, 'Reginald McKenna', 134–135; Carosso, 'The Morgan Partnerships', Unfinished Manuscript, pp. 4-32 to 4-37, Vincent Carosso Papers, ARC 1214, Pierpont Morgan Library, New York; Burk, *Britain, America, and the Sinews of War*, 63.
109 Feinstein, 'Britain's Overseas Investments in 1913'.
110 Wilkins, *History of Foreign Investment in the United States to 1914*, Chs. 5–16, quoted at 139, 165; Lewis, *America's Stake*, Chs. 2–4, 8; *History of the Ministry of Munitions*, Vol. 4, Pt. 3, 34.
111 White, *Story of Canada's War Finance*, 20.
112 'American Debts Abroad', *New York Times*, 14 October 1914, 10.
113 Wilkins, *History of Foreign Investment in the United States to 1914*, 165–166. Prevailing estimates in 1915 put the total at about $2–$3 billion. McKenna estimated British-owned American securities to total £600 million ($2.9 billion). See McKenna Evidence to the War Policy Committee, 23 August 1915, CAB 27/2, p. 136, The National Archives, Kew. Shortly thereafter, Lord Reading by contrast estimated the total sum at £400 million ($1.9 billion). See Cooper, 'Command of Gold Reversed', 214. John Bradbury allowed a larger possible range of £500–£800 million ($2.4–$3.8 billon). See Bradbury Memorandum, 9 September 1915, John Maynard Keynes Papers, T/7/65-67, King's College Library, Cambridge.
114 McKenna Memorandum, 22 July 1915, CAB 37/131/37, The National Archives, Kew; Farr, 'Reginald McKenna as Chancellor', 134.
115 Lambt, *Planning Armageddon*, 447–448.
116 Carosso, 'The Morgan Partnerships', Unfinished Manuscript, p. 4-38, Vincent Carosso Papers, ARC 1214, Pierpont Morgan Library, New York.
117 Farr, 'Reginald McKenna as Chancellor', 137.

118 Adams, *Arms and the Wizard*; Wrigley, 'Ministry of Munitions'; Lloyd-Jones and Lewis, *Arming the Western Front*, Chs. 6–7.
119 Burk, *Britain, America, and the Sinews of War*, 30.
120 Carosso, 'The Morgan Partnerships', Unfinished Manuscript, p. 3-84, Vincent Carosso Papers, ARC 1214, Pierpont Morgan Library, New York.
121 Ibid., p. 4-20.
122 *History of the Ministry of Munitions*, Vol. 2, Pt. 3, 11.
123 See Appendix II.
124 *History of the Ministry of Munitions*, Vol. 2, Pt. 3, 2.
125 Burk, *Britain, America, and the Sinews of War*, 34.
126 Ibid., 35–40; Carosso, 'The Morgan Partnerships', Unfinished Manuscript, pp. 3-98 to 3-105, Vincent Carosso Papers, ARC 1214, Pierpont Morgan Library, New York; *History of the Ministry of Munitions*, Vol. 2, Pt. 3, 45.
127 Carosso, 'The Morgan Partnerships', Unfinished Manuscript, p. 3-65, Vincent Carosso Papers, ARC 1214, Pierpont Morgan Library, New York; Neilson, *Strategy and Supply*, 102–106, 182–183.
128 'Food Higher in England', *New York Times*, 17 July 1915, 3; Broadberry and Howlett, 'The United Kingdom during World War I', 211; Paton, *Economic Position of the United Kingdom*, 12.
129 United States Senate, *Munitions Industry*, 8701; Morgan, *Studies in British Financial Policy*, 307. This number includes only British imports from the United States on private account, not government account, and is therefore likely a significant underestimate. See Appendix I.
130 Lambert, *Planning Armageddon*, 254–270, 437–454; Rappaport, *British Press and Wilsonian Neutrality*, 67–70; Grey Memorandum, 22 July 1915, CAB 37/131/36, The National Archives, Kew; Link, *Wilson: The Struggle for Neutrality*, 599–613; Devlin, *Too Proud to Fight*, 351–355.
131 House to Plunkett, 19 July 1915, Edward House Papers, 91:3131, Yale University Library, New Haven, Connecticut.
132 Link, *Papers of Woodrow Wilson*, Vol. 34, 11–12.
133 Lambert, *Planning Armageddon*, 437–454; Rappaport, *British Press and Wilsonian Neutrality*, 67–70; Grey Memorandum, 22 July 1915, CAB 37/131/36, The National Archives, Kew.
134 Carosso, 'The Morgan Partnerships', Unfinished Manuscript, p. 4-33, Vincent Carosso Papers, ARC 1214, Pierpont Morgan Library, New York.
135 'Cotton Prices in the World Wars', March 1944, *Monthly Review of Financial and Business Conditions (Fifth Federal Reserve District)*, 2–4; Devlin, *Too Proud to Fight*, 354; Paton, *Economic Position of the United Kingdom*, 52.
136 'British Credit Here May Need Cover of Allies', *Wall Street Journal*, 10 August 1915 (Morning Edition), 8, c. 1; Burk, *Britain, America, and the Sinews of War*, 55–58.

Chapter 2

1 'British Gold Shipment Less than $20,000,000', *Wall Street Journal*, 12 August 1915 (Morning Edition), 8.
2 See Carosso, 'The Morgan Partnerships,' Unfinished Manuscript, pp. 4-41 to 4-43, 4-84, Vincent Carosso Papers, ARC 1214, Pierpont Morgan Library,

New York; Horn, *Britain, France, and the Financing of the First World War*, 102–103.

3 Estimated using Morgan, *Studies in British Financial Policy*, 308.
4 In particular, Horn, *Britain, France, and the Financing of the First World War*, 106.
5 Johnson, *Collected Writings of John Maynard Keynes*, Vol. 16, 204.
6 War Trade Bureau of Research, *Export Trade Policy of the United Kingdom*, 43.
7 *Parliamentary Debates*, 88 H.C. Deb. 5 s., 944.
8 Morgan, *Studies in British Financial Policy*, 307. These figures exclude purchases made on British government account, which may have been very substantial.
9 Farr, 'Reginald McKenna as Chancellor', 137; Johnson, *Collected Writings of John Maynard Keynes*, Vol. 16, 109.
10 See Cassar, *Asquith as War Leader*; Clifford, *The Asquiths*; Jenkins, *Asquith*; and Spender and Asquith, *Life of Herbert Henry Asquith*.
11 Turner, 'Cabinets, Committees and Secretariats', 63.
12 Turner, *British Politics*, 61–64; Adams, *Bonar Law*, 187–192; Blake, *Unknown Prime Minister*, 248–252; Heffer, *Staring at God*, 231–232.
13 Lambert, *Planning Armageddon*, 459.
14 Carosso, 'The Morgan Partnerships,' Unfinished Manuscript, p. 4-43, Vincent Carosso Papers, ARC 1214, Pierpont Morgan Library, New York; Burk, *Britain, America, and the Sinews of War*, 64.
15 [McKenna] Cabinet Note, 26 August 1915, T 170/73, The National Archives, Kew.
16 Treasury Memorandum, [Late August 1915], T 170/73, The National Archives, Kew.
17 Ibid.
18 Treasury/Ministry of Munitions Correspondence, August–September 1915, T 170/73, The National Archives, Kew; Neilson, *Strategy and Supply*, 116–120.
19 'The Money Market', 4 September 1915, *Economist*, 1.
20 See Isaacs, *Rufus Isaacs*.
21 Link, *Wilson: The Struggle for Neutrality*, 616–625, quoted at 624; Carosso, 'The Morgan Partnerships,' Unfinished Manuscript, p. 4-47, Vincent Carosso Papers, ARC 1214, Pierpont Morgan Library, New York.
22 The best account is Carosso, 'The Morgan Partnerships,' Unfinished Manuscript, pp. 4-44 to 4-87, Vincent Carosso Papers, ARC 1214, Pierpont Morgan Library, New York. For US interest rates in this period, see Kemmerer, 'The War and Interest Rates', 102. Quote taken from White, *Story of Canada's War Finance*, 22. See also Horn, *Britain, France, and the Financing of the First World War*, 107–112; Burk, *Britain, America, and the Sinews of War*, 67–75.
23 United States Senate, *Munitions Industry*, 8632.

24 See, for example, 'Sell $320,000,000 of Allies Bonds', 12 December 1915, *New York Times*, 1; and 'Demand Exceeds $500,000,000 Loan', 30 September 1915, *New York Times*, 1.

25 Carosso, 'The Morgan Partnerships,' Unfinished Manuscript, pp. 4-82 to 4-87, Vincent Carosso Papers, ARC 1214, Pierpont Morgan Library, New York.

26 Johnson, *Collected Writings of John Maynard Keynes*, Vol. 16, 120; Horn, *Britain, France, and the Financing of the First World War*, 112–113; Montagu Memorandum, [15 December 1915], Montagu Papers, AS5/1/5, Trinity College Library, Cambridge. Or, as Reading put it, 'every increase of interest would further adversely affect our credit'. See Reading Memorandum, November 1915, CAB 37/136/39, The [UK] National Archives, Kew.

27 Reading Memorandum, November 1915, CAB 37/136/39, The [UK] National Archives, Kew.

28 Farr, 'Reginald McKenna as Chancellor', 138; Neilson, *Strategy and Supply*, 111–114.

29 United States Senate, *Munitions Industry*, 9232.

30 See '$1,550,000,000 of Our Shares Taken Back', 18 December 1915, *New York Times*, 12.

31 Burk, *Britain, America, and the Sinews of War*, 263.

32 United Kingdom War Office, *Statistics of the Military Effort*, 364.

33 LCES, *British Economy*, 8; Booth, *British Economy*, 124.

34 At the time, these figures were usually given in weekly recruitment rates – McKenna favoured 5,000–10,000 per week, while the conscriptionists wanted 35,000. Annualizing these figures using a fifty-two-week year, to facilitate a more meaningful comparison with the overall British labour force, gives 260,000–520,000 men per year for McKenna compared with 1,820,000 for the conscriptionists. See, for example, Cassar, *Asquith as War Leader*, 154; and Farr, 'Reginald McKenna as Chancellor', 153–154.

35 Adams and Poirier, *Conscription Controversy*, 94-99; Cassar, *Asquith as War Leader*, 150–151; Turner, *British Politics*, 64–65.

36 Farr, 'Reginald McKenna as Chancellor', 141.

37 War Policy Committee Meeting Minutes, 23 August 1915, CAB 27/2, The National Archives, Kew.

38 Calculated combining military spending figures in Broadberry and Howlett, 'United Kingdom during World War I', 216, with GDP figures from Samuel H. Williamson, 'What Was the U.K. GDP Then?', *MeasuringWorth.com*, University of Illinois-Chicago, 2017.

39 War Policy Committee Meeting Minutes, 23 August 1915, CAB 27/2, The National Archives, Kew.

40 LCES, *British Economy*, 8; Booth, *British Economy*, 124; Samuel H. Williamson, 'What Was the U.K. GDP Then?', *MeasuringWorth.com*, University of Illinois-Chicago, 2017.

41 Adams and Poirier, *Conscription Controversy*, 110.

42 Curzon Memorandum, 28 August 1915, CAB 27/2, The National Archives, Kew.

43 Wilson, *Political Diaries of C. P. Scott*, 137; Turner, *British Politics*, 74–75; Farr, 'Reginald McKenna as Chancellor', 153–154.
44 Hart, *Gallipoli*, Chs. 12–16; Erickson, *Gallipoli*, Chs. 3–4; Prior, *Gallipoli*, Chs. 17–26.
45 French, *British Strategy*, 110.
46 Watson, *Ring of Steel*, 268; DiNardo, *Breakthrough*; Stone, *Russian Army*, Ch. 7.
47 Greenhalgh, *French Army*, 77–78.
48 Gooch, *Italian Army*, Ch. 3; Schindler, *Isonzo*, Chs. 3–4.
49 Hall, 'Bulgaria in the First World War'; French, *British Strategy*, 108–110.
50 Link, *Wilson: The Struggle for Neutrality*, Ch. 13; Devlin, *Too Proud to Fight*, Chs. 10–11; Thompson, *Woodrow Wilson*, 113–115.
51 Keohane, *Party of Patriotism*, Ch. 2; Johnson, 'The Liberal War Committee'.
52 French, *British Strategy*, 110.
53 War Policy Committee Report, 19 September 1915, CAB 27/2, The National Archives, Kew.
54 Turner, *British Politics*, 78; Cassar, *Asquith as War Leader*, 152; Horne, *Labour at War*, 51, 398.
55 Asquith, *Memories*, Vol. 2, 109; Cassar, *Asquith as War Leader*, 151. See also Heffer, *Staring at God*, 288.
56 Adams and Poirier, *Conscription Controversy*, 116–118.
57 Balfour Memorandum, 19 September 1915, CAB 37/134/25, The National Archives, Kew.
58 'The Second War Budget', *Economist*, 25 September 1915, 463; *Parliamentary Debates*, 74 H.C. Deb. 5 s., 350–352; Farr, 'Reginald McKenna as Chancellor', 145–149. The projected annual government revenue before McKenna's budget was £272 million; McKenna increased that by another £107 million. See also Heffer, *Staring at God*, 286–287.
59 Keynes Handwritten Notes for Talk at Admiralty, 15 February 1917, John Maynard Keynes Papers, T/11/12-19, King's College Library, Cambridge.
60 Farr, 'Reginald McKenna as Chancellor', 136, 351 n. 41; Farr, *Reginald McKenna*, 295.
61 Johnson, *Collected Writings of John Maynard Keynes*, Vol. 16, 138–140.
62 Broadberry and Howlett, 'United Kingdom during World War I', 212; Johnson, *Collected Writings of John Maynard Keynes*, Vol. 16, 150–156.
63 Farr, 'Reginald McKenna as Chancellor', 159.
64 The British had allocated £246 million ($1.17 billion) in loans to the Allies for the period 13 October 1915–31 March 1916; see Johnson, *Collected Writings of John Maynard Keynes*, Vol. 16, 138. In fact, they managed to spend only £144.9 million ($691 million) during this period. See Keynes Memorandum, [April 1916], John Maynard Keynes Papers, T/7/126, King's College Library, Cambridge. The difference is $482 million.
65 Johnson, *Collected Writings of John Maynard Keynes*, Vol. 16, 186.
66 Lloyd George, *War Memoirs*, Vol. 2, 682–686.
67 Wilson, *Political Diaries of C. P. Scott*, 138.
68 Cassar, *Asquith as War Leader*, 153–154; Turner, *British Politics*, 67–68; Farr, 'Reginald McKenna as Chancellor', 154.

69 Turner, *British Politics*, 69–71; Adams, *Conscription Controversy*, 122–125.
70 Adams and Poirier, *Conscription Controversy*, 119–127; Heffer, *Staring at God*, 289–291.
71 Cassar, *Asquith as War Leader*, 155.
72 Balfour Memorandum, 17 October 1915, John Maynard Keynes Papers, T/1, King's College Library, Cambridge.
73 Turner, *British Politics*, 71; Adams and Poirier, *Conscription Controversy*, 125–126.
74 Bonar Law Memorandum, 25 October 1915, CAB 37/136/30, The [UK] National Archives, Kew.
75 Computed from Morgan, *Studies in British Financial Policy*, 307. These figures appear to include only imports made on private account, and not direct British government purchases, which have never been tabulated.
76 Ally, 'War and Gold'; Tooze, *Deluge*, 209–215.
77 Attard, 'Politics, Finance and Anglo-Australian Relations'.
78 White, *Story of Canada's War Finance*, 17.
79 Hall, 'Bulgaria in the First World War'.
80 Hart, *Gallipoli*, Chs. 17–19; Erickson, *Gallipoli*, Chs. 4–5; Prior, *Gallipoli*, Chs. 14–15; Clifford, 'British Intelligence and Political Leadership during the Gallipoli Campaign'.
81 Link, *Papers of Woodrow Wilson*, Vol. 34, 84–85.
82 French, *British Strategy*, 111–112.
83 Holmes, *Little Field Marshal*, 304. See also Lloyd, *Loos 1915*; Warner, *Battle of Loos*.
84 Doughty, *Pyrrhic Victory*, 188–195; Greenhalgh, *French Army*, Ch. 3.
85 Stone, *Russian Army*, Ch. 7.
86 Schindler, *Isonzo*, Chs. 5–6.
87 Link, *Wilson: The Struggle for Neutrality*, Chs. 16–17, 19; Devlin, *Too Proud to Fight*, Ch. 11.
88 Lambert, *Planning Armageddon*, 470–473; Link, *Wilson: The Struggle for Neutrality*, Ch. 20; Devlin, *Too Proud to Fight*, 356–358. Quote taken from Edward House Diaries, 2 June 1915, Yale University Library, New Haven, Connecticut.
89 Adams and Poirier, *Conscription Controversy*, 133–136; Turner, *British Politics*, 73–75; Heffer, *Staring at God*, 302–306.
90 United Kingdom War Office, *Statistics of the Military Effort*, 364.
91 Adams, *Conscription Controversy*, 136–137; Grigg, *Lloyd George: From Peace to War*, 321, 329–332; Turner, *British Politics*, 75–76.
92 Asquith, *Memories*, Vol. 2, 113; Adams and Poirier, *Conscription Controversy*, 134; Heffer, *Staring at God*, 306.
93 *Parliamentary Debates*, 77 H.C. Deb. 5 s., 213–437.
94 Taylor, *Lloyd George: A Diary*, 89; Adams and Poirier, *Conscription Controversy*, 136–137; Cassar, *Asquith as War Leader*, 160.
95 Farr, 'Winter and Discontent', 121–123; Adams and Poirier, *Conscription Controversy*, 137–140; Farr, 'Reginald McKenna as Chancellor', 233–235; Heffer, *Staring at God*, 307–308.
96 Farr, 'Reginald McKenna as Chancellor', 365–366, n. 47.

97 Trevelyan, *Grey of Fallodon*, 369–371. Though unwilling to resign, Montagu also supported McKenna: see Montagu to Asquith, 6 January 1916, Edwin Montagu Papers, AS5/1/7, Trinity College Library, Cambridge; and McKenna Memorandum, [January 1916], Edwin Montagu Papers, AS5/1/17, Trinity College Library, Cambridge.

98 Farr, 'Winter and Discontent', 122–123; Adams and Poirier, *Conscription Controversy*, 137–138; Cassar, *Asquith as War Leader*, 160–162; Waley, *Edwin Montagu*, 82; Asquith to Montagu, 28 December 1915, Edwin Montagu Papers, AS1/1/45, Trinity College Library, Cambridge; Montagu to Grey, 29, 30 December 1915, Edwin Montagu Papers, AS6/9/16, AS6/10/28, Trinity College Library, Cambridge.

99 Maurice Hankey Diaries, 30 December 1915, Churchill College Archive Centre, Cambridge; Farr, 'Winter and Discontent', 123–124; Adams and Poirier, *Conscription Controversy*, 137–138.

100 Farr, 'Reginald McKenna as Chancellor', 160.

101 Adams and Poirier, *Conscription Controversy*, 138–139; Montagu to Asquith, 3 January [1916], AS1/1/48, Edwin Montagu Papers, Trinity College Library, Cambridge.

Chapter 3

1 Neu, *Colonel House*, 185ff.

2 Edward House Diaries, 7 May 1915, Yale University Library, New Haven, Connecticut.

3 See Link, *Wilson: The Struggle for Neutrality*, Chs. 12–13, 16, 19.

4 Edward House Diaries, 21 August 1915, Yale University Library, New Haven, Connecticut.

5 Ibid., 22 August 1915.

6 Neu, *Colonel House*, 205.

7 Edward House Diaries, 28 September 1915, Yale University Library, New Haven, Connecticut; for context, see Link, *Wilson: The Struggle for Neutrality*, Ch. 19.

8 Ibid., 8, 11, 13, 14 October 1915. House had envisaged precisely this German threat to the Monroe Doctrine in his novel before the war, albeit in the form of a German-British diplomatic alliance, rather than a German victory in a European war: see House, *Philip Dru*, Ch. 28.

9 Ibid., 8, 11 October 1915.

10 Link, *Papers of Woodrow Wilson*, Vol. 35, 81–82; Devlin, *Too Proud to Fight*, 382–383; Edward House Diaries, 15 October 1915, Yale University Library, New Haven, Connecticut.

11 Link, *Papers of Woodrow Wilson*, Vol. 35, 186–187, 192; Edward House Diaries, 10–11 November 1915, Yale University Library, New Haven, Connecticut.

12 Link, *Papers of Woodrow Wilson*, Vol. 35, 254–256.

13 Edward House Diaries, 25, 27–28 November, 14–15 December 1915, Yale University Library, New Haven, Connecticut; Link, *Papers of Woodrow Wilson*, Vol. 35, 310–311, 346–347, 353, 355–357, 381–383.

14 Link, *Papers of Woodrow Wilson*, Vol. 35, 364.
15 Ibid., 381–383.
16 Ibid., 387–388.
17 Ibid., 387–388.
18 Link, *Wilson: Confusions and Crises*, 112–113.
19 Esposito, *Legacy of Woodrow Wilson*, 64. As a grammarian would put it, if the word 'moral' is read as a non-restrictive adjective, rather than as a restrictive adjective, a completely different interpretation is reached.
20 Link, *Papers of Woodrow Wilson*, Vol. 35, 80–81, 356.
21 Ibid., 311, 356.
22 Ibid., 388.
23 Tucker, *Woodrow Wilson*, 155; Devlin, *Too Proud to Fight*, 390–391; Doenecke, *Nothing Less than War*, 138–139.
24 House Diaries, 6 January 1916, Yale University Library, New Haven, Connecticut.
25 Ibid., 6 January 1916.
26 Trevelyan, *Grey of Fallodon*, 319; Devlin, *Too Proud to Fight*, 165–167, 278–279; Grey to House, 22 September 1915, Edward House Papers, 53:1664, Yale University Library, New Haven.
27 Link, *Papers of Woodrow Wilson*, Vol. 35, 466.
28 Ibid., 453–455, 457.
29 Edward House Diaries, 6 January 1916, Yale University Library, New Haven, Connecticut.
30 Adams, *Balfour*, Chs. 6–11. See also Tomes, *Balfour and Foreign Policy*; Zebel, *Balfour*; and Egremont, *Balfour*.
31 Edward House Diaries, 4 March 1915, Yale University Library, New Haven, Connecticut.
32 Ibid., 10 January 1916; Link, *Papers of Woodrow Wilson*, Vol. 35, 465–466.
33 War Committee Minutes, 28 December 1915, 13 January 1916, CAB 22/3, The National Archives, Kew; Balfour Memorandum, 21 January 1916, CAB 37/141/17, The National Archives, Kew; French, *British Strategy*, 175; Larsen, 'War Pessimism', 801.
34 Grey Memorandum, 14 January 1916, Edward Grey Papers, FO 800/96, The National Archives, Kew.
35 Wilson, *Diaries of C. P. Scott*, 165–166; Edward House Diaries, 14 January 1916, Yale University Library, New Haven, Connecticut.
36 Edward House Diaries, 14, 15 January 1916, Yale University Library, New Haven, Connecticut; Link, *Papers of Woodrow Wilson*, Vol. 35, 484–486.
37 Ibid., 15 January 1916; Link, *Papers of Woodrow Wilson*, Vol. 35, 486–488.
38 Balfour Memorandum, 19 January 1916, TNA, FO 899/3, CAB 37/141/11.
39 Edward House Diaries, 15 January 1916, Yale University Library, New Haven, Connecticut; Link, *Papers of Woodrow Wilson*, Vol. 35, 487–488; Wilson, *Political Diaries of C. P. Scott*, 179.
40 Edward House Diaries, 19 January 1916, Yale University Library, New Haven, Connecticut.
41 Proceedings of the Cabinet Committee on the Co-ordination of Military and Financial Effort, January 1916, CAB 27/4, The National Archives, Kew.
42 Farr, 'Reginald McKenna as Chancellor', 161.

43 Proceedings of the Cabinet Committee on the Co-ordination of Military and Financial Effort, January 1916, CAB 27/4, The National Archives, Kew

44 Ibid., pp. 23, 27, 38; Johnson, *Collected Writings of John Maynard Keynes*, Vol. 16, 185.

45 Proceedings of the Cabinet Committee on the Co-ordination of Military and Financial Effort, January 1916, p. 139, CAB 27/4, The National Archives, Kew.

46 Ibid., p. 38.

47 Roskill, *Hankey*, 243.

48 Proceedings of the Cabinet Committee on the Co-ordination of Military and Financial Effort, January 1916, p. 54, CAB 27/4, The National Archives, Kew.

49 Ibid., pp. 106–124.

50 Ibid., pp. 139, 201–202, 269.

51 Farr, 'Reginald McKenna as Chancellor', 236.

52 Proceedings of the Cabinet Committee on the Co-ordination of Military and Financial Effort, January 1916, pp. 201–204, 224, CAB 27/4, The National Archives, Kew.

53 Hankey to Robertson, 24 January 1916, CAB 17/159, The National Archives, Kew.

54 Proceedings of the Cabinet Committee on the Co-ordination of Military and Financial Effort, January 1916, p. 187, CAB 27/4, The National Archives, Kew.

55 Adams and Poirier, *Conscription Controversy*, 145–146.

56 Proceedings of the Cabinet Committee on the Co-ordination of Military and Financial Effort, January 1916, p. 53, CAB 27/4, The National Archives, Kew.

57 Report of the Cabinet Committee on the Co-ordination of Military and Financial Effort, January 1916, 4 February 1916, CAB 27/4, The National Archives, Kew.

58 Proceedings of the Cabinet Committee on the Co-ordination of Military and Financial Effort, January 1916, pp. 207, 269, CAB 27/4, The National Archives, Kew.

59 Montagu to Asquith, 5 February 1916, Edwin Montagu Papers, AS5/1/10, Trinity College Library, Cambridge. This letter is printed in Waley, *Edwin Montagu*, 88–89, although Waley misstates the date it was sent.

60 Runciman to McKenna, 23 January 1916, MCKN 5/9, Churchill College Archive Centre, Cambridge.

61 Edward House Diaries, 19 January 1916, Yale University Library, New Haven, Connecticut. For McKenna's friendship with Carver, see McKenna–Carver correspondence, Clifford Carver Papers, Mudd Manuscript Library, Princeton, New Jersey.

62 Maurice Hankey Diaries, 18, 22 January 1916, HNKY 1/1, Maurice Hankey Papers, Churchill College Archive Centre, Cambridge.

63 Hankey to Balfour, 25 May 1916, Add 49703, Arthur James Balfour Papers, British Library, London.

64 Hall to Spring Rice, 12 February 1916, CASR 1/44, Cecil Spring Rice Papers, Churchill College Archive Centre, Cambridge; Edward House

Diaries, 8, 13, 18 January 1916, Yale University Library, New Haven, Connecticut; Maurice Hankey Diaries, 18 January 1916, Churchill College Archive Centre, Cambridge.

65 Link, *Papers of Woodrow Wilson*, vol. 35, 483; vol. 36, 138, 166, 180, 203, 217.

66 House to Hall, 20 April 1916, Edward House Papers, 144:6220, Yale University Library, New Haven, Connecticut. For more on Gaunt, see Gaunt, *Yield of the Years*; and Delano, *Guy Gaunt*.

67 Edward House Diaries, 13 November 1915, 14 January 1916, Yale University Library, New Haven, Connecticut.

68 Link, *Papers of Woodrow Wilson*, Vol. 35, 453.

69 Hall to Keyes, 19 June 1915, Roger Keyes Papers, 82386, British Library, London.

70 Link, *Papers of Woodrow Wilson*, Vol. 35, 453, 457.

71 Ibid., 458–459, 483.

72 Maurice Hankey Diaries, 27 January 1916, Churchill College Archive Centre, Cambridge; Roskill, *Hankey*, 247.

73 Devlin, *Too Proud to Fight*, 419–420, 427; Link, *Wilson: Confusions and Crises*, 116–117, 149–150, 160–161. For a detailed account of the armed merchantmen issue, see Devlin, *Too Proud to Fight*, 410–422, 426–430; and Link, *Wilson: Confusions and Crises*, 142–194.

74 Link, *Papers of Woodrow Wilson*, Vol. 35, 462.

75 *FRUS 1916*, 150–151; Edward House Diaries, 28 January, 4 March 1916, Yale University Library, New Haven, Connecticut.

76 See, for example, '"Prepare", Wilson Pleads, 'No Man Can Be Sure of the Morrow'; Says He Is Ready to Fight for Honor', 28 January 1916, *New York Times*, 1.

77 Link, *Papers of Woodrow Wilson*, Vol. 35, 498.

78 Ibid., 36, 52.

79 Ibid., 85.

80 Devlin, *Too Proud to Fight*, 404–410.

81 Maurice Hankey Diaries, 1 February 1916, Churchill College Archive Centre, Cambridge; Roskill, *Hankey*, 247.

82 Edward House Diaries, 10 February 1916, Yale University Library, New Haven, Connecticut.

83 Maurice Hankey Diaries, 1 February 1916, Churchill College Archive Centre, Cambridge; Roskill, *Hankey*, 247; Edward House Diaries, 10 February 1916, Yale University Library, New Haven, Connecticut.

84 *FRUS: The Lansing Papers*, Vol. 1, 339.

85 Grey Memorandum, February 1916, H. H. Asquith Papers, VI:124, Bodleian Library, Oxford; Link, *Wilson: Confusions and Crises*, 160–161.

86 See Edward House Diaries, 26–29 January 1916, Yale University Library, New Haven, Connecticut; and Link, *Papers of Woodrow Wilson*, Vol. 36, 52, 85, 122–124.

87 Edward House Diaries, 7 February 1916, Yale University Library, New Haven, Connecticut.

88 'Deuxieme Entrevue Du Colonel House', 7 February 1916, Francis Bertie Papers, FO 800/181, The National Archives, Kew; Link, *Papers of Woodrow Wilson*, 149.

89 Link, *Wilson: Confusions and Crises*, 125; Devlin, *Too Proud to Fight*, 425.
90 Edward House Diaries, 10 February 1916, Yale University Library, New Haven, Connecticut; Link, *Papers of Woodrow Wilson*, Vol. 36, 166–168.
91 Edward House Diaries, 11 February 1916, Yale University Library, New Haven, Connecticut; Link, *Papers of Woodrow Wilson*, Vol. 36, 170.
92 Link, *Papers of Woodrow Wilson*, Vol. 36, 173, 180; Grey to Balfour, 18 February 1916, Edward Grey Papers, FO 800/88, The National Archives, Kew; Edward House Diaries, 10–14 February 1916, Yale University Library, New Haven, Connecticut; Devlin, *Too Proud to Fight*, 426–430.
93 Hodgson, *Woodrow Wilson's Right Hand*, 118.
94 Edward House Diaries, 11 February 1916, Yale University Library, New Haven, Connecticut.
95 Ibid., 14 February 1916.
96 Ibid., 14 January, 10, 11; 14 February 1916.
97 Taylor, *Lloyd George: A Diary*, 100.
98 Maurice Hankey Diaries, 12 February 1916, Churchill College Archive Centre, Cambridge; Hankey, *Supreme Command*, Vol. 2, 479.
99 Edward House Diaries, 14 February 1916, Yale University Library, New Haven, Connecticut.
100 Ibid., 14 February 1916.
101 Asquith to Henley, 15 February 1916, Asquith-Henley Papers, MS Eng Lett c 542/3, Bodleian Library, Oxford.
102 Edward House Diaries, 15 February 1916, Yale University Library, New Haven, Connecticut.
103 Ibid., 16, 17 February 1916.
104 Balfour to Spring Rice, 16 February 1916, CASR 1/2, Cecil Spring Rice Papers, Churchill College Archive Centre, Cambridge.
105 Hankey, *Supreme Command*, Vol. 1, 361.
106 Edward House Diaries, 17 February 1916, Yale University Library, New Haven, Connecticut.
107 Ibid., 17 February 1916.
108 Wilson inserted the word 'probably' at this point.
109 Edward House Diaries, 17 February 1916, Yale University Library, New Haven, Connecticut; Link, *Papers of Woodrow Wilson*, Vol. 36, 180; Devlin, *Too Proud to Fight*, 436–437; May, *World War and American Isolation*, 355; Link, *Wilson: Confusions and Crises*, 134–135.
110 Edward House Diaries, 21 February 1916, Yale University Library, New Haven, Connecticut; Grey Memoranda, 17, 22 February 1916, Francis Bertie Papers, FO 800/181, The National Archives, Kew.
111 Edward House Diaries, 22 February 1916, Yale University Library, New Haven, Connecticut.
112 Taylor, *Lloyd George: A Diary*, 101.
113 War Committee Minutes, 22 February 1916, CAB 22/8, The National Archives, Kew.
114 Edward House Diaries, 15, 23 February 1916, Yale University Library, New Haven, Connecticut.

115 War Committee Minutes, 22 February 1916, CAB 22/8, The National Archives, Kew.
116 Edward House Diaries, 11 February 1916, Yale University Library, New Haven, Connecticut.
117 War Committee Minutes, 22 February 1916, CAB 22/8, The National Archives, Kew. Emphasis added.
118 Edward House Diaries, 23 February 1916, Yale University Library, New Haven, Connecticut.
119 Taylor, *Lloyd George: A Diary*, 101–102.
120 Wilson, *Diaries of C. P. Scott*, 165–166, 177; Edward House Diaries, 14 January 1916, Yale University Library, New Haven, Connecticut.
121 Edward House Diaries, 23, 24, 25 February, 4 March 1916, Yale University Library, New Haven, Connecticut.
122 See Edward House Papers, file 120:4257, Yale University Library, New Haven, Connecticut.
123 Link, *Papers of Woodrow Wilson*, Vol. 36, 166–168, 180, 203.
124 Ibid., 166.
125 Ibid., 173.
126 Ibid., 180.
127 Hall to Spring Rice, 12 February 1916, CASR 1/44, Cecil Spring Rice Papers, Churchill College Archive Centre, Cambridge.
128 File HW 7/17, The National Archives, Kew.
129 Edward House Diaries, 4 March 1916, Yale University Library, New Haven, Connecticut.
130 Link, *Wilson: Confusions and Crises*, Ch. 6; Devlin, *Too Proud to Fight*, 438–447; *New York Times*, 1–8 March 1916.
131 Edward House Diaries, 4 March 1916, Yale University Library, New Haven, Connecticut.
132 Ibid., 7 March 1916; Link, *Papers of Woodrow Wilson*, Vol. 36, 266.
133 Edward House Diaries, 6 March 1916, Yale University Library, New Haven, Connecticut.

Chapter 4

1 Proceedings of the Cabinet Committee on the Co-ordination of Military and Financial Effort, January 1916, p. 139, CAB 27/4, The National Archives, Kew.
2 Douglas Haig Papers, 29 May 1916, WO 256/10, The National Archives, Kew.
3 Bertie to Grey, 28 February, 2 March 1916, Lord Hardinge of Penhurst Papers, 23, Cambridge University Library.
4 Grey to Bertie, 5 March 1916, Lord Hardinge of Penhurst Papers, 23, Cambridge University Library. Some authors have misquoted Grey as having written 'profitable friend' in place of 'possible friend'; see, for example, Williams, *Colonel House and Sir Edward Grey*, 88, 96–97, 113. This has arisen out of a copying error in Grey to Bertie, 5 March 1916, Francis Bertie Papers, FO 800/181, The National Archives, Kew. The original letter is located in the

Francis Bertie Papers, 63041, British Library, London. It confirms the copy in the Lord Hardinge of Penhurst Papers.

5 Bertie to Grey, 28 February, 2 March 1916, Lord Hardinge of Penhurst Papers, 23, Cambridge University Library.

6 Page to House, 25 May 1916, Edward House Papers, 86:2989, Yale University Library, New Haven, Connecticut.

7 Balfour to House, 2 March 1916, Edward House Papers, 10:285, Yale University Library, New Haven, Connecticut. Emphasis added.

8 Edward House Diaries, 20 March 1916, Yale University Library, New Haven, Connecticut.

9 House to Balfour, 24 March 1916, YUL, Edward House Papers, 10:285, Yale University Library, New Haven, Connecticut.

10 Devlin, *Too Proud to Fight*, 455; Moggridge, *Maynard Keynes*, 255.

11 Maurice Hankey Diaries, 6, 11, 13, 15 March 1916, Churchill College Archive Centre, Cambridge. For Montagu's relationship with Asquith, see Waley, *Edwin Montagu*, 15–115.

12 Link, *Papers of Woodrow Wilson*, Vol. 35, 266.

13 Lloyd George, *War Memoirs*, Vol. 2, 412.

14 Cooper, 'The British Response', 961.

15 House to William Wiseman, 7 July 1927, Edward House Papers, 123:4338, Yale University Library, New Haven, Connecticut.

16 Maurice Hankey Diaries, 11 March 1916, Churchill College Archive Centre, Cambridge.

17 Ibid., 14 March 1916; Hankey, *Supreme Command*, Vol. 2, 479.

18 Grey Note, 15 March 1916, H. H. Asquith Papers, II:29, Bodleian Library, Oxford.

19 Maurice Hankey Diaries, 16 March 1916, Churchill College Archive Centre, Cambridge.

20 Link, *Wilson: Confusions and Crises*, 140.

21 Montagu to Asquith, 18 March 1916, H. H. Asquith Papers, 16, Bodleian Library, Oxford.

22 Montagu to Asquith, 18 March 1916, H. H. Asquith Papers, 16, Bodleian Library, Oxford; Larsen, 'British Intelligence'.

23 War Committee Minutes, 21 March 1916, CAB 22/13 (2), The National Archives, Kew.

24 Ibid.

25 Ibid.

26 Larsen, 'British Intelligence', 702.

27 Cooper, 'The British Response', 966–967.

28 Ibid., 959, 962, 966–967.

29 Ibid., 966–967.

30 Link, *Papers of Woodrow Wilson*, Vol. 36, 443–444, 511.

31 Ibid., 443–445. House had had a previous discussion with the French Ambassador on 30 March, but had not informed him of any desire to activate the pact. See Link, *Papers of Woodrow Wilson*, Vol. 36, 387–391. Wilson and House ultimately decided not to pursue further conversations with the French. See Edward House Diaries, 12 April 1916, Yale University Library, New Haven, Connecticut.

32 Ibid., 511–512.
33 War Committee Minutes, 7 April 1916, CAB 22/15, The National Archives, Kew.
34 Maurice Hankey Diaries, 7 April 1916, Churchill College Archive Centre, Cambridge.
35 Robertson Memorandum, 21 March 1916, CAB 17/159, The National Archives, Kew.
36 Report of the Cabinet Committee on the Co-Ordination of Military and Financial Effort, 13 April 1916, p. 20, CAB 27/4, The National Archives, Kew.
37 Selborne to Curzon, 30 March 1916, Lord Curzon Papers, MSS Eur F112/117, British Library India Office Section, London.
38 Maurice Hankey Diaries, 2 May 1916, Churchill College Archive Centre, Cambridge; Report of the Cabinet Committee on the Co-Ordination of Military and Financial Effort, 13 April 1916, pp. 14, 20–21, CAB 27/4, The National Archives, Kew.
39 Report of the Cabinet Committee on the Co-Ordination of Military and Financial Effort, 13 April 1916, p. 20, CAB 27/4, The National Archives, Kew.
40 McDermott, *British Military Service Tribunals*.
41 Proceedings of the Cabinet Committee on the Co-ordination of Military and Financial Effort, April 1916, pp. 325, 338–339, CAB 27/4, The National Archives, Kew.
42 See, for example, Adams and Poirier, *Conscription Controversy*, 149–157.
43 Report of the Cabinet Committee on the Co-Ordination of Military and Financial Effort, 13 April 1916, pp. 14–15, CAB 27/4, The National Archives, Kew; Proceedings of the Cabinet Committee on the Co-ordination of Military and Financial Effort, April 1916, pp. 341–342, CAB 27/4, The National Archives, Kew.
44 Proceedings of the Cabinet Committee on the Co-ordination of Military and Financial Effort, April 1916, p. 337, CAB 27/4, The National Archives, Kew.
45 Gilbert, *Organizer of Victory*, 306–308; Heffer, *Staring at God*, 326–327.
46 Maurice Hankey Diaries, 14 April 1916, Churchill College Archive Centre, Cambridge.
47 Proceedings of the Cabinet Committee on the Co-ordination of Military and Financial Effort, April 1916, pp. 348–355, CAB 27/4, The National Archives, Kew.
48 Ibid., pp. 356–358.
49 Roskill, *Hankey*, Vol. 1, 264.
50 Army Council Memorandum, 15 April 1916, CAB 17/159, The National Archives, Kew.
51 Adams and Poirier, *Conscription Controversy*, 160.
52 Addison Diary, 17 April 1916, Christopher Addison Papers, MS.Addison dep.d.2, Bodleian Library, Oxford.
53 Adams and Poirier, *Conscription Controversy*, 159–162.
54 Harcourt Cabinet Minutes/Diary, 17 April 1916, Lewis Harcourt Papers, MS. Eng. c. 8271, Bodleian Library, Oxford.

55 Ibid.
56 Taylor, *Lloyd George: A Diary*, 105–106.
57 Wilson, *Political Diaries of C. P. Scott*, 199.
58 Addison Diary, 17 April 1916, Christopher Addison Papers, MS.Addison dep.d.2, Bodleian Library, Oxford.
59 Adams and Poirier, *Conscription Controversy*, 163–166.
60 Asquith Secret Session Speech Notes, April 1916, CAB 17/159, The National Archives, Kew; Roskill, *Hankey*, Vol. 1, 265.
61 Adams and Poirier, *Conscription Controversy*, 167–168; Heffer, *Staring at God*, 329–330.
62 Roskill, *Hankey*, Vol. 1, 266–267.
63 Grigg, *Lloyd George: From Peace to War*, 337.
64 *Parliamentary Debates*, 82 H.C. Deb. 5 s., 177.
65 Carosso, 'The Morgan Partnerships,' Unfinished Manuscript, pp. 4-96 to 4-100, Vincent Carosso Papers, ARC 1214, Pierpont Morgan Library, New York.
66 Interim Report of the Committee on War Office Expenditure, 24 March 1916, CAB 37/144/70, First Report of the Committee on War Office Expenditure, 29 May 1916, CAB 37/148/40, The National Archives, Kew.
67 First Report of the Committee on Admiralty Expenditure, 7 April 1916, CAB 37/145/16, The National Archives, Kew.
68 Addison Diary, 15 May 1915, Christopher Addison Papers, dep.d.2, Bodleian Library, Oxford.
69 Lloyd George, *War Memoirs*, Vol. 2, 684.
70 J. P. Morgan & Co. to Morgan, Grenfell, & Co. Telegram, 17 July 1916, John Maynard Keynes Papers, T/14/7, King's College Library, Cambridge.
71 Horn, *Britain, France, and the Financing of the First World War*, Ch. 6.
72 Neilson, *Strategy and Supply*, 182–185.
73 Horn, *Britain, France, and the Financing of the First World War*, quoted at 5; Neilson, *Strategy and Supply*.
74 Horn, *Britain, France, and the Financing of the First World War*, 128–129.
75 Horn, *Britain, France, and the Financing of the First World War*; Neilson, *Strategy and Supply*.
76 SDW to John Maynard Keynes, 25 May 1916, John Maynard Keynes Papers, T/14/3, King's College Library, Cambridge.
77 McKenna Memorandum, 19 May 1916, CAB 37/148/6, The National Archives, Kew.
78 Ibid.
79 Removing the underspending estimate from McKenna's figures in May gives $975 million. The actual amount was $985 million. See Johnson, *Collected Writings of John Maynard Keynes*, Vol. 16, 199.
80 Harcourt Cabinet Minutes, 25 May 1916, Lewis Harcourt Papers, MS. Eng. c. 8271, Bodleian Library, Oxford; Montagu Memorandum, [15 December 1915], Edwin Montagu Papers, AS5/1/5, Trinity College Library, Cambridge; Lambert, *Planning Armageddon*, 462. See also London Exchange Sub-Committee Memorandum, 16 November 1915, London Exchange Committee Papers, C91/1, Bank of England Archive, London.

81 'American Securities and the Exchange', 3 June 1916, *Economist*, 1057–1058. See also, for example, 'Mr. McKenna's New Tax', 30 May 1916, *Times*, 7, c. 2. Cf. Horn, *Britain, France, and the Financing of the First World War*, 133.

82 Farr, 'Reginald McKenna as Chancellor', 177.

83 McKenna to Runciman, 21 July 1916, William Runciman Papers, 149-1, University of Newcastle Robinson Library.

84 Lloyd George, *War Memoirs*, Vol. 2, 687.

85 Edwin House Diaries, 9 May 1915, 3 May 1916, Yale University Library, New Haven, Connecticut; 'Republican Party Platform of 1916', *The American Presidency Project*, University of California Santa Barbara, www.presidency.ucsb.edu.

86 Link, *Wilson: Confusions and Crises*, Ch. 9; Devlin, *Too Proud to Fight*, 476–483; Stevenson, *1917*, 16–19.

87 Link, *Papers of Woodrow Wilson*, Vol. 37, 6–7. A letter elaborating on the cable was sent on 15 May. See Link, *Papers of Woodrow Wilson*, Vol. 37, 21, 24.

88 Ibid., 43–44.

89 Ibid., 44, 57–58, 63–64.

90 Ibid., 94–95.

91 Woodward, *Military Correspondence of Field-Marshal Sir William Robertson*, 50–51.

92 Maurice Hankey Diaries, 24 May 1916, Churchill College Archive Centre, Cambridge.

93 Quoted in Hodgson, *Woodrow Wilson's Right Hand*, 107.

94 See CAB 22, The National Archives, Kew.

95 Curzon to Asquith, 24 May 1916, Lord Curzon Papers, MSS Eur F112/116, British Library India Office Section, London. Emphasis added.

96 Asquith to Curzon, 26 May 1916, Lord Curzon Papers, MSS Eur F112/116, British Library India Office Section, London.

97 Devlin, *Too Proud to Fight*, 493.

98 Cooper, 'The British Response to the House-Grey Memorandum', 964.

99 Balfour Suggested Draft Telegram, 24 May 1916, H. H. Asquith Papers, VI:127, Bodleian Library, Oxford.

100 Maurice Hankey Diaries, 23 May 1916, Churchill College Archive Centre, Cambridge.

101 Hankey to Balfour, 25 May 1916, Arthur James Balfour Papers, 49703, British Library, London; Maurice Hankey Diaries, 28 May 1916, Churchill College Archive Centre, Cambridge.

102 Maurice Hankey Diaries, 28 May 1916, Churchill College Archive Centre, Cambridge.

103 Edward House Diaries, 24 May 1916, Yale University Library, New Haven, Connecticut; Link, *Papers of Woodrow Wilson*, Vol. 37, 131.

104 Edward House Diaries, 20 May 1916, Yale University Library, New Haven, Connecticut; Link, *Papers of Woodrow Wilson*, Vol. 37, 68–69, 88–91.

105 Link, *Papers of Woodrow Wilson*, Vol. 37, 91.

106 Edward House Diaries, 19 March 1916, Yale University Library, New Haven, Connecticut.
107 Link, *Papers of Woodrow Wilson*, Vol. 37, 113–116, 118.
108 Edward House Diaries, 28 May 1916, Yale University Library, New Haven, Connecticut.
109 Link, *Papers of Woodrow Wilson*, Vol. 37, 113–116. Emphasis added.
110 Maurice Hankey Diaries, 29 May 1916, Churchill College Archive Centre, Cambridge. The paper did not cover the speech further.
111 Spring Rice to Foreign Office, 29 May 1916, FO 371/2794/102292, The National Archives, Kew.
112 Link, *Papers of Woodrow Wilson*, Vol. 36, 181.
113 'Presidential Politics', *Daily Mail*, 30 May 1916. See also, for example, 'The Association of Nations', *Westminster Gazette*, 29 May 1916, 1; 'Mr. Wilson and Peace', *The Times*, 29 May 1916, 9; 'President Wilson', *Daily Mail*, 29 May 1916, 5; 'President and Peace', *Daily Telegraph*, 29 May 1916, 9; and 'Dr. Wilson's Piecemeal', *Daily Express*, 29 May 1916, 1.
114 Link, *Papers of Woodrow Wilson*, Vol. 37, 131–132.
115 Ibid., 412–413.
116 *FRUS 1916*, 41–42.
117 Link, *Papers of Woodrow Wilson*, Vol. 37, 134–137; Edward House Diaries, 1 June 1916, Yale University Library, New Haven, Connecticut.
118 Link, *Papers of Woodrow Wilson*, Vol. 37, 177–180.
119 Ibid., 163–164, 179, 280–281.

Chapter 5

1 Cassar, *Asquith as War Leader*, 185–187; Barnett, *John Maynard Keynes*, 71; Moggridge, *Maynard Keynes*, 264.
2 For example, Grigg, *Lloyd George: From Peace to War*, 356–358; Cassar, *Asquith as War Leader*, 186–189; Jenkins, *Asquith*, 406–410.
3 McKenna to Runciman, 26 June 1916, Walter Runciman Papers, 149-1, University of Newcastle Robinson Library.
4 Lloyd-Jones, *Arming the Western Front*, Ch. 12.
5 Gilbert, *Organizer of Victory*, 343; Adams, *Arms and the Wizard*.
6 War Committee Minutes, 22 June 1916, CAB 22/32, The National Archives, Kew; Prior and Wilson, *Somme*, 34.
7 Neilson, *Strategy and Supply*, Chs. 2–3, 5.
8 Carosso, 'The Morgan Partnerships', Unfinished Manuscript, p. 3-38, Vincent Carosso Papers, ARC 1214, Pierpont Morgan Library, New York; Johnson, *Collected Writings of John Maynard Keynes*, Vol. 16, 192–193. See also Neilson, *Strategy and Supply*, Chs. 2–3, 5.
9 Carosso, 'The Morgan Partnerships', Unfinished Manuscript, p. 3-112, Vincent Carosso Papers, ARC 1214, Pierpont Morgan Library, New York.
10 Cassar, *Kitchener's War*, Ch. 23; Carosso, 'The Morgan Partnerships', Unfinished Manuscript, pp. 3-111 to 3-122, Vincent Carosso Papers, ARC 1214, Pierpont Morgan Library, New York; Neilson, *Strategy and Supply*, 184–187.

11 War Committee Minutes, 30 June 1916, CAB 42/15/15, The National Archives, Kew; Gilbert, *Organizer of Victory*, 349–350. See also Neilson, *Strategy and Supply*, 182–187, 192.

12 Though dated 29 June 1916, no mention of it was made at the War Committee meeting, so it appears to have been circulated subsequently.

13 Lloyd George Memorandum, 29 June 1916, CAB 42/15/14, The National Archives, Kew.

14 Maurice Hankey Diaries, 29 December 1915, Churchill College Archive Centre, Cambridge.

15 Lloyd George Memorandum, 29 June 1916, CAB 42/15/14, The National Archives, Kew.

16 Calculated from Samuel H. Williamson, 'What Was the U.S. GDP Then?' *MeasuringWorth.com*, University of Illinois-Chicago, 2017.

17 Johnson, *Collected Writings of John Maynard Keynes*, Vol. 16, 195.

18 United States Department of Labor, Bureau of Labor Statistics, *Retail Prices: 1907 to December, 1916*, 8.

19 See, for example, 'Fitzgerald Starts Food Embargo Fight', 22 November 1916, *New York Times*, 5, c. 3; 'Gregory Orders National Inquiry into Food Prices', 2 December 1916, *New York Times*, 1, c. 3.

20 'Cotton Prices in the World Wars', March 1944, *Monthly Review of Financial and Business Conditions (Fifth Federal Reserve District)*, 2–4.

21 See Graph 1. The loan had been sold to underwriters at $96 and to the public at $98; on 30 June 1916, the bonds were trading at $95½. See 'Bonds on Stock Exchange', 30 June 1916, *New York Times*, 16; and Burk, *Britain, America, and the Sinews of War*, 70–71.

22 Carosso, 'The Morgan Partnerships', Unfinished Manuscript, pp. V-99 to V-100, Vincent Carosso Papers, ARC 1214, Pierpont Morgan Library, New York.

23 Finance Committee Minutes, 3 July 1916, CAB 17/145, The National Archives, Kew. See also Neilson, *Strategy and Supply*, 192–193.

24 Printed in Johnson, *Collected Writings of John Maynard Keynes*, Vol. 16, 189–196.

25 Carosso, 'The Morgan Partnerships', Unfinished Manuscript, pp. 3-121 to 3-124, Vincent Carosso Papers, ARC 1214, Pierpont Morgan Library, New York; Neilson, *Strategy and Supply*, 187–191, 195–206.

26 Harcourt Cabinet Minutes, 25 May 1916, Lewis Harcourt Papers, MS. Eng. c. 8271, Bodleian Library, Oxford; Gilbert, *Organizer of Victory*, 318–334, quoted at 318.

27 Clarke, '*A Good Innings*', 156.

28 Gilbert, *Organizer of Victory*, 335–348. See also Grigg, *Lloyd George: From Peace to War*, 356–357; Rowland, *Lloyd George*, 340–343, Addison, *Four and a Half Years*, Vol. 1, 222–228; and Heffer, *Staring at God*, 400–403.

29 Gilbert, *Organizer of Victory*, 348–349; cf. Heffer, *Staring at God*, 402.

30 Dutton, *Austen Chamberlain*, 127–128.

31 Buckingham Palace Memorandum, 12 July 1916, Edwin Montagu Papers, AS5/8/268, Trinity College Library, Cambridge.

32 McKenna to Runciman, 10, 21 July 1916, Walter Runciman Papers, 149-1, University of Newcastle Robinson Library; Farr, *Reginald McKenna*, 329.

33 Addison, *Four and a Half Years*, Vol. 1, 231.
34 See, for example, Clifford, *The Asquiths*, 351–353; King to Grey, 15 July 1916, FO 800/103, The National Archives, Kew; Waley, *Edwin Montagu*, Ch. 7; and Trevelyan, *Grey of Fallodon*, 328–329.
35 Hardinge to Buchanan, December 1916, Lord Hardinge of Penhurst Papers, 28, Cambridge University Library.
36 Hardinge to Bertie, 4 October 1916, Francis Bertie Papers, 63044, British Library, London.
37 Adams and Poirier, *Conscription Controversy*, 176–179.
38 Harcourt Memorandum, 4 August 1916, CAB 42/17/3, The National Archives, Kew.
39 War Committee Minutes, 22 August 1916, CAB 42/18/4, The National Archives, Kew.
40 See Millman, *Pessimism*, 26.
41 War Committee Minutes, 22 June 1916, CAB 22/32, The National Archives, Kew; Prior and Wilson, *Somme*, 34.
42 Link, *Papers of Woodrow Wilson*, Vol. 37, 412–413.
43 Ibid., 411.
44 United Kingdom War Office, *Statistics of the Military Effort*, 258.
45 French, *British Strategy* , 204.
46 Hardinge to Buchanan, 26 August 1916, Lord Hardinge of Penhurst Papers, 24, Cambridge University Library. See also Hardinge to Buchanan, 12 July 1916, Lord Hardinge of Penhurst Papers, 23, Cambridge University Library; and Hardinge to Arthur Hardinge, 3 October 1916, Lord Hardinge of Penhurst Papers, 26, Cambridge University Library.
47 Hardinge to Rodd, 29 November 1916, Lord Hardinge of Penhurst Papers, 27, Cambridge University Library.
48 Woodward, *Field Marshal Sir William Robertson*, 32, 49–53.
49 Robertson to Haig, 29 July 1916, Douglas Haig Papers, WO 256/11, The National Archives, Kew.
50 Smith Memorandum, 1 August 1916, FO 899/4, The National Archives, Kew.
51 Prior and Wilson, *Somme*, 196.
52 Ibid., 197; Watson, *Ring of Steel*, 324; Beach, *Haig's Intelligence*, 207–208.
53 Heffer, *Staring at God*, 421.
54 Prior and Wilson, *Somme*, 197–198; Blake, *Private Papers of Douglas Haig*, 157–158.
55 Beach, *Haig's Intelligence*, Ch. 9.
56 Watson, *Ring of Steel*, 300–310, 327; Stone, *Russian Army*, Ch. 10.
57 McKenna to Runciman, 21 July 1916, Walter Runciman Papers, 149-1, University of Newcastle Robinson Library.
58 House to Lloyd George, 10 July 1916, Lloyd George to House, 31 July 1916, Edward House Papers, 70:2340, Yale University Library, New Haven, Connecticut; Edward House Diaries, 15 August 1916, Yale University Library, New Haven, Connecticut.
59 For a detailed discussion of these memoranda, see especially Rothwell, *British War Aims*, Ch. 1. See also Hanak, 'The Government, the Foreign Office, and Austria-Hungary', 168–171; and Goldstein, *Winning the Peace*, 9–13.

60 Grey to Bonar Law, 25 July 1916, Edward Grey Papers, FO 800/91, The National Archives, Kew; Paget and Tyrell Memorandum, 7 August 1916, CAB 17/160, The National Archives, Kew.
61 Spring Rice Report, 16 June 1916, Edward Grey Papers, FO 800/86, The National Archives, Kew. See also Burton, *Cecil Spring Rice*, Chs. 5–6.
62 Drummond to Spring Rice, 25 July 1916, Edward Grey Papers, FO 800/86, The National Archives, Kew.
63 *FRUS, 1916 Supplement*, 41–42; Grey to Spring Rice, 29 July 1916, Edward Grey Papers, FO 800/86, The National Archives, Kew.
64 Grey to Spring Rice, 29 July 1916, Edward Grey Papers, FO 800/86, The National Archives, Kew.
65 Hardinge to Bertie, 5 July 1916, Francis Bertie Papers, 63042, British Library, London. Copy in Lord Hardinge of Penhurst Papers, 23, Cambridge University Library.
66 Bertie to Hardinge, 13 July 1916, Lord Hardinge of Penhurst Papers, 23, Cambridge University Library. For more on Bertie, see Hamilton, *Bertie of Thame*.
67 Hardinge to Bertie, 19 July 1916, Francis Bertie Papers, 63042, British Library, London. Copy in Lord Hardinge of Penhurst Papers, 23, Cambridge University Library.
68 Bertie to Hardinge, 23 July 1916, Extract from Bertie to Grey, 29 February 1916, Bertie to Grey, 2 March 1916, Grey to Bertie, 5 March 1916, Lord Hardinge of Penhurst Papers, 23, Cambridge University Library.
69 Hardinge to Bertie, 26 July 1916, Francis Bertie Papers, 63042, British Library. Copy in Lord Hardinge of Penhurst Papers, 23, Cambridge University Library.
70 Bertie Memorandum, 10 August 1916, Francis Bertie Papers, FO 800/171, The National Archives, Kew.
71 Bertie Memorandum, 11 August 1916, Francis Bertie Papers, FO 800/171, The National Archives, Kew. Copy in Francis Bertie Papers, 63043, British Library, London.
72 Ibid.
73 Ibid.
74 Bertie Memorandum, 17 August 1916, Francis Bertie Papers, 63043, British Library, London.
75 Bertie to Asquith, 17 August 1916, Francis Bertie Papers, FO 800/190, The National Archives, Kew.
76 Bertie Memorandum, 17 August 1916, Francis Bertie Papers, FO 800/190, The National Archives, Kew.
77 See, for example, Harris, *Douglas Haig*, 253–254.
78 Drummond to Stamfordham, 15 October 1915, Grey to Stamfordham, 10 December 1915, Edward Grey Papers, FO 800/103, The National Archives, Kew.
79 Bertie to Hardinge, 24 August 1916, Edward Grey Papers, FO 800/59, The National Archives, Kew. Copy in David Lloyd George Papers, E/3/14/6, Parliamentary Archives, London.
80 Grey to Bertie, 24 August 1916, FO 371/2804, The National Archives, Kew.
81 Carnegie Endowment for International Peace Division of International Law, *Official German Documents*, 981–982.

82 Quoted in Draft 'D', Chapter 25, Hall Unpublished Autobiography, p. 2, Reginald Hall Papers, HALL 3/6, Churchill College Archive Centre, Cambridge.
83 Larsen, 'British Signals Intelligence', 55–56; Draft 'D', Chapter 25, Hall Unpublished Autobiography, Reginald Hall Papers, HALL 3/6, Churchill College Archive Centre, Cambridge, 4–6; Beesly, *Room 40*, 210.
84 See files ADM 223/745, ADM 223/774, ADM 223/776, The National Archives, Kew; Maurice Hankey Diaries, 25 August 1916, HNKY 1/1, Churchill College Archive Centre, Cambridge. Peter Freeman, relying only on the file HW 7/7, The National Archives, Kew, put this date at around 14 September 1916. The Admiralty files and Hankey's diary prove that this actually took place the preceding month. See Freeman, 'MI1(b)', 213; and Freeman, 'Zimmermann Telegram Revisited', 132.
85 Draft 'D', Chapter 25, Hall Unpublished Autobiography, Reginald Hall Papers, HALL 3/6, Churchill College Archive Centre, Cambridge, 6; Beesly, *Room 40*, 210.
86 For details on the Sussex Pledge, see Link, *Wilson: Confusions and Crises*, Ch. 9; and Devlin, *Too Proud to Fight*, Ch. 15.
87 Carnegie Endowment for International Peace Division of International Law, *Official German Documents*, 979.
88 Why Hankey believed that the cables were sometimes routed through Russia is unclear. There is no telegraph route from Buenos Aires to Stockholm via Russia, rather than Britain, that would make much sense. See Burns, 'Submarine Cable Route Maps'. Nor is there any intelligence documentation that supports the idea that some of the telegrams went via a Russian route. Larsen, 'British Signals Intelligence', 54–57.
89 Maurice Hankey Diaries, 25 August 1916, HNKY 1/1, Churchill College Archive Centre, Cambridge.
90 Laughlin to Page, 30 August 1916, Walter Hines Page Papers, 755/20, Harvard University Houghton Library, Cambridge, Massachussets. This letter is also available, with Hall's and Hardinge's names redacted, in Hendrick, *Life and Letters*, Vol. 2, 180–182.
91 French, *British Strategy*, 205.
92 Asquith to Henley, 26 August 1916, 31 August 1916, Asquith-Henley Papers, MS Eng Lett c 542/4, Bodleian Library, Oxford.
93 Link, *Papers of Woodrow Wilson*, Vol. 37, 422–424.
94 Ibid., 38, 89–93.
95 House to Clifford Carver, 22 August 1916, Clifford Carver Papers, Box 13, Princeton University Mudd Manuscript Library, Princeton, New Jersey.

Chapter 6

1 Spring Rice to Drummond Telegram, 6 September 1916, Edward Grey Papers, FO 800/86, The National Archives, Kew.
2 Edward House Diaries, 8 October 1916, Yale University Library, New Haven, Connecticut.

3 Devlin, *Too Proud to Fight*, 519. Similarly, see Edward House Diaries, 9 May 1915, Yale University Library, New Haven, Connecticut.

4 Edward House Diaries, 25 September 1916, Yale University Library, New Haven, Connecticut.

5 Link, *Papers of Woodrow Wilson*, Vol. 37, 502.

6 Harcourt Cabinet Minutes, 27 June, 2 August 1916, Lewis Harcourt Papers, MS. Eng. c. 8271, Bodleian Library, Oxford; Devlin, *Too Proud to Fight*, 502–503. See also Larsen, 'British Signals Intelligence'; and O'Halpin, 'British Intelligence in Ireland'.

7 Andrew, *Secret Service*, 247–248; Dudgeon, *Roger Casement*, 534.

8 Lambert, *Planning Armageddon*, 483–496; Devlin, *Too Proud to Fight*, 503–505; Osborne, *Britain's Economic Blockade*, 105–109, 115–121.

9 See Osborne, *Britain's Economic Blockade*, Ch. 6; and West, 'Intelligence and the Development of British Grand Strategy', Ch. 8.

10 Devlin, *Too Proud to Fight*, 505–512.

11 Link, *Wilson: Campaigns for Progressivism and Peace*, 65, 69–70; Devlin, *Too Proud to Fight*, 505–513; Messimer, *Baltimore Sabotage Cell*, Chs. 6–7; Osborne, *Britain's Economic Blockade*, 127–132, 135–136.

12 Link, *Wilson: Campaigns for Progressivism and Peace*, 65–68; Devlin, *Too Proud to Fight*, 513–517.

13 Ibid., 70–75; Devlin, *Too Proud to Fight*, 517–518.

14 Edward House Diaries, 20 September 1916, Yale University Library, New Haven, Connecticut.

15 U.S. and the Blockade: Possible Retaliatory Measures, 13 September 1916, FO 371/2795/182388, The National Archives, Kew.

16 Edward House Diaries, 3 September 1916, Yale University Library, New Haven, Connecticut.

17 The translation in *Official German Documents* reads 'up to' instead of 'by', which is slightly ambiguous. The British decrypt translates this as 'by', which demonstrates that there was no ambiguity on this point for the British to misinterpret. See note 19, below.

18 Carnegie Endowment for International Peace Division of International Law, *Official German Documents*, 984.

19 Buenos Aires to Stockholm German Decrypt, 8 September 1916, ADM 223/745, The National Archives, Kew. The wording of the translation on the decrypt differs slightly.

20 Carnegie Endowment for International Peace Division of International Law, *Official German Documents*, 984; Buenos Aires to Stockholm Decrypt, 10 September 1916, ADM 223/745. The translation in *Official German Documents* reads: 'If Wilson is reelected I consider mediatory action by him as very likely to occur before the end of the year'.

21 Madrid to Washington Decrypt, 19 July 1916, HW 7/17, The National Archives, Kew.

22 Washington to Madrid Decrypt, 23 August 1916, HW 7/17, The National Archives, Kew.

23 Edward House Diaries, 2 October 1916, Yale University Library, New Haven, Connecticut.
24 Prior and Wilson, *Somme*, 279–280; War Committee Minutes, 12 September 1916, CAB 22/48, The National Archives, Kew.
25 Hardinge to Spring Rice, 8 September 1916, Lord Hardinge of Penhurst Papers, 25, Cambridge University Library.
26 Beach, *Haig's Intelligence*, 215.
27 Torrey, *Romanian Battlefront*, Ch. 7; French, *British Strategy*, 222–223; Barrett, *Prelude to Blitzkrieg*, Chs. 2–5; Stone, *Russian Army*, Ch. 11.
28 See Woodward, *Lloyd George and the Generals*, Chs. 5–6.
29 United States Senate, *Munitions Industry*, 9232; Bradbury to Morgan's, 15 September 1916, London Exchange Committee Papers, C91/6, Bank of England Archive, London.
30 Carosso, 'The Morgan Partnerships,' Unfinished Manuscript, pp. 4-151 to 4-159, Vincent Carosso Papers, ARC 1214, Pierpont Morgan Library, New York; 'British $250,000,000 Loan Announced', 17 August 1916, *Wall Street Journal*, 1.
31 Carosso, 'The Morgan Partnerships', Unfinished Manuscript, pp. 4-182 to 4-188, Vincent Carosso Papers, ARC 1214, Pierpont Morgan Library, New York; United States Senate, *Munitions Industry*, 10778–10788; 'Collateral for $300,000,000 American Loan', 6 November 1916, London Exchange Committee Papers, C91/6, Bank of England Archive, London.
32 United States Senate, *Munitions Industry*, 8803.
33 See Thompson, *Politicians, the Press, and Propaganda*; Thompson, *Northcliffe*; and McEwen, 'Northcliffe and Lloyd George at War'.
34 Howard to C. F. Mosher, 14 December 1916, Roy Howard Papers, Indiana University School of Journalism, Bloomington.
35 Haig Diary, 2 August 1916, Douglas Haig Papers, 158, National Library of Scotland, Edinburgh.
36 Northcliffe to Joseph Conrad, 7 August 1916, Alfred Harmsworth (Lord Northcliffe) Papers, 62334, British Library, London.
37 Northcliffe to Lloyd George, 6 August 1916, Alfred Harmsworth (Lord Northcliffe) Papers, 62157, British Library, London.
38 Sassoon to Northcliffe, 19 September 1916, Alfred Harmsworth (Lord Northcliffe) Papers, 62160, British Library, London.
39 Northcliffe to Sassoon, 19 September 1916, Alfred Harmsworth (Lord Northcliffe) Papers, 62160, British Library, London.
40 Northcliffe to Sassoon, 23 September 1916, Alfred Harmsworth (Lord Northcliffe) Papers, 62160, British Library, London.
41 Northcliffe to Sassoon, [25] September 1916, Alfred Harmsworth (Lord Northcliffe) Papers, 62160, British Library, London.
42 Northcliffe to Lloyd George, 25 September 1916, David Lloyd George Papers, E/2/21/2, Parliamentary Archives, Westminster.
43 See Link, *Wilson: Campaigns for Progressivism and Peace*, 175–176; and Lloyd George to Grey, 2 October 1916, David Lloyd George Papers, E/2/13/6, Parliamentary Archives, Westminster.
44 Berlin to Washington Decrypt, 25 September 1916, HW 7/17, The National Archives, Kew. The word '(a?)' was a decryption error, and should actually

read 'proposed'; otherwise, the first paragraph was correctly decrypted. Beginning with 'To-day', the original telegram read: 'To-day or to-morrow Von Jagow will ask me to get cipher cablegram to you for Bernstorff. This cablegram he says will refer to this message and matter'. The remainder of the decrypt is correct in substance, if not in precise wording. See *FRUS, 1916 Supplement*, 55. In President Theodore Roosevelt's dispatch of 8 June 1905, Roosevelt proposed 'a meeting of Russian and Japanese plenipotentiaries … without any intermediary'. See *FRUS, 1905*, 807.

45 Joseph Grew, *Turbulent Era*, Vol. 1, 251. Original manuscript in Joseph Grew Papers, 7, Harvard University Houghton Library, Cambridge.

46 Egan to State Department, 25 September 1916, Record Group 59, State Department Decimal File 1910–1929, 763.72119/172, US National Archives and Records Administration, College Park, Maryland.

47 Haig Diary, 21 October 1916, Douglas Haig Papers, 159, National Library of Scotland, Edinburgh.

48 Wieten, *Howard and Northcliffe*, 16.

49 I have not been able to identify this person, although this possibly refers, inaccurately, to Ambassador Page.

50 See Manuscript Copy of Interview, [27 September 1916], David Lloyd George Papers, E/2/21/3, Parliamentary Archives, Westminster.

51 Crawford Memorandum, 17 September 1916, CAB 17/160, The National Archives, Kew. Crawford signed his memorandum 'C & B' – that is, 'Crawford and Balcarres', his full title. Previous authors have been unable to identify Crawford as the author of the memorandum. See, for example, Link, *Wilson: Campaigns for Progressivism and Peace*, 175–176.

52 See, for example, 'Briand Administers a Stinging Rebuke to Deputy Who Urges France to End War', *New York Times*, 20 September 1916, 1.

53 War Committee Minutes, 28 September 1916, CAB 22/52, The National Archives, Kew.

54 Howard to House, 28 September 1916, Edward House Papers, 63:1991, Yale University Library, New Haven, Connecticut.

55 Ibid.

56 See, for example, 'Never Again!', *Times*, 29 September 1916, 7, c. 3. Jeremy Black incorrectly cites this article as dating from 29 November 1916. See Black, *Great War*, 126.

57 Edward House Diaries, 30 September 1916, Yale University Library, New Haven, Connecticut.

58 Link, *Papers of Woodrow Wilson*, Vol. 38, 313–314.

59 Hardinge to Bertie, 10 October 1916, Bertie Papers, 63044, British Library, London. Copy in Hardinge Papers, 26, Cambridge University Library.

60 *Daily Mail*, 29 September 1916, 5; *Daily Express*, 29 September 1916, 1.

61 Grey to Lloyd George, 29 September 1916, David Lloyd George Papers, E/2/13/5, Parliamentary Archives, Westminster.

62 Grey to Runciman, 30 September 1916, Walter Runciman Papers, 303, University of Newcastle Robinson Library.

63 Repington, *First World War*, Vol. 1, 348–352. In 1918, Repington would move to the arch-Conservative *Morning Post*. See Repington, *First World War*, Vol. 2, Ch. 30.

64 C. P. Scott Diaries, 2–3 October 1916, C. P. Scott Papers, John Rylands University Library of Manchester. Some portions are omitted from Wilson, *Political Diaries of C. P. Scott*, 227–228. Scott wrote that McKenna said he was 'in the position now of *borrowing from* America two million pounds a day', instead of *spending* that sum. Scott clearly mistranscribed the remark; had McKenna in fact been succeeding in borrowing £2 million ($10 million) a day, the Treasury would have far less cause for anxiety.

65 Wilson, *Political Diaries of C. P. Scott*, 227–228. Other Liberals believed that there was meaningful public support for a peace by negotiation. See Martin, *Peace without Victory*, Ch. 4.

66 War Committee Minutes, 28 September 1916, CAB 22/52, The National Archives, Kew.

67 Wilson, *Political Diaries of C. P. Scott*, 227–228.

68 C. P. Scott Diary, 2–3 October 1916, C. P. Scott Papers, John Rylands University Library of Manchester.

69 Wilson, *Political Diaries of C. P. Scott*, 228.

70 Philpot, *Three Armies*, 47.

71 Wilson, *Political Diaries of C. P. Scott*, 228.

72 Clifford, *The Asquiths*, 367–369.

73 Clifford Carver Diary, 9 October 1916, Clifford Carver Papers, Princeton University Mudd Manuscript Library, Princeton, New Jersey.

74 Clifford, *The Asquiths*, 367–369.

75 *The Nation*, 30 September 1916, 805–806; *The Nation*, 7 October 1916, 10; 'The Failure of Statesmanship', *Manchester Guardian*, 30 September 1916, 6, c. 2–3; 'The Perils of Interviews', *Manchester Guardian*, 3 October 1916, 2, c. 2–3; 'Neutrals and Mediation', *Manchester Guardian*, 7 October 1916, 6, c. 5; 'We Will Win', *Westminster Gazette*, 29 September 1916, 1, c. 3; 'The Fight to Be to a Finish', *Daily Chronicle*, 29 September 1916, 3, c. 7; 'The Noblest Economy', *The Daily News and Leader*, 29 September 1916, 4, c. 2–3.

76 'The Chancellor's Ordeal', *Morning Post*, 29 September 1916, 6, c. 3–4.

77 'Keep Out of the Ring', *Daily Express*, 29 September 1916, 4, c. 3.

78 'Hands Off!', *Daily Mail*, 29 September 1916, 4, c. 2.

79 Bertie to Hardinge, 4 October 1916, Francis Bertie Papers, 63044, British Library, London.

80 Lennox, *Diary of Lord Bertie of Thame*, Vol. 2, 34–35.

81 Hardinge to Alan Johnstone, 3 October 1916, Lord Hardinge of Penhurst Papers, 26, Cambridge University Library.

82 Hardinge to Bertie, 10 October 1916, Francis Bertie Papers, 63044, British Library, London. Copy in Lord Hardinge of Penhurst Papers, 26, Cambridge University Library.

83 Hardinge to Bertie, 4 October 1916, Francis Bertie Papers, 63044, British Library, London.

84 Bertie to Hardinge, 16 October 1916, Lord Hardinge of Penhurst Papers, 25, Cambridge University Library. Copy in Francis Bertie Papers, 63044, British Library, London.

85 Hardinge to Bertie, 18, 28 October 1916, Lord Hardinge of Penhurst Papers, 25, Cambridge University Library.

86 Clifford Carver Diary, 2 October 1916, Clifford Carver Papers, Princeton University Mudd Manuscript Library, Princeton, New Jersey.
87 Carver to House, 2 October 1916, Edward House Papers, 25:780, Yale University Library, New Haven, Connecticut.
88 Edward House Diaries, 2 October 1916, Yale University Library, New Haven, Connecticut.
89 Spring Rice to Foreign Office, David Lloyd George Papers, E/3/28/1, Parliamentary Archives, Westminster.
90 Washington to Berlin German Decrypt, 5 October 1916, ADM 223/745, The National Archives, Kew.
91 See *FRUS, 1916 Supplement*, 55.
92 Taylor, *Lloyd George: A Diary by Frances Stevenson*, 114.
93 Ibid.
94 Lloyd George to Grey, 2 October 1916, David Lloyd George Papers, E/2/13/6, Parliamentary Archives, Westminster.
95 Grey to Strachey, 9 October 1916, Edward Grey Papers, FO 800/111, The National Archives, Kew.
96 War Committee Minutes, 3, 5 October 1916, CAB 22/53, CAB/54, The National Archives, Kew.
97 Montagu Memorandum, 29 August 1916, CAB 17/160, The National Archives, Kew.
98 War Committee Minutes, 5 October 1916, CAB 22/54, The National Archives, Kew; Addison, *Four and a Half Years*, 256.
99 War Committee Minutes, 5 October 1916, CAB 22/54, The National Archives, Kew; First Report of the Man-Power Distribution Board, 30 September 1916, CAB 42/21/2, The National Archives, Kew.
100 Keynes' Handwritten Notes for Talk at Admiralty, 15 February 1917, John Maynard Keynes Papers, T/11/12-19, Kings' College Library, Cambridge.
101 James Douglas Interview with Edwin Montagu, 7 November 1916, Edwin Montagu Papers, AS6/9/7-8, Trinity College Library, Cambridge.
102 US and the Blockade: Possible Retaliatory Measures, 13 September 1916, FO 371/2795/182388, The National Archives, Kew.
103 The Blockade and US Retaliatory Measures, 14 September 1916, FO 371/2795/183075, The National Archives, Kew.
104 See, for example, War Office to Foreign Office, 25 September 1916, FO 371/2795/191174, The National Archives, Kew; Link, *Wilson: Campaigns for Progressivism and Peace*, 76-80.
105 Admiralty to Foreign Office, 2 October 1916, FO 371/2795/196319, The National Archives, Kew.
106 Interdepartmental Committee on the Dependence of the British Empire on the U.S.: Summary of Results of First Meeting on Oct 3, 4 October 1916, FO 371/2795/197644, The National Archives, Kew. Similarly, see *History of the Ministry of Munitions*, Vol. 2, Pt. 3, 124–125.
107 See Dependence of the British Empire on the United States, 13 October 1916, FO 371/2796/205593, The National Archives, Kew.
108 Précis for the Army Council No. 841, Edward Stanley (Lord Derby) Papers, 27/18, Liverpool Record Office.

109 Dutton, *Odyssey of an Edwardian Liberal*, 45.
110 'Parliament and Mr. Lloyd George's Interview', *Manchester Guardian*, 10 October 1916, 2, c. 4–5. It is tempting to ascribe this to McKenna, but McKenna had spoken with Scott on 2 October, and the *Guardian* did not print anything as a result of this conversation. Presumably, McKenna had asked Scott not to. The more probable explanation is that this information came from another Liberal member of the Cabinet, who consented to allowing the *Guardian* to use it.
111 Clifford Carver Diary, 10 October 1916, Clifford Carver Papers, Princeton University Mudd Manuscript Library, Princeton, New Jersey. Interestingly, Carver never seems to have related this to House, perhaps for fear that he had overstepped his bounds. See Edward House Papers, 25:780, Yale University Library, New Haven, Connecticut.
112 'To-Day's Meeting of Parliament', *Manchester Guardian*, 10 October 1916, 3, c. 6.
113 *Parliamentary Debates*, 86 H. C. Deb. 5 s., 95-103; MacCarthy, *H. H. A.*, Vol. 1, 10.
114 Link, *Papers of Woodrow Wilson*, Vol. 35, 327; Nordholt, *Woodrow Wilson*, 171.
115 *Parliamentary Debates*, 86 H. C. Deb. 5 s., 95–103.
116 Ibid., 127–133; cf. 'Kitchener Sure Allies Will Win', *New York Times*, 10 November 1914.
117 *Parliamentary Debates*, 86 H. C. Deb. 5 s., 127–133.
118 Ibid., 134–136. Emphasis added.
119 Ibid., 134–136.
120 'Mr. Asquith's Speech', *Manchester Guardian*, 12 October 1916, 2, c. 2–3.
121 'Progress of the War', *Manchester Guardian*, 12 October 1916, 5, c. 7.
122 'The Lloyd George Interview', *Manchester Guardian*, 12 October 1916, 2, c. 4–5.
123 'The Prime Minister's Survey', *Westminster Gazette*, 12 October 1916, 1, c. 2–3.
124 'Review of the Week', *Labour Leader*, 12 October 1916, 1, c. 3.
125 *Daily Mail*, 12 October 1916, 4, c. 2.
126 *National Review*, November 1916, 298.
127 Bertie to Asquith, 16 October 1916, Francis Bertie Papers, 63044, British Library, London.
128 Lennox, *Diary of Lord Bertie of Thame*, Vol. 2, 47.
129 Asquith to Henley, 21 October 1916, Asquith-Henley Papers, MS Eng Lett c 542/4, Bodleian Library, Oxford. See also Blake, *Private Papers of Douglas Haig*, 171.
130 *Daily Mail*, 12 October 1916, 6, c. 4.
131 'Allies' War Aims', *The Daily News and Leader*, 12 October 1916, 2, c. 4.
132 'Lloyd George Hits Back at His Critics', *New York Times*, 12 October 1916, 2.
133 Parliamentary Question, 12 October 1916, FO 371/2803/207735, The National Archives, Kew.
134 Dell to Crozier, 11 October 1916, C. P. Scott Papers, 334/116, John Rylands University Library of Manchester. Some portions are omitted from Wilson, *Political Diaries of C. P. Scott*, 228–229.

135 'Mr. Lloyd George and Mediation', *Manchester Guardian*, 16 October 1916, 4, c. 6.
136 Wilson, *Political Diaries of C. P. Scott*, 229–230.
137 Grey Memorandum, 20 October 1916, printed in Link, *Wilson: Campaigns for Progressivism and Peace*, 180–182.
138 See Devlin, *Too Proud to Fight*, Chs. 17–20; Link, *Wilson, Campaigns for Progressivism and Peace*, Chs. 3–9.
139 See, for example, 'Lord Grey and the Allies' Aims', *Manchester Guardian*, 24 October 1916, 7–8.
140 'The Foundations of Peace', *Morning Post*, 25 October 1916, 6, c. 2–3.
141 House to Grey, 24 October 1916, Edward House Papers, 53:1668, Yale University Library, New Haven, Connecticut.
142 Grey to House, 2 November 1916, Edward House Papers, 53:1668, Yale University Library, New Haven, Connecticut. Emphasis added.

Chapter 7

1 Turner, *British Politics*, 128; French, *British Strategy*, 233; Stevenson, *First World War and International Politics*, 110; Millman, *Pessimism*, 29–31; Fry, *Lloyd George and Foreign Policy*, 237–238; Grigg, *Lloyd George*, 432; Cassar, *Asquith as War Leader*, 207–208; Jenkins, *Asquith*, 417–419; Lowe and Dockrill, *Mirage of Power*, 244–245; Rothwell, *British War Aims*, 53–55; Stevenson, *Cataclysm*, 121; Fest, 'British War Aims and German Peace Feelers', 288; Martin, *Peace Without Victory*, 35–36; Woodward, 'Britain's "Brass Hats"', 65. A few historians, curiously, have departed from this, but in generally brief accounts of the episode that do not engage the historiographical consensus. See Hattersley, The Great Outsider, 404; Gilbert, *Organizer of Victory*, 374–378; and Rowland, *Lloyd George*, 353.
2 War Committee Minutes, CAB 22/59-79, The National Archives, Kew; Maurice Hankey Diaries, 24 November 1916, Churchill College Archive Centre, Cambridge.
3 Quoted in Draft 'D', Chapter 25, Hall Unpublished Autobiography, p. 2, Reginald Hall Papers, HALL 3/6, Churchill College Archive Centre, Cambridge.
4 Most of the decrypts have two dates: the date of the decrypted telegram and a second (much later) date of decryption. Room 40 appears to have worked backwards from August 1916 and seems to have finished decrypting the Swedish roundabout telegrams from early 1916 in early November 1916. See file ADM 223/745, The National Archives, Kew.
5 Carnegie Endowment for International Peace Division of International Law, *Official German Documents*, 989.
6 See file ADM 223/745, The National Archives, Kew.
7 Hardinge to Rennell Rodd, 25 October 1916, Lord Hardinge of Penhurst Papers, 26, Cambridge University Library. Emphasis added. See also Hardinge to Charles Marling, 27 October 1916, Hardinge to Rodd, 2 November 1916, Hardinge to Arthur Hardinge, 7 November 1916, and

Hardinge to Esme Howard, 27 October 1916, Lord Hardinge of Penhurst Papers, 26, Cambridge University Library.

8 Carnegie Endowment for International Peace Division of International Law, *Official German Documents*, 990; Buenos Aires to Stockholm Decrypt, 22 October 1916, ADM 223/745, The National Archives, Kew.

9 Hardinge to Arthur Hardinge, 7 November 1916, Lord Hardinge of Penhurst Papers, 26, Cambridge University Library.

10 Draft 'D', Chapter 25, Hall Unpublished Autobiography, p. 2, Reginald Hall Papers, HALL 3/6, Churchill College Archive Centre, Cambridge.

11 Buenos Aires to Stockholm Decrypt, 5 October 1916, ADM 223/745, The National Archives, Kew; Carnegie Endowment for International Peace Division of International Law, *Official German Documents*, 986.

12 Carnegie Endowment for International Peace Division of International Law, *Official German Documents*, 987, 989. See also Devlin, *Too Proud to Fight*, 534–542.

13 Buenos Aires to Stockholm Decrypt, 23 May 1916, ADM 223/745, The National Archives, Kew.

14 Buenos Aires to Stockholm Decrypt, 6 June 1916, ADM 223/745, The National Archives, Kew.

15 Messimer, *Baltimore Sabotage Cell*, Ch. 12; Messimer, *Merchant U-Boat*, Ch. 13.

16 Gathen, 'Zimmermann Telegram', 15.

17 Hardinge to Rumbold, 17 November 1916, Horace Rumbold Papers, 17, Bodleian Library, Oxford.

18 Buenos Aires to Stockholm Decrypt, 17 November 1916, ADM 223/745, The National Archives, Kew.

19 Doerries, *Imperial Challenge*, Ch. 6.

20 Maurice Hankey Diaries, 18 November 1916, Churchill College Archive Centre, Cambridge. Emphasis added.

21 Maurice Hankey Diaries, 20 November 1916, Churchill College Archive Centre, Cambridge; Larsen, 'British Signals Intelligence', 60–61.

22 Buenos Aires to Stockholm Decrypt, 23 November 1916, ADM 223/745, The National Archives, Kew.

23 Buenos Aires to Stockholm Decrypt, 19 November 1916, ADM 223/745, The National Archives, Kew.

24 Berlin to Washington Decrypt, 17 November 1916, HW 7/17, The National Archives, Kew.

25 Berlin to Washington Decrypt, 22 November 1916, HW 7/17, The National Archives, Kew.

26 Edward House Diaries, 12–14 November 1916, Yale University Library, New Haven, Connecticut.

27 Edward House Diaries, 14 November 1916, Yale University Library, New Haven, Connecticut.

28 Edward House Diaries, 14–15 November 1916, Yale University Library, New Haven, Connecticut.

29 Carver to House, 3 October 1916, Edward House Papers, 25:780, Yale University Library, New Haven, Connecticut.

30 Link, *Papers of Woodrow Wilson*, Vol. 38, 497.
31 Ibid., 40, 74.
32 Ibid. 40, 60–63; House to Grey, 24 November 1916, Arthur Balfour Papers, GD433/2/75/14, National Archives of Scotland, Edinburgh; copy in Edward House Papers, 53:1668, Yale University Library, New Haven, Connecticut; Edward House Diaries, 29 November 1916, Yale University Library, New Haven, Connecticut; Devlin, *Too Proud to Fight*, 565.
33 House to Grey, 24 November 1916, Arthur Balfour Papers, GD433/2/75/14, National Archives of Scotland, Edinburgh; copy in Edward House Papers, 53:1668, Yale University Library, New Haven, Connecticut.
34 House to Grey, 24 November 1916, Arthur Balfour Papers, GD433/2/75/14, National Archives of Scotland, Edinburgh. (Postscript omitted from copy in Edward House Papers.)
35 House to Balfour, 23 November 1916, Arthur Balfour Papers, GD433/2/75/17, National Archives of Scotland, Edinburgh; copy in Edward House Papers, 10:285, Yale University Library, New Haven, Connecticut.
36 Page to House Draft, 21 November 1916, Walter Hines Page Papers, 658, Harvard University Library, Cambridge, Massachussets.
37 United States Senate, *Munitions Industry*, 8724.
38 War Committee Minutes, 28 November 1916, CAB 22/77, The National Archives, Kew.
39 United States Senate, *Munitions Industry*, 8726.
40 Printed in Johnson, *Collected Writings of John Maynard Keynes*, Vol. 16, 198–209.
41 Runciman Memorandum, 26 October 1916, CAB 24/2, The National Archives, Kew; Dewey, *British Agriculture*, 31.
42 Crawford Memorandum of War Committee Meeting, 9 November 1916, Earl of Crawford Papers, 95/4 (3), National Library of Scotland, Edinburgh.
43 Maurice Hankey Diaries, 10 November 1916, Churchill College Archive Centre, Cambridge.
44 War Committee Minutes, 9 November 1916, CAB 22/65, The National Archives, Kew.
45 Runciman Memorandum, 9 November 1916, Walter Runciman Papers, 97–98, University of Newcastle Robinson Library.
46 Crawford Memorandum, 30 October 1916, CAB 24/2, The National Archives, Kew.
47 Crawford Memorandum of a Conversation with Lloyd George, 3 November 1916, Crawford Memorandum of a Conversation with Asquith, 4 November 1916, Earl of Crawford Papers, 95/4 (3), National Library of Scotland, Edinburgh.
48 Crawford Memorandum, 30 October 1916, CAB 24/2, The National Archives, Kew. See also Crawford Memorandum, 9 November 1916, Walter Runciman Papers, 92-2, University of Newcastle Robinson Library.
49 Crawford to Asquith, 4 November 1916, Earl of Crawford Papers, 95/4 (3), National Library of Scotland, Edinburgh.
50 Vincent, *Crawford Papers*, 363. For context, see Dewey, *British Agriculture*.

51 Lloyd George Memorandum, 10 November 1916, CAB 24/2, The National Archives, Kew.
52 War Committee Minutes, 13 November 1916, CAB 22/67, The National Archives, Kew.
53 Crawford Memorandum on Cabinet, 13 November 1916, Earl of Crawford Papers, 95/4 (3), National Library of Scotland, Edinburgh.
54 *Parliamentary Debates*, 87 H. C. Deb. 5 s., 841–863.
55 Ibid., 897.
56 Ibid., 863–867, 1044–1053.
57 Ibid., 939.
58 Hankey Memorandum, 31 October, CAB 24/2, The National Archives, Kew.
59 Lansdowne's memorandum is dated 13 November, but Crawford leaves a memorandum of a conversation with Lansdowne, dated 14 November, in which Lansdowne spoke of his memorandum as though it had not yet been distributed. See Crawford Memorandum of a Conversation with Lord Lansdowne, 14 November 1916, Earl of Crawford Papers, 95/4 (3), National Library of Scotland, Edinburgh.
60 See Turner, *British Politics*, 70, 94; Duffy, *Integrity of Ireland*, 110; O'Day, *Irish Home Rule*, 271–274; Newton, *Lord Lansdowne*, Ch. 19; Heffer, *Staring at God*, 385–386.
61 Emphasis added.
62 Emphasis in original.
63 Lansdowne Memorandum, 13 November 1916, CAB 29/1, The National Archives, Kew. Emphasis added.
64 Vincent, *Crawford Papers*, 365.
65 Crawford Memorandum, 17 September 1916, CAB 17/160, The National Archives, Kew.
66 Vincent, *Crawford Papers*, 365.
67 Crawford Memorandum, 13 December 1916, Earl of Crawford Papers, 95/4 (3), National Library of Scotland, Edinburgh.
68 Trevelyan, *Grey of Fallodon*, 324; Grey to Spring Rice, 26 November 1916, FO 115/2090, The National Archives, Kew.
69 Grey to Runciman, 20 November 1916, Walter Runciman Papers, 300, University of Newcastle Robinson Library.
70 French, *British Strategy*, 233–237.
71 Riddell, *Lord Riddell's War Diary*, 223.
72 Maurice Hankey Diaries, 16 November 1916, Churchill College Archive Centre, Cambridge.
73 Lloyd George, *War Memoirs*, Vol. 2, 574–575; Hankey, *Supreme Command*, Vol. 2, 562–563.
74 Maurice Hankey Diaries, 16, 22 November 1916, Churchill College Archive Centre, Cambridge.
75 Cecil Memorandum, 27 November 1916, CAB 37/160, The National Archives, Kew.
76 Maurice Hankey Diaries, 29 November 1916, Churchill College Archive Centre, Cambridge.
77 Montagu Memorandum, 29 August 1916, CAB 17/160, The National Archives, Kew; Montagu Memorandum, [January 1917], Edwin Montagu

Papers, AS6/10/33, Trinity College Library, Cambridge. See also Larsen, 'War Pessimism in Britain', 807–808; and Swinnerton, *Arnold Bennett*, 397.

78 Maurice Hankey Diaries, 22 November 1916, Churchill College Archive Centre, Cambridge.

79 Turner, *British Politics*, 102.

80 Riddell, *Lord Riddell's War Diary*, 223; Turner, *British Politics*, 102.

81 Maurice Hankey Diaries, 22 November 1916, Churchill College Archive Centre, Cambridge.

82 Harcourt Cabinet Minutes/Diary, 6 December 1916, Lewis Harcourt Papers, MS. Eng. c. 8271, Bodleian Library, Oxford.

83 Maurice Hankey Diaries, 4 December 1916, Churchill College Archive Centre, Cambridge.

84 Taylor, *Lloyd George: A Diary*, 127.

85 Page to Wilson, 17 March 1918, Woodrow Wilson Papers, Reel 95, Library of Congress, Washington, District of Columbia.

86 Yearwood and Hazlehurst, 'Affairs of a Distant Dependency'.

87 See Fraser, 'Lord Beaverbrook's Fabrications', 151.

88 Maurice Hankey Diaries, 10 November 1916, Churchill College Archive Centre, Cambridge.

89 Wilson, *Political Diaries of C. P. Scott*, 233–238. Emphasis added. See also Hammond, *C. P. Scott*, 201.

90 Vincent, *Crawford Papers*, 366; Harcourt Cabinet Minutes, 29 November 1916, Lewis Harcourt Papers, MS. Eng. c. 8271, Bodleian Library, Oxford.

91 Asquith, *Memories and Reflections*, Vol. 2, 128.

92 Vincent, *Crawford Papers*, 366; Harcourt Cabinet Minutes, 22 November 1916, Lewis Harcourt Papers, MS. Eng. c. 8271, Bodleian Library, Oxford.

93 Rothwell, *British War Aims*, 54.

94 Robertson, *Soldiers and Statesmen*, Vol. 1, 280.

95 Robertson Memorandum, 24 November 1916, CAB 37/160/15, The National Archives, Kew.

96 Ibid. Robertson later tried to backpedal by privately assuring Lansdowne that he had not had Lansdowne personally in mind when writing this passage – a statement of dubious veracity. See Woodward, *Military Correspondence*, 119–120. Cf. Millman, *Pessimism*, 31; and Winters, 'Exaggerating the Efficacy of Diplomacy', 32.

97 Robertson Memorandum, 24 November 1916, CAB 37/160/15, The National Archives, Kew.

98 Cassar, *Asquith as War Leader*, 212.

99 'Stand Firm in the Faith', *Morning Post*, 23 November 1916, 6, c. 3–4.

100 Harcourt Cabinet Minutes, 13, 22 November 1916, Lewis Harcourt Papers, MS. Eng. c. 8271, Bodleian Library, Oxford.

101 Crawford Memoranda, 13, 29 November 1916, Earl of Crawford Papers, 95/4 (3), National Library of Scotland, Edinburgh; Vincent, *Crawford Papers*, 368–369; Montagu to Asquith, 27 November 1916, Edwin Montagu Papers, AS5/1/18, Trinity College Library, Cambridge; Harcourt Cabinet Minutes/Diary, 28 November 1916, Lewis Harcourt Papers, MS. Eng. c. 8271, Bodleian Library, Oxford.

102 Crawford Memorandum, 28 November 1916, Earl of Crawford Papers, 95/ 4 (3), National Library of Scotland, Edinburgh; Addison, *Four and a Half Years*, Vol. 1, 268–269.
103 Vincent, *Crawford Papers*, 367. See also War Committee Minutes, 23 November, CAB 22/73, The National Archives, Kew.
104 Stone, *Russian Army*, Chs. 10–11.
105 Schindler, *Isonzo*, Chs. 7–9.
106 Torrey, *Romanian Battlefront*, Chs. 9–10; Barrett, *Prelude to Blitzkrieg*, Chs. 8–9.
107 *Parliamentary Debates*, 88 H. C. Deb. 5 s., 49–100; Crawford Memorandum, 28 November 1916, Earl of Crawford Papers, 95/4 (3), National Library of Scotland, Edinburgh.
108 Crawford Memorandum, 28 November 1916, Earl of Crawford Papers, 95/ 4 (3), National Library of Scotland, Edinburgh. Presumably Crawford is referring to *Parliamentary Debates*, 23 H. L. Deb 5 s., 587–600, 675–684.
109 Letter printed in its entirety in Blake, *Unknown Prime Minister*, 307; and Spender and Asquith, *Life of Herbert Henry Asquith*, Vol. 2, 250–251.
110 McEwen, 'Struggle for Mastery', 148.
111 See, for example, McKenna, *Reginald McKenna*, 258–259; Trevelyan, *Grey of Fallodon*, 325–327; and Robbins, *Sir Edward Grey*, 321–322.
112 Blake, *Unknown Prime Minister*, 307; Spender, *Life of Herbert Henry Asquith*, Vol. 2, 250–251.
113 French, *British Strategy*, 234; Devlin, *Too Proud to Fight*, 553; Lowe and Dockrill, *Mirage of Power*, 244–245; Stevenson, *Cataclysm*, 121. See also Robbins, *Sir Edward Grey*, 343–344. Only Rothwell implies that Grey might have had any genuine concern that the war might no longer be winnable. See Rothwell, *British War Aims*, 55.
114 Grey Memorandum, 27 November 1916, CAB 37/160, The National Archives, Kew.
115 Runciman to Curzon, 8 December 1916, Lord Curzon Papers, Mss Eur F112/117, British Library India Office Section, London.
116 Roskill, *Hankey*, 315.
117 Jackson Memorandum, 16 November 1916, CAB 24/2, The National Archives, Kew. See also Roskill, *Hankey*, 314–315; and War Committee Minutes, 20 November 1916, CAB 22/70, The National Archives, Kew.
118 Asquith to Balfour, 20 November 1916, Arthur Balfour Papers, 49692, British Library, London; Roskill, *Hankey*, 320.
119 French, *British Strategy*, 248.
120 Keynes Handwritten Notes for Talk at Admiralty, 15 February 1917, John Maynard Keynes Papers, T/11/12-19, King's College Library, Cambridge.
121 Lloyd George, *War Memoirs*, Vol. 2, 686.
122 Lansdowne Memorandum, 27 November 1917, CAB 37/160, The National Archives, Kew. Emphasis added.
123 Asquith to Lansdowne, 28 November 1916, Lord Lansdowne (Bowood) Papers, 88906/20/11, British Library, London.
124 See note 1, above.
125 Adonis, 'Fitzmaurice, Henry Charles Keith Petty'.

126 Cecil Memorandum, 27 November 1916, CAB 37/160, The National Archives, Kew; Long Memorandum, 29 November, CAB 37/160, The National Archives, Kew. See also Heffer, *Staring at God*, 462.

127 Grigg, *Lloyd George*, 327; see Chapter 6, above.

128 Army Council Memorandum, 28 November 1916, CAB 37/160/25, The National Archives, Kew; Adams, *Conscription Controversy*, 184–186.

129 Turner, *British Politics*, 79; Lester, *H. H. Asquith*, 273.

130 Runciman to Asquith, 1 December 1916, Walter Runciman Papers, 149-2, University of Newcastle Robinson Library.

131 Adams, *Conscription Controversy*, 179–181.

132 Runciman to Asquith, 1 December 1916, Walter Runciman Papers, 149-2, University of Newcastle Robinson Library.

133 Cecil Memorandum, 27 November 1916, CAB 37/160, The National Archives, Kew.

134 Carosso, 'The Morgan Partnerships', Unfinished Manuscript, pp. 4-112 to 4-114, n. 439, 4-188 to 4-190, Vincent Carosso Papers, ARC 1214, Pierpont Morgan Library, New York.

135 Burk, *Britain, America, and the Sinews of War*, 83–84; Carosso, 'The Morgan Partnerships', Unfinished Manuscript, pp. 4-191 to 4-119, Vincent Carosso Papers, ARC 1214, Pierpont Morgan Library, New York; Horn, *Britain, France, and the Financing of the First World War*, 149–151; Seligman to Bradbury, 4 November 1916, London Exchange Committee Papers, C91/6, Bank of England Archive, London.

136 See Appendix II.

137 United States Senate, *Munitions Industry*, 8732–8733; Link, *Wilson: Campaigns for Progressivism and Peace*, 200; Farr, 'Reginald McKenna as Chancellor', 187. Emphasis in original.

138 White, *Story of Canada's War Finance*, 50–51.

139 Link, *Wilson: Campaigns for Progressivism and Peace*, 200; Carosso, 'The Morgan Partnerships', Unfinished Manuscript, pp. 4-201 to 4-202, Vincent Carosso Papers, ARC 1214, Pierpont Morgan Library, New York.

140 Link, *Wilson: Campaigns for Progressivism and Peace*, 200–203; Carosso, 'The Morgan Partnerships', Unfinished Manuscript, pp. 4-196 to 4-200, Vincent Carosso Papers, ARC 1214, Pierpont Morgan Library, New York; See also Soutou, *L'or et le sang*, 373–378.

141 War Committee Minutes, 28 November 1916, CAB 22/76, CAB 22/77, The National Archives, Kew; Maurice Hankey Diaries, 28 November 1916, Churchill College Archive Centre, Cambridge.

142 Asquith to Sylvia Henley, 29 November 1916, MS Eng Lett c 542/4, Asquith-Henley Papers, Bodleian Library, Oxford.

143 War Committee Minutes, 28 November 1916, CAB 22/77, The National Archives, Kew. For context on the railway wagon problem, see Brown, *British Logistics*, Chs. 4–5.

144 War Committee Minutes, 28 November 1916, CAB 22/77, The National Archives, Kew. Cf. French, *British Strategy*, 248.

145 War Committee Minutes, 28 November 1916, CAB 22/77, The National Archives, Kew.

146 Farr, 'Reginald McKenna as Chancellor', 188.
147 War Committee Minutes, 28 November 1916, CAB 22/77, The National Archives, Kew.
148 Vincent, *Crawford Papers*, 368.
149 Asquith to the King, 30 November 1916, CAB 41/37, The National Archives, Kew.
150 Vincent, *Crawford Papers*, 368–369.
151 London Exchange Committee Minutes, 28-29 November 1916, London Exchange Committee Papers, C91/17, Bank of England Archive, London; Link, *Wilson: Campaigns for Progressivism and Peace*, 203.
152 United States Senate, *Munitions Industry*, 8738–8739; Carosso, 'The Morgan Partnerships', Unfinished Manuscript, pp. 4-202 to 4-204, Vincent Carosso Papers, ARC 1214, Pierpont Morgan Library, New York.
153 Harcourt Cabinet Minutes, 29 November 1916, Lewis Harcourt Papers, MS. Eng. c. 8271, Bodleian Library, Oxford.
154 See Horn, *Britain, France, and the Financing of the First World War*, 115.
155 London Exchange Committee Minutes, 29 November 1916, London Exchange Committee Papers, C91/17, Bank of England Archive, London; Harcourt Cabinet Minutes, 29 November 1916, Lewis Harcourt Papers, MS. Eng. c. 8271, Bodleian Library, Oxford; Asquith to the King, 30 November 1916, CAB 41/37, The National Archives, Kew; Horn, *Britain, France, and the Financing of the First World War*, 152.
156 Vincent, *Crawford Papers*, 368–369.
157 Harcourt Cabinet Minutes, 29 November 1916, Lewis Harcourt Papers, MS. Eng. c. 8271, Bodleian Library, Oxford.
158 Johnson, *Collected Writings of John Maynard Keynes*, Vol 16, 211; Asquith to the King, 30 November 1916, CAB 41/37, The National Archives, Kew; Horn, *Britain, France, and the Financing of the First World War*, 152; London Exchange Committee Minutes, 7 December 1916, London Exchange Committee Papers, C91/17, Bank of England Archive, London.
159 Maurice Hankey Diaries, 30 November 1916, Churchill College Archive Centre, Cambridge.
160 Runciman, who was not a member of the War Committee, was allowed in during a different part of the meeting – it was not as if he had merely been absent that day.
161 War Committee Minutes, 30 November 1916, CAB 22/78, The National Archives, Kew; Roskill, *Hankey*, 322.
162 Maurice Hankey Diaries, 29 November 1916. Churchill College Archive Centre, Cambridge.
163 War Committee Minutes, 1 December 1916, CAB 22/79, The National Archives, Kew; Runciman to Asquith, 1 December 1916, Walter Runciman Papers, 149-2, University of Newcastle Robinson Library; Runciman to Hankey, 1 December 1916, Maurice Hankey Papers, HNKY 4/8, Churchill College Archive Centre, Cambridge.
164 McEwen, 'Struggle for Mastery', 140–141; Turner, *British Politics*, 132–133; Heffer, *Staring at God*, 462.
165 Heffer, *Staring at God*, 462.

166 War Committee Minutes, 1 December 1916, CAB 22/79, The National Archives, Kew.

167 Lloyd George Memorandum, 1 December 1916, H. H. Asquith Papers, 31, Bodleian Library, Oxford; Roskill, *Hankey*, 323.

168 Carosso, 'The Morgan Partnerships', Unfinished Manuscript, pp. 4-204, 4-213 to 4-220, Vincent Carosso Papers, ARC 1214, Pierpont Morgan Library, New York.

169 War Cabinet Minutes, 9 December 1916, CAB 37/161/9, The National Archives, Kew. (The sum is derived by adding $64 million for the week ending 1 December to $76 million for the week ending 8 December.)

170 Johnson, *Collected Writings of John Maynard Keynes*, Vol. 16, 210–211; Burk, *Britain, America, and the Sinews of War*, 87.

171 Carosso, 'The Morgan Partnerships', Unfinished Manuscript, pp. 4-210 to 4-213, 4-220 to 4-223, Vincent Carosso Papers, ARC 1214, Pierpont Morgan Library, New York.

172 London Exchange Committee Minutes, 5–6 December 1916, London Exchange Committee Papers, C91/17, Bank of England Archive, London.

173 Lloyd George Memorandum, 1 December 1916, H. H. Asquith Papers, 31, Bodleian Library, Oxford; Roskill, *Hankey*, 323.

174 Vincent, *Crawford Papers*, 370.

175 Asquith to Lloyd George, 1 December 1916, H. H. Asquith Papers, 31, Bodleian Library, Oxford.

176 Roskill, *Hankey*, 234; Adams, *Bonar Law*, 228–229; Gilbert, *Organizer of Victory*, 393–395.

177 Beaverbrook, *Politicians and the War*, Vol. 2, Ch. 17; Turner, *British Politics*, 132, 134; McEwen, 'Struggle for Mastery', 143; Rowland, *Lloyd George*, 360; Hattersley, *David Lloyd George*, 409–410; Gilbert, *Organizer of Victory*, 393; Adams, *Bonar Law*, 228. Beaverbrook's account long dominated views of these events. See Stubbs, 'Beaverbrook as Historian'; Fraser, 'Lord Beaverbrook's Fabrications'; and McEwen, 'Lord Beaverbrook'.

178 'Lloyd George to Resign', *Reynolds's Newspaper*, 3 December 1916, 1, c. 2–3.

179 Newton, *Lord Lansdowne*, 453.

180 Conservative Resolution, 3 December 1916, H. H. Asquith Papers, 31, Bodleian Library, Oxford.

181 Harcourt Cabinet Minutes/Diary, 4 December 1916, Lewis Harcourt Papers, MS. Eng. c. 8271, Bodleian Library, Oxford.

182 Ibid.

183 Roskill, *Hankey*, 325.

184 Wilson, *Political Diaries of C. P. Scott*, 246–247; Clark, '*A Good Innings*', 161. Similarly, see Addison, *Four and a Half Years*, Vol. 1, 270–271.

185 Lloyd George to Asquith, 5 December 1916, H. H. Asquith Papers, 31, Bodleian Library, Oxford.

186 Colvin, *Carson*, Vol. 3, 209–210.

187 Vincent, *Crawford Papers*, 375.

188 McEwen, 'Struggle for Mastery', 148.

189 McEwen, *Riddell Diaries*, 175.

190 Harcourt Cabinet Minutes/Diary, 4 December 1916, Lewis Harcourt Papers, MS. Eng. c. 8271, Bodleian Library, Oxford.
191 Roskill, *Hankey*, 325–326.
192 Asquith to Pamela McKenna, 3 December 1916, Reginald McKenna Papers, MCKN 9/3, Churchill College Archive Centre, Cambridge; Jenkins, *Asquith*, 443.
193 Jenkins, *Asquith*, 442.
194 'Reconstruction', 4 December 1916, *Times*, 9, c. 1–2.
195 Wrench, *Geoffrey Dawson*, 140.
196 McEwen, 'Press and the Fall of Asquith', 882; McEwen, 'Struggle for Mastery', 153–154; Turner, *British Politics*, 135; French, *British Strategy*, 237; Farr, 'Winter and Discontent', 136.
197 'The Crisis of the War and of the Ministry', *Manchester Guardian*, 4 December 1916, 4, c. 2–3; Wilson, *Political Diaries of C. P. Scott*, 243–244; Hammond, *C. P. Scott*, 205. It was reported elsewhere in the paper that Asquith had *proposed* a committee of himself, Lloyd George, Bonar Law, Carson, and Henderson, but that Lloyd George demanded Asquith's exclusion. See 'The Government to Be Reconstructed', *Manchester Guardian*, 4 December 1916, 5, c. 1.
198 Wilson, *Political Diaries of C. P. Scott*, 245.
199 Asquith to Lloyd George, 4 December 1916, H. H. Asquith Papers, 31, Bodleian Library, Oxford.
200 Lloyd George to Asquith, 4 December 1916, H. H. Asquith Papers, 31, Bodleian Library, Oxford.
201 Ibid.
202 Wilson, *Political Diaries of C. P. Scott*, 247–248.
203 'Prime Minister on Reconstruction', *Times*, 5 December 1916, 9, c. 5.
204 'The Cabinet Crisis', *Times*, 5 December 1916, 9, c. 3.
205 'Mr. Lloyd George's Suggested Cabinet', *Manchester Guardian*, 5 December 1916, 5, c. 1.
206 Roskill, *Hankey*, 326.
207 Harcourt Cabinet Minutes/Diary, 4 December 1916, Lewis Harcourt Papers, MS. Eng. c. 8271, Bodleian Library, Oxford; Herbert Samuel Memorandum, 5 December 1916, J. A. Spender Papers, 46392, British Library, London.
208 'Mr. Lloyd George's Suggested Cabinet', *Manchester Guardian*, 5 December 1916, 5, c. 1.
209 Asquith to Lloyd George, 4 December 1916, H. H. Asquith Papers, 31, Bodleian Library, Oxford.
210 Lloyd George to Asquith, 5 December 1916, H. H. Asquith Papers, 31, Bodleian Library, Oxford.
211 Wilson, *Political Diaries of C. P. Scott*, 248.
212 Lloyd George to Asquith, 5 December 1916, H. H. Asquith Papers, 31, Bodleian Library, Oxford.
213 Waley, *Edwin Montagu*, 104.
214 Lloyd George to Asquith, 5 December 1916, H. H. Asquith Papers, 31, Bodleian Library, Oxford.
215 Taylor, *Lloyd George: A Diary*, 132.

216 Asquith to Lloyd George, 5 December 1916, H. H. Asquith Papers, 31, Bodleian Library, Oxford.
217 Harcourt Cabinet Minutes/Diary, 4 December 1916, Lewis Harcourt Papers, MS. Eng. c. 8271, Bodleian Library, Oxford.
218 See Self, *Austen Chamberlain Diary Letters*, 35; Johnson, *Robert Cecil*, Ch. 3; Gilmour, *Curzon*, 491; and Cecil, *All the Way*, 136–137.
219 Turner, *British Politics*, 139; McEwen, 'Struggle for Mastery', 148; Harcourt Cabinet Minutes/Diary, 4 December 1916, Lewis Harcourt Papers, MS. Eng. c. 8271, Bodleian Library, Oxford.
220 Balfour to Asquith, 5 December 1916, Asquith to Balfour, 5 December 1916, Balfour to Asquith, 5 December 1916, Arthur Balfour Papers, 49692, British Library, London.
221 Harcourt Cabinet Minutes/Diary, 5 December 1916, Lewis Harcourt Papers, MS. Eng. c. 8271, Bodleian Library, Oxford; Bonar Law to Asquith, 5 December 1916, H. H. Asquith Papers, 31, Bodleian Library, Oxford.
222 Harcourt Cabinet Minutes/Diary, 6 December 1916, Lewis Harcourt Papers, MS. Eng. c. 8271, Bodleian Library, Oxford.
223 Roskill, *Hankey*, 327; Lewis, *Carson*, 201.
224 Stamfordham to Haldane, 5 December 1916, Haldane Memorandum, 5 December 1916, Richard Haldane Papers, National Library of Scotland, Edinburgh; Heffer, *Staring at God*, 471.
225 Roskill, *Hankey*, 327; Lewis, *Carson*, 201.
226 See Turner, *British Politics*, 141–142.
227 Turner, *British Politics*, 142–148; Heffer, *Staring at God*, 476–486; Grey to Balfour, 8 December 1916, Arthur Balfour Papers, Add. 49731, British Library, London.
228 Spender, *Life of Herbert Henry Asquith*, Vol. 2, 274.
229 For example, Turner, *British Politics*, 141.
230 Harcourt Cabinet Minutes/Diary, 6 December 1916, Lewis Harcourt Papers, MS. Eng. c. 8271, Bodleian Library, Oxford.
231 Self, *Austen Chamberlain Diary Letters*, 37.
232 Hankey Diary, 2 December 1916.
233 Cassar, *Lloyd George at War*, 268–271; David, 'Liberal Party Divided'. See also Lester, *H. H. Asquith*, 317ff.
234 Wilson, 'The Coupon and the British General Election of 1918'; Wilson, *Downfall of the Liberal Party*, Chs. 6–8; Farr, 'Waging Democracy'; Douglas, 'Background to the "Coupon" Election Arrangements'.
235 Millman, *Pessimism*, 32–41.
236 Wilson, *Political Diaries of C. P. Scott*, 241.
237 Robertson Memorandum, 31 August 1916, CAB 29/1, The National Archives, Kew.
238 Hankey, *Supreme Command*, Vol. 2, 557.

Chapter 8

1 Asquith to Henley, 6 December 1916, Asquith-Henley Papers, MS Eng Lett c 542/4, Bodleian Library, Oxford.
2 See, for example, Cassar, *Lloyd George at War*; French, *Strategy of the Lloyd George Coalition*; and Millman, *Pessimism*.

3 Strictly speaking, Lord Crawford became Lord Privy Seal, but as the full Cabinet did not meet, Crawford had no responsibilities.

4 Grey Memorandum, [Late November / Early December 1916], Edward Grey Papers, FO 800/96, The National Archives, Kew. Printed in Grey, *Twenty-Five Years*, Vol. 2, 126–129.

5 Devlin, *Too Proud to Fight*, 555.

6 Grey Memorandum, [Late November / Early December 1916], Edward Grey Papers, FO 800/96, The National Archives, Kew. Printed in Grey, *Twenty-Five Years*, Vol. 2, 126–129. See also War Committee Minutes, 21 November 1916, CAB 22/72, The National Archives, Kew.

7 Ibid.

8 'The "Peace Letter" of 1917', March 1934, *The Nineteenth Century and After*, Vol. 115, No. 685, 371; Winters, 'Exaggerating the Efficacy of Diplomacy', 32.

9 Grey to Balfour, 9 December 1916, Arthur Balfour Papers, GD433/2/75/10, National Archives of Scotland, Edinburgh. Copy in Edward Grey Papers, FO 800/96, The National Archives, Kew. Similarly, see Trevelyan, *Grey of Fallodon*, 324–325.

10 Drummond to Balfour, 11 December 1916, Arthur Balfour Papers, GD433/2/75/14, National Archives of Scotland, Edinburgh.

11 Cecil to Lloyd George, December 1916, Robert Cecil Papers, FO 800/197, The National Archives, Kew.

12 Link, *Papers of Woodrow Wilson*, Vol. 40, 185–186, 189.

13 'Signal by the President Bathes Liberty Statue in Flood of Light', *New York Times*, 3 December 1916.

14 Devlin, *Too Proud to Fight*, 566–567. Link, *Papers of Woodrow Wilson*, Vol. 40, 131–132.

15 'Belgium's Appeal to US Made Public', 17 November 1916, *New York Times*, 2; 'Belgium Appeals to Pope and Spain', 24 November 1916, *New York Times*, 1. More generally, see Pirenne, *Belgium and the First World War*, Ch. 7.

16 *FRUS, 1916 Supplement*, 70–71.

17 'Germany Defends Belgians' Transfer', *New York Times*, 9 December 1916.

18 Devlin, *Too Proud to Fight*, 567.

19 *FRUS, 1916 Supplement*, 94.

20 'The German Peace Proposals', *Manchester Guardian*, 13 December 1916, 4, c. 1–3; 'The German Peace Terms', *Manchester Guardian*, 14 December 1916, 4, c. 1–2.

21 Carnegie Endowment for International Peace Division of International Law, *Official German Documents*, 998–999; Devlin, *Too Proud to Fight*, 574.

22 See, for example, 'Reichstag Summoned', *Times*, 11 December 1916, 7, c. 6.

23 Berlin to Washington Decrypt, 10 December 1916, HW 7/17, The National Archives, Kew. This was not the only information pointing in this direction. See Kernek, 'British Government's Reactions', 726–727, n. 16.

24 Trevelyan, *Grey of Fallodon*, 325.

25 War Cabinet Minutes, 9 December 1916, CAB 23/1/1, The National Archives, Kew; London Exchange Committee Minutes, 7–8 December

1916, London Exchange Committee Papers, C91/17, Bank of England Archive, London.

26 War Cabinet Minutes, 9 December 1916, CAB 23/1/1, The National Archives, Kew.

27 Carosso, 'The Morgan Partnerships', Unfinished Manuscript, p. 4-219, Vincent Carosso Papers, ARC 1214, Pierpont Morgan Library, New York.

28 Collier, *Brasshat*, 253. See also Callwell, *Field Marshall*, Vol. 1, 306.

29 'Mr. Bonar Law on the Peace Overtures', *Manchester Guardian*, 15 December 1916, 4, c. 2–3. See also *The Nation*, 16 December 1916, 398.

30 *Parliamentary Debates*, 88 H. C. Deb. 5 s., 942.

31 Ibid., 1730–1732.

32 Drummond Memorandum, 13 December 1916, Robert Cecil Papers, FO 800/197, The National Archives, Kew.

33 Leo Amery Diary, 29 November 1917, Leo Amery Papers, AMEL 7/13, Churchill College Archive Centre, Cambridge.

34 See Spence, 'Englishmen in New York'; Troy, 'Gaunt-Wiseman Affair'; Gaunt, *Yield of the Years*; Popplewell, *Intelligence and Imperial Defence*, 237–252; Voska and Irwin, *Spy and Counter-Spy*, 29–30; Thwaites, *Velvet and Vinegar*, Chs. 11–15; Andrew, *For the President's Eyes Only*, Ch. 2; Read and Fisher, *Colonel Z*, 121; Willert, *Road to Safety*, Ch. 2; and Peterson, *Propaganda for War*, 152–158.

35 Fowler, *British-American Relations*, Chs. 1–2; Andrew, *For the President's Eyes Only*, Ch. 2; Lockhart, 'Sir William Wiseman'; Murray, *Master and Brother*, 154; Murray, *At Close Quarters*, 2; Devlin, *Too Proud to Fight*, 611–612; Burk, *Old World, New World*, 450–451; Jeffery, *MI6*, 114; Kernek, *Distractions of Peace*, 35–36.

36 William Wiseman Papers, 4:91, Yale University Library, New Haven, Connecticut.

37 Telegram No. 342, December 13, 1916, William Wiseman Papers, 4:91, Yale University Library, New Haven, Connecticut.

38 This telegram is the first example of its kind that survives, but it seems that Wiseman had been sending in foreign policy assessments for quite some time. Wiseman makes a reference to a September telegram in which he had reported that Bernstorff believed that there would be a peace move before Christmas. More importantly, however, Wiseman gives advice that only makes sense if his reports had been regularly sent to the Foreign Office and were receiving a favourable reception there. He counsels London that if it wished to retain US sympathy, Britain's 'answer should be that we are not out to haggle over territory but to right a great wrong and guarantee its non-recurrence. "Quit and indemnify Belgium and then we will discuss peace. We can have no dealings with an unrepentant [particularly bellicose German General Friedrich von] Bernhardi". Also, Wilson should be lauded in the press for refusing to be deceived'. See Telegram No. 457, 15 December 1916, William Wiseman Papers, 4:91, Yale University Library, New Haven, Connecticut. In a second example of him giving specific foreign policy advice, the following day Wiseman telegraphed a French report that Wilson believed the French and English peoples wanted peace. Wiseman urged that the

previous British Ambassador to Washington, James Bryce – a Liberal with a strong reputation in America – send Wilson a message denying this. See Telegram No. 458, 16 December 1916, William Wiseman Papers, 4:91, Yale University Library, New Haven, Connecticut.

39 Telegram No. 349, 16 December 1916, William Wiseman Papers, 4:91, Yale University Library, New Haven, Connecticut. Cf. Devlin, *Too Proud to Fight*, 610: 'There is nothing to show that the British Foreign Office were in the least interested in the [German] terms'. For Balfour's illness, see Devlin, *Too Proud to Fight*, 583–584. As late as 26 December, the Foreign Office continued to be represented (when needed) on the War Cabinet by Cecil. See War Cabinet Minutes, 26 December 1916, CAB 23/1/18, The National Archives, Kew. Balfour's first attendance at the War Cabinet did not occur until the following day. See War Cabinet Minutes, 27 December 1916, CAB 23/10/19, The National Archives, Kew.

40 Edward House Diaries, 17 December 1916, Yale University Library, New Haven, Connecticut; Telegram No. 460, [17 December 1916], William Wiseman Papers, 4:91, Yale University Library, New Haven, Connecticut.

41 Telegram No. 460, [17 December 1916], William Wiseman Papers, 4:91, Yale University Library, New Haven, Connecticut.

42 Link, *Papers of Woodrow Wilson*, Vol. 40, 262.

43 Telegram No. 350, 18 December 1916, William Wiseman Papers, 4:91, Yale University Library, New Haven, Connecticut. See also Edward House Diaries, 18 December 1916, Yale University Library, New Haven, Connecticut. Note the reference to Balfour, which again demonstrates Wiseman's direct link to the Foreign Office.

44 *Parliamentary Debates*, 88 H. C. Deb. 5 s., 1333–1336.

45 Ibid., 1358–1367.

46 Turner, *British Politics*, 186.

47 Keynes to Grant, 14 January 1917, John Maynard Keynes Papers, 57931, British Library, London.

48 *The Nation*, 23 December 1916, 433; 'The Reply to Germany', *Manchester Guardian*, 20 December 1916, 6, c. 2–3.

49 War Cabinet Minutes, 18 December 1916, CAB 23/1/10, The National Archives, Kew. The minutes do not reveal who favoured asking Germany for its terms, but given his wobble, it seems likely that Bonar Law was amongst them.

50 *FRUS, 1916 Supplement*, 98–99.

51 Edward House Diaries, 20 December 1916, Yale University Library, New Haven, Connecticut; Telegram No. 460, [17 December 1916], William Wiseman Papers, 4:91, Yale University Library, New Haven, Connecticut.

52 'The American Note', *Manchester Guardian*, 22 December 1916, 4, c. 2; 'America and the Allies', *Manchester Guardian*, 23 December 1916, 4, c. 2–3.

53 'The President's Note', *Westminster Gazette*, 22 December 1916, 1, c. 2–3; Link, *Papers of Woodrow Wilson*, Vol. 40, 333.

54 Historians have previously believed both decrypts to be of American telegrams. See Freeman, 'MI1(b)', 217–218; Ferris, 'Now That the Milk Is Spilt', 537; and Larsen, 'British Intelligence', 703.

55 Carnegie Endowment for International Peace Division of International Law, *Official German Documents*, 998–999.

56 Hardinge to Lloyd George, 14 December 1916, US Decrypt, 9 December 1916, David Lloyd George Papers, F/3/2/1, Parliamentary Archives, London. Note in particular Hardinge's use of the plural 'telegrams'.

57 Decrypt, 9 December 1916, HW 7/17, The National Archives, Kew. Importantly, his copy was also marked 'No. 128' – the number of the German original – providing unambiguous proof that the decrypt was originally German in origin.

58 Robertson to Lloyd George, 14 December 1916, David Lloyd George Papers, F/44/3/3, Parliamentary Archives, London; Hardinge to Lloyd George, 15 December 1916, David Lloyd George Papers, F/3/2/2, Parliamentary Archives, London; Berlin to Washington Decrypt, 12 December 1916, HW 7/17, The National Archives, Kew.

59 Robertson to Lloyd George, 14 December 1916, David Lloyd George Papers, F/44/3/3, Parliamentary Archives, London; Hardinge to Lloyd George, 14 December 1916, US Decrypt, 9 December 1916, David Lloyd George Papers, F/3/2/1, Parliamentary Archives, London; Hardinge to Lloyd George, 15 December 1916, F/3/2/2, Parliamentary Archives, London.

60 Wilson, *Political Diaries of C. P. Scott*, 253. Emphasis added.

61 C. P. Scott Diaries, 31 January 1917, C. P. Scott Papers, John Rylands University Library of Manchester. This may be referring to Spring Rice to Foreign Office, 5 December 1916, FO 371/2800/04727, The National Archives, Kew.

62 Kernek, 'British Government's Reactions', 749.

63 Where Hankey had always kept a near-verbatim record of the proceedings of Asquith's War Committee, he now wrote up only the War Cabinet's conclusions.

64 Cecil Memorandum, 22 December 1916, CAB 23/1/16, The National Archives, Kew.

65 War Cabinet Minutes, 21 December 1916, CAB 23/1/13, The National Archives, Kew.

66 Maurice Hankey Diaries, 24 December 1916, Churchill College Archive Centre, Cambridge.

67 Ibid.

68 Drummond Memorandum, 21 December 1916, Robert Cecil Papers, FO 800/197, The National Archives, Kew.

69 Kernek, 'British Government's Reactions', 745.

70 Telegram No. 468, 22 December 1916, William Wiseman Papers, 4:91, Yale University Library, New Haven, Connecticut.

71 Curiously, however, there are no references to Wiseman in House's diary from 21 or 22 December. See Edward House Diaries, 21–22 December 1916, Yale University Library, New Haven, Connecticut.

72 War Cabinet Minutes, 23 December 1916, CAB 23/1/16, The National Archives, Kew.

73 War Cabinet Minutes, 9 December 1916, CAB 23/1/1, The National Archives, Kew.

74 Anglo-French Conference Meeting Minutes, 28 December 1916, CAB 28/2/
   2/14, Anglo-French Conference Meeting Conclusions, CAB 28/2/2/13, The
   National Archives, Kew; Horn, *Britain, France, and the Financing of the First
   World War*, 159.
75 *FRUS, 1916 Supplement*, 117–118.
76 Edward House Diaries, 27 December 1916, Yale University Library, New
   Haven, Connecticut; Link, *Papers of Woodrow Wilson*, Vol. 40, 337.
77 Edward House Diaries, 28 December 1916, Yale University Library, New
   Haven, Connecticut; Link, *Papers of Woodrow Wilson*, Vol. 40, 337, 343, 345;
   House to Bernstorff, 28 December 1916, Edward House Papers, 12:403,
   Yale University Library, New Haven, Connecticut.
78 Bernstorff to House, 30 December 1916, Edward House Papers, 12:403,
   Yale University Library, New Haven, Connecticut; Carnegie Endowment for
   International Peace Division of International Law, *Official German
   Documents*, 1010–1011.
79 Tuchman, *Zimmermann Telegram*, 133; Nickles, *Under the Wire*, 219–220,
   n. 23; Larsen, 'British Signals Intelligence'.
80 Bernstorff to House, 10, 11 January 1917, Edward House Papers, 12:404,
   Yale University Library, New Haven, Connecticut; House to Lansing, 17, 24,
   26 January, 1917, Edward House Papers, 69:2274, Yale University Library,
   New Haven, Connecticut; Link, *Papers of Woodrow Wilson*, Vol. 40, 508;
   Edward House Diaries, 23 January 1917, Yale University Library, New
   Haven, Connecticut; Devlin, *Too Proud to Fight*, 617, 652; Boghardt,
   Zimmermann Telegram, 139.
81 Tuchman, *Zimmermann Telegram*, 104, 130.
82 Carnegie Endowment for International Peace Division of International Law,
   Official German Documents, 1279.
83 Doerries, *Imperial Challenge*, 191.
84 Carnegie Endowment for International Peace Division of International Law,
   Official German Documents, 1010.
85 See Kernek, *Distractions of Peace*, 27–28.
86 *FRUS, 1916 Supplement*, 123–124.
87 Birnbaum, *Peace Moves*, 296–299.
88 Stevenson, *1917*, 19–29; Birnbaum, *Peace Moves*, Chs. 9–10; Devlin, *Too
   Proud to Fight*, 618–622; Watson, *Ring of Steel*, Ch. 10.
89 Steffen, 'Holtzendorff Memorandum'.
90 Devlin, *Too Proud to Fight*, 594.
91 Carnegie Endowment for International Peace Division of International Law,
   Official German Documents, 1012–1013; Birnbaum, *Peace Moves*, 300–304;
   Bernstorff, *My Three Years*, 281–282.
92 *FRUS, 1917 Supplement I*, 7–8.
93 Devlin, *Too Proud to Fight*, 603.
94 Telegram No. CX 500, 16 January 1917, William Wiseman Papers, 4:91,
   Yale University Library, New Haven, Connecticut.
95 Carosso, 'The Morgan Partnerships', Unfinished Manuscript, pp. 4-224 to 4-
   229, Vincent Carosso Papers, ARC 1214, Pierpont Morgan Library,
   New York.

96 'British Loan Well Secured by Collateral', 20 January 1917, *Wall Street Journal*, 1.

97 Carosso, 'The Morgan Partnerships', Unfinished Manuscript, pp. 4-229 to 4-234, Vincent Carosso Papers, ARC 1214, Pierpont Morgan Library, New York; Burk, *Sinews of War*, 89–90.

98 Burk, *Sinews of War*, 87–90; Carosso, 'The Morgan Partnerships', Unfinished Manuscript, pp. 4-191 to 4-234, Vincent Carosso Papers, ARC 1214, Pierpont Morgan Library, New York.

99 'Requisitioning Securities', 27 January 1917, *Economist*, 134–135; London Exchange Committee Minutes, 18 December 1916, London Exchange Committee Papers, C91/17, Bank of England Archive, London.

100 No specific statistics are given for January–March 1917. A total of £76 million ($364 million) purchased for March 18–30 December 1916 can be calculated from the 1919 Report of the American Dollar Securities Committee, which was printed in the United States Senate. *Munitions Industry*, 11745–11747. The fiscal year total ending 31 March 1917 is given as $526 million (converting sterling securities at 1 £ = $4.77). See Lewis, *America's Stake*, 544. Subtracting gives $162 million. Cf. Horn, *Britain, France, and the Financing of the First World War*, 133.

101 Lewis, *America's Stake*, 544. The amount of US railroad investments in foreign hands, moreover, was almost precisely the same in January 1917 as it was in 1919. See Lewis, *America's Stake*, 532, 546. In January 1917, the figure has been estimated at $1.185 billion; in 1919, $1.285 billion.

102 Keynes Handwritten Notes for Talk at Admiralty, 15 February 1917, John Maynard Keynes Papers, T/11/12-19, King's College Library, Cambridge.

103 Keynes to Grant, 14 January 1917, John Maynard Keynes Papers, 57931, British Library, London.

104 Johnson, *Collected Writings of John Maynard Keynes*, Vol. 16, 222–223. See also Lloyd George, *War Memoirs*, Vol. 2, 684.

105 Link, *Papers of Woodrow Wilson*, Vol. 40, 477–478, 517; Edward House Diaries, 15 January 1917, Yale University Library, New Haven, Connecticut.

106 Bernstorff to House, 20 January 1917, Edward House Papers, 12:404, Yale University Library, New Haven, Connecticut.

107 See Edward House Diaries, 2, 13, 15 January 1917, Yale University Library, New Haven, Connecticut.

108 Wiseman to [Foreign Office], 16 January 1917, William Wiseman Papers, 4:91, Yale University Library, New Haven, Connecticut.

109 Link, *Papers of Woodrow Wilson*, Vol. 40, 493, 497.

110 Ibid., 477–478, 491, 493, 507–509, 516–517, 524.

111 Ibid, 508, 517; House to Bernstorff, 17 January 1917, Edward House Papers, 12:404, Yale University Library, New Haven, Connecticut; House to Lansing, 17 January 1917, Edward House Papers, 69:2274, Yale University Library, New Haven, Connecticut.

112 Link, *Papers of Woodrow Wilson*, Vol. 40, 525–527; Bernstorff to House, 18 January 1917, House to Bernstorff, 19 January 1917, Edward House Papers, 12:404, Yale University Library, New Haven, Connecticut.

113 Carnegie Endowment for International Peace Division of International Law, *Official German Documents*, 1017–1019; 1337. For context, see Devlin, *Too Proud to Fight*, Ch. 19; Birnbaum, *Peace Moves*, Chs. 10–11; and Watson, *Ring of Steel*, Ch. 10.

114 Carnegie Endowment for International Peace Division of International Law, *Official German Documents*, 1021–1050; Bernstorff, *My Three Years*, 381.

115 The last surviving decrypt demonstrating Room 40's failure to show any progress on 7500 is Bernstorff to Berlin Decrypt, 16 December 1916, ADM 223/745, The National Archives, Kew.

116 Draft 'D', Chapter 25, Hall Unpublished Autobiography, pp. 10–12, Reginald Hall Papers, HALL 3/6, Churchill College Archive Centre, Cambridge; Boghardt, *Zimmermann Telegram*, 96–97.

117 Carnegie Endowment for International Peace Division of International Law, *Official German Documents*, 1021.

118 Wiseman to [Foreign Office], 20 January 1917, William Wiseman Papers, 4:91, Yale University Library, New Haven, Connecticut.

119 Devlin, *Too Proud to Fight*, 602–604; Link, *Wilson: Campaigns for Progressivism and Peace*, 264–269.

120 Edward House Diaries, 21 January 1917, Yale University Library, New Haven, Connecticut; Link, *Papers of Woodrow Wilson*, Vol. 40, 527. Both Link and Devlin incorrectly state that House told Wiseman of the planned address. See Link, *Wilson: Campaigns for Progressivism and Peace*, 280; and Devlin, *Too Proud to Fight*, 611.

121 Edward House Diaries, 22 January 1917, Yale University Library, New Haven, Connecticut.

122 Link, *Papers of Woodrow Wilson*, Vol. 40, 533–539.

123 Ibid., 41, 55; Link, *Wilson: Campaigns for Progressivism and Peace*, 271.

124 Carnegie Endowment for International Peace Division of International Law, *Official German Documents*, 1045–1046.

125 Edward House Diaries, 23 January 1917, Yale University Library, New Haven, Connecticut; Link, *Papers of Woodrow Wilson*, Vol. 41, 18–19.

126 Carnegie Endowment for International Peace Division of International Law, *Official German Documents*, 1045–1046.

127 Hall to Wiseman, 23 January 1917, William Wiseman Papers, 4:91, Yale University Library, New Haven, Connecticut.

128 Edward House Diaries, 24 January 1917, Yale University Library, New Haven, Connecticut; Link, *Papers of Woodrow Wilson*, Vol. 41, 17. Similarly, see Montagu Memorandum, [January 1917], Edwin Montagu Papers, AS6/10/33, Trinity College Library, Cambridge.

129 Edward House Diaries, 25 January 1917, Yale University Library, New Haven, Connecticut; Link, *Papers of Woodrow Wilson*, Vol. 41, 3–4, 17.

130 Link, *Papers of Woodrow Wilson*, Vol. 41, 24–26; Edward House Diaries, 26 January 1917, Yale University Library, New Haven, Connecticut.

131 Carnegie Endowment for International Peace Division of International Law, *Official German Documents*, 1046.

132 Ibid., 1047–1048.

133 Edward House Diaries, 26 January 1917, Yale University Library, New Haven, Connecticut; Link, *Papers of Woodrow Wilson*, Vol. 41, 26, 39–40.
134 Link, *Papers of Woodrow Wilson*, Vol. 41, 26.
135 Further Notes on Conversation with [House], 26 January 1917, William Wiseman Papers, 4:91, Yale University Library, New Haven, Connecticut; Link, *Papers of Woodrow Wilson*, Vol. 41, 26–27.
136 Further Notes on Conversation with [House], 26 January 1917, William Wiseman Papers, 4:91, Yale University Library, New Haven, Connecticut; Link, *Papers of Woodrow Wilson*, Vol. 41, 26–27. These notes actually appear to be for a draft telegram to the Foreign Office; there is no proof that the telegram was actually dispatched, but it seems unlikely that Wiseman would have concealed this report.
137 Wiseman to [Foreign Office], 27 January 1917, William Wiseman Papers, 4:91, Yale University Library, New Haven, Connecticut. House records no further conversation with Wiseman on 27 January – see Edward House Diaries, 27 January 1917, Yale University Library, New Haven, Connecticut.
138 Link, *Wilson: Campaigns for Progressivism and Peace*, 281.
139 Hardinge to Sir Ralph Paget, 16 January 1917, Lord Hardinge of Penhurst Papers, 29, Cambridge University Library. Written on the same day as Telegram 157 was dispatched, it cannot tell us anything about whether the intelligence was being provided to the Foreign Office.
140 Further Notes on Conversation with [House], 26 January 1917, William Wiseman Papers, 4:91, Yale University Library, New Haven, Connecticut; Link, *Papers of Woodrow Wilson*, Vol. 41, 26–27.
141 Doerries, *Imperial Challenge*, 217–218.
142 Bernstorff to House, 31 January 1917, Edward House Papers, 12:404, Yale University Library, New Haven, Connecticut.
143 Edward House Diaries, 1 February 1917, Yale University Library, New Haven, Connecticut.
144 Bernstorff, *My Three Years*, 379.
145 Edward House Diaries, 31 January 1917, Yale University Library, New Haven, Connecticut; Bernstorff to House, 31 January 1917, Edward House Papers, 12:404, Yale University Library, New Haven, Connecticut.
146 Devlin, *Too Proud to Fight*, 626.
147 Lansing Memorandum, 4 February 1917, Robert Lansing Papers, Library of Congress, Washington, District of Columbia.

Chapter 9

1 See Shanafelt, *Secret Enemy*, Ch. 5.
2 See especially Horčička, 'Austria-Hungary, Unrestricted Submarine Warfare, and the United States' Entrance'.
3 Shanafelt, *Secret Enemy*, 106–109.
4 Manteyer, *Austria's Peace Offer*, 83–84.
5 Stevenson, *First World War and International Politics*, 140.

6 Fried, *Austro-Hungarian War Aims*, Ch. 6; Shanafelt, *Secret Enemy*, Chs. 5–6, quoted at 128.

7 Ibid., 199; Shanafelt, *Secret Enemy*, 130–131.

8 Fest, *Peace or Partition*, 68–70, 75–76.

9 United States Senate, *Munitions Industry*, 9232.

10 Carosso, 'The Morgan Partnerships', Unfinished Manuscript, pp. 4-224 to 4-240 quoted at p. 4-239, Vincent Carosso Papers, ARC 1214, Pierpont Morgan Library, New York. See also Burk, *Britain, America, and the Sinews of War*, 92–94.

11 Burk, 'Mobilization of Anglo-American Finance', 39, n. 43. For US GDP in 1916, see Samuel H. Williamson, 'What Was the U.S. GDP Then?' *MeasuringWorth.com*, University of Illinois-Chicago, 2017. For US GDP in 2019, see the US Bureau of Economic Analysis' website, www.bea.gov.

12 Unsigned to Balfour, 11 June 1917, T 172/422, The National Archives, Kew.

13 *FRUS, 1917 Supplement II*, 552–553; Link, *Wilson: Campaigns for Progressivism and Peace*, 379–380; Keynes to Chalmers and Bradbury, [February 1917], T 172/420, The National Archives, Kew; Bonar Law to Lever, 2 March 1917, T 172/421, The National Archives, Kew. A number of authors note an 8 March 1917 statement from the Federal Reserve Board supportive of foreign loans (see, for example, Devlin, *Too Proud to Fight*, 661), but given the US Treasury's stance, this statement did not actually result in any meaningful US lending to the Allies.

14 The amount of securities in British possession in July 1917 is given as $150 million. See Johnson, *Collected Writings of John Maynard Keynes*, Vol. 16, 250. British government securities sales in the second quarter of 1917 were $44 million. See United States Senate, *Munitions Industry*, 9232. Approximately $90 million in US securities was bought up by the British government during April 1917 – April 1918. See Lewis, *America's Stake*, 544. It is not clear what fraction of this was purchased after July 1917; if uncollected assets are included, at most the British had some $300 million in undeployed assets by this point.

15 Sir Hardman Lever Diary, April–July 1917, T 172/429, The National Archives, Kew; Lever to Bonar Law, 7 May 1917, T 172/424, The National Archives, Kew; Burk, 'Mobilization of Anglo-American Finance', 35–36, 39, n. 43; Burk, *Britain, America, and the Sinews of War*, 94–95, 196–201; *FRUS, 1917 Supplement II*, 536, 552–553; 'Federal Government – Receipts and Outlays: 1900 to 2003', Table No. HS-47, US Census website, www.census.gov.

16 *FRUS, 1917 Supplement II*, 549–554, quoted at 553; Burk, 'J. M. Keynes and the Exchange Rate Crisis', 412; Carosso, 'The Morgan Partnerships', Unfinished Manuscript, Reel 2 – final unnumbered pages typed by D. W. Wright, Vincent Carosso Papers, ARC 1214, Pierpont Morgan Library, New York; Burk, 'Mobilization of Anglo-American Finance', 38.

17 Shanafelt, *Secret Enemy*, 115–116.

18 Link, *Papers of Woodrow Wilson*, Vol. 36, 126.

19 Ibid., 41, 39–40.

20 Wiseman to [Foreign Office], 31 January 1917, William Wiseman Papers, 4:91, Yale University Library, New Haven, Connecticut; Edward House Diaries, 31 January 1917, Yale University Library, New Haven, Connecticut.

21 Edward House Diaries, 1 February 1917, Yale University Library, New Haven, Connecticut.

22 Ibid.

23 See Vienna-Madrid Decrypts Summary, [1917], Documents.23329/J, Imperial War Museum, London.

24 Link, *Papers of Woodrow Wilson*, Vol. 41, 39–40.

25 Edward House Diaries, 1 February 1917, Yale University Library, New Haven, Connecticut.

26 Horčička, 'Austria-Hungary, Unrestricted Submarine Warfare, and the United States' Entrance', 254–256.

27 *FRUS, 1917 Supplement I*, 104–105, 112–113. An exceptionally short Reuters dispatch had appeared in the press the previous day saying that Austria-Hungary was sending a separate note and that it would be 'along lines similar to the German note', but evidently both men had missed it. See 'Austria Sends a Separate Note on Intensified Naval Warfare', *New York Times*, 2 February 1917, 1.

28 Horčička, 'Austria-Hungary, Unrestricted Submarine Warfare, and the United States' Entrance', 255–256; Shanafelt, *Secret Enemy*, 116.

29 Link, *Papers of Woodrow Wilson*, Vol. 41, 108–112.

30 Hardinge to Stamfordham, 8 February 1917, Lord Hardinge of Penhurst Papers, 29, Cambridge University Library.

31 Devlin, *Too Proud to Fight*, 626; Edward House Diaries, 15 February 1917, Yale University Library, New Haven, Connecticut; Bernstorff, *My Three Years*, 393.

32 Draft 'D', Chapter 25, Hall Unpublished Autobiography, p. 16, Reginald Hall Papers, HALL 3/6, Churchill College Archive Centre, Cambridge. In his memoirs, Gaunt falsely claimed to have been tipped off by House of the break in relations in a dramatic telephone call ahead of the official speech, a claim that historians have largely accepted. See, for example, Boghardt, *Zimmermann Telegram*, 103. The quote used in this paragraph is taken from Hall's unpublished memoirs – almost certainly the text of the original telegram – which notably exists *without* the claim that Gaunt had any advance knowledge: 'Bernstorff *has just been given* his passports' (Emphasis added). An identical text for this telegram is provided in Hendrick, *Life and Letters*, Vol. 2, 215. Hendrick had interviewed Hall in 1921 in putting his book together and almost certainly got the text of the telegram from him. See Freeman, 'Zimmermann Telegram Revisited', 109. Gaunt's own account claims to correct the text of the document that had been previously published in *Life and Letters* based on what he says was the actual original document, which he gives as: 'Cable to Admiral Hall to be deciphered personally. The Barber [Bernstorff] *gets his papers at 2 p.m. to-day* stop I'll probably get soused stop' (Emphasis added).

Gaunt's text is demonstrably a forgery crafted to support a dramatic story that exaggerates his own importance: at the time, Reginald Hall was still a

384 Notes to pages 289–293

captain; he was not promoted to rear-admiral for nearly another three months, on 27 April 1917. See *London Gazette*, 1 May 1917, Issue 30042, 4095. Moreover, House records in his diary entry for that day that he specifically tipped off *only* Wiseman as to the impending break with Germany – noting also that he was 'finding some embarrassment in dealing with Gaunt and Wiseman … Heretofore I have given everything to Gaunt, but in his absence I found Wiseman much more satisfactory'. See Edward House Diaries, 2 February 1917, Yale University Library, New Haven, Connecticut.

33 Draft 'D', Chapter 25, Hall Unpublished Autobiography, p. 16, Reginald Hall Papers, HALL 3/6, Churchill College Archive Centre, Cambridge; Cooper, *Walter Hines Page*, 364; Boghardt, *Zimmermann Telegram*, 103.

34 Hall launched the initiative with a telegram that had been drafted, typed, encoded, and sent out by 10 o'clock on the morning of Monday, 5 February – the likelihood of that including a trip down Whitehall to the Foreign Office and back before it went out is vanishingly small. See Boghardt, *Zimmermann Telegram*, 104.

35 Link, *Papers of Woodrow Wilson*, Vol. 41, 477–478.

36 Edward House Diaries, 4 February 1917, Yale University Library, New Haven, Connecticut.

37 Link, *Papers of Woodrow Wilson*, Vol. 41, 149.

38 See Edward House Diaries, February 1917, Yale University Library, New Haven, Connecticut, quoted at 12 February 1917.

39 Shanafelt, *Secret Enemy*, 115–116; Fest, *Peace or Partition*, 53–54; Fried, *Austro-Hungarian War Aims*, 194.

40 *FRUS, 1917 Supplement I*, 38–39.

41 Link, *Papers of Woodrow Wilson*, Vol. 41, 158–159. Emphasis added.

42 War Cabinet Minutes, 18 January, CAB 23/13/1, The National Archives, Kew.

43 See also Fest, *Peace or Partition*, Ch. 2; Stevenson, *First World War and International Politics*, 139–148; and Mamatey, *United States and East Central Europe*, 52–71.

44 Washington to London Decrypt, 8 February 1917, HW 7/17, The National Archives, Kew.

45 *FRUS, 1917 Supplement I*, 38–39.

46 Maurice Hankey Diaries, 1 March 1917, Churchill College Archive Centre, Cambridge.

47 Link, *Papers of Woodrow Wilson*, Vol. 41, 211–212, 270.

48 Ibid., 270; Kernek, *Distractions of Peace*, 40; Fest, *Peace or Partition*, 53–54; Horčička, 'Austria-Hungary, Unrestricted Submarine Warfare, and the United States' Entrance', 258.

49 Boghardt, *Zimmermann Telegram*, 104–117.

50 Draft 'D', Chapter 25, Hall Unpublished Autobiography, pp. 21–22, Reginald Hall Papers, HALL 3/6, Churchill College Archive Centre, Cambridge.

51 Boghardt, *Zimmermann Telegram*, 119; Cooper, *Walter Hines Page*, 366–368.

52 Kernek, *Distractions of Peace*, 40; Fest, *Peace or Partition*, 53–54; Horčička, 'Austria-Hungary, Unrestricted Submarine Warfare, and the United States' Entrance', 258; Fried, *Austro-Hungarian War Aims*, 194.

53 Link, *Papers of Woodrow Wilson*, Vol. 41, 260, 270–273; *FRUS*, 1917 Supplement I, 55–56; Page to Wilson Draft, February 1917, Walter Hines Page Papers, 1090.5, Box 3, Journal 1917, Harvard University Houghton Library, Cambridge, Massachusetts. Emphasis in original.

54 Page to Wilson Draft, February 1917, Walter Hines Page Papers, 1090.5, Box 3, Journal 1917, Harvard University Houghton Library, Cambridge, Massachusetts. Emphasis added.

55 Page to Wilson Draft, February 1917, Walter Hines Page Papers, 1090.5, Box 3, Journal 1917, Harvard University Houghton Library, Cambridge, Massachusetts. Winston Churchill's 1942 admission to Franklin Roosevelt that Britain had been breaking American codes has been called 'unprecedented', but this is now not wholly true. See Kruh, 'British American-Cryptanalytic Cooperation'. For further context of the Ambassador's problems that plagued Anglo-American relations in this period, see Kihl, 'A Failure of Ambassadorial Diplomacy'. See also Montagu to Drummond, 26 February 1916, Edwin Montagu Papers, AS1/5/88, Trinity College Library, Cambridge.

56 Link, *Papers of Woodrow Wilson*, Vol. 41, 260, 267–268.

57 Page Diary, 24 February 1917, Walter Hines Page Papers, 1090.5, Box 3, Journal 1917, Harvard University Houghton Library, Cambridge, Massachusetts; Boghardt, *Zimmermann Telegram*, 119.

58 Link, *Papers of Woodrow Wilson*, Vol. 41, 280–282; Boghardt, *Zimmermann Telegram*, 119–121.

59 London to Washington Decrypt, 24 February 1917, HW 3/179, The National Archives, Kew. The passages on the decrypt that are marked for emphasis are the markings of the surprise of discovering what was happening for the first time: the text of the Zimmermann Telegram that Page relays, along with a long passage beginning 'Early in the war the British government obtained possession of a German cipher code'. Only those not already privy to the Zimmermann Telegram secret would have emphasized those passages of the American telegram.

60 Crocker to Hall, Undated, Washington to London Decrypt, 27 February 1917, HW 3/179, The National Archives, Kew.

61 Ramsay, *'Blinker' Hall*. Similarly, see, for example, Devlin, *Too Proud to Fight*, 653–656; Tuchman, *Zimmermann Telegram*, 183; and Link, *Wilson: Campaigns for Progressivism and Peace*, 354–359.

62 Boghardt, *Zimmermann Telegram*, Ch. 11, quoted at 180.

63 Ibid., 138, 189.

64 Kennedy, 'Thomas Boghardt'.

65 Link, *Wilson: Campaigns for Progressivism and Peace*, Ch. 9.

66 Boghardt, *Zimmermann Telegram*, 135–137; Link, *Papers of Woodrow Wilson*, Vol. 41, 288; Edward House Diaries, 26 February 1917, Yale University Library, New Haven, Connecticut.

67 Lansing Memorandum, 4 March 1917, Robert Lansing Papers, Library of Congress, Washington, District of Columbia. See also Boghardt, *Zimmermann Telegram*, 138–140.

68 Link, *Papers of Woodrow Wilson*, Vol. 41, 305.

69 Devlin, *Too Proud to Fight*, 653–654; Boghardt, *Zimmermann Telegram*, 141–144, 172–179, 191–194.
70 Link, *Wilson: Campaigns for Progressivism and Peace*, 356–377; Devlin, *Too Proud to Fight*, 656–658.
71 Horčička, 'Austria-Hungary, Unrestricted Submarine Warfare, and the United States' Entrance', 262.
72 Link, *Papers of Woodrow Wilson*, Vol. 41, 158.
73 Lansing Memorandum, 4 March 1917, Robert Lansing Papers, Library of Congress, Washington, District of Columbia.
74 Link, *Wilson: Campaigns for Progressivism and Peace*, 345.
75 Link, *Papers of Woodrow Wilson*, Vol. 41, 524–525.
76 *FRUS, 1917 Supplement I*, 62–63; Link, *Papers of Woodrow Wilson*, Vol. 41, 313.
77 Link, *Papers of Woodrow Wilson*, Vol. 41, 398–399.
78 Devlin, *Too Proud to Fight*, 642; Carnegie Endowment for International Peace Division of International Law, *Official German Documents*, 1334.
79 United States Department of Commerce, *Annual Report of the Commissioner of Navigation to the Secretary of Commerce for the Fiscal Year Ended June 30, 1917*, 64.
80 Thompson, *Woodrow Wilson*, 144, 147.
81 Devlin, *Too Proud to Fight*, 644, 652; Carosso, 'The Morgan Partnerships', Unfinished Manuscript, p. 4-241, Vincent Carosso Papers, ARC 1214, Pierpont Morgan Library, New York.
82 Carnegie Endowment for International Peace Division of International Law, *Official German Documents*, 1336; Devlin, *Too Proud to Fight*, 641–642; Kernek, *Distractions of Peace*, 40–41.
83 Link, *Papers of Woodrow Wilson*, Vol. 41, 398–399, 421–422. *FRUS, 1917 Supplement I*, 65–66. For the 'overt acts', see 'Ship Shelled and Bombed', *New York Times*, 14 March 1917; Devlin, *Too Proud to Fight*, 663–664; and Link, *Wilson: Campaigns for Progressivism and Peace*, 391, 396–397.
84 *FRUS, 1917 Supplement I*, 131–133, 161–168, 186.
85 Manteyer, *Austria's Peace Offer*, 1–31.
86 Ibid., Chs. 1–2.
87 Shanafelt, *Secret Enemy*, 128–133; Fest, *Peace or Partition*, 64–76; Manteyer, *Austria's Peace Offer*, Chs. 3–5.
88 Devlin, *Too Proud to Fight*, 665–666
89 Edward House Diaries, 27–28 March, 2 April 1917, Yale University Library, New Haven, Connecticut. For the general expectation of a request for a declaration of war, see, for example, Lever to Bonar Law, 29 March 1917, T 172/421, The National Archives, Kew.
90 Devlin, *Too Proud to Fight*, 687.
91 Link, *Papers of Woodrow Wilson*, Vol. 41, 526–527.

Conclusion

1 Farr, 'Reginald McKenna as Chancellor', 190.
2 McKenna to Carver, 2 June 1917, Reginald McKenna Papers, MCKN 9/8, Churchill College Archive Centre, Cambridge.

3 See, for example, Sharp, *David Lloyd George*, Ch. 2.
4 See, for example, Tomlinson, 'Thrice Denied'.
5 'British Strategy in a Certain Eventuality', Memorandum, 25 May 1940, CAB 66/7/48, The National Archives, Kew; Stafford, 'The Detonator Concept'; Hill, *Cabinet Decisions*, Ch. 6.
6 See Files THCR 1/20/3/5-8, Margaret Thatcher Papers, Churchill College Archive Centre, Cambridge.
7 Trevelyan, *Grey of Fallodon*, 325.
8 Proceedings of the Cabinet Committee on the Co-Ordination of Military and Financial Effort, April 1916, pp. 356–358, CAB 27/4, The National Archives, Kew.
9 Johnson, *Collected Writings of John Maynard Keynes*, Vol. 16, 200.
10 Ibid., 187.
11 Ferguson, 'How (Not) to Pay for the War'. See also Broadberry and Harrison, 'Economics of World War I', 23.
12 Watson, *Ring of Steel*, Ch. 8.
13 Johnson, *Collected Writings of John Maynard Keynes*, Vol. 16, 187.
14 See, for example, Winter, *Great War and the British People*, Chs. 4, 7; Gregory, *Last Great War*, 282–289; and Gazeley and Newell, 'First World War and Working-Class Food Consumption'.
15 See, for example, Stevenson, *French War Aims*; and Stevenson, 'French War Aims and the American Challenge'.
16 Fisk, *Inter-Ally Debts*, 348. See also Burk, *Britain, America, and the Sinews of War*, 223; and Hautcoeur, 'Was the Great War a Watershed?', 191.
17 'Federal Government—Receipts and Outlays: 1900 to 2003', Table No. HS-47, US Census website, www.census.gov.
18 Rockoff, 'Until It's Over, Over There', 333.
19 See, for example, Grant, *Forgotten Depression*; and Walton and Rockoff, *History of the American Economy*, Chs. 21–22.
20 Hankey, *Supreme Command*, Vol. 2, 564; Roskill, *Hankey*, 325–326.
21 Maurice Hankey Diaries, 8 February 1917, Churchill College Archive Centre, Cambridge.
22 Maurice Hankey Diaries, 19–20 May 1916, Churchill College Archive Centre, Cambridge.
23 Maurice Hankey Diaries, 18 March 1917, Churchill College Archive Centre, Cambridge. See also Maurice Hankey Diaries, 1 March 1917, Churchill College Archive Centre, Cambridge.
24 Maurice Hankey Diaries, 9 April 1917, Churchill College Archive Centre, Cambridge.
25 Thompson, 'Woodrow Wilson and David Lloyd George'.
26 Roskill, *Hankey*, 333.
27 Stevenson, *1917*, 45.
28 Edward House Diaries, 8 May 1915, Yale University Library, New Haven, Connecticut.
29 Maurice Hankey Diaries, 1 February 1916, Churchill College Archive Centre, Cambridge.
30 Keynes Handwritten Notes for Talk at Admiralty, 15 February 1917, John Maynard Keynes Papers, T/11/12-19, King's College Library, Cambridge.

31 Lambert, *Planning Armageddon*, Chs. 5–11; Osborne, *Britain's Economic Blockade*, Chs. 4–6; West, 'Intelligence and the Development of British Grand Strategy', Chs. 5–8; cf. Coogan, 'The Short-War Illusion Resurrected', 1060–1062.
32 Stone, *Russian Army*, Ch. 12.
33 Shanafelt, *Secret Enemy*, 110.
34 Link, *Papers of Woodrow Wilson*, Vol. 40, 528.
35 Wilson, *Political Diaries of C. P. Scott*, 233–238. See also Hammond, *C. P. Scott*, 201.
36 Lloyd George to House, 31 July 1916, Edward House Papers, 70:2340, Yale University Library, New Haven, Connecticut.
37 Wilson, *Diaries of C. P. Scott*, 165–166.

Appendix I

1 The Bank of England estimated that private gold shipments from the beginning of the war to August 1916 amounted to only £4–5 million ($20–25 million). Cunliffe to C. de Sahmen, 1 August 1916, London Exchange Committee Papers, C91/5, Bank of England Archive, London.
2 Horn, *Britain, France, and the Financing of the First World War*, 157. Similarly, see Clarke, *Locomotive of War*, Chs. 5, 7.
3 Johnson, *Collected Writings of John Maynard Keynes*, Vol. XVI, 215–222.
4 Morgan, *Studies in British Financial Policy*, 341.
5 Calculated from Johnson, *Collected Writings of John Maynard Keynes*, Vol. XVI, 258, assuming a four-week month.
6 Morgan, *Studies in British Financial Policy*, 341.
7 Johnson, *Collected Writings of John Maynard Keynes*, Vol. XVI, 185.
8 Horn, *Britain, France, and the Financing of the First World War*, 86. It is unclear whether this sum includes those on government account.
9 Calculated from Paton, *Economic Position of the United Kingdom*, 118.
10 Horn, *Britain, France, and the Financing of the First World War*, 157.
11 Johnson, *Collected Writings of John Maynard Keynes*, Vol. XVI, 238.
12 Ibid., 204, 209.
13 United States Senate, *Munitions Industry*, 8701; calculated from War Trade Board Bureau of Research, *Export Trade Policy of the United Kingdom*, 43.
14 See, for example, Barnett, *John Maynard Keynes*, Ch. 9.
15 Johnson, *Collected Writings of John Maynard Keynes*, Vol. XVI, 210–222, quoted at 222.

Appendix II

1 Maddison, *Contours of the World Economy*, 379.

Bibliography

Archival Sources

British

Bank of England Archive, London
London Exchange Committee Papers
The Bank of England, 1914–1921 (Unpublished War History)
Bodleian Library, Oxford
Christopher Addison Papers
Asquith-Henley Papers
H. H. Asquith Papers
Margot Asquith Papers
James Bryce Papers
Eyre Crowe Papers
Lionel Curtis Papers
Maurice de Bunson Papers
Lewis Harcourt Papers
Alfred Milner Papers
Gilbert Murray Papers
Arthur Ponsonby Papers
Horace Rumbold Papers
British Library, London
Arthur James Balfour Papers
Francis Bertie Papers
Robert Cecil Papers
Alfred Harmsworth (Lord Northcliffe) Papers
Roger Keyes Papers
John Maynard Keynes Papers
Horatio Kitchener Papers
Lord Jellicoe Papers
Lord Lansdowne (Bowood) Papers
Walter Long Papers
C. P. Scott Papers
J. A. Spender Papers

British Library India Office Section, London
Lord Curzon Papers
Lord Reading Papers
Cambridge University Library
Robert Crewe-Milnes (Lord Crewe) Papers
Lord Hardinge of Penhurst Papers
Churchill College Archive Centre, Cambridge
Leo Amery Papers
Beesley/McLachlan/Hirst Papers
Reginald Brett (Viscount Esher) Papers
Winston Churchill Papers
William Clarke Papers
Alexander Denniston Papers
John Fisher Papers
Auckland Geddes Papers
Reginald Hall Papers
Maurice Hankey Papers and Diaries
Reginald McKenna Papers
Philip Noel-Baker Papers
Henry S. Rawlinson Papers
Cecil Spring Rice Papers
Margaret Thatcher Papers
Hart Liddell Centre for Military Archives, King's College London
Launcelot Kiggell Papers
William Robertson Papers
John Rylands University Library of Manchester
C. P. Scott Papers and Diaries (Microfilm Publication)
Liverpool Record Office
Edward Stanley (Lord Derby) Papers
National Archives of Scotland, Edinburgh
Arthur Balfour Papers
National Army Museum, London
Reginald Brett (Viscount Esher) Papers
National Library of Scotland, Edinburgh
Earl of Crawford Papers and Diaries
Douglas Haig Papers
Richard Haldane Papers
Arthur Murray (Viscount Elibank) Papers
Parliamentary Archives, London
David Lloyd George Papers
The National Archives, Kew
Admiralty Papers (ADM)
Arthur Balfour Papers (FO 800/199-217)
Francis Bertie Papers (FO 800/159-191)
Robert Cecil Papers (FO 800/195-198)
Eyre Crowe Papers (FO 800/243)
Eric Drummond Papers (FO 800/329, 383-385)
Edward Grey Papers (FO 800/35-113)
Douglas Haig Papers (WO 256)
Sir Hardman Lever Diary (T 172/429)

Horatio Kitchener Papers (PRO 30/57)
George Macdonogh Papers (WO 106/1510-1517)
Philip Noel-Baker Papers (FO 800/249)
Arthur Nicolson Papers (FO 800/336-381; PRO 30/81)
Lord Reading Papers (FO 800/222-226)
Cecil Arthur Spring Rice Papers (FO 800/241-242)
Cabinet Office Papers (CAB)
Foreign Office Papers (FO)
Treasury Papers (T)
War Office Papers (WO)
Papers inherited by the Government Code and Cipher School (HW)
Trinity College Library, Cambridge
Edwin Montagu Papers
University of Newcastle Robinson Library
Walter Runciman Papers

Canadian

National Archives Canada, Ottawa, Ontario
[U.K.] Report on Cable Censorship during the Great War
(1914–1919), Record Group 25 f8, Volume 1073, File #81

American

Harvard University Houghton Library, Cambridge, Massachusetts
Ellis Dresel Papers
Oswald Garrison Villard Papers
Joseph Grew Papers
Walter Hines Page Papers
William Phillips Papers and Diary
Indiana University School of Journalism, Bloomington, Indiana
Roy Howard Papers (selected documents)
The Morgan Library and Museum, New York, New York
Vincent Carosso Papers
King's College Library, Cambridge
John Maynard Keynes Papers
Library of Congress, Washington, District of Columbia
Chandler Anderson Papers
Ray Stannard Baker Papers
William Jennings Bryan Papers
Frederick Dixon Papers
Roy Howard Papers
Robert Lansing Papers
Woodrow Wilson Papers
Princeton University Mudd Manuscript Library, Princeton, New Jersey
Clifford Carver Papers
US National Archives and Records Administration, College Park, Maryland
Edward Bell Papers
US State Department Archives

Yale University Library, New Haven, Connecticut
Gordon Auchincloss Papers
William Buckler Papers
Edward House Papers and Diaries
Vance McCormick Papers
Sidney Mezes Papers
Frank Polk Papers
Charles Seymour Papers
Arthur Willert Papers
William Wiseman Papers

Periodicals

Daily Chronicle
Daily Express
Daily Mail
Daily News and Leader
Economist
London Gazette
Manchester Guardian
Monthly Review of Financial and Business Conditions (Fifth Federal Reserve District)
Morning Post
The Nation
National Review
New York Times
Nineteenth Century and After
Reynolds's Newspaper
Spectator
Times
Wall Street Journal
Westminster Gazette

Codebooks

Georgetown University Lauinger Library Special Collections, Washington, DC
United States Department of State. *Cipher of the Department of State* [Gray Code]. Washington: Government Printing Office, 1918. Item Number MI-14863.
United States Department of State. *Code A1*. Washington: Government Printing Office, 1919. Item Number MI-14860.
United States Department of State. *Decode A1*. Washington: Government Printing Office, 1919. Item Number MI-14861.
United States Department of State. *Decode B1*. Washington: Government Printing Office, 1920. Item Number MI-14862.

Government Publications

Carnegie Endowment for International Peace Division of International Law. *Official German Documents Relating to the World War*. New York: Oxford University Press, 1923.

Paton, William A. *The Economic Position of the United Kingdom: 1912–1918*. Washington: Government Printing Office, 1919.

History of the Ministry of Munitions. 12 vols. London: HMSO, 1922.

United Kingdom House of Commons. *The Parliamentary Debates: Official Report: 5th Series*. London: H. M. S. O.

United Kingdom House of Lords. *The Parliamentary Debates: Official Report: 5th Series*. London: H. M. S. O.

United Kingdom War Office. *Statistics of the Military Effort of the British Empire during the Great War, 1914–1920*. London: HMSO, 1922.

United States Department of Commerce. *Annual Report of the Commissioner of Navigation to the Secretary of Commerce for the Fiscal Year Ended June 30 1917*. Washington: Government Printing Office, 1917.

United States Department of Labor, Bureau of Labor Statistics. *Retail Prices: 1907 to December, 1916*. Bulletin of the United States Bureau of Labor Statistics No. 228, Retail and Cost of Living Series No. 18. Washington: Government Printing Office, 1917.

United States Department of State. *Papers Relating to the Foreign Relations of the United States, 1905 with the Annual Message of the President Transmitted to Congress, December 5, 1905*. Washington: Government Printing Office, 1906.

Papers Relating to the Foreign Relations of the United States: The Lansing Papers 1914–1920. Washington, DC: Government Printing Office, 1939.

Papers Relating to the Foreign Relations of the United States, 1914, Supplement, the World War. Washington, DC: Government Printing Office, 1928.

Papers Relating to the Foreign Relations of the United States, 1915, Supplement, the World War. Washington: Government Printing Office, 1928.

Papers Relating to the Foreign Relations of the United States, 1916, Supplement, the World War. Washington: Government Printing Office, 1929.

Papers Relating to the Foreign Relations of the United States, 1917, Supplement 1, the World War. Washington: Government Printing Office, 1931.

Papers Relating to the Foreign Relations of the United States, 1917, Supplement 2, the World War. 2 vols. Washington: Government Printing Office, 1932.

United States Senate, Seventy-Third Congress. *Munitions Industry: Hearings before the Special Committee Investigating the Munitions Industry*. Washington, DC: Government Printing Office, 1934–1943.

War Trade Board Bureau of Research. *Export Trade Policy of the United Kingdom, 1913–1918*. Washington, DC: Government Printing Office, 1918.

Memoirs and Published Primary Sources

Addison, Christopher. *Four and a Half Years: A Personal Diary from June 1914 to January 1919*. London: Hutchinson, 1934.

Asquith, Herbert Henry. *Memories and Reflections 1852–1927*. 2 vols. London: Cassel and Company, 1928.

Bernstorff, Johann Heinrich Andreas Hermann. *My Three Years in America*. Garden City, NY: Doubleday.

Blake, Robert. *The Private Papers of Douglas Haig 1914–1919*. London: Erye & Spottiswoode, 1952.

Burns, Bill. 'Submarine Cable Route Maps'. *History of the Atlantic Cable & Undersea Communications Website*. Last accessed 12 June 2013. www.atlantic-cable.com/Maps/index.htm.

Callwell, C. E. *Field-Marshal Sir Henry Wilson: His Life and Diaries*. London: Cassell and Company, 1927.

Carosso, Vincent P. *The Morgans Private International Bankers, 1854–1913*. Cambridge, MA: Harvard University Press, 1987.

Cecil, Robert. *All the Way*. London: Hodder and Stoughton Limited, 1949.

Clarke, Alan. *'A Good Innings': The Private Papers of Viscount Lee of Fareham*. London: John Murray, 1974.

Clarke, Peter. *The Locomotive of War: Money, Empire, Power, and Guilt*. London: Bloomsbury, 2017.

David, Edward (Ed.). *Inside Asquith's Cabinet: From the Diaries of Charles Hobhouse*. London: John Murray, 1977.

Dutton, David (Ed.). *Odyssey of an Edwardian Liberal: The Political Diary of Richard Durning Holt*. Gloucesterm UK: Alan Sutton Publishing Limited, 1989.

Ewing, Alfred W. *The Man of Room 40: The Life of Sir Alfred Ewing*. London: Hutchinson, 1939.

'Some Special War Work Part I'. *Cryptologia* 4/4 (1980), 193–203.

'Some Special War Work Part II'. *Cryptologia* 5/1 (1981), 33–39.

Gaunt, Guy. *The Yield of the Years: A Story of Adventure Afloat and Ashore*. London: Hutchinson, 1940.

Grey, Sir Edward. *Twenty-Five Years: 1892–1916*. 3 vols. London: Hodder and Stoughton, 1925.

Hankey, Lord Maurice. *The Supreme Command 1914–1918*. 2 vols. London: George Allen and Unwin Limited, 1961.

House, Edward. *Philip Dru: Administrator: A Story of Tomorrow 1920–1935*. New York: B. W. Huebsch, 1912.

Lennox, Blanche Gordon (Ed.). *The Diary of Lord Bertie of Thame 1914–1918*. 2 vols. London: Hodder and Stoughton, 1924.

Link, Arthur S. (Ed.). *The Papers of Woodrow Wilson*. 69 vols. Princeton, NJ: Princeton University Press, 1966–1994.

Lloyd George, David. *War Memoirs of David Lloyd George*. London: Odhams Press, 1933–1936.

London and Cambridge Economic Service (LCES). *The British Economy: Key Statistics 1900–1964*. London: The Times Publishing Company, 1964.

MacCarthy, Desmond (Ed.). *H. H. A.: Letters of the Earl of Oxford and Asquith to a Friend*. 2 vols. London: Geoffrey Bles, 1933–1934.

Manteyer, G. (Ed.). *Austria's Peace Offer 1916–1917*. London: Constable and Company, 1921.

McEwen, J. M. (Ed.). *The Riddell Diaries: 1908–1923*. London: Athlone Press, 1986.

Repington, Charles à Court. *The First World War*. London: Constable, 1920.

Riddell, George. *Lord Riddell's War Diary 1914–1918*. London: Ivor Nicholson & Watson, 1933.

Self, Robert C. *The Austen Chamberlain Diary Letters: The Correspondence of Sir Austen Chamberlain with His Sisters Hilda and Ida, 1916–1937*. Cambridge: Cambridge University Press, 1995.

Seymour, Charles (Ed.). *The Intimate Papers of Colonel House: Arranged as a Narrative by Charles Seymour, Professor of History at Yale University*. 4 vols. London: Ernest Benn, 1926.

Swinnerton, Frank (Ed.). *Arnold Bennett: The Journals*. Hammondsworth, UK: Penguin Books, 1971.

Taylor, A. J. P. (Ed.). *Lloyd George: A Diary by Frances Stevenson*. London: Hutchinson, 1971.

Thwaites, Norman. *Velvet and Vinegar*. London: Grayson & Grayson, 1932.

Vincent, John (Ed.). *The Crawford Papers: The Journals of David Lindsay, Twenty-Seventh Earl of Crawford and Tenth Earl of Balcarres, 1871–1940*. Manchester: Manchester University Press, 1984.

Voska, Emanuel Victor, and Will Irwin. *Spy and Counter-Spy: The Autobiography of a Master-Spy*. London: George G. Harrap, 1941.

White, Thomas. *The Story of Canada's War Finance*. Montreal: n.p., 1921.

Woodward, David (Ed.). *The Military Correspondence of Field-Marshal Sir William Robertson, Chief of the Imperial General Staff, December 1915–February 1918*. London: The Army Records Society, 1989.

Secondary Works

Adams, R. J. Q. *Arms and the Wizard: Lloyd George and the Ministry of Munitions*. London: Cassell, 1978.

'Asquith's Choice: The May Coalition and the Coming of Conscription, 1915–1916'. *Journal of British History* 25/3 (1986), 243–263.

Bonar Law. London: John Murray, 1999.

Balfour: The Last Grandee. London: John Murray, 2007.

Adams, R. J. Q., and Philip P. Poirier. *The Conscription Controversy in Great Britain, 1900–18*. London: Macmillan Press, 1987.

Adonis, Andrew. 'Fitzmaurice, Henry Charles Keith Petty-, Fifth Marquess of Lansdowne (1845–1927)'. In *The Oxford Dictionary of National Biography*, C. G. Matthew, Brian Harrison, and Lawrence Goldman (Eds.). Oxford: Oxford University Press, 2004; online edition, May 2009.

Aldrich, Richard. *Hidden Hand: Britain, America, and Cold War Secret Intelligence*. London: John Murray, 2001.

GCHQ: The Uncensored Story of Britain's Most Secret Intelligence Agency. London: Harper Press, 2010.

Ally, Russell. 'War and Gold – The Bank of England, the London Gold Market, and South Africa's Gold, 1914–19'. *Journal of Southern African Studies* 17/2 (1991), 221–238.

Ambrosius, Lloyd. *Woodrow Wilson and the American Diplomatic Tradition: The Treaty Fight in Perspective*. Cambridge: Cambridge University Press, 1987.

Wilsonian Statecraft: Theory and Practice of Liberal Internationalism during World War I. Wilmington: SR Books, 1991.

Wilsonianism: Woodrow Wilson and His Legacy in American Foreign Relations. New York: Palgrave Macmillan, 2002.

Andrew, Christopher. 'Déchiffrement et diplomatie: le cabinet noir du Quai d'Orsay sous la Troisième République'. *Relations Internationales* 5 (1976), 37–64.

'Governments and Secret Services: A Historical Perspective'. *International Journal* 34/2 (1979), 167–186.

Secret Service: The Making of the British Intelligence Community. London: Heinemann, 1985.

'Secret Intelligence and British Foreign Policy, 1900–1939'. In *Intelligence and International Relations 1900–1945*, Christopher Andrew and Jeremy Noakes (Eds.). Exeter: University of Exeter, 1987, 9–28.

'The Making of the Anglo-American SIGINT Alliance'. In *In the Name of Intelligence: Essays in Honor of Walter Pforzheimer*, Hayden B. Peake and Samuel Halpern (Eds.). Washington, DC: NIBC Press, 1994, 95–109.

For the President's Eyes Only: Secret Intelligence and the American Presidency from Washington to Bush. London: HarperCollins, 1995.

'Reflections on Intelligence Historiography since 1939'. In *National Intelligence Systems: Current Research and Future Prospects*, Gregory F. Treverton and Wilhelm Agrell (Eds.). Cambridge: Cambridge University Press, 2009, 28–57.

Andrew, Christopher, and David Dilks (Eds.). *The Missing Dimension: Governments and Intelligence Communities in the Twentieth Century*. Urbana and Chicago: University of Illinois Press, 1984.

Andrew, Christopher, Richard J. Aldrich, and Wesley K. Wark (Eds.). *Secret Intelligence: A Reader*. London: Routledge, 2009.

Attard, Bernard. 'Politics, Finance and Anglo-Australian Relations: Australian Borrowing in London 1914–1920'. *Australian Journal of Politics & History* 35/2 (1989), 142–163.

Baker, Ray Stannard. *Woodrow Wilson: Life and Letters*. 8 vols. London: William Heinemann, 1935.

Balderston, T. 'War Finance and Inflation in Britain and Germany, 1914–1918'. *Economic History Review* 42/2 (1989), 222–244.

Barnett, Vincent. *John Maynard Keynes*. London: Routledge, 2013.

Barrett, Michael B. *Prelude to Blitzkrieg: The 1916 Austro-German Campaign in Romania*. Bloomington: Indiana University Press, 2013.

Beach, Jim. 'Origins of the Special Intelligence Relationship? Anglo-American Intelligence Co-operation on the Western Front, 1917–1918'. *Intelligence and National Security* 22/2 (2007), 229–249.

Haig's Intelligence: GHQ and the German Army, 1916–1918. Cambridge: Cambridge University Press, 2013.

Beaverbrook, Lord. *Politicians and the War, 1914–1916*. Hamden, CT: Archon Books, 1960.

Beesly, Patrick. *Room 40: British Naval Intelligence 1914–1918*. London: Hamish Hamilton, 1982.

Birnbaum, Karl E. *Peace Moves and U-Boat Warfare: A Study of Imperial Germany's Policy towards the United States April 18, 1916 – January 9, 1917.* Stockholm: Almqvist & Wiksell, 1958.

Black, Jeremy. *The Great War and the Making of the Modern World.* London: Continuum, 2011.

Blake, Robert. *The Unknown Prime Minister: The Life and Times of Andrew Bonar Law, 1858–1923.* London: Eyre and Spottiswoode, 1955.

Blewett, Neal. *The Peers, the Parties and the People: The General Elections of 1910.* London: Macmillan, 1972.

Boghardt, Thomas. *The Zimmermann Telegram: Intelligence, Diplomacy and America's Entry into World War I.* Annapolis, MD: Naval Institute Press, 2012.

Booth, Alan. *The British Economy in the Twentieth Century.* New York: Palgrave, 2001.

Broadberry, Stephen, and Mark Harrison. 'The Economics of World War I: An Overview'. In *The Economics of World War I*, Stephen Broadberry and Mark Harrison (Eds.) Cambridge: Cambridge University Press, 2005, 3–40.

Broadberry, Stephen, and Peter Howlett. The United Kingdom during World War I: Business as Usual? In *The Economics of World War I*, Stephen Broadberry and Mark Harrison (Ed.) Cambridge: Cambridge University Press, 2005, 206–234.

Brown, Brendon. *Monetary Chaos in Europe: The End of an Era.* London: Routledge, 2011.

Brown, Ian Malcolm. *British Logistics on the Western Front.* Westport, CT: Praeger, 1988.

Burk, Kathleen. 'Great Britain in the United States, 1917–1918: The Turning Point'. *International History Review* 1/2 (1979), 228–245.

'J. M. Keynes and the Exchange Rate Crisis of 1917.' *Economic History Review* 32/3 (1979), 405–416.

'The Mobilization of Anglo-American Finance during World War I'. In *Mobilization for Total War: The Canadian, American, and British Experience 1914–1918, 1939–1945*, N. F. Dreisziger (Ed.). Waterloo, ON: Wilfrid Laurier University Press, 1981, 23–42.

'The Treasury: From Impotence to Power'. In *War and the State*, Kathleen Burk (Ed.). London: George Allen & Unwin, 1982, 84–107.

Britain, America, and the Sinews of War, 1914–1918. Boston: George Allen & Unwin, 1985.

Morgan Grenfell, 1838–1988: The Biography of a Merchant Bank. Oxford: Oxford University Press, 1989.

Old World, New World: The Story of Britain and America. London: Little, Brown, 2007.

Burton, David H. *Cecil Spring Rice: A Diplomat's Life.* London: Associated University Presses, 1990.

Cassar, George H. *Asquith as War Leader.* London: The Hambledon Press, 1994.

Kitchener's War: British Strategy from 1914–1916. Dulles, VA Potomac Press, 2005.

Lloyd George at War, 1916–1918. London: Anthem Press, 2011.

Clifford, Brendan. '*British Intelligence and Political Leadership during the Gallipoli Campaign, September-December 1915*'. History Faculty Undergraduate Dissertation, University of Cambridge, 2015.

Clifford, Colin. *The Asquiths*. London: John Murray, 2002.

Collier, Basil. *Brasshat: A Biography of Field Marshal Sir Henry Wilson*. London: Secker & Warburg, 1961.

Colvin, Ian. *The Life of Lord Carson*. 3 vols. London: Victor Gollancz, 1932–1936.

Conyne, G. R. *Woodrow Wilson: British Perspectives, 1912–21*. London: Macmillan, 1992.

Coogan, John W. *The End of Neutrality: The United States, Britain, and Maritime Rights 1899–1915*. Ithaca, NY: Cornell University Press, 1981.

'The Short-War Illusion Resurrected: The Myth of Economic Warfare as the British Schlieffen Plan'. *Journal of Strategic Studies* 38/7 (2015), 1045–1064.

Cooper, John Milton, Jr. 'The British Response to the House-Grey Memorandum: New Evidence and New Questions'. *Journal of American History*, 59/4 (1973), 958–971.

'The Command of Gold Reversed: American Loans to Britain 1915–1917'. *Pacific Historical Review* 45/2 (1976), 209–230.

Walter Hines Page: The Southerner as American 1855–1918. Chapel Hill: University of North Carolina Press, 1977.

The Warrior and the Priest: Woodrow Wilson and Theodore Roosevelt. Cambridge: The Belknap Press of Harvard University Press, 1983.

'The United States'. In *The Origins of World War I*, Richard F. Hamilton and Holger H. Herwig (Eds.). Cambridge: Cambridge University Press, 2003, 415–442.

Woodrow Wilson: A Biography. New York: Alfred A. Knopf, 2009.

Crosby, Travis L. *The Unknown Lloyd George: A Statesman in Conflict*. London: I. B. Tauris, 2014.

David, Edward. 'The Liberal Party Divided 1916–1918'. *Historical Journal* 13/3 (1970), 509–532.

Davis, Lance, and Robert Huttenback. 'The Export of British Finance, 1865–1914'. In *Money, Finance, and Empire 1790–1960*, A. N. Porter and R. F. Holland (Eds.). London: Frank Cass, 1985, 28–76.

De Cecco, Marcello. *The International Gold Standard: Money and Empire*. New York: St. Martin's Press, 1984.

DeGroot, Gerard J. *Blighty: British Society in the Era of the Great War*. London: Longman, 1996.

Delano, Anthony. *Guy Gaunt: The Boy from Ballarat Who Talked America into the Great War*. Melbourne: Arcadia, 2017.

Devlin, Patrick. *Too Proud to Fight: Woodrow Wilson's Neutrality*. London: Oxford University Press, 1974.

Dewey, P. E. *British Agriculture in the First World War*. London: Routledge, 1989.

Dimsdale, Nicholas, and Anthony Hotson (Eds.) *British Financial Crises since 1825*. Oxford: Oxford University Press, 2014.

DiNardo, Richard L. *Breakthrough: The Gorlice-Tarnow Campaign*. Santa Barbara, CA: Praeger, 2010.

Doenecke, Justus. *Nothing Less than War: A New History of America's Entry into World War I*. Lexington: University Press of Kentucky, 2011.

Doerries, Reinhard R. *Imperial Challenge: Ambassador Count Bernstorff and German-American Relations, 1908–1917*. Christa D. Shannon (Trans.). Chapel Hill: University of North Carolina Press, 1989.

Doughty, Robert A. *Pyrrhic Victory: French Strategy and Operations in the Great War*. Cambridge, MA: Belknap Press of Harvard University Press, 2005.

Douglas, Roy. 'The Background to the "Coupon" Election Arrangements'. *English Historical Review* 86/2 (1971), 318–336.

Dudgeon, Jeffrey. *Roger Casement: The Black Diaries with a Study of His Background, Sexuality, and Irish Political Life*. Belfast: Belfast Press, 2002.

Duffy, Stephen. *The Integrity of Ireland: Home Rule, Nationalism, and Partition, 1912–1922*. Madison, WI: Fairleigh Dickinson University Press, 2009.

Dutton, David. *Austen Chamberlain: Gentleman in Politics*. New Brunswick, NJ: Transaction, 1985.

Egerton, George. 'The Lloyd George "War Memoirs": A Study in the Politics of Memory'. *Journal of Modern History* 60/1 (1988), 55–94.

Egremont, Max. *Balfour: A Life of Arthur James Balfour*. London: Collins, 1980.

Erickson, Edward. *Gallipoli*. Barnsley, UK: Pen & Sword Military, 2010.

Esposito, David M. *The Legacy of Woodrow Wilson: American War Aims in World War I*. Westport, CT: Praeger, 1996.

'Imagined Power: The Secret Life of Colonel House'. *Historian* 60/4 (1998), 741–755.

Evans, Martin Marix. *Somme 1914–18: Lessons in War*. Stroud: The History Press, 2010.

Farr, Martin. '*Reginald McKenna as Chancellor of the Exchequer 1915–1916*'. PhD Dissertation, University of Glasgow, 1998.

'A Compelling Case for Voluntarism: Britain's Alternative Strategy, 1915–1916'. *War in History* 9/3 (2002), 279–306.

Reginald McKenna: Financier among Statesmen, 1863–1916. London: Routledge, 2008.

'Waging Democracy: The British General Election of 1918 Reconsidered'. *Cercles* 21 (2011), 65–94.

'Winter and Discontent: The December Crises of the Asquith Coalition, 1915–1916'. *Britain and the World* 4/1 (2011), 109–141.

Feinstein, Charles. 'Britain's Overseas Investments in 1913'. *Economic History Review* 43/2 (1990), 288–295.

Ferguson, Niall. *The Pity of War*. London: The Penguin Press, 1998.

'How (Not) to Pay for the War'. In *Great War, Total War: Combat and Mobilization on the Western Front, 1914–1918*, Roger Chickering and Stig Förster (Eds.). Cambridge: Cambridge University Press, 2000, 409–434.

Ferris, John. 'Before "Room 40": The British Empire and Signals Intelligence, 1898–1914'. *Journal of Strategic Studies* 12/4 (1989), 431–457.

'The Road to Bletchley Park: The British Experience with Signals Intelligence, 1892–1945'. *Intelligence and National Security* 17/1 (2002), 53–84.

'"Now That the Milk Is Spilt": Appeasement and the Archive on Intelligence'. *Diplomacy and Statecraft* 19/3 (2008), 527–565.

Fest, Wilfred B. 'British War Aims and German Peace Feelers during the First World War (December 1916–November 1918)'. *Historical Journal* 15/2 (1972), 285–308.

Peace or Partition: The Habsburg Monarchy and British Policy 1914–1918. London: George Prior, 1978.

Fisk, Harvey. *The Inter-Ally Debts: An Analysis of War and Post-War Public Finance, 1914–1923.* New York: Bankers Trust Company, 1924.

Floyd, M. Ryan. *Abandoning American Neutrality: Woodrow Wilson and the Beginning of the Great War, August 1914 – December 1915.* New York: Palgrave Macmillan, 2013.

Fowler, Wilton B. *British-American Relations 1917–1918: The Role of Sir William Wiseman.* Princeton, NJ: Princeton University Press, 1969.

Fraser, Peter. 'Lord Beaverbrook's Fabrications in *Politicians and the War, 1914–1916*'. *Historical Journal* 25/1 (1982), 147–166.

'The British "Shells Scandal" of 1915'. *Canadian Journal of History* 18/1 (1983), 69–86.

Freeman, Peter. 'The Zimmermann Telegram Revisited: A Reconciliation of the Primary Sources'. *Cryptologia* 30/2 (2006), 98–150.

'MI1(b) and the Origins of British Diplomatic Cryptanalysis'. *Intelligence and National Security* 22/2 (2007), 206–228.

French, David. *British Economic and Strategic Planning 1905–1915.* London: George Allen & Unwin, 1982.

'The Rise and Fall of Business as Usual'. In *War and the State: The Transformation of the British Government, 1914–1919*, Kathleen Burk (Ed.). London: George Allen & Unwin, 1982, 7–31.

British Strategy and War Aims 1914–1916. London: Allen & Unwin, 1986.

'Watching the Allies: British Intelligence and the French Mutinies of 1917'. *Intelligence and National Security* 6/3 (1991), 573–592.

The Strategy of the Lloyd George Coalition, 1916–1918. Oxford: Clarendon Press, 1995.

Fried, Marvin. *Austro-Hungarian War Aims in the Balkans during World War I.* London: Palgrave Macmillan, 2014.

Fry, Michael. *Lloyd George and Foreign Policy: The Education of a Statesman: 1890–1916.* Montreal: McGill-Queen's University Press, 1977.

Gannon, Paul. *Inside Room 40: The Codebreakers of World War 1.* Hersham, UK: Ian Allan, 2010.

Gathen, Joachim von zur. 'Zimmermann Telegram: The Original Draft'. *Cryptologia* 31/1 (2007), 2–37.

Gazeley, Ian, and Andrew Newell. 'The First World War and Working-Class Food Consumption in Britain'. *European Review of Economic History* 17/1 (2013), 71–94.

Gilbert, Bentley Brinkerhoff. *David Lloyd George: A Political Life: The Organizer of Victory 1912–1916.* London: B. T. Batsford, 1992.

Gilmour, David. *Curzon.* London: John Murray, 1994.

Goldstein, Erik. *Winning the Peace: British Diplomatic Strategy, Peace Planning, and the Paris Peace Conference, 1916–1920.* Oxford: Clarendon Press, 1991.

Gooch, John. 'Soldiers, Strategy and War Aims in Britain 1914–1918'. In *War Aims and Strategic Policy in the Great War 1914–1918*, Barry Hunt and Adrian Preston (Eds.). London: Croom Helm, 1977, 21–40.

The Italian Army in the First World War. Cambridge: Cambridge University Press, 2014.

Grant, James. *The Forgotten Depression: 1921: The Depression That Cured Itself.* New York: Simon and Schuster, 2015.

Gregory, Adrian. *The Last Great War: British Society and the First World War.* Cambridge: Cambridge University Press, 2008.

Gregory, Ross. *Walter Hines Page: Ambassador to the Court of St. James's.* Lexington: The University Press of Kentucky, 1970.

The Origins of American Intervention in the First World War. New York: W. W. Norton & Company, 1971.

Greenhalgh, Elizabeth. *Victory through Coalition: Britain and France during the First World War.* Cambridge: Cambridge University Press, 2005.

The French Army and the First World War. Cambridge: Cambridge University Press, 2014.

Grew, Joseph. *Turbulent Era: A Diplomatic Record of Forty Years 1904–1945.* Freeport, NY: Books for Libraries Press, 1952.

Grieves, Keith. *The Politics of Manpower, 1914–1918.* Manchester: Manchester University Press, 1988.

Grigg, John. *Lloyd George: From Peace to War 1912–1916.* London: Methuen, 1985.

Hall, Richard. 'Bulgaria in the First World War'. *Historian* 73/2 (2001), 300–315.

Hamilton, Keith. *Bertie of Thame: Edwardian Ambassador.* Woodbridge, UK: Boydell Press, 1990.

Hammond, John Lawrence. *C. P. Scott of the Manchester Guardian.* London: G. Bell and Sons, 1934.

Hanak, Harry. 'The Government, the Foreign Office, and Austria-Hungary, 1914–1918'. *The Slavonic and East European Review* 47/108 (1969), 161–197.

Harris, J. P. *Douglas Haig and the First World War.* Cambridge: Cambridge University Press, 2008.

Hart, Peter. *Gallipoli.* Oxford: Oxford University Press, 2011.

Hattersley, Roy. *David Lloyd George: The Great Outsider.* London: Little, Brown and Company, 2009.

Hautcoeur, Pierre-Cyrille. 'Was the Great War a Watershed? The Economics of World War I in France'. In *The Economics of World War I*, Stephen Broadberry and Mark Harrison (Eds.). Cambridge: Cambridge University Press, 2005, 169–205.

Hazlehurst, Cameron. *Politicians at War July 1914 to May 1915.* London: Jonathan Cape, 1971.

Headrick, Daniel R. *The Invisible Weapon: Telecommunications and International Politics, 1851–1945.* Oxford: Oxford University Press, 1991.

Heckscher, August. *Woodrow Wilson.* New York: Macmillan, 1991.

Heffer, Simon. *Staring at God: Britain in the Great War.* London: Penguin Random House, 2019.

Hendrick, Burton J. *The Life and Letters of Walter H. Page*. London: William Heinemann, 1924.

Herwig, Holger H. *The First World War: Germany and Austria-Hungary 1914–1918*. London: Arnold, 1997.

Hill, Christopher. *Cabinet Decisions on Foreign Policy: The British Experience, October 1938–June 1941*. Cambridge: Cambridge University Press, 1991.

Hines, Jason. 'Sins of Omission and Commission: A Reassessment of the Role of Intelligence in the Battle of Jutland'. *Journal of Military History* 72/4 (2008), 1117–1154.

Hinsley, F. H. (Ed.). *British Foreign Policy under Sir Edward Grey*, Cambridge: Cambridge University Press, 1977.

Hodgson, Godfrey. *Woodrow Wilson's Right Hand: The Life of Colonel Edward M. House*. New Haven, CT: Yale University Press, 2006.

Holmes, Richard. *The Little Field Marshal: Sir John French*. London: Cape, 1981.

Horčička, Václav. 'Austria-Hungary, Unrestricted Submarine Warfare, and the United States' Entrance into the First World War'. *International History Review* 34/2 (2012), 245–269.

Horn, Martin. *Britain, France, and the Financing of the First World War*. Montreal and Kingston: McGill-Queen's University Press, 2002.

Horne, Alastair. *The Price of Glory: Verdun 1916*. London: Macmillan, 1962.

Horne, John N. *Labour at War: France and Britain 1914–1918*. Oxford: Clarendon Press, 1991.

Imlah, Albert H. 'British Balance of Payments and Export of Capital, 1816–1913'. *Economic History Review* 5/2 (1952), 208–239.

Isaacs, Gerald Rufus. *Rufus Isaacs: First Marquess of Reading*. 2 vols. London: Hutchinson, 1945.

James, William. *The Eyes of the Navy: A Biographical Study of Admiral Sir Reginald Hall K. C. M. G. , C. B. , L. L. D. , D. C. L.* London: Methuen, 1955.

Jeffery, Keith. *MI6: The History of the Secret Intelligence Service 1909–1949*. London: Bloomsbury, 2010.

1916: A Global History. London: Bloomsbury, 2015.

Jenkins, Roy. *Asquith*. London: Collins, 1978.

Johnson, Elizabeth. *Collected Writings of John Maynard Keynes*. Vol. 16. Cambridge: Cambridge University Press, 2013.

Johnson, Gaynor. *Robert Cecil: Politician and Internationalist*. London: Ashgate, 2013.

Johnson, Matthew. 'The Liberal War Committee and the Liberal Advocacy of Conscription in Britain, 1914–1916'. *Historical Journal* 51/2 (2008), 399–420.

Kahn, David. *The Codebreakers: The Story of Secret Writing*. New York: Macmillan Publishing, 1967.

The Reader of Gentlemen's Mail: Herbert O. Yardley and the Birth of American Codebreaking. New Haven: Yale University Press, 2004.

Kemmerer, E. W. 'The War and Interest Rates'. *American Economic Review* 9/1 (1919), 96–107.

Kennedy, Ross A. 'Woodrow Wilson, World War I, and an American Conception of National Security'. *Diplomatic History* 25/1 (2001), 1–31.

The Will to Believe: Woodrow Wilson, World War I, and America's Strategy for Peace and Security. Kent: Kent State University Press, 2009.

'Thomas Boghardt, The Zimmermann Telegram: Intelligence, Diplomacy, and America's Entry into World War I', *Intelligence and National Security* 29/2 (2014), 310–312.

Keohane, Nigel. *The Party of Patriotism: The Conservative Party and the First World War.* Farnham, UK: Ashgate, 2010.

Kernek, Sterling. 'The British Government's Reactions to President Wilson's "Peace" Note of December 1916'. *Historical Journal* 13/4 (1970), 721–766.

Distractions of Peace during War: The Lloyd George Government's Reactions to Woodrow Wilson, December 1916–November 1918. Philadelphia: American Philosophical Society, 1975.

Kihl, Mary R. 'A Failure of Ambassadorial Diplomacy'. *Journal of American History* 57/3 (1970), 636–653.

Knock, Thomas. *To End All Wars: Woodrow Wilson and the Quest for a New World.* Princeton, NJ: Princeton University Press, 1995.

Krause, Jonathan. *Early Trench Tactics in the French Army: The Second Battle of Artois, May–June 1915.* Farnham, UK: Ashgate Publishing, 2013.

Kruh, Louis. 'British American-Cryptanalytic Cooperation and an Unprecedented Admission by Winston Churchill'. *Cryptologia* 13/2 (1989), 123–134.

Lambert, Nicholas. *Planning Armageddon: British Economic Warfare and the First World War.* Cambridge, MA: Harvard University Press, 2012.

Larsen, Daniel. 'British Intelligence and the 1916 Mediation Mission of Colonel Edward M. House'. *Intelligence and National Security* 25/5 (2010), 682–704.

'War Pessimism in Britain and an American Peace in Early 1916'. *International History Review* 34/4 (2012), 795–817.

'Abandoning Democracy: Woodrow Wilson and Promoting German Democracy, 1918–1919'. *Diplomatic History* 37/3 (2013), 476–508.

'Intelligence in the First World War: The State of the Field'. *Intelligence and National Security* 29/2 (2014), 282–302.

'British Codebreaking and American Diplomatic Telegrams, 1914–1915'. *Intelligence and National Security* 32/2 (2017), 256–263.

'British Signals Intelligence and the 1916 Easter Rising in Ireland'. *Intelligence and National Security* 33/1 (2018), 48–66.

'Creating an American Culture of Secrecy: Cryptography in Wilson-Era Diplomacy'. *Diplomatic History* 44/1 (2020), 102–132.

Lester, V. Markham. *H. H. Asquith: Last of the Romans.* Lanham, MD: Lexington Books, 2019.

Levin, N. Gordon, Jr. *Woodrow Wilson and World Politics: America's Response to War and Revolution.* New York: Oxford University Press, 1968.

Levine, Naomi. *Politics, Religion, and Love: The Story of H. H. Asquith, Venetia Stanley, and Edwin Montagu, Based on the Life and Letters of Edwin Samuel Montagu.* New York: New York University Press, 1991.

Lewis, Cleona. *America's Stake in International Investments.* Washington, DC: The Brookings Institution, 1938.

Lewis, Geoffrey. *Carson: The Man Who Divided Ireland*. London: Hambledon and London, 2005.

Liddle, Peter H. *The 1916 Battle of the Somme: A Reappraisal*. London: Leo Cooper, 1992.

Lieven, Dominic. 'Keith Neilson. *Strategy and Supply: The Anglo-Russian Alliance, 1914–1917.*' *International History Review* 8/1 (1986), 149–151.

Towards the Flame: Empire, War and the End of Tsarist Russia. London: Allen Lane, 2015.

Link, Arthur S. *Wilson: The New Freedom* (Vol. 2). Princeton, NJ: Princeton University Press, 1956.

Wilson: The Struggle for Neutrality 1914–1915 (Vol. 3). Princeton, NJ: Princeton University Press, 1960.

Wilson: Confusions and Crises 1915–1916 (Vol. 4). Princeton, NJ: Princeton University Press, 1964.

Wilson: Campaigns for Progressivism and Peace 1916–1917 (Vol. 5). Princeton, NJ: Princeton University Press, 1965.

Woodrow Wilson: Revolution, War, and Peace. Arlington Heights, IL: Harlan Davidson, 1979.

Lloyd, Nick. *Loos 1915*. Stroud: Tempus, 2006.

Lloyd-Jones, Roger, and M. J. Lewis. *Arming the Western Front: War, Business and the State in Britain 1900–1920*. Abingdon, UK: Routledge, 2016.

Lockhart, John B. 'Sir William Wiseman, Bart – Agent of Influence'. *RUSI Journal* 134 (1989), 63–67.

Lowe, C. J., and M. L. Dockrill. *The Mirage of Power*. London: Routledge, 1972.

Maddison, Angus. *Contours of the World Economy, 1–2030 AD: Essays in Macro-Economic History*. Oxford: Oxford University Press, 2007.

Mamatey, Victor S. *The United States and East Central Europe 1914–1918: A Study in Wilsonian Diplomacy and Propaganda*. Princeton, NJ: Princeton University Press, 1957.

Martin, Laurence W. *Peace Without Victory: Woodrow Wilson and the British Liberals*. New Haven, CT: Yale University Press, 1958.

May, Ernest R. *The World War and American Isolation 1914–1917*. Cambridge, MA: Harvard University Press, 1959.

McDermott, James. *British Military Service Tribunals, 1916–1918*. Manchester: Manchester University Press, 2011.

McEwen, J. M. 'The Press and the Fall of Asquith'. *Historical Journal* 21/4 (1978), 863–883.

'The Struggle for Mastery in Britain: Lloyd George versus Asquith, December 1916'. *Journal of British Studies* 18/1(1978), 131–156.

'Lord Beaverbrook: Historian Extraordinary'. *Dalhousie Review* 59/1 (1979), 129–143.

'Northcliffe and Lloyd George at War, 1914–1918'. *Historical Journal* 24/3 (1981), 651–672.

McKenna, Stephen. *Reginald McKenna: 1863–1943: A Memoir*. London: Eyre & Spottiswoode Ltd, 1948.

McMahon, Paul. *British Spies and Irish Rebels: British Intelligence and Ireland, 1916–1945*. Woodbridge, UK: Boydell Press, 2008.

Messimer, Dwight R. *The Merchant U-Boat: Adventures of the Deutschland 1916–1918*. Annapolis, MD: Naval Institute Press, 1988.

The Baltimore Sabotage Cell: German Agents, American Traitors, and the U-Boat Deutschland during World War I. Annapolis, MD: Naval Institute Press, 2015.

Millman, Brock. *Pessimism and British War Policy 1916–1918*. London: Frank Cass, 2001.

Moggridge, D. E. *Maynard Keynes: An Economist's Biography*. London: Routledge, 1992.

Morgan, Edward. *Studies in British Financial Policy 1914–25*. London: Macmillan, 1952.

Murray, Arthur C. *Master and Brother: Murrays of Elibank*. London: John Murray, 1945.

At Close Quarters: A Sidelight on Anglo-American Diplomatic Relations. London: John Murray, 1946.

Neilson, Keith. *Strategy and Supply: The Anglo-Russian Alliance, 1914–1917*. London: George Allen & Unwin, 1984.

Newton, Thomas. *Lord Lansdowne: A Biography*. London: Macmillan, 1929.

Neu, Charles. *Colonel House: A Biography of Woodrow Wilson's Silent Partner*. Oxford: Oxford University Press, 2015.

Nickles, David Paull. *Under the Wire: How the Telegraph Changed Diplomacy*. Cambridge, MA: Harvard University Press, 2003.

Nordholt, Jan Willem Schulte. *Woodrow Wilson: A Life for World Peace*. Herbert H. Rowen (Trans.). Berkeley: University of California Press, 1991.

O'Day, Alan. *Irish Home Rule 1867–1921*. Manchester, UK: Manchester University Press, 1998.

O'Halpin, Eunan. 'British Intelligence in Ireland, 1914–1921.' In *The Missing Dimension: Governments and Intelligence Communities in the Twentieth Century*, Christopher Andrew and David Dilks (Eds.). Urbana: University of Illinois Press, 1984, 54–77.

Osborne, Eric W. *Britain's Economic Blockade of Germany 1914–1919*. London: Frank Cass, 2004.

Otte, Thomas. *July Crisis: The World's Descent into War, Summer 1914*. Cambridge: Cambridge University Press, 1914.

Peters, John. 'The British Government and the City–Industry Divide: The Case of the 1914 Financial Crisis'. *Twentieth Century British History* 4/2 (1993), 126–148.

Peterson, Horace Cornelius. *Propaganda for War: The Campaign against American Neutrality, 1914–1917*. Norman: University of Oklahoma Press, 1939.

Philpott, William James. *Anglo-French Relations and Strategy on the Western Front, 1914-1918*. London: Macmillan, 1996.

Bloody Victory: The Sacrifice on the Somme and the Making of the Twentieth Century. London: Little, Brown, 2009.

(Also published as: Three Armies on the Somme: The First Battle of the Twentieth Century. New York: Alfred A. Knopf, 2010.)

Pirenne, Henri. *Belgium and the First World War*. Wesley Chapel, FL: Brabant Press, 2014.

Popplewell, Richard J. *Intelligence and Imperial Defence: British Intelligence and the Defence of the Indian Empire 1904–1924*. London: Frank Cass, 1995.

Prete, Roy A. 'Joffre and the Origins of the Somme: A Study in Allied Military Planning'. *Journal of Military History* 73/2 (2009), 417–448.

Prior, Robin. *Gallipoli: The End of the Myth*. London: Yale University Press, 2009.

Prior, Robin, and Trevor Wilson. *Command on the Western Front: The Military Career of Sir Henry Rawlinson 1914-1918*. Oxford: Blackwell, 1992.

The Somme. Sydney: University of New South Wales Press, 2005.

Pugh, Martin. 'Asquith, Bonar Law, and the First Coalition'. *Historical Journal* 17/4 (1974), 813–836.

Lloyd George. London: Longman, 1988.

Ramsay, David. *'Blinker' Hall: Spymaster: The Man Who Brought America into World War I*. Stroud, UK: The History Press, 2008.

Rappaport, Armin. *The British Press and Wilsonian Neutrality*. Stanford, CA: Stanford University Press, 1951.

Read, Anthony, and David Fisher. *Colonel Z: The Life and Times of a Master of Spies*. London: Hodder and Stoughton, 1984.

Reynolds, David. *An Ocean Apart: The Relationship Between Britain and America in the Twentieth Century*. London: Hodder & Stoughton, 1988.

Britannia Overruled: British Policy and World Power in the Twentieth Century. London: Longman, 1991.

America, Empire of Liberty. London: Penguin, 2009.

Richards, Harry. 'Room 40 and German Intrigues in Morocco: Re-assessing the Operational Impact of Diplomatic Cryptanalysis during World War I'. *Intelligence and National Security* 32/6 (2017), 833–848.

Robbins, Keith. *Sir Edward Grey: A Biography of Lord Grey of Fallodon*. London: Cassell, 1971.

Roberts, Richard. *Saving the City: The Great Financial Crisis of 1914*. Oxford: Oxford University Press, 2013.

Roberston, William. *Soldiers and Statesmen, 1914–1918*. New York: Scribner, 1926.

Rockoff, Hugh. 'Until It's Over, Over There: The US Economy in World War I'. In *The Economics of World War I*, Stephen Broadberry and Mark Harrison (Eds.). Cambridge: Cambridge University Press, 2005, 310–343.

Rogan, Eugene. *The Fall of the Ottomans: The Great War in the Middle East, 1914–1920*. London: Allen Lane, 2015.

Roskill, Steven W. *Hankey: Man of Secrets*. London: Collins, 1970–1974.

Rothwell, V. H. *British War Aims and Peace Diplomacy, 1914–1918*. Oxford: Clarendon Press, 1971.

Rowland, Peter. *Lloyd George*. London: Barrie & Jenkins, 1975.

Santoni, Alberto. 'The First Ultra Secret: The British Cryptanalysis in the Naval Operations of the First World War'. *Revue Internationale d'Histoire Militaire* 63 (1985), 99–110.

Schindler, John R. *Isonzo: The Forgotten Sacrifice of the Great War*. Westport, CT: Praeger, 2001.

Schwartz, Anna J. *Money in Histrorical Perspective*. Chicago: University of Chicago Press, 2007.

Seymour, Charles. *American Diplomacy during the World War*. Baltimore: The Johns Hopkins Press, 1934.

Shanafelt, Gary W. *The Secret Enemy: Austria-Hungary and the German Alliance, 1914–1918.* New York: Columbia University Press, 1985.

Sharp, Alan. *David Lloyd George: Great Britain.* London: Haus Publishing, 2008.

Sheffield, Gary. *Forgotten Victory: The First World War: Myths and Realities.* London: Headline, 2001.

The Somme. London: Cassell, 2003.

The Chief: Douglas Haig and the British Army. London: Aurum, 2011.

Sheldon, Jack. *The German Army on the Western Front, 1915.* Barnsley, UK: Pen & Sword, 2012.

Silber, William L. *When Washington Shut Down Wall Street: The Great Financial Crisis of 1914 and the Origins of America's Monetary Supremacy.* Princeton, NJ: Princeton University Press, 2007.

Singh, Simon. *The Science of Secrecy.* London: Anchor Books, 1999.

Sloan, Geoff. 'The British State and the Irish Rebellion of 1916: An Intelligence Failure or a Failure of Response?' *Intelligence and National Security* 28/4 (2013), 453–494.

Smith, Arthur D. Howden. *Mr. House of Texas.* New York, London: Funk & Wagnalls Company, 1940.

Soutou, Georges-Henri. *L'or et le sang: Les buts de guerre économiques de la Première Guerre mondiale [Blood and Gold: The Economic War Aims of the First World War].* Paris: Fayard, 1989.

Spence, Richard B. 'Englishmen in New York: The SIS American Station, 1915–21'. *Intelligence and National Security* 19/3 (2004), 511–537.

Spender, John Alfred. *Life, Journalism and Politics.* London: Cassel and Company, 1927.

Spender, John Alfred, and Cyril Asquith. *Life of Herbert Henry Asquith, Lord Oxford and Asquith.* 2 vols. London: Hutchinson, 1932.

Stafford, David. 'The Detonator Concept: British Strategy, SOE and European Resistance after the Fall of France'. *Journal of Contemporary History* 10/2 (1975), 185–217.

Steffen, Dirk. 'The Holtzendorff Memorandum of 22 December 1916 and Germany's Declaration of Unrestricted U-boat Warfare'. *Journal of Military History* 68/1 (2004), 215–224.

Steigerwald, David. 'Historiography: The Reclamation of Woodrow Wilson?' *Diplomatic History* 23/1 (1999), 79–99.

Stevenson, David. 'French War Aims and the American Challenge'. *Historical Journal* 22/4 (1979), 877–894.

French War Aims against Germany 1914–1919. Oxford: Clarendon Press, 1982.

The First World War and International Politics. Oxford: Clarendon Press, 1988.

'The Failure of Peace by Negotiation in 1917'. *Historical Journal* 34/1 (1991), 65–86.

1914–1918: The History of the First World War. London: Penguin Books, 2004. (Also published as: *Cataclysm: The First World War as Political Tragedy.* New York: Basic Books, 2004.)

1917: War, Peace, and Revolution. Oxford: Oxford University Press, 2017.

Stone, David. *The Russian Army in the Great War: The Eastern Front, 1914–1917.* Lawrence: University Press of Kansas, 2015.

Strachan, Hew. 'The Battle of the Somme and British Strategy'. *Journal of Strategic Studies* 21/1 (1998), 79–95.

Financing the First World War. Oxford: Oxford University Press, 2004.

Stubbs, J. O. 'Beaverbrook as Historian: *Politicians and the War* Reconsidered'. *Albion* 14/3–4 (1982), 235–253.

Suttie, Andrew. *Rewriting the First World War: Lloyd George, Politics and Strategy 1914–1918*. Basingstoke, UK: Palgrave Macmillan, 2005.

Sylvest, Casper. *British Liberal Internationalism, 1880-1930: Making Progress?* Manchester, New York: Manchester University Press, 2009.

Tansill, Charles C. *America Goes to War*. Boston: Little, Brown, & Co., 1938.

Taylor, A. J. P. *Struggle for Mastery in Europe 1848–1918*. Oxford: Clarendon Press, 1954.

Thompson, J. Lee. *Politicians, the Press, and Propaganda: Lord Northcliffe and the Great War, 1914–1919*. Kent: Kent State University Press, 1999.

Northcliffe: Press Baron in Politics, 1865–1922. London: John Murray, 2000.

Thompson, John A. 'Woodrow Wilson and World War I: A Reappraisal'. *Journal of American Studies* 19/3 (1985), 325–348.

Woodrow Wilson: Profiles in Power. London: Longman, 2002.

A Sense of Power: The Roots of America's Global Role. Ithaca, NY: Cornell University Press, 2015.

'Woodrow Wilson and David Lloyd George: Uncongenial Allies'. In *Presidents and Prime Ministers: From Cleveland and Salisbury to Trump and May, 1895–2019*, Michael Patrick Cullinane and Martin Farr (Eds.). London: Palgrave Macmillan, Forthcoming.

Tomes, Jason. *Balfour and Foreign Policy: The International Thought of a Conservative Statesman*. Cambridge: Cambridge University Press, 1997.

Tomlinson, Jim. 'Thrice Denied: "Declinism" as a Recurrent Theme in British History in the Long Twentieth Century'. *Twentieth Century British History* 20/2 (2009), 227–251.

Tooze, Adam. *The Deluge: The Great War and the Remaking of the Global Order*. London: Allan Lane, 2014.

Torrey, Glenn. *The Romanian Battlefront in World War I*. Lawrence:University Press of Kansas, 2011.

Travers, Tim. *The Killing Ground: The British Army, the Western Front and the Emergence of Modern Warfare 1900–1918*. London: Allen & Unwin, 1987.

Trevelyan, George M. *Grey of Fallodon*. London: Longmans, Green and Co., 1937.

Troy, Thomas F. 'The Gaunt-Wiseman Affair: British Intelligence in New York in 1915'. *International Journal of Intelligence and Counterintelligence* 16/3 (2003), 442–461.

Tuchman, Barbara. *The Zimmermann Telegram*. London: Constable, 1958.

Tucker, Robert W. *Woodrow Wilson and the Great War: Reconsidering America's Neutrality 1914–1917*. Charlottesville: University of Virginia Press, 2007.

Turner, John. 'Cabinets, Committees and Secretariats: The Higher Direction of War'. In *War and the State*, Kathleen Burk (Ed.). London: George Allen & Unwin, 1982, 57–83.

British Politics and the Great War: Coalition and Conflict 1915–1918. New Haven, CT: Yale University Press, 1992.

Valone, Stephen J. '"There Must Be Some Misunderstanding": Sir Edward Grey's Diplomacy of August 1, 1914'. *Journal of British Studies* 27 (1988), 405–424.

Viereck, George Sylvester. *The Strangest Friendship in History: Woodrow Wilson and Colonel House*. London: Duckworth, 1933.

Waley, S. D. *Edwin Montagu: A Memoir and an Account of His Visits to India*. London: Asia Publishing House, 1964.

Wallach, Jehuda L. *Uneasy Coalition: The Entente Experience in World War I*. Westport, London: Greenwood Press, 1993.

Walton, Gary M., and Hugh Rockoff. *History of the American Economy (Thirteenth Edition)*. Boston: Cengage Learning, 2018.

Walworth, Arthur. *Woodrow Wilson*. New York: W. W. Norton &Company, 1978.

Warner, Philip. *The Battle of Loos*. London: William Kimber, 1976.

Watson, Alexander. *Ring of Steel: Germany and Austria-Hungary at War, 1914–1918*. London: Penguin, 2014.

Weber, Ralph E. *United States Diplomatic Codes and Ciphers 1775–1938*. Chicago: Precedent Publishing Inc., 1979.

Masked Dispatches: Cryptograms and Cryptology in American History, 1775–1900. Fort Meade, MD: National Security Agency, 1993.

'State Department Cryptographic Security, Herbert O. Yardley, & President Woodrow Wilson's Secret Code'. In *In the Name of Intelligence: Essays in Honor of Walter Pforzheimer*, Hayden B. Peake and Samuel Halpern (Eds.). Washington, DC: NIBC Press, 1994, 543–596.

West, Kieran. 'Intelligence and the Development of British Grand Strategy in the First World War'. PhD Dissertation, Cambridge University Library, 2011.

Wieten, Jan. *Howard and Northcliffe: Two Press Lords on the Warpath*. Bloomington: Indiana University School of Journalism, 1990.

Wilkins, Mira. *The History of Foreign Investment in the United States to 1914*. Cambridge, MA: Harvard University Press, 1989.

The History of Foreign Investment in the United States to 1914–1945. Cambridge, MA: Harvard University Press, 2004.

Willert, Arthur. *The Road to Safety: A Study in Anglo-American Relations*. London: Derek Verschoyle, 1952.

Williams, Joyce Grigsby. *Colonel House and Sir Edward Grey: A Study in Anglo-American Diplomacy*. Lanham, MD: University Press of America, 1984.

Wilson, Trevor. 'The Coupon and the British General Election of 1918'. *Journal of Modern History* 36/1 (1964), 28–42.

The Downfall of the Liberal Party. London: Collins, 1966.

(Ed.). *The Political Diaries of C. P. Scott 1911–1928*. London: Collins, 1970.

The Myriad Faces of War: Britain and the Great War, 1914–1918. Cambridge: Polity Press, 1986.

Winkler, Jonathan Reed. *Nexus: Strategic Communications and American Security in World War I*. Cambridge, MA: Harvard University Press, 2008.

'Information Warfare in World War I'. *Journal of Military History* 73/3 (2009), 845–867.

Winter, Jay. *The Great War and the British People*. Basingstoke, UK: Palgrave MacMillan, 2003.

Winters, Frank. 'Exaggerating the Efficacy of Diplomacy: The Marquis of Lansdowne's "Peace Letter" of November 1917'. *International History Review* 32/1 (2010), 25–46.

Woodward, David. 'Britain's "Brass Hats" and the Question of a Compromise Peace, 1916–1918'. *Military Affairs* 35/2 (1971), 63–68.

'David Lloyd George, A Negotiated Peace with Germany, and the Kuhlmann Peace Kite of September, 1917'. *Canadian Journal of History*, 6/1 (1971), 75–93.

Lloyd George and the Generals. Newark: University of Delaware Press, 1983.

Trial by Friendship: Anglo-American Relations, 1917–1918. Lexington: University Press of Kentucky, 1993.

Field Marshal Sir William Robertson: Chief of the Imperial General Staff in the Great War. Westport, CT: Praeger, 1998.

(Ed.). *America and World War I: A Selected Annotated Bibliography of English-Language Sources*. New York, London: Routledge, 2007.

Wrench, John Evelyn. *Geoffrey Dawson and Our Times*. London: Hutchinson, 1955.

Wrigley, Chris. 'The Ministry of Munitions: An Innovatory Department'. In *War and the State*, Kathleen Burk (Ed.). London: George Allen & Unwin, 1982, 32–56.

Yearwood, Peter. *Guarantee of Peace: The League of Nations in British Policy 1914–1925*. Oxford: Oxford University Press, 2009.

Yearwood, Peter, and Cameron Hazlehurst. '"The Affairs of a Distant Dependency": The Nigeria Debate and the Premiership, 1916'. *Twentieth Century British History* 12/4 (2001), 397–431.

Zebel, Sydney H. *Balfour: A Political Biography*. Cambridge: Cambridge University Press, 1973.

Zeman, Z. A. B. *A Diplomatic History of the First World War*. London: Weidenfeld and Nicolson, 1971.

Index

Addison, Christopher, 119–120
Aitken, Max (Lord Beaverbrook), 208
Albert I, King, 304
Alfonso XIII, King of Spain, 33, 36, 164,
  190, 250, 285, 287
Arabic, 72
Arbitrage, 17, 49–51, 323
Argentina, 35, 51, 309
Asquith, Arthur, 174
Asquith, H. H., 15, 28, 52–53, 99, 139,
  145, 173–174, 181–182, 222, 313–314
  and American mediation, 15, 94–99,
    101, 107–111, 127–130, 152, 170,
    194, 247–248
  and conscription, 58, 61–62, 64–66,
    68–70, 114–117, 119–122
  and food supply, 200
  and formation of national unity
    government, 32, 38–40, 53
  and intelligence, 192, 210
  and Lansdowne Memorandum,
    203–204, 218
  and military strategy, 98, 157, 165, 184,
    228
  and war strategy, 9, 30, 61–62, 71,
    83–88, 113–117, 119–122, 177, 188,
    307–310
  as leader of opposition, 246, 256–257
  Efforts to remove David Lloyd George as
    Minister of Munitions, 137–138,
    142–143, 314
  Fall of, 20, 188–189, 205–209, 213–215,
    224–243
  Relationship with Reginald McKenna,
    38–40
Asquith, Margot, 69, 174
Asquith, Raymond, 173–174
Australia, 38, 66, 198
Austria-Hungary, 41, 61, 67, 120, 148, 214,
  265, 292
  and peace negotiations, 20, 22, 251,
    280–283, 285–287, 300–305, 316

and submarine warfare, 287–291, 303
and Zimmermann Telegram, 299
Relations with Germany. *See Germany:*
  Relations with Austria-Hungary

Balfour, Arthur J., 16, 53, 99, 123, 189,
  213, 217, 253
  and 'Freedom of the Seas', 79, 82, 90
  and American mediation, 21, 78–80,
    82–83, 88, 94–97, 101, 106–107, 111,
    128, 131–132, 135, 196, 243,
    247–248, 261, 275–277
  and British economic dependence on
    United States, 139, 222–223, 312–313
  and conscription, 70
  and fall of Asquith, 215, 236–240
  and intelligence, 90, 155, 192, 276, 296
  and Lansdowne Memorandum, 204
  and league of nations, 79, 82,
    131–132
  and military strategy, 80, 145
  and Roger Casement, 162
  and war strategy, 18, 62, 66, 120, 177,
    196
  Use of William Wiseman, 16, 20,
    254–255, 261, 275–277
Bank of England, 25, 28, 41–43, 48, 225,
  228–229, 252, 266
Belgium, 24, 68, 131, 204, 250, 256, 264,
  304
  Prospect of restoration of, 97, 130, 182,
    254, 265, 267, 274–275, 282
Bell, Edward, 293, 296
Benedict XV, Pope, 33, 36, 190,
  250, 286
Bernstorff, Johann Heinrich von, Count,
  264, 289, 308
  and American mediation, 155, 164–165,
    175, 190–193, 251, 264–265,
    267–271, 273–279, 286–287
  and British intelligence, 35, 155,
    164–165, 175, 190–193, 257, 259, 289

411